Accelerated SQL Server 2008

Robert E. Walters, Michael Coles, Robert Rae,
Fabio Ferracchiati, and Donald Farmer

Accelerated SQL Server 2008

Copyright © 2008 by Robert Walters

ISBN-13 (pbk): 978-1-59059-969-3

ISBN-10 (pbk): 1-59059-969-1

ISBN-13 (electronic): 978-1-4302-0606-4

ISBN-10 (electronic): 1-4302-0606-3

Printed and bound in the United States of America 9 8 7 6 5 4 3 2 1

Lead Editor: Jonathan Gennick
Technical Reviewer: Fabio Ferracchiati
Editorial Board: Clay Andres, Steve Anglin, Ewan Buckingham, Tony Campbell, Gary Cornell, Jonathan Gennick, Kevin Goff, Matthew Moodie, Joseph Ottinger, Jeffrey Pepper, Frank Pohlmann, Ben Renow-Clarke, Dominic Shakeshaft, Matt Wade, Tom Welsh
Project Manager: Denise Santoro Lincoln
Copy Editor: Marilyn Smith
Associate Production Director: Kari Brooks-Copony
Production Editor: Ellie Fountain
Compositor and Artist: Kinetic Publishing Services, LLC
Proofreader: April Eddy
Indexer: Broccoli Information Management
Cover Designer: Kurt Krames
Manufacturing Director: Tom Debolski

Distributed to the book trade worldwide by Springer-Verlag New York, Inc., 233 Spring Street, 6th Floor, New York, NY 10013. Phone 1-800-SPRINGER, fax 201-348-4505, e-mail orders-ny@springer-sbm.com, or visit http://www.springeronline.com.

For information on translations, please contact Apress directly at 2855 Telegraph Avenue, Suite 600, Berkeley, CA 94705. Phone 510-549-5930, fax 510-549-5939, e-mail info@apress.com, or visit http://www.apress.com.

Apress and friends of ED books may be purchased in bulk for academic, corporate, or promotional use. eBook versions and licenses are also available for most titles. For more information, reference our Special Bulk Sales–eBook Licensing web page at http://www.apress.com/info/bulksales.

This book is dedicated to Jim Gray, whose early work with SQL Server paved the way for the enterprise-ready data platform it is today.

Contents at a Glance

PART 4 ▪▪▪ Business Intelligence in SQL Server

Contents

PART 1 ▪▪▪ Overview of SQL Server

PART 2 ▪▪▪ Enterprise Data Platform

■CHAPTER 4 High Availability 47

■CHAPTER 5 Performance 81

PART 3 ■■■ Development in SQL Server

PART 4 ■■■ Business Intelligence in SQL Server

About the Authors

ROBERT E. WALTERS is a data platform technology specialist with Microsoft. He specializes in navigating customers through the powerful features and functionality of relational databases. Rob's extensive experience with Microsoft SQL Server started more than 8 years ago, when he worked as a consultant for Microsoft Consulting Services in Denver, Colorado. Shortly after the dot-com bubble burst, Rob returned to Microsoft's headquarters and worked as a program manager in the SQL Server product unit. There, he owned various features within SQL Server, including SQL Server Agent, various management features, and the security for the database engine.

Rob coauthored *Programming Microsoft SQL Server 2005* (Microsoft Press) and *Pro SQL Server 2005* (Apress). He holds a Bachelor of Science in Electrical Engineering from Michigan State University and a Master of Business Administration from Seattle University.

When not thinking about databases, Rob enjoys spending time with his wife, children, and two Saint Bernard dogs.

MICHAEL COLES has worked in the information technology industry for more than a decade, with an emphasis on database-enabled applications. Previously, he worked in a wide range of industries, including retail, manufacturing, and insurance, to name a few. He currently serves as a database architect and applications developer for a consulting firm specializing in business intelligence solutions. Michael lives in New Jersey, and spends his spare time commuting to and from New York City.

FABIO CLAUDIO FERRACCHIATI is a prolific writer on cutting-edge technologies. Fabio has contributed to more than a dozen books on .NET, C#, Visual Basic, and ASP.NET. He is a .NET Microsoft Certified Solution Developer (MCSD) and lives in Rome, Italy. You can read his blog at http://www.ferracchiati.com. Fabio also was the technical reviewer for this book.

ROBERT RAE works as a senior technology specialist in enterprise architecture, focusing on large enterprise accounts for Microsoft. In this role, Robert helps customers better understand how to leverage Microsoft application platform capabilities within their enterprise architectures. Robert spends the vast majority of his time focused on database solutions for business intelligence, data quality, high availability, disaster recovery, and development. Prior to joining Microsoft Robert spent 12 years as president of a consulting firm that focused on enterprise integration and enabling software as a service.

 ■**DONALD FARMER** has been a member of the Microsoft Business Intelligence team for 7 years. He has worked on both the Analysis Services and Integration Services product teams. Donald is now a principal program manager for SQL Server Analysis Services, working to build the new generation of analytic technology, including predictive analysis, within the Microsoft business intelligence offering. Donald is a popular speaker at international events for both business and technical audiences, with a wide range of interests including data integration, information quality, metadata intelligence, and master data management. He is the author of a number of books and articles. Prior to joining Microsoft, Donald worked not only on business intelligence projects, but also in fields as varied as medieval archaeology and fish farming.

Acknowledgments

As most of you know, writing a technical book requires hundreds of hours of researching, outlining, writing, editing, and reviewing content. I could not have done it without the support of many people. I would like to give a special thanks to the following folks, who gave me valuable feedback and provided timely answers to questions: Dan Jones, Bill Ramos, Richard Waymire, Euan Garden, Steven Gott, Peter Saddow, Srini Acharya, Rick Negrin, Dom Arvisais, and Michiel Wories.

Most of all, I would like to thank my wife and family for giving me the support I needed to get this book done.

Thanks!

Robert E. Walters (*lead author*)

Introduction

Before I describe the contents of this book and why I think you should just take it over to the counter and buy it, I would like to give you an insider's look at the SQL Server 2008 product development cycle. I believe this insight will provide you with a deeper understanding of how SQL Server is continuing to evolve. The rest of this book will show you why SQL Server is enterprise-ready.

For the past 5 years, I was a program manager at Microsoft in the SQL Server product unit. During this time, I owned various features within the product, including SQL Server Agent, SQL Server Express, and most recently, database security.

When I joined SQL Server in 2002, the product team was in year 3 of planning and implementing the Yukon (SQL Server 2005) release. One of my first responsibilities was to own the Create Database/ Database Properties dialog in SQL Server Management Studio. After working with the user interface (UI) design team and various UI developers, we crafted the interesting grid-based dialog that you see today in Management Studio. However, arriving at the implemented Create Database dialog was not as straightforward as we wanted.

In our organization, we had separate teams writing the UI, writing the Server Management Objects (SMO) code to support the UI, and writing the code in the database engine itself. One of the more common issues we faced was the orchestration of the three separate teams working on a particular feature. Each of the three teams didn't necessarily put the same priority on the work, and this resulted in situations like having a UI that did nothing because either the SMO or database team didn't write the code to support it at the time. In the end, when it came time to ship the product, there were some features that had no UI support in SQL Server Management Studio. For example, try to manage Service Broker in Management Studio in SQL Server 2005. I will save you the time— there isn't much there.

So why am I airing our dirty laundry? Well, it's not because I want everyone to enjoy the smell. It's because I want to tell you about the dramatic improvements in efficiency that have been made, resulting in a better product for you, the SQL Server customer.

With respect to our software development issues, the upper management in the SQL Server product unit actually cared about the problems people in the product team experienced. When SQL Server 2005 was released, the management set aside a bunch of folks, locked them away (not literally), and had them come up with solutions to the problems. What came as a result was called the SQL Engineering System (SES), which has fundamentally changed the way Microsoft develops SQL Server.

As with other versions of the product, we started with the core themes of the release. In SQL Server 2008's case, these were as follows: mission-critical platform, dynamic development, beyond relational data, and pervasive business insight. These were not just marketing buzzwords, but actually meant something in the SES process. Then another, smaller group came up with scenarios that matched each of these themes. One of the scenarios I was involved with was "secure platform for data." This scenario dealt with issues around data protection. As program managers, we helped define the various improvements that would support this scenario. My specific assignments were the security-related improvements, such as transparent database encryption, Extensible Key Management, and auditing improvements. So, everything we did in the product boiled down to an improvement based on a scenario that was part of a major theme. This kept everyone focused on the common goals for the release.

To address the issues around the mechanics of software development, the SES process defined a number of other measures. One of these measures was a globally ranked improvement list (GRIL), which numbered each improvement across the entire product. The idea was one team couldn't say it had no time to help out another team if that other team was working on a higher-ranked improvement. This ascending list helped keep the hoarding of resources within teams to a minimum and allowed for better collaboration between teams. With a single ranked list, it was also possible to ensure that when an improvement was being made, all teams affected (those dealing with management tools, the database engine, setup, and so on) were brought in and contributed resources as needed.

The end result of the SES process to you, the user of SQL Server, is the following: the quality of the Community Technical Preview (CTP) releases is very high. This is because, by the time each feature is checked in, it has full SMO, tools, and SQL Server Books Online documentation. The improvements made to the product add much more value, since they interact with more parts of the product. Take Resource Governor, for example (a topic covered in Chapter 5 of this book). That improvement affected multiple teams within the product and would have failed miserably if everyone were not in sync and did not treat the feature with the same priority. Finally, it is possible for SQL Server to ship more frequently, since the quality of the code in the main code branch is near release quality.

Who This Book Is For

SQL Server 2008 is an evolution of the third generation of the SQL Server platform. With every release of the product come new features for the database administrator and developer to explore. Because we can't possibly cover absolutely everything in SQL 2008, we focus on the key features and functionality that will rapidly boost your knowledge and skills of this great product. If you know what the acronym DBA stands for and have an interest in SQL Server 2008, then this book is for you!

Valuable Resources

As a SQL Server user, you may have thought of a suggestion to enhance SQL Server, or you may have found an issue with the product. The SQL Server team has a web site that allows you to submit feedback, as well as download the latest CTP releases of the product: http://connect.microsoft.com/ sqlserver. Don't think that what you submit goes into some database and no one ever reads it. Well, never mind the first part of that statement—the comments actually do go into a database, but people from the product team really do read them! Feedback that is entered using the SQL Server Connect web site automatically goes into our issue-tracking database, and program managers and others from the respective feature areas periodically comb through the entries. So don't think you are wasting your time by submitting suggestions and issues. On the contrary, they are all read and responded to by SQL Server team members.

The Microsoft Developer Network (MSDN) forums provide an opportunity to post questions and have them answered by the community and those in the product team. The SQL Server forums can be found at http://forums.microsoft.com/msdn/default.aspx?forumgroupid=19&siteid=1. These forums are very active, with thousands of posts in each topic. The response time is quick, as members of the product team actively monitor and respond to postings.

How This Book Is Structured

This book is written in such a way that you can read through the book cover to cover or dip in and out for specific topics. It is structured into 21 chapters divided into four parts, as follows:

Part 1, Overview of SQL Server: Chapter 1 discusses the vision for SQL Server 2008, the various editions of SQL Server, and SQL Server consolidation. Chapter 2 covers SQL Server installation and configuration. The experience of installing SQL Server 2008 is completely new, and those of us who have suffered battle scars installing previous versions of SQL Server will be in for a pleasant surprise.

Part 2, Enterprise Data Platform: The eight chapters in this part cover key improvements related to relational database concepts.

- Chapter 3 covers Policy Management (PM), the new policy-based framework for SQL Server. The possibilities of PM are endless. Examples of use include allowing administrators to lock down server configurations and enforce that developers use proper naming conventions when creating their objects in the database.

- Chapter 4 is about the key high availability (HA) features in SQL Server 2008, including database snapshots, Windows clustering, SQL Server replication, and other ways to reduce downtime. However, its focus is database mirroring, the newest of the HA technologies.

- Chapter 5 explores the enhancements in SQL Server 2008 as they relate to managing and monitoring resources, increasing performance by optimizing storage, and improving query performance. Specific features covered include the Data Collector, Resource Governor, backup and data compression, and sparse column support, to name a few.

- Chapter 6 covers the core security concepts included in SQL Server, as well as the new auditing feature in SQL Server 2008.

- Chapter 7 discusses encryption capabilities in SQL Server, which have been expanded enough to make encryption a topic for its own chapter! This chapter covers encrypting data using SQL Server, as well as the new transparent database encryption and extensive key management features of SQL Server 2008.

- Chapter 8 covers automation and monitoring. The plethora of tools available in SQL Server contributes to its ease of use compared with other relational database products on the market. SQL Server 2008 includes a new PowerShell provider, as well as a new event framework called Extended Events. This chapter covers these topics, as well as others, including SQL Server Agent, maintenance plans, and SQLCMD.

- Chapter 9 is about Service Broker, which is in its second release with SQL Server 2008. This chapter provides an overview of Service Broker and discusses the key improvements in SQL Server 2008, including message priorities and the SSBDiagnose diagnostic utility.

- Chapter 10 explores the Full-Text Search (FTS) feature in SQL Server 2008, which is more integrated into the database engine than in previous versions of SQL Server.

Part 3, Development in SQL Server: The eight chapters in this part cover topics important to developers, such as Transact-SQL (T-SQL) changes and LINQ to SQL.

- Chapter 11 introduces new datatypes. SQL Server 2008 comes with a bunch of new datatypes, including types for dates and times that are time-zone aware, hierarchical types, and spatial types. You'll also learn about the new filestream feature, which allows for large objects to be stored directly on the file system, while still having the transactional consistency of the database engine.

- Chapter 12 covers T-SQL for developers. T-SQL continues to be evolved in SQL Server 2008. Investments were made in new syntax, including the MERGE statement, which is an ISO/ANSI standard-specified statement that allows users to express multiple Data Manipulation Language (DML) actions (INSERT, UPDATE, and DELETE) against a specified target table based on join conditions with a source table. This and other T-SQL enhancements are discussed in depth in this chapter.

- Chapter 13 covers T-SQL for DBAs. Locking enhancements, filtered indexes, and table partitioning are among the many features that the database administrator should be aware of and utilize in SQL Server 2008.

- Chapter 14 discusses the role of .NET inside SQL Server. It also walks through programming, debugging, and deploying a common language runtime (CLR) stored procedure.

- Chapter 15 expands on the .NET discussion in the previous chapter and includes coverage of user-defined datatypes, functions (both scalar and table-valued), aggregates, and triggers.

- Chapter 16 provides an overview of the XML technology as it relates to SQL Server. It takes a broad look at XPath and XML Schema support in SQL Server 2008, and then drills down into how to get XML into and out of the database.

- Chapter 17 investigates native XML support in SQL Server 2008, via the XML datatype. You'll learn how to create XML columns, insert data into those columns, and then retrieve that XML data using XQuery.

- Chapter 18 covers Language Integrated Query (LINQ), a Microsoft .NET Framework component that adds native data-querying capabilities to .NET languages. This chapter explores the relationship between LINQ and SQL Server.

Part 4, Business Intelligence in SQL Server: The three chapters in this part discuss the tools and features that are the business intelligence offering of Microsoft.

- Chapter 19 covers Reporting Services, an extremely popular feature within the SQL Server product. Investments in the Reporting Services engine were made in SQL Server 2008, allowing it to handle massive amounts of reporting. This chapter covers the core concepts of Reporting Services, as well as the many enhancements to Reporting Services in SQL Server 2008.

- Chapter 20 focuses on Analysis Services. Databases store data, but they become truly profitable when the data can be used and interpreted to provide business intelligence. Powered by a robust Business Intelligence Development Studio (BIDS) environment, SQL Server Analysis Services is a major player in the business intelligence market. This chapter covers the advancements in Analysis Services in SQL Server 2008.

- Chapter 21 covers SQL Server Integration Services, Microsoft's Extract, Transform, and Load (ETL) tool. This chapter guides you through all of the Integration Services concepts, including data flow, control flow, and transformation tasks, using plenty of examples. You'll learn about the new Integration Services tasks, including an enhanced lookup operator that will support more flexible levels of caching. There is also new profiling data quality functionality, which will provide advanced algorithms for identifying patterns within data values.

Errata

Apress makes every effort to make sure that there are no errors in the text or code. However, mistakes happen, and we recognize the need to keep you informed of any mistakes as they're discovered and corrected. An errata sheet will be made available on the book's main page at `http://www.apress.com`. If you find an error that hasn't already been reported, please let us know.

Contacting the Authors

You can contact the book's lead author, Rob Walters, at `Robert.Walters@Microsoft.com`.

Robert E. Walters

PART 1

■ ■ ■

Overview of SQL Server

CHAPTER 1

■ ■ ■

SQL Server 2008 Overview

The previous release of SQL Server, SQL Server 2005, was a major release. It contained a ton of new functionality, including the revision of major query-processing components within the database engine. With SQL Server 2008, the development cycle was much shorter, and the changes are not quite as dramatic. Even though the overall quantity of changes is less than those in SQL Server 2005, the improvements that were made in this new release are specific and significant, and they will absolutely be of value to your organization.

In recent years, one of the trends has been the explosion of data. This massive increase in the quantity of data can be attributed to changes in behavior by consumers and businesses. For consumers, we need to look no further than digital cameras for a great example. With digital cameras, it is now possible to take a thousand different perspectives of your favorite landmark without worrying about film or development costs. All of these digital photos take up cheap disk space and need to be managed for easy searching. As another example, consider the amount of data generated by the medical industry in its daily operations. X-rays are being created and stored in a digital format for easier portability and quicker viewing time (doctors don't need to wait for someone to fetch a patient record from the vault).

The increase of data in recent years comes with a price, and it's not the cost of hardware, as some may think. Although the hardware industry has done a great job of providing low-dollar-per-gigabyte ratios year after year, the increase in digitally born data has sweetened the deal for potential data thieves. This increased security risk, combined with the influx of regulatory compliance laws, such as the Sarbanes-Oxley Act of 2002, has influenced the security features within SQL Server. Security design has been at the core of every feature implementation in SQL Server, and the SQL Server 2008 release is no different. Most of the security-specific improvements, such as auditing and transparent data encryption, are discussed in Chapters 6 and 7 of this book.

The Vision of SQL Server 2008

SQL Server 2008 is driven by a vision consisting of four key pillars: enterprise data platform, beyond relational, dynamic development, and pervasive insight. Although some might think of these catchy names as merely marketing hype, they actually meant something to the product development team.

Microsoft changed the way SQL Server is designed and developed. Specific user scenarios were derived from these core themes, and in the end, actual improvements to the product were made relating to those scenarios. The result is a high-quality release that focuses on the key pain points and industry trends. Here, we'll take a look at each of the pillars and discuss some key features within them. These features, as well as many others, are discussed in more detail in the subsequent chapters of this book.

Enterprise Data Platform

To be classified as an enterprise-ready database means much more than being able to formulate query results really fast. An enterprise database must meet the strict service level agreements established by the organizations using SQL Server. SQL Server 2008 has made improvements in supporting high service level agreements, like the ability to hot-add CPUs. Administrators will also find installing and managing the setup of cluster nodes to be much easier. More information about SQL Server setup and configuration can be found in Chapter 2.

Being an enterprise data platform also means the data that is stored inside the database is secure. SQL Server 2008 continually builds upon its security features. For example, it enables database files to be automatically encrypted with transparent data encryption. The importance of encryption is prominent with Microsoft, opening the door for Hardware Security Module (HSM) and Enterprise Key Management (EKM) vendors to integrate natively with the encryption support in SQL Server 2008. Encrypting data with SQL Server and storing the encrypted keys within the database provide security, but a more secure solution is to store the encryption keys separately from the actual data, and that is where HSM and EKM solutions add value.

Performance has always been a key attribute of an enterprise-ready database. The Data Collector is a feature within SQL Server that gives database administrators (DBAs) the ability to collect performance-related data and store it within a database. This data can be practically anything, such as Performance Monitor counters, results from database management views, and specific queries. Having performance data reside in a database allows for easy data mining and reporting, and that is the key benefit of the Data Collector. Details on this feature are discussed in Chapter 5.

SQL Server 2008 has many new features that validate SQL Server as an enterprise data platform. These features are discussed in detail throughout Part 2 of this book.

Beyond Relational

Data managed within a data platform is more than just relational data. As data growth increases, the types of data stored are no longer the traditional integer, character, and binary values we know and love. New data structures that are important to users are movie files, audio files, and medical images, to name a few. And we not only need to store these new types of data, but we also want to be able to perform useful operations on them, such as indexing and metadata searches.

With SQL Server 2008, investments were made in a feature called *filestream*, which allows files of arbitrary size to be stored in the file system and managed from the database. This capability enables database applications to exceed the 2GB limit. We can essentially place volume-sized binaries directly into SQL Server and obtain the same seek performance we would if we were querying the file system directly, instead of through Transact-SQL (T-SQL). Filestream is discussed in detail in Chapter 11.

SQL Server 2008 also includes support for spatial datatypes. The support conforms to the OpenGIS standards and allows for easy management of global positioning system (GPS) and geographic information system (GIS) data. Having native spatial support also makes it easy and fun to work with spatial applications like Microsoft's Virtual Earth. Spatial data support is also discussed in Chapter 11.

Dynamic Development

Without developer support, platform products such as SQL Server would have died off a long time ago. Microsoft has always made developer productivity a high priority in all of its products. SQL Server 2008 is no exception.

SQL Server 2008 contains improvements in the T-SQL language (discussed in Chapter 12), as well as new date and time datatypes (discussed in Chapter 11) to fill the void that the existing ones created. SQL Server has also integrated itself with the LINQ effort within Microsoft. LINQ provides a higher level of data abstraction, making it really easy to code against disparate data sources. LINQ, as it's related to SQL Server, is discussed in detail in Chapter 18.

Pervasive Insight

Since the inception of Online Analytical Processing (OLAP) services in SQL Server 7.0, Microsoft has continually strived for a self-service business intelligence model. The idea is to allow the average employee to easily ask a business intelligence question and get the results, without needing to go through various layers of DBAs and report developers. Gradually, throughout the releases of SQL Server, we have seen more tools and features that promote this behavior.

At the core of business intelligence is SQL Server Analysis Services. New in Analysis Services are enhanced cube, dimension, and attribute designers. These designers, as well as core improvements related to the monitoring, analysis, and performance tuning of Analysis Services, continually push Microsoft's business intelligence engine further into the leader category of various industry analysts' charts. Analysis Services is discussed in Chapter 20.

In order for Analysis Services to effectively mine data, it needs a great Extract, Transform, and Load (ETL) tool. Investments with SQL Server Integration Services (the replacement for Data Transformation Services in SQL Server 2000) have continued, with the addition of capabilities such as caching transformations, enhanced lookup transformations, data profiling, and a set of expanded data sources. These exciting enhancements are discussed in Chapter 21.

Over the past few years, Microsoft has acquired a few companies in the reporting market. Some of these acquisitions, like Dundas and its graphical reporting controls, have shown up in Reporting Services in SQL Server 2008. The Reporting Services engine has also been upgraded to release its dependency on Internet Information Server (IIS), among other well-anticipated features. Chapter 19 covers Reporting Services in SQL Server 2008.

SQL Server 2008 Editions

At the time of this writing, the SQL Server 2008 editions are essentially the same as those that were available for SQL Server 2005. Five main SQL Server 2008 editions are available:

Enterprise Edition: This is primarily used for business-critical, large-scale online transaction processing (OLTP), large-scale reporting, data warehousing, and server consolidation require-ments. Enterprise Edition comes with more than 60 features that are not found in Standard Edition. Some of these features are significant enough to entice those who have always said that Standard Edition was good enough. Features found only in Enterprise Edition are data and backup compression, audits that use extended events, and Resource Governor, to name a few. The gap of features between Standard Edition and Enterprise Edition is far greater in SQL Server 2008 than it was in SQL Server 2005.

Standard Edition: This edition is primarily used for departmental applications and small to medium-sized OLTP loads. Standard Edition comes with most of the powerful reporting capa-bilities found in SQL Server Reporting Services and makes a great reporting and analytics server as well.

Workgroup Edition: This edition includes the basic SQL Server relational database capabilities, as well as some of the replication technologies. This makes Workgroup Edition good for running branch office applications and performing remote synchronization with other geographically separated servers. Workgroup Edition is considerably less expensive than Standard Edition.

Express Edition: This is the free version of SQL Server. It's ideal for learning and building desktop and small server applications, and for redistribution. Although a lot of the Enterprise Edition functionality is intentionally disabled, the actual SQL Server runtime binary (`sqlservr.exe`) is created with the exact same code base as that of SQL Server Enterprise Edition (and all other editions, for that matter). This makes Express Edition a stable, high-performance database engine for a great price.

Compact Edition: This is the other free SQL Server version, designed to be an embedded database for applications. The ideal use case for Compact Edition is building stand-alone and occasionally connected applications for mobile devices, desktops, and clients.

■**Note** Developer and Evaluation Editions expose the same functionality as Enterprise Edition, but have special licensing restrictions. For example, Microsoft does not allow you to run Developer Edition on your production server.

A Word on Server Consolidation

Currently, many of us are working in companies where the latest cost-saving initiative is that of *server consolidation*. This new buzzword is getting a lot of attention lately. You may be happy to learn that SQL Server 2008 has some features that will help if your organization decides to consolidate.

If we look at why companies consolidate, we find two key motivations behind the effort:

Reduce costs: Consolidation reduces costs through reductions in software licensing fees, technical support costs, and, ultimately, hardware expenses. By using fewer servers, we will generate less heat and consume less electricity, and in the end, we are a bit friendlier to the environment.

Reduce server management complexity: Since SQL Server is a low-cost, enterprise-ready database platform, a lot of application vendors have included SQL Server as part of their solution. This trend, in addition to the proliferation of SQL Server in the enterprise as the organization's critical database, has led to SQL Server sprawl. When the sprawl gets out of hand, administrators do not know how many SQL Server implementations are actually deployed or where a specific database actually resides. Sprawl is much more difficult to administer, secure, and update. Server consolidation can reduce this sprawl.

Now that you are sold on server consolidation, realize that you should not implement server consolidation just for the sake of doing so. If done wrong, consolidation can make things worse. Some applications will not work well in a consolidated environment, and you must ensure that proper testing has been performed before moving consolidated servers into production.

When we talk about server consolidation and SQL Server, it is important to separate the physical hardware and operating system from the software aspect of a SQL Server implementation. From a physical aspect, depending on the hardware vendor, the server can be set up to host different operating systems by physically separating resources like memory and CPU utilization. Certain operating systems have native virtualization capabilities, like Windows Server 2008 and its Hyper-V technology. Hyper-V allows you to create separate virtual machines (VMs) running within a single physical machine. With Hyper-V, you can also efficiently run multiple different operating systems—Windows, Linux, and others—in parallel, on a single server. This exciting new technology in Windows Server 2008 does give VMWare a run for the money in the virtualization market. If you are interested in consolidating via server virtualization on Windows, check out the plethora of information found at `http://www.microsoft.com/virtualization/default.mspx`.

From a database application perspective, consolidation to SQL Server means either consolidating multiple databases on a single server instance or consolidating multiple server instances across multiple physical servers, but fewer than the number of servers the organization currently has.

Generally, in consolidation, we are reducing the number of physical servers and/or software licenses needed for our organization. What an organization actually ends up with as far as how many databases live within each instance and on how many instances live on each physical server is totally dependent on the organization's architecture and the requirements and restrictions for each database.

Consolidation may have some unwanted side effects. Consider the case where we are consolidating two server instances into one. If we have different users for each of these instances, we may have inadvertently given an elevation of privilege to some user accounts with this merger. Consider the case where the sysadmin of server instance 1 has no access to server instance 2, and these two instances are merged. The sysadmin of server instance 1 now has access to the contents that were contained on server instance 2. In security lingo, this is a prime example of an elevation of privilege. Given this example, it is important to emphasize that consolidation will not only put a strain on performance with respect to disk I/O, but it also may create some security issues if not properly designed.

Realize that the final architecture and design of consolidation is only one part of the overall consolidation effort. There are a few key issues that you may need to address, depending on where you fall in terms of responsibility in your organization. Perhaps one of the most important issues is that consolidation needs a buy-in from all parts of the organization. It needs an executive sponsor to help push the monetary considerations through the upper level of management. It also needs a buy-in from the actual workers who will be performing the consolidation. To some people, consolidation means potential job loss, and in some rare circumstances, this may be true. However, in the majority of cases, consolidation will give DBAs more time to work on the more challenging issues facing their organization. With fewer servers to manage, less time needs to be devoted to the mundane tasks of database maintenance.

In addition to buy-ins, if you are a manager, you need to make sure you allocate enough time for your resources. Proper planning and execution takes time, and most DBAs don't usually have any spare free time to dedicate to consolidation.

If you are interested in or are currently involved in a consolidation effort, take a look at the Resource Governor and Policy Management features in SQL Server 2008. Resource Governor, discussed in detail in Chapter 5, gives DBAs the ability to restrict users' or applications' use of SQL Server resources like memory and CPU utilization. Resource Governor was designed to prevent runaway queries from taking over the SQL Server instance, but it also has direct benefits in the SQL Server consolidation scenario.

Policy Management (PM) is another must-consider feature to use in a consolidation effort. Discussed in detail in Chapter 3, PM allows DBAs to define policies and enforce these policies against the SQL Server instances they are managing. For example, imagine a policy that would enforce the Resource Governor settings across all the servers in your organization. Suppose that this enforcement is necessary to maintain the service level agreement that your company's information technology department has with the organization. If another administrator wanted to tweak his server to gain more CPU bandwidth for his own queries, he would be denied. PM enables a plethora of scenarios, not just for consolidation, but in security, naming consistency, and many other areas. The time invested in learning PM is well worth it.

Summary

SQL Server 2008 contains a series of improvements that target scalability, performance, availability, security, and manageability. Keep in mind that some of the improvements mentioned in this book target and benefit multiple scenarios. Data compression is a prime example. This feature, which is discussed in Chapter 5, allows users to compress the storage of data within their tables. When using data compression in the business intelligence scenario, the primary benefit is disk-space savings, since databases used for analytical processing tend to have many repeating and null values. Thus, this feature could have also been discussed in the chapter that covers Analysis Services (Chapter 20).

This book is based on the feature-complete February community technology preview (CTP) release of SQL Server 2008. As with any product that is not shipped, there may some minor changes in the user interfaces shown in this book's screenshots by the time the final version is released.

CHAPTER 2

∎∎∎

SQL Server Installation and Configuration

Those of us who have spent many years in product development might come to the conclusion that one of the least glamorous jobs is to design and code the installation and configuration of a product. This task is often contracted out to consultants, so companies can keep their most talented developers happy working on the complex logic within the product. Alternatively, a company can have great in-house people do the job, but not hire enough staff or not fund that part of the project well enough to build a high-quality setup experience. The latter seems to be the case with previous versions of SQL Server.

Microsoft has now realized that the first impression of the product is the setup and configuration experience. Microsoft has definitely invested in this experience in SQL Server 2008, and it shows. The experience of installation and configuration of SQL Server 2008 can be summarized in a single word: pleasant. Not only is the user interface clean, but there are also extra wizards that help you set up and configure the more complicated features like clustering. In general, you will find SQL Server 2008 easy to install, thanks to all the hard work that the setup team did in completely redesigning the experience for SQL Server 2008. If any Microsoft managers are reading this, please give the members of the team a few hundred dollars bonus on their next review.

This chapter covers the following topics:

- Requirements for SQL Server 2008
- Pre-upgrade tasks
- The Upgrade Advisor tool
- SQL Server 2008 installation

SQL Server Requirements

The minimum RAM required to run SQL Server is 512MB, with 1GB recommended if you are planning to use SQL Server to handle larger workloads.

For disk space, you neeed 290MB. Disk space is cheap. Even if you are installing SQL Server on a desktop machine, you probably have at least a few gigabytes free. If you are concerned that you don't have 290MB free to install just the database engine, you probably have some other problems to deal with first. The exact space requirements depend on what you install. SQL Server Books Online does a great job at enumerating specifically what each components takes as far as disk space is concerned, in an article appropriately titled "Hardware and Software Requirements for Installing SQL Server 2008." (SQL Server Books Online is available online from `http://msdn.microsoft.com`.)

SQL Server 2008 works on almost all flavors of Windows: XP, Vista, Windows Server 2003, and Windows Server 2008. But do watch out for the service pack requirements. As an example, the February Community Technology Preview (CTP) release requires Service Pack 2 if you are running SQL Server on Windows Server 2003. If your organization takes a while to move to service packs, you may want to factor this into your deployment schedule.

Upgrading to SQL Server 2008

Setup supports a direct upgrade from SQL Server 2000 and 2005. Those of you still on SQL 7.0 will need to upgrade to SQL Server 2000 or 2005 first before upgrading to SQL Server 2008. Since the product development cycle was shorter than that of SQL Server 2005, the changes and issues involved with upgrading from SQL Server 2005 to SQL Server 2008 are minimal compared with the move from SQL Server 2000 to SQL Server 2008.

You can upgrade to SQL Server in two ways:

- *Direct in-place upgrade*: SQL Server setup does the heavy lifting of updating the necessary binary files and upgrades all the attached databases to the new version's format.

- *Side-by-side upgrade*: This is sometimes referred to as a *migration*. It essentially installs a fresh SQL Server 2008 instance alongside the instance that is to be upgraded. This process is mostly manual, since the idea is for the database administrator (DBA) to copy over the databases and configuration information to the new server. Once this information is copied and attached, the DBA can verify that the applications work correctly.

The in-place upgrade is the more automated of the two options, but might not be the best option for some organizations. An in-place upgrade takes down the server for a duration of time, and without previous testing, who knows what will happen after the upgrade is complete? The positive aspect of the in-place upgrade is that when the upgrade is completed, the instance name of the new SQL Server is the same as it was pre-upgrade, so existing applications do not need to change any connection string information. With a side-by-side upgrade, the new installation uses a new instance name, so applications might need to have their connection string information changed to point to the new instance.

To help you with the upgrade, Microsoft released a free tool called Upgrade Advisor, which essentially scans your existing SQL Server instance and gives you a report on any potential issues you will have after the upgrade. But before we talk about using Upgrade Advisor, we need to discuss planning the upgrade. If you were going to simply upgrade your production servers without a plan, then you may want to consider freshening up your resumé. A plan is critical to the success of an upgrade.

Planning the Upgrade

A smooth upgrade requires a good plan. Before you upgrade, you need to prepare your environment. The pre-upgrade tasks include the following:

- *Ensure the server hardware that will host SQL Server 2008 will be sufficient.* The server hardware should meet the minimum hardware requirements, such as the amount of available RAM and disk space. The operating system on the server hardware should also contain the latest service pack or the minimum service pack required by SQL Server 2008.

- *Inventory the applications that will use the upgraded server.* This list will be used to validate that your upgrade was successful. After upgrade, run through the list and verify that all the applications work correctly, if possible.

- *Take note of the cross-edition upgrade matrix.* Some upgrade scenarios, like upgrading from SQL Server 2005 Enterprise Edition to SQL Server 2008 Standard Edition, are not supported with an in-place upgrade. SQL Server Books Online describes various upgrade scenarios in an article titled "Version and Edition Upgrades."

- *Take performance benchmarks.* In some situations, upgrading may actually decrease query performance. This is usually observed when upgrading from SQL Server 2000, since the query processor internal to the database engine was rewritten in SQL Server 2005. This rewrite causes a different query plan to be created from the queries that you issue. The good news is that most of the time, your queries will run better out of the box in SQL Server 2008. In the rare case that you find your queries running worse, it's possible to save query plans so there will be no surprises after you upgrade. This feature is described in more detail in Chapter 5.

- *Use the Upgrade Advisor tool.* Upgrade Advisor is a free, stand-alone application that connects to a SQL Server instance and performs an analysis to determine if any issues need to be addressed before upgrading. It also will analyze script and trace files. Results of this tool should be carefully reviewed and addressed before proceeding with the upgrade. The Upgrade Advisor tool is discussed in the next section.

- *Fix or work around backward-compatability issues.* The Upgrade Advisor tool will note any backward-compatibility issues. In most cases, when a feature or behavior is changed, Microsoft announces a deprecation of that feature or functionality. This deprecation will last for three releases; in the fourth release, the feature or functionality will be removed from the product. In some rare cases, Microsoft needs to modify or remove a feature without going through the formal deprecation procedure. Thus, if you used this feature and then upgraded, it's possible that your application would not work as you expected. It is important to address these backward-compatibility issues before upgrading your SQL Server instance.

- *Create a back-out plan.* If you have done your homework, the upgrade experience should go seamlessly. In the event of something going wrong during the upgrade, you may need to revert back to your original system configuration. This may involve more steps than just canceling the setup wizard. For this reason, it is good to have a formal back-out plan.

- *Understand upgrade or migration for each component within SQL Server.* When performing an upgrade of a database, most people tend to think about just the relational data. If all you are using SQL Server for is to store relational data, then either using the setup wizard to perform an in-place upgrade or migrating the data using a backup/restore or a detach/attach technique might be sufficient. However, if you use other technologies, you may need to be aware of other issues.

The last item is particularly important, because different components may have different upgrade paths. For example, if you're using Analysis Services, with an in-place upgrade, you can use the setup wizard just as you would with upgrading the database engine. To perform a migration, you can use the Migration Wizard tool available from the server node context menu off of an analysis server connection in SQL Server Management Studio. If you have Analysis Services projects written using Business Intelligence Development Studio (BIDS), you can simply import into BIDS in SQL Server 2008.

With another component within the SQL Server product, Reporting Services, the migration process is slightly different. Again, if you choose to perform an in-place upgrade, the setup wizard will perform most of the heavy lifting. If you choose to migrate, there is a list of things to do. SQL Server Books Online describes the migration of Reporting Services very well in an article entitled "How to: Migrate a Reporting Services Installation."

As you can see, it is imperative to consider all the components that you are using within the SQL Server product.

■**Note** For a definitive list of migration steps, refer to the appropriate "How to: Migrate . . ." Books Online topics. Note that at the time of this writing, not all migration topics were defined for each component.

Using Upgrade Advisor

The Upgrade Advisor (UA) tool is available on the SQL Server 2008 installation disks, in the Servers\Redist\Upgrade Advisor folder. It will also be available as a free download from http://microsoft.com/downloads.

Here, we'll walk through an example of running UA against a SQL Server 2005 instance.

1. Launch UA. You will be presented with the welcome screen, as shown in Figure 2-1.

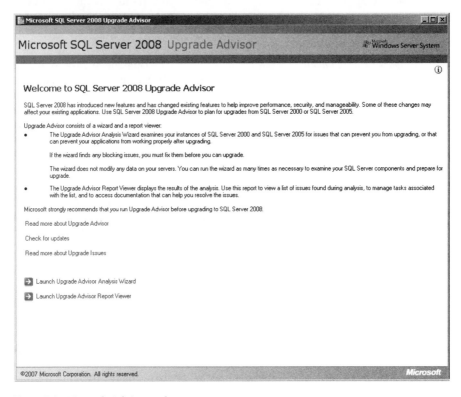

Figure 2-1. *Upgrade Advisor welcome screen*

2. Click the Launch Upgrade Advisor Analysis Wizard link. You will see the familiar welcome screen, and then the SQL Server Components page, as shown in Figure 2-2.

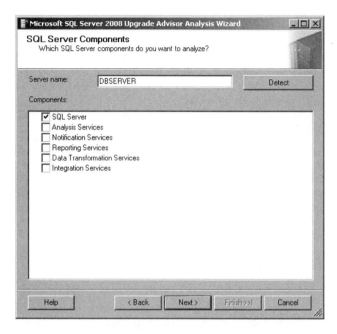

Figure 2-2. *Choosing SQL Server components*

3. Type the name of a server and click Detect. The wizard will determine the components that are installed on that instance. In this example, we are checking a SQL Server 2005 instance. We enter the server name, DBSERVER. Since all we are interested in testing is the SQL Server database engine, we check SQL Server and click Next to continue.

4. Next, you see the Connection Parameters page, as shown in Figure 2-3. Specify the instance name (PROD in this example) and the credentials used to connect to this server instance (Windows Authentication in this example). Click Next to continue.

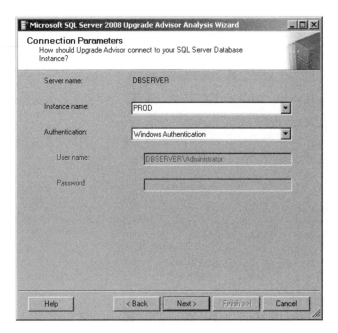

Figure 2-3. *Specifying connection parameters*

5. The next wizard page is where you select which databases to analyze, provide a separate trace file, and pass a path to SQL batch files, as shown in Figure 2-4. UA can analyze all of these items. Click Next to continue.

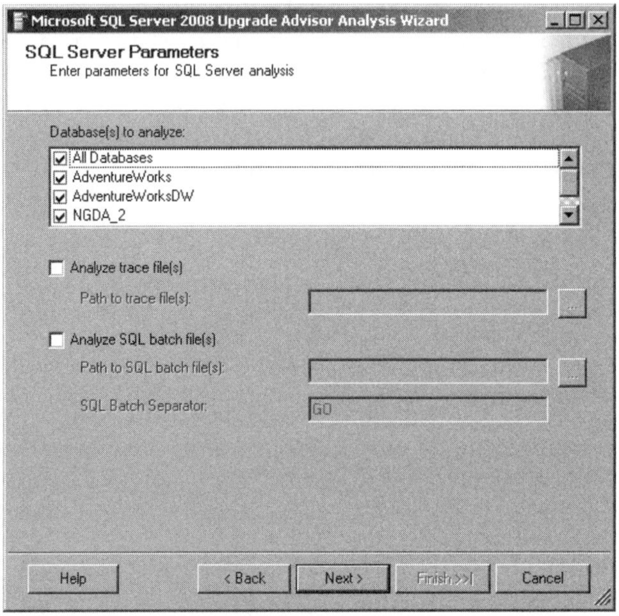

Figure 2-4. *Choosing SQL Server parameters*

6. The next page shows a summary of the options you selected. Click Next, and UA goes to work, churning through all the stored procedures, metadata, and objects within the databases you selected.

7. When the analysis is complete, UA will display the results. In our simple example, when the SQL Server 2005 instance was scanned, the wizard presented the warning shown in Figure 2-5.

Figure 2-5. *Completed UA analysis*

8. Click Launch Report. You will see a list of issues that UA found, as in the example in Figure 2-6. Each item has an Issue Resolved check box. Checking this box will remove the item from the list. This way, it's really easy to keep track of which issues are already resolved and which ones remain to be addressed.

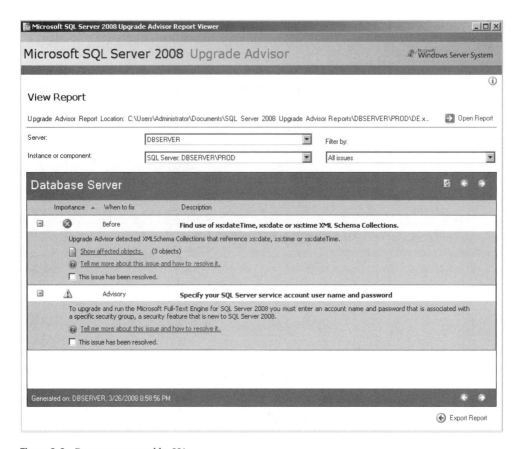

Figure 2-6. *Report generated by UA*

UA creates a directory under the My Documents folder to store its reporting information. UA allows you to analyze multiple servers. For each server analyzed, a subfolder is created. To view reports, click the Launch Upgrade Advisor Report Viewer link from the main UA screen (Figure 2-1).

■**Note** Each time you run UA against the same server, it overwrites the information saved from a prior run of UA.

You'll notice in this example that the number of issues upgrading SQL Server 2005 to SQL Server 2008 was fairly minimal. If you are upgrading from SQL Server 2000, expect the list to be a bit longer.

Performing the Upgrade

Now that you have decided on what type of upgrade you will perform and have gone through all the items in the pre-upgrade tasks list, it is time to perform the actual upgrade.

Before you go ahead and run the setup wizard, or start migrating data from your original SQL Server instance, it is important to make sure your environment is ready for the upgrade. The first task is to check the database consistency for those databases being upgraded. This is as simple as issuing a DBCC CHECKDB command against each of the databases for the instance you are upgrading.

After you've checked your databases for consistency, take a backup of all the databases in your SQL Server instance. When the backups are complete, verify the backups as well to ensure their own consistency. At this point, you are ready to start the upgrade or migration process.

In this section, we will walk through a basic installation of SQL Server 2008. Although there is a nice HTML user interface that can be brought up when you insert the SQL Server media, we chose to run the setup program directly from the Servers folder on the SQL Server installation disk.

The first thing the setup program does is to detect whether you have .NET Framework 3.5 installed. If you do not, it installs that version of the .NET Framework. Next, you are presented with the infamous license agreement to which you must agree in order to proceed. Then setup will copy some support files. Once this is complete, the real installation begins.

You will see the SQL Server Installation Center screen, as shown in Figure 2-7. From here, you can create a new installation, upgrade an existing SQL Server instance, and create or change an existing clustering configuration.

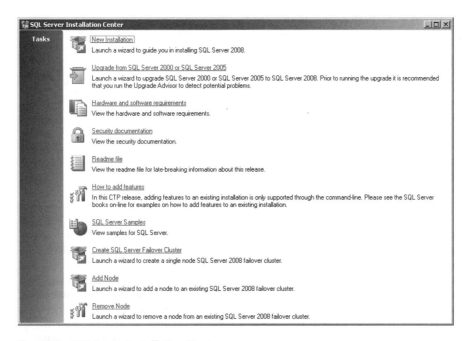

Figure 2-7. *SQL Server Installation Center screen*

Clustering support in setup is of great value. If you are running SQL Server 2008 on Windows Server 2008, you are already gaining a huge number of features, including support for up to 16 nodes and an ease on restrictions like the requirement that nodes be on the same subnet. This means that Geoclusters are now a viable option for SQL Server deployments. A *Geocluster* is a clustering config-uration where the active and passive servers are physically separated by large geographical distances.

These types of clustering configurations required special considerations during deployment. Windows Server 2008 implemented features that makes Geoclustering easier. The increased support for clusters doesn't end with what Windows Server 2008 provides to SQL Server 2008. The SQL Server Installation Center offers access to a few wizards to make it really easy for administrators to set up and maintain a clustered configuration.

In this example, we are installing a new instance of SQL Server 2008 on a server that already has SQL Server 2005 installed. This is what is known as a side-by-side configuration. When we choose New Installation from the SQL Server Installation Center screen, the New Installation Wizard starts. This wizard will immediately perform a system configuration check, as shown in Figure 2-8.

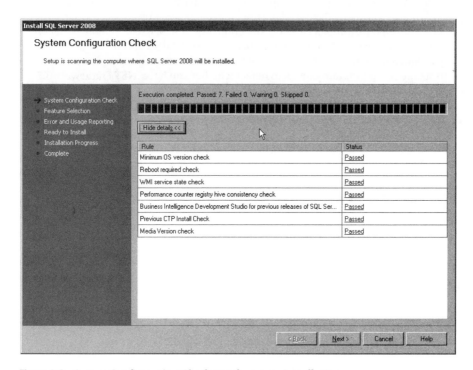

Figure 2-8. *System Configuration Check step for a new installation*

If you fail the system configuration check, you won't be able to continue installation unless you address the issue. SQL Server is fairly strict on the requirements for service packs. For example, if you are using Windows Server 2003, you must have at least Service Pack 2 installed.

Once you have passed the checks, you are ready to select which components to install, as shown in Figure 2-9. The setup program allows for a variety of configurations. You can use it to install just the client tools, SQL Server Books Online, or every feature, as shown in Figure 2-9. Once you have made your selections, the wizard will dynamically add steps as needed.

In our example, we are installing SQL Server 2008 side-by-side with SQL Server 2005. You can see the existing SQL Server instance that is already installed on this server, as shown in Figure 2-10. From this page, you can set the instance name, ID, and root directory for the new SQL Server 2008 instance.

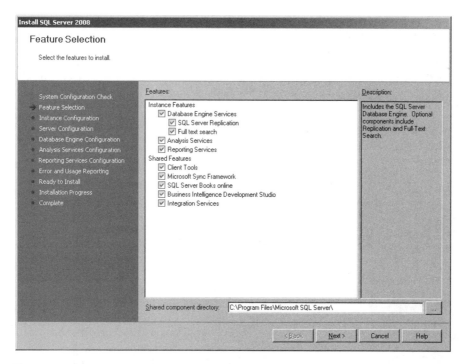

Figure 2-9. *Feature Selection step for a new installation*

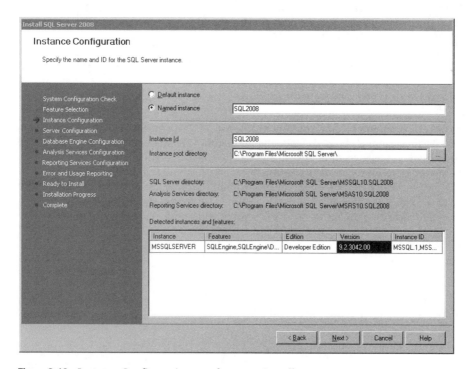

Figure 2-10. *Instance Configuration step for a new installaton*

The Server Configuration page, shown in Figure 2-11, is where you enter credentials for the various services that will be installed. This user interface is much more intuitive than in previous versions of SQL Server. You can clearly see which services are assigned to which accounts. You can even apply the same account and password to all services, using the fields at the bottom of the page. Although this is not a security best practice, if your organization allows the same credentials to be used, clicking the Apply to All button saves a lot of typing.

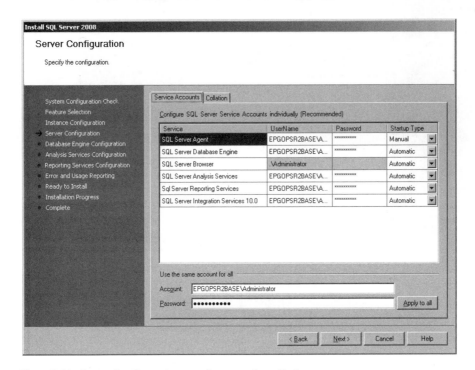

Figure 2-11. *Server Configuration step for a new installation*

The Server Configuration page also contains a Collation tab. With the SQL Server 2008 setup, you'll find that the most commonly used and configured settings are presented to you directly, and the more advanced or less used features are usually available on a different tab.

Since in this example, we requested that setup install the database engine, we are presented with a page that will allow us to provide some key configuration information, as shown in Figure 2-12. While the security mode is nothing new, having to specify a SQL Server administrator is. By default, there is no one defined to be the administrator. You must provide a valid username for this purpose.

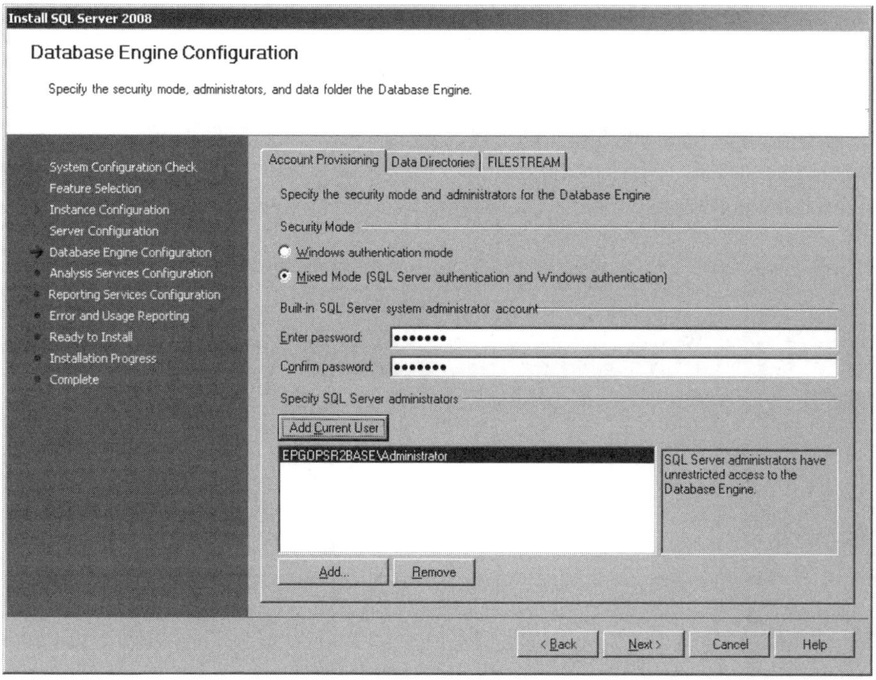

Figure 2-12. *Database Engine Configuration step for a new installation*

The Data Directories tab of the Database Engine Configuration page, shown in Figure 2-13, allows users to change the directories of all the database files. To change the root location for all directories in one shot, just change the Data Root Directory setting. This feature would never make the key bullet points of the product, yet it's subtle but useful improvements like this that make the setup experience much more pleasant than with earlier versions.

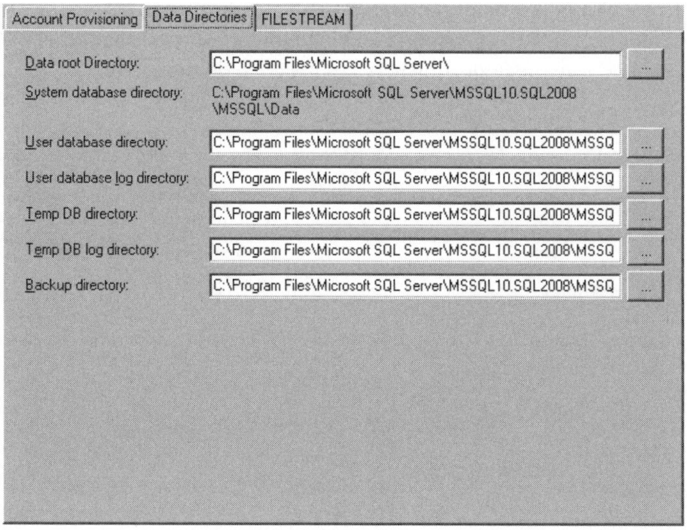

Figure 2-13. *Data Directories tab of the Database Engine Configuration page*

While there aren't a lot of options to configure with respect to Analysis Services, you can easily add the current user as an administrator, as shown in Figure 2-14. The Data Directories tab allows you to specify which directories you want to use for the data, log, temp, and backup files.

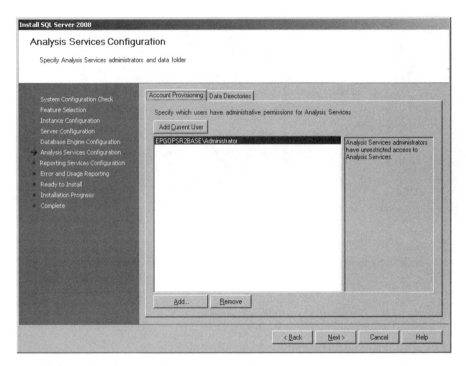

Figure 2-14. *Analysis Services Configuration step for a new installation*

Since we also wanted to install Reporting Services, the wizard added a Reporting Services Configuration page, as shown in the Figure 2-15. This page allows you to install Reporting Services and perform the configuration later, install in SharePoint mode, or install and configure Reporting Services as part of the initial installation. As with SQL Server 2005, Reporting Services contains a configuration tool that is used to configure the Reporting Services instance on the server.

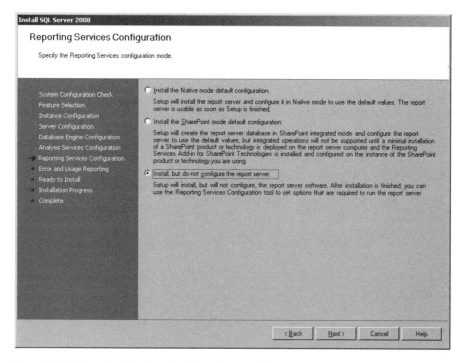

Figure 2-15. *Reporting Services Configuration step for a new installation*

The next page is the Error and Usage Reporting page. It contains two check boxes, which basically ask you if it's OK if SQL Server periodically sends usage information to Microsoft. This transmission doesn't contain any personal data. The information that is obtained is intended to answer questions about how you use the product. The results of these queries across many organizations throughout the world ultimately allow Microsoft to design a better product.

At this point, you are ready to begin installation of the product. As with other software installation procedures, you are kept up-to-date on the installation progress. If for any reason something fails to install, you will be able to read the setup log files, which are located on the installation drive under the path `Program Files\Microsoft SQL Server\100\Setup Bootstrap\Log`. The setup program will create multiple text files that you can sift through. To troubleshoot, start with the text file with the word *Summary* in it. That should give you a hint as to which component had the problem.

Summary

The installation and configuration experience has been overhauled in SQL Server 2008. Users will find a more usable user interface, with critical parameters easily configurable and more esoteric options accessible yet not cluttering up the wizard. Not only was the user interface improved, but additional wizards were implemented to help configure complicated tasks such as clustering. Installing SQL Server is a much more pleasant experience with SQL Server 2008.

PART 2

Enterprise Data Platform

CHAPTER 3

■ ■ ■

Policy Management

Policy Management (PM) is a policy-based framework for SQL Server. This book will use "PM," but the formal term has recently been changed to "policy-based management" (PBM). This policy engine can be thought of much like the group policy feature within the Windows operating system. With Windows group policies, administrators create policies like "user passwords must be a certain length" and "the client machine must not allow the installation of applications." Users and other resources can then be grouped into organizational units (OUs), and these policies can be applied to one or more OUs. PM within SQL Server allows database administrators (DBAs) to create SQL Server policies and deploy these policies across multiple servers. Examples of SQL Server policies include "ensure xp_cmdshell is never enabled on the server" and "ensure data and log files do not reside on the same drive."

Policies can be scheduled to run periodically or run on demand. In addition, the policy will either simply log the violation or proactively prevent an action from occurring by rolling back the transaction and raising an error.

In this chapter, we will cover the following topics:

- Needs addressed by PM

- Components that make up PM

- A walk-through of implementing a standardized naming convention policy

- PM administration

Needs Addressed by Policy Management

It is a fair assumption to say that each time a new SQL Server version comes out, it will have more features. As time goes on, we train ourselves on this new product, and then another one is introduced. Eventually, we will see features within the product that we never knew existed. These features will expose more controls and properties than we probably care to learn. With an increase in the amount of feature controls comes a need to manage by intent, rather than directly managing each and every knob on a feature. For an analogy, consider Internet Explorer's Tools/Options dialog box back in the version 4 days. It was basically a checked list box of every imaginable switch you could control. Enable ActiveX Controls and Enable Cookies were some of the options available. Most nontechnical people would just leave the Enable ActiveX Controls check box checked and continue web surfing, not realizing the potential security impact of that decision. Later versions of Internet Explorer have a single setting, Security Level, with the options of High, Medium, or Low. Under the covers, these are combinations of many of the switches in the earlier versions, but in a more simplified representation. PM in SQL Server 2008 addresses this need for management by intent.

Another change in the information technology industry is that of consolidation of data centers. In 2006, Hewlett-Packard announced that it planned to consolidate its 85 data centers into just 6 worldwide. With this drastic change, do you think they will be hiring more DBAs to manage these servers? Probably not many, if any at all. This increase of server management responsibilities amplifies the need for virtualized management. With virtualized management, it should be as simple as creating a server configuration and deploying this configuration across one or more servers. Virtualized management should allow DBAs the ability to define logical groups of servers and create or deploy different configurations for these various groups. PM in SQL Server 2008 addresses this need for virtualized management.

Let's face it—hiring a DBA is not cheap for companies. "Do more with less" is an often overused statement and one we all tend to live by in our day-to-day lives. This philosophy is also embedded in our database architectures. Imagine a retail company that has 50 stores across a geographic region. In each one of these stores, there is a SQL Server database replicating sales and inventory data back to the corporate headquarters. Do you think that there is a DBA staffed at each one of these retail store outlets? Probably not. Most likely, the DBAs are staffed at headquarters and responsible for maintaining the remote databases. Thus, it is critical that a system be in place to proactively ensure that the configuration of these remote servers remains consistent. PM in SQL Server 2008 addresses this need for intelligent monitoring.

Policy Management Components

PM contains a plethora of concepts and definitions. To help explain these, we'll consider a standard naming convention scenario as an example. Suppose that the development management team has come out with guidelines describing the proper naming convention to be used in your organization, with the following specific requirements:

- All table names within the Staging database must start with the characters tbl.

- Anyone attempting to issue a Data Definition Language (DDL) statement to create or alter a table with a name that does not start with tbl will have that transaction aborted.

- All tables must be created in the developer or test schema.

Keeping this scenario in mind, let's start reviewing the key components that make up PM.

Managed Targets

A *managed target* defines which entity you want to manage. These entities that PM is able to manage in SQL Server 2008 all reside within a SQL Server instance. Examples of entities include the instance of SQL Server itself, a database, a table, or a schema. Note that these entities by themselves can form a natural hierarchy.

As an example, a database contains objects like tables and stored procedures. Thus, if you define a database as a target, you have the ability to apply a set of target filters to obtain a more specific target, like "only databases that are greater than 1GB in size."

In the example, you would like a filtered database target that is described as "all tables within the Staging' database." You can create this filter using a PM condition, as described shortly.

Facets

Each managed target has various properties and behaviors associated with it. For example, a database has properties that describe things like collation, default filegroup, whether it's a snapshot, and its last backup date. PM exposes these properties through a management *facet*. Facets not only model properties of a target, but they sometimes also model behaviors. For example, a behavior within the Database Maintenance facet is DataAndBackupOnSeparateLogicalVolumes, which returns whether or not the database has its data and backup files on separate logical volumes.

Table 3-1 lists all the available facets and examples of some of the facet properties. To see a complete list of properties of a facet, select to view the properties of a facet in SQL Server Management Studio.

■**Note** Table 3-1 shows only some selected properties exposed by a particular facet. Most facets contain a plethora of properties. For the complete list of properties of a particular facet, refer to SQL Server Books Online.

Table 3-1. *Management Facets*

Facet	Examples of Facet Properties
Application Role	Date and time of role creation and modification; the default schema for the application role
Asymmetric Key	Encryption key length; encryption key algorithm; owner of the key
Audit	Audit destination, audit file path, behavior when writing an audit record fails
Backup Device	Type of backup device; path to device or filename
Cryptopgraphic Provider	Whether symmetric or asymmetric keys can be created or imported; authentication support of provider
Database	Number of active connections to database; whether Service Broker is enabled; whether change tracking is enabled; space used by data; default schema; default filegroup
Database Audit Specification	Audit name that belongs to this specification; enabled status
Database DDL Trigger	Execution context of trigger; whether trigger is enabled; whether trigger is encrypted; assembly information
Database Options	Exposes many options, including AutoShrink, AutoClose, RecoveryModel, and Trustworthy
Database Role	Whether role is fixed role or user-defined role; name and owner of role
Data File	Filename; growth properties; file size; usage information
Database Maintenance	Whether data and backup files are on separate logical volumes; dates of last backups; recovery model; database status
Database Performance	Whether data and log files are on separate logical volumes; whether collation matches master or model; whether database automatically closes or shrinks
Database Security	Whether the database trustworthy bit is set; whether the database owner is a sysadmin
File Group	Whether this filegroup is a default; whether filestream is enabled on this filegroup; the size of the filegroup; whether filegroup is read-only
Index	Fill factor; file space used; associated partition scheme
Linked Server	Name; whether it is a publisher or subscriber; query timeout
Log File	Filename; file growth; current size information
Login	Whether login is disabled; whether password is expired; whether user must change password; SID for login account
Multipart Name	Name information of an object, including name and schema
Resource Governor	Classifier Function; enabled status

Continued

Table 3-1. *Continued*

Facet	Examples of Facet Properties
Resource Pool	Maximum and minimum CPU and memory limits
Rule	Date and time of rule creation and modification; rule name and associated schema
Schema	Name and owner of schema
Server	Backup directory; audit level; default collation; whether instance is clustered; path to master database
Server Audit	Whether C2 auditing is enabled; whether default trace is enabled
Server Audit Specification	Audit name that belongs to this specification; enabled status
Server Configuration	Affinity masks; maximum memory and worker threads; query governor cost limit; whether SQLMail is enabled
Server DDL Trigger	Execution context; whether trigger is encrypted; whether trigger is system object
Server Information	Server instance collation; SQL Server edition; error log file path; whether instance is clustered; physical RAM
Server Performance	Affinity masks; whether lightweight pooling is enabled; maximum worker threads; network packet size
Server Security	Whether command shell rights are enabled only for `sysadmin` users; authenticaion mode of SQL Server; proxy accout configuration and status
Server Settings	Backup file location; number of log files used; polling behavior of Performance Monitor
Stored Procedure	Execution context; assembly information; whether the stored procedure is encrypted or system object
Surface Area Configuration	Configuration parameters that are off by default, such as whether the CLR is enabled, whether Database Mail is enabled, and whether to allow `xp_cmdshell`
Surface Area Configuration for Analysis Services	Security-related configuration settings for Analysis Services
Surface Area Configuration for Reporting Services	Security-related configuration settings for Reporting Services
Symmetric Key	Encryption key length; encryption key algorithm; owner of key
Synonym	Base server; database; schema; object
Table	Data space used; assigned filegroup, whether it has a clustered index; size of index
Trigger	Execution context; whether trigger is encrypted; whether trigger is system object; whether a deletion will fire this trigger
User	Login; user type; whether user has database access; SID
User-Defined Function	Execution context; function type; whether function is encrypted; table variable name parameter
User-Defined Type	Assembly name; collation; whether type is fixed length; whether type is nullable
View	Creation and modification information; whether view has index; whether view is encrypted; whether view is schema-bound
Workload Group	Maximum degree of parallelism; Importance
XML Schema Collection	Creation and modification information; XML Schema collection

In the standard naming convention example, you are concerned with the names of tables and the schemas where the table resides. You want a facet that exposes a name property and schema property for a table. Looking at the list of available facets in Table 3-1, you can see that the Multipart Name facet fits this description. This facet exposes these properties from any of these managed targets: stored procedures, synonyms, tables, user-defined functions, user-defined types, views, and XML Schema collections. Now that you have found your facet, it is time to create a condition.

Conditions

Facets by themselves state only the facts. For PM to be useful, we want to define certain conditions that are interesting to us as administrators, such as "when database file size is greater than 5GB" or "when schema is equal to developer." For this, we have *conditions*, which are Boolean expressions defined on a specific management facet. They specify a set of valid states of the management facet.

To create a new condition, connect to SQL Server using SQL Server Management Studio and navigate down to the Policy Management node, under the Management node of the server instance. Right-click this node and choose to create a new condition. You will see the New Condition dialog box, as shown in Figure 3-1.

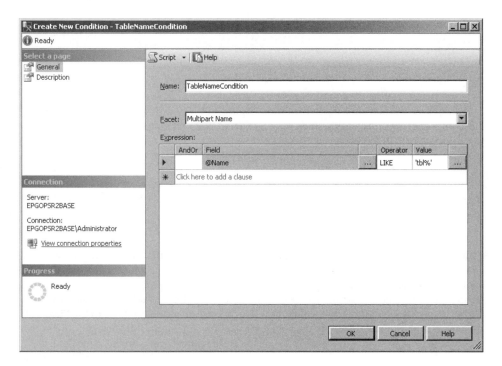

Figure 3-1. *Creating a new PM condition*

The Facet drop-down list shows all the facets listed in Table 3-1. In order to define a condition, you must specify a facet. For this example, selecte Multipart Name as the facet, and you will see the options @Name and @Schema in the grid's Field column, as shown in Figure 3-2.

Figure 3-2. *Field column showing properties of selected facet*

The Field column in the grid is populated with properties available for the selected facet. If you had selected the Backup Device facet instead, for example, the Field list would change to those properties that are exposed by the Backup Device facet. This dialog box is also smart enough to know which kinds of values apply to which fields. For example, if you selected @BackupDeviceType, the Value column would be populated with possible backup device types, as shown in Figure 3-3.

Figure 3-3. *Value column showing properties of selected field*

Returning to the sample table name condition (Figure 3-2), you want to specify the @Name field and change the operator to LIKE, since you want a partial string match, rather than an equality. Next, put the value tbl% in the Value cell of the grid.

Note In the current build of SQL Server 2008, you must enclose strings in the Value cell within single quotes. So, for the example, you must enter 'tbl%'. This may not be required in the final version of SQL Server 2008, since it is not very intuitive to the user.

At this point, you could click OK, and you would have a condition that checks only if the first three characters of the Name property are tbl. However, for the example, you need a more complex expression. You want to make sure the first three characters of the Name property are tbl *and* that the schema of the table is only within the developer schema or the test schema. To add the first schema restriction, click the AndOr cell on the next line in the grid and select AND. In the Field cell, select @Schema, and put 'developer' in the Value cell, as shown in Figure 3-4. Then click the AndOr cell below that, select OR, select @Schema in the Field cell, and enter 'test' in the Value field.

	AndOr	Field		Operator	Value	
▶		@Name	...	LIKE	'tbl%'	...
	AND	@Schema	...	=	'developer'	...
✱	Click here to add a clause					

Figure 3-4. *Building an expression using expression grid*

It is also possible to create groups of expressions. In the example, you also need to group both @Schema fields, since the logic would be incorrect if you did not. This grouping can be done by selecting both the @Schema rows, right-clicking, and selecting Group Clauses, as shown in Figure 3-5.

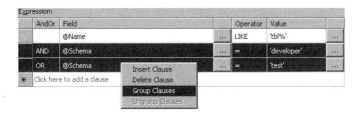

Figure 3-5. *Grouping expression clauses*

At this point, you have created a condition whose Boolean expression evaluates to true when the name of a table contains `tbl` as the first three characters and the schema for the table is either in the `developer` schema or the `test` schema. The final configuration for the condition is shown in Figure 3-6.

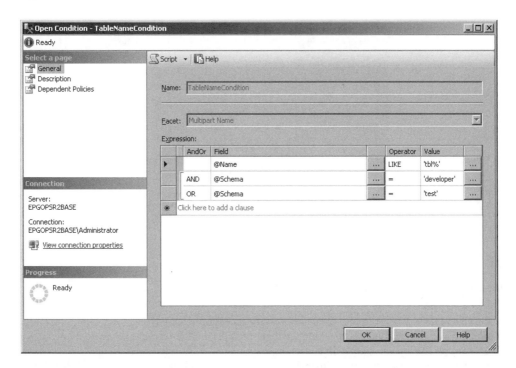

Figure 3-6. *A configured condition*

Policies

A *policy* binds a condition against its expected behavior. To create a policy, right-click the Policies node in Object Explorer and select New Policy. For this example, enter the name TableNamePolicy for the policy and select TableNameCondition for the check. You will be presented with a list of objects to apply this policy against, as shown in Figure 3-7.

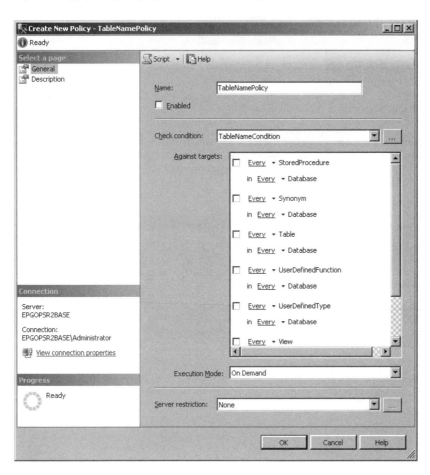

Figure 3-7. *Creating a new policy*

This list in the Against Targets box is based on the facet you selected for the condition. If you had selected a condition that was checking the database file size, for example, you would only be allowed to apply this policy against database targets.

Since this example is concerned only with tables within a database, check the Every Table check box. The *Every* words in the Against Target box are links that reveal a drop-down list that allow for further filtering. Click the Every link beneath the check box you just selected to see the list of available conditions for a database, as shown in Figure 3-8.

Figure 3-8. *Options to filter targets within the policy*

Since you want to apply this policy only for the Staging database, select New Condition. You will see the dialog box for creating a new condition, with the Database facet already selected. Finish the creation of this condition by specifying @Name = 'Staging', as shown in Figure 3-9.

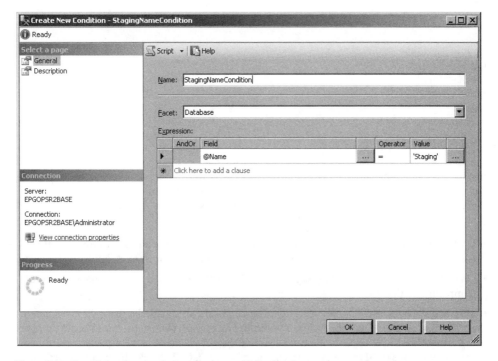

Figure 3-9. *Condition for restricting the name of the database*

■**Note** At the time of writing this chapter, when we created our StagingNameCondition, this new condition was not automatically selected under Every Database. We needed to click the Every drop-down list and select StagingNameCondition.

At this point, your Against Targets box should look like Figure 3-10.

☐ Every ▾ StoredProcedure
   in Every ▾ Database

☐ Every ▾ Synonym
   in Every ▾ Database

☑ Every ▾ Table
   in StagingNameCondition ▾ Database

☐ Every ▾ UserDefinedFunction
   in Every ▾ Database

☐ Every ▾ UserDefinedType
   in Every ▾ Database

☐ Every ▾ View
   in Every ▾ Database

☐ Every ▾ XmlSchemaCollection
   in Every ▾ Database

Figure 3-10. *Specifying the targets for the new policy*

In addition to creating your own conditions, you can use one of the predefined conditions that come as part of the SQL Server 2008 sample policies, which are described in the next section.

The Execution Mode option beneath the Against Targets list controls when the policy is applied. The choices are as follows:

- *On Demand*: When a policy is defined, it is applied only when the administrator proactively runs the policy against the server. This is the default selection for when to apply the policy.

- *On Change – Prevent*: Changes are attempted. They will be aborted if the changes are out of compliance with the policy.

- *On Change – Log Only*: Changes are attempted. A log entry is created if the policy is violated. So, the processing will proceed without error, but an event will be written into history tables in the msdb database. These tables can be viewed directly via the `syspolicy_policy_execution_history` view or `syspolicy_policy_execution_history_detail` view, or by simply selecting View History from the Policies context menu.

- *On Schedule*: The policy is checked on a scheduled basis. A log entry is created for policies that are violated. This option schedules a policy check via the SQL Server Agent. With this option, you can pick from an existing schedule or create a new schedule to run the policy check job.

For this example, choose On Change – Prevent, to abort the transaction if it violates the policy.

By default, this policy can run on any server to which it is applied. If this policy should run only on certain types of servers (for example, only when the server instance is SQL Server 2000 or only when the instance is an Enterprise Edition), you can apply a predefined condition or create your own. Use the Server Restriction drop-down list to pick the desired condition for the server type, if any.

The Create New Policy dialog box also contains a page called Description, where you can provide some extra information that will be presented when the policy has been violated. Figure 3-11 shows an example.

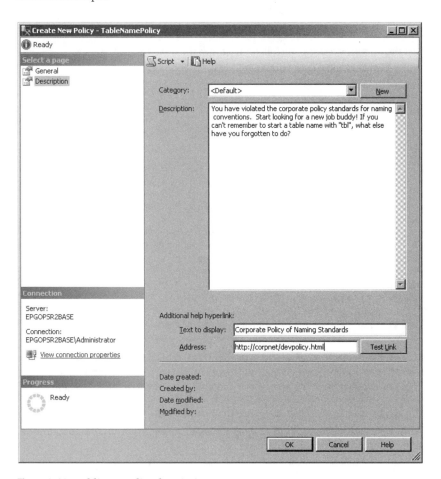

Figure 3-11. *Adding a policy description*

As a policy editor, you are free to put whatever text you deem suitable in the Description box. Obviously, one might not want to be as candid as in Figure 3-11 if this policy is defined on a live server.

You can also add a hyperlink as part of the policy violation error. This hyperlink will be displayed along with the description text.

To complete your policy definition for this example, check the Enabled check box on the General page of the dialog box. Click OK, and your policy is created and actively in use.

■**Note** By default, policies (even the predefined ones that come with SQL Server 2008) are not enabled. Thus, if you create a policy and wonder why it's not working, be sure to check that it's enabled. Object Explorer has different icons for enabled and disabled policies, so it's easy to tell by just looking at the policy list.

You can now test the policy by issuing the following commands:

```
--Test Case: Create a table in the dbo schema with name violation
CREATE TABLE developer.Orders
(order_num   INT   NOT NULL,
purchase_time   DATETIME2   NOT NULL,
order_amount   DECIMAL(2)   NOT NULL)
```

Issuing this CREATE TABLE command yields the following:

```
(local)(EPGOPSR2BASE\Administrator):
Policy 'TableNamePolicy' has been violated by
'Server/Database[@Name='foo']/Table[@Name='Orders' and @Schema='developer']'.
This transaction will be rolled back.
Policy description: 'You have violated the corporate policy for standard naming
conventions. Start looking for a new job, buddy! If you can't remember to start a
 table name with tbl.. what else have you forgotten to do?'
Additional help: 'Corporate Development Policy of Naming Standards' :
 'http://corpnet/devpolicy.html'.
(local)(EPGOPSR2BASE\Administrator): Msg 3609, Level 16, State 1,
Procedure sp_syspolicy_dispatch_event, Line 50
The transaction ended in the trigger. The batch has been aborted.
```

If we corrected the table name and called it tbl_Orders instead of Orders and left the schema of developer unchanged, the command would execute successfully, since both criteria are satisfied. We would also get this same policy violation error if the name were acceptable but the schema were not developer or test.

Policies can be deployed across multiple servers by native import and export support. Basically what is provided is the ability to script out in the policy. The resulting script is an XML document, which can easily be imported on any destination server.

Sample Policies

SQL Server 2008 comes with many predefined policies for you to use. At the time of this writing, the only way to install these policies is by importing them into SQL Server via the Import dialog box in SQL Server Management Studio, shown in Figure 3-12. To launch this dialog box, navigate to the Policies node under the Management node in Object Explorer, right-click, and select Import Policy.

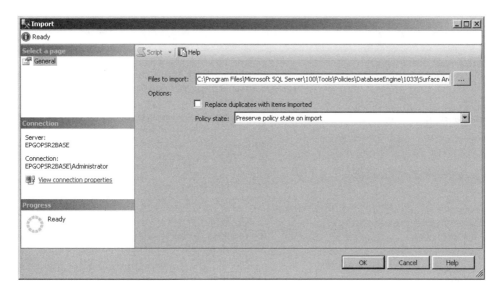

Figure 3-12. *Import dialog box*

On a default installation, the location for the sample policy files is `C:\Program Files\Microsoft SQL Server\100\Tools\Policies`. These include policies not only for the database engine, but for Analysis Services and Reporting Services as well.

Table 3-2 lists the policies that are available for the database engine to import.

Table 3-2. *SQL Server Predefined Policies*

Policy	Description
Asymmetric Key Encryption Algorithm Best Practice	Checks whether asymmetric keys were created with 1024-bit or better.
Backup and Data File Location Best Practice	Checks if database and the backups are on separate backup devices.
CmdExec Rights Secured Best Practice	Checks that only members of the `sysadmin` fixed-server role can execute CmdExec and ActiveX Script job steps. Applies only to SQL Server 2000.
Data and Log File Location Best Practice	Checks whether data and log files are placed on separate logical drives.
Database Auto Close Best Practice	Checks that the `AUTO_ CLOSE` option is off for SQL Server Standard and Enterprise Editions.
Database Auto Shrink Best Practice	Checks that the `AUTO_SHRINK` option is off for user databases on SQL Server Standard and Enterprise Editions.
Database Collation Best Practice	Looks for user-defined databases that have a collation different from the master or model databases.
Database Page Verification Best Practice	Checks if the `PAGE_VERIFY` database option is not set to `CHECKSUM` to provide a high level of datafile integrity.

Continued

Table 3-2. *(Continued)*

Policy	Description
Database Status Best Practice	Checks if the status of a database is suspect by looking for error 824. Error 824 indicates that a logical consistency error was detected during a read operation.
File Growth for SQL Server 2000 Best Practice	Checks an instance of SQL Server 2000. Warns if the datafile is 1GB or larger and is set to automatically grow by a percentage, instead of growing by a fixed size.
Guest Permissions Best Practice	Checks if permission to access the database is enabled for guest users.
Last Successful Backup Date Best Practice	Checks whether a database has recent backups.
Non-Read-only Database Recovery Model Best Practice	Checks whether the recovery model is set to the full recovery model instead of the simple recovery model for databases that are not read-only.
Public Not Granted Server Permissions Best Practice	Checks that the server permission is not granted to the Public role.
Read-only Database Recovery Model Best Practice	Checks whether the recovery model is set to simple for read-only databases.
SQL Server 32-bit Affinity Mask Overlap Best Practice	Checks an instance of SQL Server having processors that are assigned with both the affinity mask and the affinity I/O mask options.
SQL Server 64-bit Affinity Mask Overlap Best Practice	Checks an instance of SQL Server having processors that are assigned with both the affinity 64 mask and the affinity 64 I/O mask options.
SQL Server Affinity Mask Best Practice	Confirms whether the affinity mask setting of the server is set to 0.
SQL Server Blocked Process Threshold Best Practice	Checks whether the blocked process threshold option is set lower than 5 and is not disabled (0).
SQL Server Default Trace Best Practice	Checks whether default trace is turned on to collect information about configuration and DDL changes to the instance of SQL Server.
SQL Server Dynamic Locks Best Practice	Checks whether the value of the locks option is the default setting of 0.
SQL Server I/O Affinity Mask for Non-enterprise SQL Servers Best Practice	Checks that the affinity I/O mask is disabled for non-Enterprise Editions.
SQL Server Lightweight Pooling Best Practice	Checks whether lightweight pooling is disabled on the server.
SQL Server Login Mode Best Practice	Checks for Windows authentication.
SQL Server Max Degree of Parallelism Best Practice	Checks the maximum degree of parallelism option for the optimal value to avoid unwanted resource consumption and performance degradation.
SQL Server Max Worker Threads for 32-bit SQL Server 2000 Best Practice	Checks the maximum worker threads server option for potentially incorrect settings of an instance of SQL Server 2000 that is running on a 32-bit server.
SQL Server Max Worker Threads for 64-bit SQL Server 2000 Best Practice	Checks the maximum worker threads server option for potentially incorrect settings of an instance of SQL Server 2000 that is running on a 64-bit server.

Policy	Description
SQL Server Max Worker Threads for SQL Server 2005 and Above Best Practice	Checks the maximum work threads server option for potentially incorrect settings of an instance of SQL Server 2005.
SQL Server Network Packet Size Best Practice	Checks whether the value specified for the network packet size server option is set to the optimal value of 8060 bytes.
SQL Server Open Objects for SQL Server 2000 Best Practice	Checks whether the open objects server option is set to 0, the optimal value on SQL Server 2000 instances.
SQL Server Password Expiration Best Practice	Checks whether password expiration on SQL Server logins is enforced.
SQL Server Password Policy Best Practice	Checks whether password policy enforcement on SQL Server logins is enabled.
SQL Server System Tables Updatable Best Practice	Checks whether SQL Server 2000 system tables can be updated.
Surface Area Configuration for Database Engine Features	Checks surface area configuration options.
Symmetric Key Encryption for User Databases Best Practice	Checks that symmetric keys with a length less than 128 bytes do not use the RC2 or RC4 encryption algorithm.
Symmetric Key for Master Database Best Practice	Checks for user-created symmetric keys in the master database.
Symmetric Key for System Databases Best Practice	Checks for user-created symmetric keys in the msdb, model, and tempdb databases.
Trustworthy Database Best Practice	Checks whether the dbo or a db_owner is assigned to a fixed server sysadmin role for databases where the trustworthy bit is set to on.
Windows Event Log Cluster Disk Resource Corruption Error Best Practice	Detects SCSI host adapter configuration issues or a malfunctioning device error message in the system log.
Windows Event Log Device Driver Control Error Best Practice	Detects the error with event ID 11 in the system log.
Windows Event Log Device Not Ready Error Best Practice	Detects device not ready error messages in the system log.
Windows Event Log Disk Defragmentation Best Practice	Detects specific defragmentation error messages in the system log.
Windows Event Log Failed I/O Request Error Best Practice	Detects a failed I/O request error message in the system log.
Windows Event Log I/O Delay Warning Best Practice	Detects event ID 833 in the system log.
Windows Event Log I/O Error During Hard Page Fault Error Best Practice	Detects an I/O error during a hard page fault in the system log.
Windows Event Log Read Retry Error Best Practice	Detects error event ID 825 in the system log.
Windows Event Log Storage System I/O Timeout Error Best Practice	Detects error event ID 9 in the system log.
Windows Event Log System Failure Error Best Practice	Detects error event ID 825 in the system log.

Each policy that is imported will also install one or more conditions. For example, if you import the SQL Server Password Policy Best Practice, it will create a policy that references two new conditions: "Password policy enforced" and "SQL Server 2005 or later." You can use these conditions with any policy, including those that are user-defined.

Policy Management Administration

A variety of tools and features are available to help administrators manage PM. As mentioned previously in this chapter, policy history is stored in the msdb database. Along with that history, the msdb database stores almost everything PM-related, including policies and conditions. Thus, it is critical that you take regular backups of msdb to avoid losing any policy configuration information.

Policy Status

When you enable a policy, Object Explorer will show you objects that violate that policy. For example, suppose that you set your TableNamePolicy policy to only log out-of-compliance changes instead of preventing them, and then created some tables. Object Explorer might look something like Figure 3-13. As you can see, Object Explorer has a special icon for items that have violated a policy.

Figure 3-13. *Object Explorer showing objects and folders that violated one or more policies*

You can view the policies that affect any object. For example, if you right-click dbo.tblCustomers in Figure 3-13 and select Policies ➤ View Policy, you will be presented with a window that shows all the policies on the server that affect the dbo.tblCustomers table object, as shown in Figure 3-14.

In the View Policies window shown in Figure 3-14, you can see that the TableNamePolicy policy was violated. The History column provides a link to view the history of this policy, and the Evaluate column has a link to rerun the policy (in case you managed to fix the problem and want to make sure you are within compliance of the policy).

The Log File Viewer window launched from the View Policies window is the same as the viewer that can be launched from other areas in Object Explorer, as shown in Figure 3-15. This viewer reads historical information from system tables inside the msdb database and presents this data in a more readable format. The information that is contained in the history is made up of some metadata describing the policy runtime history, including when the policy was executed, the target for the policy, and some XML describing the violation if any occurred.

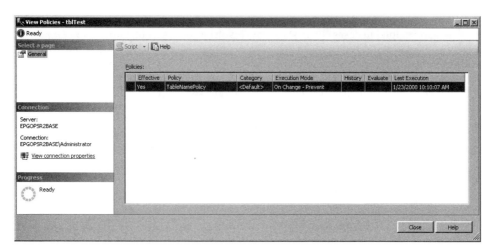

Figure 3-14. *Viewing policies for a given object*

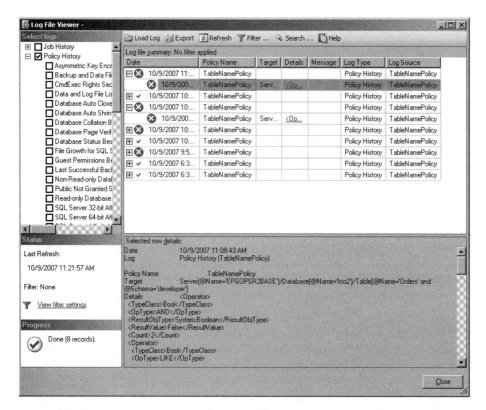

Figure 3-15. *Log File Viewer window showing policy history*

When you drill down on a specific error in the viewer, the XML that describes the error is shown. This is particularly helpful in cases where the errors involved some sort of automation. This XML describes the policy, expected values, and actual values obtained. Since XML doesn't have a lot of aesthetic qualities, and fairly simple definitions could be pages in length, a Detailed View window pops up whenever you click the Details column in the viewer. In Figure 3-15, if you clicked the highlighted Details cell, you would be presented with the window shown in Figure 3-16.

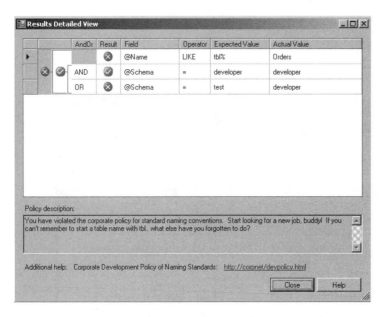

Figure 3-16. *Detailed view of policy condition and runtime results*

The Detailed View window shows exactly which part of the condition within the policy failed. In this case, the condition applies to the schema for the table to be within developer or test, and this is shown with the grouping of AND and OR on the left side of the window. Since this condition was satisfied, you see a green check for the Schema group. However, the Name condition was violated, and hence it is shown with a red *X*, indicating failure. You can see the expected value was a name that has tbl as the first three characters and the actual value was Orders, which is in violation of the policy. This may be very intuitive for simple policies, but as policy conditions get more complex, this user interface will be a welcome asset when debugging your policy violations.

PM Security

A new database role contained in msdb is called PolicyAdministratorRole. This new role allows non-sysadmin users the ability to author policies and conditions on the server.

Depending on the size of your organization, you may have multiple sysadmin users working on a server. If everyone were a trustworthy employee, we probably wouldn't have to talk about protection against sysadmin attacks. However, we live in a world full of outsourcing, and your organization's contractors may not have the same vested interest in protecting your data as you do.

So, is it possible to protect against someone with sysadmin rights to SQL Server? The answer is yes and no. Technically, it is impossible to prevent sysadmin from performing actions against SQL Server, since, in fact, that user is sysadmin and owns the SQL Server instance. The only way to protect against a dishonest sysadmin is to enable auditing on SQL Server. Some might think, "Well, the sysadmin just has to disable auditing." True, he could disable it, which will log an event that would state the fact that it was disabled. In addition, if auditing were set up to leverage the new auditing features in SQL Server 2008, as described in Chapter 6, SQL Server would write audit logs to a file-share on which the SQL Server service account has only append permission.

So, why all this discussion on protection from sysadmin in a chapter about PM? PM lives in the msdb database, and it employs technologies like DDL triggers, which can potentially be disabled or intentionally modified by a user with high enough privileges (like a sysadmin).

The moral of the story is if you don't trust your sysadmin, make sure you have proper auditing enabled or else hire a more trustworthy sysadmin. Realistically, the sysadmin can obtain data and information a lot more easily than mucking with PM, but it is important to note this as another attack surface.

Think about this: if you give someone full control of msdb, you are giving him the ability to modify your policies and conditions of PM (as well as SQL Server Agent and everything else that lives in msdb). It is important to be very vigilant about granting permissions to users.

Summary

PM is a policy-based framework for SQL Server 2008. This first version of PM allows DBAs to create policies and have these policies enforced on their SQL Server instances. Policies are based on conditions. These conditions determine the allowed state of a specific target (a SQL Server instance, a particular database, all users, and so on) with respect to a particular facet. Facets model behavior and characteristics of various targets.

The available facets are a fixed list for SQL Server 2008. Eventually, developers may be able to create their own custom facets. This capability would make it easy to create a "company best practices" facet that might include some company-specific business processes and procedures. In the meantime, the out-of-the-box facets will get most organizations on track for setting up PM and enforcing policies.

PM will drastically reduce the total cost of ownership and allow DBAs to focus on the more important things, like database architecture and database-capacity planning.

CHAPTER 4

■■■

High Availability

With SQL Server 2008, Microsoft is looking to continue its push forward into both the largest and smallest database environments in the world. Microsoft envisions a world where a single data platform can accommodate mobile applications running on handheld or embedded devices all the way up to the world's largest enterprise database environments. With features like database mirroring, database snapshots, peer-to-peer conflict detection, hot-add CPU and memory, and data partitioning, Microsoft is moving closer and closer to this vision.

In many organizations today, data availability and business continuance are of major concern. Without the data to drive it, the business can't perform its necessary functions. While making the data and the technology that houses that data highly available is a primary concern for many information technology (IT) managers, there are many barriers to achieving this high availability. The right technology is one piece of the puzzle, but high availability also is achieved by having consistent processes and well-trained people. In this chapter, we'll focus on the technology aspects provided by SQL Server to support high availability, and we'll leave the people and process as your issues to resolve.

This chapter covers the following topics:

- Database mirroring
- Database snapshots
- Windows clustering
- SQL Server replication
- Hot-add memory and CPUs
- Online index operations
- Table and index partitioning

High Availability Defined

Ask ten database administrators (DBAs) how they define high availability (HA), and you'll probably get ten different answers. We're going to throw our own (informal) definition into the hat as well.

In its simplest form, HA is about keeping your servers and their services up and running. HA is about making sure that end users do not experience hiccups in the operation of the system, and that the business can perform at an acceptable level. We use the term *acceptable level*, because one organization may consider an acceptable level to be 1 hour of downtime per week, while another may consider 1 second of downtime per week acceptable. It depends on the level of HA that you need. An effective HA strategy will ensure that the defined acceptable level of downtime is met. Downtime comes in one of the following two forms:

- *Unplanned downtime*: This is what most people are trying to avoid when they implement an HA solution. These are the dreaded crashes, power outages, "D'oh!" administrative moments (such as pushing the power button on the server by accident), and so on.

- *Planned downtime*: This includes activities like performing regular maintenance, patching, installing software, upgrading hardware, and similar tasks that you will know about in advance and can plan for accordingly. Most times, your downtime is planned rather than unplanned. Any HA strategy should try to help you minimize this type of downtime as well.

A term that goes hand in hand with HA is *disaster recovery* (DR), which is the means by which you protect your system against lost data and restore normal operations in the event of a system failure. DR is a piece of any HA strategy. Even after a disaster, you need to be able to get your system back up and running to achieve HA.

In essence, your DR strategy is your backup and restore strategy. For the highest level of DR, this involves a secondary site located some distance from the primary site. In the event that a catastrophic failure happens at the primary site, there is a failover to the secondary site. You can combine HA with DR to make servers in both the primary and secondary sites more bulletproof. DR is a key part of any overarching HA solution.

Many SQL Server technologies are available when implementing your HA/DR solutions. Database mirroring is the newest of these technologies. Other HA-related technologies include failover clustering, log shipping, and transactional replication.

Log shipping is one of the principles by which database mirroring operates. In other words, entries from a transaction log in one database are transferred and applied to another. When the database mirroring feature was originally being developed, it was called *real-time log shipping*. As development progressed, it made more sense to rename the feature to database mirroring, since, in effect, that is what the feature does. Most administrators understand disk mirroring in a Redundant Array of Inexpensive Disks (RAID) configuration, so the term *database mirroring* for SQL Server made sense.

The main advantages mirroring has over log shipping or transactional replication are that potential data loss is eliminated, automatic failover is enabled, and administration and monitoring are simplified. An interesting addition is the transparent client redirection. Without this technology, developers would need to write custom code into their application to failover gracefully.

It's true that failover clustering provides automatic failover and client redirection, but mirroring is much easier to set up and use than clustering, which also requires specialized hardware. Additionally, mirroring provides a substantial decrease in potential downtime over clustering.

Table 4-1 lists the technologies that SQL Server 2008 provides to help implement HA/DR solutions and explains the differences between each. We will look at details of each solution, especially database mirroring, in this chapter.

Table 4-1. *SQL Server HA/DR Solutions*

Area	Database Mirroring	Failover Clustering	Transactional Replication	Log Shipping
Data loss	No data loss	No data loss	Some data loss possible	Some data loss possible
Automatic failover	Yes, in HA mode	Yes	No	No
Transparent to client	Yes, autoredirect	Yes, connect to same IP	No, but Network Load Balancing (NLB) helps	No, but NLB helps
Downtime	< 3 seconds	20 seconds or more, plus database recovery	Seconds	Seconds plus database recovery
Standby read access	Yes, using database snapshot	No	Yes	Intermittently accessible
Data granularity	Database only	All system and user databases	Table or view	Database only
Masking of disk failure	Yes	No, shared disk solution	Yes	Yes
Special hardware	No, duplicate recommended	Cluster Hardware Compatibility List (HCL) hardware	No, duplicate recommended	No, duplicate recommended
Complexity	Some	More	More	More

Database Mirroring

As noted in the previous section, many of the well-known HA technologies included in SQL Server, such as failover clustering and log shipping, are very valuable but somewhat cumbersome to configure and use. Also, in many cases, they solve only half of the problem for many applications—namely, failing over the database server. This leaves the application developer in a lurch, since all applications must be programmed with special code to failover the application to a new database server in the case of a failure in the original database server.

With database mirroring, SQL Server provides both database availability and application availability through the SQL Native Access Client (SNAC) stack, which understands and can work with database mirrors.

How Database Mirroring Works

Figure 4-1 shows the basic architecture of the database mirroring technology. In the simplest deployment of database mirroring, there are two major server-side components: the *principal server instance* (principal) and the *mirror server instance* (mirror). The principal, as the name implies, contains the principal database. This is the database where you will perform your *transactions*.

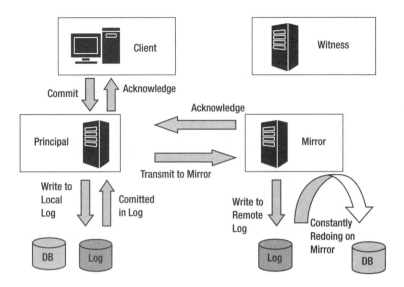

Figure 4-1. *Database mirroring architecture, with witness*

The basic idea behind database mirroring is that synchronized versions of the database are maintained on the principal and mirror. If the principal database (or the principal itself!) becomes unavailable, then the client application will smoothly switch over to the mirror database, and operation (from the users' point of view) will continue as normal.

So, a client interacts with the principal and submits a transaction. The principal writes the requested change to the principal transaction log and automatically transfers the information describing the transaction over to the mirror, where it is written to the mirror transaction log. The mirror then sends an acknowledgment to the principal. The mirror continuously uses the remote transaction log to "replicate" changes made to the principal database to the mirror database. With SQL Server 2008, a good amount of focus has been placed on the performance of handling these log records, and the following enhancements have been made:

- The data stream between the two partners is compressed. Note that SQL Server will compress the data stream between partners only when a 12.5 percent compression ratio can be achieved.

- SQL Server adds records to the mirror log asynchronously, while at the same time processing records from the log on disk.

- SQL Server has improved its efficiency around the buffers used to queue up log records when sending them to the mirror.

- When a failover occurs, SQL Server has improved the undo/redo process for transactions on the mirror (which was the principal before failure) that may not have been commited. SQL Server sends page hints to the principal early in the undo process, so that the principal can cache the pages into the send queue for the mirror.

Database mirroring runs in-process in SQL Server. Unlike replication, which is a log reader, database mirroring sends the log buffers stored in memory to the mirror before writing them to disk.

■**Note** Sometimes corruption occurs in the log files because of disk errors, failures, or other issues. With database mirroring, if the mirror is keeping up with the principal, you can avoid some of these disk-based corruptions. One caveat is that if the mirror gets behind for some reason, such as being suspended, or if you have a failover and the other server comes back online after a period of time, the principal will need to go to disk to get the older log blocks, so hardening your disks and making sure they are reliable is a must with database mirroring.

Synchronous and Asynchronous Modes

Database mirroring has a *synchronous* and an *asynchronous* mode of operation. The synchronous mode will force the principal to not consider a transaction committed until the mirror has entered the transaction into its transaction log and sent back an acknowledgment. In asynchronous mode, the principal does not wait for the mirror to acknowledge that it has received the transaction before committing. This mode is potentially faster, but you do run the risk of the two databases getting out of sync, since it is not guaranteed that a transaction actually made it to the mirror.

What happens, then, in the basic principal/mirror setup if the principal experiences a failure? Typically, the DBA will manually force service on the mirror, so that the mirror becomes the target for the application. The client is automatically and transparently (to the user) redirected to the mirror. This *transparent client redirection* is an interesting innovation. Without this technology, developers would need to write custom code into their application in order to failover gracefully to the mirror node.

If, instead, the mirror experiences a failure then, in synchronous mode or asynchronous mode, the principal database would continue to be available, but would be exposed for the period of time that the mirror is unavailable.

Let's now introduce the third server component into our mirroring architecture: the *witness server instance* (witness). Unlike the principal and the mirror, the witness does not perform any database operations—it doesn't maintain a transaction log or a mirror copy of the database. Its primary function is to allow *automatic failover* (no DBA intervention). Essentially, the witness monitors the operation of the principal and mirror, and if the principal exhibits no heartbeat response within a defined timeout period, then the witness triggers automatic failover to the mirror. Furthermore, if the mirror fails, but the principal is still in contact with the witness, the principal can continue to operate. When the witness detects that the mirror is back online, it will instruct the mirror to resynchronize with the principal.

The witness can also break any ties between the principal and the mirror to prevent split-brain scenarios, where both machines think they are the principal. For example, if both servers come up at the same time and both think they are the principal, then the witness can break the tie. When a failure happens, all participants in the mirror get a vote to decide who the principal is. Of course, if the principal itself is down, then only the mirror and the witness will vote. In this scenario, the witness and mirror would decide the mirror needs to become the principal, and the failover would occur. When the original principal comes back online, it would assume the role of mirror, and the log buffers would go from the new principal to the new mirror.

Database mirroring uses the idea of a quorum when running in synchronous mode. A *quorum* is the minimum number of partners needed to decide what to do in a mirrored set. In database mirroring, a quorum is at least two partners. The partners could be the principal and the witness, the witness and the mirror, or the principal and the mirror. A full quorum is when all three partners—principal, mirror, and witness—can communicate with one another. If at any point a partner is lost, such as the principal server, the other two partners establish a quorum and arbitrate what should happen. Each partner in the quorum gets a vote and, in the end, the witness breaks any ties between the principal and the mirror.

If, for some reason, all three partners lose communication with each other, automatic failover will not occur. You will want to make sure that your witness can always talk to your mirror over the network, since this link is crucial to making sure that automatic failover will occur.

When working with a witness, but in asynchronous mode, the principal will send the transaction details over to the mirror to commit, and commit the transaction locally. The principal does not wait for the acknowledgment from the mirror before committing. Since synchronization cannot be guaranteed in this mode, you lose the ability to perform automatic failover. Microsoft recommends that if you are going to run in asynchronous mode, you do not use a witness, since a quorum would be required, but you are not getting the benefits of the quorum, because asynchronous mode does not support automatic failover. Asynchronous mode may be suitable on occasions when you are willing to sacrifice HA for performance. Since synchronous mode requires committing on both sides, if you do not have acceptable network bandwidth, or if the mirror gets behind, your overall application performance could suffer due to delayed transaction commits.

Table 4-2 summarizes the different database mirroring modes, and the pros and cons for each mode.

Table 4-2. *Database Mirroring Modes*

Mode Name	Synchronous or Asynchronous?	Witness Present?	Pro/Con
High Availability	Synchronous	Yes	Supports automatic failover and is the most hardened. If the mirror disappears but the principal and witness are connected, operations continue. The mirror catches up when it comes back online.
High Protection	Synchronous	No	No automatic failover. If the mirror is unavailable, the principal database goes offline.
High Performance (not recommended)	Asynchronous	Yes	Fast performance, but the data is not guaranteed on the other side and there is no automatic failover. This is useful for low-bandwidth connections between the mirror and principal since performance is best. This mode requires a quorum before users can connect, so it is not recommended.
High Performance (recommended mode)	Asynchronous	No	Microsoft recommends that if you are going to run asynchronously, you run with this configuration. There is no automatic failover, and the mirror is a hot standby server but not guaranteed to be up-to-date.

Database Mirroring States

In database mirroring, your system goes through a set of database states. These states indicate the status of your mirror, and you can query for them, as you will see when we look at how to monitor database mirroring using catalog views. Table 4-3 lists the different states for databases that are part of database mirroring.

Table 4-3. *Database Mirroring States*

State	Description
SYNCHRONIZING	The beginning phase for any mirror, since this is when the principal and the mirror are synchronizing their contents. The mirror is not fully in sync with the principal yet and is lagging behind. Both principal and mirror will normally be in this state, where log records are being sent between the two and being applied on the mirror.
SYNCHRONIZED	When both the principal and the mirror are in sync. The principal is sending any changes to the mirror to be applied, and the mirror is not lagging behind. Both manual and automatic failover can occur only in this state.
SUSPENDED	Mirroring is no longer occurring, either through administrative intervention or REDO errors on the mirror. The principal is considered to be running exposed, which means that the principal is running without a partner on the other side of the mirror.
PENDING_FAILOVER	The administrator performs a manual failover but the mirror has not accepted the failover yet. This state occurs only on the principal.
DISCONNECTED	The partner has lost communications with the other partner and the witness, if the witness is present.

Automatic Page Repair

SQL Server 2008 Enterprise Edition adds some very nice functionality with regard to repairing certain SQL Server errors that are the result of failed/corrupted page reads. If a partner (principal or mirror) within a database mirroring configuration fails with one of the errors listed in Table 4-4, SQL Server will automatically try to resolve the error by replacing the page with a fresh copy that it requests from the other partner. Obviously, much care needs to be taken during this process to ensure that both partners are at a consistent state with regard to transactions, and this is automatically handled by the database mirroring session.

Table 4-4. *Errors Accounted for by Database Mirroring*

Error	Description
823	The operating system performed a cyclic redundancy check that failed.
824	Logical errors occurred.
829	A page has been marked as restore pending.

For errors reading data pages on the principal, the following actions are taken:

- An entry is entered into the suspect_pages table for the particular page in error.

- The principal server then sends the page ID and current log sequence number (LSN) to the mirror server. At the same time, the page is marked as restore pending, making it inaccessible to application queries.

- The mirror ensures that it has applied all transactions up to the provided log sequence number within the request. Once the mirror and the principal are transactionally consistent, the mirror attempts to retrieve the page identified by the page ID provided within the request. Assuming that the mirror can access the page, it is returned to the principal.

- The principal replaces the corrupted page with the new page from the mirror.

- The page is marked as restored within the suspect_pages table, and the principal applies any deferred transactions.

For errors reading data pages on the mirror, the following actions are taken:

- When a page error is detected on the mirror, the mirroring session automatically enters a SUSPENDED state.

- An entry is entered into the suspect_pages table on the mirror for the particular page in error.

- The mirror server sends the page ID principal server.

- The principal attempts to retrieve the page identified by the page ID provided within the request. Assuming that the page can be accessed, it is returned to the mirror.

- It is possible that the mirror provided the IDs of multiple corrupt pages during the request. Therefore, the mirror must receive copies of each requested page before it tries to resume the mirroring session. If all pages were provided from the principal and the mirror session is resumed, then the entries within the suspect_pages table are marked as restored. If the mirror does not receive all pages requested, then the mirroring session is left in a SUSPENDED state.

Page repairs are performed asynchronously, so requests for the corrupt page may fail while the page is being replaced. Depending on the state of the page repair, the request will return the appropriate error code (823 or 824) or error 829, which indicates the page is marked as restoring and actively being restored. It may be possible to account for this within the data access layer of your application and retry the query if you know that database mirroring is being used.

Managing Database Mirroring Using T-SQL

In this section, we'll demonstrate how to set up a mirroring architecture using Transact-SQL (T-SQL). This example uses three SQL Server server instances (principal/mirror/witness). As discussed previously, you can use only two server instances (no witness), but then you lose the ability to do automatic failovers.

MICROSOFT VIRTUAL SERVER

While you evaluate database mirroring, you have a good excuse to look at some other technologies at the same time. For example, you may not have three machines that you can use for the evaluation, and this is where technologies such as Microsoft Virtual Server (MVS) come in handy. With MVS, you can run three virtual machines on a single physical machine.

We recommend the use of MVS to evaluate database mirroring, rather than creating three instances of SQL Server on a single machine, because with the virtual technology you can do a hard shutdown of the virtual machine. In lieu of having three machines, this will provide the most realistic simulation of an "unplanned catastrophe." The database mirroring feature does support the forcing of a manual failover, but simulating a real failure is best for your evaluation.

One of the main prerequisites for setting up database mirroring is to ensure that your databases run in full recovery mode, since database mirroring uses the transaction log and requires the more extensive logging and log information created when you use full recovery mode. To do this, you can use the following ALTER DATABASE statement:

```
USE master;
GO
ALTER DATABASE YOURDATABASEHERE
SET RECOVERY FULL;
GO
```

Also, remember that nonlogged operations will not work with database mirroring, so do not use the nonlogged bulk copy program (bcp) to load data into the database.

Setting Up Connectivity

Database mirroring uses the endpoint connection model and requires that you set up endpoints so that the principal and the mirror can talk to each other. You have the option of either using the Security Support Provider Interface (SSPI), which uses Windows credentials, or using certificate-based authentication.

Using Windows-Based Authentication

If you want to use Windows-based authentication, the accounts that you use for your SQL Server service accounts involved in the database mirroring session must be in the same domain, or at least in a trusted domain. If the accounts are not in trusted domains, the connection between the principal and the mirror will fail. If you do not have trusted domains or you do not use Windows-based authentication, you must use certificates for authentication, as described in the next section.

You will also need to assign permissions to the accounts to be able to connect to the other server(s), via endpoints, and also to the database, as you will see shortly. The example in this chapter assumes that you use the same service account for all your instances.

To use Windows-based authentication, perform the following steps:

1. Create the endpoints for mirroring. To create an endpoint, you need to use the CREATE ENDPOINT statement. This statement takes the name of the endpoint, the state, the protocol, and the payload. The following example creates a new endpoint that uses a TCP payload on a particular port. This code should be run on the principal server. Make sure to give your endpoint a unique name.

```
CREATE ENDPOINT MirroringEndPoint
    STATE=STARTED
    AS TCP (LISTENER_PORT=10111)
    FOR DATABASE_MIRRORING (ROLE=PARTNER)
GO
```

■**Note** You can have only one endpoint per server instance for database mirroring. If you try to create more than one endpoint, you will receive an error.

2. Create a login, if one does not already exist, and assign CONNECT permissions to the endpoint for that login. The following code creates a login that maps to the Windows account that the witness will use to log on, and it assigns permissions on the endpoint:

```
USE master;
GO
CREATE LOGIN [YOURDOMAIN\witnessaccount] FROM WINDOWS ;
GO
GRANT CONNECT ON ENDPOINT::MirroringEndPoint TO [YOURDOMAIN\witnessaccount];
GO
```

3. Perform the same operations on the mirror, since the witness needs to be able to connect to and authenticate against both servers. The following code creates an endpoint and a user login, and assigns permissions on the mirror for the witness:

```
CREATE ENDPOINT MirroringEndPoint
    STATE=STARTED
```

```
    AS TCP (LISTENER_PORT=10111)
    FOR DATABASE_MIRRORING (ROLE=ALL)
GO
USE master;
GO
CREATE LOGIN [YOURDOMAIN\witnessaccount] FROM WINDOWS;
GO
GRANT CONNECT ON ENDPOINT::MirroringEndPoint TO [YOURDOMAIN\witnessaccount];
GO
```

4. Create an endpoint on the witness to allow the principal and the mirror to connect to the witness. This example assumes that the same Windows account is used to log on to both the principal and the mirror. The following code performs this step:

```
CREATE ENDPOINT MirroringEndPoint
    STATE=STARTED
    AS TCP (LISTENER_PORT=10111)
    FOR DATABASE_MIRRORING (ROLE=ALL)
GO
USE master;
GO
CREATE LOGIN [YOURDOMAIN\dbaccount] FROM WINDOWS;
GO
GRANT CONNECT ON ENDPOINT::MirroringEndPoint TO [YOURDOMAIN\dbaccount];
GO
```

Connecting Using Certificates

You may want to use certificates for authentication rather than Windows-based authentication for your connectivity. Certificates use the encryption technology introduced in SQL Server 2005.

■**Note** Certificates are used only for authentication and not for encrypting the communication between your principal and mirror. To learn more about encryption in SQL Server, refer to Chapter 7.

The following steps demonstrate how to create your certificates and assign them for your database mirroring authentication. You should perform these steps on the principal database server.

1. If you have not already set up your database master key for encryption, you must do that now; otherwise, you will get an error when you try to create the certificate in the database. The following T-SQL command creates the database master key, which is secured via a password that you specify:

```
CREATE MASTER KEY ENCRYPTION BY PASSWORD = '!@@@gh!2a*'
GO
```

2. Create the certificate you want to use inside your database. The following command creates a certificate using the encryption technology provided within SQL Server:

```
USE master;
CREATE CERTIFICATE HOST_ServerACert
    WITH SUBJECT = 'Server A cert for DBM';
GO
```

3. Create your endpoints to use your certificates. Notice that you pass the authentication and the encryption values to the CREATE ENDPOINT function.

```
CREATE ENDPOINT MirroringEndPoint
    STATE = STARTED
    AS TCP (
        LISTENER_PORT=10111
        , LISTENER_IP = ALL
    )
    FOR DATABASE_MIRRORING (
        AUTHENTICATION = CERTIFICATE ServerACert
        , ENCRYPTION = REQUIRED ALGORITHM RC4
        , ROLE = ALL
    );
GO
```

4. Back up the certificate and transfer it securely to your mirror database server. You can back up the certificate using the following command:

```
BACKUP CERTIFICATE ServerACert TO FILE = 'C:\ServerACert.cer';
GO
```

5. Perform steps 1 through 4 on your mirror database server, except change ServerA to ServerB for the naming. You'll need the certificate from server B copied over to server A.

6. Create a login for your mirror database and make that login have permissions to the certificate on your principal. This is for the incoming connection, as opposed to the steps you just performed for the outgoing connection. The following code creates the login and also grants connect permissions on the endpoint for database mirroring:

```
USE master
GO
CREATE LOGIN mirrorlogin WITH PASSWORD = '!@#1579212'
CREATE USER mirroruser FOR LOGIN mirrorlogin
GO
GRANT CONNECT ON ENDPOINT::MirroringEndPoint TO [mirrorlogin]
GO
```

7. Assign your user to your newly copied certificate from the mirror server. The following code creates a certificate and uses the mirror's certificate:

```
CREATE CERTIFICATE mirrorservercert
    AUTHORIZATION mirroruser
    FROM FILE = 'c:\ServerBCert.cer'
GO
```

8. Reverse the procedure in steps 6 and 7 on the mirror so that the principal can log on to it. Also, make sure to allow the witness to be able to log on to both the principal and the mirror using the same steps just outlined.

Backing Up and Restoring the Principal Database

Now that you have security and connectivity set up between your principal, mirror, and witness, you can get your database ready to go. Again, before performing the steps presented in this section, make sure your database is in full recovery mode. The first step is to back up the database so that you can move it over and restore it on the mirror. The following code will back up your principal database:

```
USE YourDB
BACKUP DATABASE YourDB
    TO DISK = 'C:\YourDB.bak'
    WITH FORMAT
GO
```

Once you copy over the database to your mirror server, you need to restore the database, which will ensure that you have the database in the same state of principal and mirror. You must make sure that you use the same name for the database on both the principal and the mirror. According to Microsoft's recommendations, the path (including the drive letter) of the mirror database should be identical to the path of the principal database. If these pathnames differ, you cannot add any files to the database. It's not required, but it will make it easier for you, since you will not need to change configuration. Also, you must restore your database using the NORECOVERY option with database mirroring. The following code restores the database on the mirror:

```
RESTORE DATABASE YourDB
    FROM DISK = 'C:\YourDB.bak'
    WITH NORECOVERY
GO
```

If you are testing database mirroring on the same server using multiple instances, or your pathnames differ between your principal and mirror for the database, you will need to restore your database with the MOVE keyword. The following code changes the restore path using the MOVE keyword:

```
RESTORE DATABASE YourDB
   FROM DISK='C:\YourDB.bak'
   WITH NORECOVERY,
      MOVE 'YourDB' TO
'C:\Program Files\Microsoft SQL Server\MSSQL.2\MSSQL\Data\YourDB_data.mdf',
      MOVE 'YourDB_log'
TO 'C:\Program Files\Microsoft SQL Server\MSSQL.2\MSSQL\Data\YourDB_Log.ldf';
GO
```

Establishing the Principal/Mirror Partnership

You will always want to make sure you configure your mirror server first to be a partner with your principal server before you configure the principal. To do this, you use the ALTER DATABASE statement with the SET PARTNER statement for the database mirroring option. The ports you set are server-wide, so if you run database mirroring on the same server using multiple instances for testing, you will want to use different ports. The following code sets the partner for the mirror to the principal using the TCP endpoint you created earlier:

```
ALTER DATABASE YourDB
    SET PARTNER =
    'TCP://YourPrincipalServer.YourDomain:10111'
GO
```

On the principal, you need to set its partner to the mirror server using the following code:

```
ALTER DATABASE YourDB
    SET PARTNER =
    'TCP://YourMirrorServer.YourDomain:10111'
GO
```

Finally, you need to set the witness. You can do this from either server. The following code performs this operation:

```
ALTER DATABASE YourDB
    SET WITNESS =
    'TCP://YourWitnessServer.YourDomain:10111'
GO
```

Changing Transaction Safety Levels

By default, database mirroring sets the transaction safety level to FULL. The FULL transaction safety level provides the highest levels of protection and availability, and it is required if you want to run in a synchronous state. If you want automatic failover, you need to have a witness server. If you do not want to run in FULL transaction safety mode, you can modify your transaction safety level using the database mirroring options offered by the ALTER DATABASE statement. The following code shows the different options you have with the ALTER DATABASE statement for database mirroring:

```
ALTER DATABASE dbname SET PARTNER { = 'Partner Server'
                                  | FAILOVER
                                  | FORCE_SERVICE_ALLOW_DATA_LOSS
                                  | OFF
                                  | RESUME
                                  | SAFETY { FULL | OFF }
                                  | SUSPEND
                                  | REDO_QUEUE ( integer { KB | MB | GB } | OFF
                                  | TIMEOUT integer
                                  }

ALTER DATABASE dbname SET WITNESS { = 'Witness Server'
                                  | OFF
                                  }
```

So, to change your transaction safety level from FULL to OFF, use the following command on the principal:

```
ALTER DATABASE dbname SET PARTNER SAFETY OFF.
```

You may want to run with your transaction safety level OFF if you want to maximize performance. Doing so shifts the session into asynchronous operating mode, which maximizes performance at the cost of safety. If the principal becomes unavailable, the mirror stops but is available as a hot standby. You need to make the failover happen to the mirror.

Adjusting the Timeout Setting

Beyond the database states listed in Table 4-3, database mirroring also implements a heartbeat between the partners in a mirror. By default, this heartbeat is sent every 2.5 seconds between the servers. If the partner does not respond after four pings, a failover is initiated. What will happen depends on whether you're running in synchronous or asynchronous mode, and whether a witness is present. See Table 4-3 for more details.

You can customize the timeout setting to either shorten or lengthen it depending on your situation. For example, you may want to lengthen the timeout setting if you have slow connectivity between your servers and do not want false failovers to occur. To change the timeout setting, use the `ALTER DATABASE` statement on the principal and set in seconds the timeout period you want, as shown in the following code:

```
ALTER DATABASE dbname SET PARTNER TIMEOUT 15
```

In high-performance mode, the timeout value cannot be changed and is always 10 seconds. In high-safety mode, the timeout can be configured. It is recommended that the timeout value be set to 10 seconds or more; otherwise, you may overload your system by having false failovers all the time due to missed ping messages.

Initiating a Failover

There may be times, such as when you are testing or after you have upgraded one of the mirror partners, that you want to manually initiate a failover, to make sure failovers will work when required. Rolling upgrades can be supported only if the physical log file format used by SQL Server does not change because of the upgrade. For example, if you want to install a Windows patch on the principal and then on the mirror, and this patch does not affect SQL Server, you can install the patch on the mirror, failover the principal to the mirror, and apply the patch on the old principal. When you're finished, you can failover the mirror back to the principal. Using this technique allows you to drastically reduce planned downtime within your database environment.

To initiate a failover manually, your mirror must be in the `SYNCHRONIZED` state. Also, you must connect to the master database before failing over the server, since you cannot be connected to the database that you are about to failover. When you issue the manual failover, the principal will disconnect clients, uncommitted transactions will be rolled back, and the last remnants of the log will be shipped over to the mirror. The mirror then becomes the principal, and the principal becomes the mirror. All your clients will need to reconnect to the new principal. To issue the failover, use the `ALTER DATABASE` statement with the `FAILOVER` option as follows on the principal server:

```
ALTER DATABASE dbname SET PARTNER FAILOVER
```

If you are running without a witness in `FULL` transaction safety mode, manual failover is the only type of failover you can perform.

If you are not running in `FULL` transaction safety mode (also called asynchronous mode), you can force a failover as well, but there may be some data loss since this mode does not guarantee that the mirror has received all the logs from the principal. To force a manual failover in this mode, you must use a different option with the `ALTER DATABASE` statement on the principal:

```
ALTER DATABASE dbname SET PARTNER FORCE_SERVICE_ALLOW_DATA_LOSS
```

The reason that database mirroring can failover very fast is that it takes advantage of the fast recovery technology in SQL Server. The mirror is constantly running `REDO` when it receives the log files from the principal. When the mirror is failed over to, it moves from `REDO` to `UNDO` and opens up the database for clients if you're using Enterprise Edition. For Standard Edition, the database is available after both `REDO` and `UNDO` are complete.

Suspending and Resuming Mirroring

There may be times when you want to suspend mirroring and then resume it later. For example, you may want to do this if you find a bottleneck in your system and want to allow the principal to quickly complete its pending transactions, and at some later point you want to apply the same changes to the mirror. In such cases, you can suspend the session, apply your changes to the principal, and then reenable the mirror once the bottleneck is removed. When you suspend a mirroring session, client connections are retained. Also, the log is not truncated, since the log will need to be sent to the mirror at some point, unless you break the mirror partnership. You will not want to suspend a mirror for a long period of time, since the principal's log file could fill up the available storage on your server.

To suspend the session, use the ALTER DATABASE statement on either partner as follows:

```
ALTER DATABASE dbname SET PARTNER SUSPEND
```

To resume the session, just change SUSPEND to RESUME:

```
ALTER DATABASE dbname SET PARTNER RESUME
```

Terminating Database Mirroring

To terminate a database mirroring partnership, you can use the following ALTER DATABASE command on either partner:

```
ALTER DATABASE dbname SET PARTNER OFF
```

When you terminate a partnership, all information about the session is removed, and each server has an independent copy of the database. The mirror database will be in a restoring state until it is manually recovered or deleted. If you want to recover the mirror database, use the RESTORE command with the WITH RECOVERY clause.

■**Caution** Remember to drop all database snapshots, which you will learn about later in this chapter, before breaking your mirror; otherwise, you will get an error stating that the database cannot be restored.

Managing Database Mirroring Using Management Studio

Rather than going through the manual steps to set up mirroring, you can perform all the same actions using SQL Server Management Studio. You can also pause and remove mirroring, as well as initiate a failover from Management Studio. Using the wizard is much easier than writing your own T-SQL code to configure mirroring; however, you get more control over your configuration using T-SQL.

To get started, launch Management Studio and select the database you want to set up as the mirror. Right-click the database and select Properties. You should see mirroring as a page type in the left navigation pane, as shown in Figure 4-2.

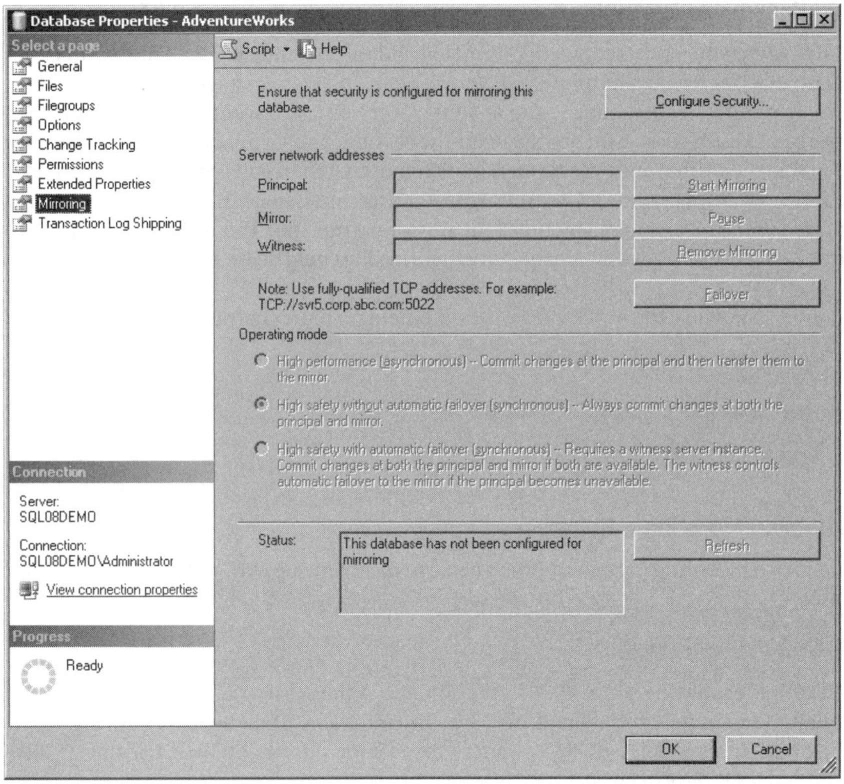

Figure 4-2. *Mirroring settings in the Database Properties dialog box*

The Configure Database Mirroring Security Wizard will step you through setting up the correct security settings for your principal, mirror, and witness, if used. The wizard will create all the endpoint settings for you automatically. Figure 4-3 shows the wizard screen where you can select which servers to configure.

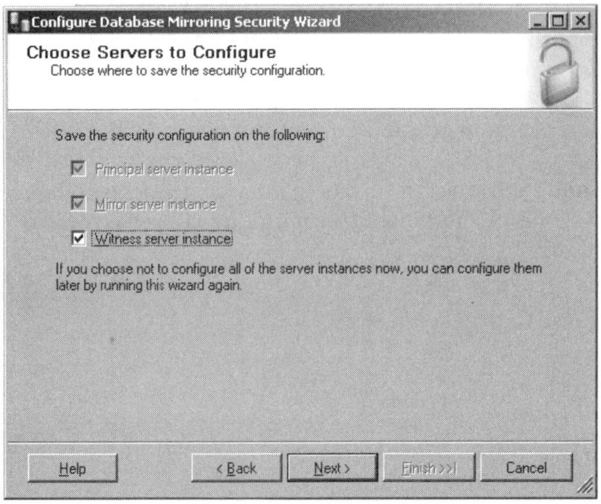

Figure 4-3. *Configure Database Mirroring Security Wizard server selection page*

Once you select the servers you want to configure, the wizard steps you through a set of questions to configure your endpoints. Note that if you are testing database mirroring using multiple instances on a single machine, you will need to specify different ports for your endpoints. Figure 4-4 shows setting the ports, encryption options, and endpoint options in the wizard.

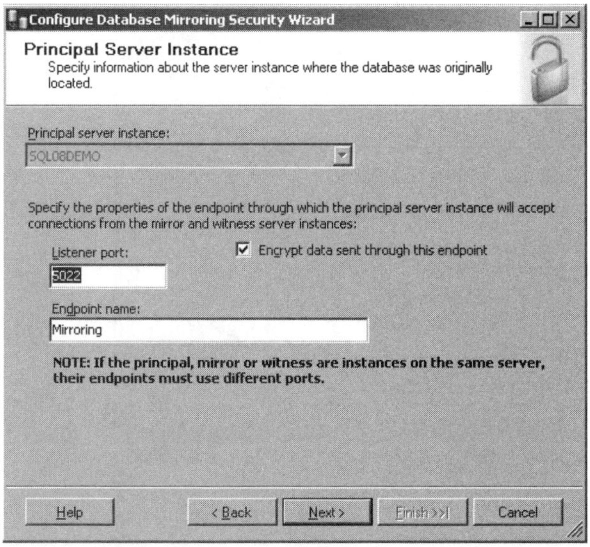

Figure 4-4. *Setting principal server instance options in the Configure Database Mirroring Security Wizard*

Next, the wizard will step you through setting the exact configuration for the remaining partners in your mirroring set. You will need to fill out the same information as you filled out for the principal (Figure 4-4).

Finally, you need to specify the SQL Server service accounts for your servers if they are different. If they are not different, you should leave the text boxes blank, as shown in Figure 4-5.

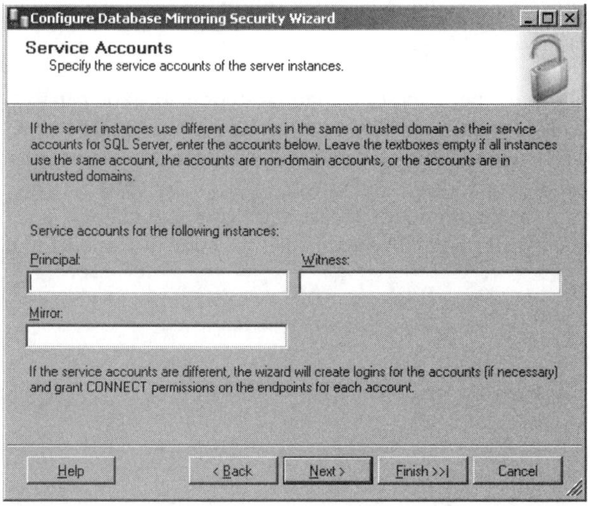

Figure 4-5. *Setting service account options in the Configure Database Mirroring Security Wizard*

Once you have done this, the wizard will complete and attempt to set up your mirroring configuration. Figure 4-6 shows the updated mirroring settings in the Database Properties dialog box once the wizard has completed.

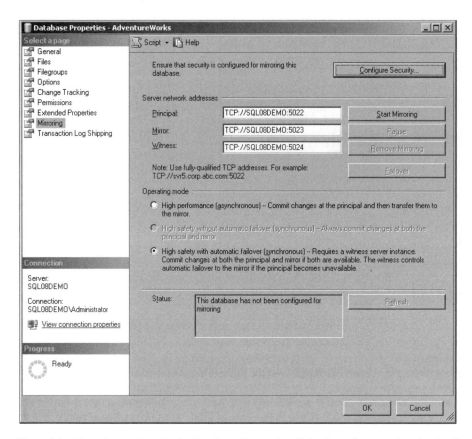

Figure 4-6. *Mirroring settings in the Database Properties dialog box after running the Configure Database Mirroring Security Wizard*

Once the wizard has completed, you'll need to perform some manual steps before you can click the Start Mirroring button in the Database Properties dialog box. You'll need to manually back up and restore your database from the principal to the mirror. Once you've restored the database with the NO RECOVERY option, you can click the Start Mirroring button. Management Studio will attempt to start database mirroring using the same commands you saw earlier to manually set up your mirror pair. Figure 4-7 shows a successfully started database mirroring session in Management Studio.

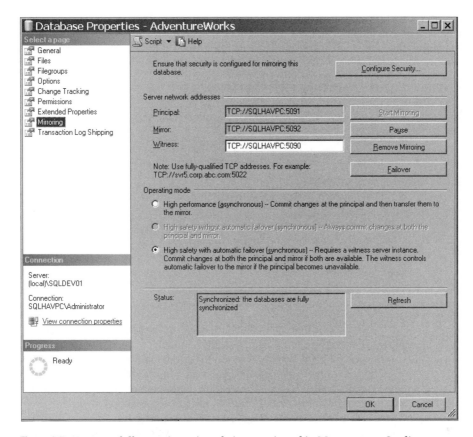

Figure 4-7. *A successfully running mirror being monitored in Management Studio*

The Mirroring section of the Database Properties dialog box will show the current state of the mirroring. You can also get a quick view of the role and status via Object Explorer, as shown in Figure 4-8.

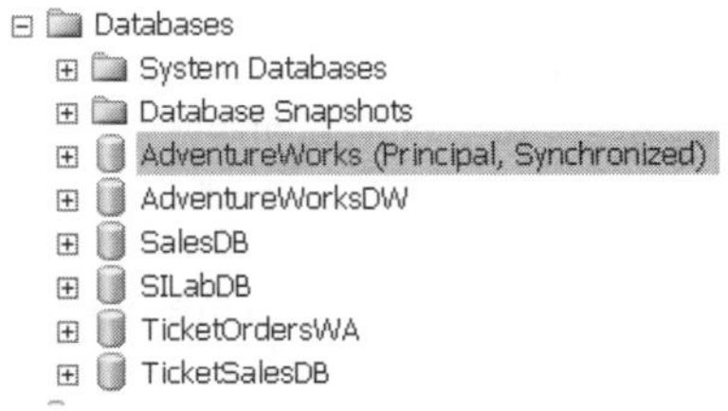

```
□ 🗀 Databases
   ⊞ 🗀 System Databases
   ⊞ 🗀 Database Snapshots
   ⊞ 🗊 AdventureWorks (Principal, Synchronized)
   ⊞ 🗊 AdventureWorksDW
   ⊞ 🗊 SalesDB
   ⊞ 🗊 SILabDB
   ⊞ 🗊 TicketOrdersWA
   ⊞ 🗊 TicketSalesDB
```

Figure 4-8. *Quick check of mirroring status in Object Explorer*

Full-Text Indexing and Mirroring

Since full-text indexing catalogs are now backed up when you back up your databases, when you restore the principal onto the mirror, the full-text catalog is restored as well. As Data Definition Language (DDL) changes are made to the principal's catalog, these changes will be reflected on the mirror.

After a failover, a crawl is automatically initiated on the mirror to update the full-text index. If you create a new catalog on the principal and the mirror cannot perform the operation for some reason, the database state will become SUSPENDED for mirroring.

Service Broker and Database Mirroring

You can use Service Broker and database mirroring together. When combining the two, you must configure Service Broker with two addresses for your route: the principal database server's address and the mirror database server's address. Service Broker will connect to both machines to see who the current principal is, and it will route the message to that principal. If the principal goes down, Service Broker will connect to the mirror, and if the mirror is now the principal, Service Broker will begin delivering messages to the new principal.

You can monitor database mirroring when combined with Service Broker by using the database mirroring Transport object, which is under the Service Broker object, which is, in turn, under the SQL Server object in Performance Monitor. One caveat, though, is that to use Service Broker with database mirroring, you must always have your transaction safety level set to FULL. See Chapter 9 for details on using Service Broker.

Client Applications and Database Mirroring

Normally, when programming your client applications for HA, you need to write a lot of special code to handle the failover of your application. With database mirroring and the .NET or SNAC SQL Server providers, transparent client redirection is automatically handled for you.

Before diving into how to change your client application to use database mirroring, we must first emphasize that transparent client redirection is not a panacea. You still will need to write good code that fails when there is an error and retries the operation. If you do not, transparent client redirection will not magically restart your transaction and complete the operation for you.

When working with transparent client redirection, you must be running the version of the SQL Server providers that comes with SQL Server. There are two modes in which you can program database mirroring: implicit and explicit.

In implicit mode, you do nothing special in your connection string code. Instead, when you first connect to a SQL Server server instance that is part of a database mirror, the SQL Server provider will cache the name of the partner server in memory. If the principal goes away, the SQL Server provider will try to connect to the new partner server on subsequent connections. If a new partner is added after the failure as a new mirror, Microsoft Data Access Components (MDAC) will cache the new partner's name as well.

With explicit mode, you need to specify the server name for the mirror in your connection string. You use the following syntax in your connection string to specify the failover partner:

```
";Failover Partner=YourServerName"
```

Even if you specify the name in the connection string, the SQL Server provider will override the name you specify with the name it retrieves from SQL Server for the failover partner. The reason to specify the partner name in the connection string is to harden your initial connection to the principal. If the SQL Server provider cannot connect to the principal to begin with and there is no partner specified in the connection string, the connection will fail. However, if there is a partner specified in the connection string, the SQL Server provider will try the failover partner for the connection.

Regardless of whether you specify the partner name in the connection string, which is a good practice, you must always specify an initial catalog or database to which to connect. If you do not, transparent client redirection will not work, and the SQL Server provider will throw an error when you attempt to create your connection.

Finally, remember that the failover partner's name is cached in memory. This means that if the application crashes or is restarted, the cached name goes away. For this reason, you will want to make it a habit to specify the failover partner name in the connection string.

Monitoring Database Mirroring

As you saw earlier, you can see the current state of the mirroring in the Mirroring section of the Database Properties dialog box in SQL Server Management Studio. SQL Server provides a variety of other ways to monitor database mirroring, including Database Mirroring Monitor, system stored procedures, catalog and dynamic management views, Performance Monitor, Profiler, and event logs.

Database Mirroring Monitor

Database Mirroring Monitor is available in SQL Server Management Studio. It encapsulates information from the database mirroring catalog views (discussed shortly) by asynchronously capturing the results from the sp_dbmmonitorupdate system stored procedure on the principal and the mirror. It presents a graphical user interface into those results, which are stored in an internal system table within msdb. Furthermore, Database Mirroring Monitor allows for an eventing subsystem through configuration of thresholds on key performance metrics.

Database Mirroring Monitor displays information regarding the partners (principal, mirror, and witness) within a mirroring session, as well as the state of the mirroring session (SYNCHRONIZED, SYNCHRONIZING, and so on) and whether there is a witness present, as shown in Figure 4-9. Database Mirroring Monitor also displays performance information about the principal and mirror server logs. To configure warning thresholds, click the Warnings tab in the Database Mirroring Monitor window. You can specify the thresholds in the Set Warning Thresholds dialog box.

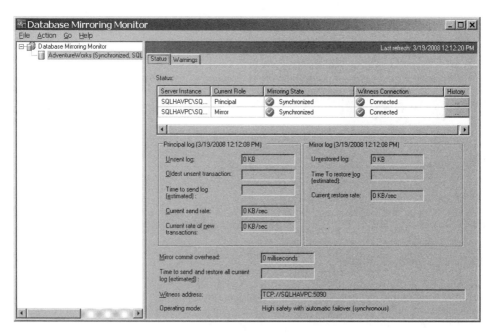

Figure 4-9. *Database Mirroring Monitor showing a synchronized session*

System Stored Procedures and Views

If you would prefer to view mirroring status information in textual format, instead of graphically with the Database Mirroring Monitor, you can run the sp_dbmmonitorresults system stored procedure to retrieve history.

SQL Server has three catalog views related to database mirroring, as well as one dynamic management view:

- sys.database_mirroring: This catalog view contains mirroring information about each database in the SQL Server instance that has mirroring enabled. You can retrieve mirroring and other information about the database using sys.databases as well.

- sys.database_mirroring_endpoints: When you need to work with endpoints, you will want to use this catalog view. Using it, you can figure out which ports your servers are listening on and make sure that you have set up your endpoints correctly. Most of the columns in this view are inherited from the sys.endpoints view. You could use sys.endpoints to view all endpoints in your system, including your database mirroring endpoints.

- sys.database_mirroring_witnesses: This catalog view contains a row for every witness role a server instance plays in a database mirroring partnership.

- sys_dm_db_mirroring_connections: As the name suggests, this dynamic management view lists information about the connections being used by database mirroring sessions.

Figure 4-10 shows using the database mirroring views from Management Studio.

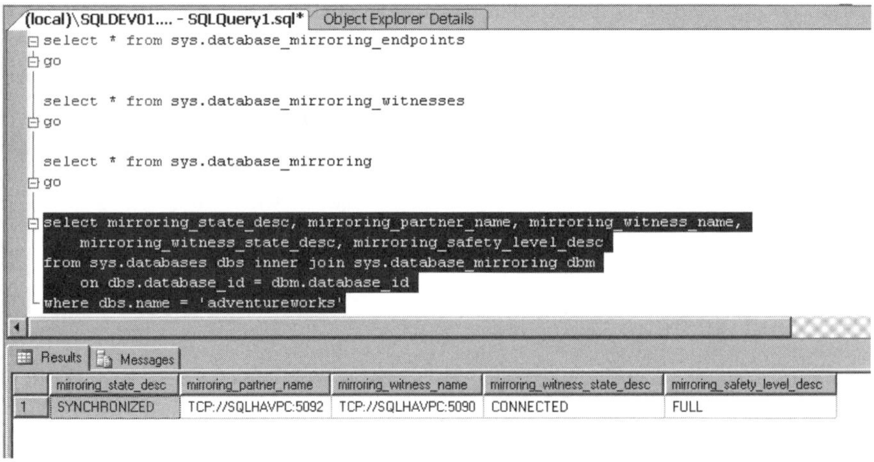

Figure 4-10. *Using the database mirroring views inside Management Studio*

Performance Monitor Counters

You can also monitor database mirroring using Performance Monitor and the database mirroring counters. You can find the Performance Monitor counters under the SQL Server: Database Mirroring object. Table 4-5 lists some of the more important Performance Monitor counters that you can use with database mirroring.

Table 4-5. *Some Database Mirroring Performance Monitor Counters*

Counter Name	Description
Bytes Received/sec	Number of mirroring bytes received per second
Bytes Sent/sec	Number of mirroring bytes sent per second
Log Bytes Received/sec	Number of log bytes received per second
Log Bytes Sent/sec	Number of log bytes sent per second
Log Send Queue	Total number of bytes of log not yet sent to the mirror
Pages Sent/sec	Number of database pages sent per second
Receives/sec	Number of mirroring messages received per second
Sends/sec	Number of mirroring messages sent per second
Transaction Delay	Average delay in transaction termination waiting for acknowledgment from the mirror

If you let Performance Monitor run and there is no transaction activity on your principal, you will see the pattern of the database mirroring pings appear in your capture. Monitor the Total Bytes Sent/sec or the Mirroring Bytes Sent/sec counter to see the pings.

Profiler

You can use Profiler to watch the changes that are happening to your databases that are part of a mirror. Profiler will not show the log being shipped from one server to another, but you will see any SQL commands sent to the current principal or any snapshots on the mirror. You can also see the state change events when roles change because of a failover. To find the database mirroring–specific event in Profiler, look under Database and select the Database Mirroring State Change option.

Event Notifications and Logs

You can use a couple of event notifications for database mirroring to support very powerful automated processing when a mirroring state changes:

- *Database Mirroring State Change*: Triggered when a state change occurs, such as a mirror becoming a principal.

- *Audit Database Mirroring Login*: Can be used to monitor security issues between the principal, mirror, and witness.

Database mirroring puts out events to the Windows Event Log and the SQL Server error log. Some events are information, such as messages telling you that database mirroring has started and what the role of the server is. You can scan the event log to quickly see what's happening with your database mirroring setup, or you can use a third-party tool to monitor the log. Database mirroring event IDs are in the 1400 range, so if you want to filter for them, you will want to filter in that range for SQL Server.

Performance Considerations for Database Mirroring

Depending on how you configure mirroring, you can expect different levels of performance. For example, if you use the FULL transaction safety level, your performance on your principal will be affected by two primary factors: the mirror's I/O ability on the transaction log and your network connection, since the network packets must make a round-trip between the principal and the mirror.

On the mirror, you will want to make sure that you have the same computing and I/O power as the principal. The reason for this is in the case of a failover. You do not want 100 percent load on a larger machine rolling over to a less capable machine. I/O throughout is also very important on the mirror, since the mirror is performing sequential log writes and singleton lookups. Make sure to put your data, log, and tempdb files on different drives that use different disk controllers, if possible.

The edition of SQL Server that you use also affects database mirroring. Even though the Standard Edition of SQL Server supports database mirroring, it has limited capabilities. The Transaction safety level must always be FULL in Standard Edition, and the mirror database server always uses a single thread for the REDO queue processing. In Enterprise Edition, one thread is created per four CPUs for the REDO queue processing.

Finally, make sure to keep your backup and restore procedures in place, even if you use database mirroring. You should back up your databases from the principal server.

Limitations of Database Mirroring

There are a few limitations with database mirroring. First and foremost is that database mirroring supports only two nodes in terms of failover support. Both log shipping and failover clustering support more than two nodes. For scale-out, read-only scenarios, you should consider peer-to-peer replication, rather than database mirroring.

You can use both log shipping and replication with database mirroring. You should make the principal database server the primary in your log shipping topology. You can then make one or more other database servers your secondary database servers that get the log shipped to them. Do not make the mirror database server your secondary database server. As for replication, you can use your principal database server as a publisher and secondary servers as subscribers.

You cannot mirror the master, msdb, temp, or model system databases. Furthermore, you must keep all your logins and jobs in sync manually, since database mirroring does not mirror your logins and jobs between servers. Also, make sure to remove all database snapshots on the mirror before breaking your mirror.

While many customers have requested this feature, you cannot back up your database from the mirror. Instead, you need to back up your databases from the principal server.

Finally, mirroring supports the relational engine only at a database level. If you want instance failover, you will need to configure mirroring for every database in an instance. Also, if you want HA for other components, such as Analysis Services and Reporting Services, you will need to use Windows clustering.

Database Snapshots and Mirroring

When you have a mirrored system, you may want to use the mirror as the server that users query to generate reports on their data, for two reasons:

- You do not want users querying your primary OLTP system, since it must handle the load for all your transactions.

- You may want to get more usage out of your mirror, since you have already invested in the hardware for the mirror.

Before we dive into a discussion about creating snapshots on your mirrors, though, there are some things you need to think about. First and foremost is that allowing users to query the mirror using snapshots will be a performance hit on the mirror. This could, in turn, slow down your entire database mirroring solution. The second consideration is that when there is a failover to the mirror, you do not want your clients querying your new principal; rather, you want to failover your snapshots and your clients to the new mirror if it's available.

How Database Snapshots Work

The easiest way to define database snapshots is to use the term *copy-on-write*. Snapshots use a copy-on-write technology, so that only changes to the database are written to the snapshot. Therefore, the entire database does not need to be copied when creating a snapshot; only the changes are copied. Now, if your entire database is changing over the lifetime of a snapshot, then your snapshot will become larger as the changes are applied.

Database snapshots are a read-only, point-in-time, static view of your database. Snapshots work at the data-page level. This means that when a data page changes, the original page is copied over to the snapshot. If the same data page is modified later, the snapshot does not change and is unaware of the new data page. To update the snapshot with the new data, you need to create a new snapshot.

When a snapshot is created, a sync log sequence number is created in the source database. SQL Server then runs recovery on the snapshot, since uncommitted transactions need to be rolled back on the snapshot. This does not affect the transactions on the source database. SQL Server creates an NTFS sparse file to hold the snapshot. NTFS sparse files work as you might guess: when they are initially created, sparse files are, in fact, *sparse*. They don't contain any data, and they grow as data is added to the file. Allocations to the sparse file are in 64KB blocks. When a copy-on-write happens, all the pages are zeroed out except for the changed data page, if a new 64KB block is allocated. When other pages change, individual pages are copied over to the 64KB block.

When an application updates a value in the database, before the new value is written, the database makes a copy of that page to the snapshot in its sparse file. SQL Server maintains a bitmap for the related sparse file so that it can quickly decide where the I/O should go on a read operation, since the snapshot or the original database may contain the correct information. When a read operation comes in, if the snapshot already contains the correct data, SQL Server will go to the snapshot for the information. If the data has not changed in the original database and therefore hasn't been copied to the snapshot, SQL Server will go to the original database to retrieve the information. No locks are taken on the original database when a read happens for a snapshot. Figure 4-11 shows this process for database snapshots.

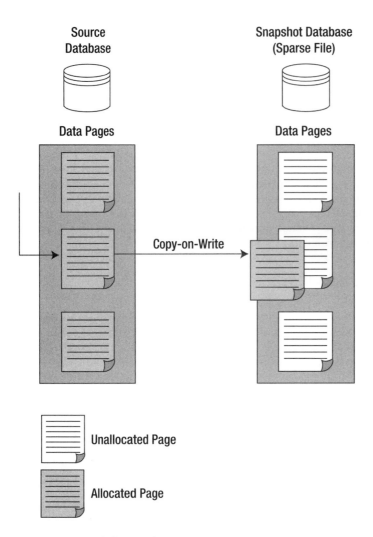

Figure 4-11. *Database snapshots*

You may be wondering how database snapshots can work with database mirroring, since the database on the mirror is restoring. Through the magic of code, database snapshots get an exclusive latch on the mirror database, so that snapshots can read the data in a mirrored database.

■**Caution** You can speed up the population of a snapshot with some routine maintenance on your source database. For example, if you rebuild an index, you may find that your snapshot will start growing very fast as the index is rebuilt. You may not have intended for this to happen, so be aware that if anything changes the source database, the snapshot will grow.

Managing Snapshots Using T-SQL

You may want to perform some common operations with snapshots using T-SQL. These include creating and deleting snapshots, as well as reverting to a snapshot.

Creating a Database Snapshot

To create a database snapshot, use the CREATE DATABASE statement with the AS SNAPSHOT OF argument. You must specify every database file of the source database. You can have multiple snapshots on your system, so that you have different point-in-time views of your databases. Note, though, that you will need to explicitly connect to the snapshot from your applications.

One best practice to follow is to use descriptive names for your snapshots so you know when they were created, just in case you have many snapshots on your system. The following example creates a snapshot of the AdventureWorks database on a mirrored server:

```
CREATE DATABASE AdventureWorks_dbss031908 ON
   ( NAME=AdventureWorks_Data,
     FILENAME= 'C:\Program Files\Microsoft SQL Server\
        MSSQL.1\MSSQL\Data\AdventureWorks_data_031908.ss')
   AS SNAPSHOT OF AdventureWorks;
```

Dropping a Database Snapshot

To drop a database snapshot, you just need to use the DROP DATABASE statement. All the sparse files associated with your snapshot will be deleted as well. The following code deletes the snapshot without affecting the source database just created:

```
DROP DATABASE AdventureWorks_dbss031908
GO
```

Reverting to a Database Snapshot

We all make mistakes. Thankfully, database snapshots can help us recover from our mistakes. When you revert to a snapshot, the pages stored in the snapshot are rewritten back to the original database. The log is also overwritten and rebuilt in the process. Any updates to the database since the snapshot was taken, from both a data and metadata standpoint, are lost, so you must be completely sure that you want to revert to the snapshot.

A number of restrictions apply when reverting a source database to a snapshot:

- You cannot revert if the source database has read-only or compressed filegroups.

- You cannot have filegroups currently offline that were online when the snapshot was taken.

- You cannot have multiple snapshots in existence when you revert. You must remove all other snapshots except the one snapshot to which you want to revert.

- You cannot revert on the mirror. If you want to revert in a database mirroring scenario, you need to be taking snapshots on the principal.

■**Caution** You may lose your metadata about mirroring if you revert to a snapshot. Also after reverting, you may need to set up your database mirroring configuration again.

You should back up your log before you revert to a snapshot. You cannot use this backup to roll forward changes after reverting, but the log may be useful in helping to understand what changes were made to the database after the snapshot was taken by using a log explorer tool. In addition, if you are using full recovery mode for your logs, you can restore the database on a separate server and use the point-in-time recovery feature to restore only up to the point that the failure or error was made. You can then bulk-export the changes and bulk-import the changes into your newly reverted database. Finally, perform a full backup of your database after you revert to the snapshot.

The following code will revert back to the snapshot created earlier:

```
RESTORE DATABASE AdventureWorks from
    DATABASE_SNAPSHOT = 'AdventureWorks_dbss031908'
GO
```

Performance Considerations When Using Snapshots on Mirrors

Some special considerations relate to using snapshots on your mirrors. Remember that if you are running with FULL transaction safety on, the principal will wait for an acknowledgment from the mirror. If you are running many snapshots that users are querying against on the mirror, that will affect the performance of both the mirror and, in turn, the principal. One of the ways that you can make your snapshots more performant is to place your snapshots on a different drive than your mirror's log. This way, the two technologies do not contend for I/O with one another.

You will also want to move the snapshots from the old mirror to the new mirror when it comes back online. This is not done automatically for you, so you will need to script the creation of the snapshots on a failure. Also, you will need to change your client applications, since the snapshot will now be on a different server.

Using and Monitoring Database Snapshots

Since snapshots look like real databases, you can easily query them for the data contained in the snapshot. Rather than specifying the source tables, you can use the tables contained in your snapshot. The following query returns a list of customers from the Customers table in the snapshot:

```
SELECT [DepartmentID]
      ,[Name]
      ,[GroupName]
      ,[ModifiedDate]
  FROM [AdventureWorks_dbss031908].[HumanResources].[Department]
GO
```

Management Studio will display the snapshots you have created. If you want to view the physical path to the database snapshot, you can use the physical_name column of the sys.master_files catalog view. Note that if you query the same column in sys.database_files, the view will always return the source database files, even if you specify the database snapshot.

To determine the actual size of the sparse files, you can use the BytesonDisk column from the fn_virtualfilestats function. This function takes a database ID and a file ID as values. The function will then return the file statistics. Also, you could use Windows Explorer to view the size of the file using the Size on Disk value from the file's Properties dialog box.

The following code returns information about the snapshot file. Notice the use of the DB_ID and FILE_IDEX functions to get the database ID and the file ID. Note that the file ID will correspond to the logical name of the file from sys.master_files. You could also retrieve both of these values from sys.master_files.

```
SELECT *
FROM fn_virtualfilestats(DB_ID(N' AdventureWorks_dbss031908'),
    FILE_IDEX(N'Northwind'));
GO
```

Programming against a database snapshot is very straightforward. Instead of connecting to the original database, you just connect to the snapshot in your connection string. The only caveat is that you will need to manually connect to a different snapshot if you want to change snapshots.

Limitations of Database Snapshots

While there are many benefits to database snapshots, you should also be aware of their limitations. The biggest one is that database snapshots are available only in the Enterprise Edition of SQL Server 2008. If you have the Express, Workgroup, or Standard Edition, you do not have access to the database snapshot functionality.

Second, the database and its snapshot must exist in the same instance. You cannot create a snapshot in a separate instance. While snapshots exist on a source database, you cannot drop, detach, or restore the source. You must first delete all snapshots for that database. Backup of the source database is unaffected by snapshots, so you can back up the database while you have active snapshots. Also, you cannot snapshot the master, tempdb, or model databases.

For the snapshot itself, remember it is a read-only copy reflecting the exact state of the source database at the creation time of the snapshot, with any uncommitted transactions rolled back. Files cannot be changed on the snapshot. Permissions are inherited from the source and cannot be changed. This is important, because if you change the permissions on the source database, these changes will not be reflected in existing snapshots. You may have users who you no longer want to have permissions on your data, but if you have snapshots, you must make sure to re-create your snapshots after changing permissions. Snapshots cannot be backed up or restored, nor can they be attached or detached. Also, you cannot create snapshots on FAT32 or RAW partitions. Finally, snapshots do not support full-text indexing, and any full-text catalogs on the source will not exist in the snapshot.

Remember that the snapshot is not an entire copy of the source database. The snapshot will go back to the source database for data that has not changed. This means that the state of the source database will affect the snapshot. If the source database goes into recovery mode, some data may not be available in the snapshot. If the source database takes a file offline, some data in the snapshot may not be available as well. If when you created the snapshot a filegroup was offline in the source and you bring it online later, it still will be considered offline in the snapshot. You will want to make sure you understand the state of both the snapshot and the source database; otherwise, you may get interesting errors from the snapshot that you may not realize are caused by the state of the source database.

Windows Clustering in SQL Server

Another way to achieve HA with SQL Server is to use Windows clustering. The main reason for discussing clustering here is to compare it to database mirroring. You can use mirroring with clustering. However, you must mirror between clusters, not within a cluster. Therefore, you could have a principal running on a two-node cluster that communicates with a mirror that runs on a separate two-node cluster.

The only thing to watch out for when using mirroring and clustering is the failover times and conflicts. For example, if you set the timeout of mirroring to 1 minute and clusters usually failover after 30 seconds, you may have clusters that failover before your mirror or vice versa. Also, you could get into some weird situations where the cluster and the mirror failover at about the same time. You definitely will want to test any configuration on which you have mirroring and clustering running together.

The main difference between mirroring and clustering is that clustering is at an instance level, while mirroring is at a database level. Mirroring does not failover other services of SQL Server or other services of the operating system. Therefore, if you use mirroring, you will need to make sure that any ancillary services that you expect to be running on the server, such as SQL Server Agent or others, must be started and running on the mirror server.

One of the benefits of mirroring as compared with clustering is that mirroring does not require special hardware, nor does it require a shared disk subsystem. Your mirrored database servers can exist in separate locations.

SQL Server Replication

SQL Server version 6.0 introduced replication as a built-in feature, and each version since then has made significant improvements or additions to the base functionality. SQL Server 2008 introduces major improvements to conflict detection in peer-to-peer replication (something that has been requested for a long time) and adds graphic replication management capabilities for the administrator.

At a very basic level, replication exists to move data and database objects between servers or between clients and servers using a wide variety of connection types, including the Internet. SQL Server Compact Edition plays an integral part when communicating with devices such as handheld scanners, Pocket PCs, and laptops that may not require, or are not capable of running, a full version of SQL Server 2008.

SQL Server implements three kinds of replication; snapshot replication, merge replication, and transaction replication. For all three types, SQL Server uses a publishing metaphor in which publishers, subscribers, distributors, publications, subscriptions, and articles all work as a coordinated unit to accomplish replication. Figure 4-12 illustrates the components of replication.

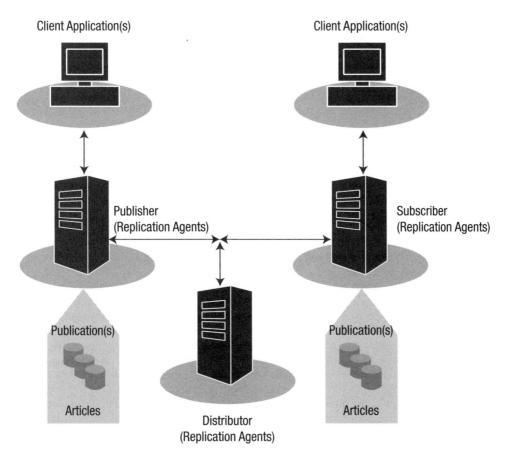

Figure 4-12. *Components of replication architecture*

Snapshot Replication

Snapshot replication distributes a point-in-time copy of the articles within the publication. Although snapshot replication is sometimes used by itself, it is most often used to initialize a subscriber for merge or transaction replication. It is important to consider the overall size of the dataset to be replicated as part of the snapshot, as the generation of the snapshot could require substantial resources on the publisher, and the application of the snapshot could require substantial resources on the subscriber.

Merge Replication

Merge replication is most often utilized in situations where data and objects are being synchronized between clients and servers that are not always in a connected state. Such is the case with sales force automation systems, point-of-sale systems, and field automation systems.

Merge replication allows many sites/devices to work independently while either connected or disconnected from the network. When the site/device is reconnected to the network, changes are synchronized between the publisher and subscriber. Consider an inventory tracking system within a large warehouse where radio frequency identification (RFID) scanners and barcode readers are used to track and count inventory. Many of these devices may be continually connected to a network;

however, it is quite possible that some of these devices will maintain a local data store using SQL Server Compact Edition and are only periodically connected to the network, at which time changes are synchronized with the publisher.

Traditionally, merge replication has allowed advanced conflict detection and processing. This is changing somewhat with SQL Server 2008, as advanced conflict detection can now be programmed within peer-to-peer transaction replication.

Transaction Replication

Transaction replication is typically used when replicating data between servers. Transaction replication is also the preferred method for replicating large amounts of data or when very low latency between the publisher and subscriber is required. Transaction replication is capable of functioning when the publisher or subscriber is a non-SQL Server database, such as Oracle.

Transaction replication can be configured with a number of different publication types, one of which is peer-to-peer transactional replication. In peer-to-peer replication, data can be maintained across a number of servers, or nodes, within the replication topology. Although transaction replication is typically used to scale out read-intensive applications, it is also possible for updates to take place within each node in the topology.

Traditionally, it has been very important to avoid conflicts for peer-to-peer replication by ensuring that the same record could not be updated on many nodes at the same time. Although it is still important to ensure that conflicts don't occur, SQL Server 2008 introduces the ability to perform conflict detection within a peer-to-peer topology. When a conflict is detected within the topology, the Distribution Agent will report a critical error, and the conflict will need to be handled manually before the topology returns to a consistent state. Although not ideal, this solution does provide an extra layer of protection by ensuring that transactions are not lost as a result of conflicts within a peer-to-peer topology.

A new Peer-to-Peer Topology Wizard makes the configuration of peer-to-peer topologies ridiculously easy. Once an initial publication is created on one of the nodes within the topology, you can use the wizard to graphically configure the remaining nodes within the topology, as shown in Figure 4-13.

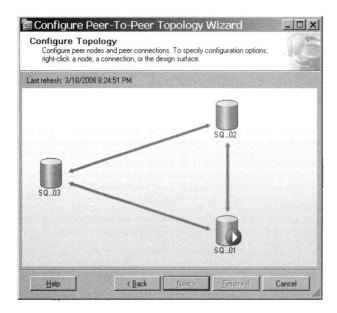

Figure 4-13. *Peer-to-Peer Topology Wizard*

Replication and Mirroring

There may be times when replication will make more sense than database mirroring for your data availability needs. For example, if you want a scale-out, read-only reporting solution, peer-to-peer replication is a much better solution than mirroring, since replication can support many peers in its topology. With mirroring, you can have only a single mirror. However, replication does not natively support failover transparently, as mirroring does. You must write your applications in such a way to understand failures in a replicated environment. Plus, replication is at the Data Manipulation Language (DML) level, while mirroring is at the log level, so you may find that mirroring has better performance in certain scenarios.

That said, you can combine mirroring and replication. You could replicate the principal using replication or even log shipping. However, this introduces a bunch of complexities that you may not want to deal with. For example, if the principal fails over and then comes back up as the mirror, replication will break, since the database will not be readable.

Reducing Planned Downtime

As mentioned at the beginning of this chapter, we are actually trying to minimize two general flavors of downtime: planned and unplanned. Combinations of the previous technologies can be used to address, and possibly eliminate, unplanned downtime. However, it has generally been accepted that some amount of planned downtime is required. However, increasingly, we are dealing with organizations that have zero tolerance for any type of downtime. Financial organizations are following the sun when it comes to data entry of things like new policies. Medical providers are increasingly leveraging SQL Server for their most mission-critical emergency room systems. This 24 × 7 business demand is eliminating the typical nightly cycle.

The SQL Server product team is helping us address these demands by allowing many operations to be performed while our databases are online and accessible by end users. These include adding a CPU or memory to a running system, as well as performing online index operations and partitioning tables and indexes.

Adding a CPU to a Running System

The ability to dynamically add CPUs (*hot-add*) to a SQL Server instance, without restarting, is a new feature available in SQL Server 2008. The following are the requirements for this feature:

- The underlying server hardware must support the ability to dynamically add a CPU without restarting, unless using virtualization or hardware partitioning.

- The operating system must be Windows Server 2008 Enterprise Edition or Windows Server 2008 Datacenter Edition. The operating system must also be a 64-bit edition.

- SQL Server 2008 Enterprise Edition must be used.

SQL Server will not automatically recognize or use a newly added CPU(s). You must use the RECONFIGURE command to enable the new CPU.

Adding Memory to a Running System

Similar to dynamically adding a CPU, you can hot-add memory to a SQL Server and use it, without needing to restart the SQL Server instance. This feature has the following requirements:

- It is available only in the 64-bit SQL Server Enterprise Edition, or the 32-bit version with Address Windowing Extensions enabled.
- The operating system must be Windows Server 2003 or 2008 Enterprise or Datacenter Edition.
- The underlying physical hardware must support the ability to dynamically add memory, unless using virtualization or hardware partitioning.

Performing Online Index Operations

SQL Server provides the ability to create, rebuild, and drop indexes online. The idea of online index operations is that users of the database are not locked from the table or index undergoing the operations. This is very different functionality than we were used to with online index operations in editions prior to SQL Server 2005, which required exclusive locks while the operation was being performed, thus ensuring that users could not change or access the data in any way.

The following is an example using the online option:

```
USE AdventureWorks;
GO
ALTER INDEX PK_SalesOrderDetail_SalesOrderID_SalesOrderDetailID
    ON Sales.SalesOrderDetail
REBUILD WITH (ONLINE = ON);
```

See the SQL Server Books Online topic "How Online Index Operations Work" for further details on implementing this technology.

Keep in mind that online index operations make extensive use of tempdb, and therefore you should ensure that tempdb is configured to Microsoft's recommended best practices.

Partitioning Tables and Indexes

Table and index partitioning provide the ability to create, modify, and delete subsets of data without affecting the integrity of the entire data collection. Partitioning is often thought of as a way to increase performance and scalability when working with large amounts of data. Although performance is typically increased, partitioning was originally designed to improve manageability of large tables and indexes.

With data partitioned into many smaller subsets, operations such as index rebuilds and individual partition backups execute much more quickly than they would against a nonpartitioned table or index. In fact, the combination of index partitioning and online index operations provides a very powerful solution for performing maintenance operations without any planned downtime.

Summary

This chapter walked you through many of the HA and DR technologies available in SQL Server. Understanding how these technologies fit into your overall HA strategy is an important step in planning your SQL Server deployment. It is quite posssible that a number of different technologies may be used in parallel to fill the needs of your SQL Server solutions. While accounting for unplanned downtime is typically the major focus of most HA initiatives, it is becoming increasingly important to reduce planned downtime to support 24×7 business operations.

CHAPTER 5

■ ■ ■

Performance

Database performance is affected by a lot of factors, including the server hardware, the operating system configuration, and the database configuration. As database administrators (DBAs) and developers, we can set only so many knobs at the hardware and operating system level to improve performance. We can have the biggest impact on our database's performance by designing an efficient database architecture using indexes and compression where appropriate. We can also design queries that leverage the latest hints, locking, and other techniques.

In this chapter, we will explore the enhancements in SQL Server 2008 as they relate to the following performance-related topics:

- Resource management
- Storage optimization
- Query performance

Managing and Monitoring Resources

Many options exist for managing and monitoring resources. Most features that ship in SQL Server expose a way to monitor their state not only through their own tool, but also from larger, enterprise-wide monitoring tools like Microsoft's System Center Operations Manager. A good example is the SQL Server Agent scheduling service. You can monitor SQL Server Agent jobs using SQL Server Management Studio or the System Center Operations Manager. With that said, Microsoft realizes that some organizations don't have the budget for these kinds of enterprise-wide management tools. In addition, some of these enterprise tools don't have the granularity that DBAs demand. SQL Server 2008 introduces some additional tools, including the Data Collector and Resource Governor, to help you monitor and manage resources in SQL Server.

Data Collector

Throughout the evolution of SQL Server, its developers have strived to improve the tools available to users to aid in performance configuration. With SQL Server 2005, the Database Tuning Advisor (DTA) tool was introduced to allow users to submit a workload and receive suggestions on how to improve the query performance. SQL Server 2008 adds the ability to easily obtain and analyze server-wide performance-related information. Obtaining this information is part of a feature called the Data Collector, which allows users to pull data from a variety of sources into a data warehouse for analysis. Sources of this information include SQL Trace events, Performance Monitor counters, and the SQL Server History and Health tool, to name a few.

The Data Collector is the plumbing that allows users to easily choose which interesting properties to monitor. It places this information in a management data warehouse, which is either a new
database that the user creates or an existing database on the server.

Once you have a common place for this data, you can do a variety of useful things with it, such
as perform analytical operations to obtain trend information and to deduce potential issues before
they occur. You can also easily communicate these findings with the rest of your organization by
creating reports from the data that was collected via Reporting Services.

Configuring the Management Data Warehouse

You can configure a management data warehouse to be used by the Data Collector via Transact-SQL
(T-SQL) stored procedures or by using the Configure Management Data Warehouse Wizard in SQL
Server Management Studio. Here, we'll walk through using the wizard.

To launch the wizard, in Object Explorer, expand the Management node, right-click the Data
Collection node, and choose Configure Management Data Warehouse. Click Next on the welcome
page to move to the Configure Management Data Warehouse Storage page, as shown in Figure 5-1.

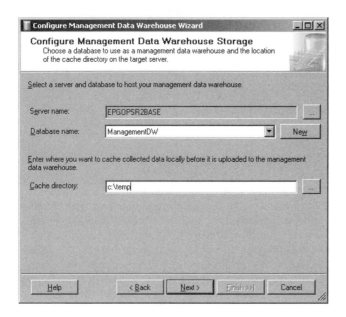

Figure 5-1. *Configure Management Data Warehouse Storage page*

Here, you can specify either a local or remote database for the destination of your data collection.
You can also optionally specify a local cache directory. Having a local cache improves performance,
since you will not be immediately writing to the data warehouse database upon acquisition of each
piece of data. This frequency of collection is a configurable property and will be discussed in the
"Adding Collection Items" section a little later in this chapter.

The next page in the wizard, shown in Figure 5-2, asks you to configure the security of the database. On this page, when you select a login in the top grid, the role membership for that selected login is shown in the bottom grid.

Figure 5-2. *Map Logins and Users page*

In Figure 5-2, User2 is selected as the login, and the bottom grid reveals this login is a member of the mdw_admin, mdw_reader, and mdw_writer roles. These are the three database roles within the management data warehouse database, and are defined as follows:

- mdw_admin: Members of this role have read, write, update, and delete access to the management data warehouse database.

- mdw_reader: Members of this role have read access to the historical data only. This role is used primarily for troubleshooting purposes.

- mdw_writer: Members of this role can upload and write data into the management data warehouse database.

In our example, we have User1 and User2. User1 was assigned just the mdw_reader role. User2 is an mdw_admin.

The next page of the wizard will provide a summary of the actions that will be performed, as shown in Figure 5-3. When you click Finish, the wizard will create or update the selected database with the objects used by the Data Collector.

Figure 5-3. *Summary page*

In addition to creating database roles and various stored procedures, the wizard will create three data collection sets: Disk Usage, Query Statistics, and Server Activity. These system-installed collection sets contain a number of collection items utilizing both the T-SQL and Performance Monitor counter collector types. They not only provide some useful information upon collection, but they are also good to use to learn more about how to create your own data collection sets. You can see the creation scripts for these collection sets by right-clicking them and selecting Script Data Collection as ➤ CREATE To ➤ New Query Editor Window.

To demonstrate using the Data Collector, we'll walk through creating your own data collection set.

Creating Collection Sets

Collection sets are containers that hold zero or more collection item objects. The set itself defines properties, such as whether the data that is obtained should be cached, how long the data should be retained before it is deleted from the warehouse, and SQL Server Agent proxy account information used by Agent jobs when collecting the data.

In SQL Server 2008, you will need to use a T-SQL stored procedure to create the collection set, since SQL Server Management Studio does not have a tool to perform this action. You use the sp_syscollector_create_collection_set stored procedure in the msdb database.

As an example, we will create a collection set called UserSession_Stats. In the next section, we will add a collection item that will simply make a call to a view and return the active sessions for the local instance of SQL Server.

■**Note** If you are following along with this example, you should copy and run the entire script as one batch, since the sp_syscollection_create_collection_set stored procedure provides output variables that are needed when you run the stored procedure to create a collection item.

```
USE msdb
GO
DECLARE @mycollection_set_id int
DECLARE @mycollection_set_uid UNIQUEIDENTIFIER

--Create collection set, the container for various collection items
EXEC [dbo].[sp_syscollector_create_collection_set] @name=N'UserSession_Stats',
@collection_mode=1, --This means noncached mode
@description=N'Collects data about user session information',
@target=N'',
@logging_level=1, --Sets logging level used by SSIS
@days_until_expiration=90,
@proxy_name=N'',
@schedule_name=N'CollectorSchedule_Every_6h', --Uses existing SQL Agent schedule
@collection_set_id=@mycollection_set_id OUTPUT,
@collection_set_uid=@mycollection_set_uid OUTPUT
```

Note a few parameters in this stored procedure:

- collection_mode: This property determines if the collection and upload are on the same or separate schedules.

- logging_level: This property is set because under the covers, a SQL Server Integration Services (SSIS) package is performing the actual data collection.

- proxy_name: The proxy account information may also be required, since you might need to establish the security context that will be used to obtain the data you are after. In this example, we are running under the sysadmin account, so we don't need to specify a proxy account.

- schedule_name: Many existing Agent schedules are available. This example uses the schedule that executes every 6 hours. You could select to run the collection on other schedules, such as every 5, 10, 15, 30, or 60 minutes. These shared schedules are created for you in SQL Agent as part of the configuration wizard.

After creating a collection set, you can add collection items for it.

Adding Collection Items

A *collection item* defines the piece of data that the user is requesting. Just as a collection set has properties associated with it, so does the collection item. One of these properties is collector type, which identifies the actual mechanism for collecting data and uploading it to the management data warehouse. SQL Server 2008 comes with three collector types out of the box: T-SQL Query Collector, SQL Trace Collector, and Performance Counters Collector.

■**Tip** To see a list of all the available collector types, query the syscollector_collector_types view in the msdb database.

You can also create your own collector types by using the sp_syscollector_create_collection_item stored procedure. For our example, we can take the output variables that came from the sp_syscollector_create_collection_set stored procedure and pass them into sp_syscollector_create_collection_item, which will create a collection item for our sample collection set. The following code does this:

```
DECLARE @mycollector_type_uid UNIQUEIDENTIFIER

SELECT @mycollector_type_uid = collector_type_uid FROM
[dbo].[syscollector_collector_types]
WHERE NAME = N'Generic T-SQL Query Collector Type';

DECLARE @collection_item_id INT

EXEC [dbo].[sp_syscollector_create_collection_item] @name=N'User_Connections',
@parameters=N'<TSQLQueryCollector><Query><Value>
SELECT COUNT(*) AS '' Active_sessions'' FROM sys.dm_exec_sessions
</Value><OutputTable>usersession_info</OutputTable></Query>
<Databases UseSystemDatabases="false" UseUserDatabases="false"/>
</TSQLQueryCollector>', @collection_item_id=@collection_item_id OUTPUT,
@frequency=5, -- How frequently we will obtain a sample data point
@collection_set_id=@mycollection_set_id,
@collector_type_uid=@mycollector_type_uid
```

The frequency parameter determines how frequently in seconds SQL Server will sample the data.

You can see that the unique identifier for the T-SQL Query Collector type was obtained from a query to the syscollector_collector_types view and passed as one of the parameters to the syscollector_create_collection_item stored procedure. The parameters parameter is where you define specifics of the query you wish to issue and where to place the query results.

Each collector type has a different schema. You can see the schema for each of these types by querying the parameter_schema column of the syscollector_collector_types view. All the available options for that collector type will be described in the schema. You can also refer to SQL Server Books Online for the options for the collector types that come with SQL Server.

With the T-SQL Query Collector, you have the option to issue the query agaist system databases, user databases, both, or none at all. Other collector types will offer different options.

Once you have defined the collection set and collection items, you are ready to start collecting the data.

Collecting Data

To start collecting data, you can issue the sp_syscollector_start_collection_set stored procedure call, or right-click the collection set and select Start Data Collection Set from the context menu. In our example, every 6 hours, we will be uploading our samples of data that were collected at 5-second intervals. When uploaded, the data it is copied into our output table usersession_info in the management data warehouse database that we defined as part of the TSQLQueryCollector parameter when we created the collection item.

After you've collected and stored some data, you can work with it in interesting ways, such as creating reports or data mining using Analysis Services. Some reports are available out of the box. A good example of this is the Server Activity History report. This is more of an interactive report, allowing users to zoom in and out of time ranges. Some of the information displayed in this report is shown in Figures 5-4 and 5-5.

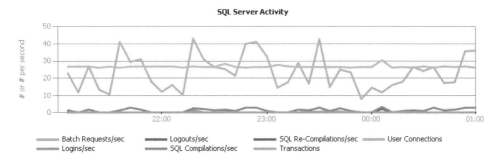

Figure 5-4. *SQL Server Activity chart within the Server Activity History report*

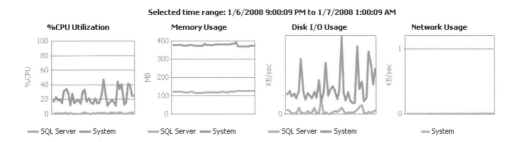

Figure 5-5. *Various counters within the Server Activity History report*

Being able to collect data and record it in one central place is very useful. Although it would be nice to have better tools to support this initial release of the Data Collector, the overall value of this feature is huge.

Resource Governor

How many times have you seen a query eat up system resources like memory and CPU for extended lengths of time? These types of runaway queries will be a thing of the past with a properly configured Resource Governor. Resource Governor allows the DBA to allocate database resources (CPU bandwidth and memory) to users and applications.

In earlier versions of SQL Server, it was not possible to differentiate workloads. Thus, an administrator query, an OLTP workload, and a report-generation query would all have the same priority to the SQL Server database engine. Not having the ability to limit or prioritize workloads can lead to a disproportionate distribution of resources and unpredictable performance.

Resource Governor in SQL Server 2008 allows the DBA to create workload groups and resource pools. The DBA can then define priorities on these workloads and assign workloads to resource pools. So, for example, you could configure a scenario where the OLTP queries take more of the CPU cycles than do your administrator queries, or you could make all your administrator queries take most of the CPU and let your users have whatever is left (after all, you're the one who uses SQL Server every day, so you deserve all of the CPU bandwidth!).

Creating Resource Pools

Resource pools represent a collection of physical resources of the server. In SQL Server 2008, resource pools define minimum and maximum values for memory and CPU utilization. A resource pool is similar to the concept of a virtual instance of SQL Server. However, a true virtual instance would include much more separation than just the division of memory and CPU utilization.

SQL Server 2008 has two predefined resource pools:

- *Internal*: The internal pool is used solely by the SQL Server database engine. System administrators cannot change or configure any settings for the internal pool.

- *Default*: The default pool will be used by all workloads that do not have a pool assigned to them. Thus, if you never configure Resource Governor in SQL Server, all your workloads will be running in the default pool. This pool cannot be altered or dropped, but unlike with the internal pool, you can alter its minimum and maximum settings.

Most of the time, system administrators will be interested in creating their own resource pools. When defining minimum and maximum values for a resource pool, keep in mind the following:

- The sum of minimum values across all pools cannot exceed 100 percent. This is because SQL Server makes every effort to ensure these minimum values are respected.

- The maximum values can be set anywhere in the range between the minimum defined and 100 percent.

Theoretically, if all pools were set to a maximum of 100 percent, it would be impossible for all workloads using those pools to achieve 100 percent. Thus, when planning your minimum and maximum values, it is important to consider the *effective maximum percentage*. To explain this concept, let's take a look at an example.

Suppose we have three user-defined resource pools, plus the internal and default pools, as shown in Table 5-1. The Effective Maximum Percentage column in the table is defined as the maximum CPU percentage, taking into consideration all the other pools defined. We calculate this percentage as the smallest, or minimum, value between the defined maximum for the pool and the difference between the defined maximum and the sum of the other minimum percentages.

Table 5-1. *Resource Pools for the Example*

Resource Pool	Minimum	Maximum	Effective Maximum Percentage
Internal	0	100	100; this value is not affected by user-defined settings
Default	0	100	= Minimum of 100 or (100–(20+50+10))=100 or 20=20
Pool1	20	70	= Minimum of 70 or (100–(50+10))=40
Pool2	50	100	= Minimum of 100 or (100–(20+10))=70
Pool3	10	50	= Minimum of 50 or (100–(20+50))=30

You can see that the effective maximum percentages are different from what we intended the maximum to be when we defined the pools originally.

To create a resource pool, use the CREATE RESOURCE POOL statement. The following code creates two resource pools:

```
CREATE RESOURCE POOL AdminQueries
WITH (MAX_CPU_PERCENT = 100)

CREATE RESOURCE POOL UserQueries
WITH (MAX_CPU_PERCENT=100)
```

This example creates the resource pools AdminQueries and UserQueries. Both of these can utilize a maximum of 100 percent of the CPU. We will show how different maximum configurations affect the pools shortly. First, we need to talk about how to determine who gets to use which resource pool.

Creating Workload Groups

We have defined pools for resources, but we don't want to assign users directly to the pools themselves, since that would be a management nightmare. Instead, we create *workload groups*. These groups allow system administrators to easily monitor resource consumption and move different workloads among different pools.

A workload group is mapped to a resource pool. A resource pool can have zero or more workload groups using the pool. A workload group provides a bucket to group user sessions. We will cover how to map user sessions to workload groups when we discuss the classifier function in the next section.

Just as there are preconfigured internal and default resource pools, there are predefined internal and default workload groups. The internal workload group is used solely by the SQL Server database engine and cannot be altered or deleted. The default workload group will be used by all user sessions that are not assigned a workload group.

To create a workload group, use the CREATE WORKLOAD GROUP statement. Continuing our example, let's create four workload groups that will use the two resource pools we defined in the previous section, as follows:

```
CREATE WORKLOAD GROUP NightlyMaintenanceTasks
USING AdminQueries

CREATE WORKLOAD GROUP AdhocAdmin
USING AdminQueries

CREATE WORKLOAD GROUP SAPUsers
USING UserQueries

CREATE WORKLOAD GROUP DailyExecReports
USING UserQueries
```

Here, we defined the NightlyMaintenanceTasks and AdhocAdmin groups to use the AdminQueries resource pool, and the SAPUsers and DailyExecReports groups to use the UserQueries resource pool. At this point, we have established which users or connections will be grouped into which workload. Now we need what is called a classifier function.

Creating a Classifier Function

A *classifier function* classifies the incoming sessions and assigns the session requests and queries to a specific workload group. The group differentiation can be identified by almost any property available in the connection string (IP address, application name, username, and so on). As an example, let's create our classifier function to behave in the following manner:

- If a user connects and has a login called SAP_Login, make him part of the SAPUsers workload group.
- If a user connects and the application name is Microsoft SQL Server Management Studio, make him part of the AdhocAdmin workload group.
- If a user is a member of the ReportUsers group, make him part of the DailyExecReports workload group.
- If a user is connecting using shared memory and is in the NightlyAdmin group, assign him to the NightlyMaintenanceTasks workload group.

The code to create this classifer function is as follows:

```
USE MASTER
GO
CREATE FUNCTION class_func_1()
RETURNS SYSNAME WITH SCHEMABINDING
BEGIN
    DECLARE @val sysname
    --Handle workload groups defined by login names
    IF 'SAP_Login' = SUSER_SNAME()
    BEGIN
        SET @val='SAPUsers';
        RETURN @val;
    END
    IF APP_NAME() = 'Microsoft SQL Server Management Studio'
    BEGIN
        SET @val='AdhocAdmin';
        RETURN @val;
    END

    IF IS_MEMBER ('ReportUsers') = 1
    BEGIN
        SET @val='DailyExecReports';
        RETURN @val;
        END

    IF ConnectionProperty('net_transport') = 'Shared memory' AND
       IS_MEMBER ('NightlyAdmin') = 1
    BEGIN
        SET @val='NightlyMaintenanceTasks';
        RETURN @val;
    END

RETURN @val;

END
```

■**Note** In the real world, your classifier function may have a bit more code than this example. That's because our example doesn't handle any special cases, such as what to do if users could fall into more than one group.

After you have defined the classifier function, you need to bind it to Resource Governor. To do this, issue the following statement:

```
ALTER RESOURCE GOVERNOR
    WITH (CLASSIFIER_FUNCTION = dbo.class_func_1)
```

Changes won't be in effect until you issue the RECONFIGURE statement, as follows:

```
ALTER RESOURCE GOVERNOR RECONFIGURE
```

At this point, we have configured our resource pools and workload groups, and have applied a classifier function for use by Resource Governor. To show the real power of this feature, let's create two connections. The first connection will be made by the SAP_Login login. Therefore, it will be part of the SAPUsers workload group and bound to the UserQueries resource pool. The second connection will be made by a system administrator who is using SQL Server Management Studio. Therefore, this connection will be part of the AdhocAdmin workload group and bound to the AdminQueries resource pool.

In order to easily see the effects of Resource Governor, you can look at the various Performance Monitor counters available.

Viewing Resource Governor Performance Monitor Counters

Both SQL Server:Resource Pools Stats and SQL Server:Workload Group Stats are new Performance Monitor performance objects in SQL Server 2008. Together, these objects provide enough information to monitor the various workloads and resource pools that you have defined.

SQL Server:Resource Pools Stats contains counters for both memory and CPU utilization. Examples include the amount of memory used by the resource pool, the system CPU usage by all requests in the resource pool, and the number of query memory grants per second occurring in the resource pool. SQL Server:Workload Group Stats contains CPU usage counters, as well as query-related information, such as the number of requests waiting in the queue due to Resource Governor limits.

To demonstrate using these counters, let's continue with our example of two resource pools and four workload groups. Launch Performance Monitor (either by typing perfmon at a command prompt or by navigating from the Control Panel to the Administrative Tools folder and selecting Performance). In Performance Monitor, right-click the graph and select Add Counter from the context menu. Select SQLServer:Resource Pools Stats from the Performance Object drop-down list, and add the "CPU usage %" counter for both the AdminQueries and UserQueries resource pools, as shown in Figure 5-6.

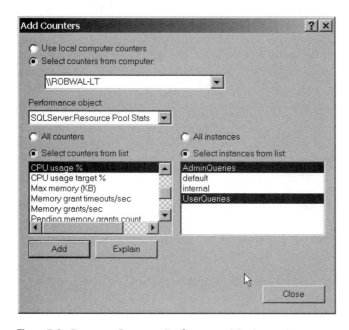

Figure 5-6. *Resource Governor Performance Monitor counters*

At this point, we are ready to apply a workload to our two connections. For lack of a better workload, let's use the following script, whose purpose is to stress the CPU by selecting the version of SQL Server a million times.

```
SET NOCOUNT ON
DECLARE @i int=10000000;
DECLARE @s varchar(100);
```

```
WHILE @i > 0
BEGIN
    SELECT @s = @@version;
    SET @i = @i - 1;
END
```

If both the SAP_Login and sysadmin users run this script on their connection, our Performance Monitor results will look like Figure 5-7.

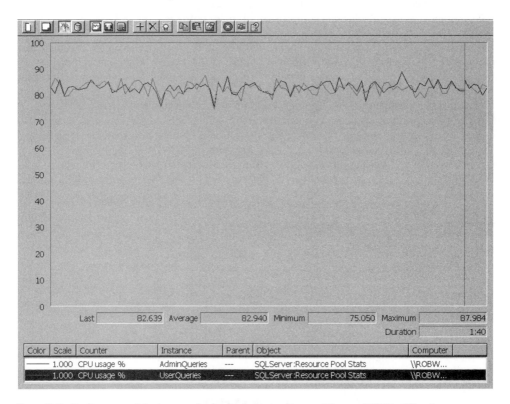

Figure 5-7. *Performance Monitor results for both connections with equal CPU utilization*

Both of our connections are competing for resources, and basically they share the same percentage of CPU utilization. You can also see that the lines are not that straight. This is because there are other services and applications that are also competing for CPU time.

Now imagine that we are starting to receive calls from our SAP users saying that their queries are running more slowly. One thing we could do is restrict our AdminQueries resource pool to use only 20 percent maximum CPU and our UserQueries to use up to 80 percent maximum CPU. To do this, we issue the following statements:

```
ALTER RESOURCE POOL UserQueries
    WITH (MAX_CPU_PERCENT = 80)

ALTER RESOURCE POOL AdminQueries
    WITH (MAX_CPU_PERCENT = 20)
```

In order for changes to become effective, we need to issue the RECONFIGURE command as well:

```
ALTER RESOURCE GOVERNOR RECONFIGURE
```

Now when we look at our Performance Monitor counters, we can see a distinct difference in the CPU utilization between the two workloads, as shown in Figure 5-8. The counters show the administrator workloads taking a significantly lower CPU utilization than the user queries, which is what we expected.

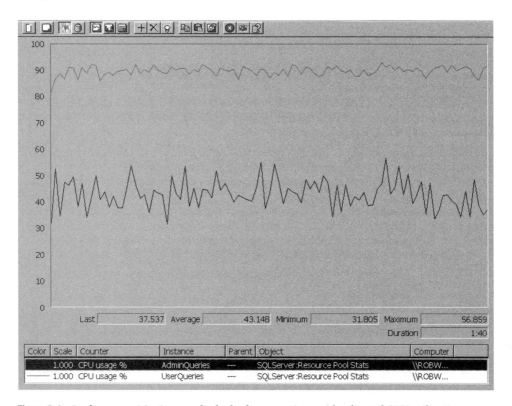

Figure 5-8. *Performance Monitor results for both connections with adjusted CPU utilization*

If you want to get a quick look at which sessions are in which workload groups, you can use one of the new Resource Governor-related dynamic management views. The following code will show this information:

```
SELECT
    s.session_id, s.login_name, s.program_name, s.group_id, g.name
FROM
    sys.dm_exec_sessions as s JOIN
    sys.dm_resource_governor_workload_groups as g
    ON s.group_id=g.group_id
WHERE
    session_id > 50
```

The result of this query against a server running the Resource Governor sample script shows the following:

```
session_id    login_name                      program_name  group_id  name
51            NT AUTHORITY\SYSTEM SQLAgent     ...           2         default
52            DOMAIN\UserAdmin                 SQLCMD        257       AdhocAdmin
53            SAP_Login                        SQLCMD        258       SAPUsers
```

Resource Governor will no doubt be an incredible asset to your organization. Up until now, some third-party applications assume they own the SQL box and tune their queries with this in mind. Now system administrators have the ability to limit memory and CPU utilization, regardless of what the applications are trying to do. Handling these runaway query scenarios is what Resource Governor is all about.

Optimizing Storage

Users and organizations continue to pile gigabytes of information into their databases. From a cost standpoint, adding extra disk storage isn't usually a roadblock for most people.

The effects of very large amounts of data are evident when performing regular database maintenance or data retrieval. As the database grows larger, and the database file and log files increase in size, so do the database backups. This not only increases the time to back up the database, but may also increase the recovery time in case of a failure. SQL Server 2008 addresses the data explosion by providing out-of-the-box support for database backup compression, as well as the ability to compress the data that is stored within the database itself.

Backup Compression

Backup compression has been a long-awaited feature within the SQL Server database engine. Until now, users who wanted to compress backups would need to purchase third-party backup solutions. In SQL Server 2008, backup compression is supported natively in the database engine for both disk and tape backup devices. This feature is available in Enterprise Edition of SQL Server. (As with all other Enterprise Edition features, if you are using a Developer or Evaluation Edition, you will still be able to use backup compression.)

You can enable backup compression by default on all database backups or for a specific backup. To enable compression for all backups, set the global server-level option 'backup compression default' to a value of 1, as shown in the following code:

```
USE master
GO
EXEC sp_configure ' backup compression default', '1';
RECONFIGURE WITH OVERRIDE;
```

To enable compression for a specific backup, specify WITH COMPRESSION as an option to the BACKUP DATABASE statement.

■**Note** Compressed and uncompressed backups cannot coexist in a media set.

To see backup compression at work, let's back up the AdventureWorks database. To compare the savings of compression, first back up the database without compression, and then do the backup with compression.

```
--Without compression
BACKUP DATABASE AdventureWorks TO DISK='C:\Backups\AdvtureWorksDB_nocompression.bak'
GO
--With compression
BACKUP DATABASE AdventureWorks TO DISK='C:\Backups\AdvtureWorksDB_compression.bak'
WITH COMPRESSION
```

Now we have two backup files on our hard disk. To see the compressed backup size and the compression ratio, issue the following query against the backupset table in msdb:

```
select ((backup_size / 1024) / 1024) as 'Backup Size (MB)',
((compressed_backup_size / 1024) / 1024) as 'Compressed Backup Size(MB)',
 (backup_size/compressed_backup_size) as 'Compression Ratio' from msdb..backupset;
```

The result of this query is as follows:

Backup Size (MB)	Compressed Backup Size(MB)	Compression Ratio
172.07519531250	172.07519531250	1.000000000000000000
172.07519531250	40.02343654589	4.299360828581752858

You can see that the database backup size was about 172MB without compression vs. 40MB with compression. The actual compression savings will depend on the type of data being compressed. For example, encrypted data stored as varbinary will not compress as well as varchar data.

Obviously, when a database is compressed, the backup file size will be smaller. Also, compressing a backup significantly reduces the elapsed time of the backup operation since a compressed backup requires less device I/O than an uncompressed backup of the same data. However, during the process of compressing a backup, the CPU usage will increase. If you are concerned how backup compression affects your server, you can watch a few performance counters: the "Device Throughput Bytes/sec" counter of the SQLServer:Backup Device object and the "Backup/Restore Throughput/sec" counter of the SQLServer:Databases object.

Overall, database compression will be a very welcome addition to the DBA's backup strategies. The end result of backup compression is savings on the physical disk file size. However, this will not do us much good if our live data is so large that performance is suffering due to costly disk I/O. The good news is that SQL Server 2008 supports data compression as well, as discussed in the next section.

Data Compression

Most organizations that utilize databases do not have just one copy of the data. Data is usually backed up and transported to some off-site location. Some data might be transferred over to a staging database and then into a data warehouse for further processing.

As the world around us keeps producing more and more digitally born data, managing that data spins out of control. Suddenly, updating an index or performing a database backup takes longer. Your database maintenance time slot may have fit before, but with more data, you may find that maintenance actions are being performed during regular office hours. Users are complaining, and you think it might be time to get your resume ready. But not so fast on that Monster.com submission. SQL Server 2008 has another tool in the toolbox to help with this data explosion. This tool is native support for data compression within tables and indexes.

Before we jump into the details of how data compression works within SQL Server, let's consider how we could reduce the size of data in a database. At a high level, we need to reduce the amount of information stored, as the bottleneck we are circumventing is disk I/O contention. One way to achieve this is to compress the datafile on the physical disk. This option would achieve our goal of reducing the data footprint; however, in a relational database environment, this would not be the best solution from a performance perspective. Since data is read in chunks from the file system, we would end up doing more compression and decompression for data that is unneeded. The other option is to store the data more efficiently within the rows and pages of the database itself. This pushes more work on the CPU for an efficient read and write of compressed data to the physical disk. Storing the data more efficiently within the database is the option most database vendors, including Microsoft, use to address the data-compression problem.

Variable-Length Decimal Storage Format

SQL Server 2008 is the first version that contains native data-compression support; however, starting with SQL Server 2005 Service Pack (SP) 2 came an improvement that was designed to reduce the storage requirements for decimal values. Microsoft found that data warehouse fact tables contained a lot of zeros and nulls, and using a normal decimal datatype to store these values, each took a good 5 bytes of storage. Add a few million rows to a fact table that contains a bunch of zeros and nulls, and you can see the advantage of introducing a way to knock down the size of the table.

The solution is to use a vardecimal storage format. This is not a new datatype; rather, it's a switch that causes the internal storage of the decimal datatype to change. When zero and null values are stored in the vardecimal storage format, they are optimized to use only 2 bytes. Other variable sizes will range anywhere from 5 to 20 bytes per value.

To take advantage of the vardecimal storage format, you need to enable the functionality both at the database level and the table level, as in the following example:

```
USE master;
GO
EXEC sp_db_vardecimal_storage_format 'AdventureWorks', 'ON';
GO
USE AdventureWorks;
GO
EXEC sp_tableoption 'Sales.SalesOrderDetail', 'vardecimal storage format', 'ON';
```

A simple call to sp_tableoption would cause existing fixed-length decimal datatype declarations to behave as variable-length decimal datatypes. The behavior is the same as the way varchar datatype variables store char information.

Converting all your decimal tables to vardecimal storage format may not always be the best solution. For example, as with using the varchar datatype, if you define a column to be varchar(10) and are almost always using the full ten characters of space allocated, then you are much better off using char(10) and saving the overhead of the extra variable offset information that is stored in the variable-length datatype.

If you were not already familiar with the vardecimal storage format in SQL Server 2005 SP2, you may be excited to give it a try on your decimal data. However, it is important to note that this feature has been deprecated starting in SQL Server 2008, which now offers row-compression support. Since row compression in SQL Server 2008 performs the same task as enabling vardecimal support, the sp_db_vardecimal_storage_format and sp_tableoption options to enable vardecimal support are deprecated.

Row Compression

The vardecimal storage format introduced in SQL Server 2005 SP2 optimized the decimal datatype by changing the underlying storage of the data while not forcing developers to change their datatype declarations in their applications. In SQL Server 2008, this optimization of the decimal fixed-length datatype has been expanded to include other numeric types and types based on them, such as int, decimal, float, datetime, and money. This new behavior is wrapped up in a feature called *row compression*. Row compression does a great job at handling zero and null values. In fact, it takes no space to store zero or null values after row compression is enabled.

SQL Server 2008 comes packed with tools that help DBAs configure and utilize the new compression feature. In addition to a Data Compression Wizard, which we will discuss a little later in this chapter, you can use the sp_estimate_data_compression_savings stored procedure to sample the data in your table and get an estimate of the compression savings. You do not need to enable compression on the entire table; compression can be enabled on a specific partition as well. This procedure enumerates all the partitions and the compression savings obtained as they relate to the object being compressed.

To help illustrate the power of sp_estimate_data_compression_savings, let's take a look at one of the larger tables in the AdventureWorks database. The SalesOrderDetail table contains more than 120,000 rows of data, taking up about 10MB of space. This table contains a mix of datatypes, including int, money, and numeric, which are all good candidates for compression. To see the savings when row compression is applied, issue this statement:

```
sp_estimate_data_compression_savings 'Sales','SalesOrderDetail',NULL,NULL,'ROW'
```

The results of this stored procedure contain eight columns. They are as follows:

object_name	schema_name	index_id	partition_number	SWCC	SWRC	SSWCC	SSWRC
SalesOrderDetail	Sales	1	1	10040	7728	9904	7624
SalesOrderDetail	Sales	2	1	3424	4136	3280	3968
SalesOrderDetail	Sales	3	1	1968	1824	1824	1696

■**Note** The actual column names for the result set of sp_estimate_data_compression have been abbreviated so the data could fit on this page. The abbreviations are SWCC: Size with current compression setting (KB), SWRC: Size with requested compression setting (KB), SSWCC: Sample size with current compression setting (KB), and SSWRC: Sample size with requested compression setting (KB).

The results show three entries for SalesOrderDetail but only one partition. This is because compression takes into consideration each of the three indexes defined on the table. An index_id of 1 represents the clustered index defined on the table. The index_id values 2 and 3 (actually, any value greater than 1) represent nonclustered indexes. (An index_id of 0 means no index is defined.) When you enable compression on a table, heap or clustered indexes will be compressed. Nonclustered indexes are not automatically compressed when you issue the compression statement. However, the results from the query show the before and after savings for all indexes.

To enable row compression on a table, you can use Data Definition Language (DDL) or the Data Compression Wizard (discussed shortly). For example, if we decided to go ahead and enable compression on the SalesOrderDetail table, we could issue the following:

```
ALTER TABLE [Sales].[SalesOrderDetail] REBUILD
WITH (DATA_COMPRESSION = ROW)
```

From the sp_estimate_data_compression_savings results, we can expect the table size to now be about 7.54MB (7728KB).

As noted, you can also compress just partitions. If we had multiple partitions and wanted to compress just a single partition, our statement would be something like the following:

```
ALTER TABLE [Sales].[SalesOrderDetail] REBUILD PARTITION=4
WITH (DATA_COMPRESSION = ROW)
```

Page Compression

Compressing data with row compression is good if you have a lot of unique data. However, if you have a lot of frequently occurring data, you still end up storing the same repeated compressed value. This is where *page compression* comes in.

■**Note** In a relational database, a *page* contains the actual data of the rows. A row can reside only in one page, with each page containing 8,060 bytes of information.

Enabling page compression reduces the amount of information on each page. It does this by utilizing column prefixes and dictionary compression.

Using column prefixes, a prefix list is stored in the page. This list contains patterns of common values per column. Consider the sample data for the Sales.SalesOrderDetail table shown in Table 5-2.

Table 5-2. *Sample Data for Sales.SalesOrderDetail Table*

ProductID	UnitCost	SalesPrice	Inventory	ProductGroupID
1	32	45	1670	1
2	32	45	1672	1
3	8	10	16	2
4	54	75	324	1

You can see that the ProductID column does not have any repeated values, and thus there are no valid column prefixes. The UnitCost column has the value 32 repeated twice, so the database engine stores the value 32 in a column prefix variable CA and replaces the contents of the data in the row to point to CA. The SalesPrice column also has a repeated value of 45. The database engine will create a column prefix value CB for the value 45 and replace the data in the row with pointers to CB.

The Inventory column initially doesn't appear to have any repeated values. However, the database engine notices that the numbers 167 are the first three digits of two rows in this column, so it will store 167 as a column prefix and label it CC. In the actual rows of data, it will place a pointer to the column prefix and the extra information. In the first row, the extra information is 0 to make the full value of 1670. In the second row, the extra information is 2 to make the full value of 1672. In the third row, the value stored is 16, which is the first two digits of our column prefix 167. The database engine has some additional smarts to recognize this and stores a pointer to CC and an indication that it should use only the first two digits in the prefix.

In the last column, ProductGroupID, the database engine will create a column prefix CD and give it a value of 1. It will then store pointers to CD wherever the value 1 is stored in any of the rows for that given column.

To recap, our column prefix values are as follows:

CA: 32

CB: 45

CC: 167

CD: 1

Our data page now resembles Table 5-3.

Table 5-3. *Data Page After Column Prefix Definitions*

ProductID	UnitCost	SalesPrice	Inventory	ProductGroupID
1	[C1]	[C2]	[C3] + 0	[C4]
2	[C1]	[C2]	[C3] + 2	[C4]
3	8	10	[C3]->2	2
4	54	75	324	[C4]

The other optimization that occurs with page compression is dictionary compression. This looks for common values stored across all columns and rows, as opposed to colunm prefixes, which consider just a given column. In our example, we have the value 1 in both the ProductID column and the ProductGroupID column. Thus, the database engine creates a dictionary entry DA with a value of 1 and replaces the value 1 in the ProductID column and the column prefix value CD in the ProductGroupID column. This page-level process continues, and in our example, we have two additional page-level dictionary entries: DB with a value of 32, and DC with a value of 2. After dictionary compression, the page will resemble Table 5-4.

Table 5-4. *Data Page After Column Prefix Definitions and Dictionary Compression*

ProductID	UnitCost	SalesPrice	Inventory	ProductGroupID
[D1]	[D2]	[C2]	[C3] + 0	[D1]
[D3]	[D2]	[C2]	[C3] + 2	[D1]
3	8	10	[C3]->2	[D3]
4	54	75	[D2] + 4	[D1]

■**Note** What we have described is conceptually what happens when you enable page compression. But be aware that there are many more optimizations and efficiencies that occur within the database engine to increase performance.

As for row compression, SQL Server 2008 has a stored procedure that estimates your savings with page-level compression: sp_estimate_data_compression_savings. Issuing the following statement will show the savings estimate for the SalesOrderDetail table in the AdventureWorks database using page compression:

```
sp_estimate_data_compression_savings 'Sales','SalesOrderDetail',NULL,NULL,'PAGE'
```

The results of this statement are as follows:

```
object_name      schema_name  index_id  partition_number SWCCS SWRCS SSWCCS SSWRCS
SalesOrderDetail Sales        1         1                10040 4928  9904   4864
SalesOrderDetail Sales        2         1                3424  4136  3280   3968
SalesOrderDetail Sales        3         1                1968  1608  1824   1496
```

As some of you may have speculated, our sample table benefitted significantly from page compression. Instead of just 7.54MB using row compression, page compression yields a table size of just 4928KB, or about 4.8MB.

As with row compression, you can enable page compression using the Data Compression Wizard (discussed next) or DDL. For example, the following code will enable page compression on the SalesOrderDetail table:

```
ALTER TABLE [Sales].[SalesOrderDetail] REBUILD
WITH (DATA_COMPRESSION = PAGE)
```

Using the Data Compression Wizard

In addition to DDL, you can use the Data Compression Wizard in SQL Server Management Studio to easily configure data compression. Under the covers, the wizard calls the same stored procedures as DDL discussed in the previous sections. If you are not a command-line junkie, you will appreciate this easy point-and-click way of configuring compression. The wizard allows you to play with different configurations in an attempt to determine which might yield better compression results.

To launch the Data Compression Wizard, in Object Explorer, right-click any table or index and select Storage ➤ Manage Compression. Figure 5-9 shows an example of using the wizard with the Sales.SalesOrderDetail table of the AdventureWorks database.

Figure 5-9. *Data Compression Wizard showing per partition compression settings*

As the wizard shows, this table has about 121,000 rows and takes about 9.8MB for the data alone. This table is definitely a good candidate for compression. By choosing different options from the Compression Type drop-down list, you can see estimates of the savings for each specific compression type. In Figure 5-9, Page is chosen as the compression type, and the wizard shows that the table would end up being about 4.8MB instead of more than 9.8MB. If you selected row compression, you would see that this table would end up being about 7.5MB, which is only a 20 percent reduction, as opposed to the more than 50 percent reduction achieved using page compression.

Monitoring Compression Performance

Two compression-specific performance monitor counters may be useful in monitoring compression performance. Both of these counters are available as part of the SQL Server:Access Methods object.

Assuming table compression is defined, when rows are added to a page, nothing out of the ordinary happens. When the page fills up and is ready to split, the database engine will perform a check to see if the kind of data that is stored will benefit from compression. This action is shown by the "Page compression attempts" counter. If page compression will be of benefit, the database engine will compress the page, and the "Page compressed/sec" counter is incremented.

Since the act of checking the data itself is a tax on the CPU, having a lot of attempts and a relatively smaller amount of actual compressions may cause delays in query execution. This situation can happen when the data stored is more unique than similar. Thus, in situations where the page compression attempts are much greater than the actual page compressions, you may want to forego compressing the tables.

■**Note** "Page compression attempts" and "Page compressed/sec" counter values are also available via the `sys.dm_db_index_operational_stats` dynamic management view.

Improving Query Performance

Reworking queries and their supporting functions (like indexes, statistics, and hints) is where you can easily make adjustments and fine-tune query performance. SQL Server has always provided tools to facilitate optimizing query performance. In this section, we will explore some of the more significant tools and capabilities available in SQL Server 2008.

Plan Guide Support

When going from one point to another, many different routes will take you to the same destination. Query plans in SQL Server describe a series of steps needed to obtain information stored in a SQL Server relational database. As with point-to-point travel, there are practically an infinite number of query plans that could be generated for a single query to obtain the same final result.

When a query is submitted to the database engine, the query optimizer evaluates possible query plans and returns what it considers the best one from a performance standpoint. Since the query optimizer in SQL Server is great but not perfect, database developers and administrators occasionally need to manually examine and tune the plans to get better performance. You can imagine the pain that would occur if you spent a lot of time tuning the query, just to have it replaced upon upgrade to a new version of SQL Server. This is what happened when users went from SQL Server 2000 to SQL Server 2005. SQL Server 2005 brought some huge changes (more than 5 years' worth of changes). In all that development work, the query optimizer had changes, and some users who fine-tuned their SQL Server 2000 queries were experiencing performance degradation after upgrading to SQL Server 2005. In SQL Server 2008, this issue is solved via the ability to freeze query plans.

Freezing query plans not only takes care of the upgrade issue, but it also can be leveraged in a few more ways that may be even more interesting to discuss. Consider the following scenarios:

- If you are software development shop and ship software that runs on the SQL Server platform, you may want to ensure that your mission-critical queries always run with the same plan.

- If you are a system administrator who is responsible for various production-level servers, you may have certain queries that are critical from a performance perspective and are willing to sacrifice a consistent query plan for a potentially better optimized query plan generated by the database engine. This sacrifice between consistency and automatic performance tuning comes as a result of SQL Server not recompiling the query based on changes to the statistics of the data.

Creating Plan Guides

Technically, a plan guide is nothing more than a database object that associates query hints with certain queries in a database. To create a plan guide, you can use the sp_create_plan_guide statement or XML Showplan data.

As an example, let's create a stored procedure that simply returns all addresses by the two-letter state that was passed in as a parameter. Our stored procedure is as follows:

```
CREATE PROCEDURE dbo.GetAddressByState
    (@State nvarchar(3))
AS
BEGIN
SELECT AddressLine1,AddressLine2, City FROM Person.Address a
INNER JOIN Person.StateProvince s ON s.StateProvinceID=a.StateProvinceID
WHERE s.StateProvinceCode=@State;
END
```

From previous testing, we know that when this stored procedure is issued, most of the time the State variable is 'WA', for Washington. To optimize this query, we can create a plan guide that optimizes for this input variable. The code to create the plan guide is as follows:

```
EXEC sp_create_plan_guide N'GetAddress_PlanGuide',
    N'SELECT AddressLine1,AddressLine2, City FROM Person.Address a
INNER JOIN Person.StateProvince s ON s.StateProvinceID=a.StateProvinceID
WHERE s.StateProvinceCode=@State;',
    N'OBJECT',
    N'dbo.GetAddressByState',
    NULL,
    N'OPTION (OPTIMIZE FOR (@State = N''WA''))';
```

To see your plan guides, use the sys.plan_guides catalog view. Issuing SELECT plan_guide_id,name,query_text,hints FROM sys.plan_guides will return the new plan guide we just created:

plan_guide_id	nname	query_text	hints
65547	GetAddress_PlanGuide	SELECT AddressLine1, AddressLine2, City FROM Person.Address a...	OPTION (OPTIMIZE FOR (@State = N'WA'))

To enable, disable, and drop plans, you can use the sp_control_plan_guide stored procedure. The plans are enabled by default when they are created. To disable the plan we just created, issue the following query:

```
EXEC sp_control_plan_guide N'DISABLE', N'GetAddress_PlanGuide';
```

In the previous plan guide creation script, we created a plan by passing the SQL statement and optimization options directly to the `sp_create_plan_guide` statement. Alternatively, you can create plan guides using XML Showplan data. Consider the following example:

```
DECLARE @xml_showplan NVARCHAR(max);
SET @xml_showplan =
(SELECT query_plan
     FROM sys.dm_exec_query_stats AS qs
     CROSS APPLY sys.dm_exec_sql_text(qs.sql_handle) AS st
     CROSS APPLY sys.dm_exec_text_query_plan(qs.plan_handle, DEFAULT, DEFAULT) AS qp
WHERE st.text LIKE
N'SELECT emp.Title,c.FirstName,c.LastName FROM HumanResources.Employee emp
JOIN Person.Contact c ON emp.ContactID=c.ContactID')

EXEC sp_create_plan_guide
    @name = N'Guide1_from_XML_showplan',
    @stmt = N'SELECT emp.Title,c.FirstName,c.LastName
        FROM HumanResources.Employee emp
        JOIN Person.Contact c ON emp.ContactID=c.ContactID;',
    @type = N'SQL',
    @module_or_batch = NULL,
    @params = NULL,
    @hints =@xml_showplan;
```

This script obtained the XML Showplan data for the given query and used it to define the hint in the query plan.

In all the examples we have discussed up until now, we have created the plan by passing the actual SQL statement and optimization information. Sometimes, this capability is satisfactory; however, if you already have a lot of tuned queries in your query cache, it is not easy to script or generate a plan based on these queries. SQL Server 2008 introduces the `sp_create_plan_from_cache` statement, which allows you to create plan guides directly from queries stored in cache.

Using Plan Guides As a Backup

In the beginning of this section, we discussed a couple scenarios of where using plan guides could be beneficial. Another possibility is to use plan guides as a backup in case your queries start to perform more poorly than expected. In that case, you can follow this game plan:

- Identify mission-critical queries. Although it is possible to tune almost every query, it is best to pick those that are frequently used or that take a long time to run. This information can be obtained easily by configuring traces in Profiler.

- Tune queries. Entire books are devoted to this subject. You can start with examining the execution plan and seeing if there are any red flags, such as the query is issuing table scans, column statistics for tables in the query are missing, and so on.

- Clear the query cache. Issuing a `DBCC FREEPROCCACHE` statement will clear all the queries in the plan cache. This statement also has the ability to selectively clear plans and even to clear all plans in a given resource pool. For more information about resource pools, see the "Resource Governor" section earlier in this chapter.

- Run queries. Executing queries will cause query plans to be generated, provided those plans do not already exist.

- Create plan guides using the `sp_create_plan_guide_from_cache` statement.

- Disable all the generated plan guides using the `sp_control_plan_guide` statement.

At this point, the plans of your optimized queries are stored. If there are performance issues in the future, you can enable these plans using the `sp_control_plan_guide` statement.

Managing Query Plans

On paper, the procedure outlined in the previous section will work great, and you can enable your saved plan guides with `sp_control_plan_guide`. However, occasionally, over time, small changes occur in the database that render these plans invalid. Reasons for invalid plans vary but commonly are due to missing indexes or changes to the physical design of the objects your queries are leveraging. To check the validity of a plan guide, you can use the `sys.fn_validate_plan_guide` function. If you want to take a more proactive stance on invalid plan guides, you can monitor two new event classes using Profiler or any other tool that listens to trace events:

- The "Plan Guide Successful" event is raised when the database engine successfully produces an execution plan for a query or batch that contains a plan guide.

- The "Plan Guide Unsuccessful" event fires when an execution plan was compiled without using a plan guide. When this event occurs, a call to `sys.fn_validate_plan_guide` might determine the cause of the issue.

To monitor plan guide usage, you can use two new performance counters, which are both part of the SQL Server:SQL Statistics performance object:

- The "Guided plan executions/sec" counter reveals the number of plan executions per second in which the query plan has been generated by using a plan guide.

- The "Misguided plan executions/sec" counter indicates when the execution plan had to be compiled because the database engine could not use the plan guide that was defined for the query or batch.

Monitoring these performance counters over time can indicate gradual performance trends due to issues with valid plan guides.

Up until now, we have shown how to use T-SQL to manage plan guides. Those who like using graphical tools will be pleased to know that SQL Server Management Studio has support for plan guides. Plan guides in Management Studio are enumerated under the Programmability node in Object Explorer. From this node, you can create new plan guides, as well as enable, disable, and even script plan guides.

Plan guides were introduced in SQL Server 2005 and have continued to evolve in SQL Server 2008 in terms of useful functionality. Those who actively monitor performance issues with their servers will find the enhancements made to plan guides very useful.

Sparse Columns

As we mentioned earlier in this chapter, data stored in fact tables tends to have a lot of nulls and empty values. In SQL Server 2008, a large effort was made in optimizing the database storage for this kind of scenario. A *sparse column* is another tool used to reduce the amount of physical storage used in a database.

When set, the SPARSE storage attribute instructs the database engine to optimize the storage of null and empty values, so that the storage requirements of these values are zero. A sparse column behaves just like any other column for all query and Data Manipulation Language (DML) operations. It is recommended that the SPARSE attribute be used when more than 90 percent of the rows of a particular column in a table currently have or are expected to have null values.

To help illustrate the space savings, let's take a look at two similar tables, both with 100,000 rows. They are created as follows:

```
CREATE TABLE NonSparseTable(a int, b int, c int, d int)
GO
CREATE TABLE SparseTable(a int, b int SPARSE, c int SPARSE, d int SPARSE)
GO

DECLARE @i int=0
WHILE @i < 100000
 BEGIN
 INSERT INTO SparseTable VALUES (@i,null,null,null)
 INSERT INTO NonSparseTable VALUES (@i,null,null,null)
 SET @i+=1
 END
```

In our example, we defined our columns as int SPARSE. Issuing an sp_spaceused statement against both tables yields the following:

Name	rows	reserved	data	index_size	unused
SparseTable	100000	1416 KB	1352 KB	8 KB	56 KB
NonSparseTable	100000	2632 KB	2600 KB	8 KB	24 KB

As you can see, although both tables contained the same data, the table with the three sparse columns takes only half as much storage space as the table without sparse columns.

Sparse columns not only save storage space, but they allow you to have more than 1,024 columns per table. It is now possible to have up to 100,000 columns per table when you use sparse columns. If you do decide to exceed the 1,024 limit, just remember that you still must have at most 1,024 non-sparse columns per table.

You can use several catalog views to determine whether a column is sparse. The is_sparse bit is exposed through the sys.columns, sys.all_columns, sys.system_columns, sys.computed_columns, and sys.identity_columns views. You can also use the COLUMNPROPERTY function to check whether a column is sparse. As an example, to determine if our column b in SparseTable is a sparse column, we can issue the following SELECT statement:

```
SELECT COLUMNPROPERTY(object_id('dbo.SparseTable'),'b','IsSparse')
```

This will return the value of 1, indicating column b is a sparse column.

Sparse columns help in reducing the storage cost, but this is not the only role they will play in database architectures, as explained in the following section.

Column Sets

The limit of the number of columns defined per table is 1,024. For most applications, this might be an acceptable limit. However, since the trend is to store data that is more and more heterogeneous in nature, there is an increasing need for databases to have tables that exceed this limit.

Consider the example of an online outdoor equipment store that sells an assortment of products, ranging from personal items like hiking boots and clothing to sports equipment like kayaks and tents. When we think about a database table design for this web site, we can imagine a product table that would list the product and searchable characteristics. These might be the size for the boots and clothing or the length and color for the kayak. Ideally, as a developer it would be easiest to simply issue queries against our table that resemble something like the following:

```
SELECT product_name WHERE product_type = 'kayak' AND length > 2 AND color = 'red'
```

or

```
SELECT product_name, fabric_type WHERE product_type='shirt' size = 'XL'
```

Designing a table schema that would work with these queries would require all possible properties—length, color, size, fabric type, and so on—to be defined as columns in the table. The main problem with this approach is that we would rapidly breach our 1,024 column limit. In addition, if we had 100 different shoes for sale, we would be taking up space by having columns like length and fabric_type that would not apply to some of our products.

To address this type of situation, SQL Server 2008 introduces *column sets*. A column set is a group of sparse columns in a table. Having a column set defined will allow operations to be easily performed on the group while still being defined as just a list of columns. In SQL Server 2008, you can have only one column set for all sparse columns defined in a table.

A column set is conceptually similar to an updatable computed column; however, a number of additional restrictions are placed on columns sets. Column sets do not have support for constraints, default values, or distributed queries that reference a column set. See SQL Server Books Online for a complete list of restrictions when using columns sets.

As an example of using a column set, let's create a Products table and insert some test data for the outdoor equipment store:

```
CREATE TABLE Products
(product_id          int,
product_name         varchar(50),
product_type         varchar(10) SPARSE,
size                 varchar(10) SPARSE,
[length]             int SPARSE,
Color                varchar(10) SPARSE,
fabric_type          varchar(50) SPARSE,
sparseColumnSet      XML COLUMN_SET FOR ALL_SPARSE_COLUMNS)
GO
INSERT INTO Products(product_id,product_name,product_type,length,color)
VALUES (1,'Really nice kayak','kayak',3,'blue')
INSERT INTO Products(product_id,product_name,product_type,size,color)
VALUES (2,'Rusty Bike','bicycle','mens','red')
INSERT INTO Products(product_id,product_name,product_type,size,color,fabric_type)
VALUES (3,'Stud Shirt','shirt','XL','white','80% cotton/20% polyester')
INSERT INTO Products(product_id,product_name,product_type,length,color)
VALUES (4,'Kozy Kayak','kayak',1,'white')
INSERT INTO Products(product_id,product_name,product_type,size,color)
VALUES (5,'Bargin Bike','bicycle','womens','pink')
INSERT INTO Products(product_id,product_name,product_type,size,color,fabric_type)
VALUES (6,'Porus Shirt','shirt','L','black','100% cotton')
```

In the last line of the table-creation script, you can see the column called sparseColumnSet, which is defined as XML COLUMN_SET FOR ALL_SPARSE_COLUMNS.

Now that we have created the table and added some values, we can see the behavior of issuing queries against this table. When we issue a SELECT * from this table, we would normally expect to see all the columns, including the last one. However, the database engine is smart enough to know that the sparseColumnSet column is actually a column set that encompasses all the sparse columns in the table. Thus, issuing SELECT * From Products yields the following:

product_id	product_name	sparsePropertySet
1	Really nice kayak	`<product_type>kayak</product_type><length>3</length><color>blue</color>`
2	Rusty Bike	`<product_type>bicycle</product_type><size>mens</size><color>red</color>`
3	Stud Shirt	`<product_type>shirt</product_type><size>XL</size><color>white</color><fabric_type>80% cotton/20% polyester</fabric_type>`
4	Kozy Kayak	`<product_type>kayak</product_type><length>1</length>`

		`<color>white</color>`
5	Bargin Bike	`<product_type>bicycle</product_type><size>womens`
		`</size><color>pink</color>`
6	Porus Shirt	`<product_type>shirt</product_type><size>L</size>`
		`<color>black</color>`
		`<fabric_type>100% cotton</fabric_type>`

The database engine has grouped all the sparse columns sets in an XML format. This behavior leads to some interesting capabilities. If you wanted to return the entire result set as XML, you could issue SELECT * FROM Products FOR XML AUTO. This would yield the following result:

```xml
<Products product_id="1" product_name="Really nice kayak">
  <sparsePropertySet>
    <product_type>kayak</product_type>
    <length>3</length>
    <color>blue</color>
  </sparsePropertySet>
</Products>
<Products product_id="2" product_name="Rusty Bike">
  <sparsePropertySet>
    <product_type>bicycle</product_type>
    <size>mens</size>
    <color>red</color>
  </sparsePropertySet>
</Products>
<Products product_id="3" product_name="Stud Shirt">
  <sparsePropertySet>
    <product_type>shirt</product_type>
    <size>XL</size>
    <color>white</color>
    <fabric_type>80% cotton/20% polyester</fabric_type>
  </sparsePropertySet>
</Products>
<Products product_id="4" product_name="Kozy Kayak">
  <sparsePropertySet>
    <product_type>kayak</product_type>
    <length>1</length>
    <color>white</color>
  </sparsePropertySet>
</Products>
<Products product_id="5" product_name="Bargin Bike">
  <sparsePropertySet>
    <product_type>bicycle</product_type>
    <size>womens</size>
    <color>pink</color>
  </sparsePropertySet>
</Products>
<Products product_id="6" product_name="Porus Shirt">
  <sparsePropertySet>
    <product_type>shirt</product_type>
    <size>L</size>
    <color>black</color>
    <fabric_type>100% cotton</fabric_type>
  </sparsePropertySet>
</Products>
```

What is most interesting about the behavior of SELECT and column sets is that you can issue direct queries to the columns and not have to worry about the underlying XML. For example, you can issue a statement that directly queries the columns in the column set. For example, you could issue this statement:

```
SELECT product_name,size,color FROM Products WHERE product_type='bicycle'
```

and get these results:

```
product_name  size    color
Rusty Bike    mens    red
Bargin Bike   womens  pink
```

As with sparse columns, an Is_Column_Set bit is exposed through the sys.columns, sys.all_columns, sys.system_columns, sys.computed_columns, and sys.identity_columns catalog views. This bit will identify whether the column is a column set.

Although SQL Server 2008 introduces only one column set per table, it is easy to see the value of these sets when tables have a large number of columns. In future versions of SQL Server, most likely further investments will be made to column sets and sparse columns to allow developers even more flexibility in their database application designs and implementations.

Summary

The end user is the ultimate consumer of our work, whether we are system administrators or developers. Their satisfaction with our products and services usually depends on how quickly the application that accesses the database can respond. SQL Server has continued to answer performance challenges that face both system administrators and developers with each new release of the product. SQL Server 2008 is no different. The features and functionality discussed in this chapter will be a welcome addition to address your performance needs and concerns.

CHAPTER 6

■ ■ ■

Security

Not so long ago, SQL Server was seen just as a desktop database, without merit in the enterprise, due to its performance, scalability, and, to some degree, security. Veteran SQL Server users can tell you that the performance and scalability have come a long way, and now SQL Server can absolutely compete toe-to-toe with all relational database products on the market today. But what about security? Microsoft has made a noticeable effort over the past five years to make SQL Server the most secure database product on the planet.

Back in 2003, there was a virus called the SQL Slammer, which caused denial-of-service attacks and a lot of bad press for SQL Server. This drove home the point that security needs to be considered by everyone and for every part of the product development process. At that time, the SQL Server team stopped development of SQL Server 2005 for about six months and reviewed every line of code in SQL Server 2000 for security vulnerabilities, creating threat models for all its features. As a result, the team released SQL Server 2000 Service Pack 3, which was an accumulation of security fixes—a roll-up of existing issues plus proactive patches on potential vulnerabilities. The payoff for this effort has been huge. If you take a look at the National Vulnerability Database (http://nvd.nist.gov/), you will see that, since 2003, SQL Server has practically no published security vulnerabilities, while other database vendors have struggled with hundreds of issues. SQL Server 2005 and 2008 build on this secure platform and provide additional security-related features and functionality.

This chapter discusses security-related features introduced in SQL Server 2005, as well as the new auditing feature in SQL Server 2008. This chapter covers the following topics:

- Disabled database engine features
- Principals and securables
- Permissions
- Code Access Security
- Auditing in SQL Server 2008

Disabled Database Engine Features

To ensure that SQL Server is as secure as possible out of the box, a number of features that represent potential security risks are disabled by default, and must be explicitly enabled before they can be used. These features include the following:

- Remote connections
- Dedicated administrator connection
- .NET Framework
- Database Mail

- SQLMail

- Service Broker

- HTTP connectivity

- Database mirroring

- Web Assistant

- xp_cmdshell XP

- Ad Hoc Remote Queries

- OLE Automation XPs

- SMO and DMO XPs

In SQL Server 2005, a graphical tool called the Surface Area Configuration Tool was provided as a way to manage the configuration for these features. In SQL Server 2008, this tool has been removed, and the replacement functionality can be accomplished using Policy-based Management. More information about Policy-based Management is available in Chapter 3. For the most part, you can enable the database engine features mentioned here using the sp_configure system stored procedure. To manage network-related options, such as remote connectivity, you use the SQL Server Configuration Manager.

Remote Connections

Starting with SQL Server 2005, by default, some SQL Server editions don't accept remote connections; they accept only connections from the local machine. This clearly reduces risks considerably, as hackers will need access to the machine, or access to another enabled service that accepts remote connections (such as an HTTP endpoint). Unfortunately, it also dramatically reduces the usefulness of SQL Server! If your server really doesn't need to accept remote connections (for example, if it's only ever accessed from ASP.NET web pages on that machine), it's a good idea to keep this setting. However, most SQL Server instances will need to be accessed from client machines that are running data-entry applications and the like. Therefore, in most cases, you'll need to enable remote connections.

To enable remote connections, navigate to the Protocols node of the instance you want to manage in SQL Server Configuration Manager (SQL CM). The right pane of SQL CM shows the available protocols. From here, you can enable, disable, or modify the properties of the protocol, such as which specific port SQL Server should listen to for requests, as shown in Figure 6-1.

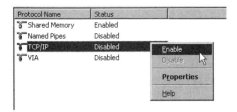

Figure 6-1. *Enabling a protocol in SQL Server Configuration Manager*

■**Note** If you are planning to accept remote connections, you may need to add the port information to the firewall installed on the server. If the firewall does not have this information, your remote connections will fail.

Dedicated Administrator Connection

The dedicated administrator connection (DAC) can be used to connect to SQL Server when the service itself is refusing connections using the regular connection protocols. The DAC listens on a dedicated port that only members of the sysadmin server role can use. Also, it's only possible to connect via the DAC from the local machine using the SQLCMD.EXE command-line tool. However, remote connections over the DAC can be enabled through the sp_configure procedure:

```
EXEC sp_configure 'remote admin connections', 1
GO
reconfigure
GO
```

■Note The sa account still exists in SQL Server 2008, but Microsoft recommends that you use the sysadmin fixed server role instead, which has the same (unlimited) powers. In addition, SQL Server installation enforces a password for the sa account, so you will not be able to use a blank password (even though having a blank password is really easy to remember).

.NET Framework

Although having the common language runtime (CLR) enabled for a database server brings much new functionality to SQL Server, it also brings potential security loopholes if not administered correctly. There are few limits to the tasks that an unsafe SQL assembly can perform if the appropriate security code isn't put in place (see the "Code Access Security" section later in this chapter); for example, with poor security, a SQL assembly could have access to the entire file system on the database server. Therefore, database administrators (DBAs) need to be especially vigilant of which actions .NET code is allowed to perform. For this reason, the CLR is disabled by default and needs to be explicitly enabled before SQL assemblies can be executed on that server.

CLR support can be enabled by executing the sp_configure stored procedure with the 'clr enabled' option. You also need to run RECONFIGURE to activate this change:

```
sp_configure 'clr enabled', 1
GO
RECONFIGURE
GO
```

Database Mail

SQL Server 2005 introduced the Database Mail replacement for SQLMail. Not only is Database Mail based on Simple Mail Transfer Protocol (SMTP), but it also leverages Service Broker for extremely fast and reliable e-mail service from SQL Server. With this flexibility and power, DBAs should be careful about who they give permissions to send mail, as it is quite easy to turn SQL Server into a spam engine. In addition, Database Mail should be configured to encrypt message contents, as messages are sent in plain text by default. This may require additional setup work for your SMTP server; however, you will mitigate packet-sniffing attacks by encrypting this channel.

Database Mail can be enabled through the Configure Database Mail Wizard, which is launched from the context menu of the Management ➤ Database Mail node in Object Explorer. Note that Database Mail relies on Service Broker, so it will work only if it's run in a database for which Service Broker has been enabled. See Chapter 9 for details about Service Broker.

SQLMail

SQLMail is the traditional mail technology built into SQL Server, and it has been replaced by Database Mail. SQLMail poses the same potential security vulnerabilities as Database Mail, but with the added risk that, because it's based on Messaging Application Programming Interface (MAPI), rather than directly on SMTP, SQLMail can read as well as send mail. This means that you need to make sure not only that any stored procedures that use SQLMail can't send data from SQL Server to people who aren't intended to access it, but also that it can't be misused to access data stored in the e-mail account of the MSSQLServer service. Even worse, because it's MAPI-based, SQLMail requires Outlook to be installed on the SQL Server machine, with all the attendant risks of viruses and worms transmitted through e-mail. Finally, SQLMail runs as an extended stored procedure in the same address space as the SQL Server process, so any failure could impact the entire server.

SQLMail can be enabled programmatically as follows:

```
EXEC sp_configure 'SQL Mail XPs', 1
GO
RECONFIGURE
GO
```

■**Note** It is strongly recommended that you use Database Mail rather than SQLMail, if possible. SQLMail has been on the deprecation list since SQL Server 2005, so it is very likely the components will be completely gone from the SQL Server binaries within the next few releases.

Service Broker, HTTP Connectivity, and Database Mirroring

Service Broker is SQL Server's asynchronous messaging technology. We will look at using Service Broker in detail in Chapter 9, including enabling it for a specific database.

If you want to create additional SQL Server services, such as Service Broker or web services, by default, SQL Server won't accept connections. To enable these, you need to explicitly create an endpoint telling SQL Server to listen or talk on a specific port.

Database mirroring is an easy-to-manage alternative to log shipping and failover clustering, and involves creating an exact copy of a database on another SQL Server instance that can be used if the primary database fails. Any updates to the primary database are replicated to the mirror database, so the copy remains exact. Again, the security liability here is that data must be transmitted over the network to the mirror server, and therefore also requires HTTP endpoints to be configured and active. For more information about configuring database mirroring, see Chapter 4.

Web Assistant

Web Assistant is a set of stored procedures that create HTML pages based on a database query. In general, Web Assistant is deprecated, and its functionality is replaced with Reporting Services. However, it is still supported for backward compatibility. To enable Web Assistant, run the following command:

```
EXEC sp_configure 'Web Assistant Procedures', 1
GO
RECONFIGURE
GO
```

xp_cmdshell XP

The `xp_cmdshell` extended procedure (XP) allows operating system commands to be executed from within the database environment. This has obvious dangers from both accidental and malicious misuse, so this procedure is disabled by default. It can be enabled through the `sp_configure` procedure:

```
EXEC sp_configure 'xp_cmdshell', 1
GO
RECONFIGURE
GO
```

In SQL Server 2005, the proxy account used when calling `xp_cmdshell` changed. In previous versions, calling `xp_cmdshell` via a SQL authenticated user would leverage the proxy account defined in the SQL Server Agent service. In SQL Server 2005 and later, the proxy credentials used for `xp_cmdshell` are set by using `sp_xp_cmdshell_proxy_account`.

Ad Hoc Remote Queries

If Ad Hoc Remote Queries are enabled, the `OPENROWSET` and `OPENDATASOURCE` functions can be used to query a remote SQL Server without setting up a linked server. These queries are harder to keep track of than linked or remote servers, as they will be buried in Transact-SQL (T-SQL) code, so Ad Hoc Remote Queries should be enabled only if your stored procedures actually make such queries. Ad Hoc Remote Queries can be enabled through the `sp_configure` procedure:

```
EXEC sp_configure 'Ad Hoc Distributed Queries', 1
GO
RECONFIGURE
GO
```

OLE Automation XPs

By default, XPs aren't permitted to call custom OLE Automation objects. We hope that in time, .NET assemblies will begin to replace C++ XPs, and DBAs will have more control over what code is running in the database. In the meantime, the DBA has no control whatsoever (except for the assurances of the developer!) over what these objects do, so OLE Automation XPs should be permitted only if necessary. To do this, you can use `sp_configure`:

```
EXEC sp_configure 'Ole Automation Procedures', 1
GO
RECONFIGURE
GO
```

SMO and DMO XPs

Server Management Objects (SMO), and its predecessor Distributed Management Objects (DMO), provide APIs for developers to perform automated administration tasks on SQL Server. There is naturally some security risk involved in permitting these, as both SMO and DMO can be used in external applications for managing SQL Server, over which the DBA has little or no control.

However, SMO and DMO are enabled by default, as two of SQL Server's management tools, Management Studio and Database Tuning Advisor (DTA), rely on them. You should therefore disable them only if you don't need these tools, and neither SMO nor DMO are used by any existing applications. They can be disabled using `sp_configure`:

```
EXEC sp_configure 'SMO and DMO XPs', 0
GO
RECONFIGURE
GO
```

Principals and Securables

The SQL Server security model relies on two fairly straightforward concepts: *principals* and *securables*. Principals are those objects that may be granted permission to access particular database objects. Securables are those objects to which access can be controlled.

Principals

Principals may represent a specific user, a role that may be adopted by multiple users, or an application. SQL Server divides principals into three classes:

- *Windows principals*: These represent Windows user accounts or groups, authenticated using Windows security.

- *SQL Server principals*: These are server-level logins or groups that are authenticated using SQL Server security.

- *Database principals*: These include database users, groups, and roles, as well as application roles.

Note that SQL Server and Windows logins apply only at the server level; you can't grant permissions on these to specific database objects. To do this, you need to create a user associated with the login. You'll see how to do this when we look at database principals.

Windows Principals

SQL Server allows you to create logins from Windows user accounts or groups. These can belong either to the local machine or to the domain. When users log on to SQL Server using Windows authentication, their current user account must either be created as a login in SQL Server or they must belong to a Windows user group that exists as a login.

To create a login from a Windows account, use the FROM WINDOWS clause in the CREATE LOGIN statement:

```
CREATE LOGIN [apress\AdventureWorks Reader]
FROM WINDOWS
WITH DEFAULT_DATABASE = AdventureWorks;
```

This will create a login for a previously set up Windows user called AdventureWorks Reader in the apress domain, and sets the default database for this login to AdventureWorks. You can also specify a DEFAULT_LANGUAGE in the WITH clause. Note that the login must have the same name as the actual Windows account.

SQL Server Principals

Whereas Windows authentication relies on the underlying operating system to perform authentication (determining who a particular user is), and SQL Server performs only authorization (determining which actions an authenticated user is entitled to perform), with SQL Server authentication, SQL Server itself performs both authentication and authorization.

As in previous versions of SQL Server, SQL Server 2008 supports both individual logins and server roles, to which multiple individual users can be assigned.

SQL Server Logins

When users connect to SQL Server using SQL Server authentication, they supply a username and password. SQL Server uses these to authenticate each user and determine the appropriate access rights. These user credentials are stored in SQL Server and are not connected at all to Windows user accounts.

In general, Windows authentication is preferred to SQL Server authentication. Because Windows authentication relies on the underlying operating system security mechanism, it doesn't require an extra password that could be compromised. In order to access SQL Server, users need to log on to Windows with an appropriate account, rather than merely supplying a username/password combination.

However, in some cases it's not possible to use Windows authentication (for example, if you're accessing SQL Server from a non-Windows operating system), and for this reason (and also for backward compatibility), SQL Server authentication is still supported in SQL Server 2008. In fact, it was slightly enhanced in SQL Server 2005; for example, by allowing Windows Active Directory password policies to be enforced.

To create a SQL Server login, use the CREATE LOGIN command with a WITH PASSWORD clause:

```
CREATE LOGIN [AdventureWorks Editor]
WITH PASSWORD = 'gsd45QK^*%demt',
     DEFAULT_DATABASE = AdventureWorks,
     CHECK_EXPIRATION = ON,
     CHECK_POLICY = ON;
```

If the password is supplied to the statement as a hash, add the HASHED keyword immediately after it; otherwise, the password will be hashed before it is stored. You can also add the MUST_CHANGE keyword after the password to stipulate that users must change their password the first time they log in. As with Windows logins, you can also specify the DEFAULT_DATABASE and/or DEFAULT_LANGUAGE for the login. Finally, you can specify whether you want domain password expiration policies and/or password complexity policies to be applied to the password (these are both ON by default); we'll look at SQL Server logins and Windows password policies shortly.

Server Roles

Server roles are predefined server-level principals that are granted a fixed set of permissions. Both SQL Server and Windows logins can be added as members of a server role; in which case, they inherit the role's permissions. Examples of server roles include dbcreator, which allows the creation of databases, and security, which manages security accounts within SQL Server.

You can use SQL Server Management Studio to manage server role memberships. Alternatively, you can use catalog views to view the list of members of a role. Although most permission and role changes are made through the ALTER Data Definition Language (DDL) statement, server role membership management still relies on the older sp_addsrvrolemember stored procedure.

Logins from Certificates and Asymmetric Keys

Starting with SQL Server 2005, you can create logins from certificates and asymmetric keys. For example, the following code creates a SQL Server certificate and then uses this to create a login:

```
CREATE CERTIFICATE awCert
ENCRYPTION BY PASSWORD = 'gwp;&569DVLq'
WITH START_DATE = '04/04/2005',
     EXPIRY_DATE = '04/04/2006',
     SUBJECT = 'caserver.apress.com'
GO

CREATE LOGIN [awCertifiedLogin]
FROM CERTIFICATE awCert
GO
```

A server login created in this way will be associated with the supplied certificate/asymmetric key. When the certificate or key is used to log on to SQL Server (for example, via an HTTPS or a Service Broker endpoint), it will be in the security context of this login. See Chapter 9 for an example of creating logins in this way to identify two Service Broker instances to each other. A login created in this manner can't be used to log on to SQL Server in the normal way through ADO.NET or Management Studio.

Windows Server 2003 and 2008 Policies

For SQL Server 2008 installations on Windows Server 2003 and Windows Server 2008 (currently Enterprise edition or above only), SQL Server can use the Windows security policies for SQL Server authentication. This means that the system administrator can stipulate that SQL Server security must meet the same standards as Windows security with regard to the following:

- *Password complexity*: Ensures that passwords used with SQL Server authentication meet a set of requirements such as containing nonalphanumeric characters.

- *Password length*: Specifies the minimum number of characters that a valid password can contain. Passwords with fewer characters won't be accepted.

- *Password history*: Ensures that users don't reuse recent passwords when their password expires and they are forced to change it.

- *Account lockout threshold*: Specifies how many chances users get to enter their password correctly before the account is locked.

- *Account lockout duration*: Specifies how long an account will be locked after users have incorrectly entered their password the number of times specified in the account lockout threshold.

- *Password age*: Specifies the maximum and minimum allowed age for a password (how long a password will be valid before the user is forced to change it, and the earliest time that a user will be allowed to change the password, respectively).

These policies will be applied only on SQL Server installations running on Windows Server 2003 or Windows Server 2008. This feature is unavailable on Windows 2000, XP, or Vista (even if the machine is on a Windows Server 2003 domain).

To test this, we'll demonstrate how to enforce a minimum length for SQL Server passwords. First, you need to set the policy on the local machine, so open the Local Security Settings MMC snap-in (Start ➤ Programs ➤ Administrative Tools ➤ Local Security Policy) or Default Domain Controller Security Settings (Start ➤ Programs ➤ Administrative Tools ➤ Domain Controller Security Policy), depending on whether or not the SQL Server machine is a domain controller.

Open the Account Policies node, and then the Password Policy node, and double-click the Minimum Password Length policy, as shown in Figure 6-2.

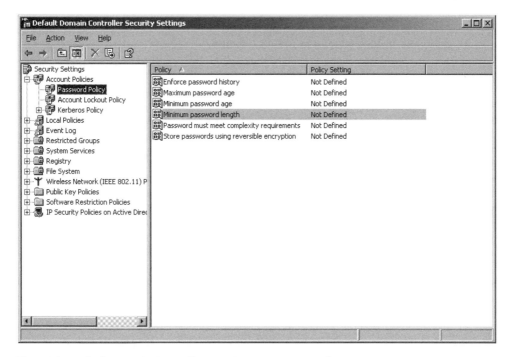

Figure 6-2. *Default Domain Controller Security Settings in Windows Server 2003*

Check the Define This Policy Setting check box and set the minimum length to six characters, as shown in Figure 6-3.

Figure 6-3. *Setting the minimum password length in Windows Server 2003*

Now if you attempt to create a SQL Server login, SQL Server will check the password against the local Windows security policy, and if the password doesn't meet the requirements of the password, the attempt will fail. To test this, create a user with an invalid password:

```
CREATE LOGIN Bob WITH PASSWORD = 'bob'
```

SQL Server will reject this command and won't create the login, because the password doesn't meet the criteria stipulated in the local Windows policy. You should now see an error message like this:

```
.Net SqlClient Data Provider: Msg 15116, Level 16, State 1, Line 1
Password validation failed. The password does not meet policy requirements
because it is too short.
```

Database Principals

Database principals are the objects that represent users to which you can assign permissions to access databases or particular objects within a database. Whereas logins operate at the server level and allow you to perform actions such as connecting to a SQL Server, database principals operate at the database level, allowing you to select or manipulate data, perform DDL statements on objects within the database, or manage users' permissions at the database level.

SQL Server 2008 recognizes three types of database principals:

- Database users
- Database roles
- Application roles

■**Note** Database groups, deprecated since SQL Server 7.0, are removed in SQL Server 2008.

Database Users

Database user principals are the database-level security context under which requests within the database are executed, and are associated with either SQL Server or Windows logins. To create a database user, you should not use the sp_adduser system stored procedure, which is now deprecated, but instead issue the CREATE USER command within the target database:

```
USE AdventureWorks
GO

CREATE USER awEditor
FOR LOGIN [AdventureWorks Editor];
GO
```

This will create a new user within the AdventureWorks database and associate this user with the AdventureWorks Editor login you created earlier. When a user with this login attempts to access the AdventureWorks database, that user will do so under the security context of the awEditor user within that database.

You can also create a user associated with a certificate or an asymmetric key:

```
CREATE USER [awCertifiedUser]
FOR CERTIFICATE awCert;
```

In this case, if a user (or an application) identified by a particular certificate or asymmetric key logs on to a web service, the query will be run in the security context of the user associated with that certificate or key.

Database Roles

As in previous versions of SQL Server, a database role principal may be either a user-defined role or a fixed database role. Database roles can be created and have permissions assigned to them (although, of course, the permissions of fixed database roles are fixed).

To create a database role, you now use the `CREATE ROLE` T-SQL statement, instead of the `sp_addrole` system stored procedure:

```
CREATE ROLE [AdventureWorks Editor]
AUTHORIZATION dbo;
```

The (optional `AUTHORIZATION` clause corresponds to the `@ownername` parameter of `sp_addrole`, and indicates the owner of the database role. Note that you still use the system stored procedure `sp_addrolemember` to add users to a user-defined role.

Application Roles

Application roles allow you to define a security context for a specific application. After the application has connected to SQL Server, it calls the `sp_setapprole` system stored procedure, and from that point, has the permissions assigned to the application role, rather than those of the user account under which the application is running. Since SQL Server 2005, application roles are created using the `CREATE APPLICATION ROLE` statement, rather than the `sp_addapprole` stored procedure:

```
CREATE APPLICATION ROLE DataEntryAppRole
WITH PASSWORD = 'gSLi87po(&$dK',
DEFAULT_SCHEMA = Sales;
```

The `DEFAULT_SCHEMA` clause is optional. We'll look at SQL Server schemas shortly, in the "Schema-Scoped Securables" section.

Object Ownership

Two key features relating to object ownership are important to understand. First is the optional `AUTHORIZATION` clause in many `CREATE` statements, which allows you to set the owner of the created object. For example, to specify that you want the new object to be owned by a user called `John`, rather than the user who is executing the statement when creating a new database role, use the following:

```
CREATE ROLE NewDbRole
AUTHORIZATION John;
```

You can also change the owner of an object using the `ALTER AUTHORIZATION` SQL statement, which takes the following form:

```
ALTER AUTHORIZATION
ON <entity_type>::<entity_name>
TO <principal_name>
```

Instead of providing the name of a principal as the new owner, you can specify `SCHEMA OWNER`, which will set the owner of the object to the owner of the schema to which it belongs.

For example, to change the owner of the role you created previously from `John` to a user called `Fred`, use the following command:

```
ALTER AUTHORIZATION
ON ROLE::NewDbRole
TO Fred;
```

Impersonation

Starting with SQL Server 2005, a user is allowed to impersonate another user for a specific block of code. This is achieved using the EXECUTE AS clause, which is added to the CREATE/ALTER statements for procedures, functions, triggers, and Service Broker queues.

Unlike the existing SETUSER, EXECUTE AS isn't restricted to members of the sysadmin fixed server role or the db_owner database role. This is important, because the impersonating account doesn't need to have access to the objects referenced in the module (the procedure, function, and so on), as long as it has permission to execute the module and the impersonated account has the requisite permissions to access the referenced objects. This means that you can force access to data through particular database objects, rather than directly through the database tables. Note that the default is for modules to be executed under the caller's account, so without impersonation, the caller wouldn't be able to access the data at all.

To see how this works, open a query window in Management Studio and create a couple of new users in the AdventureWorks database:

```
USE AdventureWorks
GO

CREATE LOGIN John WITH PASSWORD = '34r%*Fs$lK!9';
CREATE LOGIN Jane WITH PASSWORD = '4LWcm&(^o!HXk';

CREATE USER John FOR LOGIN John;
CREATE USER Jane FOR LOGIN Jane;
GO
```

Now give John SELECT permission on the database by adding that account to the db_datareader fixed database role, and permission to create stored procedures by adding him to the db_ddladmin role:

```
EXEC sp_addrolemember 'db_datareader', 'John';
EXEC sp_addrolemember 'db_ddladmin', 'John';
GO
```

Now you can create a new stored procedure that reads some data from the database. Set the EXECUTE AS clause so that the procedure will always impersonate John:

```
CREATE PROCEDURE usp_GetAddresses
WITH EXECUTE AS 'John'
AS
SELECT * FROM Person.Address;
GO
```

Use the new ALTER AUTHORIZATION command to set the owner of this procedure to the new user, John, so that the procedure has a different owner from the underlying tables. This breaks the chain of ownership and forces SQL Server to check the permissions on the underlying objects:

```
ALTER AUTHORIZATION ON usp_GetAddresses
TO John;
```

Finally, let's give Jane permission to execute this procedure (but not to access the data directly):

```
SETUSER
GRANT EXECUTE ON usp_GetAddresses TO Jane;
```

To test that this worked, switch to the user Jane and verify that you can't read data as that user:

```
SETUSER 'Jane'
SELECT * FROM Person.Address;
```

You should see this error message, confirming that Jane can't access the data directly:

```
SELECT permission denied on object 'Address', database 'AdventureWorks',
schema 'Person'.
```

Now execute the stored procedure you just created:

```
EXEC usp_GetAddresses;
```

This should run fine and return the data as expected, proving that you've forced Jane to access the data through the stored procedure by not granting her SELECT permission on the table. You can use this technique regardless of whether the ownership chain is broken between the stored procedure and the table.

As well as specifying the actual name of a user, you can also stipulate that a module should run as the CALLER (the default), the object's OWNER, or SELF (a shortcut for the name of the user account under which the object is being created or modified). This provides a great deal of flexibility when it comes to chains of ownership (when modules call other modules), as it allows you to specify in advance exactly under which user account each module should run.

Securables

Securables are the database objects to which you can control access and to which you can grant principals permissions. SQL Server 2008 distinguishes between three scopes at which different objects can be secured:

- *Server scope*: Server-scoped securables include logins, HTTP endpoints, event notifications, and databases. These are objects that exist at the server level, outside any individual database, and to which access is controlled on a server-wide basis.

- *Database scope*: Securables with database scope are objects such as users, roles, and CLR assemblies, which exist inside a particular database but not within a schema.

- *Schema scope*: This group includes those objects that reside within a schema within a database, such as tables, views, and stored procedures. A SQL Server 2005 or 2008 schema corresponds roughly to the owner of a set of objects (such as dbo) in SQL Server 2000.

Server-Scoped Securables

Server-scoped securables are objects that are unique within a SQL Server instance (for example, an instance can contain only one database of a given name, and there can be only one service listening on a given port). The following are the server-scoped objects:

- Connections

- Databases

- Event notifications

- HTTP endpoints

- Linked servers

- Logins

Permissions on server-scoped securables can be granted only to server-level principals (that is, either SQL Server logins or Windows logins), not to database-level principals such as users or roles. Also, these permissions must be granted in the master database. Any attempt to grant them within another database produces the following error:

```
Permissions at the server scope can only be granted when the current database is
master
```

Database-Scoped Securables

Database-level securables are unique to a specific database. The following are the database securables in SQL Server 2008:

- Application roles
- Assemblies
- Certificates and asymmetric/symmetric keys
- DDL events
- Full-text catalogs
- Message types
- Remote Service Bindings
- Roles
- Routes
- Schemas
- Service contracts
- Services
- Users

On each of these securables, you can apply permissions to the database-level security principals. However, if you grant permissions to a SQL Server or Windows login that doesn't have a corresponding database user principal, SQL Server will create a user with the same name for you in the current database. This doesn't apply to logins created from certificates or asymmetric keys.

Schema-Scoped Securables

A *schema* is a layer within the SQL Server security hierarchy. While schemas did exist in SQL Server 2000, they weren't distinct from the database user; each user had a corresponding schema of objects of which they were the owner, and schemas couldn't be explicitly created or named.

In SQL Server 2005 and 2008, a schema is still a collection of objects owned by a database user, but there is no longer a one-to-one link between users and schemas. A user can own more than one schema, and schemas can, if they are owned by a SQL Server role or a Windows group, be owned by more than one user.

The following objects are securable at the schema level:

- Defaults
- Functions
- Procedures
- Queues
- Rules
- Synonyms
- Tables

- Types
- User-defined aggregates
- Views
- XML Schema collections

How Schema-Level Security Works

A look at the schemas in the AdventureWorks database is instructive if you want to see how schemas are intended to be used. Each schema contains a set of objects commonly accessed by the same set of users; in this case, a department of the company, such as Sales, Production, or Human Resources. You can get a list of the schemas in a database from the sys.schemas system view:

```
USE [AdventureWorks]
SELECT * FROM sys.schemas;
```

When you add a user, you can assign a default schema for that user. For example, let's drop and re-create the user Jane from the previous example and set her DEFAULT_SCHEMA to Sales (while we're at it, we'll also add her to the db_ddladmin fixed role, so that she can create procedures in this database):

```
USE AdventureWorks
DROP USER Jane;

CREATE USER Jane FOR LOGIN Jane
WITH DEFAULT_SCHEMA = Sales;

EXEC sp_addrolemember 'db_ddladmin', 'Jane';
```

Setting the default schema means that anything Jane does will, by default, occur in this schema, so any objects she creates will be placed in the Sales schema, and any objects she references will be assumed to be in the Sales schema unless the object name is explicitly qualified by the name of the schema in which it resides. So, suppose that Jane runs this CREATE PROCEDURE statement:

```
USE AdventureWorks
GO

CREATE PROCEDURE usp_GetCustomers
AS
SELECT * FROM Customer
```

The new procedure will be placed in the Sales schema, and any user with a different default schema will need to refer to it as Sales.usp_GetCustomers. Also note that Jane can refer to the Customer table without explicitly prefixing the schema name, because it's in her default schema. If you don't specify a default schema in the CREATE USER command, it will default to dbo, as in SQL Server 2000.

Creating a New Schema

To create a schema, issue the CREATE SCHEMA command. For example, to create a schema named Finance, use this command:

```
CREATE SCHEMA Finance
```

You can also specify the database principal that owns the schema:

```
CREATE SCHEMA Finance AUTHORIZATION Jane
```

This gives Jane ownership of the schema and implicitly access to all the database objects within it, even if these aren't granted elsewhere. However, it doesn't give her permission to create objects within the schema, because DDL events are scoped at the database level, not at the schema level. See the "Managing Schema Permissions" section later in this chapter for information about how to do that.

One final point to note regarding the CREATE SCHEMA statement is that it can include nested CREATE TABLE and CREATE VIEW statements for creating tables and views within the schema, so the entire schema can be created in one go. You can also include GRANT, DENY, and REVOKE statements within the CREATE SCHEMA command.

Permissions

Permissions are the individual rights, granted (or denied) to a principal, to access a securable. As in previous SQL Server versions, you can GRANT permissions, DENY permissions, or REVOKE permissions that have already been granted. What's changed is the sheer number of permissions that you can grant—there are 181 combinations of permissions and securables!

Types of Permissions

The exact permissions that can be granted, and the format for the GRANT and DENY commands, vary according to the securable. These can be broken down into 12 groups:

- *Server permissions*: Permissions that apply to the server as a whole, such as permission to connect to the server or to an endpoint, permission to create or alter DDL or other events, and permission to access resources external to SQL Server. The controlling permission is CONTROL SERVER, which gives the grantee authority to perform any action and is effectively equivalent to adding the login to the sysadmin fixed server role.

- *HTTP endpoint permissions*: Permissions to connect to the endpoint and to control, alter, view the definition of, or take ownership of the object.

- *Certificate permissions*: Permissions to alter or control a specific certificate.

- *Database permissions*: Database-wide permissions that apply to all objects in the current database. For example, they include permissions to create, alter, and execute objects in the database; to perform select, insert, update, or delete operations in any object in the database; and to control or take ownership of the database.

- *Schema permissions*: Permissions that apply to a named schema or to all objects within the schema. They include the ability to perform select, insert, update, and delete operations on any object in the schema; to execute any procedure or function in the schema; or to control, alter, or take ownership of the schema.

- *Assembly permissions*: Permissions on a specific assembly, such as permission to execute, control, alter, or take ownership of the assembly.

- *Type permissions*: Permissions on a specific user-defined type, such as permission to execute, control, or take ownership of the type.

- *Full-text catalog permissions*: Permissions to reference, take ownership of, view the definition of, or control the catalog.

- *Service Broker permissions*: Permissions on a specific Service Broker object. These vary slightly depending on the type of object.

- *Server principal permissions*: Permissions to impersonate a given login account or to alter, view the definition of, take ownership of, or control the login.

- *Database principal permissions*: Permissions to impersonate a given user or to alter, control, or view the definition of a specific database principal.

- *Object permissions*: Permissions granted on a schema-scoped securable such as a table, view, or stored procedure, such as to execute or to perform select, delete, and other operations on the object. You can also specify ALL (or ALL PRIVILEGES) to grant all available permissions on the object.

We can't cover every permission here, so please consult SQL Server Books Online for a full list of the permissions supported by each type of object.

The basic syntax for the GRANT statement is as follows:

```
GRANT <permission>
[ON [<securable type>::]<securable>]
TO <principal>
[WITH GRANT OPTION]
[AS {<group> | <role> }]
```

The ON clause is omitted for database permissions and server permissions, which apply to the current database or server, respectively, as a whole. The <securable type>:: syntax is not used for permissions on database objects such as tables, views, and stored procedures. The WITH GRANT OPTION and AS {<group> | <role> } clauses are optional in all cases. The former gives the grantee the ability to grant the permission in turn to other principals, and the latter indicates the name of a database group or role that the granter belongs to and that has the authority to grant permissions on the securable.

The syntax for DENY and REVOKE follows the same basic format.

Managing Permissions

The preceding (necessarily somewhat condensed) information shows how much control the DBA now has in granting permissions on specific objects. A wide range of permissions is available, and with the addition of the schema to the security hierarchy comes a finer degree of control. However, in the real world, permissions don't occur singly, and managing permissions has two major complications:

- Many permissions implicitly grant other permissions, and permissions combine so that there may be multiple permissions on the same object.

- Objects call other objects, on which the principal may or may not have permissions.

Managing Schema Permissions

Schemas provide an extra layer in the authorization hierarchy that didn't exist in earlier versions of SQL Server. For example, the database-level permission to create tables or other objects doesn't actually mean anything unless you also have permission to add those objects to a specific schema, as database objects must now exist within a schema in the database. Conversely, as you saw earlier, the owner of a schema automatically has the right to perform select, delete, and other operations from objects within the schema, but not to create new objects in the schema. In order to allow that, you need to give the user the relevant permission at the database level. Here's an example:

```
USE AdventureWorks
GRANT CREATE TABLE TO Jane
```

This gives Jane the right to create tables in the database, and assuming she is the owner of the Finance schema created previously, she can now create new tables there. In order to create objects in a schema, a user needs ALTER permission on the schema, so Jane can't create tables in the Sales schema unless you grant her this permission:

```
GRANT ALTER
ON SCHEMA::Sales
TO Jane
```

As you would expect, if there's a conflict in permissions between the schema itself and an object in the schema, `DENY` overrides `GRANT`. For example, try to run this T-SQL code:

```
DENY SELECT ON SCHEMA::HumanResources TO Jane
GRANT SELECT ON HumanResources.Department TO Jane

SETUSER 'Jane'
SELECT * FROM HumanResources.Department
SETUSER
```

This denies `Jane` access to the `HumanResources` schema, but tries to grant access to the `Department` table within it, and then switches to the `Jane` user and tries to read from the table. You'll get the following error message:

```
SELECT permission denied on object 'Department', database 'AdventureWorks',
schema 'HumanResources'.
```

This means that there's no way to explicitly deny access to all but a specific set of objects in a schema. You need to either grant access only to the required object, without configuring access to the remaining objects, or explicitly deny access to each of the objects that you don't want the principal to access.

Ownership Chaining and Cross-Database Ownership Chaining

If a database object (such as a stored procedure) accesses another object (such as a table), SQL Server will skip permission checking for performance reasons if the owner of the two objects is the same. If the two objects have different owners, the chain of ownership will be broken, and SQL Server will check the permissions on the accessed object. This is the concept of *ownership chaining*.

While conceptually this works on paper, it is sometimes hard to implement in real life. Forcing the ownership of the table to the user who wrote the stored procedure, using our example, may not be suitable for some organizations. This is where using the `EXECUTE AS` clause can really be beneficial. The `EXECUTE AS` clause specifies exactly which security context you want a module, such as a stored procedure or function, to run in, as you saw in the "Impersonation" section earlier in this chapter. It also allows you to continue the chain of ownership, even across database boundaries.

Cross-database ownership chaining is used to allow access to resources on different databases without explicitly granting users access to the target database or tables within the target database. Careful planning is needed when using this feature, as enabling this feature raises some significant security concerns. For more information, read the "Ownership Chains" topic in SQL Server Books Online.

To use cross-database chaining in your SQL Server instance, you can enable it using the `sp_configure` stored procedure, and then run `RECONFIGURE`:

```
sp_configure 'cross db ownership chaining', 1
GO
RECONFIGURE
GO
```

Let's kick the tires by creating a new login called `William` and a couple new databases, with a simple table in each. These tables contain data on actual customers and on recipients who have signed up for a mailing list, for whom you have only an e-mail address. Once you've added some data to the tables, you'll write a view that performs a union query on the two tables. You will also create a user based on the William login, to whom you grant permission to access the view, but neither of the tables directly. Note that the William user must exist in both of the databases, or the query will fail.

```
CREATE DATABASE CustomerData
WITH DB_CHAINING ON

CREATE DATABASE MailingList
WITH DB_CHAINING ON
GO
CREATE LOGIN William WITH PASSWORD = '?sdj7JS3&*(%sdp_';

USE CustomerData
CREATE TABLE Customers
(
    CustomerID int IDENTITY PRIMARY KEY,
    FirstName nvarchar(255) NOT NULL,
    LastName nvarchar(255) NOT NULL,
    Email varchar(255) NOT NULL
);

INSERT INTO Customers VALUES ('John', 'Smith', 'John.Smith@somewhere.com');
INSERT INTO Customers VALUES ('Jane', 'Jones', 'JaneJ@somewhereelse.com');
GO

CREATE USER William FOR LOGIN William;
GO

USE MailingList
CREATE TABLE EmailAddresses
(
    ContactID int IDENTITY PRIMARY KEY,
    Email varchar(255) NOT NULL
);

INSERT INTO EmailAddresses VALUES('gprice@somedomain.com');
INSERT INTO EmailAddresses VALUES('fredb@anotherdomain.com');
GO

CREATE VIEW vGetAllContactEmails
AS
SELECT Email FROM EmailAddresses
UNION
SELECT Email FROM CustomerData.dbo.Customers;
GO

CREATE USER William FOR LOGIN William;
GRANT SELECT ON vGetAllContactEmails TO William;
GO

SETUSER 'William'
SELECT * FROM vGetAllContactEmails
SETUSER
```

When you set the current user to William, you should be able to access the view, even though it accesses data in another database. Because the view and the two tables it selects data from are all owned by the same user, the chain of ownership isn't broken.

Code Access Security

While T-SQL now has far more granular permissions than previously, it's still relatively crude compared with the control available with .NET. From the point of view of security, the most important aspect of .NET–SQL Server integration is that it allows the database developer to take advantage of Code Access Security (CAS). CAS is the .NET mechanism that allows developers to state explicitly which permissions their code needs to run (for example, the permission to access unmanaged code or the permission to access some part of the file system), and also to grant or deny permission to specific code to perform some action.

Four fundamental actions can be performed with CAS permissions:

- *Assert*: Asserting a permission allows a section of code to perform a given action, even if the method (which may be in a different assembly) that called the current method doesn't have that permission. The current code itself must have permission to perform the action, or the assert will fail.

- *Deny*: Denying a permission will cause any attempts further down the method call stack to perform the prohibited action or to demand the same permission to fail. However, the denial may be overridden by a subsequent call to Assert() or PermitOnly().

- *Demand*: Demanding a permission signals that the code requires this permission to run. The demand will be granted only if hasn't been denied higher up the call stack or permitted only on a different resource.

- *PermitOnly*: You can grant access to only a specific resource, and refuse access to other resources that require the same permission. PermitOnly can be overridden by an assert or a deny permission, but not by another PermitOnly.

Imperative and Declarative CAS

CAS can be implemented in two ways: declaratively, using attributes to demand and assert permissions; and imperatively, by calling methods on individual permission objects (these are defined in the System.Security.Permissions namespace, and derive from the CodeAccessPermission base class). Permissions can also be configured for entire assemblies, groups of assemblies, or even the entire local machine or domain using the CAS policy management application, caspol.exe, or the .NET Configuration Wizard.

CAS permissions are slightly misnamed—in many cases, they're actually broad groups of permissions that contain individual permissions. For example, the Security permission contains subpermissions to enable assembly execution, to allow calls to unmanaged code, and so on. To request a specific permission using imperative security, you instantiate the corresponding .NET class, passing in any parameters you need to identify precisely what your code needs permission to do, and then call the appropriate Demand(), Assert(), Deny(), or PermitOnly() method on the instance. For example, to demand Read permission on the file C:\temp.txt, use this code:

```
FileIOPermission perm = new FileIOPermission(FileIOPermissionAccess.Read,
    @"C:\temp.txt");
perm.Demand();
```

To do the same using declarative security, place .NET attributes in front of the assembly, class, or method that requires the permission, passing in the appropriate action as a SecurityAction enumeration member:

```
[FileIOPermission(SecurityAction.Demand, Read=@"C:\temp.txt")]
public static string ReadTempData()
{
    // Method body...
}
```

Using CAS with SQL Server

To see how this works in practice, let's look at a simple example. You'll write a C# DLL called `FileReader.dll` that reads a list of names of sales representatives in a text file line by line, and returns the contents as a string array. This will be called by a SQL Server assembly (`GetSalesAssem.dll`), also written in C#, which looks up these names in the AdventureWorks database and extracts the sales figures for the year to date and last year, and returns these as a result set.

Here is the code for `FileReader.cs`:

```
using System.Collections;
using System.IO;
using System.Security.Permissions;

namespace Apress.SqlServer2008.SecurityChapter
{
    public class FileReader
    {
        public static string[] ReadFile(string filename)
        {
            FileIOPermission perm = new FileIOPermission(
                                    FileIOPermissionAccess.Read, filename);
            perm.Demand();

            ArrayList names = new ArrayList();
            FileStream fs = new FileStream(filename, FileMode.Open,
                                    FileAccess.Read);
            StreamReader sr = new StreamReader(fs);
            while (sr.Peek() >= 0)
                names.Add(sr.ReadLine());
            sr.Close();
            fs.Close();

            return (string[])names.ToArray(typeof(string));
        }
    }
}
```

You use CAS to demand permission to read the file that's passed in as a parameter to the method that does the file reading. If the caller doesn't have permission to access the file, this line will throw an exception. You don't handle this exception in this class, because you want the exception to be available to the caller. You could create a new exception with its `InnerException` set to the original `Exception` object, but this involves creating an extra object that you don't really need.

Compile this C# file on the command line using the following statement:

```
csc /t:library FileReader.cs
```

Next comes the SQL Server assembly. This reads the names from the file specified in the parameter and uses these to construct a SQL statement that gathers the sales data for each employee. You then execute this statement against the server and return the results as a data reader to SQL Server:

```
using System;
using System.Data;
using System.Data.SqlClient;
using System.Data.SqlTypes;
using System.Security;
using System.Security.Permissions;
using System.Text;
using Microsoft.SqlServer.Server;
```

```csharp
namespace Apress.SqlServer2008.SecurityChapter
{
    public class SalesFetcher
    {
        public static void GetSalesForNames(SqlString filename)
        {
            try
            {
                // Create a PermissionSet to hold the permissions we want to grant
                PermissionSet perms = new PermissionSet(PermissionState.None);

                // Ensure that only correct file can be accessed through this method
                FileIOPermission ioPerm = new FileIOPermission(
                    FileIOPermissionAccess.Read, @"C:\names.txt");
                perms.AddPermission(ioPerm);

                // Permit access to SQL Server data
                SqlClientPermission sqlPerm = new SqlClientPermission(
                                                PermissionState.None);
                sqlPerm.Add("context connection=true", "",
                        KeyRestrictionBehavior.AllowOnly);
                perms.AddPermission(sqlPerm);
                perms.PermitOnly();

                // Get the names from the text file as a string array
                string[] names = FileReader.ReadFile(filename.ToString());

                // Build SQL statement
                StringBuilder sb = new StringBuilder();
                sb.Append(@"SELECT emp.EmployeeID,
                                sp.SalesYTD + sp.SalesLastYear AS RecentSales
                            FROM Sales.SalesPerson sp
                                INNER JOIN HumanResources.Employee emp
                                ON emp.EmployeeID = sp.SalesPersonID
                            WHERE sp.SalesPersonID IN
                            (
                                SELECT emp.EmployeeID
                                FROM HumanResources.Employee emp
                                    INNER JOIN Person.Contact c
                                    ON c.ContactID = emp.ContactID
                                WHERE c.FirstName + ' ' + c.MiddleName + ' ' +
                                    c.LastName
                            IN (");

                // Concatenate array into single string for WHERE clause
                foreach (string name in names)
                {
                    sb.Append("'");
                    sb.Append(name);
                    sb.Append("', ");
                }
                sb.Remove(sb.Length - 2, 2);
                sb.Append("))");

                // Execute the SQL statement and get back a SqlResultSet
                using (SqlConnection cn = new SqlConnection(
                                            "context connection=true"))
```

```
        {
            cn.Open();
            SqlCommand cmd = new SqlCommand(sb.ToString(), cn);
            SqlDataReader dr = cmd.ExecuteReader();

            // Send success message to SQL Server and return SqlDataReader
            SqlPipe pipe = SqlContext.Pipe;
            pipe.Send(dr);
            pipe.Send("Command(s) completed successfully.");
            cn.Close();
        }
    }
    catch (Exception e)
    {
        SqlPipe pipe = SqlContext.Pipe;
        pipe.Send(e.Message);
        pipe.Send(e.StackTrace);
        pipe.Send("Error executing assembly");
    }
  }
 }
}
```

This is where the power of CAS really shows itself, because you grant access to only one specific file (here, C:\names.txt) by calling PermitOnly() on your FileIOPermission object. Any attempt to access any other file through this assembly will fail. Now, in this case, you could have just hard-coded the value into the method call on the FileReader class, but CAS also lets you specify an array of files to which you want to permit access through this method; in which case, hard-coding the filename wouldn't have been an option.

As well as the FileIOPermission, notice that you also require a SqlClientPermission, which permits you to connect to SQL Server via the context connection; otherwise, calling PermitOnly on the FileIOPermission would prevent you from accessing SQL Server data. You create a new SqlClientPermission object with no permissions to connect to any SQL Server, and then call the Add method on this permission object, allowing connection on the context connection with no exceptions. It's not possible to call PermitOnly() individually on more than one permission in a method, so you need to create a PermissionSet object, add these two permissions to it, and then call PermitOnly() on the PermissionSet.

To compile this file, run the following command:

```
csc /t:library /r:FileReader.dll /r:"<path to sqlaccess.dll>" GetSalesAssem.cs
```

where <path to sqlaccess.dll> is

```
<Program Files>\Microsoft SQL Server\<MSSQL instance>\MSSQL\Binn\sqlaccess.dll
```

For example, on our system, this is the following path:

```
C:\Program Files\Microsoft SQL Server\MSSQL.1\MSSQL\Binn\sqlaccess.dll
```

Now you just need to register the assembly in SQL Server and create a procedure that will call this method. The stored procedure has one parameter, of type nvarchar, which will automatically be converted by the CLR to the corresponding .NET type (System.String), which is the type of the parameter to your .NET method:

```
USE AdventureWorks
GO
```

```
CREATE ASSEMBLY GetSalesAssem
FROM 'C:\Apress\AcceleratedSQLServer2008\Chapter6\GetSalesAssem.dll'
WITH PERMISSION_SET = EXTERNAL_ACCESS
GO

CREATE PROCEDURE uspGetSalesForNames @filename nvarchar(255)
AS EXTERNAL NAME GetSalesAssem.
    [Apress.SqlServer2008.SecurityChapter.SalesFetcher].GetSalesForNames
GO
```

To test this, create a new text file called names.txt in the root of the C:\ folder that contains the following names:

```
Michael G Blythe
Garrett R Vargas
Amy E Alberts
```

and call the new procedure:

```
EXEC uspGetSalesForNames 'C:\names.txt'
```

You should see the employee ID and sales data for each of these employees. You can check that CAS is working by making a copy of this file called names2.txt and running the procedure against that. You'll see an error message and stack trace indicating that the attempt to demand the FileIOPermission failed.

Auditing in SQL Server 2008

The need for auditing has probably existed since the days of the caveman. It's part of the sad fact that it is not possible or logical to trust everyone. Just ask the stockholders of the once powerful Enron Corporation about trust in their management.

■**Note** Enron was once a powerful leader in the energy business in the United States. Things started to turn ugly when the company admitted that it had misstated its income and that its equity value was a couple of billion dollars less than its balance sheet said. Further investigation revealed Enron had created partnerships with other companies—companies created by Enron itself. Enron used these partnerships to hide debts and losses on its trading business. In the end, Enron also took down Arthur Anderson, a once prestigious accounting firm, since that firm was responsible for auditing the Enron books.

The high-profile corruption of Enron and its accounting firm gave fuel to the creation of additional governmental legislation like the Sarbanes-Oxley (SOX) Act of 2002, which was intended to address the issues around public accounting. SOX is just one of many regulatory compliance laws. As a DBA, you may be tasked with working with a consultant to see how your company can comply with respect to the databases used in your company. Since these laws don't come out and say, "You must turn on encryption for this type of information," actual configuration of the database is left up to interpretation.

Even if you are not affected by SOX or other governmental regulations, auditing adds value in many other situations. Does your organization outsource work to third-party companies or employees? Do you ever want to know the user who is reading data from a particularly sensitive table? An effective auditing solution can answer these questions and many others.

Auditing has always been available to some degree in SQL Server. SQL Server 2005 leveraged its SQL Trace functionality and created a set of auditing classes. These trace classes enable administrators to audit events like failed login attempts and users trying to create or alter objects within the database. The SQL Server 2005 functionality was useful and effective, but a few areas needed improvement. Because auditing was exposed via SQL Trace, the logical tool to use to create and manage auditing was the SQL Server Profiler tool. Profiler is a tool designed for performance, tuning, and optimization, not auditing a database. In addition, the fact that auditing was using SQL Trace implied the performance of the system may be affected, since enabling trace on the database degrades performance to some degree.

Recognizing the importance of auditing, the SQL Server 2008 product team designed an auditing solution that addresses these concerns and provides a framework for further auditing capabilities in future SQL Server releases. DBAs no longer need to use SQL Server Profiler to create and manage audits. They can use either SQL Server Management Studio or native T-SQL. Auditing no longer uses SQL Trace. Instead, it employs a powerful new eventing subsystem in SQL Server called Extended Events. This new eventing subsystem leverages Service Broker to securely and transactionally store and forward auditing messages.

With any new features comes a variety of new objects, catalog views, and possibly some new T-SQL to learn. Auditing is no exception. If you have used auditing previously in SQL Server, it may benefit you to temporarily forget what you know. We will refer to how the new auditing in SQL Server 2008 relates to SQL Trace when we talk about specifying what to audit. Keep in mind that SQL Server Management Studio provides a variety of management dialog boxes, so you do not need to remember the T-SQL syntax.

Where to Write Audit Data

An audit needs to write records somewhere so auditors and other users with read access can review the actual auditing information. The Server Audit object defines the location of where audit data will be written. Server audits are defined at the server level, as opposed to defined for a particular database.

An audit is allowed to write to a file on the file system, the Windows Applications Log, or the Windows Security Log. Each of these options has slightly different requirements and parameters available for configuration.

Here is an example of logging audit data to a file:

```
CREATE SERVER AUDIT [CustomerProtectionAudit]
TO FILE
(    FILEPATH = N'C:\AuditLogs\'
    ,MAXSIZE = 0 MB
    ,MAX_ROLLOVER_FILES = 0
    ,RESERVE_DISK_SPACE = OFF
)
WITH
(    QUEUE_DELAY = 1000
    ,ON_FAILURE = CONTINUE
)
```

Two options are common to all auditing destinations:

QUEUE_DELAY: Since we are leveraging Service Broker behind the scenes, audit events are written to a queue. In the example here, the queue delay is 1 second (1000). This means the queue is allowed to fill up for 1 second before it is flushed to disk or to the Windows logs. This also means that if the server died unexpectedly within this 1 second, you may potentially lose auditing events. Setting the QUEUE_DELAY to 0 means synchronously writing auditing records. Those of us experienced with the word *synchronous* know that usually means slow, and setting QUEUE_DELAY to 0 will slow down your application. Your organization will need to determine if you must guarantee audit events are logged or if you are able to take a 1-, 2-, or 10-second hit in auditing records due to an unforeseen catastrophic event.

ON_FAILURE: The possible options here are CONTINUE and SHUTDOWN. CONTINUE means if for some reason audit records can't be physically written, the server instance on which auditing is defined should continue to run, just as it does 24 hours a day, 7 days a week. SHUTDOWN means that if the audit records can't be physically written, the server instance should shut down. Yes, SHUTDOWN means that users would be kicked off, transactions would be aborted, and many people may be upset, but it is all for the sake of auditing.

Sending audit events to either the Windows Application Log or the Windows Security Log does not require any special parameters. For example, here's the form for using the Windows Application Log:

```
CREATE SERVER AUDIT [CustomerProtectionAudit]
TO APPLICATION_LOG
```

Logging to the Windows Application Log is straightforward and requires no special configuration. However, logging to the Windows Security Log requires that the SQL Server service account be Local System, Local Service, Network Service, or a domain user with SeAuditPrivilege, and not an interactive user. These are requirements that come from the operating system.

When you send audit events to a file, you need to define certain behaviors, such as how big to allow the audit file to grow and where to put the file on the file system. The TO FILE parameter provides these definitions, as in the preceding example:

```
TO FILE
(    FILEPATH = N'C:\AuditLogs\'
    ,MAXSIZE = 0 MB
    ,MAX_ROLLOVER_FILES = 0
    ,RESERVE_DISK_SPACE = OFF
)
```

Notice that you do not specify a filename for the audit data, but instead specify a file path. This is because SQL Server will autogenerate a filename for the audit data. The format of the filename is composed of the audit name, the audit globally unique identifier (GUID), a file offset value, and a timestamp value. An example autogenerated pathname is as follows:

```
CustomerProtectionAudit_3986977D-1EFF-434A-8078-22B1BB22BD1D_0_ ➥
128367603342740000.sqlaudit
```

SQL Server allows you to specify both local and remote fileshares.

■**Note** You might question the performance and reasons for allowing remote fileshares. Yes, the performance will be slow. Just imagine if you specified synchronous and wrote to a remote fileshare! But consider the case where the organization wants to protect itself from DBAs (e.g., members of the sysadmin group or those with CONTROL SERVER permissions). By default, these users have access to everything and anything inside SQL Server. The only way to ensure DBAs do their job and nothing else is to define auditing and write audit events to a fileshare where the SQL Server service account and the sysadmin have nothing but append access. Now you may be thinking with your hacker's hat on and wonder why a sysadmin couldn't just stop the audit? Realize that an audit can't be started, stopped, or deleted without writing an audit event stating that the event occurred. Thus, the auditor can see a stopped audit event and start to ask questions of the DBA.

MAXSIZE is simply the maximum size you are willing to let the audit file grow to. A value of 0 means unlimited. When a file gets to a maximum size, it will roll over to a new file if you have the MAX_ROLLOVER_FILES parameter set. By default, MAX_ROLLOVER_FILES is set to 0, indicating the audit file will never roll over to a new one. To keep audit files manageable, it may be necessary to set some arbitrary limit, like 500MB or 1GB; otherwise, viewing or managing the audit file could take an extra long time. Do not worry about concatenating the files, because SQL Server has a function that will easily return the entire audit (or pieces of it) to you, without you needing to manually piece together these files. This function is called fn_get_audit_file and will be discussed later in this chapter, when we walk through an auditing example.

RESERVE_DISK_SPACE means that SQL Server will preallocate the size of the audit file on disk to that defined in MAXSIZE. This is useful for ensuring that you will have enough disk space to audit for a given period of time.

Note that other parameters are available for specifying where to log data for these T-SQL statements. Refer to SQL Server Books Online for the complete list.

What to Audit

Now that we have discussed where the audit events are written to, it might be helpful to describe exactly how to tell SQL Server what is interesting to audit. In SQL Server, we have things that happen and exist in the service instance scope, and things that happen and exist in the database scope. This is also how auditing is divided. SQL Server auditing has objects called Server Audit Specification and Database Audit Specification.

Server Audit Specifications

Server Audit Specification objects allow auditors to audit server instance information, such as failed and successful logins, whenever a login's password changes, and whenever a login's membership in a role changes. Table 6-1 shows the kinds of groups of events you can audit. See SQL Server Books Online for a complete list.

Table 6-1. *Server-Level Audit Event Groups*

Name	Description
DATABASE_CHANGE_GROUP	Occurs when a database is created, altered, or dropped. When this event is set in a Server Audit Specification, it fires whenever *any* database is created, altered, or dropped. This event is equivalent to Audit Database Management Event Class in SQL Trace.
DATABASE_OBJECT_CHANGE_GROUP	Occurs when a CREATE, ALTER, or DROP statement is executed on database objects, such as schemas. When this event is set in a Server Audit Specification, it fires whenever *any* database object is created, altered, or dropped. This could lead to very large quantities of audit records. This event is equivalent to Audit Database Object Management Event Class in SQL Trace.
LOGIN_CHANGE_PASSWORD_GROUP	Occurs whenever a login's password is changed via ALTER LOGIN or sp_password. This event group includes events from Audit Login Change Password Event Class in SQL Trace (a deprecated SQL Trace event class).
SERVER_STATE_CHANGE_GROUP	Occurs when the SQL Server service state is modified. This is equivalent to Audit Starts and Stops Event Class in SQL Trace.
SUCCESSFUL_LOGIN_GROUP	Occurs when a user has successfully logged in to SQL Server. This is equivalent to Audit Login Event Class in SQL Trace.
FAILED_LOGIN_GROUP	Occurs when a user tries to log in to SQL Server and fails. This event is equivalent to Audit Login Failed Event Class in SQL Trace.
LOGOUT_GROUP	Occurs when a user has logged out of (logged off) SQL Server. This event is equivalent to Audit Logout Event Class in SQL Trace.

From a glance at Table 6-1's Description column, you can see that the Server Audit Specification events are equivalent to SQL Trace event classes. This is not because auditing in SQL Server 2008 uses SQL Trace, but rather that internally in the engine code, where it has a path to raise a SQL Trace event, it has a path to raise an auditing event, leveraging the extended eventing infrastructure. Doing this allows for an easier upgrade for those users using SQL Trace in SQL Server 2005 for their auditing needs.

Let's take a look at an example of creating a Server Audit Specification:

```
CREATE SERVER AUDIT SPECIFICATION [ProductionServerAuditSpecification]
FOR SERVER AUDIT [CustomerProtectionAudit]
```

Notice there are no options on the CREATE SERVER AUDIT SPECIFICATION DDL other than to specify an existing Server Audit object. You must define a Server Audit object before you can define a Server Audit Specification.

In SQL Server 2008, you also must create the object first, and then ALTER it to add or remove any audit events that you wish to manage. For example, to add the FAILED_LOGIN_GROUP to the sample Server Audit Specification, issue the following:

```
ALTER SERVER AUDIT SPECIFICATION [ProductionServerAuditSpecification]
ADD (FAILED_LOGIN_GROUP)
```

You can have one or more Server Audit Specification objects defined on an instance. In addition, you can point any Server Audit Specification to any Server Audit (the place where audit records are written) you defined.

Notice that we have not talked about filtering of any kind. Once you enable the FAILED_LOGIN_GROUP, for example, you get an audit for every single failed login. In SQL Server 2008, you can't say just give me failed logins for the sa login only. This lack of filtering is only for Server Audit Specification objects. For Database Audit Specification objects, some filtering is available.

Database Audit Specifications

Database Audit Specification objects allow auditors to audit database-scoped information, such as whenever a CREATE, ALTER, or DROP statement is issued; whenever a database user is created; or whenever permissions to this user have changed. Table 6-2 shows the kinds of events you can audit. See SQL Server Books Online for the complete list.

Table 6-2. *Database-Level Audit Events*

Name	Description
DATABASE_OBJECT_ACCESS_GROUP	Occurs whenever database objects such as certificates, asymmetric keys, and symmetric keys are accessed. This event is equivalent to Audit Database Object Access Event Class in SQL Trace.
DATABASE_OWNERSHIP_CHANGE_GROUP	Occurs when you use the ALTER AUTHORIZATION statement to change the owner of a database, and the permissions required to do that are checked. This event is equivalent to Audit Change Database Owner Event Class in SQL Trace.
SELECT	Occurs whenever a SELECT statement is issued.
INSERT	Occurs whenever an INSERT statement is issued.
UPDATE	Occurs whenever an UPDATE statement is issued.
DELETE	Occurs whenever a DELETE statement is issued.
EXECUTE	Occurs whenever an EXECUTE statement is issued.

As with Server Audit Specification events, Database Audit Specification events are based on the locations of SQL Trace events, but this is not the case with all of them. Some can go a bit more granular than was possible using the SQL Trace audit event classes.

Again, for this type of auditing, you must first create the Database Audit Specification object. Then you can ALTER the object and add events:

```
CREATE DATABASE AUDIT SPECIFICATION [CustomerDatabaseAudit]
FOR SERVER AUDIT [CustomerProtectionAudit]
ALTER DATABASE AUDIT SPECIFICATION  [CustomerDatabaseAudit]
ADD (SELECT ON [dbo].[Accounts] BY Developers)
GO
```

Database Audit Specification objects do allow some degree of filtering. In this example, we want to audit SELECT on the Accounts table only when users of the Developers group are issuing the statement.

Database Audit Specification objects apply to one Server Audit object. However, you can have more than one Database Audit Specification for any given database.

Since Database Audit Specification objects live in the database and are linked to the Server Audit object via a GUID, in certain scenarios where two copies of the same database are used, such as in the case of database mirroring, you will need to use the same audit GUID for both sides of the mirror. The SERVER AUDIT DDL syntax allows for creating the Server Audit object with a specific GUID. Thus, all you need to do to support this scenario is create the Server Audit object on the mirrored server with the same GUID as the primary server.

An Auditing Example

To help illustrate the concepts described in the previous sections, we will walk through an auditing scenario. Suppose you are a senior DBA at a financial company, and your organization uses an internal application written by another team in your company. Lately, this application seems to be having some problems, and you need to allow a group of developers access to your production SQL Server installation. Since the production servers contain customer-sensitive information, you need to ensure that they do not modify or add any information. Also, the upper management wants to track all SELECT queries against the data.

Implementing Auditing

For this example, you will simplify the database architecture for the internal application and have a single database called Customers. This database will have a table defined as follows:

```
CREATE TABLE Accounts
(customer_id    INT       NOT NULL,
Balance  DECIMAL        NOT NULL,
social_sec_num         VARCHAR(13)    NOT NULL)
GO
--We should insert some interesting values as well
INSERT INTO Accounts VALUES (1,59768.34,'041-00-0000')
INSERT INTO Accounts VALUES (2,128.01,'368-11-1111')
INSERT INTO Accounts VALUES (3,59768.34,'532-22-2222')
GO
```

Next, assume you have a Windows NT group called Developers and a Windows user called User1, who is a member of this group. At this point, you want to create the SQL login and a database user for this NT group:

```
USE master
GO
```

```
CREATE LOGIN [MYCOMPANY\Developers] FROM WINDOWS
GO
USE Customers
GO
CREATE USER [Developers] FOR LOGIN [MYCOMPANY\Developers]
GO
GRANT SELECT, INSERT, UPDATE, DELETE ON [dbo].[Accounts] TO [Developers]
GO
```

Now that the accounts are created, you can create your Server Audit object:

```
CREATE SERVER AUDIT [CustomerProtectionAudit]
TO FILE
(    FILEPATH = N'C:\AuditLogs\'
     ,MAXSIZE = 0 MB
)
WITH
(    QUEUE_DELAY = 1000
     ,ON_FAILURE = SHUTDOWN
)
```

Once the Server Audit object is created, you can create a Database Audit Specification object that audits any SELECT against the Accounts table for Developers:

```
USE Customers
GO
CREATE DATABASE AUDIT SPECIFICATION [CustomerDatabaseAudit]
FOR SERVER AUDIT [CustomerProtectionAudit]
ALTER DATABASE AUDIT SPECIFICATION  [CustomerDatabaseAudit]
ADD (SELECT ON [dbo].[Accounts] BY Developers)
GO
```

Note that, by default, server audits are not enabled. Thus, in order to start receiving audit events, you need to enable them, as follows:

```
--We must be in the master database to issue the ALTER SERVER AUDIT command
USE master
GO
ALTER SERVER AUDIT [CustomerProtectionAudit]
     WITH (STATE=ON);
GO
```

At this point, you are auditing events. To simulate a live environment, you can launch SQLCMD under User1's context and issue a SELECT and an INSERT query against the Accounts table. If you want to see the auditing data, you can view this in SQL Server Management Studio, or you can use the new function fn_get_audit_file.

Using fn_get_audit_file to View Auditing Data

The new fn_get_audit_file function returns information to the user in a record-set form from audit files written to the file system. This function can return a specific audit file or a single record set containing information from all the audit files within a particular directory. In the example, since you have only one auditing file, you can view your auditing events simply by passing the path-name and the wildcard *:

```
SELECT * FROM fn_get_audit_file('c:\AuditLogs\*',null,null)
```

Alternatively, you could directly call out the audit file, like this:

```
SELECT * FROM fn_get_audit_file('c:\AuditLogs\CustomerProtectionAudit_3986977D- ➥
1EFF-434A-8078-22B1BB22BD1D_0_128367603342740000.sqlaudit',null,null)
```

If you had more than one Server Audit object writing to the same folder, you would have another file that contained another name, GUID, timestamp, and offset. If you didn't want to return this information, you could use the wildcard again. This time, placing the * just after the GUID will give you all the audit records in the folder for the given Server Audit:

```
SELECT * FROM fn_get_audit_file('c:\AuditLogs\CustomerProtectionAudit_3986977D- ➥
1EFF-434A-8078-22B1BB22BD1D*',null,null)
```

When you issue this command, you will see a row for every audit event and a plethora of columns—too many to list on a book page. What is important to note here is that, in this example, you audited SELECT, INSERT, UPDATE, and DELETE for a database user that was really a Windows NT group. The audit log will show the Windows user that accessed the command—in this case, MYCOMPANY\User1, instead of the NT group MYCOMPANY\Developers. It will also tell you the exact statements that were issued.

Managing Audits

In SQL Server 2005, there was a big push to get users off of querying the system tables directly and to use catalog views instead. Auditing follows this effort and provides a bunch of catalog views that describe each of the components of auditing.

The sys.server_audits view describes all the server audits that are defined on the server instance. This information includes the names, where they write their audit events, if they shut down on failure, and the queue delay value. The catalog views for database audits include one that describes their configuration and many others. These catalog views are sys.database_audit_specifications and sys.database_audit_specification_details.

There are also dynamic management views that can be used to show the runtime status of auditing. Check out sys.dm_server_audit_status to determine if the audit is enabled and the current file size (if auditing to a file).

For those of us who prefer to use a user interface to manage databases, SQL Server Management Studio now has support for auditing. Everything that you did via T-SQL in the previous section can be done via Management Studio. Server audits have an Audits node below the Security node of a server instance, as shown in Figure 6-4.

Figure 6-4. *Server Audits and Server Audit Specifications in Object Explorer*

You can see from Object Explorer which server audits are enabled and which are disabled by observing the icon associated with the Server Audit object name. As with most other database objects, from the context menu of a particular Server Audit object, you can enable, disable, view properties, or create a new Server Audit object. You can also view the audit history. Viewing the audit history will launch the familiar Log File Viewer dialog box, which shows the application log, security log, or the audit events from the file system.

Since Server Audit Specification objects are scoped at the server-instance level, they are also available under the Security node of the server instance. Here, you can also enable, disable, and manage your server audits.

Database Audit Specification objects are scoped to the database. To manage them, you need to navigate down the specific Database node to the Security node, as shown in Figure 6-5.

Figure 6-5. *Database Audit Specifications in Object Explorer*

As with all other audit objects in Object Explorer, you can create new database audit specifications, modify the properties, and enable and disable them by using the context menus.

Summary

SQL Server has continued to enhance its security feature set with every new release of the database engine, and SQL Server 2008 is no exception. This release of SQL Server builds on top of the major work that went into the SQL Server 2005 security feature set, with emphasis on an improved auditing and encryption story.

Auditing in SQL Server 2008 is the first step in a multirelease effort to enhance the auditing capabilities in SQL Server. Customers and governmental agencies are constantly requiring more and more granular auditing capabilities, so you can bet that SQL Server will keep up with the demands and continue to develop this feature by providing even more filtering and more reporting capabilities.

The encryption enhancements in SQL Server 2008 are significant enough for them to have their own chapter. Chapter 7 covers the encryption enhancements in SQL Server.

■ ■ ■

SQL Server Encryption

High-powered computers and cheap storage have made it possible for businesses to store unprecedented amounts of personal data about their customers. As a result, there has been a big push to secure this confidential information. Even state and federal government have gotten in on the act by passing a flurry of consumer protection and personal data privacy laws and regulations. If your organization falls under the scope of the various regulations and data privacy laws, like the Health Insurance Portability and Accountability Act (HIPAA) or the Securities and Exchange Commission's Fair and Accurate Credit Transactions Act (FACTA), you'll be pleased to know that SQL Server 2008 includes several Transact-SQL (T-SQL) extensions and built-in functions to make securing personal data in the database easier than ever.

In this chapter, we will discuss the built-in SQL Server 2008 encryption tools, covering the following topics:

- The SQL Server encryption model, including the SQL Server encryption hierarchy and the newly introduced concepts of server certificates and database encryption keys

- Transparent data encryption, which allows you to transparently encrypt an entire database at once without affecting front-end and middle-tier applications

- Extensible Key Management (EKM), which allows you to use third-party hardware security modules (HSMs) to manage enterprise encryption keys externally

- Symmetric and asymmetric encryption functions

- Generation of one-way hashes and use of certificates to digitally sign your data

- Use of security catalog views to access security metadata

- Efficiency when querying encrypted data

■Note SQL Server encryption, discussed in this chapter, is only a small part of your overall security strategy. Database-level encryption protects your data "at rest," and is your last line of defense in a total strategy. When developing your total security strategy, you should consider several factors, including physical security, database permissions, security "over the wire," and client computer and application security. A lot of confusion is caused by people who think that encrypting data at rest on their server is a complete security strategy. Be sure to consider all the different pieces of the puzzle, and don't assume that database-level encryption alone is a replacement for a complete security strategy.

Encryption Keys

The SQL Server encryption model includes built-in encryption key management patterned after the ANSI X9.17 standard. This standard defines several layers of encryption keys, which are used to encrypt other keys, which in turn are used to encrypt actual data. The layers of encryption keys defined by the ANSI X9.17 standard and the roughly analogous layers defined by SQL Server are listed in Table 7-1.

Table 7-1. *SQL Server and ANSI X9.17 Encryption Key Layers Comparison*

SQL Server Layer	ANSI X9.17 Layer	Description
Service master key (SMK)	Master Key (KKM)	Encrypts database master keys
Database master key (DMK), asymmetric keys, certificates, symmetric keys	Key Encrypting Key (KEK)	Encrypts symmetric keys
Symmetric keys	Data Key (KD)	Encrypts data

■**Note** The ANSI X9.17 standard is the "Financial Institution Key Management (Wholesale)" standard. This standard defines methods for securely storing and transferring encryption keys, an area of encryption that has been the subject of debate and research throughout the field of cryptography for decades. Encryption key management is not easy. After all, modern encryption theory has only one primary mandate: the security of a system lies with the encryption key. No matter how secure the algorithm you use to encrypt your data, if your encryption key is not properly secured, your data can be easily compromised. SQL Server's encryption key management is built on top of the secure Data Protection API (DPAPI), making it as secure as possible on a computer that runs Windows.

The service master key (SMK) is the top-level key, the granddaddy of all SQL Server keys. There is a single SMK defined for each instance of SQL Server 2008. The SMK is secured by the Windows Data Protection API (DPAPI), and it is used to encrypt the next layer of keys, the database master keys (DMKs). The SMK is automatically created by SQL Server the first time it is needed.

DMKs are used to encrypt symmetric keys, asymmetric keys, and certificates. Each database can have a single DMK defined for it.

The next layer of keys includes symmetric keys, asymmetric keys, and certificates. Symmetric keys are the primary means of encrypting data in the database. While asymmetric keys and certificates can be used to encrypt data (with some work on your part, which we will discuss in the "Asymmetric Keys" section later in this chapter), Microsoft recommends that you encrypt data exclusively with symmetric keys.

In addition to all the keys and certificates previously supported by SQL Server 2005, SQL Server 2008 introduces the concept of server certificates and database encryption keys in support of the new transparent data encryption functionality. The server certificate is simply a certificate created in the master database. The database encryption key is a special symmetric key used to encrypt an entire database at once. We'll discuss the server certificate and database encryption key in detail in the "Transparent Data Encryption" section later in this chapter. Figure 7-1 shows the SQL Server 2008 encryption key hierarchy.

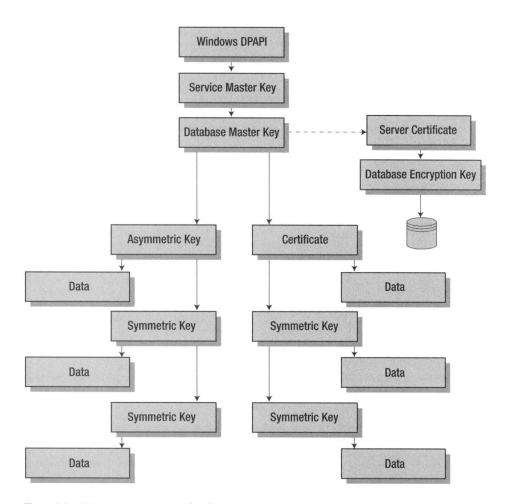

Figure 7-1. *SQL Server encryption key hierarchy*

Service Master Key

SQL Server 2008 includes the following T-SQL statements to alter, back up, and drop SMKs:

- ALTER SERVICE MASTER KEY: Allows you to change or regenerate the SMK. This statement can be used to change the SMK and to automatically decrypt and re-encrypt the entire encryption key hierarchy.

- BACKUP SERVICE MASTER KEY: Backs up your SMK to a file. The SMK is encrypted before backup and stored in encrypted format. You must supply a password to be used to encrypt the SMK backup.

- RESTORE SERVICE MASTER KEY: Restores your SMK from a file. The SMK RESTORE statement requires you to supply the same password used when you backed up the SMK. Like ALTER SERVICE MASTER KEY, the RESTORE SERVICE MASTER KEY statement regenerates the entire encryption key hierarchy.

After installing a new SQL Server 2008 instance, you should immediately back up the SMK and store it in a safe location. The BACKUP SERVICE MASTER KEY statement takes the following form:

```
BACKUP SERVICE MASTER KEY TO FILE = 'c:\MK\backup_master_key.dat'
    ENCRYPTION BY PASSWORD = 'p@$$w0rD';
```

In this example, the SMK is backed up to the file c:\MK\backup_master_key.dat, and it is encrypted with the password p@$$w0rD. The encryption password is required if you need to restore the SMK.

If you need to alter, restore from backup, or regenerate your SMK, SQL Server will attempt to decrypt and re-encrypt all keys in the encryption key hierarchy. If any of these decryptions fail, the whole process will fail. If that happens, you can use the FORCE option on the ALTER SERVICE MASTER KEY and RESTORE SERVICE MASTER KEY statements. However, be aware that if you must use the FORCE option, you can count on data loss.

Database Master Keys

As mentioned previously, the SQL Server encryption key hierarchy includes a single DMK for each database. The DMK directly encrypts asymmetric keys and certificates that can be used to encrypt symmetric keys. Symmetric keys are used, in turn, to encrypt other symmetric keys and data.

Unlike the SMK, which is generated automatically the first time it is needed, a DMK must be created explicitly with the CREATE MASTER KEY statement. SQL Server includes the following T-SQL statements to manage DMKs:

- CREATE MASTER KEY: Creates a DMK within a database. A password must be supplied to encrypt the DMK in the database when it is created.

- ALTER MASTER KEY: Allows you to regenerate your DMK or to change how the DMK is secured by adding or removing encryption by password or SMK. If you regenerate the DMK, all the keys it protects will be decrypted and re-encrypted.

- DROP MASTER KEY: Drops the DMK from the current database. If any private keys in the current database are protected by the DMK, the DROP statement will fail.

- BACKUP MASTER KEY: Backs up the DMK to a file. You must specify a password, which will be used to encrypt the DMK in the file.

- RESTORE MASTER KEY: Restores the DMK from a file. You must supply the same password you used when backing up the DMK for a RESTORE operation to succeed. You must also supply a second password to encrypt the DMK in the database after it is restored. During the restore process, SQL Server attempts to decrypt and re-encrypt all keys protected by the DMK.

- OPEN MASTER KEY: Opens the DMK so that it can be used for encryption and decryption. The DMK must be open in order for any encryption or decryption operation to succeed, although SQL Server can implicitly open your DMK when it's protected by the SMK, which we will discuss shortly.

- CLOSE MASTER KEY: Closes a DMK that was explicitly opened using OPEN MASTER KEY after you are finished using it for encryption and decryption.

The ALTER MASTER KEY and RESTORE MASTER KEY statements attempt to regenerate the hierarchy of encryption keys that the DMK protects. That is to say, these statements try to automatically decrypt and re-encrypt all encryption keys below the DMK in the hierarchy. If any of these decryptions fail, the entire ALTER or RESTORE statement will fail. The FORCE option can be used to force an ALTER or RESTORE statement to complete regardless of errors. But be warned: the FORCE option should be used only as a last resort, since it always results in data loss.

All DMK management statements require CONTROL permission on the database, and they must be executed in the context of the current database.

The following statement creates a DMK in the AdventureWorks database:

```
USE AdventureWorks;
GO
CREATE MASTER KEY
 ENCRYPTION BY PASSWORD = N'Avx3$5*!';
```

You should back up all of your DMKs and store them in safe locations as soon as you create them. You can back up the DMK with a statement like the following:

```
BACKUP MASTER KEY TO FILE = N'c:\MK\AwMasterKeyBackup.bak'
 ENCRYPTION BY PASSWORD = N'#%e3)Fr';
GO
```

If you ever need to restore the DMK, use the RESTORE MASTER KEY statement, as follows:

```
RESTORE MASTER KEY FROM FILE = 'c:\MK\AwMasterKeyBackup.bak'
 DECRYPTION BY PASSWORD = N'#%e3)Fr'
 ENCRYPTION BY PASSWORD = N'Avx3$5*!';
GO
```

When restoring a DMK, you need to supply the same password in the DECRYPTION BY PASSWORD clause that you used when you performed the BACKUP operation.

SQL Server 2008 provides two methods of securing DMKs. Using the first method requires you to explicitly supply a password when you create, alter, or restore your DMK. This password will be used to encrypt the DMK and store it in the database. If you encrypt your DMK with a password, you must supply the same password every time you need to access the keys the DMK protects. This also means you need to use the OPEN MASTER KEY and CLOSE MASTER KEY statements to explicitly open and close the DMK.

By default, SQL Server also provides a second method of securing your DMKs. When you create a DMK, it is automatically encrypted using the SMK and Triple DES algorithm, with copies stored in both the current database and the master database. This allows SQL Server to automatically open and close your DMK when it is needed, without the need for you to supply a password.

On the plus side, this automatic SMK-based security makes development easier, since you don't need to use explicit OPEN MASTER KEY and CLOSE MASTER KEY statements to open and close the DMK every time you encrypt your data. You also don't need to worry about managing, storing, and/or transmitting a password to SQL Server every time you want to perform an encryption or a decryption operation. The downside to this method (and you *knew* there would be one) is that every sysadmin can decrypt the DMK. In many businesses, this could be the deciding factor against using this feature.

You can use the ALTER MASTER KEY statement to turn off automatic encryption of your DMK by SMK, as in the following T-SQL code:

```
USE AdventureWorks;
GO
ALTER MASTER KEY
 DROP ENCRYPTION BY SERVICE MASTER KEY;
```

Dropping the DMK is as simple as executing the DROP statement:

```
DROP MASTER KEY;
```

The OPEN MASTER KEY and CLOSE MASTER KEY statements are used to open and close the DMK so that it can be used to encrypt and decrypt the other keys and certificates that it protects. These keys can then be used to encrypt and decrypt symmetric keys and data. As we noted, SQL Server can implicitly open and close your DMK if it is not encrypted by the SMK. We will describe how to use the DMK with and without automatic SMK encryption in the "Symmetric Keys" section later in this chapter.

Asymmetric Keys

SQL Server encryption provides support for asymmetric keys, which are actually composed of a pair of encryption keys: a public key and a private key. The private key can have a key length of 512, 1,024, or 2,048 bits. SQL Server provides the following statements to manage asymmetric keys:

- CREATE ASYMMETRIC KEY: Allows you to generate a new asymmetric key public key/private key pair, import the key pair from a file, or import a public key from a .NET assembly. This statement requires CREATE ASYMMETRIC KEY permissions on the database.

- ALTER ASYMMETRIC KEY: Allows you to modify the properties of an existing asymmetric key. With this statement, you can remove the private key from the public key/private key pair or change the password used to encrypt a private key in the public key/private key pair. This statement requires CONTROL permission on the asymmetric key if you are removing the private key from it.

- DROP ASYMMETRIC KEY: Drops an asymmetric key from the database. This statement requires CONTROL permission on the asymmetric key.

The algorithm/key length identifiers provided by SQL Server for use in the WITH ALGORITHM clause of the CREATE and ALTER ASYMMETRIC KEY statements are listed in Table 7-2.

Table 7-2. *Asymmetric Key Algorithm/Key Length Identifiers*

Identifier	Description
RSA_512	512-bit private key for use with RSA public key/private key encryption algorithm
RSA_1024	1,024-bit private key for use with RSA public key/private key encryption algorithm
RSA_2048	2,048-bit private key for use with RSA public key/private key encryption algorithm

When you create an asymmetric key, its private key is protected by the DMK by default. If the DMK does not exist, you must supply a password to encrypt the private key at creation time. However, if the DMK does exist, the ENCRYPTION BY PASSWORD clause of the CREATE statement is optional.

■**Note** There are no BACKUP and RESTORE statements for asymmetric keys in SQL Server 2008. If you are importing an asymmetric key from an external file or assembly, this may not be an issue. However, we recommend that you load asymmetric keys from external sources or consider using certificates if you are using SQL Server to generate public key/private key pairs for asymmetric encryption in the database. Certificates, described in the next section, have T-SQL BACKUP and RESTORE statements.

When altering an asymmetric key pair with the ALTER ASYMMETRIC KEY statement, the following rules apply:

- If you are changing the password used to encrypt the private key or if the private key is currently protected by the DMK and you want to change it to be encrypted by password, the ENCRYPTION BY PASSWORD clause is mandatory.

- If the private key is currently protected by password and you want to change it to encryption by DMK or you are changing the password used to encrypt the private key, the DECRYPTION BY PASSWORD clause is required.

SQL Server provides the built-in EncryptByAsymKey and DecryptByAsymKey T-SQL functions to encrypt and decrypt data via asymmetric keys. EncryptByAsymKey requires you to supply the asymmetric key pair ID number, obtained with the `AsymKey_ID` function. `AsymKey_ID` takes the name of the asymmetric key as a parameter and returns the `integer` ID of the key as a result. `EncryptByAsymKey` also accepts its plain text to encrypt in the form of a `char`, `nchar`, `varchar`, `nvarchar`, `binary`, or `varbinary` constant, expression, variable, or column name (in a DML statement). `EncryptByAsymKey` returns a `varbinary` result, regardless of the type of the plain text passed in.

The `DecryptByAsymKey` function decrypts data that was previously encrypted using `EncryptByAsymKey`. `DecryptByAsymKey` accepts the asymmetric key pair ID number, just like the `EncryptByAsymKey` function. It also accepts the `varbinary` encrypted text and an optional asymmetric key password, which is required if the asymmetric key is encrypted by password. The asymmetric key password can be omitted if the asymmetric key is secured by the DMK, but must be of `nvarchar` type if it is used.

Here is an example of encryption and decryption by asymmetric key:

```
CREATE ASYMMETRIC KEY SampleAsymKey
 WITH ALGORITHM = RSA_2048
 ENCRYPTION BY PASSWORD = N'B&^19!{f!5h';

DECLARE @plaintext NVARCHAR(58);
DECLARE @ciphertext VARBINARY(256);
-- Initialize the plain text
SET @plaintext = N'This is a sample plain text string';
PRINT @plaintext;
-- Encrypt the plain text
SET @ciphertext = EncryptByAsymKey (AsymKey_ID (N'SampleAsymKey'), @plaintext);
PRINT @ciphertext;
-- Decrypt the cipher text
SET @plaintext = DecryptByAsymKey (AsymKey_ID (N'SampleAsymKey'), @ciphertext,
 N'B&^19!{f!5h');
PRINT CAST(@plaintext AS NVARCHAR(MAX));

DROP ASYMMETRIC KEY SampleAsymKey;
GO
```

Although SQL Server 2008 provides the `EncryptByAsymKey` and `DecryptByAsymKey` encryption functions, Microsoft recommends that you use asymmetric keys to encrypt symmetric keys only, and use symmetric keys to encrypt your data. One reason for this is speed. Symmetric encryption is considerably faster than asymmetric encryption. Another reason for encrypting data with symmetric encryption is the limitation on the sizes of data that asymmetric encryption can handle. Table 7-3 shows the limitations of the asymmetric algorithms based on the private key lengths implemented in SQL Server 2008.

Table 7-3. *Asymmetric Algorithms, Key Lengths, and Limitations*

Algorithm	Private Key	Plain Text	Cipher Text
RSA_512	512 bits	53 bytes	64 bytes
RSA_1024	1,024 bits	117 bytes	128 bytes
RSA_2048	2,048 bits	245 bytes	256 bytes

For an asymmetric key with a private key 1,024 bits long, for instance, the `RSA_1024` algorithm will encrypt a `varchar` value with only a maximum length of 117 characters, or an `nvarchar` value with a maximum length of 58 characters. This limitation makes asymmetric encryption a poor choice for data of any considerable length. If, however, you get stuck encrypting lengthy data asymmetrically (perhaps because of business requirements, for example), you can use a work-around like the user-defined functions (UDFs) shown in the following example.

```
USE AdventureWorks;
GO

CREATE FUNCTION dbo.BigAsymEncrypt (@asym_key_name NVARCHAR(128),
 @plain_text NVARCHAR(MAX))
RETURNS VARBINARY(MAX)
AS
BEGIN

  -- Calculate the chunk size of the plain text
  DECLARE @chunk VARBINARY(512);
  DECLARE @chunksize INT;
  SELECT @chunksize = (key_length / 16) - 11
  FROM sys.asymmetric_keys
  WHERE name = @asym_key_name;

  -- Clear the cipher text result
  DECLARE @result VARBINARY(MAX);
  SET @result = CAST('' AS VARBINARY(MAX));

  -- Loop through the plain text and encrypt it in chunks
  DECLARE @i INT;
  SET @i = 1;

  WHILE @i < LEN(@plain_text)
  BEGIN
  SET @chunk = EncryptByAsymKey(AsymKey_ID(@asym_key_name),
  SUBSTRING(@plain_text, @i, @chunksize - 11));

  -- Append the chunks of cipher text to the result
  SET @result = @result + CAST(@chunk AS VARBINARY(MAX));

  -- Increment the position counter by chunk size minus 11
  SET @i = @i + @chunksize - 11;
  END;

  -- Return the result
  RETURN @result;
END
GO

CREATE FUNCTION dbo.BigAsymDecrypt (@asym_key_name NVARCHAR(128),
 @cipher_text VARBINARY(MAX),
 @password NVARCHAR(256))
RETURNS NVARCHAR(MAX)
AS
BEGIN

  -- Calculate the chunk size of the cipher text
  DECLARE @chunksize INT;
  DECLARE @chunk VARBINARY(512);
  SELECT @chunksize = (key_length / 8)
  FROM sys.asymmetric_keys
  WHERE name = @asym_key_name;
```

```
-- Initialize the result plain text
DECLARE @result NVARCHAR(MAX);
SET @result = N'';

-- Loop through the cipher text and decrypt in chunks
DECLARE @i INT;
SELECT @i = 1;
WHILE @i < DATALENGTH(@cipher_text)
BEGIN
-- Decrypt the encrypted text
SELECT @chunk = DecryptByAsymKey (AsymKey_ID (@asym_key_name),
SUBSTRING(@cipher_text, @i, @chunksize), @password);

-- Append the plain text chunk to the result
SELECT @result = @result + CAST(@chunk AS NVARCHAR(MAX));

-- Increment the chunk pointer
SET @i = @i + @chunksize;
END;

-- Return the result
RETURN @result;
END
GO
```

The `BigAsymEncrypt` function in this listing divides up the `nvarchar(max)` plain text passed into it and encrypts it in chunks. The size of the plain text chunks is equal to the number of bits in the asymmetric encryption key's private key divided by 16 (if the plain text were `varchar` instead of `nvarchar`, it would be divided by 8 instead), minus 11 bytes. The 11 extra bytes are used by the Microsoft Enhanced Cryptographic Provider for PKCS #1 padding. The UDF performs a loop, incrementing the loop counter by the calculated chunk size after each iteration. The `BigAsymDecrypt` function divides up the encrypted cipher text, decrypting it in chunks and appending the decrypted plain text chunks to the `nvarchar` result. The chunk size of the `varbinary` encrypted text is calculated as the length of the asymmetric encryption key's private key divided by 8. Here is an example of these UDFs in action:

```
USE AdventureWorks;
GO

-- This code tests the chunked asymmetric encryption functions
DECLARE @testplain NVARCHAR(MAX);
DECLARE @testcipher VARBINARY(MAX);

-- Define the plain text for testing
SET @testplain = N'"A human being is a part of a whole, called by us' +
N'''universe'', a part limited in time and space. He ' +
N'experiences himself, his thoughts and feelings as something ' +
N'separated from the rest... a kind of optical delusion of his ' +
N'consciousness. This delusion is a kind of prison for us, ' +
N'restricting us to our personal desires and to affection for a ' +
N'few persons nearest to us. Our task must be to free ourselves ' +
N'from this prison by widening our circle of compassion to ' +
N'embrace all living creatures and the whole of nature in ' +
N'its beauty." - Albert Einstein';
```

```
-- Create a test asymmetric key
CREATE ASYMMETRIC KEY SampleAsymKey
 WITH ALGORITHM = RSA_2048
 ENCRYPTION BY PASSWORD = N'B&^19!{f!5h';

-- Test the BigAsymEncrypt and BigAsymDecrypt functions
PRINT @testplain
SET @testcipher = dbo.BigAsymEncrypt (N'SampleAsymKey', @testplain);
PRINT @testcipher
PRINT dbo.BigAsymDecrypt (N'SampleAsymKey', @testcipher, N'B&^19!{f!5h');

-- Drop the test asymmetric key
DROP ASYMMETRIC KEY SampleAsymKey;
GO
```

This example uses the asymmetric encryption functions to encrypt and decrypt a large nvarchar(max) string. Although you can use methods like this to work around the asymmetric encryption size limitations, symmetric encryption is considerably faster and should generally be used to encrypt your data.

Certificates

Certificates are another tool provided by SQL Server for asymmetric encryption. A *certificate* is basically an asymmetric key public key/private key pair containing additional data describing the certificate. The additional data includes a start date, expiration date, and certificate subject. Unlike SQL Server's asymmetric keys, certificates can be backed up to and restored from files. If you need SQL Server to generate your public key/private key pairs for asymmetric encryption, the ability to create backups makes certificates a better option than asymmetric keys.

Certificates are signed by a certifying authority, which is often a trusted third party, although SQL Server can generate *self-signed* certificates as well. SQL Server supports certificates that follow the International Telecommunication Union Telecommunication Standardization Sector (ITU-T) X.509 standard (available at http://www.itu.int/ITU-T/index.phtml).

SQL Server provides the following T-SQL extensions for managing certificates:

- CREATE CERTIFICATE: Allows you to generate self-signed SQL Server certificates, load certificates from Distinguished Encoding Rules (DER)-encoded files, or create them from certificate-signed dynamic link library (DLL) files. If the ENCRYPTION BY PASSWORD clause is omitted, SQL Server will use the DMK to secure the certificate by default.

- BACKUP CERTIFICATE: Allows you to export a certificate to a file. The exported private key is encrypted with a password you supply in the ENCRYPTION BY PASSWORD clause. There is no RESTORE CERTIFICATE statement; to restore a backed-up certificate, use the CREATE CERTIFICATE statement.

- ALTER CERTIFICATE: Allows you to add or remove a private key from a certificate, change a certificate's private key, or make a certificate available for Service Broker dialogs.

- DROP CERTIFICATE: Drops an existing certificate. A certificate that is currently being used to protect symmetric keys cannot be dropped.

■**Note** SQL Server supports certificate private key lengths from 384 to 3,456 bits, in multiples of 64 bits, for private keys imported from DER-encoded files or certificate-signed DLLs. Certificate private keys generated by SQL Server are 1,024 bits long.

The following example demonstrates how to generate and back up a self-signed SQL Server certificate and its private key (which is backed up to a separate file).

```
USE AdventureWorks;
GO

CREATE CERTIFICATE SampleCert
 ENCRYPTION BY PASSWORD = N'p$@1k-#tZ'
 WITH SUBJECT = N'Sample Certificate',
 EXPIRY_DATE = N'10/31/2026';

BACKUP CERTIFICATE SampleCert
 TO FILE = N'c:\MK\BackupSampleCert.cer'
 WITH PRIVATE KEY (
 FILE = N'c:\MK\BackupSampleCert.pvk' ,
 ENCRYPTION BY PASSWORD = N'p@$$wOrd',
 DECRYPTION BY PASSWORD = N'p$@1k-#tZ'
 );

DROP CERTIFICATE SampleCert;
GO
```

To restore the backed-up certificate and its private key, you could run a CREATE CERTIFICATE statement like the following:

```
CREATE CERTIFICATE SampleCert
 FROM FILE = N'c:\MK\BackupSampleCert.cer'
 WITH PRIVATE KEY (
 FILE = N'c:\MK\BackupSampleCert.pvk',
 DECRYPTION BY PASSWORD = N'p@$$wOrd',
 ENCRYPTION BY PASSWORD = N'p$@1k-#tZ'
 );
GO
```

Microsoft recommends that certificates, like asymmetric keys, be used to encrypt your symmetric keys, and symmetric keys be used to encrypt your data. T-SQL does, however, provide the functions EncryptByCert and DecryptByCert to encrypt data using certificates.

Encryption by certificate has the same limitations on length as asymmetric encryption. The maximum length of the plain text you can pass to EncryptByCert can be calculated using this formula: *clear_text_max_bytes* = (*private_key_length_bits* / 8) – 11. The length of the encrypted text returned can be calculated using this formula: *cipher_text_bytes* = (*private_key_length_bits* / 8).

The EncryptByCert and DecryptByCert functions both require a certificate ID, which is the int ID number for a given certificate. The Cert_ID function can be used to retrieve the ID number for a certificate by name. To use Cert_ID, pass it the name of the certificate as an nvarchar or a varchar. The EncryptByCert function accepts the plain text you wish to encrypt using a certificate. The DecryptByCert function accepts the previously encrypted text you wish to decrypt. The DecryptByCert function includes a third (optional) parameter, the certificate password, which is the same password specified when you created the certificate. If the certificate is secured by the DMK, this parameter should be left out of the call to DecryptByCert.

The following example shows how to use EncryptByCert and DecryptByCert, assuming that the SampleCert certificate created earlier in this section currently exists in the AdventureWorks database.

```
USE AdventureWorks;
GO

-- Initialize the plain text
DECLARE @plain_text NVARCHAR(58);
```

```
SET @plain_text = N'This is a test!';
PRINT @plain_text;

-- Encrypt the plain text using the certificate
DECLARE @cipher_text VARBINARY(127);
SET @cipher_text = EncryptByCert(Cert_ID(N'SampleCert'), @plain_text);
PRINT @cipher_text;

-- Decrypt the cipher text using the certificate
SET @plain_text = CAST(DecryptByCert(Cert_ID(N'SampleCert'),
 @cipher_text, N'p$@1k-#tZ') AS NVARCHAR(58));
PRINT @plain_text;
GO
```

Symmetric Keys

Symmetric keys are at the bottom of the SQL Server encryption key hierarchy. A symmetric key is used to encrypt other symmetric keys or data. Because symmetric key encryption is so much faster than asymmetric encryption and does not suffer the same data-length limitations as SQL Server's asymmetric encryption implementations, Microsoft recommends encrypting your data exclusively with symmetric keys.

While asymmetric encryption requires two keys (a public key/private key pair), symmetric encryption requires only a single key to both encrypt and decrypt your data. Symmetric encryption is performed using block cipher algorithms, which encrypt your data in blocks of a constant size, and stream cipher algorithms, which encrypt your data in a continuous stream. Block cipher algorithms have a set encryption key size and encryption block size, as shown in Table 7-4.

Table 7-4. *SQL 2008 Supported Algorithms*

Algorithm	Stored Key Length	Actual Key Length	Block Size	Comments
DES	64 bits	56 bits	64 bits	
Triple_DES	128 bits	112 bits	64 bits	
Triple_DES_3KEY	128 bits	112 bits	64 bits	This option is available only for database encryption keys.
DESX	192 bits	184 bits	64 bits	
RC2	128 bits	128 bits	64 bits	
RC4	40 bits	40 bits	N/A	Microsoft recommends that you do not use RC4 to encrypt your data. RC4 is a stream cipher, so block size is not applicable.
RC4_128	128 bits	128 bits	N/A	Microsoft recommends that you do not use RC4_128 to encrypt your data. RC4_128 is a stream cipher, so block size is not applicable.
AES_128	128 bits	128 bits	128 bits	
AES_192	192 bits	192 bits	128 bits	
AES_256	256 bits	256 bits	128 bits	

You can calculate the size of the cipher text based on the length of the plain text using one of the following formulas:

- For 8-byte block ciphers like the Data Encryption Standard (DES) family, use *length of ciphertext* = 8 * ((*length of plaintext* + 8) / 8) + 36.

- For 16-byte block ciphers like the Advanced Encryption Standard (AES), use *length of ciphertext* = 16 * ((*length of plaintext* + 16) / 16) + 44.

For either formula, add 20 bytes to the total length if you use an authenticator.

THE DES FAMILY

Triple DES and DESX are both improvements to the original DES algorithm, which was authorized for use on all unclassified data by the National Security Agency in 1976. Triple DES and DESX were both introduced to reinforce the DES algorithm with minimal changes, because various weaknesses in DES have been discovered since 1994. DES uses a 56-bit key (although SQL Server uses 64 bits to store the key).

Triple DES uses two 56-bit keys, for a total key size of 112 bits (SQL Server stores it in 128 bits). The Triple_DES encryption algorithm encrypts the data with one 56-bit key, performs a decryption operation on the data with a second key, and encrypts the data again with the first key. The total effective security of Triple DES is measured at about 80 bits.

DESX performs a bitwise exclusive OR (XOR) operation with 64 bits of extra key material before performing the DES encryption, and performs a second bitwise XOR with another 64 bits of extra key material after the encryption. This makes the total key size for DESX 184 bits, although the security provided by DESX is roughly equivalent to a key length of only 118 bits. SQL Server uses 192 bits to store the 184 bits of key material.

SQL Server provides the following statements to manage symmetric keys:

- CREATE SYMMETRIC KEY: Creates a symmetric key to be used for encryption. Symmetric keys can be encrypted by certificates, asymmetric keys, passwords, or even other symmetric keys.

- ALTER SYMMETRIC KEY: Allows you to change the method of securing your symmetric keys.

- DROP SYMMETRIC KEY: Drops a symmetric key from the database. Symmetric keys cannot be dropped while they are open.

- OPEN SYMMETRIC KEY: Opens and decrypts a symmetric key for use.

- CLOSE SYMMETRIC KEY: Closes a symmetric key that was previously opened.

- CLOSE ALL SYMMETRIC KEYS: Closes all symmetric keys currently open in the current session.

SQL Server does not provide backup or restore statements for symmetric keys. Because symmetric keys are stored in the current database, they are backed up during the normal database backup process. You can also re-create a symmetric key from scratch with the CREATE SYMMETRIC KEY statement. In order to re-create a symmetric key from scratch, you must supply a KEY_SOURCE and IDENTITY_VALUE. The KEY_SOURCE is a value SQL Server hashes and performs bitwise manipulations on to generate a symmetric encryption key. If not specified, SQL Server randomly generates a KEY_SOURCE. The IDENTITY_VALUE is a value SQL Server uses to generate a key GUID. Copies of the key GUID are stored with the data the key is used to encrypt. In order to re-create a symmetric key, you must supply the same KEY_SOURCE and IDENTITY_VALUE originally used to create the key. SQL Server guarantees that supplying duplicate IDENTITY_VALUE and KEY_SOURCE values will generate an identical key.

The following example creates a symmetric key and then drops it:

```
CREATE SYMMETRIC KEY SymTest
WITH ALGORITHM = Triple_DES
ENCRYPTION BY PASSWORD = '$#ad%61*(;dsPSlk';

DROP SYMMETRIC KEY SymTest;
```

■**Tip** You can also create temporary symmetric keys by prefixing the symmetric key name with a single # in the CREATE SYMMETRIC KEY statement. The temporary symmetric key is available only to the current session and it is automatically dropped when the current session ends.

Of course, creating a symmetric key is not very useful if you can't use it to encrypt things. And as we mentioned, symmetric keys in SQL Server can be used to protect other symmetric keys or data. To protect a symmetric key with another symmetric key, use the ENCRYPTION BY SYMMETRIC KEY clause of the CREATE SYMMETRIC KEY statement. To encrypt and decrypt data, use the EncryptByKey and DecryptByKey functions. The following example creates a symmetric key, which is used to encrypt another symmetric key, which is used in turn by EncryptByKey and DecryptByKey to encrypt and decrypt some data.

```
USE AdventureWorks;
GO

-- Create a symmetric key to encrypt a symmetric key
CREATE SYMMETRIC KEY SymKey
WITH ALGORITHM = Triple_DES
ENCRYPTION BY PASSWORD = '$#ad%61*(;dsPSlk';

-- Open the key-encrypting key
OPEN SYMMETRIC KEY SymKey
DECRYPTION BY PASSWORD = '$#ad%61*(;dsPSlk';

-- Create a symmetric key to encrypt data
CREATE SYMMETRIC KEY SymData
WITH ALGORITHM = Triple_DES
ENCRYPTION BY SYMMETRIC KEY SymKey;

-- Open the data-encrypting key
OPEN SYMMETRIC KEY SymData
DECRYPTION BY SYMMETRIC KEY SymKey;

-- Initialize the plain text
DECLARE @plain_text NVARCHAR(512);
SET @plain_text = N'"Those who would give up Essential Liberty to purchase a ' +
 N'little Temporary Safety, deserve neither Liberty nor Safety." - Ben Franklin'
PRINT @plain_text;

-- Encrypt the data
DECLARE @cipher_text VARBINARY(1024);
SET @cipher_text = EncryptByKey(Key_GUID(N'SymData'), @plain_text);
PRINT @cipher_text;

-- Decrypt the data
SET @plain_text = CAST(DecryptByKey(@cipher_text) AS NVARCHAR(512));
PRINT @plain_text;

-- Close the data-encrypting key
CLOSE SYMMETRIC KEY SymData;

-- Close the key-encrypting key
CLOSE SYMMETRIC KEY SymKey;
```

```
-- Drop the symmetric keys
DROP SYMMETRIC KEY SymData;
DROP SYMMETRIC KEY SymKey;
```

■**Note** Your symmetric key must be opened before you can protect another key with it or use it to encrypt data.

The EncryptByKey function requires the key GUID of the symmetric key to encrypt your data. The symmetric key GUID can be retrieved by passing the name of the key to the Key_GUID function. The *plain_text* passed into the function is char, varchar, nchar, nvarchar, binary, or varbinary data. The return value of EncryptByKey is varbinary(8000). Block mode ciphers on SQL Server, like Triple DES and AES, automatically use an encryption mode known as *Cipher Block Chaining* (CBC) mode and random *initialization vectors* (IVs) to further obfuscate your encrypted data.

In addition, the EncryptByKey function also accepts an optional *authenticator value* to help defeat whole-value substitutions of your data. The authenticator value passed in is a sysname, which is synonymous with nvarchar(128). When an authenticator value is provided, it is encrypted together with the plain text to even further obfuscate your data. The authenticator value can be used to "tie" your encrypted data to a specific row. If you do use an authenticator, the add_authenticator parameter to EncryptByKey must be set to 1.

The DecryptByKey function accepts your encrypted data as a varbinary(8000), and returns the decrypted plain text as a varbinary(8000). If your original data was varchar or nvarchar, then you will need to CAST or CONVERT the result back to its original datatype. If you used an authenticator value when you encrypted the plain text, you must supply the same authenticator value to decrypt your cipher text. Note that you don't need to supply the Key_GUID when you call DecryptByKey. This is because SQL Server stores the key GUID with the encrypted data during the encryption process.

CBC, PADDING, AND RANDOM IV: MIXING IT UP

SQL Server provides some encryption features that further obfuscate your encrypted cipher text. CBC mode masks each block of plain text with the previously encrypted block of encrypted cipher text before encrypting it. This makes all blocks of encrypted cipher text dependent on all previous blocks, so your data is even more sensitive to even the slightest change or corruption, further mixing up your encrypted text.

Because the first block of encrypted text doesn't have a "previous block" that it can be masked with, SQL Server generates a random IV. The random IV is used to mask the first block of plain text before encryption. The random IV helps obfuscate your cipher text, but also prevents you from creating a usable index on your encrypted data. Because the IV is randomly generated, encrypting the same data with the same key twice will not generate the same result. While the random IV helps to better protect your data, it can make searching on your encrypted data much less efficient.

Block encryption algorithms produce cipher text results with a length that is a multiple of their block size. For 64-bit block algorithms like DES, the cipher text length must be a multiple of 8 bytes. 128-bit algorithms like AES produce cipher text with a length that is a multiple of 16 bytes. The problem is that not all plain text you want to encrypt is going to be a multiple of the cipher block length. SQL Server automatically pads your plain text before it encrypts it with a block cipher, ensuring that the length of the cipher text result will always be a multiple of the cipher block size.

In addition to padding your plain text before encrypting it, SQL Server stores additional metadata with your cipher text, including the following:

- The first 16 bytes are the GUID of the symmetric key that was used to encrypt the data.
- The next 4 bytes represent a version number. For SQL Server 2008, it is hard-coded as 01000000.
- The next 8 bytes for 64-bit ciphers like DES (16 bytes for 128-bit ciphers like AES) are the randomly generated IV.
- The next 8 bytes contain the various options used to encrypt the data. If the authenticator option was used, a 20-byte SHA-1 hash of the authenticator is also included.
- The rest of the cipher text is the actual encrypted data, padded out to the block size of the cipher.

When you use the `EncryptByKey` and `DecryptByKey` functions, and the symmetric key you are using to encrypt or decrypt data is protected by another key, you must explicitly open the symmetric key with the `OPEN SYMMETRIC KEY` statement. SQL Server provides the following additional functions that automatically open and decrypt your symmetric key before decrypting your data:

- `DecryptByKeyAutoAsymKey`: Decrypts your data with a symmetric key that is protected by an asymmetric key. This function automatically opens and decrypts your symmetric key with its associated asymmetric key.
- `DecryptByKeyAutoCert`: Decrypts your data using a symmetric key that is protected by a certificate. This function automatically opens and decrypts your symmetric key with its associated certificate.

Keys are available to users who have been granted access in all current SQL Server sessions at any given time (apart from temporary symmetric keys, which were mentioned earlier in this section). Each session can open and close keys independently of the other sessions. For instance, if users Joe and Lisa had open SQL Server sessions at the same time, both could use the same symmetric key simultaneously. If Joe closed the symmetric key in his session, this would have no effect on Lisa's session or her open symmetric key.

■**Note** All open keys in a session are automatically closed when the session ends.

Transparent Data Encryption

SQL Server 2008 introduces a new encryption option known as transparent data encryption (TDE). TDE encrypts every page of your entire database and automatically decrypts each page as required during access. This feature allows you to secure your entire database without worrying about the minutiae of column-level encryption. It has the added benefit of allowing you to secure your database transparently with no changes to your front-end applications. TDE does not require extra storage space, and it can generate far more efficient query plans than queries on data encrypted at the column level, since TDE allows SQL Server to use proper indexes. The downside to TDE is that it incurs additional overhead, since SQL Server must decrypt pages of data with every query. We discuss the effects of encryption on search efficiency in the "Query Efficiency" section later in this chapter.

Enabling TDE

To enable TDE and encrypt a database, you must first create a DMK and server certificate in the master database, as follows:

```
USE master;
GO

CREATE MASTER KEY
  ENCRYPTION BY PASSWORD = 'p@$$w0rd';
GO

CREATE CERTIFICATE AdvWorksCert
  WITH SUBJECT = 'Certificate to Encrypt AdventureWorks DB',
  EXPIRY_DATE = '2022-12-31';
GO
```

Notice that the master key and certificate creation statements are the same as in any other instance, except that they are created in the master database.

■**Caution** As soon as you create a server certificate, it is critical that you back it up and store the backup in a secure location. If you ever need to recover a database encrypted with TDE and you lose the server certificate, you will suffer data loss. Having a backup of the server certificate is critical for preventing data loss and interruption of business operations!

The second step is to create a database encryption key and turn on encryption in the database you want to secure. The following example turns on TDE in the AdventureWorks database.

```
USE AdventureWorks;
GO

CREATE DATABASE ENCRYPTION KEY
  WITH ALGORITHM = TRIPLE_DES_3KEY
  ENCRYPTION BY SERVER CERTIFICATE AdvWorksCert;
GO

ALTER DATABASE AdventureWorks
  SET ENCRYPTION ON;
GO
```

The new CREATE DATABASE ENCRYPTION KEY statement creates the database encryption key for the AdventureWorks database. With this statement, we specify that the database encryption key is secured by the server certificate AdvWorksCert we previously created, and we specify use of the three-key Triple DES algorithm. The algorithms available to the CREATE DATABASE ENCRYPTION KEY statement are limited to TRIPLE_DES_3KEY, AES_128, AES_192, and AES_256.

In addition to CREATE DATABASE ENCRYPTION KEY, T-SQL provides equivalent DROP and ALTER statements to manage database encryption keys. There is no backup statement, and SQL Server provides no way to export a database encryption key from your database.

To properly secure your database, TDE must take some additional steps when it is turned on. One step that TDE takes is to zero out and encrypt your database transaction log. That way, a hacker with a log reader will not be able to reconstruct your sensitive data from the logs. TDE also encrypts the tempdb database. This prevents hackers from gaining access to sensitive data temporarily stored during processing. The fact that TDE encrypts the tempdb database can slow down processing in other databases on the same server, and you might gain performance improvements by placing encrypted databases on a SQL Server instance separate from your unencrypted databases.

Choosing Between TDE and Column-Level Encryption

TDE offers the advantage of being transparent to client applications, and it does a thorough job of securing your data. A disadvantage of TDE is that it incurs CPU and memory overhead during every database access, since whole pages of data need to be decrypted for any given database access. TDE also encrypts the tempdb database, which can affect the performance of every other database on the same SQL Server instance.

Column-level encryption has the advantages of providing pinpoint precision and additional flexibility when securing your data. The main cons of column-level encryption are that it requires additional programming, so you may need to change existing client applications, and it cannot effectively utilize indexes on encrypted data to optimize queries (see the "Query Efficiency" section later in this chapter).

So with these encryption options available to secure your SQL Server data, how do you decide which to use and when? Most real-world scenarios cover a wide range of possibilities. The following are some possible scenarios and the related considerations when deciding which method to use:

- *Only a relatively small portion of your data requires encryption.* In this scenario, it makes sense to avoid the overhead of TDE in favor of the more targeted approach provided by column-level encryption. If most or all of your data needs to be encrypted, however, TDE is the method of choice.

- *You must search on encrypted columns.* Keeping in mind that search efficiency and security are opposing goals, you should make every attempt to avoid designing systems that need to search on encrypted columns. If you absolutely must search on encrypted columns, TDE will provide far better efficiency, since column-level encryption will always result in a scan.

- *Regulatory requirements dictate the requirements.* In some cases, government regulations at the local, state, and federal levels dictate how much of your data needs to be encrypted. Usually, these regulations deal with confidential consumer, credit, and health-care information. You may also have other industry-wide requirements that mandate additional protections on sensitive data. More often than not, however, the regulations will state that "confidential" data must be encrypted, and it falls on you to determine how much of your data is affected by these requirements.

- *Contractual obligations state the requirements.* When dealing with credit card companies, credit bureaus, and credit issuers of any kind, security requirements that your company must implement are often spelled out to the nth degree in contract form. These contracts might specify several key items, such as which data must be encrypted, the algorithm that must be used to encrypt and decrypt the data, and logging requirements for data changes or queries.

- *You are supporting front-end applications that cannot be changed.* It's not uncommon for information technology (IT) managers and database administrators (DBAs) to support inherited legacy databases and client applications. If the source code for the application has been long lost, or there is no time or resources to modify the existing application, it makes sense to use TDE to secure the database, since the encryption it provides is transparent to client applications.

- *You need additional flexibility during encryption.* In some instances, you may need additional flexibility, such as a hard requirement to encrypt your symmetric key with an asymmetric key instead of a certificate, or the need to specify an authenticator during encryption, or even the need to encrypt data by passphrase instead of by key. In these cases, you may need to use column-level encryption instead of TDE. This isn't as convincing a scenario as most of the others, however, and you probably would be better off revisiting the specifications if this is the deciding factor.

As DBAs, developers, and especially IT managers learn about TDE, we expect that there will be a lot of people who will decide to take the easy path by "encrypting the whole database and forgetting about it." That's unfortunate, because in many situations, that plan will amount to serious overkill and will force the server to perform a lot of unnecessary encryption and decryption, tying up server resources that could be used elsewhere. We highly recommend that you thoroughly consider the pros and cons of TDE and column-level encryption before deciding on an encryption strategy for your databases.

Extensible Key Management

In addition to TDE, SQL Server 2008 includes a new feature known as Extensible Key Management (EKM). EKM allows you to use the Microsoft Cryptographic API (CryptoAPI) for encryption and key generation.

EKM support is designed to allow third-party vendors to offer encryption key-generation hardware and other tools, known as Hardware Security Modules (HSMs). HSM vendors can offer a lot of advantages over the standard built-in encryption functionality, including hardware-accelerated encryption and decryption, bulk encryption and decryption, and additional encryption key management. An HSM might be a smart card, a USB or flash device, or a specialized external module.

The T-SQL encryption Data Manipulation Language (DML) statements, like CREATE SYMMETRIC KEY, now include the FROM PROVIDER clause and a CREATE_DISPOSITION option to provide support for third-party EKM.

EKM/HSM functionality is vendor specific, and your HSM vendor will provide specific instructions for implementing its EKM/HSM solution in your environment.

Encryption Without Keys

In addition to using certificates, asymmetric keys, and symmetric keys, you can encrypt your data using passphrases. A *passphrase* is a string or binary value from which SQL Server can derive a symmetric key to encrypt your data.

The EncryptByPassPhrase and DecryptByPassPhrase functions allow you to use this type of encryption, as in the following example:

```
DECLARE @plain_text nvarchar(1000),
  @enc_text varbinary(2000);
SET @plain_text = N'Ask not what your country can do for you...';
SET @enc_text = EncryptByPassPhrase(N'E Pluribus Unum', @plain_text);
SELECT 'Original plain text = ', @plain_text;
SELECT 'Encrypted text = ', @enc_text;
SELECT 'Decrypted plain text = ',
  CAST(DecryptByPassPhrase(N'E Pluribus Unum', @enc_text) AS nvarchar(1000));
```

EncryptByPassPhrase accepts the plain text that you want to encrypt. DecryptByPassPhrase, on the other hand, accepts the previously encrypted cipher text that will be decrypted. For both functions, you can add an authenticator value to further obfuscate your encrypted text, as follows:

```
SET @enc_text = EncryptByPassPhrase(N'E Pluribus Unum', @plain_text,
  1, N'Authentic');
```

Both functions return a varbinary(8000) value. After you use DecryptByPassPhrase, you may need to cast your result back to another datatype, such as varchar or nvarchar, as in the preceding example.

■**Note** `EncryptByPassPhrase` and `DecryptByPassPhrase` use the Triple DES algorithm to encrypt and decrypt data. You cannot choose another algorithm to encrypt and decrypt with these functions.

Hashing and Signing Data

Prior to SQL Server 2005, T-SQL included a couple of very simple, very basic hash functions: `CHECKSUM` and `BINARY_CHECKSUM`. Neither of these hash functions is *collision-free*, and both return a 32-bit hash, which is well below the minimum length recommended by cryptographic experts for secure applications.

Introduced in SQL Server 2005, the `HashBytes` function accepts the name of a hash algorithm and an input string, as follows:

```
SELECT HashBytes ('SHA1', 'Now is the time for all good men...');
```

The hash algorithm used in the example is SHA-1. You can use MD2, MD4, MD5, SHA, or SHA-1 for this parameter. The former three are the Message Digest algorithms, which generate 128-bit hashes of the input. The latter two are the Secure Hash Algorithm, which generates a 160-bit digest of the input.

The input to the `HashBytes` function is a varchar, an nvarchar, or a varbinary value. The result of `HashBytes` is always a varbinary value with a maximum length of 8,000 bytes.

■**Caution** Cryptographers recommend that you avoid the MD2, MD4, and MD5 hash algorithms for secure applications, as weaknesses have been discovered in them that could compromise your secure data.

SQL Server also provides functions to sign data with certificates and asymmetric keys, and to verify those signatures. This is useful for protecting the integrity of sensitive data, since any small change in the data will affect the signature. The `SignByCert` and `SignByAsymKey` functions sign your data with a certificate or an asymmetric key and return the signature as a varbinary. The length of the signature depends on the length of the certificate or asymmetric key's private key. A 2,048-bit private key generates a 256-byte signature; a 1,024-bit private key generates a 128-byte signature; and so on. The formats for `SignByCert` and `SignByAsymKey` are as follows:

```
SignByCert ( certificate_ID, plaintext, password )
SignByAsymKey ( asym_key_ID, plaintext, password )
```

The `SignByCert` function accepts a certificate ID, which can be retrieved with the `Cert_ID` function. The `SignByAsymKey` function accepts the asymmetric key ID, which is retrieved with the `AsymKey_ID` function. The *plaintext* parameter in both functions is the plain text to be signed—a char, a varchar, an nchar, or an nvarchar value. The *password* is the password required to decrypt the certificate or asymmetric key, if it is protected by password.

You can verify previously signed data with the `VerifySignedByCert` and `VerifySignedByAsymKey` functions, which have the following format:

```
VerifySignedByCert ( certificate_ID, plaintext, signature )
VerifySignedByAsymKey ( asym_key_ID, plaintext, signature )
```

The `VerifySignedByCert` and `VerifySignedByAsymKey` functions accept a certificate ID and an asymmetric key ID, respectively. The *plaintext* parameter of both functions is the plain text that was previously signed, and the *signature* parameter is the varbinary signature that was generated. These two functions generate the signature for the *plaintext* value and compare the newly generated signature to the *signature* you pass in to the function. Both functions return a 1 if the data matches the *signature*, or a 0 if the data and *signature* do not match.

Security Catalog Views

SQL Server 2008 provides several security catalog views and a dynamic management view, all of which can be used to retrieve information about encryption functionality. The following views are available in SQL Server 2008:

- `sys.asymmetric_keys`: This catalog view returns information about the asymmetric key pairs installed in the current database. The information returned by this view includes the name, asymmetric key ID, private key encryption type, encryption algorithm used, public key, and additional information about each installed asymmetric key pair.

- `sys.certificates`: This catalog view returns information about the certificates installed in the current database. The information returned by this view is similar to that returned by the `sys.asymmetric_keys` view. It includes the name, certificate ID, private key encryption type, name of the certificate's issuer, certificate serial number, and additional certificate-specific information (such as subject, start date, and expiration date).

- `sys.crypt_properties`: This catalog view returns a row for each cryptographic property associated with a securable in the database. The information returned about each securable includes the class of the securable, ID of the securable, encryption type used, and SHA-1 hash of the certificate or asymmetric key used to encrypt the securable.

■**Note** *Securables* in SQL Server 2008 are resources and objects for which the SQL Server database engine regulates authorization and access. Securables are divided into three scopes for which SQL Server can regulate access: Server, Database, and Schema. The Server scope includes securables like endpoints, logins, and databases. The Database scope includes users, roles, certificates, asymmetric key pairs, symmetric keys, schemas, and other Database-scoped securables. The Schema scope contains tables, views, functions, procedures, constraints, and other objects. Not all securables have cryptographic properties, but the `sys.crypt_properties` security catalog view returns information for those that do.

- `sys.dm_database_encryption_keys`: This dynamic management view returns information about the encryption state of a database and the encryption keys used in the database. Some of the values returned in the `encryption_state` column of this view are 0 if no encryption is present, 1 if the database is unencrypted, 3 when the database is encrypted, or another value indicating a database encryption or decryption action is currently in progress.

- `sys.key_encryptions`: This catalog view returns a row for every key encryption, as specified by the `CREATE SYMMETRIC KEY` statement's `ENCRYPTION BY` clause. Information returned includes the ID of the encrypted key, encryption type, and thumbprint of the certificate or symmetric key used to encrypt the key. A *thumbprint*, in terms of SQL Server 2008 security catalog views, is an SHA-1 hash of a certificate or an asymmetric key, or a GUID for a symmetric key. Several of the security catalog views return a thumbprint of certificates, asymmetric keys, or symmetric keys.

- `sys.master_key_passwords`: This catalog view returns a row for each DMK password added with the `sp_control_dbmasterkey_password` stored procedure. Each row returns an ID of the credential to which the password belongs and a GUID of the original database at creation time. The GUID is used by SQL Server to identify credentials that may contain passwords that protect the DMK in the event that automatic decryption fails. Passwords used to protect the DMKs are stored in the credential store.

- `sys.openkeys`: This catalog view returns information about all open encryption keys in the current session. Information returned includes the ID and name of the database that contains the key; IDs, names, and GUIDs of each open key; and the date and time the key was opened.

- `sys.symmetric_keys`: This catalog view returns a row for each symmetric key in the database. Information returned includes the name, ID, GUID, length, and algorithm of the symmetric key. Also returned are the ID of the principal who owns the key and the dates that the symmetric key was first created and last modified.

Query Efficiency

As we mentioned earlier in the chapter, SQL Server automatically generates a random IV to help prevent statistical analysis attacks on columns of data. The need to eliminate patterns from encrypted data is at odds with the need to index and quickly search the same data. Indexing takes advantage of these patterns to organize data for efficient search and retrieval.

A hacker who knows the relative frequency with which certain pieces of encrypted data occur in a given column could use that information to deduce even further information about it. For example, a corporate database containing employee information in a table encrypted without the use of random IVs might leak additional information from the patterns provided. Consider the `HumanResources.Employee` table in the AdventureWorks database. Most of the executive and managerial titles occur only once, while the lower-level positions may occur dozens of times. A hacker might be able to infer additional information from this pattern, including information about which employees are paid the most. The hacker might use knowledge like this to help focus his attack. SQL Server's random IV generation helps to eliminate these patterns from encrypted data. This has two main implications for T-SQL developers:

- The same IV used during encryption is required during decryption.

- The encryption functions are nondeterministic, which means that encrypting the same plain text multiple times with the same key will not generate the same encrypted text.

The nondeterministic nature of the SQL 2008 encryption functions makes it useless to index an encrypted column directly. Searching encrypted columns requires decrypting every value in the column and comparing them one by one. This is very inefficient and can be a bottleneck in your applications if your tables are large.

Some methods have been suggested for increasing the efficiency of searching encrypted data. These methods generally include storing a hash of the encrypted data for indexing. The main problem with these methods is that they reintroduce the statistical patterns eliminated by the random IVs.

You can take several approaches to strike a balance between data security and search efficiency. The most important recommendation is to *not* encrypt columns you will use heavily in your query search criteria (`WHERE` clause), sort criteria (`ORDER BY` clause), or grouping (`GROUP BY` clause).

However, sometimes you might not have a choice—you may need to encrypt a column that is part of your `WHERE` clause or other query criteria. One thing you can do to make this more efficient is to narrow down your results using other criteria involving nonencrypted columns first.

You can create a "pseudo-index" of your data by adding an additional column to your table with a one-way hash code of your plain text, and creating an index on that column. The built-in SQL Server 2008 `HashBytes` function can be used to generate a one-way MD5, SHA-1, or other hash value of your plain text and store it in the new column. Indexing this new plain text hash value column can make equality searches (using the T-SQL = operator) much more efficient. Range searches (operators like <, >, `BETWEEN`, and so on), however, cannot be used on hashed or encrypted data.

One of the implications of pseudo-indexing with a hash value is that it once again opens the door for statistical analysis attacks using the hash values as a guide. Using a hash value as an index also makes dictionary attacks against the hashed values possible. A *dictionary attack* is one in which a hacker uses a large list of plain text values to try to guess the plain text of a hashed or an encrypted value by brute force.

Another method of pseudo-indexing encrypted data is a variation on the previous method, except that it uses a hashed message authentication code (HMAC) in place of the hash value. The HMAC basically takes a "secret" value, combines it with the plain text, and generates a hash value based on that data. Although the HMAC method provides protection against dictionary attacks, it doesn't provide any additional protection against statistical analysis.

■Tip SQL Server Engine team member Raul Garcia provides an excellent example of using an HMAC code to create an "index" on your encrypted data in his blog (`http://blogs.msdn.com/raulga`).

The main thing to consider when using SQL Server's data-encryption facilities is that encryption and search efficiency are opposing goals. The purpose of encryption is data security, often at the expense of search efficiency. While you can use the methods suggested here to increase the efficiency of SQL queries on encrypted data, the hash value and HMAC index methods require more storage and can actually circumvent SQL Server's protection against statistical analysis (via random IV).

Summary

SQL Server 2008 builds on the encryption functionality introduced in SQL Server 2005, including support for TDE and EKM, which was not available in prior releases. With the ever-increasing demand for protection of personal and corporate data stored in SQL databases, SQL Server encryption support provides the mechanisms for meeting regulatory requirements and safeguarding your valuable data.

In this chapter, we discussed the built-in SQL Server 2008 encryption tools, with an introduction to the three layers of encryption keys provided by SQL Server: SMKs, DMKs, and encryption keys, as well as the newly introduced concepts of server certificates and database encryption keys. We also talked about the types of keys and certificates available to secure your data, including certificates, asymmetric key pairs, symmetric keys, and passphrases.

SQL Server offers several symmetric and asymmetric encryption algorithms to secure encryption keys and data, as well as hash generation and support for data signatures to validate content. SQL Server 2008 adds support for transparent data encryption to secure entire databases at once, and EKM, which allows you to further secure your data with third-party hardware and software tools.

In addition, SQL Server 2008 includes new encryption-related DML statements and functions, as well as security catalog views and security-related data management views, which provide thorough encryption management capabilities.

CHAPTER 8

■ ■ ■

Automation and Monitoring

SQL Server 2008 brings many advancements that will make the daily administration and maintenance of SQL Server much easier. Additionally, moves have been made to address the plethora of concerns surrounding security. Features like SQL Server Agent aren't available after a default installation unless the system administrator explicitly asks the setup to start the service automatically. Even after the SQL Server Agent service is started, users who aren't system administrators will not have access to SQL Agent unless they are associated with one of the new SQL Agent roles. As another example, system administrators will be relieved to know that they no longer need to give sysadmin rights to developers to use the Profiler tool. By granting the ALTER TRACE permission, users can now create and replay trace files. These are just a few of the many changes and enhancements made to SQL Server in this latest version.

This chapter will explore the following automation and monitoring enhancements:

- *SQL Server Agent*: The task scheduling service used by SQL Server to execute a variety of jobs, including Transact-SQL (T-SQL), replication, and maintenance tasks. This service is also used in multiserver administration as well as monitoring and responding to events such as SQL Server alerts, performance conditions, and Windows Management Instrumentation (WMI) events.

- *Maintenance plans*: Create powerful custom workflows that can handle almost any T-SQL-based maintenance scenario.

- *SQLCMD*: Short for *SQL Command*, this is a command-line tool used to connect to SQL Server and submit T-SQL queries and commands. It's a replacement for the existing ISQL and OSQL utilities found previously in SQL Server. SQLCMD takes the functionality of these tools and adds powerful features such as variables and multiple connections.

- *SQL PowerShell*: PowerShell is the next-generation scripting environment for Windows. SQL Server 2008 comes with a provider for PowerShell. This enables users to write scripts that seamlessly interact with the operating system, Microsoft Exchange, SQL Server, and any other application that provides a PowerShell provider.

- *Database Mail*: Database Mail is an enterprise solution for your database applications to send e-mail messages to users. These messages can contain a variety of contents, including query results and file attachments. Database Mail, unlike its predecessor (SQLMail), is an asynchronous mail application designed for reliability, scalability, security, and supportability.

- *Profiler*: The usefulness of one of the best performance, tuning, and optimization tools in SQL Server has improved greatly, with features like performance log correlation and replay.

- *Extended Events*: Extended Events is a new event platform for SQL Server. Originally designed only for use by Microsoft Product Support, this high-performance eventing engine allows users to rapidly obtain event information from SQL Server and write it to a variety of targets, including the new Event Tracing for Windows format.

SQL Server Agent

Picture this scenario: you've been recently hired by a startup company as the only database administrator (DBA). After helping out the developers with their table schema designs, you retreat to your desk and contemplate how to maintain the database in the long term. Naturally, the need for a backup solution pops into your mind, and you decide to perform a full database backup at midnight, followed by a differential backup 12 hours later at noon. Since the database is mostly read-only, you imagine this solution to be best. But you then ask yourself, "How can a backup database command be issued at midnight?" Although this is a startup, and hopefully one day you'll be relaxing on a Maui beach with a nice cold glass of fermented wheat and hops in your hand, you realize that sitting around until midnight every night isn't that appealing. Here is where SQL Server Agent might help you.

SQL Server Agent is a Windows service that runs continuously. Through defining and scheduling actions called *jobs*, Agent can automatically perform work against your SQL Server system. SQL Server Agent can also be used for a variety of other purposes, including to alert you of any performance events, such as the occurrence of any deadlocks.

Scheduling Agent Jobs

As an example, let's walk through how you would create a backup job and schedule it to run at midnight. You can create SQL Server Agent jobs via stored procedures or by using SQL Server Management Studio. For this example, we will use Management Studio.

Enabling SQL Server Agent

Once you connect to the SQL Server database engine, you'll notice one of three different states of the SQL Server Agent node in Object Explorer. First, if you don't see the Agent node there at all, you probably are not a member of the sysadmin role, nor are you granted any specific access to Agent. See the "Permissions for Executing Agent Jobs" section later in this chapter for more information about how to gain access to SQL Server Agent. The second state that Agent could be in is the off state. If you perform a default installation of SQL Server and don't explicitly tell the setup to start SQL Server Agent, you'll see "Agent XPs disabled" next to the SQL Server Agent node in Object Explorer.

■**Note** One of the options provided when installing SQL Server is whether to set the startup of the SQL Agent service to automatic (to start automatically when the operating system starts) or manual (the default). By default, SQL Server setup won't set the Agent service to start up automatically. With the default, the user must manually start the service through the SQL Server Configuration Manager or the Services applet in the Control Panel. Remember to change the startup type to automatic in this applet if you plan on using the SQL Agent service.

In SQL Server, a large effort was placed on restricting the surface area for security-related attacks. One of the features that was implemented was the ability to disable execution of extended stored procedures (XPs) like xp_cmdshell, xp_sendmail, and in this case, xp_sqlagent_notify. These XPs are logically grouped inside SQL Server. You can list these groups by issuing an sp_configure statement as shown here:

```
SP_CONFIGURE  'show advanced', 1
GO
RECONFIGURE
GO
SP_CONFIGURE
```

The result set returns about 60 different global configuration settings. Although most of these settings aren't related to the enabling and disabling of XPs, if you look through this list, you'll see "Agent XPs" listed. When the value is 1, Agent-specific XPs, like xp_sqlagent_notify, as well as other procedures, like those found in Server Management Objects (SMO) calls, will be enabled.

At this point, you might be wondering whether you need to manually go to the Query Editor and issue a call to enable Agent XPs when you want your SQL Agent to work. Thankfully, this isn't the case. When the SQL Server Agent service is started, it will automatically enable the Agent XPs, and when it's stopped, it will automatically disable the Agent XPs. Note that this is the only time these XP groupings will be automatically enabled and disabled. For normal use of SQL Agent, you'll never need to worry about manually changing this setting.

If you see "Agent XPs disabled" in Object Explorer, right-click it and select Start. The Agent service will automatically enable the Agent XPs, and you can now use SQL Server Agent. When SQL Server Agent is started and the Agent XPs group is enabled, Object Explorer will show the Agent node as enabled. At this point, you're ready to create your Agent job.

Creating the Agent Job

Once you're connected to SQL Server and have started the SQL Server Agent service (if necessary), expand the SQL Server Agent node. Your screen should appear as shown in Figure 8-1.

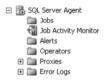

Figure 8-1. *SQL Server Agent node in Object Explorer*

To create a job, right-click the Jobs node and select New Job. This will launch the New Job dialog box, as shown in Figure 8-2.

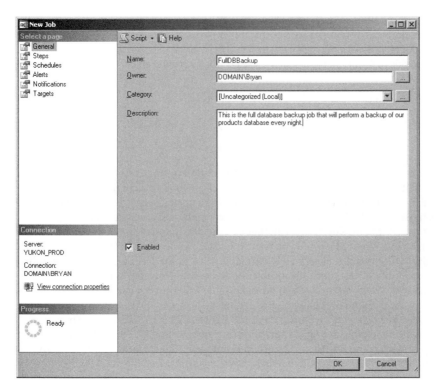

Figure 8-2. *General tab in the New Job dialog box*

The General tab allows you to enter some metadata about the job, such as its name, its description, and the owner of the job.

■**Note** Only members of the `sysadmin` role can change the owner of a job.

Referring to our original backup scenario, let's give it an appropriate name like FullDBBackup. Once you've given the job a name, you can proceed to add steps to this job. Jobs can have one or more steps to them, and each step can be of one or more of the following types: T-SQL, ActiveX Script, Operating System (CmdExec), Replication (there are actually five replication subsystems, but for the most part, these are configured using wizards and dialog boxes, and users usually don't manually create replication job steps), SQL Server Analysis Services Command and Query, and SQL Server Integration Services (SSIS) Package. Since jobs don't need to contain the same job step types, it's possible to have a job that first executes some T-SQL against SQL Server, then runs an SSIS package, and finally processes an Analysis Services cube. In this example, all we need is a single T-SQL job step. When you click the Steps tab, you're presented with a grid listing the steps within the job, as shown in Figure 8-3.

This tab allows you to add, remove, and edit job steps as well as define which job step will be executed first. Since our example has only one job step—the backup of the database itself—the first step will be the starting step. When you add or edit a step, you're presented with the New Job Step dialog box, as shown in Figure 8-4.

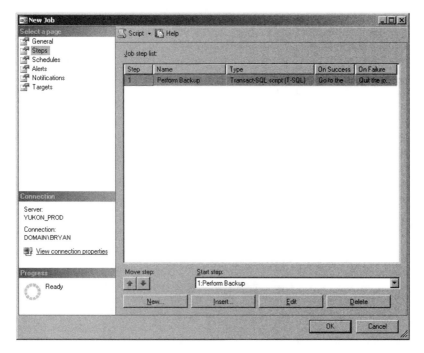

Figure 8-3. *Steps tab in the New Job dialog box*

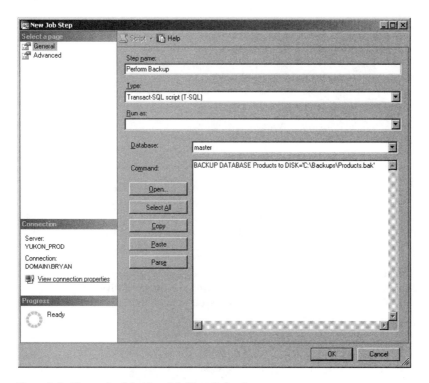

Figure 8-4. *General tab in New Job Step dialog box*

Every job step requires a unique name. Once we give this particular step a name, we can add the T-SQL script for backing up the database as the command.

After you've added the job step(s), it's time to define the schedule. In our example, we want the full database backup to occur every day at midnight. In the New Job dialog box, click the Schedules tab. You'll see another grid that lists all the schedules that will execute your job. Figure 8-5 shows how the grid looks for our database backup job. Once we've defined a schedule and clicked OK on the New Job dialog box, our database backup job is now ready for automatic execution.

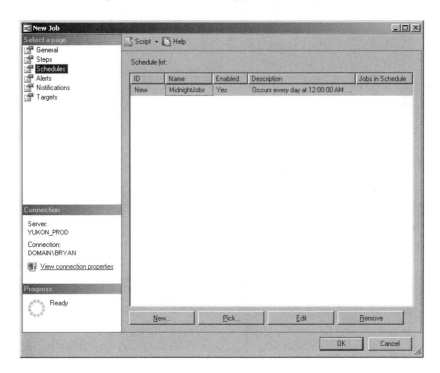

Figure 8-5. *Grid displayed on Schedules tab in New Job dialog box*

■**Note** In previous versions of SQL Server Agent, a single job could have zero or more schedules defined, and two jobs could not share the same schedule (although they could have two separate schedules defined with the same time period). In SQL Server 2005 and 2008, the same schedule can be shared among any jobs that the user owns. For more information about shared schedules, see the "Job Schedule Sharing" section later in this chapter.

As you can see from this example, SQL Server Agent provides an easy-to-use solution for routine maintenance and monitoring of SQL Server. The following sections will dive into the key features in SQL Server 2008 and provide you with potential issues related to the design and limitations to consider.

Permissions for Executing Agent Jobs

SQL Server database administrators will be pleased to note that on a default installation of SQL Server 2008, only members of the sysadmin role can create, manage, or execute SQL Server Agent jobs. Ordinary SQL users won't even see the SQL Server Agent node in the Object Explorer tree when connected to a SQL Server instance. If a user isn't a sysadmin, in order to use SQL Server Agent, that user will need to be added to one of three predefined database roles in the msdb database: SQLAgentUserRole, SQLAgentReaderRole, or SQLAgentOperatorRole.

■**Note** If you're upgrading from SQL Server 2000 to SQL Server 2008 and had Agent jobs already defined, the upgrade behavior is as follows: non-sysadmin users who owned jobs will automatically be included in the SQLAgentUserRole. This will allow the jobs to continue to run after the upgrade. Note that there are some corner-case issues with respect to upgrades that should be taken into consideration. Refer to the "Agent Upgrade" section later in this chapter for important information about this topic.

Each of these roles provides additional privileges within SQL Server Agent, starting with the most restrictive role, SQLAgentUserRole, followed by the SQLAgentReaderRole, and finally the least restrictive role, SQLAgentOperatorRole. The following tables list these new roles and the actions they can perform on Agent objects, starting with Table 8-1, which describes user role access for alert objects.

Table 8-1. *SQL Server Agent Role Access for Alert Objects*

Action	SQLAgentUserRole	SQLAgentReaderRole	SQLAgentOperatorRole
Create			
Modify			
Delete			
Enumerate			Yes
Enable/Disable			
View Properties			Yes

SQL Server Agent alerts read events generated by SQL Server and from the Windows application log. Alerts can be configured so that, based on certain criteria being met, an action will be automatically performed. These actions can be either starting an Agent job or notifying an Operator. An Operator is a SQL Agent-specific object that is basically an arbitrary name, such as BryanTheDBA, and has at least one of the following pieces of information defined: e-mail address, pager address, or net send address. An Operator can be defined on a job to be notified of job failure, or, in the case of an alert, when the alert criteria are met.

■**Note** Operators have no ties to Windows user accounts or SQL Server logins. Furthermore, the Operators we discuss here having nothing to do with the SQLAgentOperatorRole.

Table 8-2 lists user role access for Operator objects.

Table 8-2. *SQL Server Agent Role Access for Operator Objects*

Action	SQLAgentReaderRole	SQLAgentUserRole	SQLAgentOperatorRole
Create			
Modify			
Delete			
Enumerate	Yes	Yes	Yes
Enable/Disable			
View Properties			Yes

Jobs are what define the work to do in SQL Server Agent. Jobs can be run locally on the same server where SQL Server Agent is installed or remotely. When a job is set to run remotely, the sysadmin must configure one server to be the master (SQL Server Books Online documentation refers to this as the MSX server) and source of the jobs, and the rest of the servers will be targets (also known as TSX servers). Tables 8-3 and 8-4 list role access based on local or remote jobs.

Table 8-3. *SQL Server Agent Role Access for Job Objects (Local Jobs Specifically)*

Action	SQLAgentReaderRole	SQLAgentUserRole	SQLAgentOperatorRole	Comments
Create	Yes	Yes	Yes	No non-sysadmin users can change the owner of the job.
Modify	Yes	Yes	Yes	Users can modify only jobs they own.
Delete	Yes	Yes	Yes	Users can delete only jobs they own.
Enumerate	Yes	Yes	Yes	For SQLAgentReaderRole and SQLAgentOperatorRole, users can enumerate all jobs, including those owned by different users. For SQLAgentUserRole, users can enumerate only jobs they own.
Enable/Disable	Yes	Yes	Yes	For SQLAgentOperatorRole, action is supported only by calling the sp_update_job stored procedure. Users can enable/disable jobs they own. For SQLAgentOperatorRole, users can enable/disable all jobs but must do this by calling sp_update_job directly.
Start Job	Yes	Yes	Yes	For SQLAgentOperatorRole, users can start any job.
Stop Job	Yes	Yes	Yes	For SQLAgentOperatorRole, users can stop any job.

Action	SQLAgentReaderRole	SQLAgentUserRole	SQLAgentOperatorRole	Comments
View History	Yes	Yes	Yes	For SQLAgentReaderRole and SQLAgentOperatorRole, users can view history for any job. For SQLAgentUserRole, users can view history only for jobs they own.
Delete History	Yes	Yes	Yes	For SQLAgentReaderRole and SQLAgentUserRole, users can delete job history from jobs they own. For SQLAgentOperatorRole, users can delete history of any job.
View Properties	Yes	Yes	Yes	For SQLAgentReaderRole and SQLAgentOperatorRole, read-only access to all jobs.

Table 8-4. *SQL Server Agent Role Access for Job Objects (Multiserver Jobs Specifically)*

Action	SQLAgentReaderRole	SQLAgentUserRole	SQLAgentOperatorRole	Comments
Create				
Modify				
Delete				
Enumerate	Yes		Yes	
Enable/ Disable				
Start Job			Yes	
Stop Job			Yes	
View History	Yes		Yes	For SQLAgentReaderRole and SQLAgentOperatorRole, users can view history for any multiserver job.
Delete History				
Manage Target Servers				
Manage JobCategories				
View Properties	Yes		Yes	For SQLAgentReaderRole and SQLAgentOperatorRole, read-only access to all multiserver jobs.

As mentioned previously, schedules can be shared among jobs that are owned by the same user. Even sysadmins can't mix and match schedules from different users; all job and schedule "pairs" must have the same owner. Table 8-5 lists the role access for schedule objects.

Table 8-5. *SQL Server Agent User Role Access for Schedule Objects*

Action	SQLAgentReaderRole	SQLAgentUserRole	SQLAgentOperatorRole	Comments
Create	Yes	Yes	Yes	No non-sysadmin users can change the owner of the schedule.
Modify	Yes	Yes	Yes	Users can modify only schedules they own.
Delete	Yes	Yes	Yes	Users can delete only schedules they own.
Enumerate	Yes	Yes	Yes	For SQLAgentReaderRole and SQLAgentOperatorRole, users can enumerate all schedules, including those owned by different users. For SQLAgentUserRole, users can enumerate only schedules they own.
Enable/ Disable	Yes	Yes	Yes	For SQLAgentOperatorRole, action supported only by calling sp_update_schedule stored procedure. For SQLAgentUserRole and SQLAgentReaderRole, applicable only to jobs they own.
Attach and Detach	Yes	Yes	Yes	Users can only attach and detach schedules they own.
View Properties	Yes	Yes	Yes	For SQLAgentReaderRole and SQLAgentOperatorRole, read-only access to all schedules. SQLAgentUserRole can only see properties of jobs they own.

■**Note** SQL Server Agent error logs can be read by using the sp_readerrorlog stored procedure. However, the user must be a member of the securityadmin role in order to execute this stored procedure. By default, no one but sysadmins can read SQL Server Agent error logs.

Proxy Accounts

When creating a SQL Server Agent job (as described previously), as a sysadmin, you're free to add job steps of any type. For all job step types except T-SQL, when the job step is run, it's executed under the context of the SQL Server Agent service account. T-SQL job steps are a special case: they are always run under the job owner. So given this information, what if you wanted your developers who aren't sysadmins on your server to be able to schedule and execute SSIS packages? In that case, you would want to create a proxy account in SQL Server Agent for the developers.

A *proxy account* is a friendly name and a Windows credential that is stored in SQL Server. (A proxy account in SQL Server Agent contains a valid Windows credential.) Table 8-6 lists the user role access for proxy objects.

Table 8-6. *SQL Server Agent Role Access for Proxy Objects*

Action	SQLAgentReaderRole	SQLAgentUserRole	SQLAgentOperatorRole	Comments
Create				
Modify				
Delete				
Enumerate	Yes	Yes	Yes	For SQLAgentReaderRole and SQLAgentUserRole, users can enumerate only proxies that they have explicit access to. For SQLAgentOperatorRole, users can enumerate all proxies.
View Properties			Yes	Read-only access to all proxies.

The sysadmin can explicitly grant permission to use a particular proxy account to individual SQL Server logins, msdb database roles, and/or system roles. Also, this proxy can be assigned to one or more job-step types (sometimes referred to as *Agent subsystems*). Additionally, the sysadmin can define multiple proxy accounts. Each one of these proxy accounts can be used in one or more subsystems.

■**Note** In SQL Server 2008, Agent has seven subsystems in addition to the ones used for replication. One of these seven subsystems is a new one for SQL Server 2008 called PowerShell. This subsystem allows users to execute PowerShell scripts within their SQL Server Agent jobs. See the "Powershell for SQL Server" section later in this chapter for more information about the PowerShell feature.

For example, say the administrator creates a proxy account called SSISDevProxy. The administrator then assigns this new proxy account to the SSIS subsystem. He grants the SQL login, Tammie, the right to use this new proxy account. At this point, the next time Tammie logs in to SQL Server, she will be able to create a SQL Agent job with a job step of type SQL Server Integration Services Package. Under the Run As combo box, she will have the option to select SSISDevProxy as the proxy account to use when SQL Agent executes this SSIS package.

When this Agent job is executed, the Agent service will impersonate the credentials of SSISDevProxy and proceed to execute the package. In this example, there was a one-to-one-to-one relationship between user, proxy, and subsystem. However, SQL Server Agent supports a many-to-many-to-many relationship; that is, the administrator can set up many logins to many proxies to many subsystems. Figure 8-6 depicts the possibilities of defining proxy accounts. If we set up

SQL Server Agent as represented in this figure, the experiences for the three SQL logins Tammie, Gary, and George would be as follows:

- When Tammie creates an Agent job with a SQL Server Integration Services Package job-step type, she will be able to select only SSISDevProxy as a proxy to use.

- When Gary creates an Agent job with a SQL Server Integration Services Package job-step type, he can select between SSISDevProxy and SSISTestProxy because the system administrator has given him access to both of these proxies assigned to the SSIS subsystem.

- Proxy accounts themselves don't need to be assigned to just one subsystem. When George creates an Agent job with an Operating System (CmdExec) job-step type, he can select the LimitedPrivilegedProxy for use as the proxy account. However, if he created a job step of type ActiveX Script, he could also select this proxy because the system administrator had assigned this proxy to both the ActiveX Script and Operating System (CmdExec) subsystems.

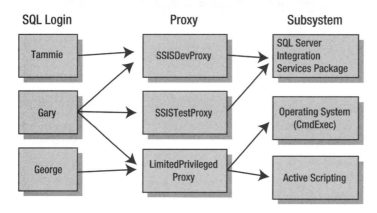

Figure 8-6. *Multiple proxy example*

The intent of the multiple proxy account feature in SQL Server Agent is to provide flexible, secure access to the Agent features.

System administrators can create proxy accounts through Object Explorer in SQL Server Management Studio or through T-SQL code. Here, we'll walk through a T-SQL example of creating a proxy account. However, if you prefer using a GUI, remember that Management Studio includes a tool that makes it easier to create and manage proxy accounts.

■**Note** You'll need to create a credential first before you can create a proxy. If you're using Object Explorer, you can create a credential by launching the New Credential dialog box and selecting New Credential from the Credentials node of the Security node.

First, create a credential in the SQL Server secure store. This credential is the actual Windows identity that the SQL Server Agent service will impersonate before it executes the job step.

```
CREATE CREDENTIAL [DevCredential]
 WITH IDENTITY='<<Domain\Username>>',
```

```
SECRET='<<password>>'
```

Next, create the Agent proxy account that references this credential, as follows:

```
USE MSDB
GO
sp_add_proxy @proxy_name = 'SSISDevProxy',
@enabled = 1,
@description = 'proxy account used by developers to test their SSIS packages',
@credential_name = 'DevCredential'
```

At this point, the proxy account is neither assigned to any subsystems nor accessible by anyone except members of the sysadmin role. Assign the proxy account to the SSIS subsystem as follows:

```
sp_grant_proxy_to_subsystem
    @proxy_name = N'SSISDevProxy',
    @subsystem_name = N'SSIS'
```

Finally, grant the SQL Server login Tammie the ability to use this new proxy account, as follows:

```
sp_grant_login_to_proxy
    @login_name = N'Tammie',
    @proxy_name = N'SSISDevProxy'
```

Now SQL Server login Tammie will be able to create a new job step of type SQL Server Integration Services Package and select SSISDevProxy as the proxy account under which to run when her package is executed.

■**Note** All subsystems use proxy accounts with the exception of the T-SQL subsystem. In this case, the Agent service can impersonate the job owner through T-SQL and doesn't need to store the user's Windows credentials separately. System administrators won't need to create a proxy account for job steps of type T-SQL.

Job Schedule Sharing

SQL Server Agent job schedules can be shared among jobs that are owned by the same user. For example, suppose you have a series of jobs that you would like to run every day at midnight. In previous versions of SQL Server, you would create a job and then create a separate schedule for each job, each executing at the same schedule time. In SQL Server 2008, you can create a single schedule (in this case, occurring every day at midnight), and attach it to one or more jobs, provided you are the owner of the jobs.

For example, suppose that, using Management Studio, Greg creates a job, Job1, with a schedule, Schedule1. Since he was told to run jobs only starting at the time defined in Schedule1 by his system administrator, Greg wants to create his second job, called Job2, with this same schedule. Greg launches the New Job dialog box in Management Studio and, after supplying the name, clicks the Schedules tab and is presented with the dialog box shown in Figure 8-7.

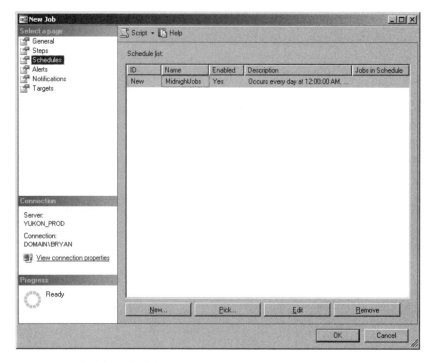

Figure 8-7. *Schedules tab of the New Job dialog box*

If Greg wanted to create a separate schedule for this job, he would simply click the New button below the grid and be presented with the New Job Schedule dialog box. However, since he wants to reuse the schedule he already created for Job1, he clicks the Pick button and is presented with the dialog box shown in Figure 8-8.

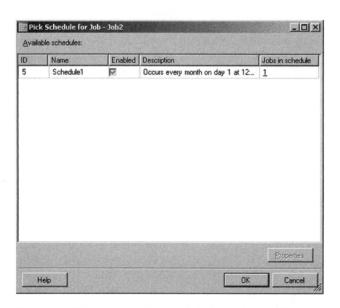

Figure 8-8. *Picking an existing schedule through the Pick Schedule for Job dialog box*

At this point, Greg can view all the jobs that are assigned to a schedule by clicking the number in the Jobs in Schedule column. Clicking this link pops up the dialog box shown in Figure 8-9.

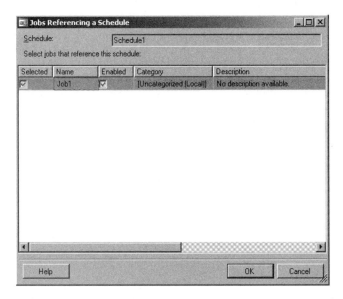

Figure 8-9. *Dialog box showing jobs that are referencing a particular schedule*

Greg can now confirm that this is the schedule he wants to reuse, as well as view the other jobs that also reference this schedule.

SQL Server Management Studio also provides a separate dialog box launched from the Jobs container node called Manage Schedules, which is shown in Figure 8-10.

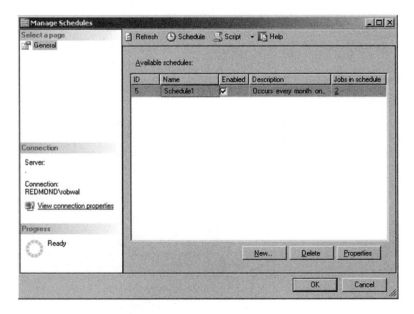

Figure 8-10. *Manage Schedules dialog box*

From this dialog box, users can see all the schedules they created and find out which other jobs reference these schedules. Users will be able to see only schedules and jobs that they own. System administrators, however, will be able to see all schedules and jobs that exist in SQL Server Agent.

Logging Agent Job-Step Output

SQL Server Agent prohibits users who are not sysadmins from logging their job-step output to the file system. However, sysadmin users can continue to use this feature. As a replacement, both non-sysadmin and sysadmin users can log job-step output to a well-known table, sysjobstepslogs, in the msdb database. Logging job-step output is available only on these specific job step types: T-SQL, CmdExec, Analysis Services Command, and Analysis Services Query.

Logging to the table is an option that can be set through the Advanced tab of the New Job Step dialog box in SQL Server Management Studio. This tab also allows you to view the log using Notepad. Alternatively, you could use the new sp_help_jobsteplog stored procedure to view this log. Just pass the job ID or job name to this stored procedure as follows:

```
USE msdb
GO
sp_help_jobsteplog @job_name='FullDBBackup'
GO
```

WMI Events and Agent Alerts

Tokens are character placeholders within T-SQL code. The use of tokens within SQL Server Agent job steps has been around in previous versions of SQL Server. At runtime, SQL Agent replaces these tokens with values such as the current date or the computer name.

■**Note** SQL Server Agent uses the $( ) token nomenclature as opposed to the brackets [ ]. It was found that using the brackets for tokens like [DATE] could clash with SQL Server's use of brackets to group object names that contain special characters.

SQL Agent responds to WMI event notifications raised by SQL Server 2008, as well as any other WMI event provider (one restriction is that events must be raised from the local server on which the Agent resides). This token is called out by the following:

```
$(WMI(X))
```

where X is the desired WMI property of the WMI event that the user wishes to insert.

SQL Server 2008 event notifications can raise WMI events from various Data Definition Language (DDL) and Data Manipulation Language (DML) statements. The following example shows how the administrator can now raise an Agent alert when someone creates a new database.

■**Note** This example can also be easily done through the SQL Server Management Studio user interface, but in the interest of introducing the parameters for the WMI events, we show it as a series of T-SQL commands.

First, let's create an Agent Operator:

```
EXEC msdb.dbo.sp_add_operator @name=N'MyAgentOperator',
                              @enabled=1,
                              @pager_days=0,
                              @netsend_address=N'robs_laptop'
GO
```

Since we supplied the netsend_address parameter, this Operator should be notified of the database creation via net send. Note that the Messenger service must be started in order for the Agent to send network messages.

Next, we'll create an Agent alert using built-in system stored procedures called sp_add_alert and sp_add_notification. This code will notify an Operator if anyone issues a CREATE DATABASE statement to SQL Server.

```
EXEC msdb.dbo.sp_add_alert @name=N'Create_Database_Alert',
                           @enabled=1,
                           @delay_between_responses=0,
                           @include_event_description_in=0,
@wmi_namespace=N'\\.\root\Microsoft\SqlServer\ServerEvents\MSSQLSERVER',
                           @wmi_query=N'SELECT * FROM CREATE_DATABASE'
GO
EXEC msdb.dbo.sp_add_notification
     @alert_name=N'Create_Database_Alert',
     @operator_name=N'MyAgentOperator',
     @notification_method = 4
GO
```

In order for SQL Server Agent to raise WMI event-based alerts, Service Broker must be enabled for msdb. If the previous example resulted in an error, try executing the following command:

```
IF(SELECT is_broker_enabled FROM sys.databases WHERE name = 'msdb')=1
ALTER DATABASE msdb SET ENABLE_BROKER
GO
```

The sp_add_alert stored procedure has two optional parameters:

- @wmi_namespace is the namespace of the desired WMI event object. If you were to create this alert through the user interface provided by Management Studio, the default path of \\.\root\Microsoft\SqlServer\ServerEvents\MSSQLSERVER is already in place for you. You may have noticed that even though the SQL Server event namespace is prepopulated, there is nothing stopping you from replacing it with any other WMI event provider. Thus, it's possible to raise Agent events on things like free disk space and all the other Win32 event providers installed on your server.

- @wmi_query is the actual WMI Query Language (WQL) query that the Agent will issue when looking for this event. In this example, we're interested in the CREATE_DATABASE event that is raised by SQL Server, so we entered SELECT * FROM CREATE_DATABASE. Although this WQL resembles T-SQL, it isn't the same.

> **■Note** A lot of resources are available on MSDN that describe how to write and use WQL. WQL resembles SQL in its syntax. In fact, it's a subset of the standard American National Standards Institute Structured Query Language (ANSI SQL) with minor semantic changes to support WMI. It's definitely worth taking the time to get to know this Windows feature. Additional information can be found online at `http://msdn.microsoft.com` (search for "Querying with WQL").

Once the preceding script has been executed, the `Operator` will be notified as shown in Figure 8-11 via a `net send` alert whenever a new database is created on the server.

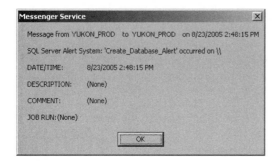

Figure 8-11. *Net send alert notification*

Agent Performance Counters

The SQL Server Agent service has a set of performance counters installed on the server. Four performance objects exist for each instance of SQL Server Agent that is installed on the server, which are defined as follows:

- *SQLAgent:Alerts*: This performance object provides information such as number of alerts activated since the Agent service started and how many alerts are raised within the last minute.

- *SQLAgent:Jobs*: This performance object describes a variety of job states, such as number of active jobs, how many jobs are queued, and the job success/failure rate as a percentage of successful/failed jobs from to the total number of executed jobs.

- *SQLAgent:JobSteps*: This performance object can determine the active and queued job steps per subsystem, in addition to the total number of step retries.

- *SQLAgent:Statistics*: Perhaps one of the more simple performance objects, this one has just one counter, Server Restarted, and describes how many times the SQL Server service was restarted during the life of the current Agent service process.

Although not an exhaustive list of everything inside the Agent service, these counters should be a starting point in monitoring the Agent service activity through Performance Monitor.

Most of the instances for these performance objects are self-explanatory, except for the Jobs object. When you select the Jobs object, you'll have the option to pick all counters or specific ones, as you can see from Figure 8-12.

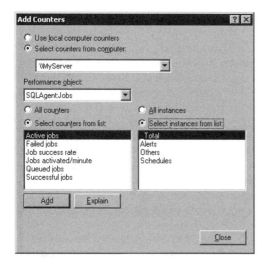

Figure 8-12. *Add Counters dialog box in Performance Montior*

In the case of the job instances, Alerts means jobs that were started by an alert, Schedules means jobs that were started by a schedule, Others means jobs that were started manually via sp_start_job, and _Total means jobs that were started by any one of these.

Agent Upgrade

If you're upgrading from SQL Server 2000, you should be aware of what happens with the SQL Server Agent service. If you're planning a new installation of SQL Server 2008 or upgrading from SQL Server 2005, this section doesn't directly apply to you; however, you may find this information educational.

Previously in this chapter, we discussed the addition of the three new database roles in the msdb database: SQLAgentReaderRole, SQLAgentUserRole, and SQLAgentOperatorRole. As with a new installation, an upgrade of SQL Agent also restricts default access to only sysadmin users. The exception to this, in the case of an upgrade, is that users who owned jobs prior to the upgrade will be automatically granted access to the SQLAgentUserRole database role in msdb. This will allow these jobs to continue to execute after the upgrade. In most cases, the jobs will continue to execute as before without any issues. There are a few exceptions that relate to jobs when the single global proxy account was set and used in the job.

As noted earlier, in early versions of SQL Server Agent, the sysadmin could define a single proxy account to use to allow non-sysadmin users to perform any of these functions:

- Execute active scripting job steps.
- Execute command shell job steps.
- Log job-step output to the file system.
- Execute the xp_cmdshell XP.

In an upgrade, the single global proxy, if defined, is created on the upgraded server and is called UpgradedProxy. Job owners who had active scripting or command shell jobs will have access to this proxy after the upgrade. Those non-sysadmin users who were logging their job output to the file system will now be upgraded to logging this output to a table. These changes will allow the jobs to continue to execute as they did previously and now provide the sysadmin the ability to configure the security context of the job step to a more granular level.

Another important note about proxies is with respect to the use of the xp_cmdshell XP. In previous versions of SQL Server, sysadmins set the proxy for this via an Agent XP, xp_sqlagent_proxy_account. In SQL Server 2008, this behavior has changed; if any of your scripts call this XP, they will need to be changed to use the new stored procedure, sp_xp_cmdshell_proxy_account, to set the proxy account for the xp_cmdshell. The link between Agent's global proxy account and the credentials that xp_cmdshell run under are now broken, which makes sense since you should not have to configure SQL Agent to use xp_cmdshell.

Another minor surprise you may notice is if you had originally configured Agent to connect to SQL Server using SQL Server authentication. In SQL Server 2008, Agent prohibits connecting back to SQL Server using SQL Server authentication. With the move to multiple proxies, Agent did away with storing credentials in the registry and now accepts only Windows authentication, which means that the Agent service account must be sysadmin on SQL Server. If you had SQL Server authentication and upgraded to SQL Server 2008, Agent will use the Agent service account to connect back to SQL Server after the upgrade is complete.

Maintenance Plans

A *maintenance plan* is a workflow of T-SQL tasks that can be scheduled to run or be executed on demand. Built upon the SSIS engine, maintenance plans provide an easy way to create workflow within your plans, to add custom T-SQL tasks in case the user interface doesn't provide the specific option you need, and to tell the user at design time what the T-SQL will look like.

Figure 8-13 shows a maintenance plan that was created to first check a database's integrity and then issue a backup database statement. If the check database integrity task failed, it would notify an Agent Operator. Notice that two different subplans are associated with this maintenance plan: one subplan is for a test database, and the other is for a development database. Although we could have easily placed these tasks within the same subplan, having multiple subplans allows you to create separate workflows and thus have these subplans run on different schedules.

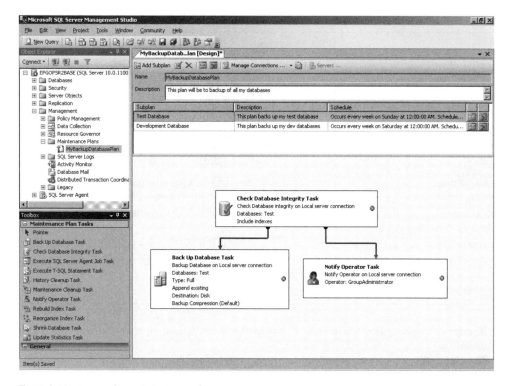

Figure 8-13. *A sample maintenance plan*

Using SQL Server Management Studio, you can create a maintenance plan either via the Maintenance Plan Wizard or through the Maintenance Plan Designer.

You can launch the Maintenance Plan Wizard by selecting Maintenance Plan Wizard from the context menu of the Maintenance Plans node in Object Explorer. To create a new plan using the Maintenance Plan Designer, simply select New Maintenance Plan from this same context menu.

Launching the Maintenance Plan Wizard will take you through a series of dialog boxes that allow you to pick and choose which tasks you would like to include as part of your plan. If you modify an existing plan or create a new plan, the Maintenance Plan Designer will open as a *document window* inside the Management Studio shell. In addition, the *toolbox* will become visible and it will, by default, locate itself beneath Object Explorer, as shown in Figure 8-13. The toolbox contains the list of all the available tasks in SQL Server 2008, as listed in Table 8-7.

Table 8-7. *Maintenance Plan Tasks*

Task	Function
Back Up Database	Performs full, differential, and transaction log backups
Check Database Integrity	Performs a database integrity check using DBCC CHECKDB
Execute SQL Server Agent Job	Launches a SQL Server Agent job
Execute T-SQL Statement	Executes any T-SQL script
History Cleanup	Deletes database backup history, maintenance plan history, and/or SQL Agent job history
Maintenance Cleanup	Deletes physical backup files
Notify Operator	Sends a message to an Agent Operator (requires Database Mail installed and configured with a default profile)
Rebuild Index	Issues an ALTER INDEX...REBUILD statement for table and view indexes
Reorganize Index	Issues an ALTER INDEX...REORGANIZE for table and view indexes
Shrink Database	Performs a shrink database command if certain parameters such as database size are met
Update Statistics	Performs an update of statistics

If you accidentally closed the toolbox, or it doesn't appear, you can open it from the View menu on the toolbar.

The Maintenance Plan Designer document window opens when you either create a new maintenance plan or modify an existing plan. This document window has two sections. The bottom half is the designer, where the actual workflow is defined. The top half is for metadata about the plan and resembles what you see in Figure 8-14.

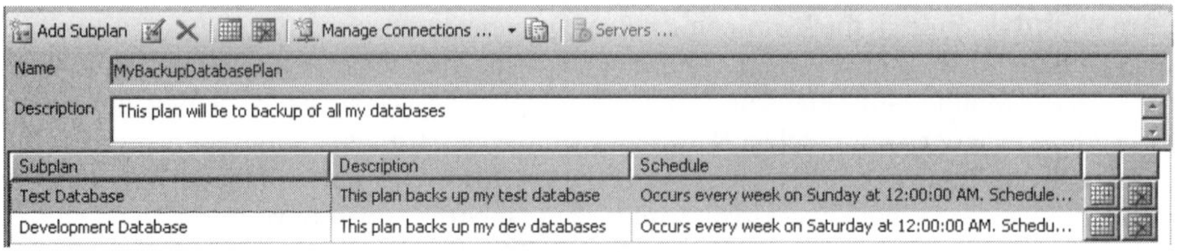

Figure 8-14. *The top half of the Maintenance Plan Designer document window*

The first issue you'll notice with this section of the designer is that the name field is read-only. When you create a new plan, you'll be asked for a plan name before you even see the designer. If you use the default name, MaintenancePlan, and later decide you want to change it, you'll need to rename it through the Object Explorer context menu. You can't change the name of the maintenance plan directly through the designer. However, the Description field below the Name field is editable; it can hold up to 512 characters.

Across the top of the document window are the following buttons (from left to right):

- *Add Subplan*: Adds a subplan to the maintenance plan.
- *Subplan Properties*: Allows you to modify the subplan name and description, and also lets you modify the subplan schedule.
- *Delete Subplan (X)*: Deletes the selected subplan.
- *Modify Subplan Schedule*: Allows you to modify the selected subplan schedule.
- *Delete Subplan Schedule*: Allows you to delete the selected subplan schedule.
- *Manage Connections*: Allows you to manage SQL Server connections, as described in the "Managing Maintenance Plan Connections" section.
- *Logging*: Allows you to set up maintenance plan logging and reporting, as explained in the "Reporting and Logging Maintenance Plans" section.

When you create a new maintenance plan, one subplan is created for you by default. This subplan has no schedule defined on it.

Scheduling Maintenance Subplans

Although you can always execute your maintenance subplans individually whenever you want, you probably will want to schedule them to be run at some particular point in the day.

To create a schedule, click the Job Schedule icon to the right of the schedule description column. This will launch the Job Schedule dialog box and allow you to define a schedule for the subplan.

In the event that you want to remove a schedule and have the plan return to being an on-demand plan only, click the icon to the right of the Job Schedule icon (the one with the red X). This will delete the schedule associated with the subplan.

Managing Maintenance Plan Connections

The Manage Connections button along the top of the Maintenance Plan Designer document window allows you to add, edit, or remove SQL Server connections. Having multiple connections allows a maintenance plan to perform work on multiple servers, with the results of the tasks rolled up in one central location on the server that is running the maintenance plan.

By default, when a user creates a maintenance plan, a single server connection is generated. This connection is to the local SQL Server on which the plan is created. If you want to perform tasks on other instances of SQL Server, you'll need to add connections.

Each subplan doesn't need to contain tasks that all connect to the same server; you could have a subplan whereby every task uses a different connection. This design makes it easier to manage and maintain multiple servers. To manage these connections, click the Connections button. This will bring up the dialog box shown in Figure 8-15.

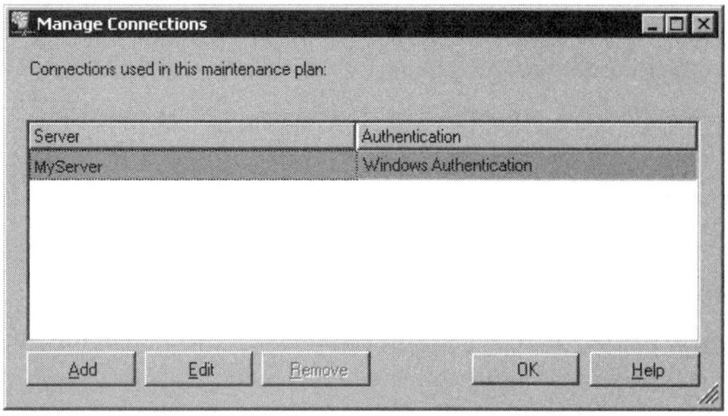

Figure 8-15. *The Manage Connections dialog box*

In Figure 8-15, notice that the Remove button is disabled for MyServer. This is because each maintenance plan requires you to have at lease one connection for the plan itself.

To add a connection to perform tasks on another SQL Server instance, click the Add button, which launches the dialog box in Figure 8-16. By default, the connection name will be blank. You're free to put in any name you would like for this connection. However, we find it easier to enter the actual server name.

Figure 8-16. *New Connection dialog box*

Once this connection is added, you can use it in any of the existing tasks as well as any new tasks that you drop on the designer surface.

Reporting and Logging Maintenance Plans

The Logging button along the top of the Maintenance Plan Designer document window, located to the right of the Manage Connections button, brings up the Reporting and Logging dialog box, as shown in Figure 8-17.

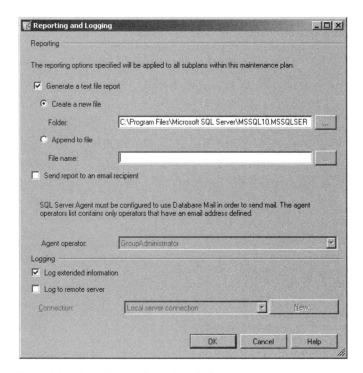

Figure 8-17. *Reporting and Logging dialog box*

With SQL Server maintenance plans, you can generate text file reports of the plan, as well as send the report to an e-mail recipient. Note that you'll need to install Database Mail in order to send the report to an Agent `Operator`.

In the Logging section of the Reporting and Logging dialog box, you'll see two check boxes:

- *Log Extended Information*: When this item is checked, all the T-SQL that gets submitted to SQL Server will be included in the maintenance plan history. It's checked by default and is useful for debugging any issues that arise from plan execution. However, depending on the size of the T-SQL script being executed, this could add a lot of data to your msdb database. To make sure your msdb database doesn't get too full, you can either uncheck this option or add a History Cleanup task that will automatically remove maintenance plan history tasks older than a certain date.

- *Log to Remote Server*: In SQL Server 2008, you can log maintenance plan information to a remote server. This option is useful if you have multiple servers that are running maintenance plans and would like to write all the logging information to a central server for easy management.

Defining Maintenance Plan Tasks

The designer surface is where you actually define what tasks are performed in your maintenance plan. To add a task, simply drag the task from the toolbox (see Table 8-7) onto the designer surface. For purposes of illustration, let's create a maintenance plan for the AdventureWorks database that first checks the database integrity (for example, whether it will issue a `DBCC CHECKDB()` against SQL Server), then on success, performs a database backup. In addition, on failure of the check, the database should notify an Agent `Operator`.

First, drag the Check Database Integrity, Backup Database, and Notify Operator tasks onto the designer surface, as shown in Figure 8-18.

Figure 8-18. *Maintenance Plan Designer designer surface*

One of the first things you may notice is the red X to the right of each of these tasks. This indicates that the task isn't configured and needs more information in order to execute—which connection to use, which database to perform the action on, and so on. Right-clicking a task brings up a context menu with the options presented in Table 8-8.

Table 8-8. *Context Menu for a Mainentance Task*

Menu Item	Function
Edit	Launches the editor dialog box for the selected task
Disable/Enable	Enables or disables the selected task
Add Precedence Constraint	Allows you to add a constraint through a dialog box; alternatively, you can click the task and drag the arrow to the destination task
Group	Allows the tasks to be grouped together
Zoom	Changes the visual appearance of the designer
Cut	Cuts the selected task
Copy	Copies the selected task to the clipboard, including the task's configuration information
Paste	Pastes the task from the clipboard
Rename	Renames the task
Delete	Deletes the selected task
Select All	Selects all tasks in the designer

To edit a task, select Edit or double-click the task. For example, double-clicking the Check Database Integrity task brings up the dialog box shown in Figure 8-19.

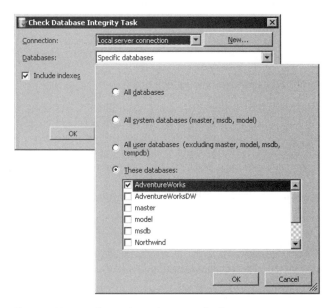

Figure 8-19. *Check Database Integrity Task dialog box*

The task dialog box may contain Connection, Databases, and Tables (or View) items. In the case of Check Database Integrity, the task needs to know only the connection and which database to check. By default, the local connection is selected; however, if you defined multiple connections, you could select one of these connections from the drop-down list or create a new connection by clicking the New button, which would bring up the New Connection dialog box (see Figure 8-16).

The Databases combo box, when dropped, shows a subdialog box that allows you to pick the databases on which to perform the action, as shown in Figure 8-20.

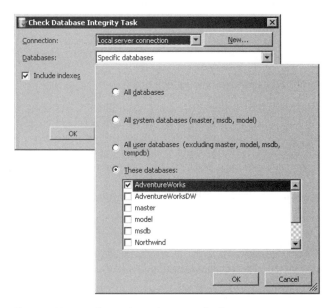

Figure 8-20. *Databases drop-down combo box*

Once you select the database or databases to perform the action on, the task may enable or disable options in the dialog box, based on whether you're performing the action on more than one database. For example, this might apply to the Back Up Database task.

Once the task is configured (that is, a connection is defined and you've selected a database and tables or views as appropriate), you may view the T-SQL that will most likely be executed at runtime against the connection. We say "most likely" because some tasks have conditions that need to be met before they are run, For example, in the case of the Shrink Database task, you define how large the database must be before shrinking, but the View T-SQL button will still always show you the T-SQL that would be executed.

Once you configure the task, the red X will disappear, and you can continue editing the other tasks.

One of the most powerful features of a maintenance plan is its ability to create workflow among the tasks. To do this, select a task, click and hold the green arrow at the bottom of the task, and drag this to another task. By default, the arrow is green, indicating On Success. To change this, simply right-click the green line and select Error or Completion for On Error or On Completion, respectively.

Once you've defined your workflow and configured the rest of your tasks, you should be able to execute your plan either via Agent, by scheduling it, or on demand, by right-clicking the plan name in Object Explorer and choosing Execute.

Maintenance plans are an important part of a DBA's daily routine. This new version of maintenance plans combines the power of the SSIS workflow engine with the usefulness of specific maintenance tasks, wrapped in an easy-to-use feature.

SQLCMD

SQLCMD, pronounced "SQL command," is a command-line tool used to connect to SQL Server and submit T-SQL queries and commands. With SQLCMD, you can perform the following:

- Execute SQL scripts against any SQL Server.

- Define and pass variables from the command line as well as within scripts.

- Use predefined system variables.

- Include multiple SQL scripts in-line.

- Dynamically change connections within the same script.

- Connect to SQL Server via the dedicated administrator connection.

SQLCMD was designed as a replacement to the existing OSQL and ISQL utilities. Of these two older utilities, only OSQL stills ships with SQL Server 2008; however, it has been deprecated since SQL Server 2005. Switching to SQLCMD from these older tools is definitely worth your time. The SQLCMD code was written from scratch, and a lot of effort was put into performance and features that promote usability, such as the ability to pass variables. SQLCMD also supports datatypes like `nvarchar(max)` and XML.

SQLCMD is designed so that the user can simply swap calls to OSQL.EXE with SQLCMD.EXE and have the script work without any modifications.

▪Note If you're directly replacing calls to SQLCMD.EXE instead of OSQL.EXE or ISQL.EXE, be aware that some parameters aren't supported and are ignored if placed on the command line. They are -D (ODBC DSN name) and -O (use old ISQL behavior).

Connecting to SQL Server

Unlike OSQL and ISQL, which used ODBC to connect to SQL Server, SQLCMD uses an OLE DB connection and allows users to make multiple connections to different servers within the same script. For example, suppose you had a few simple backup database scripts that each backed up a database on a specific server. On SERVERONE, the administrator would run this backup script to back up the ReportServer database:

```
File: backup_ReportServer.sql
BACKUP DATABASE [ReportServer] TO DISK='C:\backups\ReportServer.bak'
```

On SERVERTWO, the administrator would run this backup script to back up the Products database:

```
File: backup_Products.sql
BACKUP DATABASE [Products] TO DISK='D:\SQLServer\Backups\Products.bak'
```

In the real world, we know that administrators tend to have a lot of scripts that each performs its own functions on a specific server. With SQLCMD, you can now consolidate these into a single script using the :CONNECT command. Let's see this same scenario of backing up multiple databases using a single script:

```
File: backup_databases.sql
--Make a connection to SERVERONE using Windows Authentication
:CONNECT SERVERONE -E
--Issue a backup database command for ReportServer
BACKUP DATABASE [ReportServer] TO DISK='C:\backups\ReportServer.bak'
GO

--Make a connection to SERVERTWO using Windows Authentication
:CONNECT SERVERTWO -E
--Issue a backup database command for Products database
BACKUP DATABASE [Products] TO DISK='D:\SQLServer\Backups\Products.bak'
GO
```

Issuing the SQLCMD command sqlcmd -E -i backup_databases.sql yields the following result:

```
Sqlcmd: Successfully connected to server 'SERVERONE'.
Processed 280 pages for database 'ReportServer', file 'ReportServer' on file 4.
Processed 1 pages for database 'ReportServer', file 'ReportServer_log' on file 4.
BACKUP DATABASE successfully processed 281 pages in 0.369 seconds (6.238 MB/sec).
Sqlcmd: Successfully connected to server 'SERVERTWO'.
Processed 144 pages for database 'Products', file 'Products' on file 6.
Processed 1 pages for database 'Products', file 'Products_log' on file 6.
BACKUP DATABASE successfully processed 145 pages in 0.237 seconds (5.011 MB/sec)
```

Passing Variables

SQLCMD also provides the ability to pass variables from the command line and within the script itself. For example, assume you have a generic "backup database" script, called backup_database_generic.sql, that could be reused:

```
File: backup_database_generic.sql
:CONNECT $(myConnection)
BACKUP DATABASE $(myDatabase) TO DISK='C:\backups\$(myDatabase).bak'
```

At this point, you could call this script from the command line using the new -v parameter. This parameter tells SQLCMD that the following text is a variable, an example of which is shown here:

```
C:\>SQLCMD -E -i backup_database_generic.sql
 -v myConnection="." myDatabase="ReportServer"
```

When the backup_database_generic.sql script is run, it will have two variables defined: myConnection, which is equal to ".", and myDatabase, which is equal to "ReportServer". Alternatively, if you wanted to use variables, you also could have set the parameters within another script as shown here:

```
File: backup_database_main.sql
:SETVAR myConnection .
:SETVAR myDatabase ReportServer
```

```
:R "backup_database_generic.sql"

GO
```

When this script is executed, SQLCMD will set the `myConnection` variable to `"."` (the period is an alias for the local server—you could have used `"localhost"` or the actual name of the server as well), set the `myDatabase` variable to `"ReportServer"`, and then insert the contents of the `backup_database_generic.sql` script in-line.

Using the Dedicated Administrator Connection

SQL Server spawns a separate thread called the *dedicated administrator connection* (DAC). This connection was designed to be used by members of the `sysadmin` role in the event that they can't connect to SQL Server under normal operating conditions. There is only one connection of this type allowed per instance of SQL Server available, and it can be accessed only through SQLCMD.

To connect to SQL Server 2005 on the DAC, use the `-A` parameter in SQLCMD.

```
C:\>SQLCMD -E -S. -A
```

Creating Scripts

Although some might claim Notepad is the best text editor around, writing scripts for SQLCMD can sometimes be tedious using even this robust text editor application. For this reason, SQL Server Management Studio supports writing SQLCMD scripts.

To create a new SQL Script, open Management Studio, connect to your server, and click the New Query button. On the context menu, select New SQL Server Query. You'll now have a Query Editor window open, as shown in Figure 8-21. If you start typing SQLCMD commands in this window, you'll notice that the editor will complain, and you'll get errors if you try to execute the script.

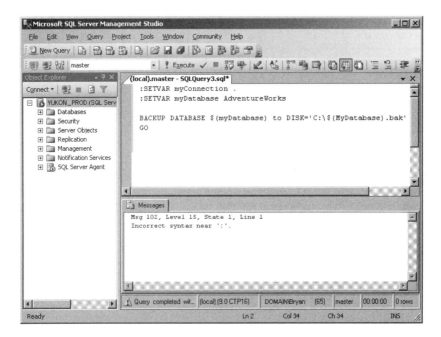

Figure 8-21. *SQL Server Management Studio not in SQLCMD mode*

These errors occur because you first need to enable SQLCMD mode in the editor. You can enable this mode by selecting SQLCMD mode from the Query menu in Management Studio. When the editor is in SQLCMD mode, you'll notice that SQLCMD-specific commands such as :SETVAR and :CONNECT are highlighted in the editor, as shown in Figure 8-22. This is to differentiate them from traditional T-SQL.

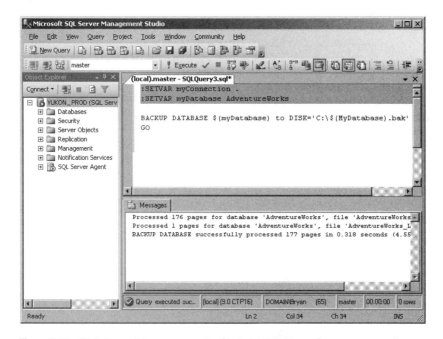

Figure 8-22. *SQL Server Management Studio in SQLCMD mode*

Once the SQLCMD mode is enabled on the editor, the script can be executed by clicking the Execute button. This will pass the script to the SQLCMD application to be interpreted instead of submitting it to the SQL Server database engine directly.

SQLCMD is a complete rewrite of the deprecated OSQL command-prompt utility. It is designed with many performance-related improvements.

PowerShell for SQL Server

PowerShell is a new command-line shell and scripting language. It offers more power and functionality than VBScript and the Windows command prompt. PowerShell will be available in Windows Server 2008 and is also available as a download (http://www.microsoft.com/windowsserver2003/technologies/management/powershell/download.mspx) for other versions of Windows.

PowerShell is designed to make it easy for vendors and developers to create providers that add value to PowerShell users. SQL Server 2008 provides a PowerShell provider that enables users to easily access SQL Server instances and SMO objects, and manage database policies within the PowerShell environment.

First, we'll provide a brief introduction to PowerShell in Windows, and then explain how to use the SQL Server PowerShell provider.

Introducing PowerShell

PowerShell was designed to make it easier for information technology administrators to manage the Windows environment. So why should we learn yet another scripting language and command line? PowerShell is the result of years of effort by the Windows team at Microsoft. They took a hard look at the current scripting experience, customer feedback, and the user experience with other, more robust scripting environments. With the knowledge obtained, they created a powerful scripting and command shell environment that finally competes with ones found in other operating systems.

The functionality of PowerShell revolves around what are called *cmdlets* (pronounced "commandlets"). You can think of cmdlets as executables that perform a specific task. PowerShell provides more than 120 cmdlets out of the box. If that is not enough, you can write your own cmdlets easily using .NET, or you can purchase third-party cmdlets.

One of the great features of PowerShell is consistency. PowerShell cmdlets always have the same format of *verb-noun*. Issuing the statement Get-Command would result in a list of all the available cmdlets. Table 8-9 shows the first 14 cmdlets listed.

Table 8-9. *Some PowerShell Cmdlets*

Name	Definition
Add-Content	Add-Content [-Path] <String[...
Add-History	Add-History [[-InputObject] ...
Add-Member	Add-Member [-MemberType] <PS...
Add-PSSnapin	Add-PSSnapin [-Name] <String...
Clear-Content	Clear-Content [-Path] <String...
Clear-Item	Clear-Item [-Path] <String[]...
Clear-ItemProperty	Clear-ItemProperty [-Path] <...
Clear-Variable	Clear-Variable [-Name] <String...
Compare-Object	Compare-Object [-ReferenceObject...
ConvertFrom-SecureString	ConvertFrom-SecureString [-String...
Convert-Path	Convert-Path [-Path] <String...
ConvertTo-Html	ConvertTo-Html [[-Property] ...
ConvertTo-SecureString	ConvertTo-SecureString [-String...
Copy-Item	Copy-Item [-Path] <String[]>...

Get-Command provides a basic definition for each cmdlet. Get-Help will return more information about a specific command. For example, issuing Get-Help Get-ChildItem gives these results:

```
NAME
    Get-ChildItem

SYNOPSIS
    Gets the items and child items in one or more specified locations.

SYNTAX
    Get-ChildItem [[-path] <string[]>] [[-filter] <string>] [-include <string[]>]
      [-exclude <string[]>] [-name] [-recurse] [-force] [<CommonParameters>]

    Get-ChildItem [-literalPath] <string[]> [[-filter] <string>]
      [-include <string[]>] [-exclude <string[]>] [-name] [-recurse]
```

```
        [-force] [<CommonParameters>]

DETAILED DESCRIPTION
        The Get-Childitem cmdlet gets the items in one or more specified locations.
        If the item is a container, it gets the items inside the container, known as
        child items. You can use the Recurse parameter to get items in all child
        containers. A location can be a file system location, such as a directory,
        or a location exposed by another provider, such as a registry hive or
        a certificate store.

RELATED LINKS
        Get-Item
        Get-Alias
        Get-Location
        Get-Process
        about_namespace

REMARKS
        For more information, type: "get-help Get-ChildItem -detailed".
        For technical information, type: "get-help Get-ChildItem -full".
```

As you can see, some information is missing here, like the definition and accepted values of parameters. You can obtain more information, including examples, by using the –default or –full option when displaying help.

As an example, let's create a script that deletes our backup files (any file that has a .BAK extension) if they are more than ten days old. The delete_backups.ps1 script is as follows:

```
#Define our variables to be used in our script
$TargetFolder = "C:\Backups"
$RetainBackups = 10
$Today = Get-Date


$LastWrite = $Today.AddDays(-$RetainBackups)
Write-Host "Removing backups from " $TargetFolder
Write-Host "Which are older than " $LastWrite

$Files = Get-Childitem $TargetFolder -include *.* -Recurse | Where
    {$_.LastWriteTime -le "$LastWrite"}

if ($Files.count -gt 0)
{
    foreach ($File in $Files)
    {
        Write-Host "Deleting File $File"
        Remove-Item $File | out-null
    }
}
else
{
    Write-Host "There are no files to delete." –foregroundcolor "Red"
}
```

PowerShell scripts have the .ps1 extension. To run this script in PowerShell, simply type the filename at the PowerShell command line—in this case, delete_backups.ps1.

As you can see from the script, the concept of an object is heavily used, without the need to define a specific datatype for each variable.

Tip For those of you looking at PowerShell script code for the first time, it can be a little scary. Luckily, Microsoft has made a lot of information about PowerShell available online, including some webcasts that do a great job at explaining scripting concepts and how to write scripts using PowerShell. These webcasts and other information can be found at http://www.microsoft.com/powershell.

If you start working with PowerShell, you may notice that familiar command-line statements like DIR, CD, MKDIR, and RMDIR work perfectly. These are not the actual executables that you would find in a regular Windows command prompt. Rather, in PowerShell they are simply aliases to similar cmdlets that perform the task. For example, the command DIR is really an alias for Get-ChildItem. You can create your own aliases as well.

At the time of this writing, PowerShell version 2.0 is in beta form and expected to be released in the near future. Version 2.0 will add even more capabilities, such as the following:

- *Script debugging*: Set breakpoints, and step into and out of scripts using the PowerShell console window itself, without the need for specialized development tool.

- *Background jobs*: Configure commands to run as asynchronous background jobs.

- *Graphical PowerShell*: See color-coding and line numbers, and use a multiple document interface.

- *Script cmdlets*: Write cmdlets using PowerShell scripts. You won't need to write them using a formal programming language like C#, Visual Basic .NET, or any other .NET language.

PowerShell is a powerful addition to the administrative capabilities of the Windows operating system. Not only does SQL Server 2008 provide out-of-the box integration, but other products like Microsoft Exchange already have support.

In our very brief discussion of PowerShell, we touched on some of the key features and benefits. We recommend that you download it and run through the plethora of tutorials and scripts available at http://www.microsoft.com/powershell.

Using SQL Server PowerShell

SQL Server 2008 contains a PowerShell provider out of the box. To launch SQL Server PowerShell, you can run SQLPS from a command line. Alternatively, you can select Start PowerShell from the context menu of a server instance in SQL Server Mangement Studio.

Those who have used the Windows command line will immediately notice the familiar text-based user interface experience. Just like the command line, PowerShell has the requirement that all providers must support a drive-qualified path. For example, if you want to perform work on your C drive on your local file system, you would access it by using the drive letter C:. And if you wanted to navigate through your SQL Server machine, you would use SQL: for the drive-qualified path.

If you launch SQL Server PowerShell from Management Studio, it automatically defaults the drive to the instance where you launched PowerShell. For example, launching it from a default instance yields the drive path to be SQL:\<server name>\DEFAULT.

Issuing Get-PSDrive at the command line results in an enumeration of the available drives in PowerShell. From Figure 8-23, you can see that three drives come with the SQL Server PowerShell provider: SQLSERVER, SQL, and SQLPolicy.

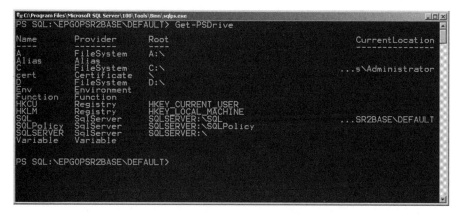

Figure 8-23. *SQL Server PowerShell showing the results of a Get-PSDrive statement*

The SQLSERVER drive is considered the root path, and beneath it are two objects: SQLPolicy and SQL. SQLPolicy is used to navigate and manage Policy Management framework objects. SQL is used to navigate SQL Server objects via the SMO hierarchy.

Using the familiar commands CD and DIR, you can easily navigate your way around the database objects. For example, to enumerate the AdventureWorks table list, you could simply do the following:

```
CD Databases\Adventureworks
```

and then this:

```
DIR Tables
```

Remember that the CD and DIR statements are not actual PowerShell commands. Rather, they are aliases to Set-Location and Get-ChildItem, respectively.

The real power of PowerShell comes with its seamless integration across multiple applications and the operating system itself. Currently, Microsoft Exchange Server 2007 and SQL Server 2008 have native providers for PowerShell. This allows you to easily obtain information within a script across these various platforms. To help illustrate this concept, let's create a simple script that obtains job information from the Windows Job Scheduler service as well as SQL Server Agent jobs, and insert this information into a table to be used for reporting. The following is the code for this example:

```
#Use WMI to obtain the AT Scheduler job list
$colItems = get-wmiobject -class "Win32_ScheduledJob"
   -namespace "root\CIMV2" -computername "."

foreach ($objItem in $colItems)
{
$JobId = $objItem.JobID
$JobStatus = $objItem.JobStatus
$JobName = $objItem.Command

#Use the SQL Provider Invoke-SqlCmd cmdlet to insert result into JobReports table
Invoke-SqlCmd -Query "INSERT INTO master..JobReports (job_engine, job_engine_id,
job_name, job_last_outcome) VALUES('NT','$JobId','$JobName','$JobStatus')"
}

#Now let's obtain the job listing from the JobServer object
Set-Location "SQL:\epgopsr2base\default\JobServer"
```

```
$jobItems = get-childitem "Jobs"

foreach ($objItem in $jobItems)
{
$JobId = $objItem.JobID
$JobStatus = $objItem.LastRunOutcome
$JobName = $objItem.Name

Invoke-SqlCmd -Query "INSERT INTO master..JobReports (job_engine,
job_engine_id, job_name, job_last_outcome) VALUES('AGENT','$JobId',
'$JobName','$JobStatus')"
}
```

This example assumes we have a table in the master database, defined as follows:

```
CREATE TABLE JobReports
(job_engine CHAR(6),
job_engine_id VARCHAR(50),
job_name VARCHAR(255),
job_last_outcome VARCHAR(50),
report_time datetime DEFAULT GETDATE())
```

After running our code, the JobReports table would be filled with entries of both the Windows AT scheduled jobs and SQL Server Agent jobs. An example result set is as follows:

job_engine	job_engine_id	job_name	job_last_outcome	report_time
NT	1	ntbackup.exe	Success	2008-01-22 15:32:29.270
NT	4	CustomApp.exe	Success	2008-01-22 15:32:29.280
AGENT	3226bb84-4e...	BackupTestDB	Succeeded	2008-01-22 15:32:29.290
AGENT	642f4e27-66...	BackupDevDB	Unknown	2008-01-22 15:32:29.300
AGENT	ddc03a7b-45...	ReIndxTestDB	Unknown	2008-01-22 15:32:29.300

In the real world, we would probably want to add much more information about the jobs, like their run times, and perhaps add the ability to obtain this information across all job servers in the enterprise. However, the main point of this example is to show how we can seamlessly obtain information from a variety of sources. Here, we obtained the AT scheduler job information via WMI.

■**Tip** PowerShell GUI WMI Explorer is a great PowerShell tool written to browse WMI classes and objects. It even provides sample code for the methods that a class exposes. This tool is well worth the time to check out. You can find an overview of the tool and a link to download it at http://thepowershellguy.com/blogs/posh/archive/2007/03/22/powershell-wmi-explorer-part-1.aspx.

The sample script obtains Agent job information by enumerating jobs within the jobs container. The properties exposed here are the same properties you would find from the Jobs object in the Microsoft.SQLServer.Management.SMO.Agent namespace. To see a list of available properties, you can simply type this:

```
Get-Item <object_name> | get-member -MemberType property
```

where *object_name* is the name of a job in our example. This command works with any object in PowerShell. Issuing this command against one of our Agent jobs yields the following results:

```
TypeName: Microsoft.SqlServer.Management.Smo.Agent.Job

Name                     MemberType Definition
----                     ---------- ----------
Category                 Property   System.String Category {get;set;}
CategoryID               Property   System.Int32 CategoryID {get;}
CategoryType             Property   System.Byte CategoryType {get;set;}
CurrentRunRetryAttempt   Property   System.Int32 CurrentRunRetryAttempt {get;}
CurrentRunStatus         Property   Microsoft.SqlServer.Management.Smo.Agent.J...
CurrentRunStep           Property   System.String CurrentRunStep {get;}
DateCreated              Property   System.DateTime DateCreated {get;}
DateLastModified         Property   System.DateTime DateLastModified {get;}
DeleteLevel              Property   Microsoft.SqlServer.Management.Smo.Agent.C...
Description              Property   System.String Description {get;set;}
EmailLevel               Property   Microsoft.SqlServer.Management.Smo.Agent.C...
EventLogLevel            Property   Microsoft.SqlServer.Management.Smo.Agent.C...
HasSchedule              Property   System.Boolean HasSchedule {get;}
HasServer                Property   System.Boolean HasServer {get;}
HasStep                  Property   System.Boolean HasStep {get;}
IsEnabled                Property   System.Boolean IsEnabled {get;set;}
JobID                    Property   System.Guid JobID {get;}
JobSchedules             Property   Microsoft.SqlServer.Management.Smo.Agent.J...
JobSteps                 Property   Microsoft.SqlServer.Management.Smo.Agent.J...
JobType                  Property   Microsoft.SqlServer.Management.Smo.Agent.J...
LastRunDate              Property   System.DateTime LastRunDate {get;}
LastRunOutcome           Property   Microsoft.SqlServer.Management.Smo.Agent.C...
Name                     Property   System.String Name {get;set;}
NetSendLevel             Property   Microsoft.SqlServer.Management.Smo.Agent.C...
NextRunDate              Property   System.DateTime NextRunDate {get;}
NextRunScheduleID        Property   System.Int32 NextRunScheduleID {get;}
OperatorToEmail          Property   System.String OperatorToEmail {get;set;}
OperatorToNetSend        Property   System.String OperatorToNetSend {get;set;}
OperatorToPage           Property   System.String OperatorToPage {get;set;}
OriginatingServer        Property   System.String OriginatingServer {get;}
OwnerLoginName           Property   System.String OwnerLoginName {get;set;}
PageLevel                Property   Microsoft.SqlServer.Management.Smo.Agent.C...
Parent                   Property   Microsoft.SqlServer.Management.Smo.Agent.J...
Properties               Property   Microsoft.SqlServer.Management.Smo.SqlProp...
StartStepID              Property   System.Int32 StartStepID {get;set;}
State                    Property   Microsoft.SqlServer.Management.Smo.SqlSmoS...
Urn                      Property   Microsoft.SqlServer.Management.Sdk.Sfc.Urn...
UserData                 Property   System.Object UserData {get;set;}
VersionNumber            Property   System.Int32 VersionNumber {get;}
```

Five cmdlets are currently available in the SQL Server PowerShell provider:

- Decode-SqlName and Encode-SqlName decode and encode special characters in SQL Server names to formats usable in PowerShell.

- Convert-UrnToPath is a useful cmdlet when coverting an SMO Uniform Resource Name (URN) value into a valid PowerShell path format.

- Evaluate-Policy is used to evaluate a Policy Management policy against a particular server instance.

- Invoke-Sqlcmd is essentially a call to the SQLCMD executable in-line within the code. We used this cmdlet in our example.

Once you have a useful script, you can run it on demand by calling it from the SQL PowerShell command line, or you can use SQL Server Agent to run it. In SQL Server 2008, Agent has a new subsystem called PowerShell. This subsystem allows users to create job steps of type PowerShell. Having a PowerShell Agent job step allows users to run PowerShell scripts as part of their jobs.

After reading about SQL Server PowerShell, you may be wondering why you should bother learning PowerShell if a T-SQL script can handle your current situation. Although T-SQL may work for you, SQL PowerShell gives you additional capabilities that may benefit you in the long term. For example, SQL PowerShell provides access to all of the capabilities of SMO, the registry, registered servers, and the Policy Management framework. Also, users of Windows or Exchange will find it really easy to integrate SQL within their management scripts. Microsoft is making a big bet with PowerShell as the future scripting engine of Windows.

Database Mail

Warning: mentioning SQLMail to some DBAs may cause undesirable reactions. The notoriously bad press that surrounded the SQLMail feature in previous versions of SQL Server can now come to an end. So can the hassles of configuring MAPI profiles, installing the Outlook client on your production server, and living with the risk of a disruptive xp_sendmail call taking down the SQL Server process.

Database Mail is an SMTP-based e-mail solution for SQL Server. This mail feature provides users with the following:

- Asynchronous mail solution
- Restricted user access to Database Mail
- Scalable Simple Mail Transfer Protocol (SMTP) server configuration
- Attachment and query restrictions

Before we dive into the Database Mail internals, let's define a few basic concepts in the Database Mail world. An *account* is name, description, and authentication information for a specific SMTP account. A group of these accounts is referred to as a *profile*. Having a group of accounts is useful, since this adds a layer of reliability, because the mail would still be sent by a different account in the profile if one particular SMTP server was down. If you're a visual person, you may see things more clearly by looking at Figure 8-24.

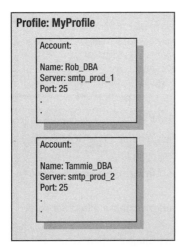

Figure 8-24. *Pictoral representation of a Database Mail profile*

Figure 8-24 shows one profile defined as MyProfile. This profile has two accounts created within it: Rob_DBA and Tammie_DBA.

When users send mail using Database Mail, they use the new stored procedure sp_send_dbmail, as in this example:

```
sp_send_dbmail      @profile_name='MyProfile',
@recipients='testuser@apress.com',
@subject='Test Message',
@body='This is the body of the message.',
@importance='HIGH'
```

One of the parameters in this stored procedure is @profile_name. When the user specifies a profile, Database Mail looks at the first account that is defined for the particular profile and attempts to send the e-mail using this account. If for whatever reason the send fails, such as when the SMTP server is offline, Database Mail will wait 100 seconds (the default Account Retry Delay setting), and then proceed down the account list and attempt to send the mail using the second account. If this account fails, it will continue to the next account, and so on. When it has reached the end of the account list, the send will fail. If you wanted Database Mail to loop back around and attempt the first account again, you could set the Account Retry Attempts setting to the number of times Database Mail will "round-robin" the account list. These global settings will be described in detail in the following section.

So are profiles just a way to group accounts? Well, sort of. There are two types of profiles: public and private. Public profiles can be accessed by any valid msdb database user. With private profiles, administrators can limit which users can use a specific profile.

Database Mail installs both configuration and mail item information in the msdb database.

Configuring Database Mail

The Database Mail Wizard can be accessed from the Configure Database Mail context menu off the Database Mail node. This wizard is used to manage accounts, profiles, and Database Mail global settings. Clicking Next on the welcome screen will bring you to the Select Configuration Task page, as shown in Figure 8-25. This page will determine which function the wizard should perform. By default, the option to configure the mail host database is selected, so you can simply click the Next button.

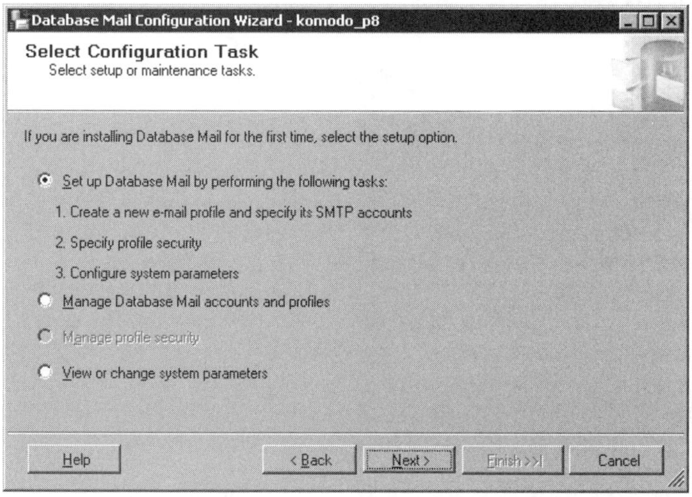

Figure 8-25. *Select Configuration Task page*

You need to have at least one profile configured in order to use Database Mail. Add a profile through the New Profile page, as shown in Figure 8-26. The profile name is what users will use when sending e-mail, so make sure it's easy to remember. The description is optional and is used to provide more information about the profile.

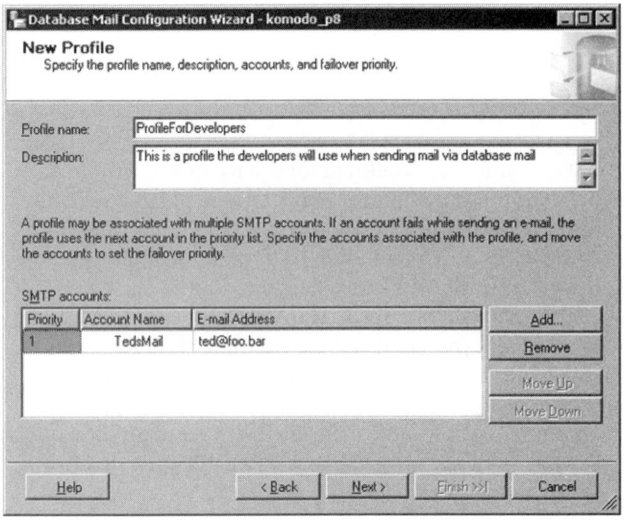

Figure 8-26. *New Profile page*

At the bottom of this page, you can define one or more accounts that this profile will use. Clicking Add will pop up a dialog box that allows you to select an existing account or create a new account. Once an account is defined, it's available for all profiles.

Clicking Next now brings you to one of the more interesting user interface conglomerations without SQL Server. The Manage Profile Security page is shown in Figure 8-27.

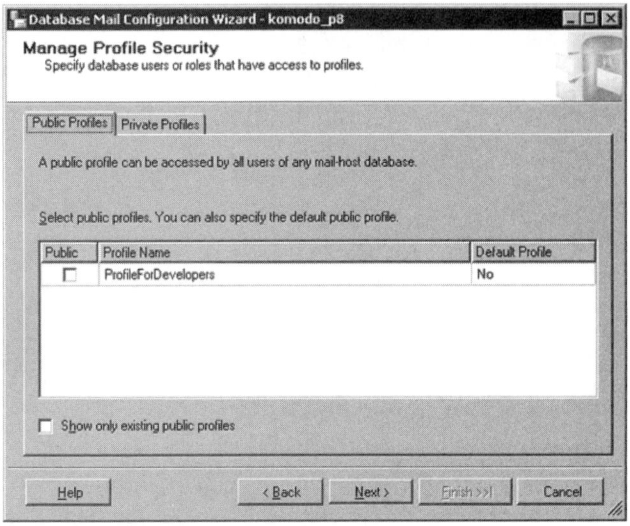

Figure 8-27. *Manage Profile Security page*

The first thing to notice about this page is it has two tabs: Public Profiles and Private Profiles. When a new profile is created, it's neither public nor private; basically only sysadmins can use this profile. If the sysadmin marks a profile as public, then any database user in the msdb database can send mail using this profile.

■Note In an effort to increase security, any non-sysadmin user who wants to use Database Mail must be added to the DatabaseMailUserRole database user role in msdb.

If you click the Private Profiles tab, you'll notice a combo box that allows you to specify a database user, as shown in Figure 8-28. From the User Name combo box, you can select any username and check the profiles to which to grant them access. Once you finish the wizard, the private profile won't generally show up unless you have the username selected in the combo box.

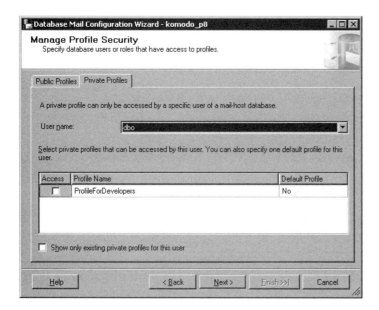

Figure 8-28. *Manage Profile Security, Private Profiles tab*

The last significant property that needs to be set on a profile is the default profile. If there are no profiles that are set for the default, users will always need to specify the @profile_name parameter in the sp_send_dbmail stored procedure call. If the sysadmin has a default profile defined, users can omit the profile, and Database Mail will use the default profile that is defined.

Clicking Next in the wizard will bring you to the last configuration page, called Configure System Parameters, shown in Figure 8-29. This page allows you to set the global settings of Database Mail. Table 8-10 describes each of these parameters.

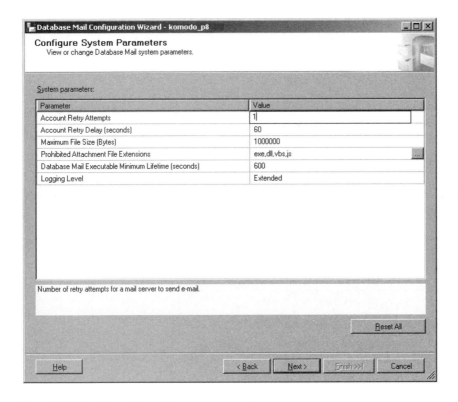

Figure 8-29. *Configure System Parameters page*

Table 8-10. *Database Mail System Parameters*

Parameter	Description
Account Retry Attempts	Number of times Database Mail will try to send the mail before declaring failure
Account Retry Delay (seconds)	Delay in between attempts to resend mail
Maximum File Size (bytes)	Maximum file size for attachments allowed per mail
Prohibited Attachment File Extensions	Determines which file extensions won't be sent
Logging Level	Amount of information saved in the log
Database Mail Executable Minimum Lifetime (seconds)	A performance-tuning option that specifies how long the Database Mail process will live before terminating due to no activity

The next page in the wizard is the summary page describing the actions that will be performed. Following that page is a progress page that will show you the live status of the actions being performed on your database.

Depending on which options you selected, you'll have a variable number of actions to be performed. In the event of a failure, the status would read "Failed," and there would be an error message hyperlink in the message column. Clicking this link may provide you with additional information about this error, provided you have an active Internet connection. This online error help feature can be seen throughout all of the SQL Server Management Studio dialog boxes and wizards.

The Database Mail feature isn't enabled by default on SQL Server. This feature can be enabled via the wizard. If you're planning on configuring Database Mail entirely through scripts and want to enable Database Mail, simply enable the Database Mail XPs parameter through the sp_configure stored procedure, as shown here:

```
SP_CONFIGURE 'show advanced', 1
GO
RECONFIGURE
GO
SP_CONFIGURE 'Database Mail XPs", 1
GO
RECONFIGURE
GO
```

After you've configured Database Mail, you're ready to send mail.

Sending Mail

For purposes of this discussion, consider an example where the administrator has created a single profile called MyDatabaseMailProfile. This profile contains two accounts: Rob_DBA using SMTP server SMTP_SVR1, and Tammie_DBA using SMTP server SMTP_SVR2.

At this point, the administrator issues the following T-SQL command:

```
Use msdb
GO
EXEC sp_send_dbmail @profile_name='MyDatabaseMailProfile',
@recipients='username@foo.bar',
@subject='Test message',
@body='This is the body of the test message.'
```

The stored procedure will first validate that the required parameters are entered, and then write the message in the sysmail_mailitems table. Having an immediate copy of the mail before it's "sent" allows the administrator to easily troubleshoot mail problems. After the mailitems entry is created, the stored procedure will call another stored procedure to create an XML document that wraps the mail. At this point, the XML document is sent to a predefined Service Broker queue. Service Broker provides queuing and reliable messaging. Using this feature allows Database Mail to asynchronously send large amounts of e-mail without disrupting other server operations.

When messages are placed on this queue, a SQL Server event notification is raised. At this point, another Service Broker queue is listening for this event, and upon reception, it will spawn the DatabaseMail90.exe process. When this process is instantiated, it obtains configuration information from msdb, pulls messages from the queue, and sends the mail. Upon completion, it will update the sysmail_mailitems table with delivery status and update the sysmail_log table. Since spawning a process is an expensive operation, the process itself will stay alive after processing all the mail items for a time period that is defined in the Database Mail global configuration settings as Database Mail Executable Minimum Lifetime. The default value is 600 seconds, or 10 minutes, and can be changed through the Database Mail Configuration Wizard, as discussed in the previous section.

SQL Profiler

SQL Profiler is the primary tool for use in performance analysis and tuning for SQL Server. It can be used to capture queries and statement events that are sent to a specific server.

For example, imagine that you're a DBA in a large organization and are tasked to find out why a particular database application is running slow. The application is an inventory management tool. This is a Win32 application that uses SQL Server as its data storage engine. Users have reported that most of the time the application works well, except for when they try to obtain a report for the quantity of items left in their inventory. You start troubleshooting this by launching Profiler, from the Performance Tools menu in SQL Server.

When Profiler is launched, you essentially have a blank screen and a menu bar. From here, you can start a new trace or load an existing trace. Since this is our first time troubleshooting in this example, let's choose New Trace from the File menu. This will cause a Connection dialog box to pop up asking on which server you want to perform a trace. We make a connection to the server that contains the Products database, which is the database that the Inventory management tool is using. Once connected, you are presented with the Trace Properties dialog box, as shown in Figure 8-30.

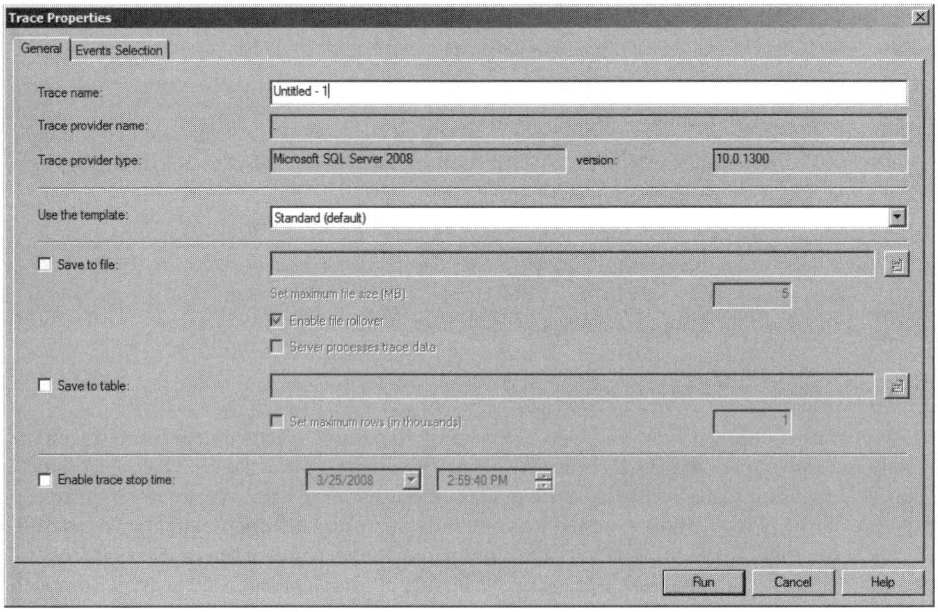

Figure 8-30. *General tab of the Trace Properties dialog box*

Here, you give the trace a name and specify where the trace should be created, in a file or in a table. Traces can also be configured to stop at a certain time, so if you had an issue that occurred at irregular intervals, you could set up a trace to run for a certain period of time in hopes of capturing some useful information.

Predefined templates are also available to help sort out which events to listen to. Eight templates are available, and if none of these is right for you, you can create your own templates. For this example, we will use the Standard (Default) template. If you click the Events Selection tab, you'll see which events and columns this particular template is using, as shown in Figure 8-31. You can add or remove events from this tab.

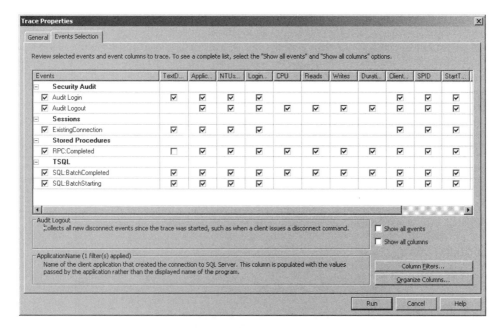

Figure 8-31. *Events Selection tab of the Trace Properties dialog box*

You can see all the available choices by checking the Show All Events and Show All Columns check boxes. To reduce the amount of unneeded data, you can optionally filter your columns by clicking the Column Filters button. Since we are looking for long-running queries in this example, let's put a filter on the Duration column to show only events that are longer than 2 seconds in duration, as shown in Figure 8-32.

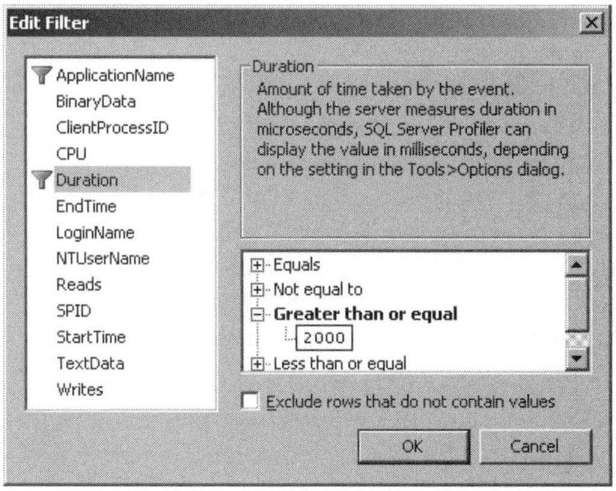

Figure 8-32. *Edit Filter dialog box*

Now that we've defined the trace, we can click Run in the Trace Properties dialog box to start recording. Once we have Profiler tracing SQL Server, we can run the problematic database application.

Assume that we ran the database application and noticed the performance problem that our users were complaining about. If we took a look at our Profiler trace, we can see the problematic T-SQL statement. If you click the row, the complete T-SQL will be displayed at the bottom of the screen, as shown in Figure 8-33.

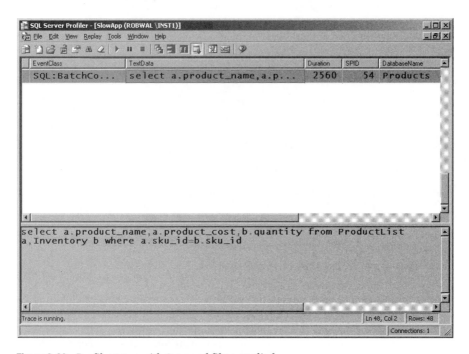

Figure 8-33. *Profiler trace with 2-second filter applied*

Now that we see that this SELECT statement was the problem, we can notify the developer of this issue or take a look at optimizing the schema using indexes.

In SQL Server, trace definitions are dynamically loaded from the server. This allows Profiler to adjust its event selection based on the server it's connecting to. For example, if in a future service pack, a new event is created or modified, Profiler will be able to adapt these new settings to its list of available events. Having a dynamic trace definition also makes it easier to add new server types from which to capture traces. Profiler can also trace and replay events from Analysis Services.

There could be times when a Profiler user would want to automate trace collection, trace manipulation, and trace replay. This would allow users to establish performance benchmarks against their applications. There is now a set of objects under the Microsoft.SqlServer.Management.Trace namespace that allows users to programmatically achieve this.

Performance Monitor Correlation

Profiler can import Performance Monitor data and correlate it to a specific trace. The combination of these two technologies gives users a useful way to observe system performance and trace events simultaneously.

■Note You can't correlate both Performance Monitor and trace events live. You must have already captured the trace file and Performance Monitor data before you can correlate them in Profiler.

As an example, suppose we want to see if sending large amounts of Database Mail affects the CPU process. First we set up a Profiler trace to capture the Database Mail stored procedure calls, just as we did previously in this chapter by selecting File ➤ New Trace. On the Events Selection tab, make sure to include at least the SQL:BatchCompleted event.

Before we start the trace, we need to define the Performance Monitor counter log that will be used to capture our Performance Monitor objects. To create a new counter log, open the Performance Monitor tool and select New Log Settings from the Counter Log node. Since we are interested in processor utilization but aren't quite sure which counter to include, let's include the Processor object of the local server. Click the Add Objects button and select this object in the Add Objects dialog box, as shown in Figure 8-34. Also include the Database Mail objects using the same Add Objects dialog box.

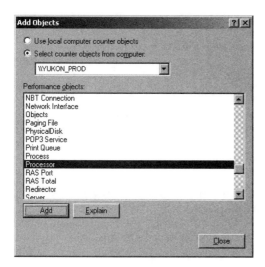

Figure 8-34. *Add Objects dialog box in Performance Monitor*

At this point, we can now start both the Profiler trace and Performance Monitor logging. Our environment is now set up so that we can execute a Database Mail script that will send 100 e-mail messages. After the script is executed, we stop the Performance Monitor log and save the trace file.

Now that we have both a performance log and trace file, we can use Profiler to correlate these two logs based on time. To do this, we first load the trace file using Profiler.

To load Performance Monitor data, select File ➤ Import Performance Data. Next, select the performance counter log file that was just created. Profiler asks us which counters we want to correlate at this point. For this example, we'll select % Processor Time and SendMailRequests. Once this selection is made, Profiler will show both the trace file and performance counters on the same screen, as shown in Figure 8-35.

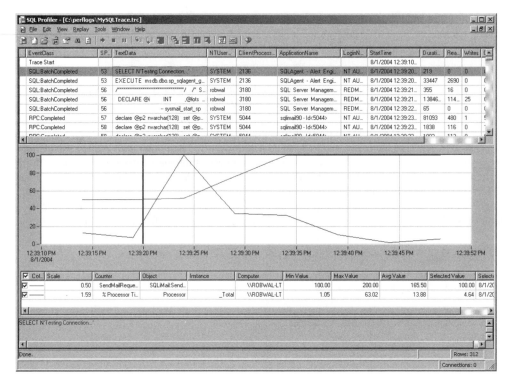

Figure 8-35. *Profiler showing Performance Monitor correlation*

The vertical line in the performance counter window correlates with the time of the event that is selected in the event grid. For example, if you wanted to know which statement was being executed when the CPU was at its peak, you could click the peak, and the event grid would highlight the statement that executed at that time. The reverse case is also true: if you select an event in the grid, the red line will move to the time period in the Performance Monitor log that contained this event.

Users can also zoom in and out of the Performance Monitor graph. This can be done by clicking the start time and dragging the mouse to the desired end time location. Once the mouse button is released, the Performance Monitor graph will adjust and show only the selected time period. The context menu of the Performance Monitor graph gives you the ability to zoom out or to show all the Performance Monitor data available.

Showplan

Showplan is a feature of SQL Server that allows you to obtain information about the data-retrieval methods chosen by the SQL Server query optimizer. Showplan appears in the form of an execution plan that includes information such as the execution cost of specific statements and queries. The actual plan information comes in the form of XML from the SQL Server database engine. The Profiler user interface interprets this information and forms the familiar Showplan execution as seen in SQL Server Management Studio.

To enable the Showplan feature in Profiler, select the Showplan XML event under the Performance category, as shown in Figure 8-36. Once this event is selected, the Events Extraction Settings tab will show up in the Trace Properties dialog box. This tab allows you to save the XML Showplan data separately to a file. You can also load the Showplan data in Management Studio for further analysis.

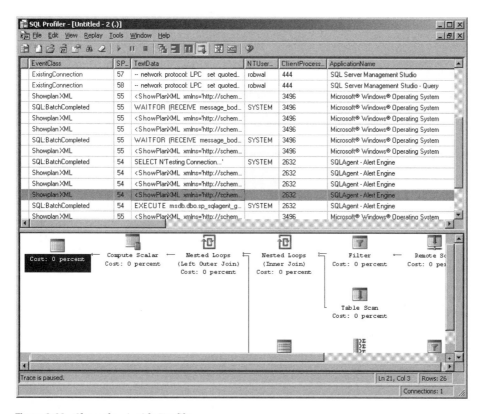

Figure 8-36. *Showplan inside Profiler*

To manually save the current trace file for offline access, select File ➤ Save As ➤ Trace XML File. Later, you can load this trace file and view the saved Showplan by selecting File ➤ Open ➤ Trace File.

■**Note** You'll need to change the Files of Type setting from SQL Profiler trace files (`*.trc`) to XML files (`*.xml`) in order to load trace files saved as XML.

Showplans can become quite large and are difficult to view in a single screen. When a Showplan exceeds the size of the visible screen, a + button appears toward the bottom-right side of the Showplan output. When clicked, a small pop-up window shows a bird's-eye view of the entire plan, as shown in Figure 8-37. The image was not intended to be completely legible; rather, it's designed to show an outline of the complete plan.

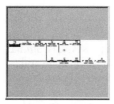

Figure 8-37. *Showplan navigational aid*

You can move the smaller rectangle around using the mouse, which allows you to select the part of the plan that you want to see. This is a small but useful feature for those larger-than-life plans.

Deadlock Visualization

When Profiler captures this event, it shows the `<deadlock-list>` tag in the TextData column. To display a graphical visualization, simply click the row, and it will appear at the bottom of the screen, as shown in Figure 8-38.

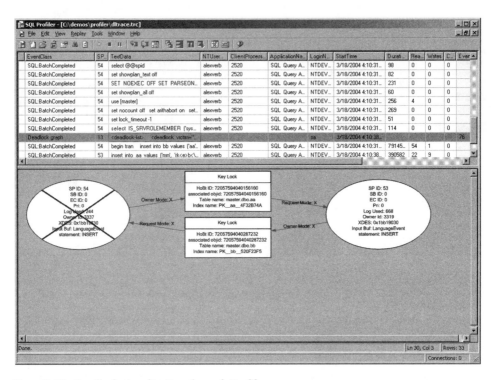

Figure 8-38. *Deadlock visualization through Profiler*

Each ellipse is a process within SQL Server. In this example, we can see that both service process (SP) IDs 54 and 53 are trying to acquire the same lock. In the end, SP ID 54 was chosen as the victim, and its actions were rolled back. The rectangles show the resource IDs and some additional information about the object. As with Showplan XML, the deadlock graph can also be saved to a file separately through the same Events Extraction Settings tab of the Trace Properties dialog box. SQL Server Management Studio can also load the graph in its user interface for further analysis.

Extended Events

Extended Events (EE) is a general event-handling infrastructure used within server systems. Similar to other event-based subsystems like SQL Trace, EE is primarily used to monitor server state and as a tool to diagnose issues in SQL Server. EE leverages the Event Tracing for Windows (ETW) feature within the operating system. This allows for event data captured from SQL Server to be correlated with data from the operating system, as well as any other applications that write ETW logs. Together, the EE services and objects create an infrastructure that is by far the most flexible and efficient eventing engine available within SQL Server. The performance of EE is many times better than that of SQL Trace.

EE events are designed to be available within the SQL Server engine itself and optionally within your own custom DLL. However, for SQL Server 2008, you will be able to use only EE events defined in the packages that come with SQL Server 2008. You will not be able to leverage EE on its own outside SQL Server.

Extended Events Components

At a high level, EE is composed of events, targets (event consumers), and actions. These pieces are all autonomous, such that the event engine has no knowledge of specific individual events that it processes. The event and corresponding target and action information are defined by the process that uses the eventing engine. The flexible design of this feature allows for any target to process any event and any event can write to any target.

A *module* is the actual binary that exposes one or more package objects. Since, as developers, we cannot add our own modules in SQL Server 2008, there is not much else to discuss with respect to modules other than that a few are installed by the SQL Server database engine and Reporting Services.

Packages

A *package* with respect to EE has no relation to packages in SSIS. This is yet another example of an overused term in SQL Server.

■**Note** Early designs of the new auditing feature in SQL Server 2008 used the term *audit packages* for the server-level audit container, but some folks on the product team thought using this term would be confusing because of the existence of SSIS packages. Apparently, the consistency police did not catch up with the EE team.

A package in EE is a container for events, targets, actions, and the other objects and structures used in an EE solution. This relationship between the package and the rest of the supporting objects in EE are shown in Figure 8-39.

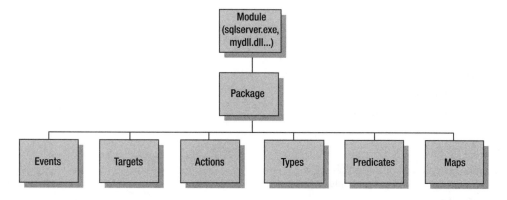

Figure 8-39. *Extended Events components*

Packages are uniquely identified by a name and GUID. In SQL Server, a number of packages are installed and available by default. Using the sys.dm_xe_packages dynamic management view, you can see the list of installed packages, including the GUID and module information. Querying this view just for the name and description yields the following:

```
Name         Description
--------     ----------------------------------------------------------------------
package      Default package. Contains all standard types, maps, compare operators,
             actions and targets
sqlos        Extended events for SQL Operating System
sqlserver    Extended events for Microsoft SQL Server
SecAudit     Security Audit Events
XeCommPkg    Cluster communication stack events
XeCMPkg      Configuration Manager Events
XeDvmPkg     Data Virtualization Manager and Agent Events
```

Each one of these packages contains a unique list of events, targets, actions, types, predicates, and maps. Don't worry about being bound to using only a single package within an EE session; you can easily mix and match events and targets among packages.

Events

Event is another overloaded term in SQL Server. When someone talks about an event, we need to ask ourselves if they are referring to a SQL Trace event, an event within Event Notifications, or one of any of the many other eventing capabilities in SQL Server.

In EE, events are similar to SQL Trace events, in that they are basically points in the engine code. Whether the start of a batch or a user login, all of these interesting points in the database engine code contain events. This is where the similarity between SQL Trace and EE ends, as events in EE are built upon an entirely different architecture.

To obtain a list of the available events, you can query the sys.dm_xe_objects dynamic management view. More than 200 events come with the preinstalled packages in SQL Server 2008. Here are just a few:

- Database started
- Database stopped
- Error log written
- Checkpoint has begun
- Checkpoint has ended
- Deadlock
- SQL statement starting
- SQL statement completed

Targets

Targets are event consumers and can be written to either synchronously or asynchronously. Targets can process these events individually or process a buffer full of them. These capabilities are available on a per-target basis.

To obtain a list of the available targets, you can query the sys.dm_xe_objects dynamic management view. A total of 13 targets come preinstalled in SQL Server 2008. Here is a sampling:

- ETW synchronous target
- Asynchronous ring buffer
- Asynchronous security audit NT security log target
- Asynchronous security audit file target

Actions

Actions are code that runs on the thread that fired the event. They are used to capture stack dumps, to inspect event data, and even to add data from outside the event's payload.

To obtain a list of the available actions, you can query the `sys.dm_xe_objects` dynamic management view. A total of 35 actions come preinstalled in SQL Server 2008. A sample list is as follows:

- Collect SQL text
- Collect client application name
- Collect NT username
- Collect current task execution time

Predicates

Since firing an event is expensive, *predicates* exist to help evaluate conditions prior to the firing of the event. Predicates are full Boolean expressions that evaluate to true or false.

There are two types of predicates: those that use local event data and those that use global state data or data that is not directly a part of the event itself. Some examples of global data include the session ID and SP ID of the connection context. Predicates also can store state, allowing scenarios where you can keep a counter such that when events occur, you can fire them every other time or every nth time. This is good to use if you have events that fire frequently and, for performance reasons, want to obtain a sample of the data, as opposed to record every single event data point.

Event Sessions

Event sessions are bindings between events and targets. Events themselves can be leveraged in multiple sessions, but the actions and predicates are defined on a per-session basis.

Extended Events Example: Detecting Deadlocks

As an example of using EE, we will create a lock condition between two users. We can create an event session that will listen for a `sqlserver.lock_deadlock` event within the AdventureWorks database. When this event is received, it will be placed in a ring buffer. In addition to the event information, we are requesting the actual SQL command be included as part of the event. The following code will create our event session:

```
CREATE EVENT SESSION AdventureWorksDeadLocks
ON SERVER
ADD EVENT sqlserver.lock_deadlock
   (ACTION (sqlserver.sql_text)
    WHERE sqlserver.database_id = 7)
ADD TARGET package0.ring_buffer
   ( SET max_memory=1024)
GO
ALTER EVENT SESSION AdventureWorksDeadLocks ON SERVER
STATE=START
GO
```

Next, we will create the deadlock using two user connections. Assume both User1 and User2 have appropriate access to the AdventureWorks database and Sales.CurrencyRate table. First, User1 issues these statements:

```
USE AdventureWorks
GO
BEGIN TRAN
UPDATE Sales.CurrencyRate SET AverageRate=2 where CurrencyRateID=1
```

Next, User2 issues these statements:

```
USE AdventureWorks
GO
BEGIN TRAN
UPDATE Sales.CurrencyRate SET AverageRate=2 where CurrencyRateID=1
```

To create the deadlock, User1 issues this statement:

```
SELECT * FROM Sales.CurrencyRate
```

Once we issue the last SELECT statement, we will have a deadlock, and SQL Server will choose a deadlock victim. When this happens, an event will be raised and sent to our ring buffer target. To see a list of the targets, you can query the sys.dm_xe_session_targets dynamic management view. Since we are using the ring buffer as a target, the actual event data is written in XML form to the target_data column of this view. Reading that column, we can see some valuable information including the SQL text. An abbreviated result set for the target_data column is as follows:

```
<RingBufferTarget eventsPerSec="166" processingTime="12" totalEventsProcessed="1"
eventCount="1" droppedCount="0" memoryUsed="512">
 <event name="lock_deadlock" package="sqlserver" id="70" version="1"
 timestamp="2008-01-16 23:19:45.403">
 ...
 <data name="mode">
  <type name="lock_mode" package="sqlserver" />
  <value>5</value>
 <text>
 <![CDATA[ LCK_M_X ]]>
  </text>
  </data>
 <data name="owner_type">
  <type name="lock_owner_type" package="sqlserver" />
  <value>1</value>
 <text>
 <![CDATA[ Transaction ]]>
  </text>
  </data>
 <data name="transaction_id">
  <type name="int64" package="package0" />
  <value>196350</value>
  <text />
  </data>
 <data name="database_id">
  <type name="uint16" package="package0" />
  <value>7</value>
  <text />
  </data>
...
 <action name="sql_text" package="sqlserver">
```

```
<type name="unicode_string" package="package0" />
<value>
<![CDATA[ BEGIN TRAN    UPDATE Sales.CurrencyRate SET AverageRate=2
where CurrencyRateID=1
]]>
</value>
<text />
</action>
...
</event>
</RingBufferTarget>
```

From this target data, we can obtain important information, including the lock ID, lock type, and SQL text that caused the deadlock.

This example used the ring buffer as a place to target events. The real power of EE comes with writing to the trace target for ETW. ETW is the next version of the tracing capabilities for Windows, available starting with Windows Server 2008. Having the ability to write to ETW trace files allows you to easily correlate events that happened in the operating system with events that happened in SQL Server, as well as any other provider that writes to ETW.

■**Note** At the time of this writing, new tools for ETW, called xperf and xperfinfo, are not yet available, but should be a part of Windows Server 2008. If you are interested in correlating SQL Server and operating system-level data, these tools promise to make that task really easy.

EE is a powerful and somewhat complicated event platform within the SQL Server engine. Here, we have just scratched the surface of what you can do with it. EE's applications reach far beyond just performance tuning—after all, this feature was originally implemented for use only by the Microsoft Product Support team. Late in the product cycle, the product team made a decision to expose interfaces into the feature and allow users to leverage the power of EE. Now that these interfaces are public, be on the lookout for really creative performance and troubleshooting designs that take advantage of EE; they should be appearing in the near future.

Summary

SQL Server provides some additional features and functionality that make it easier for DBAs to manage their servers. SQL Server Agent provides multiple proxy accounts, allowing system administrators the ability to define with more granularity access to SQL Server Agent and its related subsystems.

The maintenance plan feature gives a whole new meaning to management in SQL Server. With workflow and easy ability to configure maintenance tasks, DBAs now have an easier and more flexible way of performing scheduled server maintenance.

In addition to maintenance plans, scripts are a large part of the everyday life of a DBA. SQL-CMD, the replacement for ISQL.EXE and OSQL.EXE, provides better performance and some added features like variables. Variables allow users to easily reuse scripts and make the overall management experience easier.

SQL Server 2008 includes a provider for PowerShell, enabling users to seamlessly incorporate SQL Server commands within their PowerShell scripts.

Database Mail is a mail system that has made sending mail from SQL Server incredibly reliable and fast. Improper use of Database Mail could result in the world's best spam engine, so buyer beware.

SQL Profiler brings together a variety of technologies, such as Performance Monitor correlation, to extrapolate a fairly accurate image of actual server resource utilization and bottlenecks.

EE is a new eventing platform based on ETW. Users of this new eventing platform can expect much better performance results than those gained by using SQL Trace.

As you've seen in this chapter, the automation enhancements made in SQL Server 2008 show Microsoft's commitment to compete in the enterprise database market.

CHAPTER 9

■■■

Service Broker

One of the most important new features of SQL Server 2005 was Service Broker. Service Broker is a message-queuing technology that is native to SQL Server and allows developers to integrate SQL Server fully into distributed applications. Service Broker provides an asynchronous system for database-to-database communication; it allows a database to send a message to another database without waiting for the response, so the application will continue to function if the remote database is temporarily unavailable.

As with all message-queuing systems, Service Broker applications work by sending messages containing data to a queue. The messages will be stored on the queue until the system has the resources available to process them and perform any actions that the messages demand. This helps to ensure the scalability of the application by using resources efficiently, as messages are guaranteed to be processed at some point, even if they can't be processed immediately.

SQL Server 2008 provides additional support for Service Broker in SQL Server Management Studio, including a new diagnostic tool used to analyze the configuration of Service Broker.

In this chapter, we'll start by taking a high-level look at Service Broker, discussing the architecture of Service Broker applications and examining some sample scenarios where Service Broker can help you improve the robustness or scalability of your applications. We'll then get down to the details of creating Service Broker applications, looking at the new objects that you need to create in SQL Server and writing a simple example to show how to use these in practice. We'll then drill down into a couple of more advanced topics, including how to specify the way Service Broker should route messages and how it provides security for messages. We'll then work through a more complex example that demonstrates these advanced techniques. Next, we'll look at setting message priorities, and finally, troubleshooting Server Broker with the SSBDiagnose command-line utility.

In this chapter, we'll cover the following topics:

- The Service Broker architecture
- Scenarios for using Service Broker
- SQL Server Service Broker objects
- Service Broker routing
- Service Broker security
- Message priority
- Service Broker diagnostics

What Is Service Broker?

As intimated in the chapter introduction, Service Broker is message queuing for SQL Server. It provides a means by which you can send an asynchronous, transactional message from within a database to a queue, where it will be picked up and processed by another service. The sending and receiving services could be in separate instances of SQL Server, so the availability of the receiving service can't be guaranteed. However, because Service Broker places the message in a queue, you know that the message will eventually be picked up, even if the remote service isn't currently online.

Service Broker Architecture

The Service Broker architecture is essentially a straightforward client/server architecture. A Service Broker application consists of a client service that initiates a conversation and a receiving service that receives and processes the messages. Each service is associated with a particular queue, which it can send messages to, retrieve messages from, or both. The relationship between the services and the queue is defined by a *contract*, which specifies which type of messages the initiating and target services can send to the queue. The exchange of messages between the two services is called a *dialog conversation* (or simply a *dialog*). The fundamental architecture of a Service Broker application is shown in Figure 9-1.

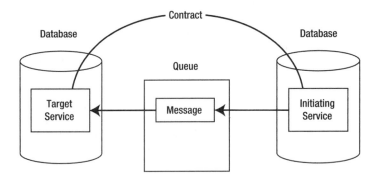

Figure 9-1. *The Service Broker architecture*

Services

A *service* is an endpoint for a Service Broker conversation. A service can be either an initiating service, which starts the conversation by sending a message to the queue, or a target service, which retrieves messages from the queue. A service is associated with a single queue (although queues can be associated with multiple services) and with a contract, which stipulates which type of messages it can send to the queue. Thus, the service is used to enforce the contract for a conversation. SQL Server also uses services to identify the queues to deliver messages to and to route messages through, and to authorize connections to remote services.

Queues

A *queue* is a depository for messages. Queues can be associated with multiple services, which can send and/or retrieve messages in the queue. A queue can also be associated with a stored procedure, which will execute when a message arrives in the queue. This gives you the option of processing messages as soon as they arrive in the queue, but it is also possible to process the messages by scheduling a SQL Server Agent job to run recurrently or when the CPUs are idle.

If the receiving service and sending service are in the same SQL Server instance, they can share the same queue; otherwise, they will need to be associated with different queues. If the receiving queue is in another instance of SQL Server, or if it isn't active for message receipt, the message will be placed in the *transmission queue* for the database that the sending service belongs to until the message can be delivered to the queue. Similarly, incoming messages will be sent to the transmission queue of the receiving database if the target queue isn't active for message receipt. You can see the messages currently in the transmission queue through the `sys.transmission_queue` system view. It's useful to check this queue when debugging Service Broker applications, as unsent messages remain here, and the `transmission_status` column may contain an error message explaining why the message wasn't sent.

Messages

Each *message* is represented by a row in the queue. The format of messages is defined by the message type, which is specified in the contract between two services. The message type can require that messages be empty, well-formed XML or XML that is valid according to a specific schema, or that no validation is to occur—in which case, the messages in a conversation can contain any data, including binary data. There are also special messages that all services receive, regardless of the contract:

- *Error messages*: These are defined as messages of type `http://schemas.microsoft.com/SQL/ServiceBroker/Error`, and they are validated as well-formed XML. They consist of a root element called `<Error>`, with child elements representing the code and description of the error. Once an error has been generated for a conversation, no further messages can be sent on that conversation.

- *End Dialog messages*: These are empty messages of type `http://schemas.microsoft.com/SQL/ServiceBroker/EndDialog` and indicate that a service is ending the conversation without error.

- *Dialog Timer messages*: These are empty messages of type `http://schemas.Microsoft.com/SQL/ServiceBroker/DialogTimer`, which are placed in a queue to indicate that a conversation timer has expired.

Dialog Conversations

A *dialog conversation* represents the exchange of messages between two services. Messages in a dialog are delivered to the queue in the order in which they are sent. When an application processes a message from a queue, it may send another message to the queue, and it can indicate that this forms part of the same conversation. The conversation continues until one of the participating applications explicitly ends the conversation or sends an error message. However, each participant in the conversation must issue an `END CONVERSATION` command, or the dialog will remain in the database (you can view the active conversations through the `sys.conversation_endpoints` system view).

The initiating application can indicate a maximum lifetime for the application, after which each side will place a timeout error in the queue and refuse further messages. Each participant in a conversation can also specify one *conversation timer* per conversation. When a conversation timer expires, SQL Server places a Dialog Timer message in the queue, as a prompt for the application to perform a specific action (such as executing a stored procedure).

Conversation Groups

Each dialog belongs to a *conversation group*. If an application accesses information from two or more services, it may need to relate these conversations to each other; it can do this by including the second conversation in the same conversation group as the first (this doesn't affect the applications at the other end of the conversations, as conversation groups aren't shared and the other applications may group the conversations as they wish). Service Broker includes the ID for the conversation group in all incoming messages in that conversation, so that the application can determine which messages from the remote services belong together.

For example, suppose you have a service that is used to process employee vacation requests and that retrieves information about the employee making the request from one service and information about the timelines for current projects from another service. It uses the data from these two services to decide whether or not to grant the request for that employee at that time. This application can use the conversation group ID to ensure that it processes the correct employee data together with the related project data.

Conversation groups are locked when a message is being sent or retrieved on that group. This helps to ensure exactly once in order (EOIO) delivery.

Contracts

The message types that each participant in a conversation is permitted to send are specified in the *contract* for that conversation. The two services in the conversation will be bound by the same contract. If the two services are in different databases, then identical contracts must be created in each database. The contract stipulates which types of messages the initiating service and the receiving service can send, and which types can be sent by either service. The contract *must* include at least one message type that can be sent by the initiating service (or by either service, which obviously includes the initiating service); otherwise, there is no way for the conversation to be initiated.

The Service Broker Endpoint

If the two services in a conversation are in different instances of SQL Server, you need to create a Service Broker *endpoint*, which will accept incoming and outgoing TCP/IP connections on a specific port. A SQL Server instance can contain only one Service Broker endpoint, which is shared between all services in the instance.

Remote Service Bindings

Remote Service Bindings are used to establish the security context under which an initiating service connects to a remote service in a different instance of SQL Server. The Remote Service Binding uses a certificate associated with the specified database user account to connect to the remote instance.

Routes

Service Broker uses routes to locate a service to which it is sending a message. If no route is explicitly associated with a service, by default, Service Broker will deliver the message within the current instance. A route contains the name of the service it is used to connect to, the ID of the Service Broker instance that hosts the service, and the network address of the remote Service Broker endpoint.

Service Broker Scenarios

Now that you've seen the various parts that make up a Service Broker application and how Service Broker works at a high level, a basic question remains: what do you actually use Service Broker for?

Service Broker brings two things to the table that ordinary SQL Server modules don't possess: guaranteed delivery of messages and asynchronicity. Without Service Broker, if you attempt to connect to a remote instance of SQL Server (for example, using a linked server), and that server isn't available, you must roll back the transaction and let the operation fail. With Service Broker, you can simply send a message to the queue and go on about your business, safe in the knowledge that when the server comes back online, it will be able to pick up the message and process it. Also, if you want to execute some complex processing within a module without Service Broker, you need to wait until that processing has completed before the module will continue executing. Service Broker allows the module to send a message and continue executing. The message can be processed at a later time, perhaps when the CPU is idle or during out-of-office hours.

Naturally, Service Broker also comes with an overhead, so it isn't an appropriate solution if you need an immediate response or if an application is time-critical. It wouldn't make any sense to use Service Broker to perform a simple SELECT query on a remote database. It's also worth bearing in mind that, if you use Service Broker for database updates, it could result in data conflicts, as the update may not be performed immediately.

The following are some possible scenarios for Service Broker applications:

- *Asynchronous triggers*: If a trigger requires resource-intensive processing that isn't time-critical, it makes sense to use Service Broker. The trigger can simply place a message on the queue and return without needing to wait for the processing to complete.

- *Bulk processing*: If a module requires extensive processing, such as bulk-data processing, Service Broker can avoid the potential performance degradation of running this immediately at busy times of the day. Instead, it can send a message to a queue, and a stored procedure can run as a SQL Server Agent job that will process any messages in the queue at a more convenient time.

- *Distributed order processing*: The other advantage of Service Broker—the guaranteed delivery of messages—makes it a good option for applications that involve order processing, where the order doesn't need to be fulfilled immediately, but it's vital that the order be delivered. This is particularly the case if orders are taken and fulfilled by different systems (for example, orders are taken at a local branch and dispatched from a central warehouse), where the availability of the remote system isn't guaranteed at the time the order is taken.

Creating Service Broker Applications

Now that you've learned what Service Broker is and what it's for, let's delve into the details of creating Service Broker applications. The exact number of steps you need to perform to do this varies, for example, on whether the conversation takes place within a single instance of SQL Server or whether the messages that will be sent are defined by an XML schema. For a single-instance application with validated XML messages, ten steps are involved:

1. Enable Service Broker for the database.
2. Create a master key for the database.
3. Create one or more XML SCHEMA COLLECTIONs to validate messages sent to the queue.
4. Define message types based on the schema(s).
5. Define the contract for the application.
6. Create a Service Broker program (for example, a stored procedure) to process messages that are sent to the queue.
7. Create the queue.

8. Create the target service.

9. Create the initiating service.

10. Create a program to initiate the conversation by sending a message to the queue.

Let's look at these individual steps before putting everything together into a simple Service Broker application. We'll skip steps 2 and 3 until we actually get to the example, as there's nothing specific to Service Broker about these, and we'll cover creating the target and initiating services (steps 8 and 9) and their associated stored procedures together.

Enabling Service Broker

Before Service Broker can be used in a database, you need to alter the database to enable Service Broker:

```
ALTER DATABASE database_name SET ENABLE_BROKER;
```

There's obviously some security risk in this, simply because it opens up another possible line of attack for a hacker trying to get into your database. However, unless you explicitly create a Service Broker endpoint, Service Broker won't accept connections from outside the instance. You also need to enable Service Broker in a database if you want to use Database Mail within that database.

Creating Message Types

Before you can create a contract for your Service Broker application, you need to define the message types that can be used in the conversation. The following is the syntax for the CREATE MESSAGE TYPE command:

```
CREATE MESSAGE TYPE message_type_name
VALIDATION = validation_type
```

The VALIDATION clause has four possible options:

- EMPTY: The message must not contain any data.
- NONE: The message is not validated and may contain any or no data.
- WELL_FORMED_XML: The message must consist of a well-formed XML document.
- VALID_XML WITH SCHEMA COLLECTION schema collection name: Messages of this type must conform to the schema(s) contained in the specified collection. If a message doesn't conform to this schema, it will be rejected and not placed on the queue; instead, an XML-formatted error message will be sent to the queue.

Creating Contracts

A *contract* consists of a list of the message types that can be included in the conversation, together with the service(s) that can send them. The basic syntax for creating a contract is as follows:

```
CREATE CONTRACT contract_name
    message_type_name SENT BY sending_service [, ...]
```

The CREATE CONTRACT statement specifies the message types that a conversation can accept and the service(s) that can send those messages. For each message type, you must also include a SENT BY clause, which indicates the services that can send messages of that type. The following are the possible values for SENT BY:

- `INITIATOR`: Only the service that started the conversation can post messages of this type.

- `TARGET`: Only the service that processes the messages on the queue can post messages of this type.

- `ANY`: Either of the two services in the conversation can send this type of message.

Instead of specifying a named message type, you can alternatively use the identifier `[DEFAULT]`, which indicates a default message type (with no validation) sent by either of the two services.

As we noted earlier, each contract must include at least one message type that may be sent by the initiator (for example, is `SENT BY` either `INITIATOR` or `ANY`).

Creating Queues

The command for creating a queue is perhaps the most complex of the new Transact-SQL (T-SQL) commands used to create Service Broker objects:

```
CREATE QUEUE queue_name
WITH
    STATUS = ON | OFF,
    RETENTION = ON | OFF,
    ACTIVATION
    (
        STATUS = ON | OFF,
        PROCEDURE_NAME = queue_sproc_name,
        MAX_QUEUE_READERS = integer,
        EXECUTE AS SELF | OWNER | user_name
    )
ON [DEFAULT] | filegroup_name
```

The `WITH` clause is optional, but if included, it can have a number of subclauses (again, all of these are optional):

- `STATUS`: This subclause indicates whether or not the queue is originally enabled.

- `RETENTION`: If this subclause is set to `OFF` (the default), any messages that are processed will be removed from the queue. Otherwise, the messages will be left on the queue, but their status will be updated to indicate that they have been processed.

- `ACTIVATION`: This subclause indicates whether a procedure will be executed on the arrival of a message in the queue. Here, you can specify the `STATUS` (whether the procedure will be activated automatically or not), the `PROCEDURE_NAME` (the SQL Server identifier for the service program), the maximum number of instances of the service program that can be created to process the queue, and the user to execute the procedure as. This can be one of `SELF` (the currently logged-in user), `OWNER` (the user account that owns the queue), or a username as a string.

Lastly, you can optionally specify an `ON` clause, which specifies the filegroup on which to create the queue. Alternatively, you can use `[DEFAULT]` to specify the default filegroup for the database.

Creating Services

You need to specify two pieces of information when you create a service: the queue with which the service is associated and the conversations in which it can participate. The conversations are specified through the contracts, so the `CREATE SERVICE` command looks like this:

```
CREATE SERVICE service_name
    ON QUEUE queue_name
    contract_name [, ...]
```

Contracts are used to indicate to other services which conversations the service can take part in, so they need to be supplied only if the service receives messages. If no contracts are specified, the service will be able to initiate conversations, but not to retrieve any responses.

Instead of naming a user-defined contract, you can use the identifier [DEFAULT] to specify the default contract, which allows either service to send unvalidated messages.

Creating Service Broker Stored Procedures

The most complex part of writing a Service Broker application, unsurprisingly, is creating the programs (typically stored procedures or triggers) that send and receive the messages. Initiating and target service applications obviously differ in that only the initiating service needs to begin a conversation, but otherwise the tasks that they need to perform are similar.

Initiating a Conversation

The first task in a conversation is for the initiating service to open up a dialog using the BEGIN DIALOG CONVERSATION command. This takes a local variable of type UNIQUEIDENTIFIER that will be populated with a handle you can use to identify the new conversation. You use this when you actually send a message on the conversation. BEGIN DIALOG CONVERSATION has three mandatory clauses:

- FROM SERVICE: The SQL Server identifier for the initiator service. Note that this is *not* surrounded by quotes.

- TO SERVICE: The name of the receiving service, as a string.

- ON CONTRACT: The SQL Server identifier for the contract that binds the two services.

Optionally, you can also specify that this conversation will belong to an existing conversation group. To associate a new dialog with an existing conversation group, supply either the ID for that group or the ID for another conversation in the group:

```
BEGIN DIALOG CONVERSATION @dialogHandle
    FROM SERVICE initiating_service
    TO SERVICE receiving_service
    ON CONTRACT contract_name
    WITH RELATED_CONVERSATION = conversation_ID
```

or

```
...
    WITH RELATED_CONVERSATION_GROUP = conversation_group_ID
```

You can include two other pieces of information in the WITH clause. You can specify a LIFETIME timeout period, after which the conversation will be closed. You also can include an ENCRYPTION option to state whether the message must be encrypted. By default, this is ON, which means that an error will occur if encryption isn't correctly configured. If it is OFF, encryption will still be used if configured, but otherwise the messages will be sent unencrypted. Messages sent to another service in the same SQL Service instance are never encrypted.

Sending Messages to a Queue

Once your conversation dialog is open, you can start to send messages to the queue. To do this, use the SEND command:

```
SEND
  ON CONVERSATION dialog_handle
  MESSAGE TYPE message_type_name
  (message_body)
```

The dialog handle will be the variable that you received from the BEGIN DIALOG CONVERSATION command or from a RECEIVE command that was used to retrieve messages from a queue. Both the *message_type_name* and the *message_body* can be omitted. The former can be omitted if the message is of the default type (requiring no validation); the *message_body* should be omitted if the message type is EMPTY. Otherwise, the message body is enclosed in parentheses, and it can contain any data, including binary data.

Retrieving Messages from a Queue

To retrieve a message from a queue, use the RECEIVE statement:

```
RECEIVE [TOP n]
  column_name [, ...]
  FROM queue_name
  INTO table_variable
  [WHERE conversation_handle = dialog_handle |
       conversation_group_id = conversation_group_id]
```

This retrieves the messages in the queue as rows into the supplied table variable. You can optionally limit the messages retrieved by specifying the maximum number of messages in the TOP clause and by restricting the messages returned to a specific conversation or conversation group.

The information about each message is contained in columns in the returned result set, and you specify the information you want to retrieve just as you do for a SELECT statement: by including the column names in the RECEIVE statement. The full list of columns in the result set returned from the RECEIVE command is shown in Table 9-1.

Table 9-1. *Columns Returned from the RECEIVE Command*

Column	Datatype	Description
status	tinyint	The status of the message. This will always be 0 for a message that has been retrieved. The full list of values is as follows: 0: Ready 1: Received message 2: Not yet complete 3: Retained sent message
queuing_order	bigint	The number of the message within the queue.
conversation_group_id	uniqueidentifier	The ID of the conversation group to which this message belongs.
conversation_handle	uniqueidentifier	The dialog handle for the conversation to which this message belongs.
message_sequence_number	bigint	The sequence number of the message within the conversation.
service_name	nvarchar(512)	The name of the conversation target service.
service_id	int	The ID of the conversation target service.
service_contract_name	nvarchar(256)	The name of the contract for the conversation.

Continued

Table 9-1. *Continued*

Column	Datatype	Description
service_contract_id	int	The ID of the contract for the conversation.
message_type_name	nvarchar(256)	The name of the message type for the message.
message_type_id	int	The ID of the message type for the message.
validation	nchar(2)	The type of validation used for the message. The possible values are as follows: E: Empty N: None X: XML
message_body	varbinary(MAX)	The body of the message.
message_id	uniqueidentifier	The ID of the message.

By default, the RECEIVE statement will return an empty result set if no messages are present in the queue. You can alter this behavior by wrapping the statement in a WAITFOR statement:

```
WAITFOR
(
    RECEIVE ...
) [, TIMEOUT timeout]
```

This causes the RECEIVE statement to wait for the timeout period (in milliseconds) until a message arrives. If the timeout period expires, an empty result set will be returned. To wait indefinitely, omit the TIMEOUT clause, or specify a value of –1.

Ending a Conversation

When your application wants to close the conversation, both sides should explicitly end the dialog:

```
END CONVERSATION dialog_handle
    [WITH ERROR = error_code DESCRIPTION = error_description]
    [WITH CLEANUP]
```

Use the WITH ERROR clause if you want to throw an error, passing in an error code (of type int) and description (of type nvarchar(3000)). This will cause Service Broker to send an Error message to the queue, which can then be handled by the other participant in the conversation. If the END CONVERSATION command is issued without a WITH ERROR clause, Service Broker places an End Dialog message on the queue to inform the remote service that the conversation is closed. However, the remote application still needs to end its side of the conversation. Once it has done this, Service Broker will remove all messages belonging to this conversation from the queue.

The WITH CLEANUP clause is used to remove any messages from a queue when it isn't possible to end the conversation normally, usually because the remote service isn't available. If the conversation is ended WITH CLEANUP, the remote service isn't informed that the conversation is ending.

Conversation Timeouts

We stated earlier in the chapter that a Service Broker application can issue one conversation timer per dialog, which will cause Service Broker to place a Dialog Timer message in the queue after a specific timeout period has elapsed. To do this, use the BEGIN CONVERSATION TIMER command:

```
BEGIN CONVERSATION TIMER(dialog_handle)
    TIMEOUT = timeout
```

Here, *dialog_handle* is the ID for the conversation that the timer will be placed on, and *timeout* is the timeout period in seconds, after which the message will be placed in the queue.

A Simple Service Broker Example

The easiest way to see how these components relate to each other is to walk through an example. To demonstrate the concepts, we'll start with a very simple example. We use only one database, although Service Broker has been designed to aid asynchronous communications distributed across multiple databases. This Service Broker application will process vacation requests from employees. Employees will call a stored procedure, passing in their employee ID number, their e-mail address, the number of hours of vacation they want to take, and the start time and date they plan to take the vacation. This will send a message to a specially created queue. When this message is processed, you will merely perform some rudimentary validation, and then use Database Mail (which itself uses Service Broker) to send an e-mail to the employee, indicating whether the request was successful.

The Service Broker application will have the following components:

- A MESSAGE TYPE to represent the XML-formatted messages that will be stored on the queue.

- An XML SCHEMA COLLECTION that will be used to validate messages as they arrive on the queue.

- A QUEUE to store the vacation requests before they are processed.

- A CONTRACT to define the message types that can be stored on the queue and the services that can send messages to the queue.

- One SERVICE that acts as the endpoint that initiates a conversation by sending a message to a queue and another that acts as the endpoint for retrieving messages from the queue.

- A stored procedure that will be called by an end user (or, more likely, an application) to make a vacation request.

- Another stored procedure for processing messages on the queue. This will be called automatically by Service Broker whenever messages arrive on the queue.

Before creating these objects, you need to enable Service Broker in the AdventureWorks database:

```
ALTER DATABASE AdventureWorks SET ENABLE_BROKER;
```

You then need to create a master key for the AdventureWorks database, which Service Broker will use as the session key for the conversation:

```
CREATE MASTER KEY
ENCRYPTION BY PASSWORD = 'sl38!Gk$^&wMv';
```

Next, create the schema that you will use to validate the holiday requests:

```
CREATE XML SCHEMA COLLECTION
[http://schemas.apress.com/AcceleratedSQL2008/HolidayRequestSchema]
AS N'<?xml version="1.0" ?>
<xs:schema xmlns:xs="http://www.w3.org/2001/XMLSchema">
    <xs:element name="vacationRequest">
        <xs:complexType>
            <xs:sequence minOccurs="1" maxOccurs="1">
                <xs:element name="employeeId" type="xs:integer" />
                <xs:element name="email" type="xs:string" />
                <xs:element name="startTime" type="xs:dateTime" />
                <xs:element name="hours" type="xs:integer" />
            </xs:sequence>
        </xs:complexType>
    </xs:element>
</xs:schema>';
```

Note that, as its name suggests, an XML SCHEMA COLLECTION object can hold more than one schema, so you can validate an XML document against multiple schemas in one go. In this case, however, you just need to ensure that your messages meet the simple criteria laid out in this single schema. Also notice that, following Microsoft's practice, you've named the schema using a Uniform Resource Name (URN).

This schema specifies that each message will consist of a root element called <vacationRequest>, which contains one instance each of the child elements <employeeId>, <email>, <startTime>, and <hours>. For example, the following message requests one day's vacation (8 hours) starting on July 26, 2004, for the employee with an ID of 140 and e-mail address of laura1@adventure-works.com:

```
<?xml version="1.0" encoding="utf-16"?>
<vacationRequest>
    <employeeId>140</employeeId>
    <email>laura1@adventure-works.com</email>
    <startTime>2004-08-01T09:00:00+00:00</startTime>
    <hours>8</hours>
</vacationRequest>
```

Now you can create a Message Type object from this schema collection:

```
CREATE MESSAGE TYPE [http://schemas.apress.com/AcceleratedSQL2008/HolidayRequest]
VALIDATION = VALID_XML WITH SCHEMA COLLECTION
    [http://schemas.apress.com/AcceleratedSQL2008/HolidayRequestSchema];
```

You want validation to occur against our schema, so you set VALIDATION to VALID_XML WITH SCHEMA COLLECTION, passing in the name of the XML SCHEMA COLLECTION object that you've just created.

Next, you define the contract for the conversations that will take place between your initiating service and receiving service:

```
CREATE CONTRACT
    [http://schemas.apress.com/AcceleratedSQL2008/HolidayRequestContract]
(
    [http://schemas.apress.com/AcceleratedSQL2008/HolidayRequest]
    SENT BY INITIATOR
);
```

This contract stipulates that only the initiating service will be sending messages to the queue and that it will send messages of only your HolidayRequest type.

Receiving Service

Now you need to define the two services that will be used to send and process the messages. First, you'll create a stored procedure to handle any messages that are sent to the queue. Once you have the message, you'll just close the conversation, as you don't want to send any information back to the initiating service.

As stated at the outset, the processing you'll perform is minimal. You'll simply check whether the employee has enough hours of vacation entitlement left (assuming an annual entitlement of 20 days or 160 hours, which we just made up for the purposes of this example), and that the employee has given enough notice (at least one week in advance of the desired vacation start date). You then e-mail the employee, either stating that the request has been granted or giving the reason for rejecting it.

```
CREATE PROCEDURE usp_ProcessHolidayRequest
AS
DECLARE @msgBody    XML(
    [http://schemas.apress.com/AcceleratedSQL2008/HolidayRequestSchema]),
        @convID     uniqueidentifier,
```

```
        @email      varchar(50),
        @employeeID int,
        @hours      int,
        @startTime  DateTime,
        @hoursTaken int,
        @msgType    nvarchar(256);

DECLARE @msgTable TABLE
(
    message_body          varbinary(max),
    conversation_handle uniqueidentifier,
    message_type_name    nvarchar(256)
);
BEGIN
    WAITFOR
    (
        RECEIVE TOP (1) message_body, conversation_handle, message_type_name
        FROM HolidayRequestQueue
        INTO @msgTable
    ), TIMEOUT 2000;

    SET @msgBody = (SELECT TOP (1) CAST(message_body AS XML) FROM @msgTable);
    SET @convID = (SELECT TOP (1) conversation_handle FROM @msgTable);
    SET @msgType = (SELECT TOP (1) message_type_name FROM @msgTable);
    END CONVERSATION @convID;

    IF @msgType = 'http://schemas.apress.com/AcceleratedSQL2008/HolidayRequest'
        BEGIN
            SET @email = @msgBody.value('data(//email)[1]', 'varchar(50)');
            SET @hours = @msgBody.value('data(//hours)[1]', 'int');
            SET @startTime = @msgBody.value('data(//startTime)[1]', 'datetime');
            SET @employeeID = @msgBody.value('data(//employeeId)[1]', 'int');
            SET @hoursTaken = (SELECT VacationHours FROM HumanResources.Employee
                                WHERE EmployeeID = @employeeID);

            IF @hoursTaken + @hours > 160
                EXEC msdb.dbo.sp_send_dbmail
                    @profile_name = 'Default Profile',
                    @recipients = @email,
                    @subject = 'Vacation request',
                    @body = 'Your request for vacation has been refused because you
have insufficient hours remaining of your holiday entitlement.';
            ELSE IF @startTime < DATEADD(Week, 1, GETDATE())
                EXEC msdb.dbo.sp_send_dbmail
                    @profile_name = 'Default Profile',
                    @recipients = @email,
                    @subject = 'Vacation request',
                    @body = 'Your request for vacation has been refused because you
have not given sufficient notice. Please request holiday at least a week in
advance.';
            ELSE
                BEGIN
                    UPDATE HumanResources.Employee
                        SET VacationHours = VacationHours + @hours;
                    EXEC msdb.dbo.sp_send_dbmail
                        @profile_name = 'Default Profile',
                        @recipients = @email,
```

```
                    @subject = 'Vacation request',
                    @body = 'Your request for vacation has been granted.';
            END
        END
END
```

The first task here is to retrieve the message from the queue, which you do with a `RECEIVE` statement:

```
WAITFOR (
        RECEIVE TOP (1) message_body, conversation_handle, message_type_name
        FROM HolidayRequestQueue
        INTO @msgTable
), TIMEOUT 2000;
```

Notice that you wrap the `RECEIVE` statement in a `WAITFOR` statement to ensure that the procedure will wait for the specified `TIMEOUT` value (in milliseconds, so 2 seconds in this case) for a message to arrive. The `RECEIVE` clause retrieves the body and type of the first message in the queue and the ID of the conversation it belongs to into a table variable called `@msgTable`.

Once you have the message shredded into a table variable, you can extract the message body from it and cast it to the XML datatype, and you can also retrieve the message type to ensure you have the right sort of message, and the dialog handle, which you need to close the conversation:

```
SET @msgBody = (SELECT TOP (1) CAST(message_body AS XML) FROM @msgTable);
SET @convID = (SELECT TOP (1) conversation_handle FROM @msgTable);
SET @msgType = (SELECT TOP (1) message_type_name FROM @msgTable);
END CONVERSATION @convID;
```

Then you check that the message is of the correct type. If so, you use XQuery and the `value()` method of the XML datatype to extract the individual values (the employee's ID and e-mail address, and the start time and duration of the planned vacation) into local variables.

Next, you query the `HumanResources.Employee` table to see how many hours of vacation the employee has already taken, and perform checks to determine whether or not to grant the vacation. If the vacation is granted, you update the `VacationHours` of that employee and e-mail the employee to confirm you're granting the request; otherwise, you just e-mail the employee stating the reason why you're refusing the request.

■**Note** Database Mail must be enabled, or this procedure won't compile. See Chapter 8 for information about installing Database Mail.

Once you've defined the message type for your service and the stored procedure that will process the messages, you can create the queue to hold the messages:

```
CREATE QUEUE HolidayRequestQueue
WITH
    STATUS = ON,
    RETENTION = OFF,
    ACTIVATION
    (
        STATUS = ON,
        PROCEDURE_NAME = usp_ProcessHolidayRequest,
        MAX_QUEUE_READERS = 5,
        EXECUTE AS SELF
    );
```

You set the queue to activate immediately and not to retain messages when they are retrieved by your stored procedure. The `ACTIVATION` clause ensures that your service program will execute whenever a message is sent to the queue.

You're now ready to create the service itself:

```
CREATE SERVICE
  [http://schemas.apress.com/AcceleratedSQL2008/HolidayRequestProcessorService]
ON QUEUE HolidayRequestQueue
(
  [http://schemas.apress.com/AcceleratedSQL2008/HolidayRequestContract]
);
```

The service simply acts as a link between the queue and one or more contracts, so no new information is introduced here, and the syntax is self-explanatory.

Initiating Service

You've now arranged the processing of messages in the queue, but as yet, you don't have any way to send messages to it. To do this, you need to create another service and a procedure that initiates a dialog and sends a message to the queue when an employee requests a vacation.

The code to create the initiator service is identical (except for the name) to the code for the processor service:

```
CREATE SERVICE
  [http://schemas.apress.com/AcceleratedSQL2008/HolidayRequestInitiatorService]
ON QUEUE HolidayRequestQueue
(
  [http://schemas.apress.com/AcceleratedSQL2008/HolidayRequestContract]
);
```

Again, you're simply associating the `HolidayRequestContract` with your queue.

The last task is to create the stored procedure that will send a message to the queue:

```
CREATE PROCEDURE usp_RequestHoliday
    @employeeId int,
    @email varchar(50),
    @hours int,
    @startDate varchar(50)
AS
DECLARE @dialogHandle uniqueidentifier,
        @body           nvarchar(1000),
        @msg            XML,
        @date           nvarchar(100)
BEGIN
    SET @body = N'<?xml version="1.0"?>
<vacationRequest>
    <employeeId>' + CAST(@employeeID AS varchar) + '</employeeId>
    <email>' + @email + '</email>
    <startTime>' + @startDate + '</startTime>
    <hours>' + CAST(@hours AS nvarchar) + '</hours>
</vacationRequest>';
    SET @msg = CAST(@body AS XML)
```

```
  BEGIN DIALOG CONVERSATION @dialogHandle
    FROM SERVICE
  [http://schemas.apress.com/AcceleratedSQL2008/HolidayRequestInitiatorService]
    TO SERVICE
    'http://schemas.apress.com/AcceleratedSQL2008/HolidayRequestProcessorService'
    ON CONTRACT
    [http://schemas.apress.com/AcceleratedSQL2008/HolidayRequestContract];

  SEND ON CONVERSATION @dialogHandle
    MESSAGE TYPE [http://schemas.apress.com/AcceleratedSQL2008/HolidayRequest]
    (@msg);
  END CONVERSATION @dialogHandle;
END
```

This procedure takes four parameters—the information that you'll pass into the message. You use this information to build an XML document that conforms to the schema you specified for your message type as nvarchar, and then cast this to the XML datatype.

Now you're ready to start the conversation. To do this, use the BEGIN DIALOG [CONVERSATION] statement, specifying the initiating and target services and the contract, and retaining a reference to the ID for the conversation. You use this ID to send a message to the remote service, specifying your HolidayRequest message type and passing in the XML-typed variable that contains the body of the message. Once you've sent this, your stored procedure has done its work, so you just close the conversation.

This completes our simple Service Broker example. To test it, execute this stored procedure, for example:

```
EXEC usp_RequestHoliday 140, 'someone@somewhere.com', 8,
                        '2004-08-01T09:00:00+00:00'
```

Note that, to make testing much easier, the e-mail address is passed in separately, instead of being looked up in the database. This means you can supply your own e-mail address instead of using the one that corresponds to the EmployeeID you pass in. Also, note that the start date is passed in as a string in XSD dateTime format ('yyyy-mm-ddThh:mm:ss+timezone offset').

Service Broker Routing and Security

Although we demonstrated the fundamental concepts of Service Broker using a single database on a single instance of SQL Server, Service Broker is designed to be able to communicate between different instances. At this point, security also becomes an issue, because you need to ensure that you can authenticate users from another instance of SQL Server. And since you might be transferring sensitive data over the network, the data sent between the two services may need to be encrypted.

Creating Distributed Service Broker Applications

You need to do three extra things to create a secure distributed Service Broker application:

- Create a Service Broker endpoint in each instance to allow Service Broker to listen for incoming messages and send messages outside the instance.

- Create a route to tell Service Broker where to find the remote service.

- Create a Remote Service Binding to provide the security credentials that the initiating service will provide so that the remote service can authenticate it.

You'll also need to create certificates and database master keys in order to provide the credentials that will be used for authentication to the remote service and for encryption of the messages sent over the network. Service Broker distinguishes between two types of security: *transport security*, which is used to specify which Service Broker instances can communicate with each other, and *dialog security*, which is used to encrypt messages in a conversation and operates at the user level. You specify the type of transport security when you create the Service Broker endpoint. Dialog security is configured using Remote Service Bindings.

Creating a Service Broker Endpoint

The syntax for creating a Service Broker endpoint is as follows:

```
CREATE ENDPOINT endpoint_name
STATE = STARTED | STOPPED | DISABLED
AS TCP
(
   LISTENER_PORT = port_number,
   LISTENER_IP = ALL | (ip_address)
)
FOR SERVICE_BROKER
(
   AUTHENTICATION = authentication_options,
   ENCRYPTION = DISABLED | SUPPORTED | REQUIRED
      ALGORITH algorithm,
   MESSAGE_FORWARDING = ENABLED | DISABLED,
   MESSAGE_FORWARD_SIZE = forward_size
)
```

All the Service Broker subclauses are optional, as is the LISTENER_IP subclause. If this subclause is omitted, Service Broker will listen on all available IP addresses. If an IP address is given, it can be either a traditional four-part IP address, or an IP version 6 (IPv6) address. The default TCP port for Service Broker is 4022.

The AUTHENTICATION subclause allows you to specify whether to use Windows authentication (the default) or a named certificate to provide credentials to the remote service. It takes the following form:

```
AUTHENTICATION = WINDOWS [NTLM | KERBEROS | NEGOTIATE] |
                 CERTIFICATE cert_name |
                 WINDOWS [NTLM | KERBEROS | NEGOTIATE] CERTIFICATE cert_name |
                 CERTIFICATE cert_name WINDOWS [NTLM | KERBEROS | NEGOTIATE]
```

If you choose Windows authentication, you can also specify whether to use the NTLM or KERBEROS protocol, or let Windows NEGOTIATE which protocol to use. The default is NEGOTIATE. If you use a named certificate, that certificate must be a valid certificate in the master database, it must be signed with the database master key, and the current date must be between its start and expiration dates. If both Windows and a certificate are specified, Service Broker will attempt to use the first authentication method in the list, and if that fails, it will try the second one.

The ENCRYPTION options are fairly self-explanatory. If it's DISABLED, Service Broker will never encrypt dialogs; if it's REQUIRED, dialogs will always be encrypted; and if it's SUPPORTED, dialogs will be encrypted only when the remote endpoint supports encryption. If encryption is used, a Remote Service Binding *must* exist in the database for the remote service, or the dialog will fail.

If you're using encryption, you can also specify the algorithm(s) that will be supported. This can be one of the following:

- RC4 (the default)
- AES
- RC4 AES
- AES RC4

As with the authentication options, if two algorithms are listed, preference will be given to the one listed first.

Finally, you can also specify whether or not Service Broker will forward messages received by this endpoint to another address (MESSAGE_FORWARDING = ENABLED) or simply discard any messages it receives that are intended for another instance. If message forwarding is enabled, you can additionally specify the maximum space (in megabytes) that may be used to store messages for forwarding.

Creating Routes

Service Broker uses routes to determine where to send messages destined for a particular service that isn't hosted on the current instance of SQL Server. If the remote endpoint supports message forwarding, the route doesn't need to point to the actual destination—it can simply point to the next hop, and from there it will be forwarded using another route.

The syntax for creating a route is as follows:

```
CREATE ROUTE route_name
WITH
    SERVICE_NAME = remote_service_name,
    BROKER_INSTANCE = uniqueidentifier,
    LIFETIME = route_lifetime,
    ADDRESS = next_hop_address,
    MIRROR_ADDRESS = mirror_address
```

The only option that's actually required is the address for the next hop. This takes the form 'TCP://hostaddress:port', where hostaddress is the hostname, IP address, or NetBIOS name of the machine that hosts the remote Service Broker instance, and port is the TCP port number on which the remote Service Broker endpoint is listening. You can also specify 'LOCAL' for the local SQL Server instance or 'TRANSPORT' for an address specified in the name of the remote service. If 'TRANSPORT' is used, you cannot specify the service name or broker instance ID in the CREATE ROUTE command.

If the database that hosts the remote service is mirrored, you should also specify the MIRROR_ADDRESS, to ensure that messages will be sent to the mirror database if the other database can't be reached. If the MIRROR_ADDRESS is specified, you *must* include the service name and the broker instance ID.

The SERVICE_NAME is the name of the remote service that this route is used to send messages to. If included, this must be exactly the same as the name of the service in the remote database. However, it can also be omitted. If you omit the SERVICE_NAME, this route will match all services, but it will have a lower priority than routes that name a service, so it won't be used to send messages to a service that is explicitly associated with a specific route.

The BROKER_INSTANCE specifies the ID of the remote instance of Service Broker that this route points to. You can find this ID by running the following query in the remote database:

```
SELECT service_broker_guid
FROM sys.databases
WHERE database_id = DB_ID()
```

Finally, the LIFETIME clause allows you to stipulate the number of seconds for which this route will remain active. After this time has elapsed, SQL Server will discard the route. By default, routes never expire.

Creating Remote Service Bindings

The last new Service Broker object we need to look at is the Remote Service Binding, which contains the security credentials that Service Broker uses to connect to a remote service (Remote Service Bindings are never used to connect to a service in the local instance).

The syntax for the CREATE REMOTE SERVICE BINDING command is as follows:

```
CREATE REMOTE SERVICE BINDING binding_name
   TO SERVICE remote_service_name
   WITH USER = user_name, ANONYMOUS = ON | OFF
```

This creates a binding between the specified service and the given database user (or application role), so that whenever Service Broker connects to the service, it will exchange the session encryption key for the dialog using a certificate associated with the specified database principal.

The only optional part of this statement is the ANONYMOUS clause, which allows you to indicate whether Service Broker should connect to the remote service as the specified user (ANONYMOUS = OFF) or it should connect as a member of the public fixed server role. The default is OFF.

Distributed Service Broker Example

Now that you've seen how to create the new objects you'll need for dialog security and message routing, let's build a more complex application that uses these objects to communicate between services in separate instances of SQL Server on different machines. This example builds on the previous vacation request example, but as well as adding an extra service to demonstrate routing and dialog security, you'll also combine two conversations into a conversation group to exercise this functionality.

As in the previous example, the application will be started by calling a stored procedure within the AdventureWorks database that sends a message to a VacationRequestService including the ID and e-mail address of the employee, and the start time and number of hours of the planned vacation. This fires the service program stored procedure, which starts off two new Service Broker conversations: one to request the number of hours' leave remaining for that employee and another requesting the number of active projects that that employee will be working on over the period. This latter service is hosted in a Projects database, on another machine. These services send messages back to the processing service, and another stored procedure is run on the queue for this service to retrieve the response messages and send an e-mail to the employee, depending on the responses from the two services. Figure 9-2 shows the architecture for this application. (Admittedly, this is somewhat more complex than it really needs to be, but that's the only way to see more of Service Broker's functionality and to understand how services communicate with each other in more realistic scenarios.)

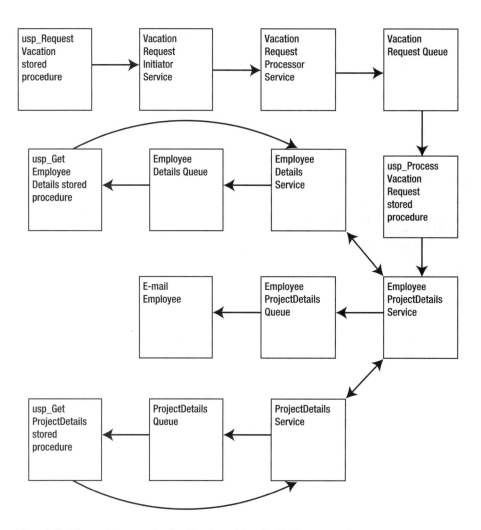

Figure 9-2. *The architecture for the distributed Service Broker example*

As this application will be distributed over two machines, we'll look at the objects that need to be created on each machine in turn. The majority of the objects will be in the instance that hosts the AdventureWorks database (in this case, this machine is called ecspi.julianskinner.local), so we'll look at the Projects database (on our example system, this is on a machine called peiriantprawf. julianskinner.local) before we tackle AdventureWorks. However, first you need to set up the Service Broker endpoints on the two machines.

Setting Up the Service Broker Endpoints

You'll use certificates to authenticate between the two instances, so before you create the Service Broker endpoint for the instance that will host the Projects database, you need to create a certificate that is signed with the master key for the master database:

```
USE master
GO
```

```
CREATE MASTER KEY ENCRYPTION BY PASSWORD = 'gs53&"f"!385';
GO

CREATE CERTIFICATE projEndpointCert
WITH SUBJECT = 'peiriantprawf.julianskinner.local',
    START_DATE = '01/01/2008',
    EXPIRY_DATE = '01/01/2009'
ACTIVE FOR BEGIN_DIALOG = ON;
GO
```

When you create a new certificate without specifying a password or a file to take the key from, it will be signed with the database master key.

Now you can create the endpoint:

```
CREATE ENDPOINT ServiceBrokerEndpoint
    STATE = STARTED
    AS TCP (LISTENER_PORT = 4022)
    FOR SERVICE_BROKER
    (
        AUTHENTICATION = CERTIFICATE projEndpointCert,
        ENCRYPTION = SUPPORTED
    );
```

You start the endpoint listening using the STATE clause and use the default TCP port of 4022. If your machine has a firewall, you'll need to allow traffic through this port. You'll use the certificate you've just created to authenticate, and you'll support but not require encryption of the dialogs over this endpoint. You won't allow anonymous connections, so you don't include an ANONYMOUS subclause in the SERVICE_BROKER options.

In order for the two instances to authenticate each other, you need to install this certificate in the instance that hosts AdventureWorks and also create a certificate there that you will install in the Projects instance. First, save the certificate you just created to a file so you can copy it to the AdventureWorks machine:

```
BACKUP CERTIFICATE projEndpointCert TO FILE =
        'C:\Apress\AcceleratedSQL2008\Chapter9\projEndpointCert.cer';
```

Now copy this file to the AdventureWorks machine and install it into that instance of SQL Server:

```
USE master
GO

CREATE CERTIFICATE projEndpointCert
FROM FILE = 'C:\Apress\AcceleratedSQL2008\Chapter9\projEndpointCert.cer';
```

Next, you need to create the Service Broker endpoint for this instance:

```
CREATE MASTER KEY ENCRYPTION BY PASSWORD = '45Gme*3^&fwu';
GO

CREATE CERTIFICATE awEndpointCert
WITH SUBJECT = 'ecspi.julianskinner.local',
    START_DATE = '01/01/2008',
    EXPIRY_DATE = '01/01/2009'
ACTIVE FOR BEGIN_DIALOG = ON;
GO

CREATE ENDPOINT ServiceBrokerEndpoint
    STATE = STARTED
```

```
AS TCP (LISTENER_PORT=4022)
FOR SERVICE_BROKER
(
    AUTHENTICATION = CERTIFICATE awEndpointCert,
    ENCRYPTION = SUPPORTED
);
```

You can now grant permissions to the remote service to connect to this endpoint. To do this, you need to create a login from the certificate and then grant that login CONNECT permission on the endpoint:

```
CREATE LOGIN sbLogin
FROM CERTIFICATE projEndpointCert;
GO

GRANT CONNECT ON ENDPOINT::ServiceBrokerEndpoint TO sbLogin;
GO
```

You need to repeat these steps in the Projects instance, so you'll back up this certificate to a file:

```
BACKUP CERTIFICATE awEndpointCert
TO FILE = 'C:\Apress\AcceleratedSQL2008\Chapter9\awEndpointCert.cer';
```

Then you'll copy the awEndpointCert.cer file generated over to the Projects machine, install it in SQL Server, create a login from the certificate, and grant it permission to connect to the Service Broker endpoint:

```
CREATE CERTIFICATE awEndpointCert
FROM FILE = 'C:\Apress\AcceleratedSQL2008\Chapter9\awEndpointCert.cer';
GO

CREATE LOGIN sbLogin
FROM CERTIFICATE awEndpointCert;
GO

GRANT CONNECT ON ENDPOINT::ServiceBrokerEndpoint
TO sbLogin;
GO
```

You now have certificates installed in both instances that allow the two Service Broker instances to authenticate each other, so they can make the initial connection. This provides transport security, but it doesn't yet allow messages to be sent with dialog security. To do this, you need to create yet more certificates—this time associated with database users—and again install these in both instances. But first, you need to create the Projects database.

The Projects Database and ProjectDetailsService

You've set up the endpoints, and now you can start to create the database-level objects. As mentioned earlier, you need to create far fewer objects in the Projects database, so you'll start there.

The Projects Database

The Projects database consists of three tables: a project table with columns for the project's name, start date, and end date; an employee table that contains the first and last names of the employee and the employee's e-mail address; and a projectemployee table that is used to join the other two tables in a many-to-many relationship. You'll also add one row to each table, so you have some data to play with. The e-mail address you use for the employee should be a real address from which you can receive mail:

```
CREATE DATABASE Projects;
GO

USE Projects
GO

ALTER DATABASE Projects SET ENABLE_BROKER;
GO

CREATE TABLE Project
(
   ProjectID   int IDENTITY PRIMARY KEY,
   ProjectName nvarchar(100),
   StartDate   datetime,
   EndDate     datetime
);

CREATE TABLE Employee
(
   EmployeeID  int IDENTITY PRIMARY KEY,
   FirstName   nvarchar(256),
   LastName    nvarchar(256),
   Email       nvarchar(512)
);

CREATE TABLE ProjectEmployee
(
   ProjectID   int FOREIGN KEY REFERENCES Project(ProjectID),
   EmployeeID  int FOREIGN KEY REFERENCES Employee(EmployeeID)
);
GO

INSERT INTO Project VALUES
   ('Accelerated SQL Server 2008', '01/01/2008', '10/15/2008');
INSERT INTO Employee VALUES ('John', 'Doe', 'JohnDoe@apress.com');
INSERT INTO ProjectEmployee VALUES (1, 1);
GO
```

The ProjectDetailsService

Now you can start to create the ProjectDetailsService. First, you'll create the message types handled by this service and their associated schemas. There will be one message type for the request, which is basically very similar to the HolidayRequest type in the previous example, except that you don't include the EmployeeID, as the IDs in the Projects database are unrelated to those in AdventureWorks. The second message type is sent in response and will contain a <projectResponse> root element, under which will be an <activeProjects> element. The <activeProjects> element will contain the number of projects the employee is working on over the time spanned by the planned vacation, as well as the e-mail address and the start time, which you return in the response so that the procedure that processes the responses has access to this data:

```
CREATE XML SCHEMA COLLECTION
    [http://schemas.apress.com/AcceleratedSQL2008/ProjectRequestSchema]
AS N'<?xml version="1.0" ?>
<xs:schema xmlns:xs="http://www.w3.org/2001/XMLSchema">
   <xs:element name="projectRequest">
     <xs:complexType>
```

```
            <xs:sequence minOccurs="1" maxOccurs="1">
                <xs:element name="email" type="xs:string" />
                <xs:element name="startTime" type="xs:dateTime" />
                <xs:element name="hours" type="xs:integer" />
            </xs:sequence>
        </xs:complexType>
    </xs:element>
</xs:schema>';

CREATE XML SCHEMA COLLECTION
    [http://schemas.apress.com/AcceleratedSQL2008/ProjectResponseSchema]
AS N'<?xml version="1.0" ?>
<xs:schema xmlns:xs="http://www.w3.org/2001/XMLSchema">
    <xs:element name="projectResponse">
        <xs:complexType>
            <xs:sequence minOccurs="1" maxOccurs="1">
                <xs:element name="email" type="xs:string" />
                <xs:element name="startTime" type="xs:dateTime" />
                <xs:element name="activeProjects" type="xs:integer" />
            </xs:sequence>
        </xs:complexType>
    </xs:element>
</xs:schema>';

CREATE MESSAGE TYPE
    [http://schemas.apress.com/AcceleratedSQL2008/ProjectRequestMessage]
VALIDATION = VALID_XML WITH SCHEMA COLLECTION
    [http://schemas.apress.com/AcceleratedSQL2008/ProjectRequestSchema];

CREATE MESSAGE TYPE
    [http://schemas.apress.com/AcceleratedSQL2008/ProjectResponseMessage]
VALIDATION = VALID_XML WITH SCHEMA COLLECTION
    [http://schemas.apress.com/AcceleratedSQL2008/ProjectResponseSchema];
```

Next, you'll create the contract for the service:

```
CREATE CONTRACT
    [http://schemas.apress.com/AcceleratedSQL2008/ProjectServiceContract]
(
    [http://schemas.apress.com/AcceleratedSQL2008/ProjectRequestMessage]
        SENT BY INITIATOR,
    [http://schemas.apress.com/AcceleratedSQL2008/ProjectResponseMessage]
    SENT BY TARGET
);
```

This stipulates that the only messages that can be sent on this conversation are the ProjectRequestMessage, sent only by the initiator, and the ProjectReponseMessage, sent only by the receiving service.

The next task is to write the activation stored procedure, which will be called whenever a message arrives on the queue:

```
CREATE PROCEDURE usp_GetProjectDetailsForEmployee
AS
DECLARE @msgBody      XML(
            [http://schemas.apress.com/AcceleratedSQL2008/ProjectRequestSchema]),
        @convID       uniqueidentifier,
        @email        varchar(512),
        @hours        int,
```

```
        @startTime      datetime,
        @endTime        datetime,
        @projectCount   int,
        @response       XML(
            [http://schemas.apress.com/AcceleratedSQL2008/ProjectResponseSchema]),
        @respText       nvarchar(1000),
        @msgType        nvarchar(256);

DECLARE @msgTable TABLE
(
    message_body        varbinary(max),
    conversation_handle uniqueidentifier,
    message_type_name   nvarchar(256)
);
BEGIN
    WAITFOR
    (
        RECEIVE TOP (1) message_body, conversation_handle, message_type_name
        FROM ProjectServiceQueue INTO @msgTable
    ), TIMEOUT 2000;

    SET @msgBody = (SELECT TOP (1) CAST(message_body AS XML) FROM @msgTable);
    SET @msgType = (SELECT TOP (1) message_type_name FROM @msgTable);
    SET @convID = (SELECT TOP (1) conversation_handle FROM @msgTable);
    IF @msgType =
        'http://schemas.apress.com/AcceleratedSQL2008/ProjectRequestMessage'
    BEGIN
        SET @email = @msgBody.value('data(//email)[1]', 'varchar(50)');
        SET @hours = @msgBody.value('data(//hours)[1]', 'int');
        SET @startTime = @msgBody.value('data(//startTime)[1]', 'datetime');
        SET @endTime = DATEADD(week, @hours/40, @startTime)

        SET @projectCount = (SELECT COUNT(*)
        FROM Project p
            INNER JOIN ProjectEmployee pe
            ON p.ProjectID = pe.ProjectID
                INNER JOIN Employee e
                ON pe.EmployeeID = e.EmployeeID
        WHERE e.Email = @email
            AND (p.StartDate < @startTime AND p.EndDate > @startTime)
            OR (p.StartDate < @endTime AND p.EndDate > @endTime)
            OR (p.StartDate > @startTime AND p.EndDate < @endTime));

        SET @respText = N'<?xml version="1.0"?>
<projectResponse>
    <email>' + @email + '</email>
    <startTime>' + CONVERT(nvarchar, @startTime, 126) + '+00:00</startTime>
    <activeProjects>' + CAST(@projectCount AS nvarchar) + '</activeProjects>
</projectResponse>';

        SET @response = CAST(@respText AS XML);
        SEND ON CONVERSATION @convID
            MESSAGE TYPE
                [http://schemas.apress.com/AcceleratedSQL2008/ProjectResponseMessage]
            (@response);
```

```
        END CONVERSATION @convID;
    END;
END;
GO
```

This isn't too different from the activation stored procedure from the first example. You retrieve the body of the first message on the queue and the ID for the conversation it belongs to, read the data into variables, and, if the message is of the correct type, use this to work out how many projects that employee will be working on at that time (using the e-mail address to identify the employee). Once you have that, you embed it in a ProjectDetailsResponseMessage and send the data back to the initiator service on the same conversation. Finally, you end the dialog.

Once you have the activation stored procedure, you can create the queue and the service:

```
CREATE QUEUE ProjectServiceQueue
WITH
    STATUS = ON,
    RETENTION = OFF,
    ACTIVATION
    (
        STATUS = ON,
        PROCEDURE_NAME = usp_GetProjectDetailsForEmployee,
        MAX_QUEUE_READERS = 5,
        EXECUTE AS SELF
    )

CREATE SERVICE [http://schemas.apress.com/AcceleratedSQL2008/ProjectDetailsService]
ON QUEUE ProjectServiceQueue
(
    [http://schemas.apress.com/AcceleratedSQL2008/ProjectServiceContract]
);
```

Next, you need to create a route, so that Service Broker knows where to find the initiating service to send replies to:

```
CREATE ROUTE EmployeeProjectDetailsRoute
WITH
    SERVICE_NAME =
        'http://schemas.apress.com/AcceleratedSQL2008/EmpProjDetailsService',
    ADDRESS = 'TCP://ecspi:4022';
GO
```

This associates the name of the remote service, which must be exactly the same as its name in the AdventureWorks database (service names are case sensitive), with a TCP address, including the name or IP address of the host machine and the port on which the SQL Server endpoint for the instance is configured to listen. For both instances, you use the default port 4022.

That almost completes your work on this instance of SQL Server, except for the little matter of dialog security, which we'll address shortly.

The AdventureWorks Side of the Conversation

We'll look at creating the EmpProjDetailsService that initiates the conversation with the ProjectDetailsService later, but for now, we need to create a couple of objects in the AdventureWorks database for the two services to be able to talk to each other.

First, create the message types and contract for the conversation in the AdventureWorks database, using exactly the same code as for the Projects database. It's important that the names of these objects are exactly the same in both databases, or the messages won't be sent to the queue.

Next, create the route so this instance of Service Broker will be able to find the `ProjectDetailsService`. The code for this is very similar to the code for the route you just created in the Projects database:

```
CREATE ROUTE ProjectDetailsRoute
WITH
    SERVICE_NAME =
                'http://schemas.apress.com/AcceleratedSQL2008/ProjectDetailsService',
    ADDRESS = 'TCP://peiriantprawf:4022';
GO
```

The EmployeeDetailsService

Next, let's turn our attention to the `EmployeeDetailsService`. The conversation architecture for this service is similar to that for the `ProjectDetailsProcessorService`, except that both initiating and target services will be in the same database. The application will send an `EmployeeRequestMessage` giving an employee ID and the number of hours requested, and the service will return an `EmployeeResponseMessage` indicating the total number of hours of vacation that employee will have taken if it's granted.

Start by creating the message types and associated XML schemas:

```
USE AdventureWorks
GO

CREATE XML SCHEMA COLLECTION
    [http://schemas.apress.com/AcceleratedSQL2008/EmployeeRequestSchema]
AS N'<?xml version="1.0" ?>
<xs:schema xmlns:xs="http://www.w3.org/2001/XMLSchema">
    <xs:element name="employeeRequest">
        <xs:complexType>
            <xs:sequence minOccurs="1" maxOccurs="1">
                <xs:element name="id" type="xs:integer" />
                <xs:element name="hours" type="xs:integer" />
            </xs:sequence>
        </xs:complexType>
    </xs:element>
</xs:schema>';

CREATE XML SCHEMA COLLECTION
    [http://schemas.apress.com/AcceleratedSQL2008/EmployeeResponseSchema]
AS N'<?xml version="1.0" ?>
<xs:schema xmlns:xs="http://www.w3.org/2001/XMLSchema">
    <xs:element name="employeeResponse">
        <xs:complexType>
            <xs:sequence minOccurs="1" maxOccurs="1">
                <xs:element name="id" type="xs:integer" />
                <xs:element name="hoursVacation" type="xs:integer" />
            </xs:sequence>
        </xs:complexType>
    </xs:element>
</xs:schema>';

CREATE MESSAGE TYPE
    [http://schemas.apress.com/AcceleratedSQL2008/EmployeeRequestMessage]
VALIDATION = VALID_XML WITH SCHEMA COLLECTION
    [http://schemas.apress.com/AcceleratedSQL2008/EmployeeRequestSchema];
```

```
CREATE MESSAGE TYPE
    [http://schemas.apress.com/AcceleratedSQL2008/EmployeeResponseMessage]
VALIDATION = VALID_XML WITH SCHEMA COLLECTION
    [http://schemas.apress.com/AcceleratedSQL2008/EmployeeResponseSchema];
```

The contract that conversations on this service will follow looks like this:

```
CREATE CONTRACT
    [http://schemas.apress.com/AcceleratedSQL2008/EmployeeServiceContract]
(
   [http://schemas.apress.com/AcceleratedSQL2008/EmployeeRequestMessage]
       SENT BY INITIATOR,
   [http://schemas.apress.com/AcceleratedSQL2008/EmployeeResponseMessage]
       SENT BY TARGET
);
```

The activation stored procedure for this service simply takes the employee ID from the top message in the queue and uses this to find the number of hours vacation taken by that employee. You then add this value to the number of hours of vacation request, wrap up the total in an EmployeeResponseMessage together with the employee's ID, and send it back to the initiating service:

```
CREATE PROCEDURE usp_GetHoursVacation
AS
DECLARE @msgBody      XML(
          [http://schemas.apress.com/AcceleratedSQL2008/EmployeeRequestSchema]),
        @response     XML(
          [http://schemas.apress.com/AcceleratedSQL2008/EmployeeResponseSchema]),
        @convID       uniqueidentifier,
        @empID        int,
        @hours        int,
        @hoursTaken   int,
        @totalHours   int,
        @msgType      nvarchar(256),
        @respText     nvarchar(1000);

DECLARE @msgTable TABLE
(
   message_body        varbinary(max),
   conversation_handle uniqueidentifier,
   message_type_name   nvarchar(256)
);
BEGIN
   WAITFOR
   (
      RECEIVE TOP (1) message_body, conversation_handle, message_type_name
      FROM EmployeeDetailsQueue INTO @msgTable
   ), TIMEOUT 2000;

   SET @msgBody = (SELECT TOP (1) CAST(message_body AS XML) FROM @msgTable);
   SET @convID = (SELECT TOP (1) conversation_handle FROM @msgTable);
   SET @msgType = (SELECT TOP (1) message_type_name FROM @msgTable);

   IF @msgType =
      'http://schemas.apress.com/AcceleratedSQL2008/EmployeeRequestMessage'
   BEGIN
      SET @empID = @msgBody.value('data(//id)[1]', 'int');
      SET @hours = @msgBody.value('data(//id)[1]', 'int');
      SET @hoursTaken = (SELECT VacationHours FROM HumanResources.Employee
```

```
                              WHERE EmployeeID = @empID);
      SET @totalHours = @hoursTaken + @hours;
      SET @respText = N'<?xml version="1.0"?>
<employeeResponse>
   <id>' + CAST(@empID AS nvarchar) + '</id>
   <hoursVacation>' + CAST(@totalHours AS nvarchar) + '</hoursVacation>
</employeeResponse>';

      SET @response = CAST(@respText AS XML);
      SEND ON CONVERSATION @convID
         MESSAGE TYPE
[http://schemas.apress.com/AcceleratedSQL2008/EmployeeResponseMessage]
         (@response);

      END CONVERSATION @convID;
   END;
END;
GO
```

Finally, you can create the queue and the service:

```
CREATE QUEUE EmployeeDetailsQueue
WITH
   STATUS = ON,
   RETENTION = OFF,
   ACTIVATION
   (
      STATUS = ON,
      PROCEDURE_NAME = usp_GetHoursVacation,
      MAX_QUEUE_READERS = 5,
      EXECUTE AS SELF
   )

CREATE SERVICE [http://schemas.apress.com/AcceleratedSQL2008/EmployeeDetailsService]
ON QUEUE EmployeeDetailsQueue
(
   [http://schemas.apress.com/AcceleratedSQL2008/EmployeeServiceContract]
);
```

The Main Service Program

The next task is to write another service that will initiate conversations with these two services within a conversation group. This conversation is similar to the one in the first example in this chapter, so the message type, schema, and contract should look pretty familiar:

```
CREATE XML SCHEMA COLLECTION
    [http://schemas.apress.com/AcceleratedSQL2008/VacationRequestSchema]
AS N'<?xml version="1.0" ?>
<xs:schema xmlns:xs="http://www.w3.org/2001/XMLSchema">
   <xs:element name="vacationRequest">
      <xs:complexType>
         <xs:sequence minOccurs="1" maxOccurs="1">
            <xs:element name="employeeId" type="xs:integer" />
            <xs:element name="email" type="xs:string" />
            <xs:element name="startTime" type="xs:dateTime" />
            <xs:element name="hours" type="xs:integer" />
         </xs:sequence>
      </xs:complexType>
```

```
    </xs:element>
</xs:schema>'

CREATE MESSAGE TYPE [http://schemas.apress.com/AcceleratedSQL2008/VacationRequest]
VALIDATION = VALID_XML WITH SCHEMA COLLECTION
    [http://schemas.apress.com/AcceleratedSQL2008/VacationRequestSchema]

CREATE CONTRACT
    [http://schemas.apress.com/AcceleratedSQL2008/VacationRequestContract]
(
    [http://schemas.apress.com/AcceleratedSQL2008/VacationRequest]
    SENT BY INITIATOR
)
GO
```

Then comes the activation stored procedure. Here, you read the first message from the VacationRequestQueue and read the data in the message into local variables. You begin a new dialog with the EmployeeDetailsService and send a message including the employee ID and the number of hours of vacation request. You then open another conversation within the same group to find out from the remote ProjectDetails service how many projects the employee will be working on during the vacation period. Including these two conversations in the same group ensures that Service Broker will match the two pieces of data for the same employee. As you've seen, these two services send response messages on the same conversations containing the data you requested. These messages will be placed on the queue associated with the EmpProjDetailsService and will be picked up later by another stored procedure. Therefore, you don't end the conversations at this time:

```
CREATE PROCEDURE usp_ProcessVacationRequest
AS
DECLARE @msgBody        XML(
            [http://schemas.apress.com/AcceleratedSQL2008/VacationRequestSchema]),
        @empRequest     XML(
            [http://schemas.apress.com/AcceleratedSQL2008/EmployeeRequestSchema]),
        @projRequest    XML(
            [http://schemas.apress.com/AcceleratedSQL2008/ProjectRequestSchema]),
        @empRequestBody  nvarchar(1000),
        @projRequestBody nvarchar(1000),
        @msgType         nvarchar(256),
        @convID          uniqueidentifier,
        @empConvID       uniqueidentifier,
        @projConvID      uniqueidentifier,
        @email           varchar(50),
        @employeeID      int,
        @hours           int,
        @startTime       DateTime;

DECLARE @msgTable TABLE
(
    message_body            varbinary(max),
    conversation_handle     uniqueidentifier,
    message_type_name       nvarchar(256)
);

BEGIN
    WAITFOR
    (
        RECEIVE TOP (1) message_body, conversation_handle, message_type_name
        FROM VacationRequestQueue INTO @msgTable
```

```
    ), TIMEOUT 2000;

    SET @msgBody = (SELECT TOP (1) CAST(message_body AS XML) FROM @msgTable);
    SET @convID = (SELECT TOP (1) conversation_handle FROM @msgTable);
    SET @msgType = (SELECT TOP (1) message_type_name FROM @msgTable);
    END CONVERSATION @convID;

    IF @msgType = 'http://schemas.apress.com/AcceleratedSQL2008/VacationRequest'
    BEGIN
        SET @email = @msgBody.value('data(//email)[1]', 'varchar(50)');
        SET @hours = @msgBody.value('data(//hours)[1]', 'int');
        SET @startTime = @msgBody.value('data(//startTime)[1]', 'datetime');
        SET @employeeID = @msgBody.value('data(//employeeId)[1]', 'int');

        SET @empRequestBody = N'<?xml version="1.0"?><employeeRequest>
    <id>' + CAST(@employeeID AS varchar) + '</id>
    <hours>' + CAST(@hours AS varchar) + '</hours>
</employeeRequest>';
        SET @empRequest = CAST(@empRequestBody AS XML)

        SET @projRequestBody = N'<projectRequest>
    <email>' + @email + '</email>
    <startTime>' + CONVERT(nvarchar, @startTime, 126) + '+00:00</startTime>
    <hours>' + CAST(@hours AS varchar) + '</hours>
</projectRequest>';
        SET @projRequest = CAST(@projRequestBody AS XML)

        BEGIN DIALOG CONVERSATION @empConvID
            FROM SERVICE
        [http://schemas.apress.com/AcceleratedSQL2008/EmpProjDetailsService]
            TO SERVICE
              'http://schemas.apress.com/AcceleratedSQL2008/EmployeeDetailsService'
            ON CONTRACT
              [http://schemas.apress.com/AcceleratedSQL2008/EmployeeServiceContract];

        SEND ON CONVERSATION @empConvID
            MESSAGE TYPE
                [http://schemas.apress.com/AcceleratedSQL2008/EmployeeRequestMessage]
            (@empRequest);

        BEGIN DIALOG CONVERSATION @projConvID
            FROM SERVICE
        [http://schemas.apress.com/AcceleratedSQL2008/EmpProjDetailsService]
            TO SERVICE
              'http://schemas.apress.com/AcceleratedSQL2008/ProjectDetailsService'
            ON CONTRACT
              [http://schemas.apress.com/AcceleratedSQL2008/ProjectServiceContract]
            WITH RELATED_CONVERSATION = @empConvID, ENCRYPTION=OFF;

        SEND ON CONVERSATION @projConvID
            MESSAGE TYPE
                [http://schemas.apress.com/AcceleratedSQL2008/ProjectRequestMessage]
            (@projRequest);
    END
END;
GO
```

You now create the EmpProjDetailsService and its associated queue where the response messages will be sent:

```
CREATE QUEUE EmployeeProjectDetailsQueue
WITH STATUS = ON, RETENTION = OFF;

CREATE SERVICE
    [http://schemas.apress.com/AcceleratedSQL2008/EmpProjDetailsService]
ON QUEUE EmployeeProjectDetailsQueue
(
    [http://schemas.apress.com/AcceleratedSQL2008/EmployeeServiceContract],
    [http://schemas.apress.com/AcceleratedSQL2008/ProjectServiceContract]
);
```

You don't set an activation procedure for the queue, because you'll pick up messages at set times. The service has two contracts, as it communicates with both the EmployeeDetailsService and the ProjectDetailsService.

You also need to create the queue to which the initial message that makes the vacation request is sent and the receiving service for this conversation:

```
CREATE QUEUE VacationRequestQueue
WITH
    STATUS = ON,
    RETENTION = OFF,
    ACTIVATION
    (
        STATUS = ON,
        PROCEDURE_NAME = usp_ProcessVacationRequest,
        MAX_QUEUE_READERS = 5,
        EXECUTE AS SELF
    );

CREATE SERVICE
    [http://schemas.apress.com/AcceleratedSQL2008/VacReqProcessorService]
ON QUEUE VacationRequestQueue
(
    [http://schemas.apress.com/AcceleratedSQL2008/VacationRequestContract]
);
GO
```

With that done, only a few tasks are left. You need to create the procedure that will process the response messages sent to the EmployeeProjectDetailsQueue, and you need to set up dialog security so that your two databases know who they're talking to. Finally, you need to create the initiating service and the stored procedure that kicks off the whole thing.

Reading the Response Messages

The real processing for the example is performed in the usp_ReadResponseMessages stored procedure, which reads the messages in the EmployeeProjectDetailsQueue by conversation group, stores the data from these messages into local variables, determines whether to grant the vacation, and e-mails the employee with the verdict:

```
CREATE PROCEDURE usp_ReadResponseMessages
AS
DECLARE @empMsgBody   XML(
            [http://schemas.apress.com/AcceleratedSQL2008/EmployeeResponseSchema]),
        @projMsgBody  XML(
            [http://schemas.apress.com/AcceleratedSQL2008/ProjectResponseSchema]),
```

```
          @groupId        uniqueidentifier,
          @empConvId      uniqueidentifier,
          @projConvId     uniqueidentifier,
          @activeProj     int,
          @hours          int,
          @empId          int,
          @email          nvarchar(50),
          @startTime      datetime;
DECLARE @msgTable TABLE
(
    message_body           varbinary(max),
    message_type_name      nvarchar(256),
    conversation_handle    uniqueidentifier
);
BEGIN
    WAITFOR
    (
       GET CONVERSATION GROUP @groupID
       FROM EmployeeProjectDetailsQueue
    ), TIMEOUT 500;
    WHILE @groupID IS NOT NULL
    BEGIN
       WAITFOR
       (
          RECEIVE message_body, message_type_name, conversation_handle
          FROM EmployeeProjectDetailsQueue INTO @msgTable
       ), TIMEOUT 2000;

       IF (SELECT COUNT(*) FROM @msgTable) > 0
       BEGIN
          SET @empMsgBody = (SELECT TOP (1) CAST(message_body AS XML)
             FROM @msgTable
             WHERE message_type_name =
           'http://schemas.apress.com/AcceleratedSQL2008/EmployeeResponseMessage');
          SET @empConvID = (SELECT TOP (1) conversation_handle FROM @msgTable
             WHERE message_type_name =
           'http://schemas.apress.com/AcceleratedSQL2008/EmployeeResponseMessage');
          SET @hours = @empMsgBody.value('data(//hoursVacation)[1]', 'int');
          SET @empId = @empMsgBody.value('data(//id)[1]', 'int');

          SET @projMsgBody = (SELECT TOP (1) CAST(message_body AS XML)
             FROM @msgTable
             WHERE message_type_name =
             'http://schemas.apress.com/AcceleratedSQL2008/ProjectResponseMessage');
          SET @projConvID = (SELECT TOP (1) conversation_handle FROM @msgTable
             WHERE message_type_name =
             'http://schemas.apress.com/AcceleratedSQL2008/ProjectResponseMessage');
          SET @activeProj = @projMsgBody.value('data(//activeProjects)[1]',
                                         'int');
          SET @email = @projMsgBody.value('data(//email)[1]', 'varchar(50)');
          SET @startTime = @projMsgBody.value('data(//startTime)[1]', 'datetime');

          IF @hours > 160
             EXEC msdb.dbo.sp_send_dbmail
                @profile_name = 'Default Profile',
                @recipients = @email,
```

```
                    @subject = 'Vacation request',
                    @body = 'Your request for vacation has been refused because you
have insufficient hours remaining of your holiday entitlement.';
            ELSE IF @startTime < DATEADD(Week, 1, GETDATE())
                EXEC msdb.dbo.sp_send_dbmail
                    @profile_name = 'Default Profile',
                    @recipients = @email,
                    @subject = 'Default Profile',
                    @body = 'Your request for vacation has been refused because you
have not given sufficient notice. Please request holiday at least a week in
advance.';
            ELSE IF @activeProj > 1
                EXEC msdb.dbo.sp_send_dbmail
                    @profile_name = 'Default Profile',
                    @recipients = @email,
                    @subject = 'Vacation request',
                    @body = 'Your request for vacation has been refused because you
have too many active projects at that time.';
            ELSE
                BEGIN
                    UPDATE HumanResources.Employee
                        SET VacationHours = @hours
                        WHERE EmployeeID = @empId;
                    EXEC msdb.dbo.sp_send_dbmail
                        @profile_name = 'Default Profile',
                        @recipients = @email,
                        @subject = 'Vacation request',
                        @body = 'Your request for vacation has been granted.';
                END

            END CONVERSATION @empConvID;
            END CONVERSATION @projConvID;
        END;

        WAITFOR
        (
            GET CONVERSATION GROUP @groupID
            FROM EmployeeProjectDetailsQueue
        ), TIMEOUT 500;
    END;
END;
GO
```

You use a new command in this procedure, GET CONVERSATION GROUP, which populates a variable of type uniqueidentifier with the ID for the next available conversation group in the queue. Like RECEIVE, this command can be enclosed in a WAITFOR statement to wait for messages to be sent to the queue if none are already on it. You therefore start by calling GET CONVERSATION GROUP and iterating through the available conversation groups until this returns null. For each conversation group, you receive all available messages into a table variable. Note that the RECEIVE command retrieves messages from only one conversation group. Once you have retrieved the messages, you select the messages of the EmployeeResponseMessage and ProjectResponseMessage types (there should be only one each of these for each conversation group), store the data in these messages into local variables, make a decision based on these values whether or not to grant the vacation, and e-mail the result to the employee.

You would probably run this procedure at set times as a SQL Server Agent job, but for convenience, you'll just run it manually to test the example.

Let's now proceed to set up dialog security.

Setting Up Dialog Security

The certificates that you created earlier exist at the server level and identify the two Service Brokers to each other, but they don't identify the users in the database, nor are they used to encrypt individual messages. To do that, you need to configure dialog security for your conversation.

Dialog security requires you to create a user in each database that corresponds to a user in the remote database. This user must have CONNECT permission to the remote database, as well as SEND permission on the service. Note that the activation stored procedures for a queue don't execute in the caller's context, so the remote users don't need permission to access data.

For this example, you'll connect as dbo in each case. This means that you need to create a user (called projUser in this example) in the AdventureWorks database that represents dbo in the Projects database, and a user (called awUser) in the Projects database that represents dbo in AdventureWorks. These dbo users must be the owners of the services that participate in the conversation, and they must own private keys. The corresponding remote users, projUser and awUser, must be the owners of certificates that correspond to these private keys, so that Service Broker can identify the certificate sent by the remote service with a local user. Finally, you also need to create a Remote Service Binding in the initiating service to tell Service Broker which user to connect to the remote service as. This process should become clearer as we walk through the steps needed to set up dialog security.

To start, create a certificate for the dbo user in the Projects database and save that to file so you can install it into AdventureWorks. The certificate is not permitted to be password protected, so you'll encrypt it with the master key for the database (which you need to create in any case for dialog security to work):

```
USE Projects
GO

CREATE MASTER KEY ENCRYPTION BY PASSWORD = 'gs53&"f"!385';
GO

CREATE CERTIFICATE projUserCert
WITH SUBJECT = 'peiriantprawf.julianskinner.local',
     START_DATE = '01/01/2008',
     EXPIRY_DATE = '01/01/2009'
ACTIVE FOR BEGIN_DIALOG = ON;
GO

BACKUP CERTIFICATE projUserCert TO FILE =
       'C:\Apress\AcceleratedSQL2008\Chapter9\projUserCert.cer'
```

Next, create the projUser user in the AdventureWorks database, install this certificate with that user as its owner (using the AUTHORIZATION clause to set the owner), and grant the user the necessary permissions. In this case, you create the user from an existing login:

```
USE AdventureWorks
GO

CREATE USER projUser FOR LOGIN login_name;
GO

CREATE CERTIFICATE projUserCert
AUTHORIZATION projUser
FROM FILE = 'C:\Apress\AcceleratedSQL2008\Chapter9\projUserCert.cer';
GO

GRANT CONNECT TO projUser;
GRANT SEND ON
```

```
    SERVICE::[http://schemas.apress.com/AcceleratedSQL2008/EmpProjDetailsService]
TO projUser;
```

You also need to create a certificate to identify the dbo user in AdventureWorks, which will be associated with the awUser user in the Projects database, and save this to file so that it can be installed into Projects. The remote service needs to identify itself to the initiating service as the owner of that service (dbo in this case), so this user must own a certificate containing a private key in the AdventureWorks database that has a corresponding certificate in Projects. Again, you'll encrypt this with the master key for the database, so you need to create that first (obviously, don't include this step if you've already created a master key for the AdventureWorks database):

```
CREATE MASTER KEY ENCRYPTION BY PASSWORD = '45Gme*3^&fwu';
GO

CREATE CERTIFICATE awUserCert
WITH SUBJECT = 'ecspi.julianskinner.local',
     START_DATE = '01/01/2008',
     EXPIRY_DATE = '01/01/2009'

BACKUP CERTIFICATE awUserCert TO FILE =
        'C:\Apress\AcceleratedSQL2008\Chapter9\awUserCert.cer';
```

While you're in AdventureWorks, you also need to create a Remote Service Binding to tell Service Broker which user to connect as:

```
CREATE REMOTE SERVICE BINDING ProjectDetailsServiceBinding
TO SERVICE 'http://schemas.apress.com/AcceleratedSQL2008/ProjectDetailsService'
WITH USER = projUser;
```

This tells Service Broker to identify itself to the ProjectDetailsService using the certificate owned by the projUser database user.

Finally, you need to create a new user in the Projects database to represent dbo in AdventureWorks, install the awUserCert certificate in the Projects database with your new user as its owner, and grant the user permissions to connect to the database and send messages to the ProjectDetailsService service. Again, you'll create the user from a preexisting login:

```
CREATE USER awUser FOR LOGIN login_name;
GO

CREATE CERTIFICATE awUserCert
AUTHORIZATION awUser
FROM FILE = 'C:\Apress\AcceleratedSQL2008\Chapter9\awUserCert.cer';
GO

GRANT CONNECT TO awUser;
GRANT SEND ON
    SERVICE::[http://schemas.apress.com/AcceleratedSQL2008/ProjectDetailsService]
TO awUser;
GO
```

■**Note** If the database user who owns the EmpProjDetailsService already owns a certificate in the Adventure-Works database, that certificate may be sent to the ProjectDetailsService instead of the certificate you've just created. In that case, dialog security will fail, as the remote Service Broker instance won't recognize the certificate and thus won't be able to associate it with a user. To rectify this, either install any existing certificates in the Projects database or change their owner in the AdventureWorks database with the ALTER AUTHENTICATION statement.

The Initiator Service

The final tasks are to create the initiator service and the stored procedure that will send the initial message. In both cases, these are practically identical to the equivalent objects in the first example; only the names have changed:

```
CREATE SERVICE
    [http://schemas.apress.com/AcceleratedSQL2008/VacReqInitiatorService]
ON QUEUE VacationRequestQueue
(
    [http://schemas.apress.com/AcceleratedSQL2008/VacationRequestContract]
);
GO

CREATE PROCEDURE usp_RequestVacation
    @employeeId int,
    @email varchar(50),
    @hours int,
    @startDate varchar(50)
AS
DECLARE @dialogHandle uniqueidentifier,
        @body          nvarchar(1000),
        @msg           XML,
        @date          nvarchar(100)
BEGIN
    SET @body = N'<?xml version="1.0"?>
<vacationRequest>
    <employeeId>' + CAST(@employeeID AS varchar) + '</employeeId>
    <email>' + @email + '</email>
    <startTime>' + @startDate + '</startTime>
    <hours>' + CAST(@hours AS nvarchar) + '</hours>
</vacationRequest>';
    SET @msg = CAST(@body AS XML)

    BEGIN DIALOG CONVERSATION @dialogHandle
        FROM SERVICE
          [http://schemas.apress.com/AcceleratedSQL2008/VacReqInitiatorService]
        TO SERVICE
          'http://schemas.apress.com/AcceleratedSQL2008/VacReqProcessorService'
        ON CONTRACT
          [http://schemas.apress.com/AcceleratedSQL2008/VacationRequestContract];

    SEND ON CONVERSATION @dialogHandle
      MESSAGE TYPE [http://schemas.apress.com/AcceleratedSQL2008/VacationRequest]
      (@msg);
    END CONVERSATION @dialogHandle;
END;
```

Run the application by executing this stored procedure within the AdventureWorks database:

```
EXEC usp_RequestVacation 140, 'someone@somewhere.com', 8,
                     '2005-08-01T09:00:00+00:00'
```

The e-mail address you pass in should be the one entered into the employee table of the Projects database.

After waiting a short while, run the usp_ReadResponseMessages procedure to process the responses that should have been sent to the EmployeeProjectDetailsQueue:

```
EXEC usp_ReadResponseMessages
```

As before, the address you passed in should shortly receive an e-mail granting or denying the request.

Message Priorities

In the SQL Server 2005 Service Broker architecture, messages are given equal priority across all conversations. Most other messaging systems, like Microsoft Message Queuing (MSMQ), provide a way to set priorities on the messages, so more important messages get processed first. This type of message priority was added in SQL Server 2008.

Message priorities in Service Broker are defined at the conversation level. The conversation priority will affect the order in which messages from different conversations will be sent and the order in which they will be received. To illustrate this point and the capability of conversation priority, let's work through an example.

For this example, create a database called SBTest and configure it for use with Service Broker, as follows:

```
ALTER DATABASE SBTest SET enable_broker

ALTER DATABASE SBTest SET HONOR_BROKER_PRIORITY ON

CREATE MASTER KEY ENCRYPTION BY PASSWORD='wnMaz5a123123'
```

As you've learned in this chapter, you need to alter the database to enable Service Broker and to provide a master key for use in encrypting the transmission of the message. To tell Service Broker to use conversation priorities, you enable this functionality at the database level through a new SET parameter called HONOR_BROKER_PRIORITY.

Next, create a simplified Service Broker configuration that has two contracts: one for customer orders and the other for internal procurement orders.

```
CREATE MESSAGE TYPE GenericMessage VALIDATION = NONE

CREATE CONTRACT MyCustomerMessageContract
(GenericMessage SENT BY INITIATOR)

CREATE CONTRACT MyInternalMessageContract
(GenericMessage SENT BY INITIATOR)

CREATE QUEUE SenderQueue

CREATE QUEUE ReceiverQueue

CREATE SERVICE Sender  ON QUEUE SenderQueue

CREATE SERVICE Receiver ON QUEUE ReceiverQueue
(MyCustomerMessageContract,MyInternalMessageContract)
```

At this point, you have configured Service Broker enough to send and receive messages. You have not defined any specific priority, so you expect the behavior to be that of SQL Server 2005.

Now, let's create a stored procedure that will send a message through either the MyCustomerMessageContract or the MyInternalMessageContract:

```
CREATE PROCEDURE SendMessageToQueue
@MyType NVARCHAR(10)
AS
DECLARE @conversationHandle UNIQUEIDENTIFIER
DECLARE @message NVARCHAR(100)
```

```
BEGIN

IF (@MyType='C')
  BEGIN
  BEGIN DIALOG @conversationHandle
  FROM SERVICE Sender
  TO SERVICE 'Receiver'
  ON CONTRACT MyCustomerMessageContract
  SET @message = 'CustomerOrder';
  END
    ELSE
  BEGIN
    BEGIN DIALOG @conversationHandle
    FROM SERVICE Sender
    TO SERVICE 'Receiver'
    ON CONTRACT MyInternalMessageContract
    SET @message = 'InternalOrder';
  END;

  SEND  ON CONVERSATION @conversationHandle
MESSAGE TYPE GenericMessage (@message);

END
```

Now you are ready to fill up the queue with some information. Executing the following code will populate our queue with a variety of customer (identified by passing 'C') and internal procurement orders (identified by anything else; in this case, 'I').

```
exec SendMessageToQueue 'I'
exec SendMessageToQueue 'I'
exec SendMessageToQueue 'I'
exec SendMessageToQueue 'I'
exec SendMessageToQueue 'C'
exec SendMessageToQueue 'C'
exec SendMessageToQueue 'I'
exec SendMessageToQueue 'I'
exec SendMessageToQueue 'C'
exec SendMessageToQueue 'I'
```

Now issue the following query to look at the messages on the queue:

```
SELECT priority, CONVERT(NVARCHAR(max), message_body) AS 'Order Type'
 FROM ReceiverQueue
```

This will result in the following result set:

Priority	Order Type
5	InternalOrder
5	InternalOrder
5	InternalOrder
5	InternalOrder
5	CustomerOrder
5	CustomerOrder
5	InternalOrder
5	InternalOrder
5	CustomerOrder
5	InternalOrder

This reflects the order in which the messages were submitted. You can see that if you enable the database to honor Service Broker priorities but do not assign any conversation priorities, by default, the conversations will be assigned the priority of 5. Service Broker priorities range from 1 to 10, with 10 being the highest.

Currently, if you went through and submitted the following command ten times:

```
RECEIVE CONVERT(NVARCHAR(max), message_body) AS 'Message',
priority as 'Priority' FROM ReceiverQueue
```

you would get the order of messages coming off the queue in the same order as they were returned by the preceding query.

Now, let's create a priority for each of the two types of contracts. The procurement_order priority will be set to 1, since it is not as important as processing customer orders, which will be set to 10:

```
CREATE BROKER PRIORITY procurement_order
FOR CONVERSATION
SET (CONTRACT_NAME=MyInternalMessageContract,
PRIORITY_LEVEL=1)

CREATE BROKER PRIORITY customer_order
FOR CONVERSATION
SET (CONTRACT_NAME=MyCustomerMessageContract,
PRIORITY_LEVEL=10)
```

Let's put the messages back on the queue:

```
exec SendMessageToQueue 'I'
exec SendMessageToQueue 'I'
exec SendMessageToQueue 'I'
exec SendMessageToQueue 'I'
exec SendMessageToQueue 'C'
exec SendMessageToQueue 'C'
exec SendMessageToQueue 'I'
exec SendMessageToQueue 'I'
exec SendMessageToQueue 'C'
exec SendMessageToQueue 'I'
```

Next, query the queue again:

```
SELECT priority, CONVERT(NVARCHAR(max), message_body) AS 'Order Type' FROM
ReceiverQueued
```

You will see the following output:

Priority	Order Type
1	InternalOrder
1	InternalOrder
1	InternalOrder
1	InternalOrder
10	CustomerOrder
10	CustomerOrder
1	InternalOrder
1	InternalOrder
10	CustomerOrder
1	InternalOrder

Now when you pick off a message from the queue, you will receive the highest priority messages first. Issuing the following statement ten times:

```
RECEIVE CONVERT(NVARCHAR(max), message_body) AS 'Message',
priority as 'Priority' FROM ReceiverQueue
```

yields the following order:

```
CustomerOrder
CustomerOrder
CustomerOrder
InternalOrder
InternalOrder
InternalOrder
InternalOrder
InternalOrder
InternalOrder
InternalOrder
```

Setting priorities affects the transmission order of messages from different conversations, as well as the order in which a conversation group is received off a queue.

A new catalog view called `sys.conversation_priorities` will display which priorities are associated with which conversations.

Troubleshooting Service Broker Using SSBDiagnose

You may need to check whether Service Broker is set up correctly. Consider the case where you have deployed your application to another environment. Unless you actually try to run the application, there is no easy way to do a sanity check to see if the Service Broker configuration is valid. For this, and other situations where you need to troubleshoot Service Broker configurations, you can use the SSBDiagnose, a command-line utility that is new in SQL Server 2008.

The SSBDiagnose tool goes through a series of predefined steps and reports its findings back to the user. For example, it will check whether the service exists and if the queue exists and is enabled. The tool will also analyze the security configuration of Service Broker and report back issues such as invalid certificates or that the certificate-mapped user doesn't have SEND permission on the service. In addition to security, the tool also looks at endpoints and routes if the dialog is not local to one instance.

The SSBDiagnose utility has two main sections of parameters. The first one describes general options, including which server to connect to and which credentials to use. It also gives an option to output the results of the utility in XML format; the default is just plain text.

To demonstrate using SSBDiagnose, let's continue the example from the previous section, involving a send and receive queue in the SBTest database. To give something useful to SSBDiagnose to diagnose, disable the receive queue (ReceiverQueue). Then issue the SSBDiagnose statement as follows:

```
SSBDiagnose -E -d SBTest FROM SERVICE Sender TO SERVICE Receiver
```

By default, the results are output in text format:

```
29914 EPGOPSR2BASE    SBTest          Queue dbo.ReceiverQueue is disabled
1 Errors, 0 Warnings
```

If you chose to output the results in XML format (obtained by specifying the –XML parameter), they would look like this:

```
<?xml version="1.0" encoding="IBM437" ?>
<diagnostics>
<banner title="Service Broker Diagnostics Tool" product="Microsoft SQL Server"
 version="10.0.1068.0 ((SQL_Main).070816-1112 )" />
<diagnostic code="29914" level="Error" server="DEV1" database="SBTest"
 object="dbo.ReceiverQueue">Queue dbo.ReceiverQueue is disabled</diagnostic>
</diagnostics>
```

Having the results come back as XML allows for some interesting applications. For example, you could run this tool as part of a maintenance schedule, and the output could be sent to another application for automatic processing. Can you imagine an autocorrecting facility, where the queue would be automatically enabled in this situation?

Summary

In this chapter, we've taken a fairly superficial look at Service Broker (out of necessity). Service Broker is a complex message queuing technology for SQL Server, and in the space of one chapter, it's not possible to go into great depth. Instead, we've concentrated on the main elements of creating Service Broker applications, with a couple of reasonably practical examples to get you started with the technology as quickly as possible.

In this chapter, we explained what Service Broker is and situations it can be used in. You learned about the Service Broker architecture and the new database objects for building Service Broker applications, as well as Service Broker routing and security. To explore the Service Broker functionality, we walked through creating both a simple, single-instance Service Broker application and a more complex, cross-instance Service Broker application.

Next, you learned how to use the new SQL Server 2008 feature for setting Service Broker conversation priorities. Finally, we covered the new SSBDiagnose utility and how it can help both administrators and developers troubleshoot Service Broker implementations.

CHAPTER 10

████

Integrated Full-Text Search

SQL Server first introduced Full-Text Search (FTS) capabilities in the SQL Server 7.0 release. Since its introduction, FTS has undergone several refinements and changes to make it faster, more powerful, more flexible, and easier than ever to configure and implement. The newest version of SQL Server FTS, known as Integrated Full-Text Search (iFTS), provides tools to efficiently perform linguistic searches against a wide range of documents and other data stored in SQL Server databases.

In this chapter, we will discuss several aspects of SQL Server 2008 iFTS, including the following:

- Creation of full-text catalogs and full-text indexes
- Use of `FREETEXT`, `CONTAINS`, `FREETEXTTABLE`, and `CONTAINSTABLE` to perform full-text searches against documents, XML data, and textual data columns
- Use of advanced iFTS options, including:
  - Complex search expressions using `AND`, `OR`, and `AND NOT`
  - Inflectional forms and thesaurus synonyms searches using `FORMSOF`
  - Proximity searches using `NEAR`
  - Weighted searches using `ISABOUT` term
- Thesaurus-based word expansion and substitution
- Use of stoplists
- New stored procedures, catalog views, and dynamic management functions to make iFTS administration easier than ever

Creating Full-Text Catalogs and Indexes

SQL Server 2008 iFTS allows you to efficiently search character data stored in `char`, `nchar`, and `nvarchar` columns. It can also be used to search binary content in `varbinary` columns, and XML data in `xml` datatype columns.

■**Note** SQL Server 2008 iFTS can also be used to search columns declared using the deprecated text, ntext, and image datatypes. It is recommended, however, that you use the new SQL Server varchar(max), nvarchar(max), and varbinary(max) datatypes instead.

Before you can take advantage of iFTS's powerful search capabilities, you need to create a full-text catalog and one or more full-text indexes. You can create these either through SQL Server Management Studio or by using Transact-SQL (T-SQL) statements.

Using the GUI to Create a Full-Text Catalog and Index

Using Management Studio, you can easily create full-text catalogs and full-text indexes. Here, we'll walk through creating a full-text catalog for the AdventureWorks database and a full-text index on the Production.ProductModel table.

Creating a Full-Text Catalog

To create the full-text catalog, in Object Explorer, expand the Storage node under the target database, right-click the Full Text Catalogs node, and select New Full-Text Catalog from the context menu, as shown in Figure 10-1.

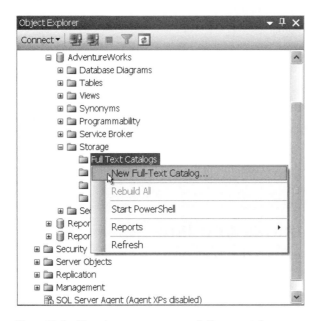

Figure 10-1. *Choosing to create a new full-text catalog*

You'll be presented with the New Full-Text Catalog dialog box. In this dialog box, you select a name for your new full-text catalog, the full-text catalog owner, an accent-sensitivity setting, and whether this full-text catalog will be designated your default full-text catalog. The accent-sensitivity setting determines whether or not iFTS differentiates between characters with and without accent marks. Figure 10-2 shows the entries for creating a catalog named AdvFTCatalog for this example.

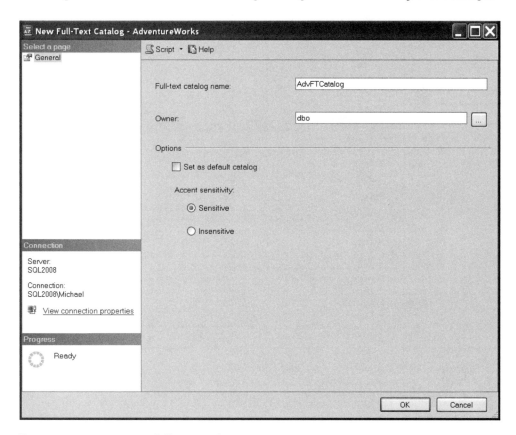

Figure 10-2. *Creating a new full-text catalog*

Once you've created your full-text catalog, it's time to define one or more full-text indexes on tables in your database.

Creating a Full-Text Index

Management Studio includes a Full-Text Indexing Wizard to guide you through creating a full-text index. Follow these steps to use the wizard:

1. Right-click a table in Object Explorer and select Full-Text Index ➤ Define Full-Text Index, as shown in Figure 10-3.

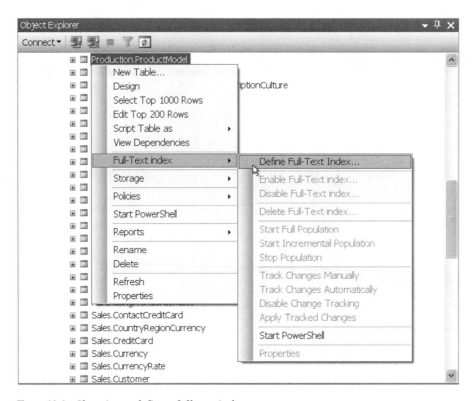

Figure 10-3. *Choosing to define a full-text index*

2. The welcome screen for the SQL Server Full-Text Indexing Wizard appears, as shown in Figure 10-4. Click Next to continue.

3. The Full-Text Indexing Wizard asks you to choose a single-column unique index from your source table, as shown in Figure 10-5. This index provides iFTS with a means of relating full-text index entries back to rows in the source table. Very often, you will see an integer primary key, usually a surrogate key, used as the index of choice for iFTS. In this example, we've used the `integer` primary key of the table, `PK_ProductModel_ProductModelID`.

Figure 10-4. *Starting the Full-Text Indexing Wizard*

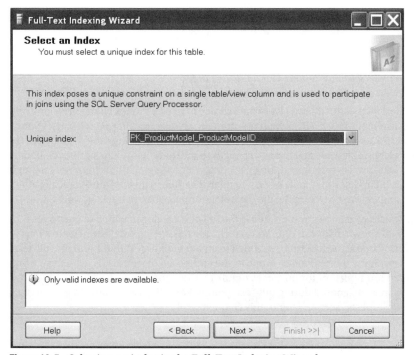

Figure 10-5. *Selecting an index in the Full-Text Indexing Wizard*

4. The wizard next asks you to select the table columns to index. You can add any character-based, binary, or large object (LOB) datatype columns to your full-text index. In Figure 10-6, we've chosen to add the `CatalogDescription`, `Instructions`, and `Name` columns of the table to the full-text index. These particular columns hold XML data and character-type data.

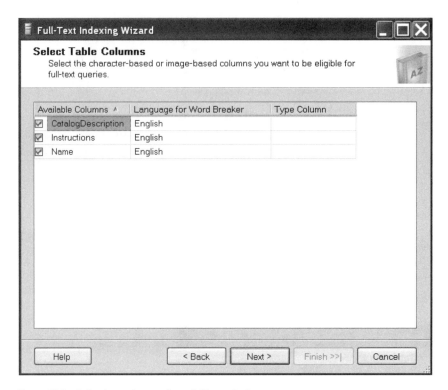

Figure 10-6. *Selecting columns for a full-text index*

5. The next step of the wizard gives you a choice of full-text index change-tracking options, as shown in Figure 10-7. The default is automatic change tracking, which causes your full-text index to automatically update whenever data in the underlying table is changed. If you have a very large table and expect many changes to the underlying data, automatic updates might use a lot of system resources during peak production times. If this is the case, you might decide to kick off updates manually or on a regular schedule instead of automatically after every data update. For our example, the default automatic change tracking works well.

6. The wizard next allows you to choose the full-text catalog in which to create your full-text index, as shown in Figure 10-8. You can choose an existing catalog or create a new one. You can also choose the filegroup on which to create the full-text index and the full-text stoplist to use with the full-text index. Stoplists are composed of stopwords, which are words considered unimportant for purposes of full-text searches—words like *the, an, and,* and *to*. Stopwords are ignored during full-text queries. We'll discuss stoplists in greater detail in the "Using Stoplists" section later in this chapter.

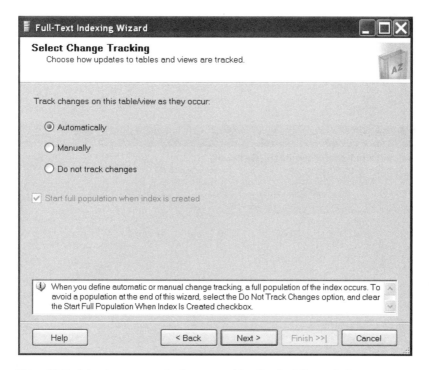

Figure 10-7. *Selecting automatic change tracking for the full-text index*

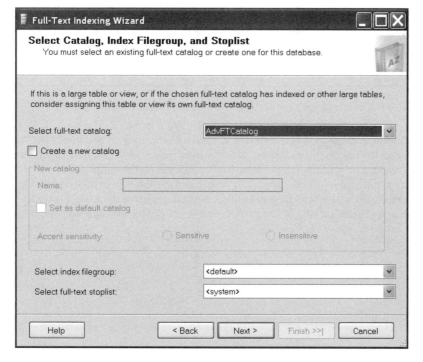

Figure 10-8. *Assigning a full-text index to a full-text catalog*

7. Optionally, you can define population schedules for tables and full-text catalogs, as shown in Figure 10-9. This option is useful if you've decided not to use automatic full-text index change tracking and want to schedule updates for off-peak times, or if you just want finer-grained control over the full-text index population process. Since we've gone with the default automatic change tracking in the example, we don't need to define a population schedule.

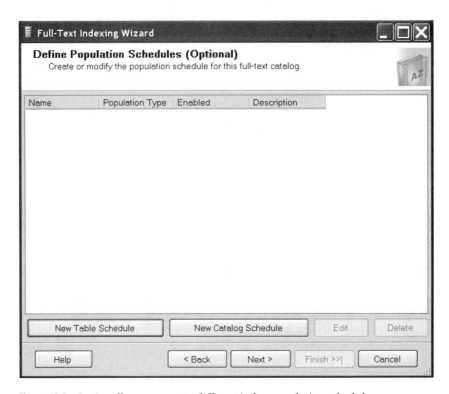

Figure 10-9. *Optionally, you can set a full-text index population schedule.*

8. The final step of the Full-Text Indexing Wizard is a summary screen that allows you to review all the options you selected as you worked your way through the wizard's screens. This is strictly an informational screen, but it provides you the option to go back to previous screens if you made a mistake or want to make a change before your full-text index is created. Clicking Finish on this screen creates your full-text index in the database. Figure 10-10 shows the Full-Text Indexing Wizard summary screen produced by the example.

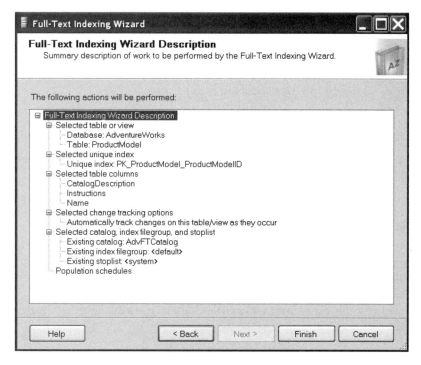

Figure 10-10. *Full-Text Indexing Wizard summary screen*

After you click Finish in the Full-Text Indexing Wizard, a progress screen is displayed, showing the success or failure of the full-text index creation process. Figure 10-11 shows that the full-text index in the example was successfully created.

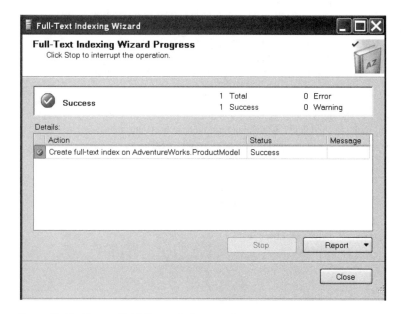

Figure 10-11. *Successful full-text index creation*

■**Note** The full-text index is an index, but it is not like standard SQL Server clustered and nonclustered table indexes. While SQL Server uses b-tree structures to store nonclustered indexes on tables, full-text indexes are stored as inverted index structures. SQL Server uses the single-column unique index on the table that you choose in the Full-Text Indexing Wizard to relate full-text index entries back to table entries. In this way, SQL Server can bridge the efficiency of full-text indexes with the power of relational indexes.

Using T-SQL to Create a Full-Text Catalog and Index

It's often necessary to script full-text catalog and full-text index creation. There are a number of reasons to script your full-text catalog and index creation, including the following:

- Many organizational information technology policies require database changes to be checked into a source-control database to maintain proper source code management and version control.

- Many database administrators (DBAs) demand that database creation and updates be scripted so they can be propagated uniformly across multiple servers or promoted consistently through different environments like development, quality assurance (QA), user acceptance testing (UAT), and production.

- You may just be the type of person who prefers the fine-grained control that T-SQL code gives you.

To create the same full-text index as in the example in the previous section, use the CREATE FULLTEXT CATALOG statement:

```
CREATE FULLTEXT CATALOG AdvFTCatalog
ON FILEGROUP [PRIMARY]
WITH ACCENT_SENSITIVITY = ON
AUTHORIZATION [dbo];
```

The CREATE FULLTEXT CATALOG statement specifies the full-text catalog name, which must be unique among full-text catalog names in the current database. This example specifies that the full-text catalog will be created on the PRIMARY filegroup, accent sensitivity will be turned on, and the owner is dbo (via the AUTHORIZATION clause). We create the full-text catalog on the PRIMARY filegroup, since the AdventureWorks database has only a single filegroup by default. In production environments, Microsoft recommends creating an additional filegroup just for full-text catalogs.

■**Note** Unlike previous versions of SQL Server, full-text catalogs in SQL Server 2008 are not created in a separate directory in the file system. They are created in the filegroup that you specify as part of the database itself. The IN PATH option from prior versions is still recognized, but it has no effect in SQL Server 2008. If you have code that uses this deprecated option, plan to change it as soon as possible.

After you create the full-text catalog with T-SQL you need to create one or more full-text indexes on it. The CREATE FULLTEXT INDEX statement fills this need:

```
CREATE FULLTEXT INDEX ON Production.ProductModel
(
  Name LANGUAGE 1033,
  CatalogDescription LANGUAGE 1033,
  Instructions LANGUAGE 1033
)
KEY INDEX PK_ProductModel_ProductModelID
```

```
ON (AdvFTCatalog)
WITH
(
  CHANGE_TRACKING AUTO,
  STOPLIST = SYSTEM
);
GO

ALTER FULLTEXT INDEX ON Production.ProductModel
ENABLE;
GO
```

As in the Full-Text Indexing Wizard example in the previous section, this `CREATE FULLTEXT INDEX` statement creates a full-text index on the `Name`, `CatalogDescription`, and `Instructions` columns of the `Production.ProductModel` table. The single-column unique index used by the full-text index is specified in the mandatory `KEY INDEX` clause. As in the previous example, we've used the `integer` primary key of the table, `PK_ProductModel_ProductModelID`.

Each column in the example has the optional `LANGUAGE` identifier included, specifying a locale identifier (LCID) of 1033, which indicates US English. We've also specified automatic change tracking and usage of the default system stoplist.

▌Tip You can get a complete list of languages and LCIDs supported by iFTS by querying the `sys.fulltext_languages` catalog view.

The `ALTER FULLTEXT INDEX` statement enables the full-text index we just created on the `Production.ProductModel` table. Additional full-text index management functionality is exposed by the `ALTER FULLTEXT INDEX` and `DROP FULLTEXT INDEX` statements. You can use `ALTER FULLTEXT INDEX` to enable or disable a full-text index; set the change-tracking mode for a full-text index; change the stoplist used by a full-text index; and start, stop, pause, or resume a full-text index population. The following code starts a full population of the `Production.ProductModel` table's full-text index.

```
ALTER FULLTEXT INDEX ON Production.ProductModel
START FULL POPULATION;
GO
```

One you've created your full-text catalog and full-text indexes, you can take advantage of them with SQL Server's full-text search predicates and functions.

Querying with iFTS

SQL Server provides four ways to query a full-text index. The `FREETEXT` and `CONTAINS` predicates can be used to retrieve rows that match a given search criteria from a table, in much the same way that the `EXISTS` predicate returns rows that meet specific criteria. The `FREETEXTTABLE` and `CONTAINSTABLE` functions return rowsets with two columns: `KEY`, which is a row identifier (the unique index value specified when the full-text index was created), and `RANK`, which is a relevance rating. Here, we'll demonstrate how to use these predicates and functions for iFTS queries.

FREETEXT Predicate Searches

The FREETEXT predicate allows you to search a character-based column, or columns, of a full-text index for words that match inflectional and thesaurus expansion and replacement forms of a free-text search string. The FREETEXT predicate accepts a column name or list of columns, a free-text search string, and an optional LCID, and performs the following steps:

- It uses a word-breaker to break a free-text string into individual words.

- It stems the words, using inflectional forms.

- It identifies expansions and replacements for words based on the FTS language-specific thesaurus.

Because it is a predicate, FREETEXT can be used in the WHERE clause of a SELECT query. All rows for which the FREETEXT predicate returns true (a match) are returned when FREETEXT is used.

The following is a sample FREETEXT query that uses the full-text index created on the AdventureWorks Production.ProductModel table in the previous section:

```
SELECT *
FROM Production.ProductModel
WHERE FREETEXT(*, N'bike');
```

The wildcard character (*) used inside the FREETEXT predicate parentheses indicates that all columns included in the full-text index should be searched for a match. The second FREETEXT parameter is the word you want to match. The query returns ten matching rows from the Production.ProductModel table.

The new integration of the full-text query engine with the SQL Server query engine provides a more efficient full-text search experience than previous versions of FTS. iFTS integration allows SQL Server to take advantage of new operators, such as the Table Valued Function [FulltextMatch] operator (shown in Figure 10-12), which replaces the expensive Remote Scan operator in SQL Server 2005.

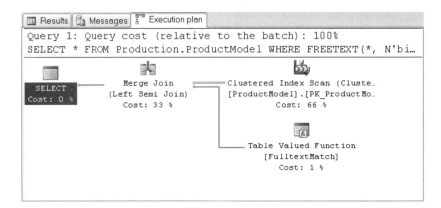

Figure 10-12. *FREETEXT query execution plan*

The FREETEXT predicate finds both exact and approximate matches of words, using two methods:

- By stemming words to locate inflectional forms of a word

- By performing word expansions and replacements based on language-specific thesaurus files, as explained in the "Managing Thesaurus Files" section later in this chapter

The FREETEXT predicate and FREETEXTTABLE function (described shortly) automatically stem words to find inflectional forms. The inflectional forms of a word include plural nouns, verb conjugations, and other variants of a word. The following example demonstrates a FREETEXT query that performs automatic stemming of the word *ride*. The inflectional forms of *ride* include the verb conjugations *rides*, *rode*, *ridden*, and *riding*, as well as the nouns *rider* and *riders*.

```
SELECT *
FROM Production.ProductModel
WHERE FREETEXT(CatalogDescription, N'ride', LANGUAGE 1033);
```

This query retrieves all rows that contain inflectional forms of the word *ride* in the CatalogDescription column. Inflectional forms that are matched in this query include the plural noun *riders* and the verb *riding*. In this FREETEXT query, the CatalogDescription column is identified by name to restrict the search to a single column, and the LANGUAGE specifier is used to indicate LCID 1033, which is US English. The results include six rows that match inflectional forms of the word ride. You can replace the word ride in the FREETEXT predicate with any of the inflectional forms we listed previously, and you will get the same results.

CONTAINS Predicate Searches

The CONTAINS predicate allows more advanced full-text searching options than the FREETEXT predicate. Like FREETEXT, the CONTAINS predicate accepts a column name or list of columns, a search condition, and an optional language identifier as parameters. The power of CONTAINS comes from its ability to handle sophisticated search conditions, as opposed to the simple search strings that FREETEXT accepts. In addition to searching for a simple word or phrase, you can use CONTAINS to search for a word or phrase prefix, a word in proximity to another word, inflectional generations or thesaurus synonyms of words, or combinations of search criteria.

A simple CONTAINS predicate is a basic keyword search, similar to FREETEXT. Unlike FREETEXT though, CONTAINS will not automatically search for inflectional forms of a word or thesaurus synonyms. The following example demonstrates a simple CONTAINS query that returns three rows.

```
SELECT *
FROM Production.ProductModel
WHERE CONTAINS(CatalogDescription, N'ride', LANGUAGE 1033);
```

To tell CONTAINS to use inflectional forms or thesaurus synonyms, use the FORMSOF generation term in your search condition. The next example performs a CONTAINS search on the Name and CatalogDescription columns of the Production.ProductModel table.

```
SELECT *
FROM Production.ProductModel
WHERE CONTAINS((Name, CatalogDescription), N'FORMSOF(INFLECTIONAL, shift)',
  LANGUAGE 1033);
```

The results include two rows that contain matches for inflectional forms of the word *shift* (like *shifting*). Use the FORMSOF(THESAURUS, ...) format to return matches for synonyms of words, as defined in your language-specific thesaurus files (discussed in the "Managing Thesaurus Files" section later in this chapter).

The CONTAINS predicate allows you to combine simple search terms by using the AND (&), AND NOT (&!), and OR (|) Boolean operators. (Note that there is no support for an OR NOT Boolean operator.) The following is a CONTAINS query with two search terms combined with the OR keyword.

```
SELECT *
FROM Production.ProductModel
WHERE CONTAINS(Name, N'FORMSOF(INFLECTIONAL, tour) OR mountain');
```

The results of this sample query, which retrieves all rows containing inflectional forms of the word *tour* (like *touring*) or the word *mountain* in the Name column, are shown in Figure 10-13.

	ProductModelID	Name	CatalogDescription	Instructions	rowguid	ModifiedDate	
1	5	HL Mountain Frame	NULL	NULL	FDD540...	2001-06-01 ...	
2	7	HL Touring Frame	NULL	<root xmln...	D60ED2...	2005-05-16 ...	
3	8	LL Mountain Frame	NULL	NULL	65BF3F...	2002-11-20 ...	
4	10	LL Touring Frame	NULL	<root xmln...	66C638...	2005-05-16 ...	
5	14	ML Mountain Frame	NULL	NULL	0D48C5...	2002-06-01 ...	
6	15	ML Mountain Frame-W	NULL	NULL	AA7769...	2002-06-01 ...	
7	18	Mountain Bike Socks	NULL	NULL	36B1A7...	2001-06-01 ...	
8	19	Mountain-100	<?xml-stylesheet ...	NULL	FCA066...	2001-06-01 ...	
9	20	Mountain-200	NULL	NULL	3B78ED...	2002-06-01 ...	
10	21	Mountain-300	NULL	NULL	ECDDD...	2002-06-01 ...	

Figure 10-13. *Partial results of CONTAINS query with compound search term*

CONTAINS also supports prefix searches using the wildcard asterisk (*) character. Place the search word or phrase in double quotes, followed immediately by the * character to specify a prefix search. Here is a simple prefix search to retrieve all rows that have a word that starts with the prefix *road* in the Name column.

```
SELECT *
FROM Production.ProductModel
WHERE CONTAINS(Name, N'"road*"');
```

The partial results of this query are shown in Figure 10-14.

	ProductModelID	Name	CatalogDescription	Instructions	rowguid	ModifiedDate	
1	8	HL Road Frame	NULL	NULL	4D332EC...	1998-05-02 ...	
2	9	LL Road Frame	NULL	NULL	DDC67A2...	2001-06-01 ...	
3	16	ML Road Frame	NULL	NULL	3494E8FF...	2001-06-01 ...	
4	17	ML Road Frame-W	NULL	NULL	CA18ECF...	2002-06-01 ...	
5	25	Road-150	<?xml-stylesheet ...	NULL	94FFB702...	2001-06-01 ...	
6	26	Road-250	NULL	NULL	3770C5E3...	2002-06-01 ...	
7	27	Road-350-W	NULL	NULL	DFE49035...	2003-06-01 ...	
8	28	Road-450	<?xml-stylesheet ...	NULL	8456BB94...	2001-06-01 ...	
9	29	Road-550-W	NULL	NULL	F85F84F2...	2002-06-01 ...	
10	30	Road-650	NULL	NULL	42E1C597...	2001-06-01 ...	

Figure 10-14. *Partial results of CONTAINS prefix search*

The CONTAINS predicate also supports proximity searches via the NEAR keyword (or ~ operator). NEAR will return matches for words that are close to one another in the source columns. The following demonstrates a NEAR proximity search that looks for instances of the word *aluminum* that occur close to the word *blueprint*. The results consist of four rows that contain these words in proximity to one another.

```
SELECT *
FROM Production.ProductModel
WHERE CONTAINS(Instructions, N'aluminum NEAR blueprint');
```

A proximity search using NEAR will fail if the words are too far apart. For the CONTAINS predicate, words are considered close to one another if they are found within approximately 50 words of each other.

FREETEXTTABLE and CONTAINSTABLE Function Searches

The FREETEXTTABLE and CONTAINSTABLE functions both operate like their similarly named predicate counterparts, but return result sets consisting of a table with two columns: KEY and RANK. The KEY column contains the key index values relating back to the unique index to matching rows in the source table. The RANK column contains relevance rankings as determined by iFTS.

Like the FREETEXT predicate, FREETEXTTABLE accepts a single column name or column list to limit the search, a free-text search string, and an optional language identifier. FREETEXTTABLE also accepts an optional parameter, *top_n_by_rank*, which limits the rows returned to a specific number ordered by RANK values. Here is an example of a FREETEXTTABLE query:

```
SELECT *
FROM FREETEXTTABLE(Production.ProductModel, *, N'aluminum', LANGUAGE 1033, 5) ft
INNER JOIN Production.ProductModel pm
  ON ft.[KEY] = pm.ProductModelID;
```

The FREETEXTTABLE function in this example joins back to the source table, Production. ProductModel, via the KEY column. The query also uses the *top_n_by_rank* option to limit the results to the top five ranking matches. The query returns five rows in descending order by the RANK column.

The CONTAINSTABLE function has the same search capabilities as the CONTAINS predicate. Like the CONTAINS predicate, the CONTAINSTABLE function accepts the name of the source table, a single column name or list of columns, a CONTAINS-style search condition, and an optional language identifier. The CONTAINSTABLE function also accepts an optional *top_n_by_rank* parameter, which limits the results returned to a specific number of rows ordered by RANK. The following example demonstrates the CONTAINSTABLE function in a simple keyword search that retrieves KEY and RANK values for all rows containing an inflectional form of the word *tour* (like *touring*). The results are shown in Figure 10-15.

```
SELECT *
FROM CONTAINSTABLE(Production.ProductModel, [Name],
  N'FORMSOF(INFLECTIONAL, tour)');
```

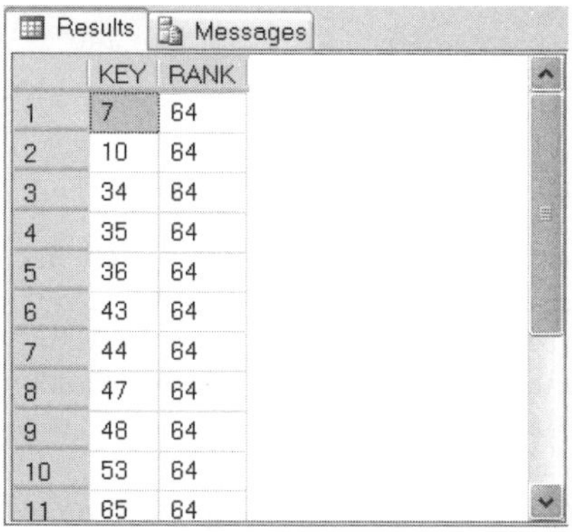

	KEY	RANK
1	7	64
2	10	64
3	34	64
4	35	64
5	36	64
6	43	64
7	44	64
8	47	64
9	48	64
10	53	64
11	65	64

Figure 10-15. *Partial results of the CONTAINSTABLE query with inflectional forms*

Among the host of CONTAINS options supported by CONTAINSTABLE is the ISABOUT term, which assigns weights to the matched words it locates. With ISABOUT, each search word is assigned a weight value between 0.0 and 1.0. CONTAINSTABLE applies the weight to the relevance rankings returned in the RANK column. The following example shows two contrasting CONTAINSTABLE queries:

```
SELECT ct.[RANK], ct.[KEY], pm.[Name]
FROM CONTAINSTABLE(Production.ProductModel, Instructions,
  N'washer OR weld OR polish') ct
INNER JOIN Production.ProductModel pm
  ON ct.[KEY] = pm.ProductModelID
ORDER BY ct.[RANK] DESC;

SELECT ct.[RANK], ct.[KEY], pm.[Name]
FROM CONTAINSTABLE(Production.ProductModel, Instructions,
  N'ISABOUT(washer WEIGHT(1.0), weld WEIGHT(0.5), polish WEIGHT(0.1))') ct
INNER JOIN Production.ProductModel pm
  ON ct.[KEY] = pm.ProductModelID
ORDER BY ct.[RANK] DESC;
```

The first query returns all products with the words *washer*, *weld*, or *polish* in their Instructions column. The second query uses ISABOUT to assign each of these words a weight between 0.0 and 1.0, which is then applied to the result RANK for each row. The results, shown in Figure 10-16, demonstrate how ISABOUT weights can rearrange the rankings of your CONTAINSTABLE query results.

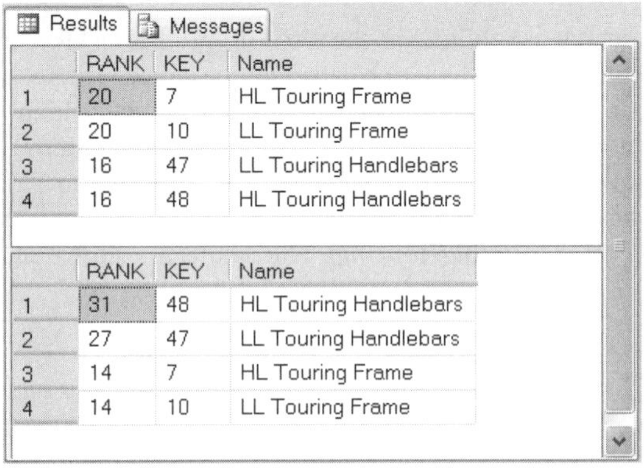

	RANK	KEY	Name
1	20	7	HL Touring Frame
2	20	10	LL Touring Frame
3	16	47	LL Touring Handlebars
4	16	48	HL Touring Handlebars

	RANK	KEY	Name
1	31	48	HL Touring Handlebars
2	27	47	LL Touring Handlebars
3	14	7	HL Touring Frame
4	14	10	LL Touring Frame

Figure 10-16. *Using ISABOUT to change result set rankings*

Managing Thesaurus Files

As you've seen in the previous sections, the FREETEXT predicate and FREETEXTTABLE function automatically perform word stemming for inflectional forms and thesaurus expansions and replacements. The CONTAINS predicate and CONTAINSTABLE function require you to explicitly state that you want inflectional forms and thesaurus expansions and replacements by using FORMSOF. While inflectional forms include verb conjugations and plural forms of words, thesaurus functionality is based on user-managed XML files that define word replacement and expansion patterns.

Each language-specific thesaurus is located in an XML file in the MSSQL\FTDATA directory of your SQL Server installation. The thesaurus files are named using the format ts*nnn*.xml, where *nnn* is a three-letter code representing the language. The tsenu.xml file, for instance, is the US English thesaurus.

To demonstrate the iFTS thesaurus capabilities, we'll begin by creating a new full-text index on the `Production.Product` table using the following code:

```
CREATE FULLTEXT INDEX ON Production.Product
(
  Name LANGUAGE 1033,
  Color LANGUAGE 1033
)
KEY INDEX PK_Product_ProductID
ON (AdvFTCatalog)
WITH
(
  CHANGE_TRACKING AUTO,
  STOPLIST = SYSTEM
);
GO

ALTER FULLTEXT INDEX ON Production.Product
ENABLE;
GO
```

Editing Thesaurus Files

You can edit the thesaurus XML files with a simple text editor or a more advanced XML editor. For this example, we opened the `tsenu.xml` thesaurus file in Notepad, made the appropriate changes, and saved the file back to the `MSSQL\FTDATA` directory. The contents of the `tsenu.xml` file, after our edits, are as follows:

```
<XML ID = "Microsoft Search Thesaurus">
  <thesaurus xmlns = "x-schema:tsSchema.xml">
    <diacritics_sensitive>0</diacritics_sensitive>
    <expansion>
      <sub>thin</sub>
      <sub>flat</sub>
    </expansion>
    <replacement>
      <pat>brick</pat>
      <pat>cherry</pat>
      <pat>magenta</pat>
      <pat>maroon</pat>
      <pat>rose</pat>
      <pat>salmon</pat>
      <pat>vermilion</pat>
      <sub>red</sub>
    </replacement>
  </thesaurus>
</XML>
```

The `diacritics_sensitive` section of the thesaurus file indicates whether accent marks are replaced during expansion and replacement. For instance, if `diacritics_sensitive` is set to 1, the words *resume* and *resumé* are considered equivalent for purposes of the thesaurus. When `diacritics_sensitive` is set to 0, these two words are considered different.

The `expansion` section indicates substitutions that should be applied during the full-text query. The word being searched is expanded to match the other words in the expansion set. In the example, if the user queries for the word *thin*, the search is automatically expanded to include matches for the word *flat* and vice versa. An expansion set can include as many substitutions as you care to define, and the thesaurus can contain as many expansion sets as you need. The following FREETEXT query demonstrates the expansion sets in action, and Figure 10-17 shows the results.

```
SELECT ProductID, Name
FROM Production.Product
WHERE FREETEXT(*, N'thin');
```

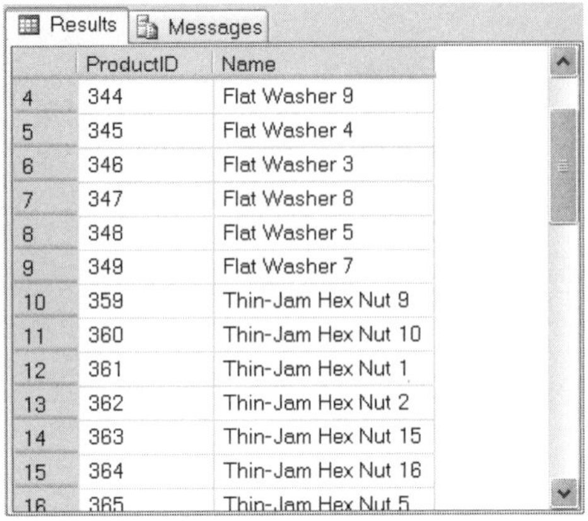

	ProductID	Name
4	344	Flat Washer 9
5	345	Flat Washer 4
6	346	Flat Washer 3
7	347	Flat Washer 8
8	348	Flat Washer 5
9	349	Flat Washer 7
10	359	Thin-Jam Hex Nut 9
11	360	Thin-Jam Hex Nut 10
12	361	Thin-Jam Hex Nut 1
13	362	Thin-Jam Hex Nut 2
14	363	Thin-Jam Hex Nut 15
15	364	Thin-Jam Hex Nut 16
16	365	Thin-Jam Hex Nut 5

Figure 10-17. *Partial results of full-text query with expansion sets*

The replacement section of the thesaurus file indicates replacements for words that are used in a full-text query. In the example, we've defined several patterns, such as *brick* and *cherry*, which will be replaced with the word *red*. The result is that a full-text query for these replacement patterns will be converted internally to a search for *red*. The following is a FREETEXT query that uses the replacement patterns defined in the thesaurus.

```
SELECT ProductID, Name, Color
FROM Production.Product
WHERE FREETEXT(*, N'brick');
```

Figure 10-18 shows the results. You can use any of the replacement patterns defined in the thesaurus file in the full-text query to get the same results.

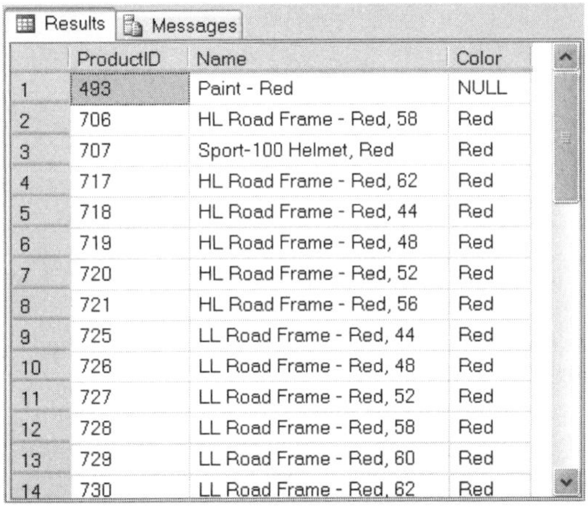

	ProductID	Name	Color
1	493	Paint - Red	NULL
2	706	HL Road Frame - Red, 58	Red
3	707	Sport-100 Helmet, Red	Red
4	717	HL Road Frame - Red, 62	Red
5	718	HL Road Frame - Red, 44	Red
6	719	HL Road Frame - Red, 48	Red
7	720	HL Road Frame - Red, 52	Red
8	721	HL Road Frame - Red, 56	Red
9	725	LL Road Frame - Red, 44	Red
10	726	LL Road Frame - Red, 48	Red
11	727	LL Road Frame - Red, 52	Red
12	728	LL Road Frame - Red, 58	Red
13	729	LL Road Frame - Red, 60	Red
14	730	LL Road Frame - Red, 62	Red

Figure 10-18. *Results of full-text query with replacement sets*

Reloading a Thesaurus

In previous versions of SQL Server, the FTS thesaurus files were loaded once when the full-text engine service was started. There was no documented way to dynamically reload the FTS thesaurus file without stopping and restarting the full-text engine service. SQL Server 2008 provides a new system stored procedure, `sys.sp_fulltext_load_thesaurus_file`, which allows you to reload thesaurus files without the hassle of stopping and restarting services. Once you have the modified `tsenu.xml` file in the `MSSQL\FTDATA` directory, you can load it using the following statement:

```
EXEC sys.sp_fulltext_load_thesaurus_file 1033;
```

The `sys.sp_fulltext_load_thesaurus_file` takes an LCID as a parameter. You can get a full list of supported LCIDs by querying `sys.fulltext_languages`.

SQL SERVER 2008 IFTS ARCHITECTURE CHANGES

SQL iFTS architecture has been changed significantly from previous versions of FTS. In prior versions of SQL Server, FTS was implemented via separate processes like SQL Server 2005's `MSFTESQL.EXE` full-text engine service. `MSFTESQL.EXE` provided a large chunk of the full-text engine functionality by performing tasks such as full-text indexing, full-text engine query processing, and filter daemon management.

SQL Server 2008 does away with `MSFTESQL.EXE`, moving its functionality directly into the `SQLSERVR.EXE` engine process. SQL Server 2008 includes a filter daemon host process, `FDHOST.EXE`, which replaces the full-text engine filter daemon process (`MSFTEFD.EXE`) in SQL Server 2005. These two processes interact with each other, and with the SQL Server query engine, to provide iFTS functionality. The SQL Server 2008 process (`SQLSERVR.EXE`) contains five major iFTS components:

- Full-text query
- Gatherer
- Indexer
- Full-text engine query processor
- Filter daemon process manager

The filter daemon host process (`FDHOST.EXE`) consists of two main components: filters and word-breakers. This new level of integration with the SQL Server query engine promises to make iFTS more efficient and easier to manage and administer than previous iterations of SQL Server FTS.

Using Stoplists

Previous versions of FTS provided system-defined lists of "noise words," which were used to ignore commonly occurring words that don't help the search, such as *the*, *a*, and *an*. The noise-word implementation in previous versions stored the noise words in text files in the file system. SQL Server 2008 introduces a new implementation of the classic noise words, known in iFTS as *stopwords*.

Stopwords are managed inside the SQL Server database using structures known as *stoplists*. You can use the system-supplied stoplists or create and manage your own stoplists through the `CREATE FULLTEXT STOPLIST`, `ALTER FULLTEXT STOPLIST`, and `DROP FULLTEXT STOPLIST` statements. The following statement creates a stoplist based on the system stoplist:

```
CREATE FULLTEXT STOPLIST AdvStoplist
FROM SYSTEM STOPLIST;
GO
```

Stoplists are far more flexible than the old noise-word lists, since you can add words to your stoplists. Consider AdventureWorks product model searches where the word *adventure* appears in several of the XML Instructions columns. We can add the word *adventure* to the previously created stoplist with the ALTER FULLTEXT STOPLIST statement, and then associate the stoplist with the full-text index on the Production.ProductModel table via the ALTER FULLTEXT INDEX statement, as follows:

```
ALTER FULLTEXT STOPLIST AdvStoplist
ADD N'adventure' LANGUAGE 1033;
GO

ALTER FULLTEXT INDEX ON Production.ProductModel
SET STOPLIST AdvStoplist;
GO
```

After application of the newly created stoplist, a full-text query against the Production.ProductModel table for the word *adventure*, as follows, will return no results:

```
SELECT *
FROM Production.ProductModel
WHERE FREETEXT(*, N'adventure');
```

Searching Documents

In addition to searching textual data stored in text-based columns of a database, iFTS can be used to search documents stored in the database. As with database searches, you need a full-text index for the document you want to search.

Creating a Full-Text Index for Documents

You can create a full-text index for a document using a variation of the CREATE FULLTEXT INDEX statement. A statement that creates a full-text index for the Production.Document table follows:

```
CREATE FULLTEXT INDEX ON Production.Document
(
  Document  TYPE COLUMN FileExtension LANGUAGE 1033
)
KEY INDEX PK_Document_DocumentNode
ON (AdvFTCatalog)
WITH
(
  CHANGE_TRACKING AUTO,
  STOPLIST = SYSTEM
);
GO
```

This version is very similar to the CREATE FULLTEXT INDEX statement for a database, with one slight difference. In this variation, the varbinary(max) Document column is specified as the column to include in the full-text index. Immediately following the column name is the TYPE COLUMN clause, followed by a column containing the document type. The FileExtension column is specified in this instance. This column contains document types of .doc, which indicates a Microsoft Word document. The type column is particularly important, since it tells SQL Server which filter should be used to extract indexable information from the document.

You can query the sys.fulltext_document_types catalog view to get a list of all the supported document types and their associated extensions.

Querying Documents

The AdventureWorks sample database has a table called `Production.Document`, which contains Microsoft Word documents in a `varbinary(max)` column named `Document`. The AdventureWorks database comes with a full-text index already created on the `Document` column of the `Production.Document` table, so we can skip the full-text index creation statement for this example. The following sample `FREETEXT` query locates documents that have the word *safe* in them. It returns the two documents shown in Figure 10-19.

```
SELECT DocumentNode, Title, DocumentSummary
FROM Production.Document
WHERE FREETEXT (*, N'safe');
```

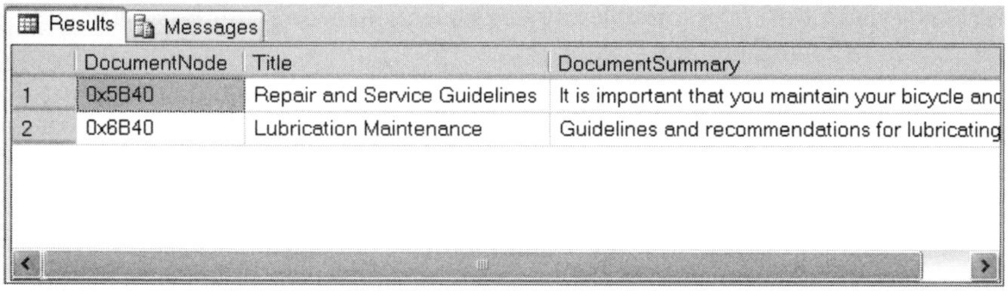

Figure 10-19. *Results of the full-text document query*

Managing iFTS

SQL Server 2008 provides new features to make configuration and administration of iFTS easier than ever. So far in this chapter, we've covered several of the new features in iFTS, including the tighter integration with the SQL query engine, the new T-SQL keywords for full-text catalog and full-text index creation and management, and the flexible new stopwords and stoplist management. In addition to the stored procedures and catalog views and functions, SQL Server 2008 provides some iFTS-specific data management functions and views.

While there are several stored procedures available for backward compatibility with previous versions of SQL Server, most of them are deprecated and should not be used for future development. Instead, you'll want to use the equivalent T-SQL statements, catalog views, and dynamic management views. These deprecated features are well-documented in SQL Server Books Online, so we'll focus instead on the new functionality in SQL Server 2008.

■**Caution** Starting with SQL Server 2005, Microsoft has deprecated many of the FTS-specific stored procedures that were available in SQL Server 2000. While they might be handy for quickly porting old SQL Server 2000 FTS administration scripts to SQL Server 2008, many of these features will be removed in a future version of SQL Server. If you use these stored procedures in your scripts or applications, it's a good idea to start preparing to get rid of them and using the T-SQL FTS-specific DDL statements and catalog views instead.

SQL Server 2008 introduces two new stored procedures to aid in iFTS management:

- The `sys.sp_fulltext_load_thesaurus_file` procedure allows you to reload thesaurus files without needing to stop and restart services.

- The `sys.sp_fulltext_resetfdhostaccount` procedure updates the Windows username and password that SQL Server uses to start the new filter daemon service.

A big issue for developers who used FTS in prior versions of SQL Server was the lack of transparency. Basically, everything that FTS did was well hidden from view, and developers and administrators had to troubleshoot FTS issues in the dark. SQL Server 2008 introduces some new catalog views and dynamic management functions that make iFTS more transparent (good news for SQL Server iFTS developers and administrators):

- If you're experiencing iFTS query performance issues, the `sys.fulltext_index_fragments` catalog view might provide some insight. With this catalog view, SQL Server reports full-text index fragments and their status. You can use the information in this catalog view to decide if it's time to reorganize your full-text index.

- The `sys.fulltext_stoplists` and `sys.fulltext_stopwords` catalog views let you see the user-defined stopwords and stoplists defined in the current database. The information returned by these catalog views is useful for troubleshooting issues with certain words being ignored (or not being ignored) in full-text queries.

- The `sys.fulltext_system_stopwords` catalog view returns a row for every stopword in the system stoplist, which is useful information if you want to use the system stoplist as the basis for your own stoplists.

- The `sys.dm_fts_parser` function accepts a full-text query string, an LCID, a stoplist ID, and an accent-sensitivity setting. It returns the results produced by the word-breaker and stemmer for any given full-text query. This information is very useful if you need to troubleshoot, or if you just want to better understand exactly how the word-breaker and stemmer affect your queries.

The following is a simple demonstration of the `sys.dm_fts_parser` function, which produces the results shown in Figure 10-20.

```
SELECT *
FROM sys.dm_fts_parser(N'FORMSOF(FREETEXT, go)', 1033, NULL, 0);
```

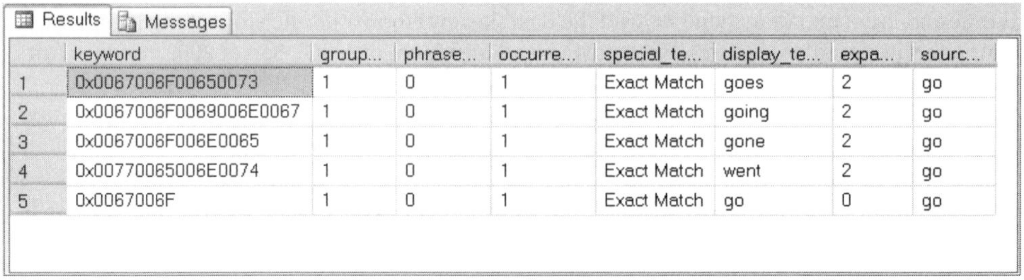

	keyword	group...	phrase...	occurre...	special_te...	display_te...	expa...	sourc...
1	0x0067006F00650073	1	0	1	Exact Match	goes	2	go
2	0x0067006F0069006E0067	1	0	1	Exact Match	going	2	go
3	0x0067006F006E0065	1	0	1	Exact Match	gone	2	go
4	0x00770065006E0074	1	0	1	Exact Match	went	2	go
5	0x0067006F	1	0	1	Exact Match	go	0	go

Figure 10-20. *Results of word-breaking and stemming a full-text query for "go"*

Summary

SQL Server 2008 improves upon the FTS capabilities previously available in SQL Server 2005. The SQL Server 2008 model provides several performance and manageability enhancements, including new Data Definition Language (DDL) statements, built-in support for a wider variety of languages, and tighter integration with the SQL Server query engine, among other improvements.

The new tools and features covered in this chapter make iFTS setup, configuration, and administration easier than ever. The tighter integration with the SQL Server query engine will enhance iFTS performance and provide a more efficient full-text search platform than any prior version of SQL Server.

PART 3

Development in SQL Server

CHAPTER 11

■■■

New Datatypes in SQL Server 2008

While the native datatypes like varchar, int, float, and datetime are at the foundation of almost all solutions, some issues arise when working with these types. The issues mainly involve the limitations of these datatypes when trying to manipulate them to fit a particular common situation. For example, if you were designing a table schema that included a list of employees and wanted to use this table to query a list of managers and their direct reports, you could write a query that used a self join. The solution could also involve using common table expressions or other approaches, all of which are composed of the native datatypes within SQL Server. SQL Server 2008 has a hierarchyid datatype that knows about hierarchical data like employee/manager relationships. The new datatypes in SQL Server 2008 are designed to address these kinds of key user scenarios.

In this chapter, we'll cover the following topics:

- Spatial datatype support, which includes GEOMETRY and GEOGRAPHY datatypes, as well as spatial indexing support

- New date and time support, which includes very flexible date and time types (we are no longer restricted to a lower bound of year 1753 or to 3.33 milliseconds of precision, for example)

- The hierarchyid datatype, which is great for applications that deal with a lot of hierarchical data

- The new filestream attribute to varbinary(max), which allows you to store large objects in the file system and have these files integrated within the database

Spatial Support in SQL Server 2008

Consider the task of storing the geographical coordinates of Boston, Massachusetts: latitude of 42.358543396 and longitude of –71.0595703125. To do this within a relational database, you could just use float datatypes. However, what if you wanted to store the boundary of ZIP code 02113 (in the downtown Boston area)? Now you would add some more floats to define the polygon for the ZIP code. Those would be easy enough to store, but when it comes to doing something with this information, unless you roll your own solution, simply storing the values isn't very useful. Interacting with other applications, such as via a web service, is even more difficult with no standard way of representing spatial information. Wouldn't it be great if there were a standard format so other users and applications could interact with a common spatial format? Well, there is a standard.

The Open Geospatial Consortium, Inc. (OGC) is an international industry consortium of more than 350 companies, government agencies, and universities, who all collaborate and develop publicly available interface specifications. These specifications, called OpenGIS Specifications, support interoperable solutions that "geo-enable" the web, wireless, and location-based services, as well as mainstream information technology (IT). The main idea is to empower developers to make complex spatial information and services accessible and useful, so that the information can be easily shared among any applications that are willing to conform to OpenGIS. SQL Server's spatial implementation is based on these specifications.

Spatial support within SQL Server is actually composed of two datatypes:

- GEOMETRY is about mapping data on a two-dimensional plane (x and y coordinate system).

- GEOGRAPHY is about storing information relating to the Earth's surface.

Let's look at both of these types in more detail.

The GEOMETRY Type

The GEOMETRY datatype is a system .NET common language runtime (CLR) datatype in SQL Server. This type represents data in a two-dimensional Euclidean coordinate system. For those of us who might not remember grade school math, two-dimensional Euclidean coordinates are also known as *plane geometry*. Plane geometry addresses things like points, lines, circles, polygons, and any shape that can live on a two-dimensional x-y plane.

Internally, spatial data is stored as binary within SQL Server. When extracting an ASCII text representation of spatial data, SQL uses the well-known text (WKT) representation defined by the OGC in Section 3.2.5 of the Simple Features Specification for SQL (http://portal.opengeospatial.org/files/?artifact_id=829). Some examples of the WKT representation of spatial data are shown in Table 11-1.

Table 11-1. *Examples of Well-Known Text Representation of Spatial Data*

Geometry Type	WKT Representation	Description
Point	POINT (10 15)	A point
Multipoint	MULTIPOINT (10 10, 50 50)	A multipoint with two points
LineString	LINESTRING (10 10,20 20,31 35)	A line string with three points
Polygon	POLYGON ((10 10, 10 20, 20 20, 20 15, 10 10))	A polygon
GeomCollection	GEOMETRYCOLLECTION ((POINT (10 15), LINESTRING (10 10,20 20))	A collection of a point and line

The function that returns the WKT representations shown in Table 11-1 is STAsText(). However, this is not the only function that supports geometry spatial data. There are actually more than 60 functions that support the GEOMETRY type (as well as the GEOGRAPHY type). Table 11-2 lists some of these functions.

Table 11-2. *Some Functions That Support the GEOMETRY and GEOGRAPHY Types*

Function	Description
STAsText	Returns the OpenGIS WKT representation of the stored geometric type value.
STGeometryType	Returns the friendly name (i.e., POINT or LINESTRING) of the stored geometric type value.
STGeomFromText	Constructs a geometry value for a given value in WKT format.
STArea	Returns the sum of the areas of all surfaces defined in the geometric type value.
STSrid	Returns the spatial reference ID (SRID) of the value stored in the geometric type.

Function	Description
STIntersects	Returns true if a given geometric value intersects with another; otherwise, it returns false. This method returns null if the SRID of this instance does not match the SRID of the other instance.
STTouches	Returns true if a given geometric value touches another; otherwise, it returns false. This method returns null if the SRID of this instance does not match the SRID of the other instance.
STWithin	Returns true if a given geometric value is within another; otherwise, it returns false. This method returns null if the SRID of this instance does not match the SRID of the other instance.
STDistance	Returns the shortest distance between a point in a given geometric value and a point in another value. This method returns null if the SRID of this instance does not match the SRID of the other instance.
GeomFromGML	Constructs a geometry value for a given value in Geography Markup Language (GML) format.
AsGML	Returns the geometric value in GML format.

Each geometric type has an SRID. All methods that operate on multiple spatial data values require that the SRIDs of the data match. Functions that compare or manipulate multiple geometric data values will fail when these data values contain different SRIDs.

The complete list of functions that support the GEOMETRY type can be found in SQL Server Books Online.

Let's consider the problem of storing the boundaries of ZIP codes and doing something useful with that information. Figure 11-1 shows the fictitious ZIP code area you'll use for this example. For simplicity, the actual coordinates are presented as integers.

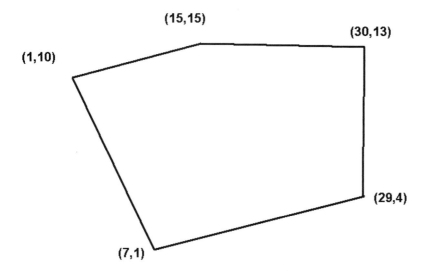

Figure 11-1. *Fictitious ZIP code boundaries*

First, create a table to store the geometry data of the ZIP code:

```
CREATE TABLE ZipCodes
(ID           INT        PRIMARY KEY,
ZipGeometry   GEOMETRY    NOT NULL,
ZipAsText     AS          ZipGeometry.STAsText()
)
```

The second column, ZipGeometry, will store the ZIP code, and you add a computed column that will display your geometry data as text, for convenience.

The next step is to populate this table with the data points shown in Figure 11-1:

```
DECLARE @ZipData GEOMETRY
SET @ZipData = geometry::STGeomFromText('POLYGON((1 10,
 15 15, 30 13, 29 4, 7 1, 1 10))', 0)

INSERT INTO ZipCodes
VALUES ('1',GEOMETRY::STGeomFromText('POLYGON((1 10,
 15 15, 30 13, 29 4, 7 1, 1 10))', 0))
```

The STGeomFromText() function takes OpenGIS WKT and stores it as binary within the SQL Server storage engine. In this case, you are storing a polygon that outlines a ZIP code.

Now that you have defined the ZIP code boundaries, you can perform various operations with that data using many of the built-in functions. For example, the following code snippet uses STArea() to get the area of the ZIP code:

```
DECLARE @ZipData GEOMETRY;
SET @ZipData=(SELECT ZipGeometry from ZipCodes where id=1)
SELECT @ZipData.STArea() as 'Area of zipcode'
```

```
Area of zipcode
----------------------
288.5

(1 row(s) affected)
```

What if the town decided to build a new high school at point 10, 10 and wanted to make sure this was within the ZIP code? The following code snippet applies the STWithin() function to answer this question:

```
DECLARE @HighSchool GEOMETRY
SET @HighSchool=GEOMETRY::STGeomFromText('POINT(10 10)',0);

IF (@HighSchool.STWithin(@ZipData)=1)
    SELECT 'School is within ZipCode'
ELSE
    SELECT 'School is outside of ZipCode'
```

```
----------------------
School is within ZipCode

(1 row(s) affected)
```

What if an elementary school is within the ZIP code area, and the town wants to know what the distance between this and the new high school will be? To answer this question, use the STDistance() function:

```
DECLARE @ElementarySchool GEOMETRY
SET @ElementarySchool=GEOMETRY::STGeomFromText('POINT(12 8)',0);
SELECT @ElementarySchool.STDistance(@HighSchool)
```

```
---------------------
2.82842712474619

(1 row(s) affected)
```

A river runs through the town. The planning and zoning committee wants to know if this river touches the border of the ZIP code. The following code snippet answers this question using STTouches():

```
DECLARE @River GEOMETRY
SET @River=GEOMETRY::STGeomFromText('LINESTRING(.5 12, 1 10, 1 8, .5 3, 0 0)',0)
SELECT @River.STTouches(@ZipData)
```

```
-----
1

(1 row(s) affected)
```

The function STTouches() returns 1 if the defined LINESTRING touches the polygon of the ZIP code defined in @ZipData. If not, the function returns 0.

These are just a sampling of the many functions that are available to the GEOMETRY type in SQL Server 2008. In addition to these functions, which manipulate or analyze the actual geometric values, a few functions help import or export the data values themselves. The previous examples used STGeomFromText(), which inputs the OpenGIS WKT format and stores this value as binary within the SQL Server storage engine. Another group of functions interacts with XML data. XML data that describes geographic data is called Geography Markup Language (GML). SQL Server has a restricted implementation of the OpenGIS GML model for SQL Server 2008. It is restricted in that it does not contain every single element defined in the model, but it does contain most of the frequently used elements, like Point, Polygon, and so on.

To see how GML works within SQL Server, let's create a stored procedure that accepts two inputs: an XML input and an integer. The XML input will be an XML instance in GML format that describes a point. The integer will tell which ZIP code to compare. The function will determine if the point supplied via GML is within the ZIP code specified by the integer. Here is the stored procedure:

```
CREATE PROCEDURE IsInZipCode(@ZipGML as xml,@ZipCode as int)
AS
BEGIN
    DECLARE @ZipData GEOMETRY;
    SET @ZipData=(SELECT ZipGeometry from ZipCodes where id=@ZipCode)

    DECLARE @PointAsGML GEOMETRY;
    SET @PointAsGML=GEOMETRY::GeomFromGml(@ZipGML,0)
    --SELECT @PointAsGML.STWithin(@ZipData)

    IF (@PointAsGML.STWithin(@ZipData)=1)
    SELECT 'Within Zipcode'
ELSE
    SELECT 'Outside of Zipcode'
END
```

Let's test this stored procedure by creating an XML variable and populating it with a point 10, 10. This point should be within the ZIP code with the ID of 1 (the only ZIP code added to the table).

```
DECLARE @MyPoint XML
SET @MyPoint='<Point xmlns="http://www.opengis.net/gml"><pos>10 10</pos></Point>'
EXEC IsInZipCode @MyPoint,1
```

```
--------------
Within Zipcode

(1 row(s) affected)
```

Here, you've added a simple `Point`, but you could have created any arrangement of `LineStrings`, `Polygons`, or anything else—after all, it's just XML.

The `GEOMETRY` datatype examples shown thus far have been inside Transact-SQL (T-SQL) code. Since the spatial datatypes are system-defined user-defined types (UDTs) written using the CLR, it is also possible to call these functions using .NET. The `GEOMETRY` type is named `SqlGeometry` and lives in the `Microsoft.SqlServer.Server.Types` namespace.

The GEOGRAPHY Type

The Earth is not a sphere, as some may think. It actually bulges at the equator due to its rotation. (For those still in disbelief, check out this discussion on the shape of Earth at `http://www.josleys.com/show_gallery.php?galid=313`.) If the Earth were a perfect consistent mass, the resulting shape due to this rotation would be an ellipsoid. However, the Earth is not a perfect mass, and thus not a perfect ellipsoid. Specialists in this field of study refer to this imperfect ellipsoid of Earth as a *geoid*.

`GEOGRAPHY` is the geodetic type, describing spatial objects on a geodetic plane (such as the Earth surface) and providing the corresponding operations on it. This datatype describes points in terms of longitude and latitude, and is often used to represent global positioning system (GPS) coordinates. Again, each object is associated with an SRID that encodes information about the standard that has been used (for example, WGS 84 for US GPS data).

`GEOGRAPHY` is very similar to `GEOMETRY`, and we can almost get away with one spatial datatype instead of two, but there are significant inherent semantic differences between working in the plane and working on an ellipsoid. For example, while we do not care about ring direction for polygons on the plane, we must take them into account on the sphere. Additionally, separating the two types allows the database engine to create more efficient indexes.

As it is prohibitive to compute distances using the real Earth, we need to create a computational model. If we consider all the mathematical models available today, a spherical model is a better choice than the plane, but the error is still substantial. The geoid would give us incredibly accurate results, but its computations are very complex, and the performance of our application may suffer. The best bet is for `GEOGRAPHY` to model its computations against an ellipsoid model.

The `GEOGRAPHY` datatype's functions are the same as with `GEOMETRY`. The difference between the two is that when you specify `GEOGRAPHY`, you are usually specifying points in terms of latitude and longitude. Also, the calculations that are performed will provide values as points on an ellipsoid, rather than as points in a plane. This is significant since, as the distances get larger, the error in calculation gets larger. Consider the case where an airline flies from Boston, Massachusetts to Seattle, Washington. If you calculated a flight plan using the Earth on a plane, you would end up traveling many more air miles than when calculating the distance taking into consideration the curvature of the Earth (flying up near the Canadian border is a shorter distance).

How Time Has Changed in SQL Server

In previous versions of SQL Server, options for date and time storage and manipulation rested on the datetime and smalldatetime datatypes. These types have some fairly significant limitations for certain types of applications. For one thing, the date range on a datetime datatype is January 1, 1753, to December 31, 9999. What if the application you were developing needed to store historical information that occurred previous to 1753? Another limitation is the 3.33 millisecond accuracy limit inherent to the datetime type. Not only is this not acceptable to some scientific and financial applications, but it isn't even in sync with the kind of time granularity you could achieve from the Windows operating system or from date and time types within the .NET Framework.

Finally, after years of asking, SQL Server now has a much better way to handle dates and times.

New Date and Time Datatypes

SQL Server 2008 introduces four new datatypes related to date and time: DATE, TIME, DATETIMEOFFSET, and DATETIME2. Together, these datatypes break down the barriers of the 1753 year limit, enable developers to leverage time-zone information, and provide precision second recording, down to 100-nanosecond granularities.

Each of the new date and time types is designed to be just another datatype in SQL Server. All Data Manipulation Language (DML) and Data Definition Language (DDL) statements, variables, stored procedures, and anything else you can think of within SQL that uses a datatype will work with these new types.

Two of the more common functions that are used with dates and times are CAST and CONVERT. In previous versions of SQL Server, when users issued CAST and CONVERT statements against a column that contained an index, the index was not leveraged and a table scan resulted. This obviously created some performance issues in certain situations. For SQL Server 2008, this behavior changed. When using the new date and time types with CAST and CONVERT commands, the SQL Server database engine will use an index if one is available.

When down-level clients, such as SQL Server 2000 and 2005 users, request date and time values from any of the new datatypes via Server Management Objects (SMO), they will receive text-string representations of the stored values. This is a great alternative to simply erroring out. These new datatypes have full support via the SQL Native Client (SNAC) library, which consists of OLE DB and ODBC support. In addition, the next version of ADO.NET (code-named Orcas) will fully support these new datatypes.

Now let's take a closer look at each of these new types.

The DATE Type

The new DATE type just stores the date itself. It is based on the Gregorian calendar and handles years from 1 to 9999.

If you were designing a schema for an employee table, what datatype would you use for entities like birthday or employee hire date? Chances are you might use datetime. That would work, but you would also be storing some additional time-related information that you didn't need. The datetime datatype also uses 6 bytes of storage. The new DATE type uses only 3 bytes. Those 3 bytes may not seem like a big savings, but multiply that by everywhere in your schema that you just need a date, spread that savings across an organization, and you will definitely see the benefit.

Some of you may be suggesting that where you just want to store the month, day, and year and are concerned about storage size, you could use tinyints (1 byte) for the month and day and a smallint (2 bytes) for the year. This would reduce your storage size to 4 bytes, which is still greater than the 3 bytes required for the DATE type. Even if you could further optimize the storage using integers, once you did this, you would need to do extra work within your application if you wanted to use the internal functions that support dates and times, like DATEPART, DATENAME, DATEDIFF, and DATEADD. These functions are all set to work with the new date and time datatypes in SQL Server 2008.

Now let's take a look at an example using the new DATE datatype. The default string literal for DATE is YYYY-MM-DD. This format complies with the SQL standard form as well as ISO 8601.

```
DECLARE @today      DATE
DECLARE @newyears   DATE

SET @today    =    SYSDATETIME()
SET @newyears =    '2007-12-31'

SELECT @today as 'Today',
    DATEADD(week,1,@today) as
        'One week from today',
    DATEDIFF(day,@today,@newyears) as
        'Days until New Years Day',
    DATALENGTH(@today) as 'Size in bytes'
```

```
Today       One week from today  Days until New Years Day  Size in bytes
----------  -------------------  ------------------------  ----------------
2007-08-24  2007-08-31           129                       3

(1 row(s) affected)
```

This example shows the new DATE type working seamlessly with the existing date functions (DATEADD and DATEDIFF). If the morning coffee is still doing its job, you might have also noticed a new system function in this example. SYSDATETIME() is one of five new built-in functions for SQL Server 2008. Its function is to return the current database system timestamp as a DATETIME2(7) type. We will discuss DATETIME2 and the new built-in system functions a little later in this section.

The TIME Type

The new TIME(n) type stores time with a range of 00:00:00.0000000 through 23:59:59.9999999. If you are intimate with existing time operations in SQL Server, you may be excited to note the precision allowed with this type. TIME supports seconds down to 100 nanoseconds. The n in TIME(n) defines this level of fractional second precision, from 0 to 7 digits of precision. Consider the following code:

```
DECLARE @time_now_0 time(0)
DECLARE @time_now_1 time(1)
DECLARE @time_now_2 time(2)
DECLARE @time_now_3 time(3)
DECLARE @time_now_4 time(4)
DECLARE @time_now_5 time(5)
DECLARE @time_now_6 time(6)
DECLARE @time_now_7 time(7)

SET @time_now_0=SYSDATETIME()
SET @time_now_1=SYSDATETIME()
SET @time_now_2=SYSDATETIME()
SET @time_now_3=SYSDATETIME()
SET @time_now_4=SYSDATETIME()
SET @time_now_5=SYSDATETIME()
SET @time_now_6=SYSDATETIME()
SET @time_now_7=SYSDATETIME()
```

```
SELECT @time_now_0 as 'Current Time', datalength(@time_now_0) as 'Size in bytes'
UNION ALL
SELECT @time_now_1,datalength(@time_now_1)
UNION ALL
SELECT @time_now_2,datalength(@time_now_2)
UNION ALL
SELECT @time_now_3,datalength(@time_now_3)
UNION ALL
SELECT @time_now_4,datalength(@time_now_4)
UNION ALL
SELECT @time_now_5,datalength(@time_now_5)
UNION ALL
SELECT @time_now_6,datalength(@time_now_6)
UNION ALL
SELECT @time_now_7,datalength(@time_now_7)
```

```
Current Time       Size in bytes
----------------   -------------
20:01:45.0000000   3
20:01:44.8000000   3
20:01:44.8000000   3
20:01:44.8040000   4
20:01:44.8035000   4
20:01:44.8035300   5
20:01:44.8035340   5
20:01:44.8035344   5

(8 row(s) affected)
```

This oversimplified example creates eight time variables, each with its own precision. Next, it assigns the current system time to each of these variables. Finally, it displays the results to the user.

You can see that the storage for the TIME is variable (between 3 and 5 bytes), depending on the precision you requested when you defined the datatype.

As with the DATE type, TIME is supported by the existing date- and time-related functions like DATEDIFF and DATEADD.

The DATETIMEOFFSET Type

DATETIMEOFFSET(n) is the time-zone-aware version of a datetime datatype. The name will appear less odd when you consider what it really is: a date + a time + a time-zone offset. The offset is based on how far behind or ahead you are from Coordinated Universal Time (UTC) time. As an example, the Eastern Standard Time (EST) zone is UTC –05:00, or 5 hours behind UTC. This is set according to the time defined in the operating system. Figure 11-2 shows an EST zone setting.

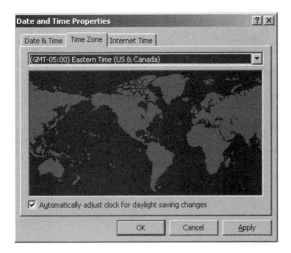

Figure 11-2. *The Windows Date and Time Properties dialog box shows the time-zone setting*

SYSDATETIMEOFFSET(), one of the new system functions, displays the date and time and the time-zone offset:

```
SELECT SYSDATETIMEOFFSET() AS 'Current Date, time and offset'
GO
```

```
Current Date, time and offset
----------------------------------
2007-08-24 20:23:50.1587968 -04:00

(1 row(s) affected)
```

This code was executed on the same server on which the screenshot in Figure 11-2 was taken. Can you find the discrepancy? I will pause and hum the jingle of *Jeopardy* for a moment.

When we ran the SYSDATETIMEOFFSET command, the offset reported -04:00, which is only 4 hours. But a 5-hour offset was defined in the Windows operating system. Why is this? The answer is daylight saving time. The screenshot and code were run in August, in an area of the United States that honors daylight saving time and thus pushes the clocks ahead an hour. SQL Server does not know anything about daylight saving time. The time that is being reported is coming directly from the operating system.

For SQL Server to take daylight saving time into account would require a live, active database of all the areas and governments that support it, and to continually update this database. It is not that this couldn't be done; it is just that the people in the SQL Server product team decided daylight saving time adjustment wasn't worth the effort in this release. The work-around is to obtain this information from either the .NET Framework or the Windows operating system, which already handles the issue of daylight saving time.

The storage of DATETIMEOFFSET(*n*) depends on the precision (*n*) specified, much like the TIME type discussed in the previous section. This size will be between 8 and 10 bytes. The offset itself has a possible range of −14:00 to 14:00.

The DATETIME2 Type

DATETIME2(*n*) is an extension of the datetime type in earlier versions of SQL Server. Ideally, this type would have been called TIMESTAMP, to conform to the ANSI SQL Standard type it represents. However, SQL Server already has a timestamp type, which has nothing to do with the SQL Standard one. Thus, the SQL Server team had to come up with a new, highly creative name. They ended up with DATETIME2.

This new datatype has a date range covering dates from January 1 of year 1 through December 31 of year 9999. This is a definite improvement over the 1753 lower boundary of the datetime datatype. DATETIME2 not only includes the larger date range, but also has a timestamp and the same fractional precision that TIME type provides. With these capabilities, you might think this type is the same as what is provided by the DATETIMEOFFSET type. The difference between DATETIME2 and the DATETIMEOFFSET type is that DATETIME2 does not contain time-zone information.

A DATETIME2(*n*) type can take between 6 and 8 bytes of storage, depending on the fractional seconds precision defined (the (*n*)). This type is the best one to use when upgrading an application that had previously used the datetime type. Not only is it fully compliant with the ANSI SQL Standard, but it is fully aligned with the .NET DateTime type.

New Date and Time System Functions

Along with the new date and time types, SQL Server 2008 introduces five new date- and time-related system functions. Three of these functions—SYSDATETIME, SYSUTCDATETIME, and SYSDATETIMEOFFSET—return a timestamp of the system in a variety of formats. The remaining two functions—TODATETIMEOFFSET and SWITCHOFFSET—display and manipulate the time-zone offset of a given date and time value.

The SYSDATETIME Function

The SYSDATETIME() function returns the system timestamp as a DATETIME2(7) value without any time-zone offset information. The value is derived from the operating system where the SQL Server instance is running.

```
SELECT SYSDATETIME() as 'Current date and time',
DATALENGTH(SYSDATETIME()) as 'Size in bytes'
```

```
Current date and time       Size in bytes
--------------------------  -------------
2007-08-24 23:51:29.2372064  8

(1 row(s) affected)
```

The SYSUTCDATETIME Function

The SYSUTCDATETIME() function is similar to the SYSDATETIME() function, except that it returns the system timestamp in UTC format.

```
SELECT SYSUTCDATETIME() as 'Current date and time',
DATALENGTH(SYSUTCDATETIME()) as 'Size in bytes'
```

```
Current date and time       Size in bytes
--------------------------  -------------
2007-08-25 03:55:07.7499712  8

(1 row(s) affected)
```

The SYSDATETIMEOFFSET Function

The SYSDATETIMEOFFSET() function is similar to both SYSDATETIME() and SYSUTCDATETIME(), in that it returns the system timestamp. In addition to the date, time, and fractional second precision, this function returns the time-zone information of the operating system that SQL Server instance is running on in the form of a DATETIME2(7) value.

```
SELECT SYSDATETIMEOFFSET() as 'Current date and time',
DATALENGTH(SYSDATETIMEOFFSET()) as 'Size in bytes'
```

```
Current date and time                   Size in bytes
--------------------------------        -------------
2007-08-25 00:04:47.6595136 -04:00      10

(1 row(s) affected)
```

The TODATETIMEOFFSET Function

The TODATETIMEOFFSET() function converts a local date, time, and time-zone offset value to a date-time offset UTC value.

```
DECLARE @DateWithoutOffset   DATETIME2
DECLARE @DateWithOffset      DATETIMEOFFSET

SET @DateWithoutOffset=sysdatetime() --SYSDATETIME contains no offset information

SET @DateWithOffset=TODATETIMEOFFSET(@DateWithoutOffset,'-03:00')

SELECT @DateWithoutOffset AS 'Without Offset',
  @DateWithOffset AS 'With offset added'
```

```
Without Offset                 With offset added
--------------------------     ----------------------------------
2007-08-25 00:25:14.8397072    2007-08-25 00:25:14.8397072 -03:00

(1 row(s) affected)
```

From this example, you can see that this function can be useful in adding time-zone information to existing date-time information.

The SWITCHOFFSET Function

The SWITCHOFFSET() function gives the user a new date, time, and time-zone-adjusted value based on a given date and the specific offset desired. As an example, suppose you stored the start time of a particular movie in the database as August 25, 2007, at 01:30 AM Pacific Standard Time (–07:00 adjusted for daylight saving time). You want to know what time this will start on the East Coast. You can use the SWITCHOFFSET() function to determine this:

```
DECLARE  @show_time  DATETIMEOFFSET
SET      @show_time  ='2007-08-25 01:30 -07:00'

SELECT @show_time
 AS 'Movie start time in Pacific timezone',
SWITCHOFFSET(@show_time,'-04:00')
  AS 'Movie start time in Eastern timezone'
```

```
Movie start time in Pacific timezone  Movie start time in Eastern timezone
------------------------------------  ------------------------------------
2007-08-25 01:30:00.0000000 -07:00    2007-08-25 04:30:00.0000000 -04:00

(1 row(s) affected)
```

We've bolded the time values here to highlight the work this function performs. From the result text, you can see that the movie starts 3 hours later, at 04:30 AM.

A New Hierarchical Datatype

Hierarchical data may be in organizational charts, file and folder lists, product catalogs, forum threads, and so on. Hierarchical data is defined as a set of data items that are related or ranked against each other. In simplest terms, a parent-child relationship is a form of hierarchy. The parent can have zero or more children, those children can have zero or more children, and so on.

Within SQL Server, you can handle hierarchical information in a few different ways:

- Use the XML datatype. This requires all of the applications and users that interact with the data to use XML. However, XML is an industry standard and is great for interacting with heterogeneous environments.

- Store the data in a relational table and use SELF JOIN statements to dynamically create the structure. This can lead to potentially complex T-SQL statements, which are difficult to manage and maintain.

- Use the new hierarchyid datatype available in SQL Server 2008.

The hierarchyid datatype is great for applications that deal with a lot of hierarchical data. It allows you to perform relational operations with hierarchical data. Many built-in functions support the new hierarchyid datatype.

The hierarchyid datatype is not a native datatype like DATE and TIME. Rather, it is a system-defined UDT. This new type is stored in Microsoft.SqlServer.Types.dll and is created within the Microsoft.SqlServer.Types namespace. *System-defined* implies that you cannot delete, rename, or otherwise mess up this type.

Given that hierarchyid is technically a CLR UDT, you might expect that the CLR must be enabled to use it with SQL Server. However, since hierarchyid is a system-defined type, you do not need to explicitly enable the CLR within SQL Server to use it.

Let's consider the organizational structure of a fictional company called The Bureaucratic Corporation, represented in Figure 11-3.

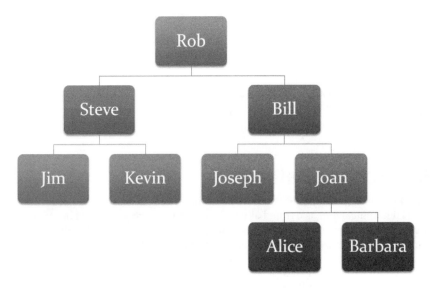

Figure 11-3. *Organizational chart for The Bureaucratic Corporation*

Suppose that you are tasked with storing this organizational chart in SQL Server using the new hierarchyid type. After creating the database, you create the Employees table, as follows:

```
CREATE TABLE Employees
(node hierarchyid PRIMARY KEY CLUSTERED,
level AS node.GetLevel() PERSISTED,
employee_id INT UNIQUE,
employee_name VARCHAR(30) NOT NULL)
```

Notice that you created a computed column using the deterministic function GetLevel(). This function returns the level in the hierarchy of the node value. In the example, the root node, Rob, is considered level 0. Steve and Bill are level 1, and following this down the tree, Alice and Barbara are considered level 3.

Once the table is created, the root node can be added as follows:

```
INSERT INTO Employees VALUES (hierarchyid::GetRoot(),5000,'Rob')
```

GetRoot() is another deterministic function that returns the root value of the node. Since you will be referencing the employees by employee_id, you'll use employee_id numbers that start with 5000, so as to not be confused with the node levels, which will be integers starting with 0.

Once you have the root node in place, you can continue and build the organizational structure. First, a disclaimer: as with any programmatic implementation, there are different ways to arrive at the same result. The examples here are oversimplistic and are not optimized by any stretch of the imagination. They are merely intended to clearly demonstrate the core concepts.

To add a subordinate to the root node, Rob, you will use the GetDescendants built-in function. This function returns a child node that is a descendant of the parent. In this case, there are no children of this parent, so this function will return the value of the first child.

```
--First let's declare some variables for use in temporarily storing the nodes
DECLARE @ManagerNode hierarchyid
DECLARE @Level hierarchyid

--Employee_ID of 5000 is the root node, "Rob"
SELECT @ManagerNode=node FROM Employees WHERE employee_id=5000
--GetDescendant will now return the first child "/1"
--since there are no other children defined
INSERT INTO Employees VALUES (@ManagerNode.GetDescendant(NULL, NULL),5001, 'Bill')
```

In the example, the root node, Rob, is considered level 0 and is represented in a text form as /. When Bill was added, he was the first child of the root node and was given the value /1. Similarly, when you add Steve, another child node, his value will be /2.

```
--Employee_ID of 5001 is Bill
SELECT @Level=node FROM Employees WHERE employee_id=5001
--We are passing (Bill,NULL) to GetDescendant. This will
--give us the node value of the next child after Bill
--Likewise if we passed (NULL,Bill) GetDescendant would
--return the node value of the child previous to Bill
--(think inserting a child before Bill)
INSERT INTO Employees VALUES
  (@ManagerNode.GetDescendant(@Level, NULL),5002, 'Steve')
```

It is important to note the textual representation of the node itself. The following query will display the organizational structure at this point:

```
SELECT node.ToString() AS NodeAsString,
node as NodeAsBinary,
node.GetLevel() AS Level,
employee_id,
employee_name
FROM Employees
```

NodeAsString	NodeAsBinary	Level	employee_id	employee_name
/	0x	0	5000	Rob
/1/	0x58	1	5001	Bill
/2/	0x68	1	5002	Steve

(3 row(s) affected)

As you build the rest of the organizational structure, the string representation as it relates to the organization is shown graphically in Figure 11-4.

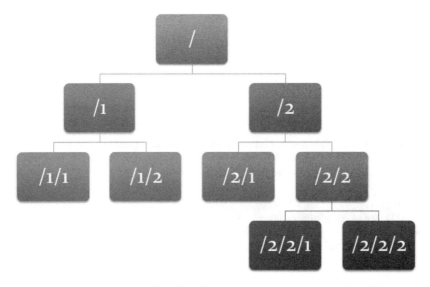

Figure 11-4. *Organizational chart for The Bureaucratic Corporation showing node names*

You can see from Figure 11-4 that, as you add a direct report, Jim under Steve, Jim's node is displayed as /2/1. The rest of the code is as follows:

```
SELECT @Level=node FROM Employees WHERE employee_id=5002
INSERT INTO Employees VALUES (@Level.GetDescendant(NULL, NULL),5003, 'Jim')
--Now we have Steve, the manager stored in @Level
--We inserted Jim as a direct report and now need
--another variable to store Jim since we are going
--to insert another direct report (child) under Steve, the manager.
DECLARE @child1 hierarchyid
--Employee_ID of 5003 is Jim
SELECT @child1=node FROM Employees WHERE employee_id=5003
--GetDescendant will return the value of the next node after Jim
INSERT INTO Employees VALUES (@Level.GetDescendant(@child1, NULL),5004, 'Kevin')

--Now we are repeating the pattern, grab Bill's node in @Level
SELECT @Level=node FROM Employees WHERE employee_id=5001
--The first child of Bill is NULL,NULL, we want to put Joseph there
INSERT INTO Employees VALUES (@Level.GetDescendant(NULL,NULL),5005, 'Joseph')
--Grab Joseph's node
SELECT @child1=node FROM Employees WHERE employee_id=5005
--Insert Joan as a direct report of Bill
INSERT INTO Employees VALUES (@Level.GetDescendant(@child1,NULL),5006, 'Joan')

--Alice is a direct report of Joan. Using the same pattern grab Joan's node
SELECT @Level=node FROM Employees WHERE employee_id=5006
--Put Alice as the first direct report (child) of Joan
INSERT INTO Employees VALUES (@Level.GetDescendant(NULL,NULL),5007, 'Alice')
--Grab Alice's node
SELECT @child1=node FROM Employees WHERE employee_id=5007
--Insert Barabara as a direct report of Joan
INSERT INTO Employees VALUES (@Level.GetDescendant(@child1,NULL),5008, 'Barbara')
```

Now running the organization query results in the following:

```
NodeAsString  NodeAsBinary  Level    employee_id employee_name
------------  ------------  -----    ----------- -------------
/             0x            0        5000        Rob
/1/           0x58          1        5001        Bill
/1/1/         0x5AC0        2        5005        Joseph
/1/2/         0x5B40        2        5006        Joan
/1/2/1/       0x5B56        3        5007        Alice
/1/2/2/       0x5B5A        3        5008        Barbara
/2/           0x68          1        5002        Steve
/2/1/         0x6AC0        2        5003        Jim
/2/2/         0x6B40        2        5004        Kevin

(9 row(s) affected)
```

Taking a look at this organization, you can see that it's too flat to make a good bureaucratic company. You need more layers of management, so let's use the built-in Reparent() function to move Joan's organization to report under Kevin.

```
DECLARE @level hierarchyid
DECLARE @OldParent hierarchyid
DECLARE @NewParent hierarchyid

SELECT @Level=node from Employees where employee_id=5006 -- Joan
SELECT @OldParent=node from Employees where employee_id=5001 -- Move from Bill
SELECT @NewParent=node from Employees where employee_id=5004 -- To Kevin

UPDATE Employees
SET node = @Level.Reparent(@OldParent, @NewParent)
WHERE node = @Level
```

When you requery the organization list, you see the following:

```
NodeAsString  NodeAsBinary  Level    employee_id employee_name
------------  ------------  -----    ----------- -------------
/             0x            0        5000        Rob
/1/           0x58          1        5001        Bill
/1/1/         0x5AC0        2        5005        Joseph
/1/2/1/       0x5B56        3        5007        Alice
/1/2/2/       0x5B5A        3        5008        Barbara
/2/           0x68          1        5002        Steve
/2/1/         0x6AC0        2        5003        Jim
/2/2/         0x6B40        2        5004        Kevin
/2/2/2/       0x6B5A        3        5006        Joan

(9 row(s) affected)
```

Can you spot a problem?

When you issued the Reparent() function, it worked, but not as some of us might have thought. The Reparent() function literally took Joan's node and placed it under Kevin's, but left all of Joan's direct reports without a manager (that is, Joan was /1/2, but this no longer exists). This behavior is an important concept when using hierarchyid. It is up to the developer to handle this behavior, if it is actually a problem in your situation.

When using hierarchyid, you can create indexes on top of the type. Two kinds of indexes may be useful to the sample application. A depth-first index will store all the nodes together and will be useful in reporting all employees reporting to a specific manager. A breadth-first index stores all the level nodes together, so queries reporting all direct reports of a specific manager will benefit from this type of index.

When you created the table, you created a depth-first index on the node column because it was created with a primary key constraint. To create the breadth-first index, you can issue the command on the node and level columns together, similar to this type of syntax:

```
create index Breadth on Employees(node,level)
```

The hierarchyid datatype allows for easy storage and management of hierarchical data. Not only are these functions available through T-SQL scripts, but they can be accessed in CLR stored procedures and functions as well.

Filestream Support

In the world of databases, the growth of data is increasing year after year. These new data items are not the traditional integers and text that we find in spreadsheets and reports; rather, the data is made up of digitally born medical images, music and video data files, and the like. With all these different kinds of data, it is becoming increasingly difficult to perform useful tasks, such as metadata searches or basic database management. SQL Server 2008 has a solution to this problem.

From a developer standpoint, dealing with heterogeneous data has always been a challenge. In SQL Server, we have two basic options to address the issue.

One option is for the developer to store the files in the file system and maintain a pointer to the file within the database. This solution works in cases where the file could be larger than 2GB and where fast streaming performance of the file is required. For those fairly new to databases, reading directly from the file system offers better streaming performance than reading the same data through the database. This is due to the fact that the database engine must manage locks on the table, even if the user is just reading the data.

Before you go off and design your new applications following this approach, it is important to note the downside of trying to maintain consistency between the files on the file system and the metadata about those files stored in the database. First, any changes that are made to the files directly through the file system are not detected by the database and will need to be addressed in your database application. Second, the administrators will have the heavy burden of trying to determine the appropriate security to apply to the file given the context of the data user. These are just some of the issues in a tedious, development-intensive solution that up until SQL Server 2005 was really the only answer to the problem.

SQL Server 2005 introduced the VARBINARY(MAX) datatype, which allows any arbitrary large object up to 2GB in size to be stored directly in the database. This mitigated a lot of user scenarios that required the use of the file system and gave developers a less error-prone database storage option for their large objects. Still, even with being able to store these large objects within the database, developers gave up on the streaming performance of the file system and faced a hard limit of 2GB for the storage of the data.

If it were a perfect world, wouldn't it be great if we could leverage the streaming performance of the file system in addition to the transactional consistencies of the database in one big, happy solution? Well, although this world is far from perfect, the new FILESTREAM attribute to VARBINARY(MAX) may just be the one feature that causes you to see the world with a different perspective. With FILESTREAM, you can have it all and even cake for dessert, without gaining an ounce on the waistline. Actually, no one can make promises about your waistline—not even Weight Watchers—but with FILESTREAM, you will be able to at least store large objects in the file system and have these files integrated within the database.

Integration is the key to the value of FILESTREAM. With integration, when database backups are performed, the files are included in the backups. Since these files are stored in the file system, the size limit of storage within the database is the size of the volume on the disk. Thus, there is no longer a 2GB limit. Also, the security of these files is managed via SQL Server security features, so if database users have access to the table, they can access the contents of the file, without the Windows administrator needing to give them specific privileges. To top off the list of these benefits, developers can leverage the Win32 file APIs against the data stored within the database to essentially give them the performance of the file system within the database.

The only significant downside to FILESTREAM is the requirement that the drive volume that has the files must be in NTFS format.

FILESTREAM is best used when the objects that are being stored are larger than 1MB and when fast read access is important. Also, FILESTREAM will be beneficial when your database applications perform their application logic within the middle tier. For smaller objects (less than 1MB), storing VARBINARY(MAX) large objects within the database may give you better streaming performance.

Enabling Filestream Functionality

Before filestream functionality can be used, it must be enabled using the sp_filestream_configure_ system stored procedure. This stored procedure has two parameters: enable_level and share_name. The enable_level parameter supports one of four values, as defined in Table 11-3.

Table 11-3. *@enable_level Definitions*

enable_level Value	Description
0	Default value. Filestream functionality is disabled.
1	Filestream works only for T-SQL access.
2	Filestream works for both T-SQL and local file system access.
3	Filestream works for T-SQL and local and remote file system access.

To get started, enable filestream functionality for both T-SQL and file system access, as follows:

```
sp_filestream_configure @enable_level = 2
```

If you used a value of 3 instead, you would be able to provide a name for a fileshare located on the Windows server hosting your SQL Server instance. This share could then be used by remote clients who want to access the filestream data.

■**Note** At the time of this writing, using sp_filestream_configure is the method for enabling filestreams. By the time SQL Server 2008 ships, this functionality will be replaced with an option in sp_configure. Refer to the help topic for sp_configure in SQL Server Books Online for the exact syntax.

When you enable filestream functionality on the server, one of the things that happens is the creation of a fileshare. If you issue a NET SHARE statement in your command window, you can see the newly created fileshare, called MSSQLSERVER, created by SQL Server for use with filestreams. The result of this statement is as follows:

```
Share name      Resource                                          Remark
----------      --------                                          -------------------
ADMIN$          C:\WINDOWS                                        Remote Admin
IPC$                                                              Remote IPC
C$              C:\                                               Default share
MSSQLSERVER     \\?\GLOBALROOT\Device\RsFx0100\.\MSSQLSERVER      SQL Server
                                                                  FILESTREAM share
```

From a quick look at the resource that is being shared, you can see that the MSSQLSERVER share isn't your traditional folder in the file system. What is happening here is SQL Server has a special driver used by the operating system that allows SQL Server to expose and manage a fileshare. Since SQL Server owns and manages this fileshare, it allows for applications to leverage the powerful streaming support of Win32 APIs while working in the context of a SQL Server transaction.

A Filestream Example

To help illustrate the power of SQL Server's filestream support, let's consider a scenario involving an online pet shop database that stores images in a database. In this example, you will create a database application called PetPhotoManager that will connect to a SQL Server instance and upload and view pictures stored in a table. First, you will create a database called OnlinePetStore, which contains a table called Pets that stores pictures of all the animals on the web site. Then you will write an application that will allow you to upload pictures to SQL Server, as well as read pictures and display them on a WinForm. These pictures will be stored as VARBINARY(MAX) and leverage the FILESTREAM attribute.

Creating the Database

Using FILESTREAM requires the designation of a special filegroup in the database. The filestream filegroup cannot be the primary filegroup, and you cannot specify the SIZE, MAXSIZE, or FILEGROWTH parameters of this filegroup, since it's really just a file directory. The following database-creation code defines a filegroup called FileStreamPhotos, and the statement CONTAINS FILESTREAM follows the FILEGROUP definition. This extra statement designates this filegroup to be one that contains filestream data.

```
CREATE DATABASE OnlinePetStore
ON PRIMARY
    (
    NAME = OnlinePetStore_data
    ,FILENAME = 'C:\data\FileStreamDB_data.mdf'
    ,SIZE = 10MB
    ,MAXSIZE = 50MB
    ,FILEGROWTH = 15%
    ),
FILEGROUP FileStreamPhotos CONTAINS FILESTREAM DEFAULT
    (
    NAME = PetPhotos
    ,FILENAME = 'C:\data\photos'
    )
LOG ON
    (
    NAME = OnlinePetStore_log
    ,FILENAME = 'C:\log\FileStreamDB_log.ldf'
    ,SIZE = 5MB
```

```
,MAXSIZE = 25MB
,FILEGROWTH = 5MB
)
```

This database-creation script indicates that the folder used to store filestream data will be C:\data\photos. In order for the database engine to accept this, the C:\data folder must exist, and the c:\data**photo** folder must not exist prior to execution of this script.

After you create the database, you are ready to define the simple Pets table that will be used to store the pet photographs:

```
USE OnlinePetStore
GO
CREATE TABLE Pets(
pet_id INT NOT NULL,
FSRowGuidColumn UNIQUEIDENTIFIER
  NOT NULL ROWGUIDCOL UNIQUE DEFAULT NEWID(),
pet_name VARCHAR(50) NOT NULL,
pet_photo VARBINARY(MAX) FILESTREAM)
```

Notice the first two bold statements. The first one is a column definition for a UNIQUEIDENTIFIER that has a designator for a GUID-based unique ID column called ROWGUIDCOL. FILESTREAM requires that you specify a ROWGUIDCOL; failure to do so means FILESTREAM won't work.

■**Note** You must define a ROWGUIDCOL within the same table as the filestream data.

The next bolded line demonstrates how to define a filestream column. The example has a column called pet_photo whose datatype is defined as VARBINARY(MAX) with the FILESTREAM attribute. Filestream columns can be only of type VARBINARY(MAX) in SQL Server 2008.

With the database objects created, you can now create the application that will insert and select filestream data.

Creating the Application

Before diving into the code, there are a few disclaimers to make. This example is written to demonstrate how one goes about accessing and managing filestream data. To keep the code brief, we intentionally skipped necessary things, like optimizing the code by creating helper classes and implementing more elaborate error-handling routines. And to keep things interesting, the code is written with a security bug. After we present the code, we will talk about this bug, even though it's not specific to SQL Server filestream data.

The PetPhotoManager application will be run from the command line and accept two options:

- The /upload option will allow the user to type the name of the pet and the local file path to a picture of the pet.

- The /view option will allow the user to view the picture of a pet whose photo is stored in the Pets table.

The core part of this application revolves around two functions: UploadPhoto() and ViewPhoto(). The following is the PetPhotoManager C# application.

```
using System;
using System.Collections.Generic;
using System.Linq;
using System.Text;
using System.IO;
```

```csharp
using System.Runtime.InteropServices;
using Microsoft.Win32.SafeHandles;
using System.Data.SqlClient;
using System.Windows.Forms;
using System.Drawing;

namespace PetPhotoManager
{
    class Program
    {
        public static string strPet_Name = "";
        public static string strPhoto_Location = "";

        static void Main(string[] args)
        {

            if (args == null || args.Length == 0 || args.Length > 3)
            {
                Console.WriteLine("PetPhotoManager examples:\n\n");
                Console.WriteLine("PetPhotoManager /upload [pet_name]
                    [photo_location]\n");
                Console.WriteLine("PetPhotoManager /view [pet_name]\n");
                return;
            }

            strPet_Name = args[1].ToString();

            if (args[0] == "/upload")
            {
                strPhoto_Location = args[2].ToString();
                UploadPhoto();
                return;
            }
            else if (args[0] == "/view")
            {
                ViewPhoto();
            }
        }

        private static void UploadPhoto()
        {
            try
            {

                //Open a connection to the OnlinePetStore database
                string strCommand = "";
                SqlConnection con = new SqlConnection
                    ("server=.;database=OnlinePetStore;integrated security=true");
                con.Open();
                //We need to create a GUID that will be used
                //as the unique identifier for the row
                Guid NewGuid = Guid.NewGuid();
                //Create an entry in the table for our new pet
                strCommand = "INSERT INTO Pets VALUES(CAST('" + NewGuid +
                    "' AS UNIQUEIDENTIFIER),'" + strPet_Name + "',0)";
                SqlCommand MySQLCommand = new SqlCommand(strCommand, con);
                MySQLCommand.ExecuteNonQuery();
```

```
//Now query to get the filestream fileshare and transaction context
strCommand = "SELECT pet_photo.PathName()," +
"GET_FILESTREAM_TRANSACTION_CONTEXT() FROM Pets " +
"WHERE FSRowGuidColumn=CAST('" + NewGuid + "' AS UNIQUEIDENTIFIER)";
SqlTransaction SQLTrans = con.BeginTransaction();
MySQLCommand.CommandText = strCommand;
MySQLCommand.Transaction = SQLTrans;

SqlDataReader rdr = MySQLCommand.ExecuteReader();
if (rdr.Read())
{
    //Variables for the filestream path, transaction context
    //and length
    string path = (string)rdr[0];
    byte[] txnContext = (byte[])rdr[1];
    int length = txnContext.Length;

    //It is best practice to close the DataReader
    //before calling OpenSqlFilestream
    rdr.Close();

    SafeFileHandle handle = OpenSqlFilestream(
    (string)path,
    1, // 1=Write access
    0,
    txnContext,
    (UInt32)length,
    new LARGE_INTEGER_SQL(0));

    //Destination
    FileStream writeBlob = new FileStream(handle,
        FileAccess.Write);

    //Source
    FileStream readPhoto = new FileStream(strPhoto_Location,
        FileMode.Open, FileAccess.Read);

    //Define block size, 512K is what NTFS is.
    const int blockSize = 1024 * 512;

    // Stream bytes from a local file into a sql table
    // via a Filestream!
    byte[] buffer = new byte[blockSize];
    int bytesRead;
    while ((bytesRead =
        readPhoto.Read(buffer, 0, buffer.Length)) > 0)
    {
        writeBlob.Write(buffer, 0, bytesRead);
    }

    writeBlob.Close();
    readPhoto.Close();
    SQLTrans.Commit();

    Console.WriteLine("\n" + strPhoto_Location +
        " inserted into Pets table.\n");
```

```
            }
            con.Close();
        }
        catch (Exception E)
        {
            Console.WriteLine("Error: " + E.Message.ToString());
        }

        return;
    }
    private static void ViewPhoto()
    {
        string strCommand = "";

        try
        {
            //Create connection to OnlinePetStore database
            SqlConnection con = new SqlConnection
                ("server=.;database=OnlinePetStore;integrated security=true");
            con.Open();
            SqlTransaction SQLTrans = con.BeginTransaction();

            //Get the network share path for the photo and transaction context
            strCommand = "SELECT pet_photo.PathName()," +
                "GET_FILESTREAM_TRANSACTION_CONTEXT() FROM Pets " +
                "WHERE pet_name='" + strPet_Name + "'";
            SqlCommand MySQLCommand =
                new SqlCommand(strCommand, con, SQLTrans);

            SqlDataReader rdr = MySQLCommand.ExecuteReader();
            if (rdr.Read())
            {

                //Fill variables with information from the query
                //This is the path name and the transaction context
                string path = (string)rdr[0];
                byte[] txnContext = (byte[])rdr[1];
                int length = txnContext.Length;

                //Its a best practice to close the Datareader
                //before calling OpenSqlFilestream
                rdr.Close();

                SafeFileHandle handle = OpenSqlFilestream(
                (string)path,
                0, // 0=Read access
                0,
                txnContext,
                (UInt32)length,
                new LARGE_INTEGER_SQL(0));

                //Create a FileStream object based on the handle from sql
                FileStream readBlob = new FileStream(handle, FileAccess.Read);

                //Create our Windows Form a Picture Box control
                System.Windows.Forms.Form frmPicture = new Form();
                frmPicture.Height = 480;
```

```
                    frmPicture.Width = 640;
                    frmPicture.Top = 100;
                    frmPicture.Left = 100;
                    frmPicture.Text = "Displaying " + strPet_Name;

                    PictureBox pb = new PictureBox();
                    //Create the image from our sql filestream
                    pb.Image = Image.FromStream(readBlob);
                    pb.Size = frmPicture.Size;
                    pb.SizeMode = PictureBoxSizeMode.StretchImage;

                    frmPicture.Controls.Add(pb);

                    frmPicture.ShowDialog();

                    readBlob.Close();
                }
                else
                {
                    Console.WriteLine("No record for " + strPet_Name +
                        " in the Pets table.\n");
                }
                con.Close();

            }
            catch (Exception E)
            {
                Console.WriteLine("Error: " + E.Message.ToString());
                return;
            }
            return;
        }

        [DllImport("sqlncli10.dll", SetLastError = true, CharSet = CharSet.Unicode)]
        public static extern SafeFileHandle OpenSqlFilestream(
                    string FilestreamPath,
                    UInt32 DesiredAccess,
                    UInt32 OpenOptions,
                    byte[] FilestreamTransactionContext,
                    UInt32 FilestreamTransactionContextLength,
                    LARGE_INTEGER_SQL AllocationSize);

        [StructLayout(LayoutKind.Sequential)]
        public struct LARGE_INTEGER_SQL
        {
            public Int64 QuadPart;
            public LARGE_INTEGER_SQL(Int64 quadPart) { QuadPart = quadPart; }
        }
    }
}
```

To use this application, upload a photo with a statement like this:

```
PetPhotoManager /upload Zeus C:\pictures\Zeus.jpg
```

To retrieve the photo, issue a statement like this:

```
PetPhotoManager /view Zeus
```

You'll see a WinForm window containing a picture of the pet, as in the example in Figure 11-5.

Figure 11-5. *PetPhotoManager view pet window (showing the author's St Bernard, Zeus, recently shaved for the summer)*

Let's start the analysis by looking at the UploadPhoto function. After making the connection to the database, you create a GUID and insert this GUID and a pet's name into the Pets table. This code snippet is as follows:

```
Guid NewGuid = Guid.NewGuid();
 strCommand = "INSERT INTO Pets VALUES(CAST('" + NewGuid +
   "' AS UNIQUEIDENTIFIER),'" + strPet_Name + "',0)";
```

Having a GUID for each row is a requirement for SQL filestream data. Once you have this entry in the table, you want to query this entry and obtain two important pieces of information:

- The path to the photo that is stored in the table. This path is based on the Uniform Naming Convention (UNC) name that you saw when you issued the NET SHARE statement earlier in this chapter.

- The transaction context, which is essentially a token that represents the transaction of the active session.

The SELECT statement to obtain this information is as follows:

```
strCommand = "SELECT pet_photo.PathName()," +
"GET_FILESTREAM_TRANSACTION_CONTEXT() FROM Pets " +
"WHERE FSRowGuidColumn=CAST('" + NewGuid + "' AS UNIQUEIDENTIFIER)";
```

After you have the path and transaction context, you can use the OpenSqlFilestream() function:

```
                SafeFileHandle handle = OpenSqlFilestream(
                (string)path,
                1, // 1=Write access
                0,
                txnContext,
                (UInt32)length,
                new LARGE_INTEGER_SQL(0));
```

The OpenSqlFilestream() function allows for both read and write access to the file. The handle that is returned can then be used directly in Win32 APIs. You can see the true power of SQL filestreams by the simple file copy that follows the OpenSqlFilestream statement:

```
FileStream writeBlob = new FileStream(handle, FileAccess.Write);
FileStream readPhoto = new FileStream(strPhoto_Location,
FileMode.Open, FileAccess.Read);
.
.
.

while ((bytesRead =
    readPhoto.Read(buffer, 0, buffer.Length)) > 0)
{
    writeBlob.Write(buffer, 0, bytesRead);
}
```

Here, you have two FileStream objects, named readPhoto and writeBlob, which are the source and destination, respectively. The source FileStream object is created with the handle obtained via the SQL filestream, and the destination FileStream object is created by passing the local filename directly into the API.

To view the photo, the process is similar to uploading the photo, in that you need to obtain the pathname and transaction context from the Pets table for the given pet name requested. The SELECT statement is as follows:

```
SELECT pet_photo.PathName(),GET_FILESTREAM_TRANSACTION_CONTEXT()
 FROM Pets WHERE pet_name='" + strPet_Name + "'";
```

Once you have this information, you can pass it into an OpenSqlFilestream() statement and request read access, as follows:

```
SafeFileHandle handle = OpenSqlFilestream(
(string)path,
0, // 0=Read access
0,
txnContext,
(UInt32)length,
new LARGE_INTEGER_SQL(0));
```

Now with a read handle, you can create a FileStream object based on the handle obtained from SQL.

```
FileStream readBlob = new FileStream(handle, FileAccess.Read);
```

To display the actual photo, you simply created a Windows Form, included a Picture Box control, and bound the image using the .FromStream() function, as follows:

```
PictureBox pb = new PictureBox();
pb.Image=Image.FromStream(readBlob);
```

Although this example is fairly simple, you can see the power of being able to leverage the streaming performance of Win32 API calls against data stored in SQL Server.

Before we conclude this discussion, we need to address the security bug that is present in the sample code. By now, you should have at least browsed the entire code listing for the PetPhotoManager application. If you haven't done so, go back and see if you can spot a common security vulnerability.

One of the most common and easiest exploits to SQL Server is the SQL-injection attack. In the example, you take the user input stored in strPet_name and in the UploadPhoto() function, insert this pet name directly into the SQL statement, as follows:

```
strCommand = "INSERT INTO Pets VALUES(CAST('" +
  NewGuid + "' AS UNIQUEIDENTIFIER),'" + strPet_Name + "',0)";
```

To exploit this, all you need to do is modify the parameters you are passing into the PetPhotoManager application.

Let's have this harmless photo-viewer application create a SQL login and give it `sysadmin` access:

```
PetPhotoManager.exe /upload "hack',0);CREATE LOGIN Hacker WITH
 PASSWORD='asdfasdf';EXEC master..sp_addsrvrolemember @loginame =
 N'Hacker', @rolename = N'sysadmin';--" c:\demo\blah.jpg
```

When SQL Server executes the `INSERT` statement, to SQL it looks like the following:

```
INSERT INTO Pets VALUES
(CAST('0e87d864-f6ab-4e0e-b8c8-4b409d79f9e6' AS UNIQUEIDENTIFIER),
'hack',0);CREATE LOGIN Hacker WITH PASSWORD='asdfasdf';
EXEC master..sp_addsrvrolemember @loginame = N'Hacker',
@rolename = N'sysadmin';--',0)
```

The key to note here is that the call is wrapped up nicely by appending the rest of the name followed by the closing apostrophe and `,0)`, so the `INSERT` statement is happy. Now all you need to do is append whatever code you desire. In this case, it is to create a login called `Hacker` and grant `sysadmin` access to the new login. To wrap things up, you just need to put in two dashes (`--`) at the end, indicating whatever else is just a comment. In this case, the rest of the `',0)` that the real application appended is now a comment.

There are a few lessons here. Never run under elevated privileges. If the application wasn't running as a `sysadmin`, you wouldn't have this particular problem. However, the exploit is still here.

To mitigate the SQL-injection attack, you could cleanse the data before allowing the variable to be used within the statement. This would include removing characters like the comment dashes and limiting the number of characters of the variable. A more secure solution would be to wrap the `INSERT` statement inside a stored procedure. Your code to call the stored procedure would then look something like this:

```
SqlCommand command = new SqlCommand("createPhotoEntry",connection);
command.CommandType = CommandType.StoredProcedure;
command.Parameters.Add("@pet_Name",SqlDbType.Text);
command.Parameters[0].Value = strPet_Name;
command.Parameters.Add("@photo_Path",SqlDbType.Text);
command.Parameters[0].Value = strPhoto_Location;
SqlDataReader dataReader = command.ExecuteReader();
```

■**Note** For an in-depth discussion of SQL injection, check out the "Web Application and SQL Injection" article on SecurityDocs.com (`http://www.securitydocs.com/library/3587`).

Summary

SQL Server 2008 brings with it a few new key datatypes that provide various solutions. These address situations that had developers and administrators creating some magic behind the scenes to make things like hierarchical relationships within data and a time measurement of nanoseconds work. With SQL Server 2008, these kinds of requirements are easier to implement.

Improvements in BLOBs were also addressed in a feature called filestream. Filestream offers the streaming performance of the file system while still leveraging powerful database capabilities like transactions and backup/restore.

These datatypes will not do your work for you. However, they give you another tool to effectively create solutions that involve dates and times, hierarchical relationships, and spatial-aware applications.

CHAPTER 12

■■■

T-SQL Enhancements for Developers

With all of the excitement around the .NET programming extensions to SQL Server, it would be easy to overlook any new changes to Transact-SQL (T-SQL). As a matter of fact, Microsoft continues to make investments in T-SQL with each new release of the product.

In this chapter, we have grouped our feature discussions into two major categories:

- Notable Data Manipulation Language (DML) features, such as extensions to the FROM clause and the new MERGE statement

- General development, like procedures, functions, and table-valued parameters

The examples in this chapter, and subsequent chapters, will be applicable to the AdventureWorks database. For those of you not already familiar with AdventureWorks, it is a much larger database and has far more realistic data and is far more normalized than previous efforts. The AdventureWorks database can be downloaded from http://www.codeplex.com/MSFTDBProdSamples.

Notable DML Features

DML in SQL Server continues to evolve throughout each release. The following features are available to make querying against SQL Server easier for the user:

- *Old-style outer joins deprecated*: "=*" in a WHERE clause will raise an error.

- *Common table expressions*: This ANSI 99 feature allows for recursion and code simplification.

- TOP: This operator allows you to do parameterized row counts, and works with more DML than just SELECT.

- FROM *clause extensions*: Join types improve usability of derived tables and table-based functions.

- OUTPUT *clause*: Use this clause to get information about data that has changed.

- *Ranking functions*: Find positional information within a result set through these functions.

- EXCEPT *and* INTERSECT: These set operators provide the ability to compare sets of like data.

- *Synonyms*: These give you the ability to provide alternate names for database objects.

- MERGE: This allows users to express multiple DML actions (such as inserts and updates) in one statement

Each of these changes (especially the common table expressions) will make the base DML statements (INSERT, UPDATE, DELETE, and SELECT) far more powerful and functional.

Old-Style Outer Joins Deprecated

This one should probably be in the title of the book, as it is going to be the most painful of all changes. Microsoft has said over and over, and book authors and experts (not always the same group, mind you) have said over and over: stop using non-ANSI-style joins; they will not be supported in a future version. Well, the future is now. Consider the following query:

```
USE AdventureWorks  --this is the default unless otherwise mentioned
GO
SELECT *
FROM   Sales.salesPerson AS salesPerson,
       Sales.salesTerritory AS salesTerritory
WHERE  salesPerson.territoryId *= salesTerritory.territoryId
```

Trying this query will give you the following (really long and very descriptive) error message that says it as good as we could:

```
Msg 4147, Level 15, State 1, Line 5
The query uses non-ANSI outer join operators ("*=" or "=*"). To run this query
without modification, please set the compatibility level for current database to 80
or lower, using stored procedure sp_dbcmptlevel. It is strongly recommended to
rewrite the query using ANSI outer join operators (LEFT OUTER JOIN, RIGHT OUTER
JOIN). In the future versions of SQL Server, non-ANSI join operators will not be
supported even in backward-compatibility modes.
```

So what does this mean? It means that you need to rewrite your queries using ANSI join operators:

```
SELECT *
FROM   Sales.salesPerson AS salesPerson
           LEFT OUTER JOIN sales.salesTerritory AS salesTerritory
               ON salesPerson.territoryId = salesTerritory.territoryId
```

Note that this restriction is only for outer joins, not for inner joins. The following works just fine and likely always will:

```
SELECT   *
FROM     Sales.salesPerson AS salesPerson,
         Sales.salesTerritory AS salesTerritory
WHERE    salesPerson.territoryId = salesTerritory.territoryId
```

Clearly, you should code this using an INNER JOIN, but the preceding will work because this syntax is required for correlated subqueries.

■**Note** This may be an issue for many people who have not heeded the warnings over the years about the new join syntax. However, the old-style joins will still work if you change back into 80 Compatibility Mode (2000) or earlier using the sp_dbcmptlevel system stored procedure.

Common Table Expressions

The primary purpose of common table expressions (CTEs) is code simplification. They are loosely analogous to views in that they are defined as a single SELECT statement.

Once defined, CTEs are used exactly like views. To illustrate, we'll take a look at a very simple example. The following query defines a CTE named simpleExample that contains a single column and row. Then a simple SELECT statement is issued to return the data defined by the CTE.

```
WITH simpleExample AS
(
     SELECT 'hi' AS columnName
)

SELECT  columnName
FROM    simpleExample
```

which returns the following:

```
columnName
----------
hi
```

What makes the CTE significantly different from a view is that the CTE is not created as an object in the database and therefore is only available for this single statement. So in this sense, it will be treated by the compiler more or less as if you had coded a derived table (a named table expression that exists only for the duration of a query) as follows:

```
SELECT  columnName
FROM    (SELECT 'hi' AS columnName) AS simpleExample
```

This is an obviously simple example, but it serves to illustrate the basics of CTEs. If you needed to reference a given derived table in your query multiple times, this method would be of great help, since instead of recoding the query over and over, you would simply reference the CTE name. If the derived table were very large, it would *greatly* simplify the final query, so debugging the final result will be much easier.

The performance of the CTE should be on par with using derived tables. If you have queries where you use multiple derived queries, such queries will be evaluated multiple times. The same would be true for CTEs. In some cases, it will be better to use a temporary table to store the results of the query that you will use in the CTE, especially for complex CTEs that are used multiple times in a query.

There are two common uses for CTEs:

- *Simplify complex queries*: To encapsulate complex code in a way to make code cleaner

- *Create recursive queries*: To implement hierarchies traversing code in a single query (something not possible previously)

Simplifying Complex Queries

Consider the following scenario: the client needs a query that has subqueries to calculate salesperson totals for the year to date, compare that value to entire sales for the company, and then compare the salespeople's sales to their quota for the year.

First, consider how this would be done using the SQL Server 2000 syntax. Each subset could be implemented as a derived table in a single query.

```
--In SQL Server 2000
SELECT  CAST(c.LastName + ', ' + c.FirstName AS varchar(30)) AS SalesPerson
    ,
--YEAR TO DATE SALES
        (SELECT amount
        FROM ( SELECT soh.SalesPersonID, sum(sod.LineTotal) as amount
               FROM   Sales.SalesOrderHeader soh
                  JOIN Sales.SalesOrderDetail sod
                  ON sod.SalesOrderID = soh.SalesOrderID
```

```
        WHERE   soh.Status = 5 -- complete
        and  soh.OrderDate >= '20040101'
        GROUP  by soh.SalesPersonID) as YTDSalesPerson
    WHERE YTDSalesPerson.salesPersonId = salesperson.SalesPersonID) AS YTDSales,

--PERCENT OF TOTAL
      (SELECT amount
      FROM (SELECT soh.SalesPersonID, sum(sod.LineTotal) AS amount
            FROM   Sales.SalesOrderHeader soh
                JOIN Sales.SalesOrderDetail sod
                ON sod.SalesOrderID = soh.SalesOrderID
            WHERE   soh.Status = 5 -- complete
            AND  soh.OrderDate >= '20040101'
            GROUP  BY soh.SalesPersonID) AS YTDSalesPerson
    WHERE YTDSalesPerson.salesPersonId = salesperson.SalesPersonID) /
        (SELECT SUM(amount)
        FROM (SELECT soh.SalesPersonID, sum(sod.LineTotal) AS amount
            FROM   Sales.SalesOrderHeader soh
                JOIN Sales.SalesOrderDetail sod
                ON sod.SalesOrderID = soh.SalesOrderID
            WHERE   soh.Status = 5 -- complete
            AND  soh.OrderDate >= '20040101'
            GROUP  BY soh.SalesPersonID) AS YTDSalesPerson
        ) AS percentOfTotal,

--COMPARE TO QUOTA
      (SELECT amount
      FROM (SELECT soh.SalesPersonID, sum(sod.LineTotal) AS amount
            FROM   Sales.SalesOrderHeader soh
                JOIN Sales.SalesOrderDetail sod
                ON sod.SalesOrderID = soh.SalesOrderID
            WHERE   soh.Status = 5 -- complete
            AND  soh.OrderDate >= '20040101'
            GROUP  BY soh.SalesPersonID)AS YTDSalesPerson
    WHERE YTDSalesPerson.salesPersonId = salesperson.SalesPersonID) -
    salesPerson.SalesQuota          AS MetQuota

  FROM    Sales.SalesPerson AS salesPerson
          JOIN HumanResources.Employee AS e
            ON salesPerson.salesPersonId = e.employeeId
          JOIN Person.Contact as c
            ON c.contactId = e.contactId
```

Of real interest here are the bold parts of the code. It is the same subquery over and over. This is a beast of a query to follow, and not overly pleasant to write. You may also be thinking that each of the derived tables could be implemented as a view, but if this is the only situation where they will be used, the management overhead of implementing three views in a production environment would not be worth the effort. You might also use a temp table, which is what we generally end up doing when we come upon this sort of situation. This is not necessarily the best way to implement something so complex in SQL Server 2000, but it was the only way to do it in one statement (a goal for writing powerful SQL, but not always readable or maintainable code).

Now let's reformulate this query using the new CTE syntax. As demonstrated in the following query, you define two CTEs to replace the derived table and the main table to produce the exact same results, with semantically the exact same query as in the previous example, only clearer to understand.

```
-- SQL Server  CTE syntax
WITH YTDSalesPerson
AS
(
    SELECT soh.SalesPersonID, SUM(sod.LineTotal) AS amount
    FROM   Sales.SalesOrderHeader soh
            JOIN Sales.SalesOrderDetail sod
              ON sod.SalesOrderID = soh.SalesOrderID
    WHERE  soh.Status = 5 -- complete
      AND  soh.OrderDate >= '20040101'
    GROUP  BY soh.SalesPersonID
),
SalesPersonInfo
AS
(
    SELECT  salesPersonId, SalesQuota AS salesQuota,
            CAST(c.LastName + ', ' + c.FirstName AS varchar(30)) AS SalesPerson
    FROM    Sales.SalesPerson AS s
             JOIN HumanResources.Employee AS e
               ON s.salesPersonId = e.employeeId
             JOIN Person.Contact AS c
               ON c.contactId = e.contactId
)
SELECT SalesPersonInfo.SalesPerson,
       (SELECT amount
        FROM YTDSalesPerson
        WHERE YTDSalesPerson.salesPersonId = salespersonInfo.SalesPersonID)
           AS YTDSales,

       (SELECT amount
        FROM YTDSalesPerson
        WHERE YTDSalesPerson.salesPersonId = salespersonInfo.SalesPersonID)
        / (SELECT SUM(amount) FROM YTDSalesPerson) AS percentOfTotal,

       (SELECT amount
        FROM YTDSalesPerson
        WHERE YTDSalesPerson.salesPersonId = salespersonInfo.SalesPersonID) -
        salesPersonInfo.SalesQuota         AS MetQuota

FROM   SalesPersonInfo
```

While this is still no beginner query, it is much easier to read and understand than the previous version. Not to mention that you can now test the CTE code by simply executing the following:

```
WITH YTDSalesPerson
AS
(
    SELECT soh.SalesPersonID, SUM(sod.LineTotal) AS amount
    FROM   Sales.SalesOrderHeader soh
            JOIN Sales.SalesOrderDetail sod
              ON sod.SalesOrderID = soh.SalesOrderID
    WHERE  soh.Status = 5 -- complete
      AND  soh.OrderDate >= '20040101'
    GROUP  BY soh.SalesPersonID
)
SELECT  *
FROM    YTDSalesPerson
```

You can use this instead of having to deal with pulling out large sections of code from your original query. And say you make a correction or change to the calculation. It changes once, and all usages change. All this without having to persist any data or objects. SQL Server does the real work! Consider also that the "black boxed" CTE works independently of the main query, so after testing it, you won't need to worry if this part of the query works as you debug the larger query.

Using CTEs for Recursive Queries

The second use of CTEs allows for recursive hierarchies to be navigated without the need for complex recursion logic done manually. Hierarchies are common in real-world situations, such as employees and managers (managers are employees), or in manufacturing with parts within other parts (an automobile engine is a part, but it also consists of a lot of other parts inside).

■Note Hierarchies can also be created using the new `hierarchyid` datatype. This datatype provides additional functionality above what users can do with CTEs. The `hierarchyid` datatype is described in more detail in Chapter 11.

Using T-SQL, it was previously complicated to build queries that dealt with hierarchies. If the number of levels in a hierarchy was known beforehand, it was possible to use self joins, but even that approach was very cumbersome. If you had unlimited numbers of levels, it was practically impossible. CTEs can make hierarchies manageable.

BASIC TREE HANDLING IN T-SQL

In dealing with tree structures in T-SQL, we use an algorithm to deal with the tree breadthwise, rather than depth-wise. For example, consider the following tree:

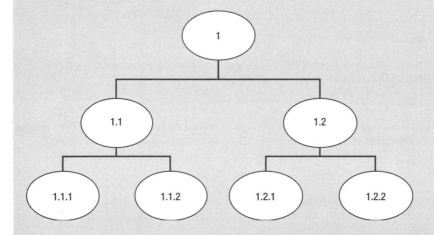

In functional programming languages, it would have been common to recursively traverse a tree one node at a time, touching one node at a time. So you would go from node 1, to 1.1, to 1.1.1, back to 1.1, to 1.1.2, back to 1.1, back to 1, on to 1.2, and so on. This works great for pointer-based languages, but in relational languages like T-SQL, a much better algorithm is to access all the children of a node in one query, then all the children of these nodes, and so on. So we would get node 1, then 1.1 and 1.2, and finally 1.1.1, 1.1.2, 1.2.1, and 1.2.2. It is a fantastic algorithm for dealing with sets, but in the following code sample, you will see that it was not very clean to implement in SQL Server 2000.

Take a look at an example that uses the Employee table in the AdventureWorks database. This is a classic example of a single-parent hierarchy with the managerId column identifying all employees who report to a specified manager. Let's look at a typical breadthwise hierarchical query used in SQL Server 2000 to retrieve all employees who reported to the manager whose managerId was 140.

```
-- SQL Server 2000 example

DECLARE @managerId int
SET @managerId = 140

 --holds the output tree level, which lets us isolate a level in the looped query
DECLARE @outTable table (employeeId int, managerId int, treeLevel int)

 --used to hold the level of the tree we are currently at in the loop
DECLARE @treeLevel as int
SET     @treelevel = 1

 --get the top level
 INSERT INTO @outTable
 SELECT employeeId, managerId, @treelevel as treelevel
 FROM   HumanResources.employee AS Employee
 WHERE  (Employee.managerId = @managerId)

 WHILE (1 = 1) --imitates do...until construct
   BEGIN

     INSERT INTO @outTable
     SELECT Employee.employeeId, Employee.managerId,
            treelevel + 1 AS treelevel
     FROM   HumanResources.employee AS Employee
              JOIN @outTable AS ht
                ON Employee.managerId = ht.employeeId
     --this where isolates a given level of the tree
     WHERE  EXISTS(    SELECT  *
                       FROM    @outTable AS holdTree
                       WHERE   treelevel = @treelevel
                         AND   Employee.managerId = holdtree.employeeId)

     IF @@rowcount = 0
       BEGIN
          BREAK
       END

     SET @treelevel = @treelevel + 1
   END

SELECT    Employee.employeeid,Contact.lastname,Contact.firstname
FROM      HumanResources.Employee AS Employee
            INNER JOIN @outTable ot
                ON Employee.employeeid = ot.employeeid
            INNER JOIN Person.Contact AS Contact
                ON Contact.contactId = Employee.contactId
```

Using CTEs, however, gives a much cleaner implementation:

```
-- SQL Server 2008 syntax
DECLARE @managerId int
SET @managerId = 140;
```

```
WITH EmployeeHierarchy (employeeid, managerid)
AS
(
    SELECT employeeid, managerid
    FROM   HumanResources.Employee AS Employee
    WHERE  ManagerID=@managerId

    UNION ALL

    SELECT Employee.employeeid, Employee.managerid
    FROM   HumanResources.Employee AS Employee
           INNER JOIN EmployeeHierarchy
             ON Employee.managerid= EmployeeHierarchy.employeeid)
SELECT  Employee.employeeid,Contact.lastname,Contact.firstname
FROM       HumanResources.Employee AS Employee
           INNER JOIN EmployeeHierarchy
               ON Employee.employeeid = EmployeeHierarchy.employeeid
             INNER JOIN Person.Contact AS Contact
                 ON Contact.contactId = Employee.contactId
```

So let's take this query apart and look at how it works. First, we define the name of the CTE and define the names of the columns that will be output:

```
WITH EmployeeHierarchy (employeeid, managerid)
AS
(
```

■**Tip** You may have noticed that we did not declare the names in previous examples. The column names being returned is optional, just as with views.

The first query gets the top level in the hierarchy. It is not required that it return only a single row, but in our case, we are getting all rows where the managerId= 140; that is, all people who work for managerId = 140. We are using a variable here to keep it equivalent to the SQL Server 2000 example.

```
    SELECT employeeid, managerid
    FROM   HumanResources.Employee AS Employee
    WHERE  managerid=@managerId
```

Then use UNION ALL to connect these rows to the next specified set:

```
    UNION ALL
```

■**Note** Recursive CTEs require a top-level statement and a UNION ALL. Without these, you will get a syntax error from the compiler.

UNION ALL does not specify duplicates to be removed, so you will need to be careful to avoid cyclical relationships in your data. The problem comes when you might have a child row that may also be a predecessor to itself.

For example, consider the following table of data:

```
employeeid    managerid
-----------   -----------
1             3
3             5
5             1
```

The manager of employee 1 is employee 3. Then when you get the manager for employee 3, it is employee 5, and then employee 5's manager is 1. So when you get to the next row, you would end up in an infinite loop, because you would find that the manager of 1 is 3, and you would just keep going until you hit the nesting limit of SQL Server code (32).

So now we get to the cool part. We get the children of the rows we got in the first part of the query by the name of the CTE—in our case, EmployeeHierarchy. This is how the recursion works. It joins to itself, but again contains itself (hence, the recursive nature of a query calling itself). It continues on until no employeeid is a manager of anyone else (down to where the real work gets done!).

```
    SELECT Employee.employeeid, Employee.managerid
    FROM   HumanResources.Employee AS Employee
             INNER JOIN EmployeeHierarchy
                 on Employee.managerid= EmployeeHierarchy.employeeid
)
```

Finally, we use the CTE. The loop happens without us even noticing from the outside by materializing the set of rows, then joining that to the full Employee table. The result is all persons who report to a given manager.

```
SELECT   Employee.employeeid,Contact.lastname,Contact.firstname
FROM     HumanResources.Employee AS Employee
           INNER JOIN EmployeeHierarchy
               ON Employee.employeeid = EmployeeHierarchy.employeeid
             INNER JOIN Person.Contact AS Contact
                 ON Contact.contactId = Employee.contactId
```

Before we leave CTEs altogether, there is one more really neat thing that you can do with them. In the query that gets the top level of the hierarchy, you can introduce values into the CTE that you can manipulate throughout the iterations of the query. The following query extends the query to include a level indicator and a hierarchy of the employee's managers, up to the top manager for the employee. In the recursive part of the CTE, you put code to add one for each level. In our case, we increment the tree level by one, and then we add the employeeid from the level to the hierarchy. We use varchar(max) since we don't know just how big the hierarchy will be.

```
DECLARE @managerId int
SET @managerId = 140;

WITH EmployeeHierarchy(employeeid, managerid, treelevel, hierarchy)
AS
(
    SELECT employeeid, managerid,
           1 AS treeevel, CAST(employeeid AS varchar(max)) AS hierarchy
    FROM   HumanResources.Employee AS Employee
    WHERE managerid=@managerId

    UNION ALL
```

```
    SELECT Employee.employeeid, Employee.managerid,
          treelevel + 1 AS treelevel,
          hierarchy + '\' +CAST(Employee.employeeid AS varchar(20)) AS hierarchy
    FROM   HumanResources.Employee AS Employee
            INNER JOIN EmployeeHierarchy
              ON Employee.managerid= EmployeeHierarchy.employeeid
)

SELECT  Employee.employeeid,Contact.lastname,Contact.firstname,
        EmployeeHierarchy.treelevel, EmployeeHierarchy.hierarchy
FROM    HumanResources.Employee AS Employee
         INNER JOIN EmployeeHierarchy
              ON Employee.employeeid = EmployeeHierarchy.employeeid
           INNER JOIN Person.Contact AS Contact
                ON Contact.contactId = Employee.contactId
ORDER BY hierarchy
```

Running this returns the following:

employeeid	lastname	firstname	level	hierarchy
103	Barber	David	1	103
139	Liu	David	1	139
130	Walton	Bryan	2	139\130
166	Tomic	Dragan	2	139\166
178	Moreland	Barbara	2	139\178
201	Sheperdigian	Janet	2	139\201
216	Seamans	Mike	2	139\216
59	Poe	Deborah	2	139\59
94	Spoon	Candy	2	139\94
30	Barreto de Mattos	Paula	1	30
154	Chen	Hao	2	30\154
191	Culbertson	Grant	2	30\191
47	Johnson	Willis	2	30\47
70	Martin	Mindy	2	30\70
82	Luthra	Vidur	2	30\82
71	Kahn	Wendy	1	71
274	Word	Sheela	2	71\274
164	Sandberg	Mikael	3	71\274\164
198	Rao	Arvind	3	71\274\198
223	Meisner	Linda	3	71\274\223
231	Ogisu	Fukiko	3	71\274\231
233	Hee	Gordon	3	71\274\233
238	Pellow	Frank	3	71\274\238
241	Kurjan	Eric	3	71\274\241
244	Hagens	Erin	3	71\274\244
261	Miller	Ben	3	71\274\261
264	Hill	Annette	3	71\274\264
266	Hillmann	Reinout	3	71\274\266

So now we have our hierarchy, it is sorted by manager, and we know how far away an employee is from the manager we passed in as a parameter.

CTEs will be helpful in cleaning up code for sure, but more important, recursive queries will be far easier to deal with than ever before.

TOP

The TOP operator is used to specify the number of rows returned by a query. In previous versions of SQL Server, TOP required a literal. So if you needed to parameterize the number of values to return when a statement was coded, the alternative was to use SET ROWCOUNT @<variableName> to restrict the rows returned. This, however, affected *all* following T-SQL statements. It was also an issue that you needed to reset ROWCOUNT to 0 after every statement you used it on, or big problems would occur when you started affecting only a couple of rows in subsequent statements.

TOP affects only a single statement, and now it allows a variable to set the number of rows affected. For example, you can return a variable set of rows based on a variable from the AdventureWorks Person.Contact table.

```
DECLARE @rowsToReturn int

SELECT  @rowsToReturn = 10

SELECT  TOP(@rowsToReturn) * --note that TOP requires parentheses to accept
                            --parameters but not for constant
FROM    HumanResources.Employee
```

If the value of the TOP parameter is invalid, such as a null value or a negative value, SQL Server will return an error. In SQL Server, you may update views that are defined using the TOP operator. However, after you update the values that show up in the view, the rows may vanish from the view.

Beyond parameterization, another change to the TOP operator is that it will work with INSERT, UPDATE, and DELETE (again with parameters if desired).

■Note When using TOP on INSERT, UPDATE, or DELETE statements, you must put parentheses around the expression, even if it is a literal.

For example, say you have a table and you want to insert the top five rows from a result set (in this case, one that just has seven values from a UNION statement). You can do this with INSERT TOP (N):

```
CREATE TABLE testTop
(
        value   int PRIMARY KEY
)
INSERT TOP (5) INTO testTop
SELECT  *   --this derived table returns seven rows
FROM    (SELECT 1  AS value  UNION SELECT 2  UNION SELECT 3 UNION SELECT 4
            UNION SELECT 5 UNION SELECT 6 UNION SELECT 7) AS sevenRows
GO
SELECT  *
FROM    testTop
GO
```

The derived table contains seven rows, but the TOP operator on the INSERT statement means that this will return only five of them:

```
value
-----------
1
2
3
4
5
```

Now, you can use TOP on an UPDATE to change two rows only:

```
UPDATE TOP (2) testTop
SET     value = value * 100

SELECT  *
FROM    testTop
```

which returns the following:

```
value
-----------
3
4
5
100
200
```

Finally, using DELETE, you can remove three rows from the table:

```
DELETE TOP(3) testTop
GO

SELECT * FROM testTop
```

which results in this output:

```
value
-----------
100
200
```

Each of these techniques is basically only good when you are trying to batch-modify a set. So you can do something like this:

```
INSERT TOP (10) otherTable (batchTableId, value)
FROM   batchTable
WHERE  NOT EXISTS ( SELECT *
                    FROM   otherTable
                    WHERE  otherTable.batchTableId = batchTable.batchTableId)
```

It is not a technique that will be extremely useful, but it is a much more elegant solution than using SET ROWCOUNT, because it is clear to the query processor from which statement you intend to limit the number of rows. Any other statements in any subordinate objects like triggers do not need to be subject to the limitation, as was the case with ROWCOUNT.

This example has a pretty big "gotcha" that may not be completely obvious to you. Notice there was no mention of which rows would be modified or deleted. As cannot be stated too many times, tables are unordered sets, and modification statements have no ORDER BY clause to order the set they deal with. It will literally just INSERT, UPDATE, or DELETE whatever number of rows you state, purely at the will of the optimizer. (SQL Server Books Online goes so far as to state that the rows affected when TOP is used will be "random," which, while technically true, is perhaps pushing it.) It stands to reason that whichever rows are easiest to modify, these rows will be the ones chosen. This is unlike how the SELECT statement returns the rows based on an ORDER BY clause if one is present, and it can be a bit confusing. Consider this example:

```
CREATE TABLE top10sales
(
 salesOrderId int,
 totalDue  MONEY
)

INSERT  TOP (10) top10sales
SELECT salesOrderId, totalDue
FROM Sales.salesOrderHeader
ORDER BY totalDue DESC
```

Ten rows from the Sales.SalesOrderHeader table will be returned and inserted, but they will not be the top ten highest values. For this, you can use the following:

```
INSERT top10sales
SELECT TOP (10) salesOrderId, totalDue
FROM   Sales.salesOrderHeader
ORDER    BY totalDue DESC
```

Now the values in the top10sales table are the top ten values in Sales.SalesOrderHeader.totalDue.

The value of adding TOP to the INSERT, UPDATE, and DELETE statements is to facilitate batching operations. For example, you might want to delete a large number of rows from a table, a few at a time, to keep the transaction small, thereby assisting in maintaining concurrent use of the table, with a small number of locks. So you could execute the following:

```
BEGIN TRANSACTION
DECLARE @rowcount int
SET @rowcount = 100
WHILE (@rowcount = 100)  --if it is less than 100, we are done, greater than 100
  BEGIN                   --cannot happen
        DELETE TOP(100) sales.salesOrderHeader
        SET @rowcount = @@rowcount
  END
ROLLBACK TRANSACTION --we don't want to actually delete the rows
```

Note that using TOP is the preferred way of acting on only a fixed number of rows, rather than using SET ROWCOUNT <N>. SET ROWCOUNT is deprecated and will be removed in the next version of SQL Server.

So, the TOP operator accepts variables as well as literal values and can be used with INSERT, UPDATE, and DELETE statements. This is a good addition, but bear in mind that TOP is merely a filter that tells SQL Server that once it starts processing rows, it needs to return only a portion of the rows that the query would return. If the number is hard-coded, it can help in optimization of the query. Using a variable means that the optimizer will need to assume you want all rows. This could have performance implications.

Extensions to the FROM Clause

SQL Server allows the FROM clause to extend the way you can manipulate data with the SELECT, INSERT, UPDATE, and DELETE SQL statements. The FROM clause supports the following:

- APPLY *operator*: CROSS APPLY and OUTER APPLY aid with use of user-defined functions.

- *Random data sampling*: This enables you to return random sets of rows from a table.

- *Pivoting data*: The PIVOT operator allows you to easily rotate the columns in a table to rows.

Join Types

One particular annoyance in early versions of SQL Server was that derived tables could not be correlated to other sets in the FROM clause. For example, the following type of query would not have been allowed:

```
SELECT Product.productNumber, SalesOrderAverage.averageTotal
FROM   Production.Product AS Product
         JOIN      (    SELECT AVG(lineTotal) AS averageTotal
                        FROM Sales.SalesOrderDetail as SalesOrderDetail
                        WHERE Product.ProductID=SalesOrderDetail.ProductID
                        HAVING COUNT(*) > 1
                   ) AS SalesOrderAverage
```

Of course, for the most part, a normal query like this was not a great problem because this query could easily be rewritten as an inner join. However, in SQL Server 2000, Microsoft added table-valued user-defined functions, for which rewriting as a join was not possible. The following example seems natural:

```
SELECT Product.productNumber, SalesOrderAverage.averageTotal
FROM   Production.Product AS Product
         JOIN dbo.getAverageTotalPerProduct(product.productId)
                                                      AS SalesOrderAverage
```

but this is also illegal. Instead, the function would need to be coded to return all rows for all products, which would probably not perform well at all, especially if you had a great many products.

This was one of the most frustrating problems with using table-based functions in SQL Server 2000. The APPLY operator allows queries of this style to make optimal use of derived tables and scalar functions. The operator injects column data from the left-hand table source into the right-hand source (valued function or derived table). There are two forms of APPLY:

- CROSS APPLY: Returns only a rowset if the right table source returns data for the parameter values from the left table source columns.

- OUTER APPLY: Just like an outer join, returns at least one row from the left table source, even if no rowset is returned from the right.

■Note The names of the join types will likely be confusing. OUTER APPLY seems very much like an OUTER JOIN, since a row is returned for each left table source, regardless of what is returned in the right table source (note that LEFT and RIGHT are not allowed). However, CROSS APPLY seems quite wrong. A CROSS JOIN would return all rows in the left table source and all rows in the right table source. CROSS APPLY seems more like it should be called an inner apply, but this is not the case.

In the next block of code, we use the `CROSS APPLY` operator to execute the derived table once per row in the `Production.Product` table. The subquery gets only one row, which is the average amount for a sale of that product. If it hasn't been sold yet, an empty result set would be the result of the `CROSS APPLY` operation, and the `Production.Product` row would not be returned:

```
SELECT Product.productNumber, SalesOrderAverage.averageTotal
FROM    Production.Product AS Product
          CROSS APPLY (    SELECT AVG(lineTotal) AS averageTotal
                           FROM Sales.SalesOrderDetail AS SalesOrderDetail
                           WHERE Product.ProductID=SalesOrderDetail.ProductID
                           HAVING COUNT(*) > 0
                           ) AS SalesOrderAverage
```

This returns the following results (truncated for readability):

```
productNumber               averageTotal
-----------------------     ----------------------------------------
BB-7421                     81.650630
BB-9108                     183.775014
BC-M005                     9.990000
BC-R205                     8.990000
BK-M18B-40                  679.055917
BK-M18B-42                  693.944595
BK-M18B-44                  647.416582
BK-M18B-48                  678.707431
BK-M18B-52                  644.185253
BK-M18S-40                  641.530154
BK-M18S-42                  626.030041
BK-M18S-44                  619.874742
BK-M18S-48                  627.573507
BK-M18S-52                  683.637900
BK-M38S-38                  945.020248
>> result set truncated <<
```

The real power of `CROSS APPLY` is with user-defined functions. Instead of a derived table, let's create a function that returns the value of the largest sale of a given product from the `Sales.SalesOrderDetail` table.

```
CREATE FUNCTION production.getAverageTotalPerProduct
(
    @productId int
)
RETURNS @output TABLE (unitPrice DECIMAL(10,4))
AS
    BEGIN
        INSERT  INTO @output (unitPrice)
        SELECT AVG(lineTotal) AS averageTotal
        FROM Sales.SalesOrderDetail AS SalesOrderDetail
        WHERE SalesOrderDetail.ProductID = @productId
        HAVING COUNT(*) > 0

        RETURN
    END
```

Now the statement can be rewritten as follows:

```
SELECT Product.ProductNumber, AverageSale.UnitPrice
FROM   Production.Product AS Product
            CROSS APPLY
                    Production.getAverageTotalPerProduct(product.productId)
                                                            AS AverageSale
```

This returns the same results as previously. Obviously, your multistatement table-valued functions would usually be a lot more complex than this (otherwise, why bother to make it a function?), but for the purposes of this example, this allows us to make use of the function in a very nice format that is usable, and should have good performance. (Clearly what performs well enough varies on a case-by-case basis. Don't take anyone's word for it—test, test, and test some more.)

In the previous example, any product rows where there were no matching unit sales were not included in the output. We change this to an OUTER APPLY to get back all rows in the product table, and NULLs for the unit price column where there have been no sales:

```
SELECT Product.ProductNumber, AverageSale.UnitPrice
FROM   Production.Product AS Product
            OUTER APPLY
                    Production.getAverageTotalPerProduct(product.productId)
                                                            AS AverageSale
```

Products that don't have any associated sales will return no rows, but you still get a row for each product:

```
ProductNumber           UnitPrice
----------------------- ----------------------------------------
AR-5381                 NULL
BA-8327                 NULL
BB-7421                 81.6506
BB-8107                 NULL
BB-9108                 183.7750
BC-M005                 9.9900
BC-R205                 8.9900
BE-2349                 NULL
BE-2908                 NULL
BK-M18B-40              679.0559
BK-M18B-42              693.9446
BK-M18B-44              647.4166
BK-M18B-48              678.7074
BK-M18B-52              644.1853
BK-M18S-40              641.5302
>> resultset truncated <<
```

■**Note** Using CROSS APPLY or OUTER APPLY allows a derived table or a table-valued function to have parameters applied for each row, making table-valued functions tremendously more useful.

Random Data Sampling

Sometimes it is desirable to get an idea about the distribution of data in a table, but it is impractical because there is just too much data. Obviously, it is seldom necessary to look at every piece of data to get an idea of how the data looks in the table. Take elections, for an example. An exit poll needs to sample only a small proportion of the population in order to predict the outcome with a high degree of accuracy.

TABLESAMPLE lets you get a random set of rows. You can specify either a percentage of the table or a given number of rows to return. However, what you will likely find weird about this operator is that it seldom returns exactly the same number of rows.

In the next example, the query returns a different selection of rows each time it is executed. What seems odd is just how large the variance in the row count will be. For this query, it typically will be between 1,800 and 3,000, which is approximately 2 percent of the number of rows in the Sales.SalesOrderDetail table, as there are 118,990 in the version of the table we are using and 2 percent is 2,379.

```
SELECT  *
FROM    Sales.SalesOrderDetail TABLESAMPLE SYSTEM (2 PERCENT)
```

There is also an option to get a more exact count of rows:

```
SELECT  *
FROM    Sales.SalesOrderDetail TABLESAMPLE SYSTEM (500 rows)
```

Again, however, it will not actually return only 500 rows; in testing, the count has been between 200 and 800. If you want to get back the same results each time you run one of these queries, you can specify the REPEATABLE option and a fixed seed for the randomizer:

```
SELECT  *
FROM    Sales.SalesOrderDetail TABLESAMPLE SYSTEM (500 rows) REPEATABLE (123456)
```

Given the same seed, you will get the same rows back. One thing to note here: this is not like the repeatable read isolation level. If another user makes changes to the data in the table, you will not get back the exact same rows. It is only true for a given "version" of the table.

As you've seen, these commands will not return the exact same number of rows each time, even when you specify a certain number of rows! This behavior has to do with the random nature of the TABLESAMPLE operator, and that the samples are done in a single pass through the table. It should not hurt your queries, but if you need an exact number of rows for a test, you could INTERSECT two table samples (INTERSECT is new and covered later in this chapter in the "EXCEPT and INTERSECT" section) and use TOP to get your set.

Pivoting Data

Excel has had pivot tables for quite some time, allowing users to rotate a table in such a way as to turn rows into columns, and back again. In SQL Server, two relational operators give some of the same functionality to T-SQL. These operators are PIVOT and UNPIVOT.

PIVOT

One thing that was almost impossible to do in T-SQL was to take a set of rows and pivot them to columns. The PIVOT operator allows you to rotate the columns in a table to rows.

As a very simple example (as simple as it can be anyhow), consider the following table of data, which we will call SalesByMonth. (We put it in the Sales schema; if you are not building this in the AdventureWorks database, you may need to create the schema using the command CREATE SCHEMA Sales.)

```
CREATE TABLE Sales.SalesByMonth
(
    year char(4),
    month char(3),
    amount MONEY,
    PRIMARY KEY (year, month)
)
```

```
INSERT INTO Sales.SalesByMonth (year, month, amount)
VALUES('2007','Jan',   789.0000)
INSERT INTO Sales.SalesByMonth (year, month, amount)
VALUES('2007','Feb',   389.0000)
INSERT INTO Sales.SalesByMonth (year, month, amount)
VALUES('2007','Mar',  8867.0000)
INSERT INTO Sales.SalesByMonth (year, month, amount)
VALUES('2007','Apr',   778.0000)
INSERT INTO Sales.SalesByMonth (year, month, amount)
VALUES('2007','May',    78.0000)
INSERT INTO Sales.SalesByMonth (year, month, amount)
VALUES('2007','Jun',     9.0000)
INSERT INTO Sales.SalesByMonth (year, month, amount)
VALUES('2007','Jul',   987.0000)
INSERT INTO Sales.SalesByMonth (year, month, amount)
VALUES('2007','Aug',   866.0000)
INSERT INTO Sales.SalesByMonth (year, month, amount)
VALUES('2007','Sep',  7787.0000)
INSERT INTO Sales.SalesByMonth (year, month, amount)
VALUES('2007','Oct', 85576.0000)
INSERT INTO Sales.SalesByMonth (year, month, amount)
VALUES('2007','Nov',   855.0000)
INSERT INTO Sales.SalesByMonth (year, month, amount)
VALUES('2007','Dec',  5878.0000)

INSERT INTO Sales.SalesByMonth (year, month, amount)
VALUES('2008','Jan',     7.0000)
INSERT INTO Sales.SalesByMonth (year, month, amount)
VALUES('2008','Feb',  6868.0000)
INSERT INTO Sales.SalesByMonth (year, month, amount)
VALUES('2008','Mar',   688.0000)
INSERT INTO Sales.SalesByMonth (year, month, amount)
VALUES('2008','Apr',  9897.0000)
```

Most likely, this would not be representative of a table in your database, but instead the final output of a query that summarized the data by month. While this is the natural format for a set-based query, it is not likely that the user will want to look at the data this way; for starters, it is ordered strangely (alphabetic order because of the clustered index on the key!), but even if it were ordered by month, it would still be pretty ugly. It is likely the desired output of this data might be like this:

```
Year   Jan         Feb          Mar          ...
-----  ----------  -----------  -----------
2007   789.0000    389.0000     8867.0000    ...
2008   7.0000      6868.0000    688.0000     ...
```

Using SQL Server 2000 coding techniques, the query would look something along these lines:

```
SELECT year,
       SUM(case when month = 'Jan' then amount else 0 end) AS 'Jan',
       SUM(case when month = 'Feb' then amount else 0 end) AS 'Feb',
       SUM(case when month = 'Mar' then amount else 0 end) AS 'Mar',
       SUM(case when month = 'Apr' then amount else 0 end) AS 'Apr',
       SUM(case when month = 'May' then amount else 0 end) AS 'May',
       SUM(case when month = 'Jun' then amount else 0 end) AS 'Jun',
       SUM(case when month = 'Jul' then amount else 0 end) AS 'Jul',
       SUM(case when month = 'Aug' then amount else 0 end) AS 'Aug',
```

```
          SUM(case when month = 'Sep' then amount else 0 end) AS 'Sep',
          SUM(case when month = 'Oct' then amount else 0 end) AS 'Oct',
          SUM(case when month = 'Nov' then amount else 0 end) AS 'Nov',
          SUM(case when month = 'Dec' then amount else 0 end) AS 'Dec'
FROM    Sales.SalesByMonth
GROUP   BY year
```

Not terribly hard to follow, but pretty messy if you start to need more information. Using the new PIVOT operator, the code is changed to this:

```
SELECT Year,[Jan],[Feb],[Mar],[Apr],[May],[Jun],
          [Jul],[Aug],[Sep],[Oct],[Nov],[Dec]
FROM (
    SELECT year, amount, month
    FROM      Sales.SalesByMonth ) AS SalesByMonth
    PIVOT  ( SUM(amount) FOR month IN
            ([Jan],[Feb],[Mar],[Apr],[May],[Jun],
             [Jul],[Aug],[Sep],[Oct],[Nov],[Dec])
    ) AS ourPivot
ORDER BY Year
```

The most important part of this query is this:

```
    PIVOT  ( SUM(amount) FOR month IN
            ([Jan],[Feb],[Mar],[Apr],[May],[Jun],
             [Jul],[Aug],[Sep],[Oct],[Nov],[Dec])
```

It produces a value for each of the columns in the IN clause that matches values in the month column. This is done via the SUM (amount) FOR month section. The moderately confusing part is that it groups on the columns that are not a part of the PIVOT statement. Since year was not in an aggregate, it grouped the pivot on year. Suppose we remove year from the query as follows:

```
SELECT [Jan],[Feb],[Mar],[Apr],[May],[Jun],
       [Jul],[Aug],[Sep],[Oct],[Nov],[Dec]
FROM (      SELECT amount, month
            FROM   Sales.SalesByMonth ) AS SalesByMonth
    PIVOT  ( SUM(amount) FOR month IN
            ([Jan],[Feb],[Mar],[Apr],[May],[Jun],
             [Jul],[Aug],[Sep],[Oct],[Nov],[Dec])
    ) AS ourPivot
```

The result is that it groups on all rows:

Jan	Feb	Mar	...
796.0000	7257.0000	9555.0000	...

When you need to store variable attributes in your schema and you cannot determine all of the data requirements at design time, PIVOT is excellent. For example, a store that has many products may have very different attributes for each product. Instead of having different tables with different attributes for each type of product (a management nightmare), you implement a table that allows for varying properties to be created and a value associated with them. Building these "property" or "attribute" tables is an easy technique for associating values with a product, but writing queries to deliver to the client can be very cumbersome.

■**Note** This kind of schema is generally only a good idea in extreme circumstances when the data is very variable. If the schema can at all be predicted, it is important to go ahead and do a full design. A good example of where this sort of schema is useful is for storing the operating data from networking routers. They have tons of properties, and each model has slightly different ones.

As an example, let's extend the `Person.Contact` table by creating a `Person.ContactProperty` table that contains properties that you might not know when the schema is designed. We will store the person's dog's name, hair color, and car style:

```
CREATE TABLE Person.ContactProperty
(
    ContactPropertyId int identity(1,1) PRIMARY KEY,
    ContactId       int REFERENCES Person.Contact(contactid),
    PropertyName  varchar(20),
    PropertyValue SQL_VARIANT,
    UNIQUE (contactid, propertyname)
)

INSERT Person.ContactProperty (contactid, propertyname, propertyvalue)
VALUES(1,'dog name','Fido')
INSERT Person.ContactProperty (contactid, propertyname, propertyvalue)
VALUES(1,'hair color','brown')
INSERT Person.ContactProperty (contactid, propertyname, propertyvalue)
VALUES(1,'car style','sedan')

INSERT Person.ContactProperty (contactid, propertyname, propertyvalue)
VALUES(2,'dog name','Rufus')
INSERT Person.ContactProperty (contactid, propertyname, propertyvalue)
VALUES(2,'hair color','blonde')

INSERT Person.ContactProperty (contactid, propertyname, propertyvalue)
VALUES(3,'dog name','Einstein')
INSERT Person.ContactProperty (contactid, propertyname, propertyvalue)
VALUES(3,'car style','coupe')
```

If we look at the data in a basic T-SQL statement:

```
SELECT   CAST(Contact.firstname + ' ' + Contact.lastname AS varchar(30)) AS Name,
         ContactProperty.propertyname, ContactProperty.propertyvalue
FROM     Person.Contact AS Contact
             INNER JOIN Person.ContactProperty AS ContactProperty
                 ON  ContactProperty.contactid = Contact.contactid
```

then we get the typical result set of a row per attribute:

name	propertyname	propertyvalue
Gustavo Achong	dog name	Fido
Gustavo Achong	hair color	brown
Gustavo Achong	car style	sedan
Catherine Abel	dog name	Rufus
Catherine Abel	hair color	blonde
Kim Abercrombie	dog name	Einstein
Kim Abercrombie	car style	coupe

It will usually be more desirable to display this data as a single row in the user interface or report. To do this currently, you would need to navigate the results and pivot the rows themselves. Not that this is always the wrong way to go. Data formatting is usually best done using the presentation layer, but in some cases, doing this in the data layer will be best; depending on what kinds of clients are being used, or if you need to use the data in a different SQL query, data in this row-per-attribute format may be troublesome to deal with.

Instead, we can use the PIVOT operator to take the propertyname values and rotate the data to provide a single row per contact. We use a derived table, selecting all of the columns required in the PIVOT from our ContactProperty table. We then pivot this, getting the attribute values by propertyname for each contactid.

```
SELECT  CAST(Contact.firstname + ' ' + Contact.lastname AS varchar(30)) AS name,
        pivotColumns.* --demonstrating that * works, it should not
                       --be done this way in production code
FROM    Person.Contact AS Contact
        INNER JOIN (SELECT contactid, propertyname,propertyvalue
                   FROM   Person.ContactProperty AS property)
                                                           as PivotTable
        PIVOT( MAX(propertyvalue)
               FOR propertyname IN ([dog name],[hair color],[car style]))
                                                           AS PivotColumns
             ON Contact.contactid = PivotColumns.contactid
```

We are getting the maximum value of the propertyvalue column for the rotated value, since only one value can be non-null. We are not restricted to only one unique value for the rotation, and this allows all sorts of aggregation to take place, making the PIVOT operator incredibly powerful. Then we specify the column that contains the values that we will pivot around. In our example, we are using the propertyname column, specifying the values that will become the columns in our output. The query output is as follows (noting that there is a null value where there was no value for a given property):

```
name                              contactid    dog name              hair color
------------------------------    -----------  --------------------  -------------------
Gustavo Achong                    1            Fido                  brown
Catherine Abel                    2            Rufus                 blonde
Kim Abercrombie                   3            Einstein              NULL

car style
-------------------
sedan
NULL
coupe
```

Note that we just used the first three contactid values from the Person.Contact table for this example.

■Note PIVOT takes a vertical set and converts it to a horizontal schema, allowing you to flatten a result set to make it easier to consume by a client.

UNPIVOT

The (almost) opposite effect of PIVOT is, not surprisingly, UNPIVOT. Less useful on a day-to-day-basis, this is a fantastic tool to have when doing data conversions or dealing with poorly designed databases. Going back to the set of data we created with our SalesByMonth query, using the INTO clause, we create a table of data called dbo.SalesByYear:

```
SELECT Year,[Jan],[Feb],[Mar],[Apr],[May],[Jun],
         [Jul],[Aug],[Sep],[Oct],[Nov],[Dec]
INTO  Sales.SalesByYear
FROM (
    SELECT year, amount, month
    FROM   Sales.SalesByMonth ) AS SalesByMonth
    PIVOT  ( SUM(amount) FOR month IN
             ([Jan],[Feb],[Mar],[Apr],[May],[Jun],
              [Jul],[Aug],[Sep],[Oct],[Nov],[Dec])
    ) AS ourPivot
ORDER BY Year
```

which contains the following output:

Year	Jan	Feb	Mar	...	
2007	789.0000	389.0000	8867.0000	...	...
2008	7.0000	6868.0000	688.0000	...	...

Now, to get this back to the original format, we can use a query like the following:

```
SELECT  Year, CAST(Month AS char(3)) AS Month, Amount
FROM    Sales.SalesByYear
        UNPIVOT (Amount FOR Month IN
          ([Jan],[Feb],[Mar],[Apr],[May],[Jun],
           [Jul],[Aug],[Sep],[Oct],[Nov],[Dec])) AS unPivoted
```

which returns this output:

```
Year Month Amount
---- ----- ------------------------------
2007 Jan   789.0000
2007 Feb   389.0000
2007 Mar   8867.0000
2007 Apr   778.0000
2007 May   78.0000
2007 Jun   9.0000
2007 Jul   987.0000
2007 Aug   866.0000
2007 Sep   7787.0000
2007 Oct   85576.0000
2007 Nov   855.0000
2007 Dec   5878.0000
2008 Jan   7.0000
2008 Feb   6868.0000
2008 Mar   688.0000
2008 Apr   9897.0000
```

This is another really nice addition to what T-SQL can do natively and will come in handy in quite a few cases. One thing you should note, however: UNPIVOT is not exactly the opposite of PIVOT. Null values in the table will not be returned as rows in the UNPIVOTed output. So, if we had the following table:

```
Year    Jan        Feb        Mar         ...
-----   ------     ----------  ----------
2007    NULL       NULL       8867.0000    ...
2008    7.0000     6868.0000  688.0000     ...
```

we would not get rows in our output like the following:

```
Year Month Amount
---- ----- -----------------------------
2007 Jan   NULL
2007 Feb   NULL
2007 Mar   8867.0000
...
```

The first two rows would not exist in the output.

OUTPUT

In SQL Server, an OUTPUT clause can be used as part of DML statements to assist in auditing changes made during the statement. The OUTPUT clause specifies a statement to output a result set of changes to a table variable.

Just as with triggers, you use the inserted and deleted tables to access the rows that have been modified in a statement and the data that is being deleted.

For example, change firstname in the Person.Contact table to the reverse of the original value. Note the BEGIN TRANSACTION and ROLLBACK TRANSACTION statements to avoid corrupting the data in the Person.Contact table.

```
BEGIN TRANSACTION

DECLARE @changes table (change varchar(2000))

UPDATE TOP (10) Person.Contact
SET    firstname = Reverse(firstname)
OUTPUT 'Was: ''' + DELETED.firstname +
               ''' Is: ''' + INSERTED.firstname + ''''
INTO   @changes

SELECT *
FROM   @changes

ROLLBACK TRANSACTION
--note that local variable tables are not affected by transactions!
```

This returns the following (assuming you haven't already made changes to the data in the Person.Contact.firstname column):

```
change
----------------------------------------------------------------
Was: 'Gustavo' Is: 'ovatsuG'
Was: 'Catherine' Is: 'enirehtaC'
Was: 'Kim' Is: 'miK'
Was: 'Humberto' Is: 'otrebmuH'
Was: 'Pilar' Is: 'raliP'
Was: 'Frances' Is: 'secnarF'
Was: 'Margaret' Is: 'teragraM'
Was: 'Carla' Is: 'alraC'
Was: 'Jay' Is: 'yaJ'
Was: 'Ronald' Is: 'dlanoR'
```

■Note The OUTPUT clause gives you the ability to access the changes from a DML statement without building triggers or any other method.

This is a very interesting new feature, and you can see some interesting potential uses, such as scanning the outputted table to see if certain changes were made, although audit trails will still be easier to implement using triggers.

Ranking Functions

Ranking functions are used to assist you in adding positional information to your result set—for example, the position of a row within a set that you are returning.

■Note We have also seen ranking functions referred to as *windowed functions*. Either terminology is fine.

Briefly, let's demonstrate this sort of operation using SQL Server 2000 code. Let's consider finding the position of a row within our set. This can be done easily using a subquery. Using the AdventureWorks database, consider the Person.Contact table. To demonstrate, we will rank the order of the contact names, using first name first, so there are duplicates. Obviously, in a production system, you would likely never do this sort of thing, but the point of doing this here is to get a small set of data that we can work with to demonstrate how the ranking functions work. We will be using the following view to limit our sets for each query.

```
CREATE VIEW contactSubset
AS
    SELECT  TOP 20 *
    FROM    Person.Contact
    WHERE   firstname LIKE 'b%'
```

So we execute the following:

```
SELECT  firstname,
        (   SELECT COUNT(*)
            FROM    contactSubset AS c
            WHERE   c.firstname < contactSubset.firstname) + 1 AS RANK
FROM    contactSubset
ORDER   BY firstname
```

which returns the following:

```
firstname                                           RANK
-------------------------------------------------   -----------
Barbara                                             1
Barbara                                             1
Barbara                                             1
Baris                                               4
Bart                                                5
Benjamin                                            6
Bernard                                             7
Betty                                               8
Bev                                                 9
Blaine                                              10
Bob                                                 11
Bradley                                             12
Brenda                                              13
Brenda                                              13
Brian                                               15
Brian                                               15
Bridget                                             17
Brigid                                              18
Bruno                                               19
Bruno                                               19
```

The subquery gives us position or rank by counting the number of employees in a copy of Employee that has names that are less than the current name in alphabetic ordering. It works great, and it is not too messy, but what if we need two criteria? For the purposes of our example, say we want to use the last name of our contacts. The query gets more and more complex:

```
SELECT    firstname, lastname,
          (   SELECT COUNT(*)
              FROM   contactSubset AS c
              WHERE  c.lastname < contactSubset.lastname
                OR   (c.lastname = contactSubset.lastname
                      AND c.firstname< contactSubset.firstname)
                  ) + 1 AS orderNumber
FROM      contactSubset
ORDER     BY lastname, firstname
```

In SQL Server, we have these four significant functions:

- ROW_NUMBER: Returns the row number of a row in a result set.

- RANK: Based on some chosen order of a given set of columns, gives the position of the row. It will leave gaps if there are any ties for values. For example, there might be two values in first place, and then the next value would be third place.

- DENSE_RANK: Same as RANK but does not leave gaps in the sequence. Whereas RANK might order values 1,2,2,4,4,6,6, DENSE_RANK would order them 1,2,2,3,3,4,4.

- NTILE: Used to partition the ranks into a number of sections; for example, if you have a table with 100 values, you might use NTILE(2) to number the first 50 as 1, and the last 50 as 2.

For each of these functions, you must specify an OVER clause, which basically specifies a sorting criterion that the functions will assign their ranking values. It does not need to be the same ordering as the ORDER BY clause, and when it is not, the results will be interesting. There is also an optional PARTITION BY criterion that you can apply to the OVER clause that allows you to break up the sections into different groups. This will be demonstrated at the end of this section.

As an example, look again at our contact subset:

```
SELECT  firstname,
        ROW_NUMBER() OVER (ORDER BY firstname) AS 'ROW_NUMBER',
        RANK() OVER (ORDER BY firstname) AS 'RANK',
        DENSE_RANK() OVER (ORDER BY firstname) AS 'DENSE_RANK',
        NTILE(4) OVER (ORDER BY firstname) AS 'NTILE(4)'
FROM    contactSubSet
ORDER   BY firstname
```

This returns the following:

FirstName	ROW_NUMBER	RANK	DENSE_RANK	NTILE(4)
Barbara	1	1	1	1
Barbara	2	1	1	1
Barbara	3	1	1	1
Baris	4	4	2	1
Bart	5	5	3	1
Benjamin	6	6	4	2
Bernard	7	7	5	2
Betty	8	8	6	2
Bev	9	9	7	2
Blaine	10	10	8	2
Bob	11	11	9	3
Bradley	12	12	10	3
Brenda	13	13	11	3
Brenda	14	13	11	3
Brian	15	15	12	3
Brian	16	15	12	4
Bridget	17	17	13	4
Brigid	18	18	14	4
Bruno	19	19	15	4
Bruno	20	19	15	4

You can see that we now have a ROW_NUMBER column that gives a unique ranking for each row, based on the ordering criteria specified. The RANK function assigns a ranking value to each row. It simply counts the number of rows with a lower value than the current one according to the ordering criteria. When ordering by first name, there are four values "lower" than Bart (three instances of Barbara and a Baris), so Bart gets a rank of 5. This will inevitably leave "gaps" in the ranking numbers. DENSE_RANK counts only distinct values; Bart gets a DENSE_RANK of 3, since only two distinct groups precede it.

Finally, NTILE breaks up the set into a number of different groups, based on a parameter (we show it set to 4 in this example). NTILE groups will have exactly the same number of values in a group if it is possible to split them evenly (for example, two groups of 10 for 20 rows, three groups of 3 for 9 rows, and so on). This is true even if all the values in the table are the same. Otherwise, some groups may have fewer members.

We can specify multiple ordering criteria in the ORDER BY clause, as follows:

```
SELECT    firstname, lastname,
          ROW_NUMBER() OVER (ORDER BY firstname, lastname) AS 'ROW_NUMBER',
          RANK() OVER (ORDER BY firstname,lastname) AS 'RANK',
          DENSE_RANK() OVER (ORDER BY firstname,lastname) AS 'DENSE_RANK',
          NTILE(4) OVER (ORDER BY firstname,lastname) AS 'NTILE(4)'
FROM      contactSubSet
ORDER     BY firstname
```

Executing this, we get the following:

firstname	lastname	ROW_NUMBER	RANK	DENSE_RANK	NTILE(4)
Barbara	Calone	1	1	1	1
Barbara	Decker	2	2	2	1
Barbara	German	3	3	3	1
Baris	Cetinok	4	4	4	1
Bart	Duncan	5	5	5	1
Benjamin	Becker	6	6	6	2
Bernard	Duerr	7	7	7	2
Betty	Haines	8	8	8	2
Bev	Desalvo	9	9	9	2
Blaine	Dockter	10	10	10	2
Bob	Gage	11	11	11	3
Bradley	Beck	12	12	12	3
Brenda	Barlow	13	13	13	3
Brenda	Diaz	14	14	14	3
Brian	Goldstein	15	15	15	3
Brian	Groth	16	16	16	4
Bridget	Browqett	17	17	17	4
Brigid	Cavendish	18	18	18	4
Bruno	Costa Da Silva	19	19	19	4
Bruno	Deniut	20	20	20	4

This gives us pretty much the same results, but now since there are no duplicates, the values for RANK and DENSE_RANK are the same as the ROW_NUMBER values.

What makes these functions so incredibly useful is that all of the ORDER BY clauses need not be the exact same. You can even have the same criteria ascending and descending in the same query:

```
SELECT    firstname,
          ROW_NUMBER() OVER (ORDER BY firstname) AS ASCENDING,
          ROW_NUMBER() OVER (ORDER BY firstname DESC) AS DESCENDING
FROM      contactSubSet
ORDER     BY firstname
```

The preceding code returns the following:

firstname	ascending	descending
Barbara	1	18
Barbara	2	19
Barbara	3	20
Baris	4	17
Bart	5	16
Benjamin	6	15
Bernard	7	14
Betty	8	13
Bev	9	12
Blaine	10	11
Bob	11	10
Bradley	12	9
Brenda	13	7
Brenda	14	8
Brian	15	5
Brian	16	6

Bridget	17	4
Brigid	18	3
Bruno	19	1
Bruno	20	2

■**Note** Note that while the descending rows seem out of order, they are actually not, since the three values for Barbara (and the other duplicates) can be ordered in either direction. It could make using the rows interesting, so if it was important for 1 to correspond to 20 in the other column, using unique columns for ordering would be required.

As we mentioned earlier, there is also a PARTITION clause you can apply to your OVER clause that will let you apply the ranking functions to individual groups in the data. In our sample data, we have several people who have the same first name. If we wanted to include rankings of names in the subsets, in our case first name, we can change our query from earlier to be as follows:

```
SELECT    firstname, lastname,
          ROW_NUMBER()OVER ( PARTITION BY firstname ORDER BY lastname) AS
                                                     'ROW_NUMBER',
          RANK()OVER ( PARTITION BY firstname ORDER BY lastname) AS 'RANK',
          DENSE_RANK()OVER ( PARTITION BY firstname ORDER BY lastname) AS
                                                     'DENSE_RANK',
          NTILE(2) OVER ( PARTITION BY firstname ORDER BY lastname) AS
                                                     'NTILE(2)'
FROM      contactSubSet
ORDER     BY firstname
```

This returns the following:

firstname	lastname	ROW_NUMBER	RANK	DENSE_RANK	NTILE(2)
Barbara	Calone	1	1	1	1
Barbara	Decker	2	2	2	1
Barbara	German	3	3	3	2
Baris	Cetinok	1	1	1	1
Bart	Duncan	1	1	1	1
Benjamin	Becker	1	1	1	1
Bernard	Duerr	1	1	1	1
Betty	Haines	1	1	1	1
Bev	Desalvo	1	1	1	1
Blaine	Dockter	1	1	1	1
Bob	Gage	1	1	1	1
Bradley	Beck	1	1	1	1
Brenda	Barlow	1	1	1	1
Brenda	Diaz	2	2	2	2
Brian	Goldstein	1	1	1	1
Brian	Groth	2	2	2	2
Bridget	Browqett	1	1	1	1
Brigid	Cavendish	1	1	1	1
Bruno	Costa Da Silva	1	1	1	1
Bruno	Deniut	2	2	2	2

Now you can see that the row numbers and rankings are based on the firstname groups, not the entire set. It isn't hard to see that by combining various OVER clauses, you can build very complex queries very easily.

The ranking functions are going to be incredibly valuable assets when writing many types of queries. They will take the place of many of the tricks that have been used for adding sequence numbers to sets, especially when dealing with partitioned sets. Understand, however, that there is no order to SQL sets. The data may be in the table in any order, and unless you specify an ORDER BY clause, the data that is returned to your client may be ordered by ROW_NUMBER, and it may not. For starters, you can include more than one ROW_NUMBER call in your query that has different ordering.

For example, say you want to see the top ten products for raw sales last year (assuming the year is 2008 right now) and you want to see them grouped into quartiles. This is very easy to write using the RANK and NTILE functions.

```
WITH salesSubset AS
(
    SELECT  Product.Name AS Product,  SUM(SalesOrderDetail.lineTotal) AS total
    FROM    Sales.SalesOrderDetail  AS SalesOrderDetail
            JOIN Sales.SalesOrderHeader AS SalesOrderHeader
                ON SalesOrderHeader.SalesOrderId = SalesOrderDetail.SalesOrderId
                    JOIN Production.Product AS Product
                        ON Product.ProductId = SalesOrderDetail.ProductId
        WHERE   orderDate >= '1/1/2007' AND orderDate < '1/1/2008'
        GROUP   BY Product.Name
)
SELECT  Product, Total,
        RANK() OVER (ORDER BY Total DESC) AS 'RANK',
        NTILE(4) OVER (ORDER BY Total DESC) AS 'NTILE(4)'
FROM    salesSubset
```

This returns the following:

Product	Total	RANK	NTILE(4)
Mountain-200 Black, 38	1327957.407668	1	1
Mountain-200 Black, 42	1139429.487144	2	1
Mountain-200 Silver, 38	1136622.492744	3	1
Mountain-200 Silver, 46	1029170.763900	4	1
Mountain-200 Silver, 42	1011486.176127	5	1
Mountain-200 Black, 46	1011074.368428	6	1
Road-350-W Yellow, 48	897217.963419	7	1
Road-350-W Yellow, 40	840970.646693	8	1
Touring-1000 Blue, 60	835290.155817	9	1
Touring-1000 Yellow, 60	826141.287192	10	1
Touring-1000 Blue, 46	810708.725268	11	1
<results truncated>			

This is probably a more efficient thing to do using Analysis Services, but you often need this kind of ad hoc query against the OLTP database. These functions add tremendous power to the SQL language. Be careful with them, however, since they do not actually have to do with the order of the table itself; rather, they calculate a position within a set, which is specified in the OVER clause.

You cannot use the ranking functions in a WHERE clause, so you will have to use a derived table or a CTE to preprocess the query. For example, say we wanted to only look at the bottom 10 percent of sales, we can change our query to use NTILE with a parameter of 10 (10 equal groups) and get only those in group 10:

```
WITH salesSubset AS
(
    SELECT  Product.Name AS Product,  SUM(SalesOrderDetail.lineTotal) AS Total
    FROM    Sales.SalesOrderDetail  AS SalesOrderDetail
```

```
                     JOIN Sales.SalesOrderHeader AS SalesOrderHeader
                   ON SalesOrderHeader.SalesOrderId = SalesOrderDetail.SalesOrderId
                     JOIN Production.Product AS Product
                   ON Product.Productid = SalesOrderDetail.Productid
          WHERE    orderDate >= '1/1/2007' AND orderDate < '1/1/2008'
           GROUP   BY Product.Name
)
SELECT  *
FROM    (SELECT  Product, Total,
                   RANK() OVER (ORDER BY total DESC) AS 'RANK',
                   NTILE(10) OVER (ORDER BY total DESC) AS 'NTILE(10)'
          FROM    salesSubset) AS productOrders
WHERE   [NTILE(10)] = 10
```

With NTILE, if you put a tiling number greater than the number of values in the set, you will get a sequential number for all of the rows, in the proper order for the data, but you will not get all groups in the data. It can be confusing.

■**Note** T-SQL has added the standard SQL functions ROW_NUMBER, RANK, DENSE_RANK, and NTILE. They make coding statements that require ordering far easier, as well as bring T-SQL a bit closer to standard SQL in addition to PL/SQL and DB2 SQL, which already have them.

EXCEPT and INTERSECT

EXCEPT and INTERSECT are new clauses that are in the same family as UNION in that they are used to combine multiple disparate query results into a single result set. They give you the ability to do a few more interesting sorts of things with the data. As you know, UNION takes two sets of data that are shaped the same (same columns, same datatypes, or types that can be coerced into the same type) and lets you combine them. EXCEPT and INTERSECT have the same requirements to have the sets be alike, but they do different operations on them:

- EXCEPT: Takes the first set of data and compares it with the second set. Only values that exist in the first set, but not in the second, are returned.

- INTERSECT: Compares the two sets and returns only rows that each set has in common.

As an example, suppose that we have a table that has a list of users and the projects that they have worked on (the actual table may be less readable, but the concept is the same):

```
CREATE TABLE projectPerson
(
     personId    varchar(10),
     projectId   varchar(10),
     PRIMARY KEY (personId, projectId)
)
GO

INSERT INTO projectPerson VALUES ('joeb','projBig')
INSERT INTO projectPerson VALUES ('joeb','projLittle')
INSERT INTO projectPerson VALUES ('fredf','projBig')
INSERT INTO projectPerson VALUES ('homerr','projLittle')
INSERT INTO projectPerson VALUES ('stevegr','projBig')
INSERT INTO projectPerson VALUES ('stevegr','projLittle')
GO
```

So we can see that joeb worked on projBig and projLittle. Now we can write the following queries. Using UNION, we could see who worked on one project or both projects:

```
SELECT personId
FROM   projectPerson
WHERE  projectId = 'projBig'
UNION
SELECT personId
FROM   projectPerson
WHERE  projectId = 'projLittle'
```

This returns the following:

```
personId
----------
fredf
homerr
joeb
stevegr
```

What if we want to see who worked only on projLittle but not projBig? This was pretty ugly in SQL Server 2000:

```
SELECT  personId
FROM   projectPerson AS projLittle
WHERE  projectId = 'projLittle'
  AND NOT EXISTS (   SELECT *
                     FROM    projectPerson AS projBig
                     WHERE  projBig.projectId = 'projBig'
                       AND  projBig.personId = projLittle.personId)
```

In SQL Server 2008, we can run the following:

```
--worked on projBig but not projLittle
SELECT personId
FROM   projectPerson
WHERE  projectId = 'projLittle'
EXCEPT
SELECT personId
FROM   projectPerson
WHERE  projectId = 'projBig'
```

This returns the following:

```
personId
----------
homerr
```

Finally, say we want to see who worked only on both projects. In SQL Server 2000, we needed to run the query we did for INTERSECT, and then UNION the result with the opposite, which is just too messy to be of value here. In SQL Server 2008, the query is very straightforward:

```
SELECT personId
FROM   projectPerson
WHERE  projectId = 'projBig'
INTERSECT
SELECT personId
```

```
FROM   projectPerson
WHERE  projectId = 'projLittle'
```

This returns the following:

```
personId
----------
joeb
stevegr
```

■**Note** T-SQL has added the relational operators INTERSECT and EXCEPT to make determining characteristics about like sets easier to perform.

Synonyms

Synonyms give you the ability to assign different names to objects. You can alias object names; for example, using the Employee table as Emp. You can also shorten names. This is especially useful when dealing with three and four part names; for example, shortening server.database.owner.object to object.

Synonyms can be created for the following objects:

- Tables (including temporary tables)
- Views
- Stored procedures (CLR and T-SQL)
- Replication filter procedures
- Extended stored procedures (XPs)
- Table-valued functions (CLR and T-SQL)
- SQL scalar functions (CLR and T-SQL)
- User-defined aggregate functions (CLR)

The command for creating a synonym is quite simple:

```
CREATE SYNONYM <synonym name> FOR <object name>
```

For example, in the AdventureWorks database, say we wanted access to the AdventureWorks. HumanResources.Employee table. We might create an Emp synonym, like this:

```
CREATE SYNONYM Emp FOR AdventureWorks.HumanResources.Employee
```

Now to see all of the employees, we use the following:

```
SELECT * from Emp
```

Finally, we drop the synonym:

```
DROP SYNONYM Emp
```

Synonym security is much like stored procedure security in previous versions. If the object used is owned by the same owner, and the user has rights to the synonym, then it is the same as giving this user rights to the object (only via use of the synonym, not the base object). If the object and synonym have different owners, then the security chain is broken, and rights to the base object must be checked.

For example, let's create a new login and user in the AdventureWorks database:

```
CREATE LOGIN Bryan WITH PASSWORD = 'Bryan1'
CREATE USER Bryan FOR LOGIN Bryan
```

Now, we will create a synonym and a view on the Sales.Customer table.

```
CREATE SYNONYM synSecure FOR Sales.Customer
GO
CREATE VIEW viewSecure --as a contrasting example
AS
SELECT *
FROM Sales.Customer
GO
```

Then we will grant all rights on each to user Bryan on these two objects:

```
GRANT SELECT,INSERT,UPDATE,DELETE ON synSecure to Bryan
GRANT SELECT,INSERT,UPDATE,DELETE ON viewSecure to Bryan
```

Now, change the security context to user Bryan and try to select from the base table:

```
EXECUTE AS LOGIN='Bryan'
SELECT * FROM Sales.Customer
```

This returns the expected error:

```
Msg 229, Level 14, State 5, Line 1
SELECT permission denied on object 'Customer', database 'AdventureWorks',
schema 'Sales'.
```

while both of these will return the entire table:

```
SELECT * FROM viewSecure
SELECT * FROM synSecure
```

This works because both the synonym and the object are owned by the same user, in this case, dbo. If you want to change the owner of an object or a schema, use the ALTER AUTHORIZATION command.

■**Note** Synonyms give you the capability to reference objects using different names for simplification or encapsulation.

MERGE

The MERGE statement is an ISO/ANSI standard-specified statement that allows users to express multiple DML actions (INSERT, UPDATE, and DELETE) against a specified target table based on join conditions with a source table. Some of you may be curious as to why we need a special statement to do these kinds of operations when we could just simply wrap them within a transaction. The main benefit is performance, since the data is processed only once.

To help illustrate MERGE, consider the simple example where we have a FactProductPurchaseHistory table in a data warehouse, which tracks the last time a particular product was purchased and the total quantity of that particular product that has been sold. This information will aid business analysts in determining if a particular product is not selling well. To support our example, let's start by creating a Products table, which is simply a list of products with a primary key; a ProductPurchase table, which is a list of all purchases; and a FactProductPurchaseHistory table, which will be used to store the summary information. The code is as follows:

```
CREATE TABLE Products
(ProductID int PRIMARY KEY,
ProductName varchar(100) NOT NULL)

CREATE TABLE ProductPurchase
(FK_ProductID int REFERENCES Products(ProductID),
PurchaseDate date,
Quantity int)

INSERT INTO Products VALUES (1,'High caffeine coffee')
INSERT INTO Products VALUES (2,'Blow-out resistant diapers')
INSERT INTO Products VALUES (3,'Spit-up proof baby formula')
INSERT INTO Products VALUES (4,'Automatic midnight baby feeder')
INSERT INTO Products VALUES (5,'Newborn baby simulator')

INSERT INTO ProductPurchase VALUES (1,'1/1/2008',1)
INSERT INTO ProductPurchase VALUES (1,'1/2/2008',1)
INSERT INTO ProductPurchase VALUES (1,'1/3/2008',2)
INSERT INTO ProductPurchase VALUES (2,'1/1/2008',5)
INSERT INTO ProductPurchase VALUES (2,'1/2/2008',3)
INSERT INTO ProductPurchase VALUES (2,'1/3/2008',7)
INSERT INTO ProductPurchase VALUES (3,'1/1/2008',5)
INSERT INTO ProductPurchase VALUES (3,'1/2/2008',4)
INSERT INTO ProductPurchase VALUES (3,'1/3/2008',8)
INSERT INTO ProductPurchase VALUES (4,'1/1/2008',12)
INSERT INTO ProductPurchase VALUES (4,'1/2/2008',15)
INSERT INTO ProductPurchase VALUES (5,'1/1/2008',1)

CREATE TABLE FactProductPurchaseHistory
(ProductID int,
LastPurchaseDate date,
TotalQuantity int)
```

At this point, we have a scenario where some products were purchased in the first few days of January, and we are now ready to create a fact table based on this information. At a high level, the MERGE statement works as follows:

```
MERGE <target_table>
USING <table_source>
ON <search_criteria>
<merge_clause>
```

The *merge_clause* consists of keyword combinations such as WHEN MATCHED, WHEN NOT MATCHED, and WHEN SOURCE NOT MATCHED. This *merge_clause*, in addition to the granularity available by being able to define search criteria, allows the MERGE functionality to be a valuable part of your database applications.

Now we are ready to issue our MERGE statement to create our fact table. The MERGE code is as follows:

```
MERGE FactProductPurchaseHistory AS fpph
USING (SELECT DISTINCT FK_ProductID,  MAX(PurchaseDate) AS 'PurchaseDate',
  SUM(Quantity) AS 'Quantity' FROM ProductPurchase GROUP BY FK_ProductID)
AS src
ON (fpph.ProductID = src.FK_ProductID)
WHEN MATCHED AND fpph.LastPurchaseDate < src.PurchaseDate THEN
    UPDATE SET fpph.LastPurchaseDate = src.PurchaseDate,
      fpph.TotalQuantity=src.Quantity
```

```
WHEN NOT MATCHED THEN
    INSERT (ProductID, LastPurchaseDate,TotalQuantity)
    VALUES (src.FK_ProductID, src.PurchaseDate, src.Quantity);
```

If you are reading about MERGE for the first time, there is a lot to digest in this kind of statement, so let's break it down. We want to merge our fact table FactProductPurchaseHistory with the ProductPurchase table. Part of the performance of MERGE relies on the fact that it passes through the data only once. Because of this, MERGE does not allow multiple updates to the same row (that is, we can't update row 1 in the FactProductPurchaseHistory table and then later on, in the same MERGE statement, update it again). This is why in our USING clause we build a query that groups together the product IDs, the most recent date, and the total quantity of purchases within the ProductPurchase table.

Since there are no records in our FactProductPurchaseHistory table, when we execute the MERGE statement, the WHEN NO MATCHED clause will be used, as opposed to WHEN MATCHED. After executing this MERGE statement, we can see the results using a simple SELECT statement:

```
SELECT p.ProductName, h.LastPurchaseDate,h.TotalQuantity
    FROM FactProductPurchaseHistory h, Products p
    WHERE h.ProductID = p.ProductID
```

Executing this SELECT statement against our new fact table yields the following:

ProductName	LastPurchase	DateTotalQuantity
High caffeine coffee	2008-01-03	4
Blow-out resistant diapers	2008-01-03	15
Spit-up proof baby formula	2008-01-03	17
Automatic midnight baby feeder	2008-01-02	27
Newborn baby simulator	2008-01-01	1

At this point, this is nothing a simple INSERT INTO statement couldn't already do for us. What is interesting now is what happens tomorrow when we want to update the fact table. Suppose this table was a million records long. How long would it take to drop and re-create? To illustrate the capability of MERGE, let's add some values simulating some additional purchases:

```
INSERT INTO ProductPurchase VALUES (1,'1/4/2008',2)
INSERT INTO ProductPurchase VALUES (2,'1/4/2008',5)
INSERT INTO ProductPurchase VALUES (5,'1/4/2008',1)
```

Now when we execute the MERGE statement again, it will run through the WHEN MATCHED clause, since we already have the products in the fact table. The WHEN MATCHED clause will run the UPDATE statement to update the quantity and last purchase date. This clause also includes search criteria: AND fpph.LastPurchaseDate < src.PurchaseDate. Without this extra condition, we would always be running through the WHEN MATCHED clause for each entry in the fact table.

After executing the MERGE statement again, the SELECT statement against our new fact table yields the following:

ProductName	LastPurchase	DateTotalQuantity
High caffeine coffee	2008-01-04	6
Blow-out resistant diapers	2008-01-04	20
Spit-up proof baby formula	2008-01-03	17
Automatic midnight baby feeder	2008-01-02	27
Newborn baby simulator	2008-01-04	2

As you can see, only the three affected rows were updated in a single pass through the data itself.

MERGE is a powerful new feature that provides a more efficient way to perform multiple DML operations. In this example, we described a data warehousing scenario. However, MERGE is flexible and can add value in many other scenarios.

General Development

In addition to the commands you use to define your DDL and DML, T-SQL supports commands to implement functional code in stored procedures, functions, triggers, and batches. Several changes and new features have been introduced for T-SQL commands:

- *Error handling*: Some ability to deal with errors in T-SQL code.

- .WRITE *extension to the* UPDATE *statement*: Easy mechanism to support chunked updates to (max) datatypes: varchar(max), nvarchar(max), and varbinary(max).

- EXECUTE: Extensions to EXECUTE to specify a server from which to execute the code.

- *Code security context*: Extensions to procedure and function declarations to specify security context.

- *.NET declarations statements*: Extensions to declare .NET assemblies for use in T-SQL.

- *T-SQL syntax enhancements*: Improvements associated with declaring and setting variables within the same statement.

- *Table value parameters*: Table structures can be passed as parameters in user-defined functions and stored procedures.

Error Handling

For as long as any T-SQL programmer can remember, error handling has been the weakest part of writing T-SQL. The story in SQL Server starting in 2005 got far better, as SQL Server now supports the use of TRY...CATCH constructs for providing rich error handling.

Before we show you the TRY...CATCH construct, we'll establish how this would need to be done in SQL Server 2000. We'll create the following two tables (again, if you're following along, create these tables in your own database, or simply in tempdb):

```
CREATE SCHEMA Entertainment
    CREATE TABLE TV
(
    TVid int PRIMARY KEY,
    location varchar(20),
    diagonalWidth int
            CONSTRAINT CKEntertainment_tv_checkWidth CHECK (diagonalWidth >= 30)
)

GO

CREATE TABLE dbo.error_log
(
    tableName SYSNAME,
    userName SYSNAME,
    errorNumber int,
    errorSeverity int,
    errorState int,
    errorMessage varchar(4000)
)
GO
```

In previous versions of SQL Server, logging and handling errors were ugly. You needed to query the @@error system variable to see if a runtime error had occurred, and then you could do what you wanted. Generally speaking, we like to include a facility for logging that an error occurs, like this:

```
CREATE PROCEDURE entertainment.tv$insert
(
        @TVid                   int,
        @location               varchar(30),
        @diagonalWidth     int
)
AS
DECLARE @Error int

    BEGIN TRANSACTION

    --insert a row
    INSERT entertainment.TV (TVid, location, diagonalWidth)
    VALUES(@TVid, @location, @diagonalWidth)

    --save @@ERROR so we don't lose it.
    SET @Error=@@ERROR
    IF @Error<>0
      BEGIN
        -- an error has occurred
        GOTO ErrorHandler
      END

    COMMIT TRANSACTION

GOTO ExitProc

ErrorHandler:
    -- roll back the transaction
    ROLLBACK TRANSACTION
    -- log the error into the error_log table
    INSERT dbo.error_log (tableName, userName,
                        errorNumber, errorSeverity ,errorState ,
                        errorMessage)
      VALUES('TV',suser_sname(),@Error,0,0,'We do not know the message!')
ExitProc:
GO
```

Now suppose we execute the procedure with an invalid parameter value disallowed by our CHECK constraint:

```
exec entertainment.tv$insert @TVid = 1, @location = 'Bed Room', @diagonalWidth = 29
```

Since our table has a CHECK constraint making sure that the diagonalWidth column is 30 or greater, this returns the following:

```
Msg 547, Level 16, State 0, Procedure tv$insert, Line 13
The INSERT statement conflicted with the CHECK constraint
"CKEntertainment_tv_checkWidth". The conflict occurred in database "AdventureWorks"
,table "TV", column 'diagonalWidth'.
The statement has been terminated.
```

Checking the error log table, we see that the error was logged, though the information is somewhat useless:

```
SELECT * FROM dbo.error_log
```

tableName	userName	errorID	errorNumber	errorSeverity	errorState
TV	DOMAINNAME\LBDAVI	1	547	0	0

errorMessage
We do not know the message!

Error handling quickly becomes a rather large percentage of the code with repetitive blocks of code used to check for an error. Even worse, we could not stop this message from being sent to the client. So the burden of deciding what went wrong was placed on the client, based on using these error messages. Needless to say, error handling in SQL Server 2000 and earlier was a real pain, and this often lead to applications *not* using CHECK constraints.

TRY...CATCH lets us build error handling at the level we need, in the way we need to, by setting a region where if any error occurs, it will break out of the region and head to an error handler. The basic structure is as follows:

```
BEGIN TRY
     <code>
END TRY
BEGIN CATCH
     <code>
END CATCH
```

So if any error occurs in the TRY block, execution is diverted to the CATCH block, and the error can be dealt with. For example, take a look at the following simple example:

```
BEGIN TRY
     RAISERROR ('Something is amiss',16,1)
END TRY
BEGIN CATCH
     SELECT ERROR_NUMBER() AS ERROR_NUMBER,
            ERROR_SEVERITY() AS ERROR_SEVERITY,
            ERROR_STATE() AS ERROR_STATE,
            ERROR_MESSAGE() AS ERROR_MESSAGE
END CATCH
```

In the TRY block, all we are doing is raising an error. Running this, we get the following:

ERROR_NUMBER	ERROR_SEVERITY	ERROR_STATE	ERROR_MESSAGE
50000	16	1	Something is amiss

Notice when you execute this, you never see the following:

```
Msg 50000, Level 16, State 1, Line 1
Something is amiss
```

Now let's look at a more detailed and interesting example. First, we clear the tables we have built for our examples:

```
DELETE FROM entertainment.TV --in case you have added rows
DELETE FROM dbo.error_log
```

Next, we recode the procedure to employ TRY and CATCH blocks. Far less code is required, and it is much clearer what is going on.

```
ALTER PROCEDURE entertainment.tv$insert
(
    @TVid          int,
    @location      varchar(30),
    @diagonalWidth int
)
AS
    SET NOCOUNT ON
    BEGIN TRY
        BEGIN TRANSACTION
        INSERT TV (TVid, location, diagonalWidth)
                VALUES(@TVid, @location, @diagonalWidth)
        COMMIT TRANSACTION
    END TRY
    BEGIN CATCH
        ROLLBACK TRANSACTION
        INSERT dbo.error_log (tableName, userName,
                            errorNumber, errorSeverity ,errorState ,
                            errorMessage)
        VALUES('TV',suser_sname(),ERROR_NUMBER(),
                ERROR_SEVERITY(), ERROR_STATE(), ERROR_MESSAGE())
        RAISERROR ('Error creating new TV row',16,1)
    END CATCH
```

Execution goes into the TRY block, starts a transaction, and then creates rows in our table. If it fails, we fall into the CATCH block where the error is sent to the log procedure as it was in the previous example. The difference is that we get access to the error information, so we can insert meaningful information, rather than only the error number.

Now execute the procedure and check the error log table.

```
exec entertainment.tv$insert @TVid = 1, @location = 'Bed Room',
                            @diagonalWidth = 29
GO
SELECT * FROM dbo.error_log
GO
```

This returns the error message we created:

```
Msg 50000, Level 16, State 1, Procedure tv$insert, Line 18
Error creating new TV row
```

And from the SELECT from the error log, we get the full error message:

tableName	userName	errorID	errorNumber	errorSeverity	errorState
TV	COMPASS.NET\LBDAVI	4	547	16	0

```
errorMessage
--------------------------------------------------------------------------------
 The INSERT statement conflicted with the CHECK constraint
"CKEntertainment_tv_checkWidth". The conflict occurred in database "AdventureWorks"
, table "TV", column 'diagonalWidth'.
```

So we can avoid showing the "ugly" error message and try to give a better message. It is not perfect, but it is leaps and bounds above what we had. The main limitation is that we will need to do some messy work to translate that constraint to a usable message. But at least this message was not sent to the user.

But this is not all. TRY...CATCH blocks can be nested to give you powerful error-handling capabilities when nesting calls. For example, say we create the following procedure:

```
CREATE PROCEDURE dbo.raise_an_error
AS
 BEGIN
      BEGIN TRY
           raiserror ('Boom, boom, boom, boom',16,1)
      END TRY
      BEGIN CATCH  --just catch it, return it as a select,
                   --and raise another error
         SELECT ERROR_NUMBER() AS ErrorNumber,
               ERROR_SEVERITY() AS ErrorSeverity,
               ERROR_STATE() AS ErrorState, ERROR_LINE() AS ErrorLine,
               ERROR_PROCEDURE() AS ErrorProcedure,
               ERROR_MESSAGE() AS ErrorMessage
               RAISERROR ('Error in procedure raise_an_error',16,1)
      END CATCH
 END
GO
```

So all this procedure will do is raise an error, causing our CATCH block to start, select the error as a result set, and then reraise the error. This reraising of the error causes there to be a single point of impact for error handling. You can decide what to do with it when you call the procedure. For example, consider the following batch that we will use to call this procedure:

```
SET NOCOUNT ON
BEGIN TRY
    EXEC raise_an_error --@no_parm = 1 (we will uncomment this for a test
    SELECT 'I am never getting here'
END TRY
BEGIN CATCH
    SELECT ERROR_NUMBER() AS ErrorNumber, ERROR_SEVERITY() AS ErrorSeverity,
           ERROR_STATE() AS ErrorState, ERROR_LINE() AS ErrorLine,
           ECAST(ERROR_PROCEDURE() AS varchar(30)) AS ErrorProcedure,
            CAST(ERROR_MESSAGE() AS varchar(40))AS ErrorMessage
END CATCH
```

Running this simply causes an error to be raised by the subordinate procedure. We get two result sets. First, we get this:

ErrorNumber	ErrorSeverity	ErrorState	ErrorLine	ErrorProcedure
50000	16	1	5	raise_an_error

ErrorMessage
Boom, boom, boom, boom

And then we get this:

ErrorNumber	ErrorSeverity	ErrorState	ErrorLine	ErrorProcedure
50000	16	1	12	raise_an_error

ErrorMessage
Error in procedure raise_an_error

Uncomment the `@no_parm = 1` bit from the statement, and you will see that that error is trapped and the message `Procedure raise_an_error has no parameters and arguments were supplied.` is returned as a result set.

If you want to ignore errors altogether, you can include an empty CATCH block:

```
SET NOCOUNT ON
BEGIN TRY
    exec raise_an_error @no_parm = 1
    select 'hi'
END TRY
BEGIN CATCH
END CATCH
```

You can also see that, in all cases, the code never executes the `select 'hi'` statement. There is no RESUME type of action in the TRY...CATCH way of handling errors.

While there is an error raised because of the invalid parameter, it is not visible to the caller. So it is incredibly important that you make certain that a CATCH handler is included, unless you really don't want the error raised.

The one type of error that will not be handled by the TRY...CATCH mechanism is a syntax error. Consider the following:

```
SET NOCOUNT ON
BEGIN TRY
    EXEEC procedure --error here is on purpose!

END TRY
BEGIN CATCH
END CATCH
```

This returns the following:

```
Msg 102, Level 15, State 1, Line 3
Incorrect syntax near 'exeec'.
```

The only case where TRY...CATCH captures syntax errors is when used in an EXECUTE (`'<SQL code>'`) situation. Suppose you execute the following:

```
SET NOCOUNT ON
BEGIN TRY
    EXEC ('seeelect *')

END TRY
BEGIN CATCH
      SELECT  ERROR_NUMBER() AS ErrorNumber, ERROR_SEVERITY() AS ErrorSeverity,
              ERROR_STATE() AS ErrorState, ERROR_LINE() AS ErrorLine,
              cast(ERROR_PROCEDURE() AS varchar(60)) AS ErrorProcedure,
              cast(ERROR_MESSAGE() AS varchar(550))AS ErrorMessage
END CATCH
```

In this case, an error will be returned via the SELECT statement in the CATCH block.

One of the limitations that you will need to deal with is when you are doing several operations in the same batch. For example, consider our tv$insert procedure. Instead of inserting a single row, let's say we are going to insert two rows:

```
      ...
      BEGIN TRANSACTION
      INSERT TV (TVid, location, diagonalWidth)
      VALUES(@TVid, @location, @diagonalWidth)
      --second insert:
      INSERT TV (TVid, location, diagonalWidth)
      VALUES(@TVid, @location, @diagonalWidth / 2 )

      COMMIT TRANSACTION
      ...
```

How would we tell the two inserts apart if one of them had an error? It would not be possible, as either statement could break the rules of the TV table's CHECK constraint. In this case, one possible way to deal with this would be a custom error message value. So you might do something like this:

```
ALTER PROCEDURE entertainment.tv$insert
(
      @TVid                   int,
      @location               varchar(30),
      @diagonalWidth      int
)
AS
    SET NOCOUNT ON
    DECLARE @errorMessage varchar(2000)
    BEGIN TRY
            BEGIN TRANSACTION
            SET @errorMessage = 'Error inserting TV with diagonalWidth / 1'
            INSERT TV (TVid, location, diagonalWidth)
            VALUES(@TVid, @location, @diagonalWidth)

            --second insert:
            SET @errorMessage = 'Error inserting TV with diagonalWidth / 2'
            INSERT TV (TVid, location, diagonalWidth)
            VALUES(@TVid, @location, @diagonalWidth / 2 )

            COMMIT TRANSACTION
    END TRY
      BEGIN CATCH
```

```
                ROLLBACK TRANSACTION
                INSERT dbo.error_log VALUES('TV',suser_sname(),
                        ERROR_NUMBER(),ERROR_SEVERITY(),
                        ERROR_STATE(), ERROR_MESSAGE())
                RAISERROR (@errorMessage,16,1)
        END CATCH
GO
```

Now we can execute it:

```
exec entertainment.tv$insert @TVid = 10, @location = 'Bed Room',
                        @diagonalWidth = 30
```

This returns the following:

```
Msg 50000, Level 16, State 1, Procedure tv$insert, Line 28
Error inserting TV with diagonalWidth / 1
```

Let's try it with a number big enough to satisfy it, but not when it is divided by two:

```
exec entertainment.tv$insert @TVid = 11, @location = 'Bed Room',
                        @diagonalWidth = 60
```

This returns the following:

```
Msg 50000, Level 16, State 1, Procedure tv$insert, Line 28
Error inserting TV with diagonalWidth / 2
```

The key here (other than we really like to watch TV and don't like small ones) is to make sure to give your CATCH block enough information to raise a useful error. Otherwise the error messages you may produce using the new error handling will not be all that much better than what we had before.

Error handling in SQL Server is *vastly* improved over previous versions, but it is going to take a big mindshift to get us there. Once you start blocking errors from a client that has expected errors in the past, you may break code by trying to fix it. So careful study and some reengineering will likely be in order to properly start using the new error-handling capabilities.

■**Note** The new TRY and CATCH blocks make safe coding easier for handling errors, including stopping error messages from ever making it to the client.

.WRITE Extension to the UPDATE Statement

In older versions of SQL Server, modifying the data in text and image columns was a real beast using T-SQL code. There were arcane READTEXT and WRITETEXT commands to do "chunked" reads and writes (just reading and writing part of a value to save the resources of fetching huge amounts of data). Starting with SQL Server 2005, the use of the text and image types is being deprecated for the new (max) datatypes: varchar(max), nvarchar(max), and varbinary(max). text and image are still available, but their use should be phased out in favor of the far better (max) types.

For the most part, you can treat the (max) datatypes just like their regular 8,000-byte or less counterparts, but if you are dealing with very large values, this may not be desired. Each of the (max) types can store up to 2GB in a single column. Imagine having to fetch this value to the client, make some changes, and then issue an UPDATE statement for a two-character change? RAM is cheap, but not cheap enough to put 4GB on all of your machines. So we can do a "chunked" update of the data in the row using a new extension to the UPDATE statement. (Note that you can do chunked reads simply by using the substring function.)

As an example, consider the following simple table with a varchar(max) column:

```
CREATE TABLE testBIGtext
(
    testBIGtextId  int PRIMARY KEY,
    value          varchar(max)
)
```

Now we create a new value simply as an empty string:

```
INSERT INTO testBIGtext
VALUES(1,'')
```

Next, we just build a loop and, using .WRITE, we put some text into the value at an offset for some length. Note that the offset must be less than or equal to the current length of the value in the column. The syntax is shown here:

```
UPDATE <tableName>
SET    <(max)columnName>.WRITE(<scalar value>, <offset in column>,<# of bytes>
WHERE ...
```

Then we just start a loop and write 1,000 of each letter of the alphabet into the value column:

```
DECLARE @offset int
SET @offset = 0
WHILE @offset < 26
 BEGIN
      UPDATE testBIGtext
        --the text I am writing is just starting at the letter A --> char(97)
        --and increasing by adding the value of offset to 97 char(97) = a
        --char (98) = b. It is also used as the offset in the varchar(max) column
        --It is multiplied by the length of the data being written to fill a
        --pattern of aaabbbccc...zzz only with a 1000 of each
      SET value.write(replicate(char(97 + @offset),1000),@offset*1000, 1000)
      WHERE  testBIGTextId = 1

      SET @offset = @offset + 1
 END
```

Everything else is just plain SQL. Run the following to make sure our data is in there:

```
SELECT testBIGtextId, len(value) AS CharLength
FROM  testBIGtext
```

This returns the following:

```
testBIGtextId  CharLength
-------------  --------------------
1              26000
```

This is a tremendous win for SQL programmers. You can easily work with long datatypes using normal functions, *plus* there's a chunking mechanism, so that when you have a column holding a couple hundred megabytes of information, you don't need to replace the whole thing in one operation.

■**Note** .WRITE allows for writing "chunks" of data into a large varchar(max), nvarchar(max), or varbinary(max) column.

EXECUTE

The EXECUTE command in previous versions of SQL Server could be used only to execute SQL on the same server. In SQL Server, EXECUTE has an AT parameter to specify that the command be executed on a linked server.

To see this in action, let's set up our local server as a remote linked server. We will create a linked server using sp_addlinkedserver, call it LocalLinkedServer, and point this to our instance of SQL Server:

```
--note: if you are not running SQL Server as the default instance, you may
--have to change where we have specified localhost to point to your server instance
EXECUTE sp_addlinkedserver   @server='LocalLinkedServer', @srvproduct='',
                             @provider='SQLOLEDB', @datasrc='localhost'

--enable the linked server to allow remote procedure calls
EXECUTE  sp_serveroption 'LocalLinkedServer','RPC OUT',True
```

Now we can execute our T-SQL on the linked server by specifying AT and the linked server name:

```
EXECUTE('SELECT * FROM AdventureWorks.Production.Culture') AT LocalLinkedServer
```

The query is executed on the linked server and the results returned. The AT parameter applies only to using EXECUTE on batches of statements, not on explicit stored procedure or function calls.

You can then use sp_dropserver to get rid of the linked server:

```
EXECUTE sp_dropserver LocalLinkedServer
```

■**Note** The EXECUTE command allows the specifying of a linked server to send the T-SQL commands to by using the AT keyword.

For completeness, we need to mention that a method of executing a batch of commands on another SQL Server already exists: using sp_executesql. It has the added benefit of allowing for parameter and return values. This procedure can also be called remotely, as follows:

```
EXECUTE ourLinkedServer.master.dbo.sp_executesql
               @statement = N'SELECT * FROM AdventureWorks.Production.Culture'
```

Code Security Context

The EXECUTE AS clause on a procedure or function declaration allows you to define the security context in which a stored procedure or function (other than in-line table-valued functions) is executed. Without this clause, the object executes in the security context of the CALLER. Note that this does not affect the execution of the procedure *unless* there is a break in the ownership chain. Any object owned by the creator of the procedure will be available to the user.

The syntax of this clause is as follows:

```
CREATE PROCEDURE <procedureName>
[parameters]
WITH EXECUTE AS <option>
AS
     <Procedure definition>
```

It is the same syntax when used for functions. There are four possible values for the EXECUTE AS option:

- EXECUTE AS CALLER (the default)
- EXECUTE AS SELF
- EXECUTE AS OWNER
- EXECUTE AS USER=<*username*>

You can also execute one of these as a stand-alone command to change the context of who is executing the procedure back to the CALLER if needed. One additional statement is included: REVERT to go back to the context set in the WITH clause of the procedure declaration.

As an example, we're going to create a user, named mainOwner, and then a procedure that uses the EXECUTE AS option on a procedure to show the basics of EXECUTE AS.

We'll start by creating several users, tables, and procedures:

```
--this user will be the owner of the primary schema
CREATE LOGIN mainOwner WITH PASSWORD = 'mainOwnery'
CREATE USER mainOwner FOR LOGIN mainOwner
GRANT CREATE SCHEMA TO mainOwner
GRANT CREATE TABLE TO mainOwner

--this will be the procedure creator
CREATE LOGIN secondaryOwner WITH PASSWORD = 'secondaryOwnery'
CREATE USER secondaryOwner FOR LOGIN secondaryOwner
GRANT CREATE SCHEMA to secondaryOwner
GRANT CREATE PROCEDURE TO secondaryOwner
GRANT CREATE TABLE TO secondaryOwner

--this will be the average user who needs to access data
CREATE LOGIN aveSchlub WITH PASSWORD = 'aveSchluby'
CREATE USER aveSchlub FOR LOGIN aveSchlub
```

Then we change to the context of the main object owner, create a new schema, and create a table with some rows:

```
EXECUTE AS USER='mainOwner'
GO
CREATE SCHEMA mainOwnersSchema
GO
CREATE TABLE  mainOwnersSchema.person
(
    personId    int constraint PKtestAccess_person primary key,
    firstName   varchar(20),
    lastName    varchar(20)
)
GO

INSERT INTO mainOwnersSchema.person
VALUES (1, 'Paul','McCartney')
INSERT INTO mainOwnersSchema.person
VALUES (2, 'Pete','Townsend')
GO
```

Next, this user gives SELECT permission to the secondaryOwner user:

```
GRANT SELECT on mainOwnersSchema.person to secondaryOwner
```

Then we set the context to the secondary user to create the procedure:

```
REVERT  --we can step back on the stack of principals,
        --but we can't change directly to secondaryOwner
```

```
GO
EXECUTE AS USER = 'secondaryOwner'
GO
```

Then we create a schema and another table:

```
CREATE SCHEMA secondaryOwnerSchema
GO
CREATE TABLE secondaryOwnerSchema.otherPerson
(
    personId    int constraint PKtestAccess_person primary key,
    firstName   varchar(20),
    lastName    varchar(20)
)
GO

INSERT INTO secondaryOwnerSchema.otherPerson
VALUES (1, 'Rocky','Racoon')
INSERT INTO secondaryOwnerSchema.otherPerson
VALUES (2, 'Sally','Simpson')
GO
```

Next, we create two procedures as the secondary users: one for the WITH EXECUTE AS as CALLER, which is the default, then SELF, which puts it in the context of the creator—in this case, secondaryOwner:

```
CREATE PROCEDURE   secondaryOwnerSchema.person$asCaller
WITH EXECUTE AS CALLER --this is the default
AS
SELECT  personId, firstName, lastName
FROM    secondaryOwnerSchema.otherPerson --<-- ownership same as proc
SELECT  personId, firstName, lastName
FROM    mainOwnersSchema.person  --<-- breaks ownership chain
GO

CREATE PROCEDURE secondaryOwnerSchema.person$asSelf
WITH EXECUTE AS SELF  --now this runs in context of secondaryOwner,
                      --since it created it
AS
SELECT  personId, firstName, lastName
FROM    secondaryOwnerSchema.otherPerson --<-- ownership same as proc

SELECT  personId, firstName, lastName
FROM    mainOwnersSchema.person  --<-- breaks ownership chain
GO
```

Next, we grant rights on the procedure to the aveSchlub user:

```
GRANT EXECUTE ON secondaryOwnerSchema.person$asCaller to aveSchlub
GRANT EXECUTE ON secondaryOwnerSchema.person$asSelf to aveSchlub
```

Then we change to the context of aveSchlub:

```
REVERT
GO
EXECUTE AS USER = 'aveSchlub'
GO
```

and execute the procedure:

```
--this proc is in context of the caller, in this case, aveSchlub
EXECUTE secondaryOwnerSchema.person$asCaller
```

which gives us the following output:

```
personId    firstName             lastName
----------- --------------------  --------------------
1           Rocky                 Racoon
2           Sally                 Simpson
Msg 229, Level 14, State 5, Procedure person$asCaller, Line 4
SELECT permission denied on object 'person', database 'tempdb', schema
'mainOwnersSchema'.
```

Next, we execute the `asSelf` variant:

```
--secondaryOwner, so it works
EXECUTE secondaryOwnerSchema.person$asSelf
```

which gives us the following output:

```
personId    firstName             lastName
----------- --------------------  --------------------
1           Rocky                 Racoon
2           Sally                 Simpson

personId    firstName             lastName
----------- --------------------  --------------------
1           Paul                  McCartney
2           Pete                  Townsend
```

What makes this different is that when the ownership chain is broken, the security context we are in is the `secondaryUser`, not the context of the caller, `aveSchlub`. This is a really cool feature, as we can now give users temporary rights that will not even be apparent to them, and will not require granting any permissions.

It is not, however, a feature that should be overused, as it could be all too easy to just build your procedures in the context of the database owner. One nice side effect of this is that we could use it instead of chaining, by setting `EXECUTE AS` to a user who can access a different database directly, so the system user may have rights to the database, but the executing user cannot. These are just the basics; `EXECUTE AS` is discussed in more detail in Chapter 6.

.NET Declarations

.NET is tightly integrated with SQL Server. .NET integration is covered in greater depth in Chapter 14. In this section, we are simply going to cover the commands to make assemblies available for use in T-SQL code.

Assembly Maintenance

Prior to using .NET assemblies in T-SQL code, you must declare and load them from the dynamic link library (DLL) file. `CREATE ASSEMBLY` loads a managed class into SQL Server memory space so that the common language runtime (CLR) database objects (discussed in the next section) can be created.

The syntax of the `CREATE ASSEMBLY` command is as follows:

```
CREATE ASSEMBLY <assemblyName> FROM <assemblyLocation>
```

Here is an example:

```
CREATE ASSEMBLY dateObject FROM 'C:\projects\bin\Debug\setDate.dll'
```

After loading, the assembly can be subsequently removed using the DROP ASSEMBLY command:

```
DROP ASSEMBLY dateObject
```

An assembly cannot be dropped if any CLR database objects reference it. These references can be seen in Management Studio by right-clicking the assembly.

CLR Database Objects

Once an assembly has been created as an operating system file and created as a database object, it can then be used to declare objects, including stored procedures, functions, triggers, user-defined types, and user-defined aggregate functions. The syntax of CREATE and ALTER for the T-SQL objects also includes the ability to reference CLR objects instead of T-SQL. The following is the basic syntax for these CLR extensions:

```
[CREATE][ALTER] DBOBJECTTYPE ([parameters])
                        AS EXTERNAL NAME assembly_name:class_name
```

For example, to create a procedure that points to a .NET assembly that has been created as an object on the SQL Server—in this case, a fictitious one called getDateValueString—we could build the following procedure:

```
CREATE PROCEDURE dateString
(
    @dateValue datetime output
) AS EXTERNAL NAME  dateObject:utf8string::getDateValueString
```

The following commands are affected by this change:

- CREATE/ALTER PROCEDURE
- CREATE/ALTER FUNCTION
- CREATE/ALTER TRIGGER
- CREATE/ALTER TYPE
- CREATE/ALTER AGGREGATE

This has been just a very brief introduction to the new SQL Server commands that revolve around .NET integration. As noted earlier, .NET integration is discussed in much more detail in Chapter 14 of this book.

Declaring and Setting Variables

How many times have you wanted to declare and set a variable all in the same statement? Developers who have worked with T-SQL may be mystified why they could never issue a statement like this:

```
DECLARE @iCounter int = 0;
```

Well, ladies and gentlemen, in SQL Server 2008, we can now finally declare and set variables within the same statement. A small feature, no doubt, but a very useful one indeed.

In addition to initializing the variable, improvements have also been made to perform arthimetic operations on the variables themselves:

```
INSERT dbo.Counters

    VALUES (@iCounter+1);
```

The value of Counters would be the value 1 after executing this statement. You can also use the +=, -=, *=, and /= operators. Taking our initial @iCounter declaration, let's use the new += operator, as follows:

```
UPDATE dbo.Counters
    SET Counter+=1;
```

The result of Counters would now be 2.

Passing Table-Valued Parameters

In earlier versions of SQL Server, stored procedures and user-defined functions allowed only scalar parameters to be passed. For most cases, this was acceptable. But in certain circumstances, this limitation led to the same stored procedure or function being called multiple times to perform a single task.

Consider the scenario where a customer is submitting an order on a web site. The order may be for multiple products. When the order is submitted, a server-side stored procedure is used to process the shopping cart list. Before SQL Server 2008, this stored procedure would accept the order items individually, and performance was slow. In SQL Server 2008, developers can now pass a table as a parameter to stored procedures and user-defined functions. In our scenario, this would allow the entire shopping cart to be passed to the stored procedure for processing in one trip, as opposed to potentially many round-trips to the server.

To be fair to pre-2008 database application designs, you could save on some round-trips by creating some sort of order item array or a special proprietary BLOB and pass that as a single parameter, but in the end, you would end up with a lot of complex code to maintain. SQL Server 2008 is able to easily and efficiently pass table structures to stored procedures and user-defined functions, without all this complex code to maintain.

Now that you are sold on the value of table-valued parameters, it's time to explain how to create and use them. Table-valued parameters are defined via a new user-defined table type. Let's continue our shopping cart scenario and assume that we have a stored procedure that will simply update the inventory at the warehouse given a specific order. Instead of calling this stored procedure for every single order item, we want to leverage table-valued parameters and pass a table containing all the products in the shopping cart. We need to first create a Products table that will contain three products and the number remaining in inventory, as follows:

```
CREATE TABLE Inventory
(product_id int PRIMARY KEY,
product_name varchar(50) NOT NULL,
quantity int DEFAULT(0))
GO
INSERT INTO Inventory VALUES (1,'Meat flavored dog shampoo',150)
INSERT INTO Inventory VALUES (2,'Generic canine nail clippers',261)
INSERT INTO Inventory VALUES (3,'Canine paw scissors',89)
GO
```

We should now create a user-defined table type that describes the table we wish to pass to our stored procedure:

```
CREATE TYPE OrderType AS
TABLE(order_item_id int PRIMARY KEY,
product_id int NOT NULL,
quantity int NOT NULL CHECK (quantity >= 1),
gift_wrap BIT DEFAULT (0))
```

Looking at the type-creation code, you may notice that you can have most of the constraints that you could otherwise use within a regular CREATE TABLE definition The most significant exception is foreign keys, which are not allowed in user-defined table types.

> ■**Note** A list of all user-defined table types is available via a system catalog view called `sys.table_types`.

It is important to note a few restrictions about user-defined table types:

- They can be used only as input parameters to user-defined functions and stored procedures.
- They cannot be used as `OUTPUT` parameters.
- They cannot be defined within the body of the user-defined function or stored procedure.
- They must be defined independently.

In SQL Server 2008, table value parameters are read only within the stored procedure or user-defined function. Outside these functions, you can treat table types like any other table, and `INSERT`, `UPDATE`, and `DELETE` as needed.

At this point in our example, we are ready to create the `UpdateInventory` stored procedure:

```
CREATE PROCEDURE UpdateInventory (@myOrder OrderType READONLY)
AS
BEGIN
UPDATE Inventory
SET Inventory.quantity-=mo.quantity
FROM Inventory
        INNER JOIN @myOrder mo
        ON (mo.product_id = Inventory.product_id)
END
```

Notice that the `READONLY` keyword is used for the `@myOrder` table variable. This is because the `READONLY` keyword is required in SQL Server 2008 to identify table variables. Within the code of the stored procedure, we are treating the `@myOrder` table variable like any other table. This procedure simply updates the inventory of each product by decrementing it by the value of the quantity ordered. Finally, to test our procedure, we can do the following:

```
DECLARE @myOrder OrderType
INSERT INTO @myOrder VALUES(1,1,10,0)
INSERT INTO @myOrder VALUES(2,3,5,0)
EXEC UpdateInventory @myOrder
```

The Inventory table before running the `UpdateInventory` stored procedure is as follows:

product_id	product_name	quantity
1	Meat-flavored dog shampoo	150
2	Generic canine nail clippers	261
3	Canine paw scissors	89

The Inventory table after running the `UpdateInventory` stored procedure is as follows:

product_id	product_name	quantity
1	Meat-flavored dog shampoo	140
2	Generic canine nail clippers	261
3	Canine paw scissors	84

We can see that the meat-flavored dog shampoo has decreased by ten units, and the canine paw scissors units have decreased by five, as these were the values defined in our order.

User-defined table types are fully supported in ADO.NET 3.0 via a new parameter type called SqlDbType.Structured. They are also supported in the ODBC and OLE DB client stacks via a new parameter type called SQL_SS_TABLE. When clients pass table variables to SQL Server, the content gets passed by value. When table variables are used within SQL Server, they are passed by reference for maximum performance gain.

For those of you who have a lot of experience with SQL Server, you may be wondering why you couldn't just use BULK INSERT instead of going through all this code. In some circumstances, it may be better to use BULK INSERT. Generally, using BULK INSERT is better when your mission is purely to insert data, especially from a file. If you want to use joins or do special business logic, you should consider leveraging table value parameters within you database application.

Summary

In this chapter, we looked at a bunch of features that have enhanced the developer experience with T-SQL. Some of these enhancements are not drastic changes, but several of them will affect the way you code objects in important ways:

- *Error handling*: SQL Server continues to be improved in the area of error handling.

- *CTEs*: Using them will make some complex queries leaner, and make hierarchies easier to deal with.

- APPLY *join operator*: Table-based user-defined functions can now take columns as parameters so they can be effectively used in the FROM clause of queries.

- *Ranking functions*: These are powerful functions that let you add sequence information about your sets.

- .WRITE *on* UPDATE *statement*: This allows for chunked updates of large text objects using T-SQL rather than READTEXT and WRITETEXT. (No pointers to deal with in code!)

- OUTPUT *clause*: This provides a cool way to see what changes are made to a table without a trigger.

- *Synonyms*: These allow you to virtually rename any object in SQL Server.

- INTERSECT *and* EXCEPT: These are set-based operators that work like UNION for finding rows that are in both sets (INTERSECT) or the differences between two sets (EXCEPT).

- PIVOT *and* UNPIVOT: These operators give you the ability to shift the rows of a table to the columns (PIVOT) and back again (UNPIVOT).

- DECLARE *and* SET: You can now easily declare and initialize variables in one line.

- *Additional operator support*: You can now leverage the +=, -=, *=, and /= operators within T-SQL.

- MERGE *statement*: This statement allows for multiple DML statements to be executed in one pass through the data.

- *Table-valued parameters*: These allow developers to pass tables as parameters to stored pro-cedures and user-defined functions.

All of these changes extend an already good language and make it better, giving you power to manipulate data in faster and more convenient ways.

CHAPTER 13

■■■

T-SQL Enhancements for DBAs

The number of new features and functionality coming into SQL Server exceeds those that are being removed and deprecated. This increases the need for database administrators (DBAs) to continually learn new features and eventually manage them in a production environment. The makers of SQL Server realize this imbalance, and with each new release of SQL Server, they supply a bevy of new Transact-SQL (T-SQL) commands to make the jobs (and lives) of DBAs easier and working with the database system more efficient.

In this chapter, we'll discuss these new features and changes, as well as other important information that is critical for success as a DBA in today's complex database environments. This chapter covers the following topics:

- Lock escalation control
- Catalog and dynamic management views
- New Performance Monitor triggers
- DDL triggers
- Indexing and performance enhancements
- Snapshots
- Data-integrity enhancements

Locking Enhancements

The whole point of locking is to optimize for better concurrency. Imagine what life in the database world would be like if there were no locking. Chances are once you had more than one user utilizing the database, you would run into many problems like dirty reads and phantom values.

SQL Server 2008 includes shared, update, exclusive, intent, schema, and bulk update locks. The lock manager within the SQL Server database engine is responsible for managing all these types of locks in all the different transactions. Since holding a lock is not the best thing to do from a performance standpoint, you always want to lock at the most granular level, like at a row level. You can imagine the amount of memory and CPU resources that are required by the lock manager when it's trying to lock at the lowest level, given potentially thousands of transactions a second. To help alleviate this strain on resources, the lock manager will escalate a lock (for example, from row to table level) given certain circumstances. In general, if a single T-SQL statement acquires at least 5,000 locks on a single nonpartitioned table (or index), or if the lock manager is running short on memory, the lock manager will issue an escalation. (The specific conditions are spelled out in SQL Server Books Online.)

In SQL Server 2008, the `ALTER TABLE` statement has a `SET` option for `LOCK_ESCALATION` with three possible values:

- `TABLE`: When set to `TABLE` (the default), the behavior of the lock manager is the same as in previous versions of SQL Server, in that the escalation will be from a row or page to a table lock, regardless of how many partitions are in the table.

- `DISABLE`: When `LOCK_ESCALATION` is set to `DISABLE`, the lock manager will not escalate most of the time. There are a few corner cases where the SQL Server database engine absolutely needs a lock to protect data integrity, but for the most part, no escalations take place.

- `AUTO`: The `AUTO` option will add a lot of value for those users who partition their tables. When set to `AUTO`, the lock manager will lock the heap or B-tree of the partition instead of the table. Once escalated to a heap or B-tree of the partition, it will never escalate again to the table level. If the table is not partitioned and `LOCK_ESCALATION` is set to `AUTO`, the escalation will be to the table level.

If you use partitions and currently have locking issues, you should definitely consider changing the lock escalation to `AUTO` as follows:

```
ALTER TABLE [MyTable] SET (LOCK_ESCALATION = AUTO)
```

You may be pleasantly surprised at the reduction in locking issues after changing to `AUTO` lock escalation.

Metadata Views

Most SQL Server DBAs do not exactly relish the idea of having to crawl through the system tables. The tasks of remembering the various types of `id` columns (which are often misleadingly named) and attempting to decode columns like `xtype` are often error-prone and not a productive use of the DBA's time. For those of you who are still used to accessing system tables directly, you may be quite comfortable issuing queries like the following:

```
SELECT
    so.name AS theTable,
    sc.name AS theColumn,
    st.name AS theType
FROM sysobjects so
JOIN syscolumns sc ON so.id = sc.id
JOIN systypes st ON sc.xtype = st.xtype
WHERE
    so.type = 'U'
```

Not only is this query tedious to write and read, the fact that you are accessing system tables directly is a big Microsoft no-no. The reason Microsoft is so strict on this policy has to do with the need for internal changes. If the SQL Server developers document an object or a function like a table, view, or stored procedure, they cannot simply change it at the next release to comply with a new feature, as this would break a lot of users' applications. Thus, they must formally announce the feature or function as deprecated and wait three releases before they can actually change it or remove it from the product. To give Microsoft the flexibility of changing things freely under the covers, SQL Server exposes a series of catalog views, which are views on top of some system objects. The idea is that the catalog views will never change, so if you write your database applications and scripts using these views, then nothing will break when you upgrade your database application to the next version of SQL Server.

Taking our previous system table query example, let's see this in terms of catalog views:

```
SELECT
    t.name AS theTable,
    c.name AS theColumn,
    ty.name AS theType
FROM sys.tables t
JOIN sys.columns c ON t.object_id = c.object_id
JOIN sys.types ty ON c.system_type_id = ty.system_type_id
```

It's not just the lack of a WHERE clause that makes this query more readable; it's the little differences, like primary key column names that actually make sense!

Starting with SQL Server 2005, the system tables are deprecated, having been replaced by two new sets of views. For backward-compatibility purposes, the system tables from previous versions of SQL Server are also still around, in the form of a third set of views. The system tables themselves are now hidden from direct user contact, but should you have legacy code written against them, you'll find that queries will still work and applications will not break; the views do a good job of mimicking the tables' functionality. However, the new metadata views offer much greater usability.

Tables describing objects (for example, sysobjects and syscolumns) have been replaced by a set of views called the *catalog views*. Tables describing system state (for example, syscacheobjects and syslocks) are now represented by a set of views called the *dynamic management views*. And the older tables themselves can now be found in a set of views appropriately called the *compatibility views*. The ANSI standard INFORMATION_SCHEMA views are also still around, but due to the fact that so much of the functionality in SQL Server is not ANSI-compliant, these views fail to provide much value in SQL Server.

Compatibility Views

All of the SQL Server system tables have been migrated into a collection of views in the sys schema (see Chapter 6 for more on schemas) called the *compatibility views*. You should attempt to migrate existing code away from the compatibility views, and start using catalog views instead.

Querying the views works the same as with previous versions of SQL Server. SELECT * FROM sysobjects still returns information about objects in the current database. SELECT * FROM sysindexes still returns information about indexes. However, some columns have been deprecated, so you should carefully test existing code before migrating it to SQL Server 2008. For instance, in SQL Server 2000, the keys column of the sysindexes system table contained a list of the columns that made up the index. But in SQL Server 2005 and 2008, that column will always be null. Other columns in the sys.indexes view that are not quite backward-compatible are dpages, reserved, used, rowmodctr, maxirow, and statblob. Code that uses these columns should be rewritten to use the sys.indexes view.

Catalog Views

The catalog views are repositories for "static" metadata. They contain data about both server-wide and database-specific objects, including logins, tables, and stored procedures, as opposed to more "dynamic" data, such as locks and the state of the procedure cache. You'll find that they are both more comprehensive and user-friendly than the system tables were. For instance, the sysindexes system table contained a column called indid that would hold various codes depending on the index type: 0 meant the table was a heap; 1 was a clustered index; and a value greater than 1 was a nonclustered index, unless it was 255, in which case it wasn't an index at all, but an indication that the table had a large object (TEXT or IMAGE) column!

With catalog views, these cryptic values are gone, and the indid column has been replaced in the sys.indexes catalog view by a column called type_desc. This column can contain the following self-explanatory character values: HEAP, CLUSTERED, NONCLUSTERED, and XML—quite an improvement. To find a list of all heap tables (tables without clustered indexes) in a SQL Server database, use the following query:

```
SELECT
    OBJECT_NAME(object_id) AS theTable
FROM sys.indexes
WHERE
    type_desc = 'HEAP'
```

Many other improvements have been made. For instance, almost all code numbers have been replaced by English-character strings, and bitmasks and other internal structures have been replaced by normalized tables. One enhancement in particular that many DBAs will enjoy is the addition of a column called `modify_date` to the `sys.objects` views and other views that inherit from it (including `sys.procedures` and `sys.views`). No more trying to pinpoint the last time someone ran an `ALTER` on one of the database objects.

Table 13-1 lists some of the key system tables and the catalog views that now expose the same information.

Table 13-1. *System Tables and Their Catalog View Equivalents*

System Table	Catalog View(s)	Description
syscolumns	sys.columns, sys.computed_columns, sys.foreign_key_column, ssys.identity_columns	The sys.columns view contains information about every column in every table in the current database. The other views can be used to get information about specific types of columns.
syscomments	sys.sql_modules, also see the OBJECT_DEFINITION function	The sys.sql_modules view and the OBJECT_DEFINITION function allow DBAs to get the definition of T-SQL stored procedures, triggers, functions, and views.
sysconstraints	sys.check_constraints, sys.default_constraints, sys.key_constraints	These views contain information about column- and table-level CHECK, DEFAULT, PRIMARY KEY, and FOREIGN KEY constraints.
sysdatabases	sys.databases	This view contains information about every database on the server.
sysdepends	sys.sql_dependencies	This view helps DBAs determine which objects are dependent on other objects in the system. For instance, SQL Server will attempt to determine which tables are referenced by which stored procedures and expose that mapping in this view. Note that this view is not guaranteed to contain all dependencies in the system; due to late binding and dynamic SQL, some references may not be present at the time of object creation.
sysfiles	sys.database_files	This view exposes information about the physical files that back the current database.
sysforeignkeys	sys.foreign_keys, sys.foreign_key_columns	These views contain data about FOREIGN KEY constraints.
sysindexes	sys.indexes	This view contains information about which indexes have been created on which tables in the current database.

System Table	Catalog View(s)	Description
sysindexkeys	sys.index_columns	This view, used in conjunction with sys.indexes, allows DBAs to determine which columns participate in indexes.
syslogins	sys.sql_logins	This view exposes data about system logins.
sysobjects	sys.objects, sys.procedures, sys.tables, sys.views, sys.triggers	The sys.objects view contains information about every user object in the current database. For information about specific object types, the sys.procedures, sys.tables, sys.views, or sys.triggers view can be used.

Table 13-1 is by no means a comprehensive list of the available catalog views. Virtually every type of object available in SQL Server has an associated catalog view. To see a complete list, navigate to the System Views node in Object Explorer in SQL Server Management Studio, as shown in Figure 13-1 (note that in this image, Object Explorer's filter is being used to limit results to objects in the sys schema). Throughout the rest of this chapter, we'll mention various catalog views in the context of helping to manage the new features discussed.

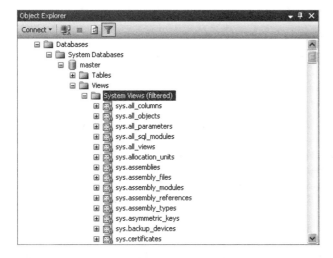

Figure 13-1. *Catalog views appear in Management Studio under the System Views node in Object Explorer.*

Dynamic Management Views and Functions

Whereas the catalog views contain data about "static" objects, the dynamic management views and functions help the user investigate the ever-changing state of the server. Note that the dynamic management functions are really nothing more than parameterized views—they are not used for modifying data. These views and functions are, like the catalog views, collected in the sys schema, but they are prefixed with dm_. Although these views also replace and improve upon system table functionality from previous versions of SQL Server, the change that will excite most DBAs is the number of new metrics now available.

The dynamic management views have been named extremely well for browsing. Those prefixed with `dm_exec` contain data relating to actively executing processes. `dm_os` views contain operating system–related data. `dm_tran` views refer to transaction state data. `dm_broker` and `dm_repl` views contain data for Service Broker and replication, respectively. The dynamic management views are available in SQL Server Management Studio under the System Views node, as shown in Figure 13-2 (note that in this image, Object Explorer's filter is being used to limit results to objects with `dm_` in their name).

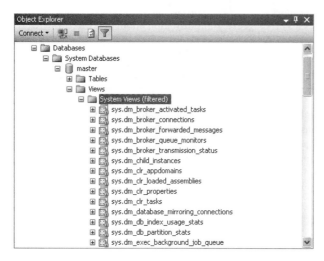

Figure 13-2. *Dynamic management views appear in Management Studio under the System Views node in Object Explorer.*

Viewing Query Plans

One of the most useful functions is `dm_exec_query_plan`. This function shows an XML representation of query plans for cached and active queries, and can take as input the `plan_handle` value exposed by three of the dynamic management views. The first of these views, `dm_exec_requests`, exposes information about which queries are active at the time the view is queried. The second, `dm_exec_query_stats`, stores aggregate statistics about stored procedures and functions, such as last execution time and total working time—it's a very useful view! And the `dm_exec_cached_plans` view replaces the older `syscacheobjects` system table, with data about compiled query plans.

As an example, to see the query plans for all active requests with valid plan handles, the following T-SQL could be used:

```
SELECT thePlan.query_plan
FROM sys.dm_exec_requests
OUTER APPLY sys.dm_exec_query_plan(plan_handle) thePlan
WHERE plan_handle IS NOT NULL
```

■**Note** See Chapter 12 for information about the OUTER APPLY relational operator.

Once an XML query plan has been retrieved, it can be saved to a file with the extension `.sqlplan`. Double-click the file, and it will open in SQL Server Management Studio, displayed as a graphical query plan. This feature will prove quite useful for both archiving baseline query plans before performance-tuning work and for remote troubleshooting. The XML can be opened with any instance of SQL Server Management Studio, and it does not require connectivity to the server that generated it for graphical display.

Monitoring Memory Using Dynamic Management Views

Although SQL Server manages memory automatically, it is still an important job for DBAs to monitor their SQL Server implementations and identify memory-usage trends. These trends may show potential operational failures or performance degradation as more and more applications are requesting resources. SQL Server 2008 introduces a series of memory-related dynamic management views to aid in tracking memory usage.

Operating System Memory

SQL Server is limited by the memory restrictions imposed by the operating system. Two new dynamic management views enable you to retrieve operating system–related memory usage information: `sys.dm_os_sys_info` and `sys.dm_os_sys_memory`.

`sys.dm_os_sys_info` displays general memory information, such as the amount of physical and virtual memory available. `sys.dm_os_sys_memory` provides a lot more information. A query of this view will reveal not only the physical memory available, but also the state of the system via the memory-resource notification bits. The memory-resource notification bits are bits that are set by the operating system to indicate the state of the memory resource (via the high memory signal and the low memory signal). The following are some columns in the `sys.dm_os_sys_memory` view:

total_phys	avail_phys	sys_cache	sys_hi_signal	sys_low_signal
537064	88960	135212	1	0

■Note The `sys.dm_os_sys_memory` view returns ten columns in total. Here, we've abbreviated the display to only five columns, to fit on the page. The last column in the view is `system_memory_state_desc`, which provides a human-readable string description of the current memory state. In our example, the value for `system_memory_state_desc` is "Available physical memory is high."

SQL Server Process Memory

The `sys.dm_os_process_memory` view provides a complete picture of the process address space of SQL Server. The values are obtained through direct calls to the operating system and, in general, are not altered by SQL Server internal methods. Information that can be obtained from this dynamic management view includes the amount of virtual address space that is currently free, the number of page faults incurred by the SQL Server process, the percentage of committed memory in the working set, and many other interesting data points.

SQL Server's Memory Manager

The memory manager for SQL Server is internal functionality to manage memory allocations within the SQL Server process. Observing the difference between process memory counters from `sys.dm_os_process_memory` and various internal counters from other dynamic management views, such as `sys.dm_os_memory_brokers`, can indicate memory use of external components in the SQL Server memory space. Many other dynamic management views dig even deeper into the core of SQL Server's memory. It takes a lot of experience and knowledge to fully understand and utilize the information returned by these powerful views. If you are feeling adventurous, you can reference

SQL Server Books Online for the complete description of functionality for those dynamic management views previously mentioned and three new memory-related views in SQL Server 2008: `sys.dm_os_memory_nodes`, `sys.dm_os_memory_brokers`, and `sys.dm_os_nodes`.

Notable SQL Server Performance Monitor Counters

SQL Server has exposed various Performance Monitor counters for a couple of releases. Obtaining the values for these counters could be achieved programmatically via Windows API calls and other ways that aren't very T-SQL friendly. With the introduction of dynamic management views came a view that could easily return Performance Monitor counters via T-SQL: `sys.dm_os_performance_counters`.

SQL Server has continued to evolve over the past few releases and now has a plethora of features. With many of these features come extra Performance Monitor counters. If you take a look at the list of counters available in SQL Server 2008, you will see many more than were provided with previous versions of SQL Server. Some of the more notable features that now have expanded counters are Service Broker, Resource Governor, and Database Mirroring. Together, these new counters can provide additional insight into the operations of SQL Server.

One other notable Performance Monitor counter doesn't have much to do with performance, availability, or any other of the sweet topics DBAs and managers like to talk about. However, this counter is probably just as important in some ways. It's called Deprecated Features.

As we've mentioned, Microsoft is pushing a lot of new features into the product and deprecating old ones. The company is now getting serious with its deprecation policy, and really will be physically removing the old bits from the SQL Server executable. This means that if your database applications or configuration still rely on deprecated features and functionality, they won't work in a future version of SQL Server—guaranteed. Since breaking backward compatibility is very bad from a product experience standpoint, Microsoft has made an effort to simplify determining if your database application is using anything deprecated. Before you upgrade, you can always use the SQL Server Upgrade Advisor to get a summary of potential upgrade issues, which would include using deprecated features within scripts. The other way to track deprecated feature usage is to use the Deprecated Features Performance Monitor counter. Issuing the following statement yields about 220 deprecated items at the time of this writing:

```
SELECT * FROM sys.dm_os_performance_counters
  WHERE object_name = 'SQLServer:Deprecated Features'
```

DDL Triggers

A common security requirement for database projects is the ability to audit any kind of change to the data. Although triggers as implemented in past versions of SQL Server made this very easy for data modification (inserts and updates), it was quite difficult to audit changes to the underlying schema. DDL triggers are the answer to this problem.

■**Note** New features in SQL Server 2008 like Policy Management (covered in Chapter 3) rely heavily on DDL triggers.

A DDL trigger can be defined at either a server-wide or database-wide granularity, and triggers can be set to fire for creation, alteration, or deletion of virtually every SQL Server object type. Unlike DML triggers, there are no `inserted` or `updated` tables, and the `update()` function does not apply. Instead, data about the event that fired the trigger can be obtained via the `eventdata()` function.

DDL triggers are created, altered, and dropped using the same T-SQL statements as DML triggers, with a slightly different syntax. DDL triggers, like DML triggers, can also be managed using catalog views (more information on this is presented later in the section "Enumerating DDL Triggers Using Catalog Views").

Creating and Altering DDL Triggers

The syntax for creating or altering a DDL trigger is as follows:

```
{ CREATE | ALTER } TRIGGER trigger_name
ON { ALL SERVER | DATABASE }
[ WITH <ddl_trigger_option> [ ...,n ] ]
{ FOR | AFTER } { event_type | event_group } [ ,...n ]
AS { sql_statement [ ...n ] | EXTERNAL NAME < method specifier > }
[ ; ]

<ddl_trigger_option> ::=
    [ ENCRYPTION ]
    [ EXECUTE AS Clause ]

<method_specifier> ::=
    assembly_name.class_name.method_name
```

Note that unlike DML triggers, DDL triggers are not defined on database objects and cannot be defined as INSTEAD OF triggers.

DDL triggers can be specified on either an ALL SERVER or a DATABASE level, and the { event_type | event_group } section controls which event will cause the trigger to fire. If a trigger is created ON ALL SERVER, it will fire for any event for which it's defined, on any database on the entire server. On the other hand, a trigger created on ON DATABASE will fire only if the event occurs in the database in which it was created.

The ALL SERVER and DATABASE levels have their own event types and event groups for which triggers can be defined. Database-level events such as CREATE_TABLE cannot be used for a server-level trigger, and server-level events such as ALTER_LOGIN cannot be used for a database-level trigger. The following server-level events can be used for DDL triggers:

- CREATE|ALTER|DROP LOGIN

- CREATE|DROP HTTP ENDPOINT

- GRANT|DENY|REVOKE SERVER ACCESS

- CREATE|ALTER|DROP CERT

All other events that can be used for DDL triggers are database-level events. These include events such as CREATE|ALTER|DROP TABLE, CREATE|ALTER|DROP TRIGGER, and so on. Every DDL event that can occur in the database can be caught using a DDL trigger. A complete list of the events available to DDL triggers can be found in the SQL Server Books Online topic "Event Groups for Use with DDL Triggers."

One particularly useful event group is the DDL_DATABASE_LEVEL_EVENTS catchall. This group includes all DDL events that can occur in a database, and it is useful for situations in which a DBA might wish to either log or block all changes to a database. For instance, the following DDL trigger, which can be created in any database, will roll back any DDL modifications a user attempts to make, unless the trigger itself is dropped or disabled:

```
CREATE TRIGGER NoChanges
ON DATABASE
FOR DDL_DATABASE_LEVEL_EVENTS
```

```
AS
    SELECT 'DDL IS NOT ALLOWED IN THE CURRENT DATABASE!'
    SELECT 'TO ALLOW DDL, DROP THE NoChanges trigger.'
    ROLLBACK
```

Dropping DDL Triggers

Dropping DDL triggers is slightly different than dropping DML triggers, as the trigger's scope must be specified in the statement. The syntax for dropping a DDL trigger is as follows:

```
DROP TRIGGER trigger_name [ ,...n ]
ON { DATABASE | ALL SERVER } [ ; ]
```

It's important to remember the additional ON clause when working with DDL triggers. Failing to include it will yield an error message stating that the specified trigger does not exist. This can be frustrating when you know that the trigger exists, but the system insists that it can't be found.

Enabling and Disabling DDL Triggers

DDL triggers, like DML triggers, can be enabled and disabled. In SQL Server this is done via two statements: ENABLE TRIGGER and DISABLE TRIGGER. These statements have similar syntax to DROP TRIGGER:

```
{ ENABLE | DISABLE } TRIGGER trigger_name
ON { DATABASE | SERVER } [ ; ]
```

Note that although DDL triggers can be enabled or disabled only by using these statements, DML triggers can still be enabled or disabled using ALTER TABLE.

Enumerating DDL Triggers Using Catalog Views

For obtaining information about database DDL triggers, DBAs can use the catalog views sys.triggers and sys.trigger_events. Server-level triggers can be enumerated using sys.server_triggers and sys.server_trigger_events. The sys.triggers and sys.server_triggers views have the same column definitions, except for two columns in the sys.triggers view that do not apply to DDL triggers: is_not_for_replication and is_instead_of_trigger. The events tables, on the other hand, have the same column definitions.

The parent_class_desc column can be used to differentiate DDL triggers from DML triggers when querying sys.triggers. The following query will return the name and creation date of all DDL triggers in the current database:

```
SELECT
  name,
  create_date
FROM sys.triggers
WHERE parent_class_desc = 'DATABASE'
```

The events views are related to the triggers views by the object_id column. To find out which events the active server-level triggers in the system will be fired on, use the following query:

```
SELECT
  tr.name,
  ev.type_desc
FROM sys.server_triggers tr
JOIN sys.server_trigger_events ev ON tr.object_id = ev.object_id
WHERE tr.is_disabled = 0
```

Programming DDL Triggers with the eventdata() Function

Without a way to figure out under exactly which conditions the trigger fired, DDL triggers would be relatively useless for tasks such as logging the events taking place in a database and when they are occurring. To provide this functionality, SQL Server includes the eventdata() function. This function returns an XML document containing information about the event that fired the trigger.

Each event can return data using a different XML schema, but they all share common base schemas. Server-level events use the following base schema:

```
<EVENT_INSTANCE>
  <EventType>name</EventType>
  <PostTime>date-time</PostTime>
  <SPID>spid</SPID>
  <ServerName>server_name</ServerName>
  <LoginName>login</LoginName>
</EVENT_INSTANCE>
```

Database-level events add a UserName element:

```
<EVENT_INSTANCE>
  <EventType>name</EventType>
  <PostTime>date-time</PostTime>
  <SPID>spid</SPID>
  <ServerName>server_name</ServerName>
  <LoginName>login</LoginName>
  <UserName>user</UserName>
</EVENT_INSTANCE>
```

Various elements appear in the schemata for events as appropriate. For instance, the object-based events (CREATE_TABLE, ALTER_PROCEDURE, and so on) add elements for DatabaseName, SchemaName, ObjectName, and ObjectType, and a TSQLCommand element that contains SetOptions and CommandText elements.

By querying the XML document, it's possible to determine every aspect of the event that fired the trigger. For instance, the following trigger echoes back the username, table name, and CREATE TABLE syntax used every time a table is created or altered in the database:

```
CREATE TRIGGER ReturnEventData
ON DATABASE
FOR CREATE_TABLE, ALTER_TABLE
AS
  DECLARE @eventData XML
  SET @eventData = eventdata()

  SELECT
    @eventData.query('data(/EVENT_INSTANCE/UserName)') AS UserName,
    @eventData.query('data(/EVENT_INSTANCE/ObjectName)') AS ObjectName,
    @eventData.query('data(/EVENT_INSTANCE/TSQLCommand/CommandText)') AS CommandText
```

■**Note** For more information about working with XML documents in SQL Server, see Chapters 16 and 17.

Of course, this trigger doesn't have to just select and return the data. The data can just as easily be inserted into a logging table:

```
CREATE TABLE DDLEventLog
(
  EventDate DATETIME NOT NULL,
```

```
  UserName SYSNAME NOT NULL,
  ObjectName SYSNAME NOT NULL,
  CommandText VARCHAR(MAX) NOT NULL
)
GO

CREATE TRIGGER ReturnEventData
ON DATABASE
FOR CREATE_TABLE, ALTER_TABLE
AS
  DECLARE @eventData XML
  SET @eventData = eventdata()

  INSERT DDLEventLog (EventDate, UserName, ObjectName, CommandText)
  SELECT
    GETDATE() AS EventDate,
    @eventData.value('data(/EVENT_INSTANCE/UserName)[1]', 'SYSNAME')
      AS UserName,
    @eventData.value('data(/EVENT_INSTANCE/ObjectName)[1]', 'SYSNAME')
      AS ObjectName,
    @eventData.value('data(/EVENT_INSTANCE/TSQLCommand/CommandText)[1]',
      'VARCHAR(MAX)') AS CommandText
```

The event data can also be parsed and used to make decisions about what course of action to take. For instance, if you have a table called DontDropMe, you could write the following trigger to keep it from being dropped:

```
CREATE TRIGGER DontDropDontDropMe
ON DATABASE
FOR DROP_TABLE
AS
  DECLARE @eventData XML
  SET @eventData = eventdata()

  DECLARE @objectName VARCHAR(MAX)
  SET @objectName =
    CONVERT(VARCHAR(MAX), @eventData.query('data(/EVENT_INSTANCE/ObjectName)'))

  IF @objectName = 'DontDropMe'
  BEGIN
    PRINT 'You cannot drop DontDropMe!'
    ROLLBACK
  END
```

Since the transaction is rolled back if the object name is DontDropMe, it's impossible to drop that table when the DontDropDontDropMe trigger is applied to the database. When using DDL triggers for this type of object-level protection, remember that the trigger fires after the event has finished, but before the transaction has committed. If a large transaction has taken place and needs to be rolled back, excessive locking could occur. Proceed with caution until (we hope) you see instead-of DDL triggers implemented in a future version of SQL Server.

Indexing and Performance Enhancements

SQL Server contains a variety of performance features that DBAs can exploit. These include table and index partitioning, filtered indexes, persisted computed columns, and many more features.

The types of indexes available in the SQL Server 2008 relational engine are essentially the same as those available in previous versions, with the addition of a specialized XML index and spatial index types. The basic index types are clustered and nonclustered. Both types of indexes are implemented internally using a variant of a B-tree data structure. A clustered index reorganizes the base data pages of the indexed table, whereas a nonclustered index is created in separate data pages. A table in SQL Server can have a single clustered index and up to 249 nonclustered indexes.

Clustered indexes are generally used to support primary keys and should be used to index "narrow" columns or groups of columns—many sources recommend that clustered index key columns should not exceed a total of 16 bytes per row. This is due to the fact that the key column data will be repeated in the leaf nodes of every nonclustered index.

Nonclustered indexes are, by default, used to support unique keys. They are also used for other types of indexes added for query performance. It's important for DBAs to remember not to go overboard when creating nonclustered indexes. Each data update of a column that participates in a nonclustered index will need to be written once to the base table and once to the index pages. Creating too many nonclustered indexes can, therefore, have a negative impact on data-modification performance.

Online Indexing

A common problem in high-availability scenarios is how and when to perform operations such as index creation, which might decrease response times or totally block other transactions. As it's often impossible to predict all indexes that a system might require once it goes live, it's important to be able to apply these changes to the production system. SQL Server provides this capability using its online indexing feature.

Creating, altering, and dropping clustered indexes produces schema modification locks that block other processes from reading and writing to the table. And creating and altering nonclustered indexes produces shared locks that block other processes from writing. Both of these can be avoided using the online indexing feature. Using this feature will allow other processes to continue normal operations, but performing the indexing operation may be quite a bit slower than in offline mode. If it's important that other processes should be able to continue normal operations during indexing— for instance, when indexing a table in an active OLTP database—this feature should be used. If concurrency is not important, the default offline indexing mode can be used to more quickly complete indexing operations.

To use the online indexing option, use the WITH clause for CREATE INDEX, ALTER INDEX, or DROP INDEX:

```
CREATE INDEX ix_Table
ON Table (Column)
WITH (ONLINE = ON)
```

The default value for the ONLINE option is OFF.

Note that this option is not available for indexing operations on tables containing LOB datatypes (TEXT, NTEXT, and IMAGE) or when creating XML indexes.

Controlling Locking During Index Creation

To further control the effects of indexing on other processes that might be attempting to access the data simultaneously, SQL Server allows the DBA to specify whether the indexing process can use row- or page-level locks. Tweaking these options can improve concurrency when creating indexes in live production systems, but beware: overriding what might be the query optimizer's best option can mean that index creation will take a much longer time. These options should be used only in specific situations in which problems are occurring due to lock contention during index creation. In most cases, they should be left set to their default values.

The DBA can turn off row locking using the `ALLOW_ROW_LOCKS` option:

```
CREATE INDEX ix_Table
ON Table (Column)
WITH (ALLOW_ROW_LOCKS = OFF)
```

Page locking can be turned off using the `ALLOW_PAGE_LOCKS` option:

```
CREATE INDEX ix_Table
ON Table (Column)
WITH (ALLOW_PAGE_LOCKS = OFF)
```

The default value for both of these options is `ON`, meaning that both row- and page-level locks are allowed. You can combine the options with each other or the `ONLINE` option by separating the options with a comma:

```
CREATE INDEX ix_Table
ON Table (Column)
WITH (ONLINE = ON, ALLOW_ROW_LOCKS = OFF, ALLOW_PAGE_LOCKS = OFF)
```

Creating Indexes with Additional Columns Included

Before SQL Server 2005, DBAs could add columns to nonclustered indexes to "cover" affected queries. For instance, consider the following table and index:

```
CREATE TABLE DatabaseSystems
(
  DatabaseSystemId INT,
  Name VARCHAR(35),
  IsRelational CHAR(1),
  IsObjectOriented CHAR(1),
  SupportsXML CHAR(1),
  FullSpecifications VARCHAR(MAX)
)

CREATE NONCLUSTERED INDEX IX_Name
ON DatabaseSystems (Name)
```

A DBA might want to query this table to find out which databases with names starting with *S* also happened to support XML:

```
SELECT Name, SupportsXML
FROM DatabaseSystems
WHERE Name LIKE 'S%'
AND SupportsXML = 'Y'
```

While the `LIKE` predicate is satisfied by the index, the database engine still has to do a lookup on the base table to get the `SupportsXML` column. To eliminate the additional lookup and "cover" the query (that is, support all of the columns from the table used in the query), the index can be dropped and a new one created to include the `SupportsXML` column:

```
DROP INDEX IX_Name
CREATE NONCLUSTERED INDEX IX_Name_SupportsXML
ON DatabaseSystems(Name, SupportsXML)
```

The query engine can now get all of the data to satisfy the query from the nonclustered index, without ever looking up data in the table itself.

But what if `IX_Name` had been a unique index? Or what if the DBA wanted to cover queries that included the `FullSpecifications` column? Solving the first problem would require creating a new index and leaving the previous one, which would end up wasting space. And indexing the `FullSpecifications` column was not possible at all. Indexes in SQL Server 2000 could contain only up to 900 bytes per row. Indexing a large varchar was simply not an option.

SQL Server now includes an indexing option designed to solve these problems. DBAs can specify additional columns to be included in a nonclustered index, using the INCLUDE keyword. Included columns are nonindexed but are included in the data pages along with the indexed data, such that they can be used to cover queries. There are no restrictions on width beyond those already enforced at the table level, and uniqueness can be specified for the indexed columns.

To create a unique index that covers the query, use the following:

```
CREATE UNIQUE NONCLUSTERED INDEX IX_Name
ON DatabaseSystems(Name)
INCLUDE (SupportsXML)
```

An index could also be created that would cover queries for either SupportsXML or FullSpecifications, or both:

```
CREATE UNIQUE NONCLUSTERED INDEX IX_Name
ON DatabaseSystems(Name)
INCLUDE (SupportsXML, FullSpecifications)
```

Keep in mind that creating large indexes that include many large columns can both use a lot of disk space and require massive amounts of I/O when updating or inserting new rows. This is due to the fact that any columns included in a nonclustered index will have their data written to disk twice: once in the base table and once in the index. When using this option to eliminate clustered index lookups, test to ensure that the additional disk strain will not be a problem when writing data.

Altering Indexes

SQL Server 2000 introduced a method of altering an existing index by creating a new one in its place, using the WITH DROP_EXISTING option. This option is especially useful for altering existing clustered indexes as it incurs less overhead than dropping and re-creating the index, by allowing the index to be modified without rebuilding existing nonclustered indexes.

SQL Server makes index alteration a first-class T-SQL operation. The ALTER INDEX syntax, while similar to that of CREATE INDEX, does not support altering an index's column list; the WITH DROP_EXISTING option of CREATE INDEX still must be used for that. However, ALTER INDEX offers much additional functionality.

In the following sections, you'll see how a DBA can use ALTER INDEX to defragment an index (replacing DBCC INDEXDEFRAG), rebuild an index (replacing DBCC DBREINDEX), and disable an index.

Defragmenting an Index

As indexes age, insertion and deletion of noncontiguous data can take its toll and cause fragmentation to occur. Although minor amounts of fragmentation won't generally hurt performance, it's a good idea to occasionally defragment indexes to keep databases running as smoothly as possible. *Defragmentation*, also known as *index reorganization*, defragments data within data pages, but does not move data pages between extents. Since only data within pages is moved, very little blocking will occur during the defragmentation process, and data can remain available to other processes. However, because extents are not fragmented, this may not be an effective method for defragmenting larger, heavily fragmented indexes. For those situations, index rebuilding is necessary (see the next section, "Rebuilding an Index," for more information).

To determine the level of fragmentation of an index, the dynamic management function sys.dm_db_index_physical_stats can be used. The column avg_fragmentation_in_percent returns the percentage of fragmented data. Unlike DBCC SHOWCONTIG, extent and logical scan fragmentation are not displayed separately. Instead, the avg_fragmentation_in_percent column shows extent fragmentation for heap tables and logical scan fragmentation for tables with clustered indexes or when displaying information about nonclustered indexes.

Although there is no hard and fast rule, a common recommendation is to keep index fragmentation below 10 percent whenever possible. Microsoft recommends defragmenting indexes that are 30 percent or less fragmented and rebuilding indexes that are more than 30 percent fragmented.

To identify indexes in the current database that have more than 10 percent fragmentation, the following query can be used:

```
SELECT
  OBJECT_NAME(i.object_id) AS TableName,
  i.name AS IndexName,
  ips.avg_fragmentation_in_percent
FROM sys.dm_db_index_physical_stats(DB_ID(), NULL, NULL, NULL, 'DETAILED') ips
JOIN sys.indexes i ON
  i.object_id = ips.object_id
  AND i.index_id = ips.index_id
WHERE ips.avg_fragmentation_in_percent > 10
```

The arguments to the `sys.dm_db_index_physical_stats` function are database ID, table ID, index ID, partition ID, and scan mode. In this example, `DB_ID()` is passed for the database ID, which tells the function to scan tables in the current database. `NULL` is passed for table ID, index ID, and partition ID, so that the function does not filter on any of those criteria. Finally, a detailed scan is used. Possible scan modes are `LIMITED` (the default), `SAMPLED`, and `DETAILED`. `LIMITED` scans only parent-level nodes and is therefore the fastest scan mode. `SAMPLED` scans parent-level nodes and a percentage of leaf nodes based on the number of rows in the table. `DETAILED` samples all nodes and is therefore the slowest scan method.

Once a fragmented index is identified, it can be defragmented using `ALTER INDEX` with the `REORGANIZE` option. The following query will defragment the index `IX_CustomerName` on the table `Customers`:

```
ALTER INDEX IX_CustomerName
ON Customers
REORGANIZE
```

Rebuilding an Index

Index defragmentation reorganizes only the leaf-level nodes of an index. Unfortunately, there are times when that isn't enough to eliminate index fragmentation, and the entire index needs to be rebuilt. The `REBUILD` option of `ALTER INDEX` can be used to facilitate this process. This is equivalent to the functionality of the deprecated `DBCC DBREINDEX` function.

Rebuilding an index is, by default, an offline operation, because pages and extents are being shuffled. When rebuilding a clustered index, the base table will be locked for the duration of the rebuild, and when rebuilding a nonclustered index, the index will be unavailable during the rebuild. However, `ALTER INDEX` includes an online indexing option to get around this problem. To rebuild the index `IX_CustomerName` on table `Customers` using the online indexing option, use the following query:

```
ALTER INDEX IX_CustomerName
ON Customers
REBUILD
WITH (ONLINE=ON)
```

The `ONLINE` option works by indexing the data outside the data pages in which the data resides, applying deltas for any data modifications, and then updating pointers from the old index to the new index. Because this operation occurs in a separate area, online reindexing will use approximately twice as much disk space as offline reindexing. The process can also be slower, in the case of databases that are very update intensive, due to the additional overhead associated with tracking data changes.

This option is therefore best used for databases that require very high availability; if downtime is acceptable, the ONLINE option will provide no benefit.

Disabling an Index

SQL Server offers an intriguing feature for indexing, namely the ability to disable indexes. This feature generated plenty of speculation as to when and where it should be used. The reality is that this feature was not created for DBAs. Rather, Microsoft included it to make updates and service packs easier to apply. There are no performance benefits or any other "hot topic" uses for disabling an index. Nonetheless, this feature can be handy in some situations.

Disabling a nonclustered index deletes the index's data rows but keeps its metadata—the index's definition—intact. Disabling a clustered index, on the other hand, keeps the data but renders it inaccessible until the index is reenabled. And disabling a nonclustered index that is being used to enforce a primary key or unique constraint will disable the constraint.

To disable an index, use ALTER INDEX with the DISABLE option:

```
ALTER INDEX IX_CustomerName
ON Customers
DISABLE
```

The index can be reenabled using the REBUILD option:

```
ALTER INDEX IX_CustomerName
ON Customers
REBUILD
```

Note that rebuilding a disabled index will require only as much disk space as the index requires, whereas rebuilding a nondisabled index requires twice the disk space: disk space for the existing index and disk space for the new, rebuilt index.

So when should index disabling be used? There are a few circumstances in which it will prove useful. A common task during Extract, Transform, and Load (ETL) processes is dropping indexes before doing bulk data loads, and then re-creating the indexes at the end of the process. Index disabling will lead to fewer code changes; there will be no need to update the ETL code when index definitions change.

Another scenario is systems with low disk space that need indexes rebuilt. Since rebuilding a disabled index takes up half the space compared to rebuilding a nondisabled index, this could prove useful in tight situations. However, note that unlike rebuilding a nondisabled index using the ONLINE option, a disabled index will not be available for online operations during the rebuild process.

A final possible use of index disabling is for testing various index configurations in situations in which the query optimizer isn't necessarily making the correct choice. Disabling and reenabling indexes should make this process a bit less painful for DBAs, by providing an automatic "backup" of the indexes being worked with.

Using Filtered Indexes

A traditional index on one or more columns covers all the rows within those columns. For the majority of cases, this may be what you need. But consider the case where a table contains a lot of columns with only a few non-null values. Creating an index on such a column would result in a larger than needed index and would take up precious CPU cycles and DBA time when index maintenance is needed. Instead, create a *filtered index*, which indexes only those rows meeting criteria that you specify. Thus, you can choose to index only the rows having non-null values in the columns being indexed. Filtered indexes can also be used in situations where you have heterogenous columns that contain categories of data or when you query columns that have ranges of values such as dollar amounts, times, and dates.

To help illustrate the value of filtered indexes, consider the scenario of a hardware store that wishes to use a database to store inventory data. The table schemas designed for this business include an Inventory and a ProdCat table. The Inventory table contains all the products that the store sells. These products are grouped into categories like Garden, Electrical, and Hardware. The tables are defined as follows:

```
CREATE TABLE ProdCat
(product_category_id          INT           PRIMARY KEY,
product_category_name         VARCHAR(30)   NOT NULL)

CREATE TABLE Inventory
(product_name          VARCHAR(30)   NOT NULL,
quantity               INT           NOT NULL,
product_category       INT           REFERENCES ProdCat(product_category_id))

INSERT INTO ProdCat VALUES (1,'Garden')
INSERT INTO ProdCat VALUES (2,'Electrical')
INSERT INTO ProdCat VALUES (3,'Hardware')
```

■Note To force SQL Server to actually leverage the index and not do table scans, we had to populate the Inventory table with about 12,000 rows.

The hardware store's database application queries the Inventory table quite frequently for the current inventory of garden accessories. To help the performance of the queries, you would want to create an index on the product_name and quantity columns. If you created a regular nonclustered index, the index would contain not only the Garden category information, but also Electrical and Hardware, since it's an index for all the rows. To get an even bigger performance gain, you can create a filtered index.

To create the filtered index, use the CREATE INDEX statement followed by the filter predicate. Here is the filtered index definition for the hardware store example:

```
CREATE NONCLUSTERED INDEX NC_Categories
    ON Inventory(product_name,quantity)
    WHERE product_category=1
```

Creating this index and running this simple statement

```
SELECT product_name,quantity FROM Inventory WHERE product_category=1
```

yields a query that runs about six times faster than if no index were defined.

Filtered indexes do have a few restrictions:

- They can be created only as nonclustered indexes

- They are not allowed on views unless they are persisted views.

- They cannot be created on XML indexes or full-text indexes.

- They cannot reference a computed column or a user-defined type column (this implies filtered indexes don't work with the new hierarchyid and spatial datatypes).

Even with these restrictions, filtered indexes lower index maintenance costs and storage requirements by targeting specific sets of data.

Filtered indexes are supported by SQL Server Management Studio as well as the Database Tuning Advisor (DTA) tool. DTA will analyze a workload against SQL Server and give you recommendations to improve performance. Filtered indexes are included as part of the suggestions in DTA.

Using Filtered Statistics

Filtered statistics are created automatically with the same filter predicate whenever users create a filtered index, as described in the previous section. However, you can manually create a filtered statistic using the CREATE STATISTIC statement. Queries on subsets of data that contain nonindexed columns benefit from creating a filtered statistic. Filtered statistics on a subset of rows can improve the accuracy of the statistics that the query optimizer uses for the query plan. Filtered statistics can also be effective with queries that select from correlated columns.

The syntax for creating filtered statistics is similar to creating a nonfiltered statistic. Here is an example:

```
CREATE STATISTICS Quantity
    ON Inventory(Quantity)
WHERE product_category=2;
```

Using Statistics for Correlated Datetime Columns

SQL Server includes an optimization to assist with queries on tables that share similar datetime data. When turned on, extra statistics will be generated for datetime columns. Joining two tables, each with datetime columns that share a foreign key reference, may allow the query optimizer to be able to determine a better plan using the additional statistics.

For instance, the AdventureWorks sample database contains a table of orders called Sales.SalesOrderHeader and a table of corresponding order detail (line items) called Sales.SalesOrderDetail. Each table contains a datetime column, ModifiedDate.

Assume that for auditing purposes, it's a business requirement of Adventure Works Cycles that any modification to an order detail row happens within 24 hours of a modification to the corresponding order header row. This would mean that all ModifiedDate values in the Sales.SalesOrderDetail table would fall into a range between the order header's modified date and 24 hours later. The query optimizer could potentially use this fact to improve performance of certain queries.

A requirement for the optimizer being able to use correlated datetime statistics is that at least one of the tables' datetime columns must be the key column for a clustered index. Since neither table includes the ModifiedDate column in its clustered index, one of the clustered indexes would need to be altered in order to use this optimization.

Once statistics are turned on and the correct indexes are in place, the query optimizer will be able to use the statistics to help drive better query plans. For instance, given the Sales.SalesOrderHeader and Sales.SalesOrderDetail tables, a user might want to see all orders modified in the last 24 hours and their corresponding line items, using the following query:

```
SELECT *
FROM Sales.SalesOrderHeader SOH
JOIN Sales.SalesOrderDetail SOD ON SOH.SalesOrderId = SOD.SalesOrderId
WHERE SOH.ModifiedDate >= DATEADD(hh, -24, GETDATE())
```

If date correlation is enabled and the correct indexes are in place, the query optimizer can analyze the datetime statistics for these two tables and determine that data for the ModifiedDate column of the SalesOrderHeader table is always 24 hours or less before the ModifiedDate column of the corresponding rows in the SalesOrderDetail table. This can allow the query to be internally rewritten into the following, possibly more efficient, format:

```
SELECT *
FROM Sales.SalesOrderHeader SOH
JOIN Sales.SalesOrderDetail SOD ON SOH.SalesOrderId = SOD.SalesOrderId
WHERE SOH.ModifiedDate >= DATEADD(hh, -24, GETDATE())
AND SOD.ModifiedDate >= DATEADD(hh, -24, GETDATE())
AND SOD.ModifiedDate <= GETDATE()
```

This form of the query can take advantage of a clustered index that involves the SalesOrderDetail's ModifiedDate column, thereby possibly avoiding an expensive clustered index lookup operation. This will be especially advantageous as the dataset in each table grows larger and the date columns become more highly selective.

To turn on date correlation statistics for the AdventureWorks database, the following T-SQL would be used:

```
ALTER DATABASE AdventureWorks
SET DATE_CORRELATION_OPTIMIZATION ON
```

Note that when performing this action, the database must not have any users connected or the only connection should be the one running the ALTER DATABASE statement.

Once the optimization is enabled, it will be automatically maintained by the query engine. Due to the extra work involved, there is a performance penalty for inserts or updates, so make sure to test carefully before rolling this into production environments. To find out if a database has date correlation turned on, query the is_date_correlation_on column of the sys.databases catalog view:

```
SELECT
    Name,
    is_date_correlation_on
FROM sys.databases
```

The column is_date_correlation_on will have a value of 1 if date correlation is turned on for a database; otherwise, it will have a value of 0.

Improving Performance of Ordering for Tertiary Collations

For situations in which string case sensitivity is unimportant from a uniqueness perspective but necessary for sorting purposes, SQL Server supports so-called *tertiary collations*. String data defined with these collations will be ordered based on case sensitivity (uppercase letters will sort before lowercase letters). However, grouping by or using the distinct operator on such a column will result in uppercase and lowercase letters being treated identically.

For example, take the following table, which includes an indexed, tertiary-collated column:

```
CREATE TABLE Characters
(
  CharacterString CHAR(3)
    COLLATE SQL_Latin1_General_CP437_CI_AI
)

CREATE CLUSTERED INDEX IX_Characters
ON Characters (Characterstring)

INSERT Characters VALUES ('aaa')
INSERT Characters VALUES ('Aaa')
```

Selecting the data from this table using an ORDER BY clause on the CharacterString column will result in two rows being returned. The row with the value 'Aaa' will sort first, followed by the row with the value 'aaa'. However, selecting the data from this table using the DISTINCT option returns only a single row. Only sorting is case sensitive. Grouping and uniqueness operations are not case sensitive.

Ordering a tertiary-collated column requires an intermediate step during which weights for each character are determined. This step is expensive, so users have the ability to precalculate the weights using the TERTIARY_WEIGHTS function.

Selecting data from the table ordered by CharacterString requires an intermediate computation and sort, even though the data in the index is already sorted, as indicated by the execution plan for an ordered SELECT statement on this table, shown in Figure 13-3.

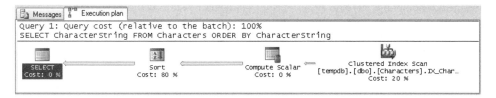

Figure 13-3. *Sorting on tertiary-collated columns requires an intermediate step.*

The solution to this problem is to create a computed column using the TERTIARY_WEIGHTS function and add it to the index to be used for sorting. The table and index should have been created this way:

```
CREATE TABLE Characters
(
  CharacterString CHAR(3)
    COLLATE SQL_Latin1_General_CP437_CI_AI,
  CharacterWeights AS (TERTIARY_WEIGHTS(CharacterString))
)

CREATE CLUSTERED INDEX IX_Characters
ON Characters
(
  CharacterString,
  CharacterWeights
)
```

As Figure 13-4 illustrates, the intermediate sort is no longer required.

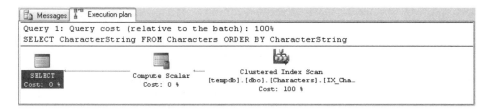

Figure 13-4. *When a computed column using the TERTIARY_WEIGHTS function is used in the index, the intermediate step is no longer required.*

Table and Index Partitioning

A common requirement in dealing with larger datasets is the ability to split the data into smaller chunks to help improve performance. Performance degradation becomes apparent once tables reach larger sizes, and splitting data across files and disks is one way to help databases scale. Although previous versions of SQL Server supported various means of partitioning data—either manually or via features like partitioned views—doing so has always been somewhat of a headache-inducing experience. Partitioning in versions prior to SQL Server 2000 meant splitting data across multiple tables, and then writing application code that could properly navigate the partitions. Things got better with SQL Server 2000's partitioned views feature, but it was difficult to swap data in or out of the partitions without affecting data availability.

Today, SQL Server makes data partitioning much easier, thanks to the inclusion of a partitioning strategy that allows the server to automatically handle partitioning of tables and indexes based on range data. Partition ranges are defined using functions called *partition functions*, and ranges are assigned to one or more filegroups using partition schemes. After a function and scheme are created, tables and indexes can use them for partitioning data. In this section, we'll examine how to use these features to build better-performing databases.

Partition Functions

Partition functions are the means by which the DBA can control which ranges of data will be used to enforce partition boundary values. These functions map partitions based on a datatype and ranges of values for that datatype, but they do not actually partition anything. Due to the fact that they only define partitions, partition functions are reusable; a single function can be used to partition many tables or indexes using the same ranges. The basic syntax for creating a partition function is as follows:

```
CREATE PARTITION FUNCTION partition_function_name(input_parameter_type)
AS RANGE [ LEFT | RIGHT ]
FOR VALUES ( [ boundary_value [ ,...n ] ] )
[ ; ]
```

Partition functions must take a single input parameter (a column) of a specific datatype—multicolumn partition functions are not supported. The function is defined in terms of ranges, and the LEFT or RIGHT designator controls the placement of the actual boundary value. For a LEFT function, each partition will be defined as containing all values less than or equal to its upper bound. For a RIGHT function, each partition will be defined as containing all values less than its upper bound; the boundary value itself will go into the next partition.

Partition ranges cannot be designed to constrain input values to a given range. Values that fall below the lowest bound will be placed into the lowest partition. Values that fall above the highest bound will be placed into an automatically generated partition for values above that bound. For example, to create a partition function based on fiscal quarters of 2008, the following T-SQL could be used:

```
CREATE PARTITION FUNCTION pf_FiscalQuarter2008 (DATETIME)
AS RANGE RIGHT FOR VALUES
('20080401', '20080701', '20081001', '20090101')
```

This function actually creates five partitions. The first partition contains every value less than April 1, 2008 (remember, RANGE RIGHT defines less-than values; if you wanted to include midnight for April 1, 2008, you could use a RANGE LEFT partition). The second, third, and fourth partitions contain all values less than July 1, 2008, October 1, 2008, and January 1, 2009, respectively. The final, implicit partition contains all values greater than or equal to January 1, 2009.

Partition Schemes

Partition schemes are the means by which the boundary values defined in partition functions can be mapped to physical filegroups. The DBA has the option of either mapping all of the partitions from a function into the same filegroup (using the ALL option) or specifying a filegroup for each partition individually. The same filegroup can be used for multiple partitions.

The basic syntax for creating a partition scheme is as follows:

```
CREATE PARTITION SCHEME partition_scheme_name
AS PARTITION partition_function_name
```

```
[ ALL ] TO ( { filegroup_name | [PRIMARY] } [ ,...n] )
[ ; ]
```

To specify that all partitions from the partition function pf_FiscalQuarter2008 (defined in the preceding section) should be mapped to the primary filegroup, the following T-SQL would be used:

```
CREATE PARTITION SCHEME ps_FiscalQuarter2008_PRIMARY
AS PARTITION pf_FiscalQuarter2008
ALL TO ([PRIMARY])
```

This example uses the ALL option to map all of the partitions to the same filegroup. It should also be noted that the primary filegroup is always specified using square brackets when defining partition schemes.

If the DBA wanted to map the first two partitions to the filegroup Q1Q2_2008 and the other three partitions to the filegroup Q3Q4_2008, the following T-SQL would be used:

```
CREATE PARTITION SCHEME ps_FiscalQuarter2008_Split
AS PARTITION pf_FiscalQuarter2008
TO (Q1Q2_2008, Q1Q2_2008, Q3Q4_2008, Q3Q4_2008, Q3Q4_2008)
```

Note that this example assumes that the filegroups have already been created in the database using ALTER DATABASE ADD FILEGROUP. Also be aware that multiple schemes can be created for a single function, so if there are several objects in a database that should be partitioned using the same data ranges but that should not share the same filegroups, multiple functions do not need to be created.

Creating Partitioned Tables and Indexes

Once partition functions and schemes have been defined, the DBA can begin using them to partition tables and indexes, which is, of course, the point to this whole exercise. CREATE TABLE and CREATE INDEX both have an ON clause that has been used in previous editions of SQL Server to specify a specific filegroup in which the table or index should be created. That clause still functions as before, but it has now been enhanced to accept a partition scheme.

Given the partition function and schemes created in the previous sections for fiscal quarters in 2008, the following T-SQL could be used to create a partitioned table to record sales amounts, partitioned by the time of the sale:

```
CREATE TABLE SalesAmounts
(
  SalesAmountId INT NOT NULL PRIMARY KEY NONCLUSTERED,
  SalesAmount NUMERIC(9,2) NOT NULL,
  SalesDate DATETIME NOT NULL
)
GO

CREATE CLUSTERED INDEX IX_SalesAmounts_SalesDate
ON SalesAmounts (SalesDate)
  ON ps_FiscalQuarter2008_Split (SalesDate)
```

The table is created using a nonclustered primary key, leaving the table itself available for indexing using a clustered index. Since a table's clustered index organizes the data in the entire table, creating the cluster on the partition range partitions the entire table.

Data from this table will now be partitioned based on the ps_FiscalQuarter2008_Split range function, using SalesDate as the partitioning column. Data for any date less than July 1, 2008, will be put into the Q1Q2_2008 partition; data for any date greater than or equal to July 1, 2008, will be put into the Q3Q4_2008 partition. Likewise, when selecting data from this table using the SalesDate column as a predicate in the WHERE clause, the query engine will need to seek only the necessary partitions for the requested data.

Creating a partitioned index is very similar to creating a partitioned table; the ON clause is used to specify a partition scheme. For instance, to create a nonclustered index on the SalesAmounts table for seeking SalesAmount values, the following T-SQL syntax could be used:

```
CREATE INDEX IX_Amount
ON SalesAmounts
(
  SalesAmount
)
ON ps_FiscalQuarter2008_PRIMARY (SalesDate)
```

This index will be partitioned on the SalesDate column, and because the partition scheme ps_FiscalQuarter2008_PRIMARY was specified, all five partitions will be maintained in the primary filegroup. Note that the partitioning column, SalesDate, need not be included in the index.

Adding and Removing Partitions

In addition to creating new partitioned tables and indexes, SQL Server also exposes capabilities for DBAs to partition existing tables, modify range boundaries of existing functions and schemes, and swap data in and out of partitions.

Partitioning an existing table can be done in one of two ways. The easier method is to create a clustered index on the table, partitioned using whatever partition scheme the DBA wishes to employ. The other method requires manipulation of partition functions and will be covered in the next section, "Modifying Partition Functions and Schemes."

Assume that in the same database that contains the SalesAmounts table and related partition function and schemes there exists the following table, which contains times that customers visited the store:

```
CREATE TABLE Visitors
(
  VisitorId INT NOT NULL,
  VisitDate DATETIME NOT NULL,
  CONSTRAINT PK_Visitors
    PRIMARY KEY (VisitorId, VisitDate)
)
```

The DBA might wish to partition this table using the same scheme as the sales data, such that data in similar date ranges will share the same filegroups. This table already has a clustered index, implicitly created by the PK_Visitors primary key constraint. To partition the table, the constraint must be dropped. The constraint then must be re-created using a partition scheme. The following T-SQL code accomplishes that:

```
SET XACT_ABORT ON

BEGIN TRANSACTION
  ALTER TABLE Visitors
  DROP CONSTRAINT PK_Visitors

  ALTER TABLE Visitors
  ADD CONSTRAINT PK_Visitors
    PRIMARY KEY (VisitorId, VisitDate)
  ON ps_FiscalQuarter2005_Split (VisitDate)
COMMIT
```

To avoid inconsistent data, the entire operation should be carried out in a single transaction. SET XACT_ABORT is used to guarantee that runtime errors in the transaction will force a rollback.

Converting this table back to a nonpartitioned table can be done using either the reverse operation (dropping the partitioned clustered index and re-creating the index nonpartitioned) or by modifying the partition function to have only a single partition.

Modifying Partition Functions and Schemes

Partition functions can be altered in two primary ways. Ranges can be "merged" into other ranges (dropped) or new ranges can be "split" off of existing ranges (added). Removing ranges using the `MERGE` keyword is quite straightforward; splitting new ranges using the `SPLIT` keyword can be a bit more involved, as the partition scheme must also be altered in order to handle the new partition.

For example, if the DBA wished to eliminate the range from `pf_FiscalQuarter2008` ending on September 30, thereby creating a larger range that ends on December 31, the following T-SQL would be used:

```
ALTER PARTITION FUNCTION
pf_FiscalQuarter2008()
MERGE RANGE ('20081001')
```

The range specified in a merge must be exactly convertible to a range boundary that exists in the partition function. As a result of a merge operation, the data will be merged into the next partition, and the partition scheme(s) associated with the function will be updated appropriately. As mentioned earlier, this can be one way of departitioning a table: alter the associated partition function, merging the ranges until only a single partition remains.

Splitting a partition function to create new range boundaries requires first altering the associated scheme(s) to provide a "next-used" filegroup, which will receive the additional partition range data. Remember that a partition scheme must have exactly the same number of filegroups as its underlying function has ranges.

To add a next-used filegroup to a partition scheme—in this case, specifying that additional partitions can be placed in the primary filegroup—the following T-SQL could be used:

```
ALTER PARTITION SCHEME ps_FiscalQuarter2008_Split
NEXT USED [PRIMARY]
```

Once the scheme has been appropriately altered, the partition function itself can have an additional range added. To add a range to `pf_FiscalQuarter2008` for all of 2009 (not minding that the function is now misnamed), the following T-SQL could be used:

```
ALTER PARTITION FUNCTION
pf_FiscalQuarter2008()
SPLIT RANGE ('20100101')
```

Remember that because the function is a `RANGE RIGHT` function, this new range boundary ends on December 31, 2009. Data from this range will be placed into the primary filegroup, as that was the next-used partition defined before it was created.

Switching Tables Into and Out of Partitions

DBAs can move data into partitions from unpartitioned tables and out of partitions back into unpartitioned tables. The former can be useful for data-loading processes, as data can be bulk-loaded into an unindexed table and then switched into a partitioned structure. The latter can be useful for data archival or other purposes.

Assume that the following staging table has been created for 2009 visitor data:

```
CREATE TABLE VisitorStaging_2009
(
  VisitorId INT NOT NULL,
  VisitDate DATETIME NOT NULL
)
```

This table has the same exact schema as the Visitors table partitioned using the ps_FiscalQuarter2008_split function. It should also have been created on whatever filegroup the DBA wishes it to eventually end up on as part of the partition scheme. For the sake of this example, that will be assumed to be the primary filegroup.

Once data for the 2009 time period has been bulk-loaded into the table, the same indexes and constraints must be created on the staging table as exist on the Visitors table. In this case, that's only the PRIMARY KEY constraint:

```
ALTER TABLE VisitorStaging_2009
ADD CONSTRAINT PK_Visitors_2009
  PRIMARY KEY (VisitorId, VisitDate)
```

A CHECK constraint must also be created on the table to guarantee that the data falls within the same range as the partition into which the table will be switched. This can be done with the following T-SQL for this example:

```
ALTER TABLE VisitorStaging_2009
ADD CONSTRAINT CK_Visitors_06012009_12012010
  CHECK (VisitDate >= '20090101' AND VisitDate < '20100101')
```

Once the CHECK constraint is in place, the table is ready to be switched into the new partition. First, the partition boundary number for the new partition should be queried from the sys.partition_functions and sys.partition_range_values catalog views:

```
SELECT rv.boundary_id
FROM sys.partition_functions f
JOIN sys.partition_range_values rv ON f.function_id = rv.function_id
WHERE rv.value = CONVERT(datetime, '20100101')
  AND f.name = 'pf_FiscalQuarter2008'
```

This value can then be plugged into the SWITCH TO option of ALTER TABLE. In this case, the boundary ID is 4, so the following T-SQL switches the VisitorStaging_2009 table into that partition:

```
ALTER TABLE VisitorStaging_2009
SWITCH TO Visitors PARTITION 4
```

The data from the staging table can now be logically queried from the Visitors partitioned table. The staging table can be deleted.

Switching tables out of partitions is much easier. Assuming that the DBA wanted to switch the data back out of the partition just switched into from the staging table, the DBA could re-create the staging table—again, on the same partition and with the same clustered index, but this time without using a CHECK constraint. Once the empty table is in place, the data can be switched out of the partition using the following T-SQL:

```
ALTER TABLE Visitors
SWITCH PARTITION 4 TO VisitorStaging_2009
```

Managing Table and Index Partitions

Management of table and index partitions is similar to management of tables and indexes, with one major difference: it's possible to reindex a specific partition in a table, should the DBA not wish to reindex the entire table at once. In addition, SQL Server includes a series of catalog views to assist with enumerating and viewing data related to partitions.

Rebuilding an index for a specific partition number is very similar to rebuilding an entire index, with the addition of a new clause to the ALTER INDEX syntax: the PARTITION clause. This clause takes a partition number as input. For instance, to rebuild partition 4 of the PK_Visitors index on the Visitors table—assuming that the index is partitioned—the following T-SQL would be used:

```
ALTER INDEX PK_Visitors
ON Visitors
REBUILD
PARTITION = 4
```

The `ONLINE` option and other indexing options are also available. This functionality can help DBAs to more accurately pinpoint and eliminate performance bottlenecks in large partitioned tables.

Three catalog views are provided to assist with viewing partition function data:

- The `sys.partition_functions` view contains data about which partition functions have been created.

- The `sys.partition_range_values` view, used with the `sys.partition_functions` view in an example in a previous section, contains the actual ranges specified for a function.

- The `sys.partition_parameters` function contains information about the parameter datatype used for a function.

The `sys.partition_schemes` view contains information about schemes. The `sys.partitions` and `sys.partition_counts` views contain data about the actual mapping between tables and their partitions, including row counts, used data pages, reserved data pages, and various other statistics. Refer to SQL Server Books Online for a list of available columns in these views.

Using Indexed Views

Although indexed views are still fairly restrictive (DBAs cannot use subqueries, derived tables, and many other constructs), they have been made slightly more flexible with each release of SQL Server. The query optimizer can match more query types to indexed views. These include scalar expressions, such as `(ColA + ColB) * ColC`, and scalar aggregate functions, such as `COUNT_BIG(*)`. For instance, the following indexed view could be created in the AdventureWorks database, indexed on the `OrderTotal` column:

```
CREATE VIEW Sales.OrderTotals
WITH SCHEMABINDING
AS
  SELECT
    SalesOrderId,
    SubTotal + TaxAmt + Freight AS OrderTotal
  FROM Sales.SalesOrderHeader
GO

CREATE UNIQUE CLUSTERED INDEX IX_OrderTotals
ON Sales.OrderTotals
(OrderTotal, SalesOrderId)
```

The query optimizer will now be able to consider queries such as the following for optimization by using the indexed view:

```
SELECT SalesOrderId
FROM Sales.SalesOrderHeader
WHERE SubTotal + TaxAmt + Freight > 300
```

This optimization also includes better matching for queries against indexes that use user-defined functions.

Using Partition-Aligned Indexed Views

Indexed views are powerful because query result sets are materialized immediately and persisted in physical storage in the database, which saves the overhead of performing costly operations like joins or aggregations at execution time. Up until the release of SQL Server 2008, indexed views were of little use in the table-partitioning scenario, because it was very difficult to switch in or out a partition to an underlying table that had an indexed view defined on it. To use indexed views with partitions, users needed to drop the indexed view, switch partitions, and then re-create the view. This solution could take quite some time to complete. SQL Server 2008 solves this problem with the introduction of partition-aligned indexed views.

Partitions are switched in and out of tables via the ALTER TABLE statement with the SWITCH option. This DDL transfers subsets of data between source and target tables quickly and efficiently. There are a number of requirements when using this statement. For example, the source and target tables (and views) must share the same filegroup. To avoid frustration when trying to switch partitions, see SQL Server Books Online's enumeration of the requirements, under the "Transferring Data Efficiently by Using Partition Switching" topic.

There are no special DDL statements to support partition-aligned index views; rather, the indexed view simply works when you SWITCH the partitions. If you use partitions in your database and need indexed views, this feature will definitely be a welcome addition in your environment.

Persisting Computed Columns

In certain situations, it can be useful to create columns whose values are computed dynamically by the SQL Server engine when referenced in a query, rather than inserted with an explicit value. Prior versions of SQL Server included the computed column feature for this purpose. Computed columns were able to be indexed, and the data existed within the index to be used for seeking or by queries covered by the index. However, a noncovered query that needed the same data would not be able to use the value persisted within the index, and it would have to be rebuilt dynamically at runtime. For complex computed columns, this can become a serious performance drain.

To eliminate this problem, the PERSIST keyword is used when creating a computed column in SQL Server. Its behavior is simple enough. Instead of the column's value being calculated at runtime, it is calculated only once, at insert or update time, and stored on disk with the rest of the column data.

To add a new persisted computed column to a table, the following T-SQL could be used, assuming that dbo.VeryComplexFunction() is a very complex function that is slowing down SELECT statements:

```
ALTER TABLE SalesData
  ADD ComplexOutput AS
    (dbo.VeryComplexFunction(CustomerId, OrderId))
    PERSISTED
```

Note that existing computed columns cannot be made persisted; they must be dropped and re-created as persisted computed columns. Likewise, persisted computed columns cannot be altered back into regular computed columns. They also will need to be dropped and re-created.

To determine which computed columns are persisted, query the is_persisted column of the sys.computed_columns catalog view. is_persisted will have a value of 1 if the column is persisted and 0 otherwise. For instance, the following query shows which columns of which tables in the current database are persisted computed columns:

```
SELECT OBJECT_NAME(object_id), name
FROM sys.computed_columns
WHERE is_persisted = 1
```

Snapshots

A common problem in database systems is that of blocking and concurrency. The system needs to ensure that a reader gets consistent data, so writes cannot take place during a read. Unfortunately, larger systems often fall victim to huge scalability bottlenecks due to blocking problems. DBAs must constantly do battle with queries, attempting to control lock granularities and transaction lengths in order to keep blocking to a minimum. But after a while, many give up and take an easier route, risking getting some inconsistent data from time to time by using "dirty reads," the READ UNCOMMITTED transaction isolation level, or the NOLOCK table hint.

Those days have come to an end with the SNAPSHOT isolation level and database snapshots features within the SQL Server database engine. These features provide mechanisms for readers to get consistent, committed data, while allowing writers to work unabated. Simply put, this means no more blocking and no more inconsistent data.

Snapshots represent the best of both worlds, but they have a cost. DBAs will pay a disk I/O penalty when using these new features due to the overhead of maintaining previous versions of rows.

SNAPSHOT Isolation Level

The SNAPSHOT *isolation level* can best be described as a combination of the consistency of the REPEATABLE READ isolation level with the nonblocking characteristics of the READ UNCOMMITTED isolation level. Transactions in the SNAPSHOT isolation level will not create shared locks on rows being read. And repeated requests for the same data within a SNAPSHOT transaction guarantee the same results.

This nonblocking behavior is achieved by storing previous committed versions of rows in the tempdb database. When an update or a delete operation occurs, the previous version of the row is copied to tempdb and a pointer to the previous version is left with the current version. Readers that started transactions before the write and that have already read the previous version will continue to read that version. Meanwhile, the write can occur, and other transactions will see the new version.

This is a definite improvement over the behavior of either the REPEATABLE READ or READ UNCOMMITTED isolation levels. The REPEATABLE READ isolation level creates shared locks for the duration of the read transaction, thereby blocking any writers. And the READ UNCOMMITTED isolation level, while not creating locks, will also not return consistent, committed data if there are updates occurring at the same time that the transaction is reading the data.

Due to its being used as a repository for maintaining data changes, the tempdb database will see greatly increased activity when the SNAPSHOT isolation level is used for write-intensive databases. To avoid problems, the isolation level should not be enabled by DBAs arbitrarily. Specific behaviors that indicate that the isolation level may be helpful include performance issues due to blocking, deadlocked transactions, and previous use of the READ UNCOMMITTED isolation level to promote increased concurrency. Before enabling the isolation level in a production environment, test carefully to ensure that tempdb can handle the additional load.

In addition to the SNAPSHOT isolation level, the READ COMMITTED isolation level can be enhanced to behave like SNAPSHOT isolation for individual queries not within a transaction. The enhanced version is called READ COMMITTED SNAPSHOT.

Enabling SNAPSHOT Isolation for a Database

Use of the SNAPSHOT isolation level is not allowed by default in SQL Server databases. Enabling it for production databases should be done only after careful testing in a development or quality-assurance environment. The row-versioning feature that allows the isolation level to work requires stamping every row in the database with a 14-byte structure that includes a unique identifier and a pointer to the previous versions of the row in tempdb. The extra 14-byte overhead per row and the work required to maintain the previous versions can add up to quite a bit of extra disk I/O, which is why the feature is OFF by default (except in the master and msdb system databases, in which it is ON by default; these databases are small enough that the additional I/O will not cause problems). If you don't actually need row-versioning capabilities, do not turn it on.

Two options are available for enabling row versioning in a database. One is for the SNAPSHOT isolation level itself. The second is for the READ COMMITTED SNAPSHOT isolation level. Both of these are options on ALTER DATABASE, and both are OFF by default. No users can be connected to the database when enabling or disabling row versioning. The READ_COMMITTED_SNAPSHOT option cannot be enabled in the master, tempdb, or msdb system databases.

For example, to allow the SNAPSHOT isolation level to be used for a database called Sales, the following T-SQL would be used:

```
ALTER DATABASE Sales
SET ALLOW_SNAPSHOT_ISOLATION ON
```

For the READ COMMITTED SNAPSHOT isolation level, the following T-SQL would be used:

```
ALTER DATABASE Sales
SET READ_COMMITTED_SNAPSHOT ON
```

Note that these options are independent of each other—either or both can be on for a database. However, since they use the same row-versioning mechanism behind the scenes, turning a second one on once the first is enabled will incur no additional overhead.

To disable either of these options, simply change the flag to OFF:

```
ALTER DATABASE Sales
SET ALLOW_SNAPSHOT_ISOLATION OFF
```

To find out which databases allow the SNAPSHOT isolation level or use the READ COMMITTED SNAPSHOT isolation level, you can query the sys.databases catalog view. The snapshot_isolation_state and is_read_committed_snapshot_on columns will contain 1 if either option is enabled or 0 otherwise. The view can be queried for the Sales database using the following T-SQL:

```
SELECT
    name,
  snapshot_isolation_state,
  is_read_committed_snapshot_on
FROM sys.databases
```

Enabling SNAPSHOT Isolation for a Transaction

Once the SNAPSHOT isolation level is turned on for a database, it can be set for a transaction using SET TRANSACTION ISOLATION LEVEL SNAPSHOT. Its behavior as compared to other isolation levels is best illustrated with a hands-on example.

The following table is created in a database with row versioning enabled:

```
CREATE TABLE TestSnapshot
(
  ColA INT,
  ColB VARCHAR(20)
)

INSERT TestSnapshot (ColA, ColB)
VALUES (1, 'Original Value')
```

Now assume that two SQL Server Management Studio connections are open to the database. In the first, the following T-SQL is executed:

```
SET TRANSACTION ISOLATION LEVEL SNAPSHOT

BEGIN TRANSACTION

SELECT ColB
FROM TestSnapshot
WHERE ColA = 1
```

This query returns the value `'Original Value'` for ColB.

With the transaction still running, the following T-SQL is executed in the second connection:

```
UPDATE TestSnapshot
SET ColB = 'New Value'
WHERE ColA = 1
```

This update will execute successfully and will return the message `'(1 row(s) affected)'`. Had the REPEATABLE READ isolation level been used in the first connection, the update would have been blocked waiting for the transaction to finish.

Back in the first window, the SELECT can be run again. It will still return the value `'Original Value'`, even though the actual value has been updated. Had the transaction been using the READ UNCOMMITTED isolation level, results would not be consistent between reads and the value returned the second time would have been `'New Value'`.

This is a very simple example to show the power of the SNAPSHOT isolation level to deliver consistent yet nonblocking results. It represents a very powerful addition to SQL Server's arsenal.

Handling Concurrent Writes in the SNAPSHOT Isolation Level

Although SNAPSHOT provides consistent repeated reads like the REPEATED READ isolation level, it has a very different behavior when it comes to writing data. Should a SNAPSHOT isolated transaction read some data and then attempt to update it after another transaction has updated it, the entire SNAPSHOT transaction will be rolled back. This is similar to a deadlock and will need to be handled the same way in production code.

To illustrate this behavior, we'll use the same TestSnapshot table from the previous example. In this case, however, suppose that the goal is to select some data into a temporary table, perform some very complex logic, and then update the table. First, the data is inserted into a temporary table:

```
SET TRANSACTION ISOLATION LEVEL SNAPSHOT

BEGIN TRANSACTION

SELECT ColB
INTO #Temp
FROM TestSnapshot
WHERE ColA = 1
```

The temporary table, #Temp, now contains a row with the value `'Original Value'`. As before, another transaction is operating on the TestSnapshot table in another connection with an update:

```
UPDATE TestSnapshot
SET ColB = 'New Value'
WHERE ColA = 1
```

After this, the first transaction has completed its complex logic and attempts to do an update of its own:

```
UPDATE TestSnapshot
SET ColB = 'Even Newer Value'
WHERE ColA = 1
```

Unfortunately, this results in the following error:

```
Msg 3960, Level 16, State 1, Line 1
Cannot use snapshot isolation to access table 'TestSnapshot' in database 'Sales'.
Snapshot transaction aborted due to update conflict. Retry transaction.
```

So what's the moral of this story? Treat any SNAPSHOT transaction that performs data updates exactly like transactions that are susceptible to deadlocks. Put code in place around these transactions to ensure that when this error occurs, an appropriate course of action will be taken.

Using the READ COMMITTED SNAPSHOT Isolation Level

Similar to the SNAPSHOT isolation level is the READ COMMITTED SNAPSHOT isolation level. This isolation level is actually a modification of the default behavior of the READ COMMITTED isolation level. By turning this option on, any single read query within an implicit or explicit READ COMMITTED transaction will behave like a snapshot read—but only for the duration of the query. So repeatable reads do not occur, but consistency is guaranteed.

Again, this is best illustrated through an example using the TestSnapshot table. Assume the database has READ COMMITTED SNAPSHOT enabled. The following query is run on one connection:

```
SET TRANSACTION ISOLATION LEVEL READ COMMITTED

SELECT ColB
FROM TestSnapshot
WHERE ColA = 1
```

This, of course, returns 'Original Value'. Now in a second connection, another transaction is started, but not committed:

```
BEGIN TRANSACTION

UPDATE TestSnapshot
SET ColB = 'New Value'
WHERE ColA = 1
```

Rerunning the select in the first connection will return 'Original Value' again, because the second transaction has not committed—no blocking occurs, as in the normal READ COMMITTED isolation level. However, as soon as the second transaction commits, the first connection will now see the updated value.

READ COMMITTED SNAPSHOT can be a good balance for databases that have a lot of read activity of data that is regularly updated, where consistency is important but repeatable results within a single transaction are not.

Database Snapshots

Like the SNAPSHOT isolation level, database snapshots give DBAs a way of presenting a consistent view of data at a certain time. However, whereas the SNAPSHOT isolation level provides this for only small amounts of data (the data involved in a given transaction), database snapshots provide a frozen replica of the database at the time the snapshot was created. This can be helpful for situations in which DBAs need to provide timestamped data for reporting or auditing purposes.

What differentiates database snapshots from other methods of providing this same functionality (such as taking a backup) is that database snapshots have no data when they're first created, and they are therefore created almost instantaneously. This is made possible by a scheme similar to that which allows the SNAPSHOT isolation level to work.

Instead of copying all of the data from the source database, the database snapshot begins life as nothing more than a pointer to the original database. As data changes in that database, the older versions of rows are migrated into the snapshot database, but at any time, the snapshot database is only as large as the amount of data that has changed since it was created. Of course, this works the other way around as well. A database snapshot can grow to be as big as the original database was at the moment the snapshot was created, so ensure that enough disk space exists to provide room for growth. DBAs should also attempt to place snapshot databases on separate physical disks from production databases, to reduce contention due to additional write operations when changes are migrated into the snapshot.

Creating Database Snapshots

Database snapshots are created using `CREATE DATABASE` with the `AS SNAPSHOT OF` option. To create a snapshot, each logical filename from the original database must appear in the definition for the snapshot, exactly as it was originally defined. The physical filename should be changed to have the `.ss` extension, but drives or paths can also be changed.

A recommended naming scheme for database snapshots is the same name as the database, followed by `_Snapshot`, optionally followed by the date and time the snapshot was created. This naming scheme should help users more quickly determine which snapshot they require for a task. It's also recommended that the snapshot's physical filenames be similarly timestamped, to make disk management easier.

As an example, assume that there is a database called Sales, with two filegroups, `SalesPrimary` and `SalesPrimary_01`. It's September 1, 2008. The following T-SQL could be used to create the snapshot:

```
CREATE DATABASE Sales_Snapshot_20080901
ON
  (NAME = SalesPrimary,
    FILENAME = 'F:\Data\SalesPrimary_20070901.ss'),
  (NAME = SalesPrimary_01,
    FILENAME = 'F:\Data\SalesPrimary_01_20070901.ss')
AS SNAPSHOT OF Sales
```

Once a snapshot is created, it will appear to clients to be a read-only database and will persist until it is explicitly dropped using `DROP DATABASE`. The base database cannot be dropped until all referencing snapshots are dropped. Any number of snapshots can be created for a database, allowing DBAs to keep a running tally of data states, as disk space allows. Remember that these databases will grow as data changes in the base database.

Reverting to a Database Snapshot

Along with providing a readily available view of the database at a specific point in time, snapshots can be used as a fail-safe in case of accidental data corruption. Please note that *using database snapshots is no replacement for a solid backup plan*. However, there are times when reverting to a snapshot could be very useful. For instance, imagine a scenario in which a development team is testing a data-upgrade script. These kinds of development tasks generally require the DBA to restore a database, run a version of the update script, regression test, and repeat the process iteratively as bugs are discovered. Using a database snapshot and reverting will decrease a lot of the downtime required for these kinds of tasks and generally make life easier for the DBA.

Reverting to a snapshot is similar to restoring from a backup. For instance, to revert the Sales database from a snapshot created on September 1, 2008, the following T-SQL could be used:

```
RESTORE DATABASE Sales
FROM
  DATABASE_SNAPSHOT = Sales_Snapshot_20080901
```

A few restrictions apply. A restore from a snapshot can occur only if the database has just one snapshot. So if multiple snapshots have been created, those other than the one to be restored from will need to be dropped. The database can have no full-text indexes. Finally, during the restore process, both the database and the snapshot will be unavailable for use.

Data-Integrity Enhancements

Microsoft has recently provided two interesting features within the SQL Server database engine:

- A checksum-based data page verification scheme, in addition to the torn-page detection option from previous versions of SQL Server
- The ability to put a database into an emergency, administrator-only access mode

We detail both features in the sections that follow.

Verifying a Database's Pages

The ALTER DATABASE statement includes syntax for page verification, with two options: one to enable torn-page detection and a newer checksum verification option. The checksum verification can detect most of the same types of failures as torn-page detection, as well as various hardware-related failures that torn-page detection cannot. However, it is more resource intensive than the older option, so as with any other change, you should test it carefully before rolling it out to production environments.

Enabling the checksum-based page verification scheme for a database called Sales could be done with the following T-SQL:

```
ALTER DATABASE Sales
SET PAGE_VERIFY CHECKSUM
```

To enable torn-page detection, use the TORN_PAGE_DETECTION option:

```
ALTER DATABASE Sales
SET PAGE_VERIFY TORN_PAGE_DETECTION
```

Note that only one of the two page-verification types can be enabled at any given time. To turn off page verification altogether, use the NONE option:

```
ALTER DATABASE Sales
SET PAGE_VERIFY NONE
```

To determine the current page-verification setting for a given database, use the page_verify_option column of sys.databases:

```
SELECT page_verify_option
FROM sys.databases
WHERE name = 'abc'
```

The column will have a value of 0 if the NONE option is set, 1 for the TORN_PAGE_DETECTION option, and 2 for the CHECKSUM option.

Putting a Database into an Emergency State

Unfortunately, even with data page verification and a very stable database management system like SQL Server, problems do sometimes occur. Should a problem arise, the DBA can set the database to the new emergency state.

This state makes the database read-only and restricts access to members of the sysadmin fixed server role. Although this sounds like a combination of the read-only and restricted user modes, there is a very important enhancement available with the emergency state option. This option can be set on databases marked suspect, thereby allowing the DBA to get in and fix errors or pull out vital data if errors cannot be fixed.

To set the database to the emergency state, use the EMERGENCY option of ALTER DATABASE. To set this mode for a database called Sales, the following T-SQL would be used:

```
ALTER DATABASE Sales
SET EMERGENCY
```

To turn off the emergency state, use the ONLINE option:

```
ALTER DATABASE Sales
SET ONLINE
```

Summary

With each new release of SQL Server comes a significant number of new features for DBAs to learn and effectively use in their environments. SQL Server 2008's release cycle was not as long as that of SQL Server 2005, so a lot of effort was spent in adding value to key features. These include more dynamic mangement views returning memory information, filtered indexes, and partition-aligned indexed views. Together, these additions and changes continue to improve the experience of the DBA and keep SQL Server competitive with all the other enterprise relational databases on the market today.

CHAPTER 14

■■■

.NET Integration

Truly devoted (or is it insane?) SQL Server programmers might think back wistfully on days spent debugging extended stored procedures, yearning for those joyfully complicated times. The rest of us, however, remember plunging headfirst into a process that always felt a lot more esoteric than it needed to be and never quite lived up to the functionality we hoped it could provide.

SQL Server 7.0 introduced the idea of *extended stored procedures* (XPs), which are dynamic link libraries (DLLs)—usually written in C++—that can be used to programmatically extend SQL Server's functionality. Unfortunately, programming and debugging XPs are quite difficult for most users. Additionally, their use gives rise to many issues, such as memory leaks and security concerns, that make them less than desirable. Luckily, XPs are a thing of the past (or are deprecated, at the very least), and starting with SQL Server 2005, programmers have much better options with tightly integrated common language runtime (CLR) interoperability. Developers can now use any .NET language they feel comfortable with to create powerful user-defined objects within SQL Server. Note, however, that only C#, Visual Basic .NET (VB .NET), and Managed C++ are officially supported languages. Although other languages can be used, getting them to work properly may require a bit of additional effort.

In this chapter, programming with CLR objects will be introduced with a step-by-step tour through development of a CLR stored procedure. Also discussed will be the .NET object model provided for SQL Server CLR development, best practices for developing CLR objects, and various deployment issues. Chapter 15 builds upon this foundation, covering all of the other types of objects that can be created in SQL Server using .NET: CLR user-defined types, CLR user-defined functions, CLR aggregates, and CLR triggers.

This chapter covers the following topics:

- SQL Server .NET integration
- The SQL Server .NET programming model
- CLR stored procedures
- CLR routine deployment

■Note Both this chapter and Chapter 15 assume familiarity with .NET programming using the C# language. Those readers who haven't yet picked up .NET skills should consider starting with Andrew Troelsen's excellent book, *Pro C# 2008 and the .NET 3.5 Platform, Fourth Edition* (Apress, 2007).

Introduction to SQL Server .NET Integration

SQL Server developers have had few choices in the past when it came to doing things in the database for which Transact-SQL (T-SQL) wasn't especially well suited. This includes such things as complex or heavily mathematical logic, connecting to remote services or data stores, and manipulating files and other non–SQL Server–controlled resources. Although many of these tasks are best suited for operation on the client rather than within SQL Server, sometimes system architecture, project funding, or time constraints leave developers with no choice—business problems must be solved in some way, as quickly and cheaply as possible. XPs were one option to help with these situations, but as mentioned in this chapter's introduction, these are difficult to write and debug, and are known for decreasing server stability. Another option was to use the sp_OA (Object Automation) stored procedures to call COM objects, but this has its own issues, including performance penalties and dealing with COM "DLL hell" if the correct versions are not registered on the SQL Server.

CLR integration does away with these issues and provides a structured, easy-to-use methodology for extending SQL Server in a variety of ways.

Why Does SQL Server Host the CLR?

There are some things that T-SQL just isn't meant to do. For instance, it's not known as a language that excels at accessing data from web services. Another good example is data structures. T-SQL contains only one data structure: the table. This works fine for most of our data needs, but sometimes something else is needed, such as an array or a linked list. And although these things can be simulated using T-SQL, it's messy at best.

The CLR is a managed environment, designed with safety and stability in mind. Management means that memory and resources are automatically handled by the runtime. It is very difficult (if not impossible) to write code that will cause a memory leak. Management also means that SQL Server can control the runtime if something goes wrong. If SQL Server detects instability, the hosted runtime can be immediately restarted.

This level of control was impossible with the XP functionality in earlier versions of SQL Server. XPs were often known for decreasing the stability of SQL Server, as there was no access control—an unwitting developer could all too easily write code that could overwrite some of SQL Server's own memory locations, thereby creating a time bomb that would explode when SQL Server needed to access the memory. Thanks to the CLR's "sandboxing" of process space, this is no longer an issue.

The CLR builds virtual process spaces within its environment, called *application domains*. This lets code running within each domain operate as if it had its own dedicated process, and at the same time isolates virtual processes from each other. The net effect in terms of stability is that if code running within one application domain crashes, the other domains won't be affected; only the domain in which the crash occurred will be restarted by the framework, and the entire system won't be compromised. This is especially important in database applications. Developers certainly don't want to risk crashing an entire instance of SQL Server because of a bug in a CLR routine.

When to Use CLR Routines

T-SQL is a language that was designed primarily for straightforward data access. Developers are often not comfortable writing complex set-based solutions to problems, and they end up using cursors to solve complex logical problems. This is never the best solution in T-SQL. Cursors and row-by-row processing aren't the optimal data-access methods. Set-based solutions are preferred.

When non–set-based solutions are absolutely necessary, CLR routines are faster. Looping over a SqlDataReader can be much faster than using a cursor. And complex logic will often perform much better in .NET than in T-SQL. In addition, if routines need to access external resources such as web services, using .NET is an obvious choice. T-SQL is simply not adept at handling these kinds of situations.

When Not to Use CLR Routines

It's important to remember an adage that has become increasingly popular in the fad-ridden world of information technology in the past few years: "To a hammer, everything looks like a nail."

Just because you can do something using the CLR doesn't mean you should. For data access, set-based T-SQL is still the appropriate choice in virtually all cases. Access to external resources from SQL Server, which CLR integration makes much easier, is generally not appropriate from SQL Server's process space. Think carefully about architecture before implementing such solutions. External resources can be unpredictable or unavailable—two factors that aren't supposed to be present in database solutions!

In the end, it's a question of common sense. If something doesn't seem to belong in SQL Server, it probably shouldn't be implemented there. As CLR integration matures, best practices will become more obvious. For the meantime, take a minimalist approach. Overuse of the technology will cause more problems in the long run than underuse.

How SQL Server Hosts .NET: An Architectural Overview

The CLR is completely hosted by SQL Server. Routines running within SQL Server's process space make requests to SQL Server for all resources, including memory and processor time. SQL Server is free to either grant or deny these requests, depending on server conditions. SQL Server is also free to completely restart the hosted CLR if a process is taking up too many resources. SQL Server itself is in complete control, and the CLR is unable to compromise the basic integrity that SQL Server offers.

Why Managed Objects Perform Well

SQL Server CLR integration was designed with performance in mind. Compilation of CLR routines for hosting within SQL Server is done using function pointers in order to facilitate high-speed transitions between T-SQL and CLR processes. Type-specific optimizations ensure that routines are just-in-time (JIT) compiled, so no further cost is associated with their invocation.

Another optimization is streaming of result sets from CLR *table-valued functions* (which will be covered in detail in the next chapter). Unlike some other rowset-based providers that require the client to accept the entire result set before work can be done, table-valued functions are able to stream data a single row at a time. This enables work to be handled in a piecemeal fashion, thereby reducing both memory and processor overhead.

Why CLR Integration Is Stable

SQL Server both hosts and completely controls the CLR routines running within the SQL Server process space. Since SQL Server is in control of all resources, routines are unable to bog down the server or access unavailable resources, as XPs could.

Another important factor is the HostProtection attribute. This attribute allows methods to define their level of cross-process resource interaction, mainly from a threading and locking point of view. For instance, synchronized methods and classes (for example, System.Collections.ArrayList. Synchronized) are decorated with the Synchronization parameter of the attribute. These methods and classes, as well as those that expose a shared provider state or manage external processes, are disallowed from use within the SQL Server–hosted CLR environment, based on permission sets chosen by the DBA at deployment time. Permission sets are covered in more detail later in this chapter, in the section "Deploying CLR Routines."

DBAs supporting the CLR features in SQL Server should realize that this is no longer the world of XPs. These objects can be rolled out with a great deal of confidence. And as will be discussed later in this chapter, the DBA has the final say over what access the CLR code will have once it is deployed within the server.

SQL Server .NET Programming Model

ADO.NET, the data-access technology used within the .NET Framework, has been enhanced to oper-ate within routines hosted by SQL Server 2008. These enhancements are fairly simple to exploit. For most operations, the only difference between coding on a client layer or within the database will be modification of a connection string. Thanks to this, .NET developers will find a shallow learning curve when picking up SQL CLR skills. And when necessary, moving code between tiers will be rela-tively simple.

Enhancements to ADO.NET for SQL Server Hosting

CLR stored procedures use ADO.NET objects to retrieve data from and write data to the database. These are the same objects you're already familiar with if you use ADO.NET today: `SqlCommand`, `SqlDataReader`, `DataSet`, and so on. The only difference is that these can now be run in SQL Server's process space (in-processes) instead of only on a client.

When accessing SQL Server via an ADO.NET client, the `SqlConnection` object is instantiated, and a connection string is set, either in the constructor or using the `ConnectionString` property. This same process happens when instantiating an in-process connection, but the connection string has been rewired for SQL Server. Using the connection string `"Context connection=true"` tells SQL Server to use the same connection that spawned the CLR method as the connection from which to perform data access.

This means, in essence, that only a single change is all that's necessary for migration of the majority of data-access code between tiers. To migrate code into SQL Server, classes and methods will still need to be appropriately decorated with attributes describing how they should function (see the "Anatomy of a Stored Procedure" section later in this chapter), but the only substantial code change will be to the connection string! Virtually all members of the `SqlClient` namespace—with the notable exception of asynchronous operations—will work within the SQL Server process space.

The other major code difference between CLR routines and ADO.NET programming on clients is that inside CLR routines, the developer will generally want to communicate back to the session that invoked the routine. This communication can take any number of forms, from returning scalar values to sending back a result set from a stored procedure or table-valued function. However, until SQL Server 2005, the ADO.NET client did not include mechanisms for communicating back to the session. Now these are available through the `Microsoft.SqlServer.Server` namespace.

Overview of the .NET Namespaces for SQL Server

The `Microsoft.SqlServer.Server` namespace was added to the .NET Framework to facilitate data-base integration. This namespace contains the methods and attributes necessary to create CLR routines within SQL Server, and perform manipulation of database objects within those routines. The `Microsoft.SqlServer.Server` namespace contains attributes for defining managed routines, as well as ADO.NET methods specific to the SQL Server provider.

In order for classes and methods to be defined as hosted CLR routines, they must be deco-rated with attributes to tell SQL Server what they are. These attributes include, among others, `SqlProcedureAttribute` for defining CLR stored procedures and `SqlFunctionAttribute` for CLR user-defined functions. All of these attributes will be explained in detail in the next chapter.

The namespace also contains ADO.NET methods that allow CLR routines to communicate back to the session that invoked them. What can be communicated back depends on the type of CLR routine. For instance, a stored procedure can return messages, errors, result sets, or an integer return value. A table-valued user-defined function, on the other hand, can return only a single result set.

When programming CLR routines that need to return data, an object called SqlContext is available. This object represents a connection back to the session that instantiated the CLR routine. Exposed by this object is another object, SqlPipe. This is the means by which data is sent back to the caller. Sending properly formatted messages or result sets "down the pipe" means that the calling session will receive the data.

Note that not all SqlContext features are available from all routine types. For instance, a scalar user-defined function cannot send back a result set. Developers must remember to carefully test CLR routines; using a feature that's not available won't result in a compile-time error! Instead, an error will occur at runtime when the system attempts to use the unavailable feature. It's very important to keep this in mind during development in order to avoid problems once routines are rolled out to production systems.

Programming a CLR Stored Procedure

Now that the basic overview of what's available is complete, it's time to get into some code! The example used in this chapter will be a dynamic cross-tabulation of some sales data in the AdventureWorks sample database that's included with SQL Server 2005 and 2008. Given the data in the Sales.SalesOrderHeader and Sales.SalesOrderDetail tables, the goal will be to produce a report based on a user-specified date range, in which the columns are sales months and each row aggregates total sales within each month, by territory.

Before starting work on any CLR routine, the developer should ask, "Why should this routine be programmed using the CLR?" Remember that in most cases, T-SQL is still the preferred method of SQL Server programming, so give this question serious thought before continuing.

In this case, the argument in favor of using a CLR routine is fairly obvious. Although this problem can be solved using only T-SQL, it's a messy prospect at best. In order to accomplish this task, the routine first must determine in which months sales occurred within the input date range. Then, using that set of months, a query must be devised to create a column for each month and aggregate the appropriate data by territory.

This task is made slightly easier than it was in previous versions of SQL Server, thanks to the inclusion of the PIVOT operator (see Chapter 12 for more information about this operator). This operator allows T-SQL developers to more easily write queries that transform rows into columns, a common reporting technique known as either *pivoting* or *cross-tabulating*. However, PIVOT doesn't provide dynamic capabilities, so the developer still needs to perform fairly complex string concatenation to get things working. Concatenating strings is tricky and inefficient in T-SQL. Using the .NET Framework's StringBuilder class is a much nicer prospect. Avoiding complex T-SQL string manipulation is argument enough to do this job within a CLR routine.

Once the determination to use a CLR routine has been made, the developer next must ask, "What is the appropriate type of routine to use for this job?" Generally speaking, this will be a fairly straightforward question; for instance, a CLR user-defined type and a CLR user-defined trigger obviously serve quite different purposes. However, the specific problem for this situation isn't so straightforward. There are two obvious choices: a CLR table-valued function and a CLR stored procedure.

The requirement for this task is to return a result set to the client containing the cross-tabulated data. Both CLR table-valued functions and CLR stored procedures can return result sets to the client. However, as will be discussed in the next chapter, CLR table-valued functions must have their output columns predefined. In this case, the column list is dynamic; if the user enters a 3-month date range, up to four columns will appear in the result set—one for each month in which there were sales, and one for the territory sales are being aggregated for. Likewise, if the user enters a 1-year date range, up to 13 columns may be returned. Therefore, it isn't possible to predefine the column list, and the only choice is to use a CLR stored procedure.

Starting a Visual Studio 2008 SQL Server Project

Once you have decided to program a CLR routine, the first step is to start Visual Studio 2008 and create a new project. Figure 14-1 shows the menu option to pick to launch the New Project Wizard.

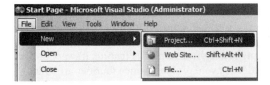

Figure 14-1. *Opening a new project in Visual Studio*

Visual Studio includes a project template for SQL Server projects, which automatically creates all of the necessary references and can create appropriate empty classes for all of the SQL Server CLR routine types. Although you could use a Class Library template instead and do all of this manually, that's not an especially efficient use of time. So we definitely recommend that you use the SQL Server Project template when developing CLR routines.

■**Note** Although Visual Studio 2005 contains the SQL Server Project templates, at the time of this writing, Visual Studio 2008 does not come with it. The templates will be available as a separate download or in Service Pack 1 of Visual Studio 2008.

Figure 14-2 shows the SQL Server Project template being chosen from the available database project templates. On this system, only C# has been installed; on a system with VB .NET, the same option would appear under that language's option tree.

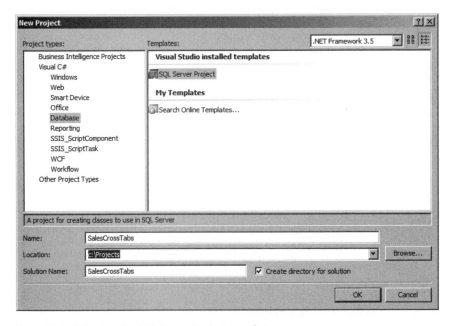

Figure 14-2. *Selecting the SQL Server Project template*

This project has been named `SalesCrossTabs`, since it's going to contain at least one cross-tabulation of sales data (perhaps more will be added in the future). A single SQL Server project can contain any number of CLR routines. However, it's recommended that any one project logically group only a small number of routines. If a single change to a single routine is made, you should not need to reapply every assembly referenced by the database.

After clicking the OK button, you are presented with the New Database Reference dialog box, as shown in Figure 14-3. By specifying a connection at this point, the project is easier to deploy and test from within the Visual Studio environment. For this example, we are making a connection to the AdventureWorks database on our local server.

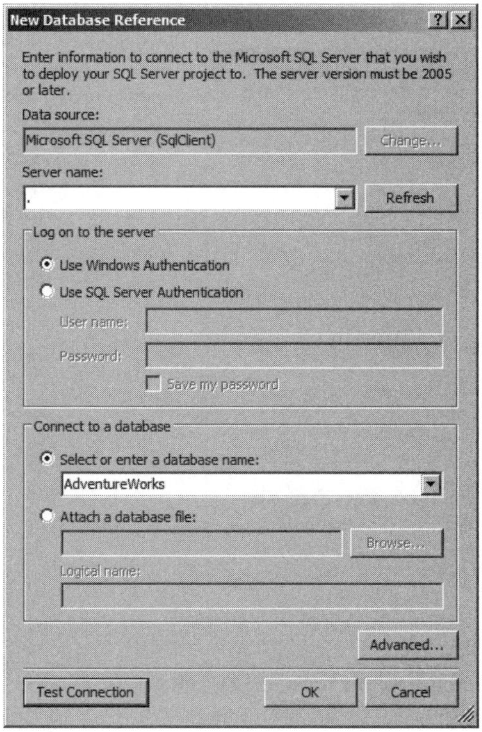

Figure 14-3. *Create a new database reference if the correct one doesn't already exist.*

At this point, a new, blank project has been created and is ready to have some code added. Right-click the project name in Solution Explorer, click Add, and then click Stored Procedure, as shown in Figure 14-4.

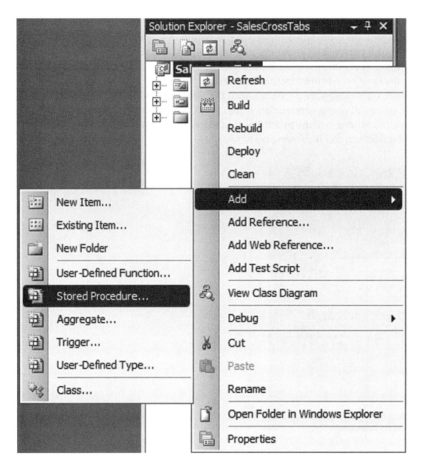

Figure 14-4. *Adding a stored procedure to the project*

The final step in adding the new stored procedure is to name it. Figure 14-5 shows the window that will appear after clicking Stored Procedure. The Stored Procedure template is selected, and the procedure has been named GetSalesPerTerritoryByMonth. Developers should remember that, just as in naming T-SQL stored procedures, descriptive, self-documenting names go a long way toward making development and maintenance easier.

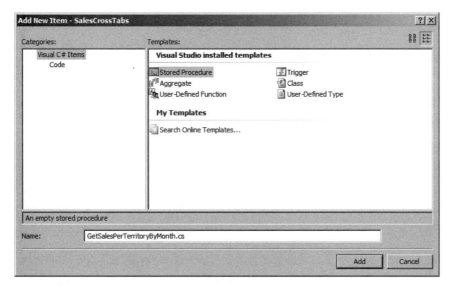

Figure 14-5. *Naming the stored procedure*

Anatomy of a Stored Procedure

After the new stored procedure has been added the project, the following code will be appear in the editing window:

```
using System;
using System.Data;
using System.Data.SqlClient;
using System.Data.SqlTypes;
using Microsoft.SqlServer.Server;

public partial class StoredProcedures
{
    [Microsoft.SqlServer.Server.SqlProcedure]
    public static void GetSalesPerTerritoryByMonth()
    {
        // Put your code here
    }
};
```

Notice that the Microsoft.SqlServer.Server and System.Data.SqlTypes namespaces have been automatically included in this project. Both of these namespaces have very specific purposes within a routine and will be necessary within most SQL Server CLR projects.

The Microsoft.SqlServer.Server namespace is necessary, as previously mentioned, for the attributes that must decorate all routines to be hosted within SQL Server. In this case, the GetSalesPerTerritoryByMonth method has been decorated with the SqlProcedure attribute. This indicates that the method is a stored procedure. The method has also been defined as static. Since this method will be called without an object instantiation, it would not be available if not defined as static. The Microsoft.SqlServer.Server namespace is also included in order to provide access to the calling context, for data access and returning data.

The `System.Data.SqlTypes` namespace provides datatypes that correspond to each of the SQL Server datatypes. For instance, the equivalent of SQL Server's `INTEGER` datatype isn't .NET's `System.Int32` datatype. Instead, it's `SqlTypes.SqlInt32`. Although these types can be cast between each other freely, not all types have direct equivalents. Many of the SQL Server types have slightly different implementations than what would seem to be their .NET siblings. For that reason, and to provide some insulation in case of future underlying structural changes, it's important to use these types instead of the native .NET types when dealing with data returned from SQL Server, including both parameters to the routine and data read using a `SqlDataReader` or `DataSet` object.

Aside from the included namespaces, note that the return type of the `GetSalesPerTerritoryByMonth` method is `void`. SQL Server stored procedures can return either 32-bit integers or nothing at all. In this case, the stored procedure won't have a return value. That's generally a good idea, because SQL Server will override the return value should an error occur within the stored procedure; so output parameters are considered to be a better option for returning scalar values to a client. However, should a developer want to implement a return value from this stored procedure, the allowed datatypes are `SqlInt32` and `SqlInt16`.

Adding Parameters

Most stored procedures will have one or more parameters to allow users to pass in arguments that can tell the stored procedure which data to return. In the case of this particular stored procedure, two parameters will be added to facilitate getting data using a date range (one of the requirements outlined in the section "Programming a CLR Stored Procedure"). These parameters will be called `StartDate` and `EndDate`, and each will be defined as type `SqlDateTime`.

These two parameters are added to the method definition, just like parameters to any C# method:

```
[Microsoft.SqlServer.Server.SqlProcedure]
public static void GetSalesPerTerritoryByMonth( SqlDateTime StartDate,
                                                SqlDateTime EndDate)
{
    // Put your code here
}
```

In this case, these parameters are required input parameters. Output parameters can be defined by using the C# `ref` (reference) keyword before the datatype. This will then allow developers to use SQL Server's `OUTPUT` keyword in order to get back scalar values from the stored procedure.

Unfortunately, neither optional parameters nor default parameter values are currently supported by CLR stored procedures.

Defining the Problem

At this point, the stored procedure is syntactically complete and could be deployed as is; but of course, it wouldn't do anything! It's time to code the meat of the procedure. But first, it's good to take a step back and figure out what it should do.

The final goal, as previously mentioned, is to cross-tabulate sales totals per territory, with a column for each month in which sales took place. This goal can be accomplished using the following steps:

1. Select a list of the months and years in which sales took place, from the `Sales.SalesOrderHeader` table.

2. Using the list of months, construct a query using the `PIVOT` operator that returns the desired cross-tabulation.

3. Return the cross-tabulated result set to the client.

The Sales.SalesOrderHeader table contains one row for each sale, and includes a column called OrderDate—the date the sale was made. For the sake of this stored procedure, a distinct list of the months and years in which sales were made will be considered. The following query returns that data:

```
SELECT DISTINCT
    DATEPART(yyyy, OrderDate) AS YearPart,
    DATEPART(mm, OrderDate) AS MonthPart
FROM Sales.SalesOrderHeader
ORDER BY YearPart, MonthPart
```

Once the stored procedure has that data, it needs to create the actual cross-tab query. This query needs to use the dates from Sales.SalesOrderHeader. For each month, it should calculate the sum of the amounts in the LineTotal column of the Sales.SalesOrderDetail table. And of course, this data should be aggregated per territory. The TerritoryId column of the Sales.SalesOrderHeader table will be used for that purpose.

The first step in creating the cross-tab query is to pull the actual data required. The following query returns the territory ID, order date formatted as *YYYY-MM*, and total line item amount for each line item in the SalesOrderDetail table:

```
SELECT
    TerritoryId,
    CONVERT(char(7), h.OrderDate, 120) AS theDate,
    d.LineTotal
FROM Sales.SalesOrderHeader h
JOIN Sales.SalesOrderDetail d ON h.SalesOrderID = d.SalesOrderID
```

Figure 14-6 shows a few of the 121,317 rows of data returned by this query.

	TerritoryId	theDate	LineTotal
1	5	2001-07	2024.994000
2	5	2001-07	6074.982000
3	5	2001-07	2024.994000
4	5	2001-07	2039.994000
5	5	2001-07	2039.994000
6	5	2001-07	4079.988000
7	5	2001-07	2039.994000
8	5	2001-07	86.521200
9	5	2001-07	28.840400
10	5	2001-07	34.200000

Figure 14-6. *Unaggregated sales data*

Using the PIVOT operator, this query can be turned into a cross-tab. For instance, to report on sales from June and July of 2004, the following query could be used:

```
SELECT
    TerritoryId,
    [2004-06],
    [2004-07]
FROM
(
    SELECT
        TerritoryId,
        CONVERT(char(7), h.OrderDate, 120) AS YYYY_MM,
        d.LineTotal
    FROM Sales.SalesOrderHeader h
```

```
       JOIN Sales.SalesOrderDetail d ON h.SalesOrderID = d.SalesOrderID
) p
PIVOT
(
    SUM (LineTotal)
    FOR YYYY_MM IN
    (
        [2004-06],
        [2004-07]
    )
) AS pvt
ORDER BY TerritoryId
```

Figure 14-7 shows the results of this query. The data has now been aggregated and cross-tabulated. Note that a couple of the values are null, which indicates a territory that did not have sales for that month.

	TerritoryId	2004-06	2004-07
1	1	779625.967724	10165.250000
2	2	240725.227509	NULL
3	3	298101.019968	NULL
4	4	993295.830953	9155.300000
5	5	269604.574888	113.960000
6	6	717837.710783	10853.700000
7	7	316740.799297	3491.950000
8	8	349467.104000	3604.830000
9	9	711086.975552	9234.230000
10	10	688354.968664	4221.410000

Figure 14-7. *Cross-tabulated sales data*

In the actual stored procedure, the tokens representing June and July 2004 will be replaced by tokens for the actual months from the input date range, as determined by the StartDate and EndDate parameters and the first query. Then the full cross-tab query will be concatenated. All that's left from the three steps defined previously is to return the results to the caller. You have a couple of choices for how to tackle that challenge.

Using the SqlPipe

As mentioned in previous sections, SqlContext is an object available from within the scope of CLR routines. This object is defined in the Microsoft.SqlServer.Server namespace as a sealed class with a private constructor, so you don't create an instance of it; rather, you just use it. The following code, for instance, is invalid:

```
//This code does not work -- the constructor for SqlContext is private
SqlContext context = new SqlContext();
```

Instead, just use the object as is. To use the SqlPipe, which is the object we need for this exercise, the following code might be used:

```
//Get a reference to the SqlPipe for this calling context
SqlPipe pipe = SqlContext.Pipe;
```

So what is the SqlPipe object? This object allows the developer to send data or commands to be executed from a CLR routine back to the caller.

The Send() Method

The Send() method, which as you can guess is used to actually send the data, has three overloads:

- Send(string message) sends a string, which will be interpreted as a message. Think InfoMessage in ADO.NET or the messages pane in SQL Server Management Studio. Sending strings using Send() has the same effect as using the T-SQL PRINT statement.

- Send(SqlDataRecord record) sends a single record back to the caller. This is used in conjunction with the SendResultsStart() and SendResultsEnd() methods to manually send a table a row at a time. Getting it working can be quite a hassle, and it's really not recommended for most applications. See the section "Table-Valued User-Defined Functions" in the next chapter for a much nicer approach.

- Send(SqlDataReader reader) sends an entire table back to the caller, in one shot. This is much nicer than doing things row by row, but also just as difficult to set up for sending back data that isn't already in a SqlDataReader object. Luckily, this particular stored procedure doesn't have that problem. It uses a SqlDataReader, so this method can be used to directly stream back the data read from the SQL Server.

The Send() methods can be called any number of times during the course of a stored procedure. Just like native T-SQL stored procedures, CLR procedures can return multiple result sets and multiple messages or errors. But by far the most common overload used will be the one that accepts SqlDataReader. The following code fragment shows a good example of the utility of this method:

```
command.CommandText = "SELECT * FROM Sales.SalesOrderHeader";
SqlDataReader reader = command.ExecuteReader();
SqlContext.Pipe.Send(reader);
```

In this fragment, it's assumed that the connection and command objects have already been instantiated and the connection has been opened. A reader is populated with the SQL, which selects all columns and all rows from the Sales.SalesOrderHeader table. The SqlDataReader can be passed to the Send() method as is, and the caller will receive the data as a result set.

Although this example is quite simplistic, it illustrates the ease with which the Send() method can be used to return data back to the caller when the data is already in a SqlDataReader object.

The ExecuteAndSend() Method

The problem with sending a SqlDataReader back to the caller is that all of the data will be marshaled through the CLR process space on its way back. Since, in this case, the caller generated the data (it came from a table in SQL Server), it would be nice to be able to make the caller return the data on its own—without having to send the data back and forth.

This is where the ExecuteAndSend() method comes into play. This method accepts a SqlCommand object, which should have both CommandText and Parameters values (if necessary) defined. This tells the calling context to execute the command and process the output itself.

Letting the caller do the work without sending the data back is quite a bit faster. In some cases, performance can improve by up to 50 percent. Sending all of that data between processes is a lot of work. But this performance improvement comes at a cost; one of the benefits of handling the data within the CLR routine is control. Take the following code fragment, for example:

```
command.CommandText = "SELECT * FROM Sales.ERRORSalesOrderHeader";
try
{
    SqlDataReader reader = command.ExecuteReader();
    SqlContext.Pipe.Send(reader);
}
catch (Exception e)
```

```
{
    //Do something smart here
}
```

This fragment is similar to the fragment discussed in the previous Send() method example. It requests all of the rows and columns from the table, and then sends the data back to the caller using the Send() method. This work is wrapped in a try/catch block. The developer, perhaps, can do something to handle any exceptions that occur. And indeed, in this code block, an exception will occur. The table Sales.ERRORSalesOrderHeader doesn't exist in the AdventureWorks database.

This exception will occur in the CLR routine—the ExecuteReader() method will fail. At that point, the exception will be caught by the catch block. But what about the following code fragment, which uses the ExecuteAndSend() method:

```
command.CommandText = "SELECT * FROM Sales.ERRORSalesOrderHeader";
try
{
    SqlContext.Pipe.ExecuteAndSend(command)
}
catch (Exception e)
{
    //Do something smart here
}
```

Remember that the ExecuteAndSend() method tells the caller to handle all output from whatever T-SQL is sent down the pipe. This includes exceptions. So in this case, the catch block is hit, but by then it's already too late. The caller has already received the exception, and catching it in the CLR routine isn't especially useful.

So which method, Send() or ExecuteAndSend(), is appropriate for the sales cross-tabulation stored procedure? Given the simplicity of the example, the ExecuteAndSend() method makes more sense. It has greater performance than Send(), which is always a benefit. And there's really nothing that can be done if an exception is encountered in the final T-SQL to generate the result set.

Putting It All Together: Coding the Body of the Stored Procedure

Now that the techniques have been defined, putting together the complete stored procedure is a relatively straightforward process.

Recall that the first step is to get the list of months and years in which sales took place, within the input date range. Given that the pivot query will use date tokens formatted as *YYYY-MM*, it will be easier to process the unique tokens in the CLR stored procedure if they're queried from the database in that format. So the query used will be slightly different from the one shown in the "Defining the Problem" section. The following code fragment will be used to get the months and years into a SqlDataReader object:

```
//Get a SqlCommand object
SqlCommand command = new SqlCommand();

//Use the context connection
command.Connection = new SqlConnection("Context connection=true");
command.Connection.Open();

//Define the T-SQL to execute
string sql =
    "SELECT DISTINCT " +
        "CONVERT(char(7), h.OrderDate, 120) AS YYYY_MM " +
    "FROM Sales.SalesOrderHeader h " +
    "WHERE h.OrderDate BETWEEN @StartDate AND @EndDate " +
```

```
    "ORDER BY YYYY_MM";
command.CommandText = sql.ToString();

//Assign the StartDate and EndDate parameters
SqlParameter param =
    command.Parameters.Add("@StartDate", SqlDbType.DateTime);
param.Value = StartDate;
param = command.Parameters.Add("@EndDate", SqlDbType.DateTime);
param.Value = EndDate;

//Get the data
SqlDataReader reader = command.ExecuteReader();
```

This code uses the same SqlCommand and SqlDataReader syntax as it would if this were being used for an ADO.NET client. Keep in mind that this code won't work unless the System.Data.SqlClient namespace is included with a using directive. The only difference between this example and a client application is the connection string, which tells SQL Server that this should connect back to the caller's context instead of a remote server. Everything else is the same—the connection is even opened, as if this were a client instead of running within SQL Server's process space.

As a result of this code, the reader object will contain one row for each month in which sales took place within the input date range (that is, the range between the values of the StartDate and EndDate parameters). Looking back at the fully formed pivot query, you can see that the tokens for each month need to go into two identical comma-delimited lists: one in the outer SELECT list and one in the FOR clause. Since these are identical lists, they only need to be built once. The following code handles that:

```
//Get a StringBuilder object
System.Text.StringBuilder yearsMonths = new System.Text.StringBuilder();

//Loop through each row in the reader, adding the value to the StringBuilder
while (reader.Read())
{
    yearsMonths.Append("[" + (string)reader["YYYY_MM"] + "], ");
}

//Close the reader
reader.Close();

//Remove the final comma in the list
yearsMonths.Remove(yearsMonths.Length - 2, 1);
```

A StringBuilder is used in this code instead of a System.string. This makes building the list a bit more efficient. For each row, the value of the YYYY_MM column (the only column in the reader) is enclosed in square brackets, as required by the PIVOT operator. Then a comma and a space are appended to the end of the token. The extra comma after the final token is removed after the loop is done. Finally, SqlDataReader is closed. When working with SqlDataReader, it's a good idea to close it as soon as data retrieval is finished in order to disconnect from the database and save resources.

Now that the comma-delimited list is built, all that's left is to build the cross-tab query and send it back to the caller using the ExecuteAndSend() method. The following code shows how that's done:

```
//Define the cross-tab query
sql =
    "SELECT TerritoryId, " +
            yearsMonths.ToString() +
    "FROM " +
    "(" +
```

```
        "SELECT " +
            "TerritoryId, " +
            "CONVERT(char(7), h.OrderDate, 120) AS YYYY_MM, " +
            "d.LineTotal " +
        "FROM Sales.SalesOrderHeader h " +
        "JOIN Sales.SalesOrderDetail d " +
            "ON h.SalesOrderID = d.SalesOrderID " +
        "WHERE h.OrderDate BETWEEN @StartDate AND @EndDate " +
    ") p " +
    "PIVOT " +
    "( " +
        "SUM (LineTotal) " +
        "FOR YYYY_MM IN " +
        "( " +
            yearsMonths.ToString() +
        ") " +
    ") AS pvt " +
    "ORDER BY TerritoryId";

//Set the CommandText
command.CommandText = sql.ToString();

//Have the caller execute the cross-tab query
SqlContext.Pipe.ExecuteAndSend(command);

//Close the connection
command.Connection.Close();
```

Note that we are using the same command object as we did for building the comma-delimited list of months in which sales took place. This command object already has the StartDate and EndDate parameters set; since the cross-tab query uses the same parameters, the parameters collection doesn't need to be repopulated. Just like when programming in an ADO.NET client, the connection should be closed when the process is finished with it.

At this point, the CLR stored procedure is completely functional as per the three design goals, so it's ready for a test drive.

Testing the Stored Procedure

Visual Studio makes deploying the stored procedure to the test SQL Server quite easy. Just right-click the project name (in this case, SalesCrossTabs) and click Deploy, as shown in Figure 14-8.

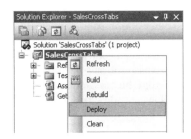

Figure 14-8. *Deploying the assembly to the test server*

Once the procedure is deployed, testing it is simple. Log in to SQL Server Management Studio and execute the following batch of T-SQL:

```
USE AdventureWorks
GO

EXEC GetSalesPerTerritoryByMonth
    @StartDate = '20040501',
    @EndDate = '20040701'
GO
```

If everything is properly compiled and deployed, this should output a result set containing cross-tabulated data for the period between May 1, 2004, and July 1, 2004. Figure 14-9 shows the correct output.

TerritoryId	2004-05	2004-06	2004-07
1	837807.162368	779625.967724	513.140000
2	168740.205705	240725.227509	NULL
3	249727.190221	298101.019968	NULL
4	1007034.715534	993295.830953	248.140000
5	264907.861900	269604.574888	NULL
6	533267.247946	717837.710783	472.150000
7	766232.284720	316740.799297	178.940000
8	407253.815030	349467.104000	149.230000
9	551630.604000	711086.975552	221.730000
10	407520.435480	688354.968664	51.460000

Figure 14-9. *Cross-tabulated sales data for the period between May 1, 2004, and July 1, 2004*

Note that running the stored procedure might result in the following message:

```
Execution of user code in the .NET Framework is disabled. Use
sp_configure "clr enabled" to enable execution of user code in the .NET Framework.
```

If this happens, execute the following batch of T-SQL to turn on CLR integration for the SQL Server:

```
USE AdventureWorks
GO

EXEC sp_configure 'clr enabled', 1
RECONFIGURE
GO
```

Using the sp_configure system stored procedure to enable CLR integration is required before CLR routines can be run in any database. Keep in mind that enabling or disabling CLR integration is a serverwide setting.

Once the stored procedure is running properly, it will appear that the stored procedure works as designed! However, perhaps some deeper testing is warranted to ensure that the procedure really is as robust as it should be. Figure 14-10 shows the output from the following batch of T-SQL:

```
USE AdventureWorks
GO

EXEC GetSalesPerTerritoryByMonth
    @StartDate = '20050501',
    @EndDate = '20050701'
GO
```

```
Msg 50000, Level 16, State 1, Line 1
No data present for the input date range.
Msg 6522, Level 16, State 1, Procedure GetSalesPerTerritoryByMonth, Line 0
A .NET Framework error occurred during execution of user defined routine or aggregate
System.Data.SqlClient.SqlException: No data present for the input date range.
System.Data.SqlClient.SqlException:
    at System.Data.SqlClient.SqlConnection.OnError(SqlException exception, Boolean bre
    at System.Data.SqlClient.SqlInternalConnection.OnError(SqlException exception, Boo
    at System.Data.SqlClient.SqlInternalConnectionSmi.ProcessMessages()
    at System.Data.SqlClient.SqlCommand.RunExecuteNonQuerySmi(Boolean sendToPipe)
    at System.Data.SqlClient.SqlCommand.InternalExecuteNonQuery(DbAsyncResult result,
    at System.Data.SqlClient.SqlCommand.ExecuteToPipe(SmiContext pipeContext)
    at Microsoft.SqlServer.Server.SqlPipe.ExecuteAndSend(SqlCommand command)
    at StoredProcedures.GetSalesPerTerritoryByMonth(SqlDateTime StartDate, SqlDateTime
```

Figure 14-10. *Attempting to cross-tabulate sales data for the period between May 1, 2005, and July 1, 2005*

Debugging the Procedure

What a difference a year makes! Luckily, since this stored procedure is being coded in Visual Studio, the integrated debugging environment can be used to track down the problem. In Solution Explorer, expand the Test Scripts node and double-click Test.sql. This will open a template that can contain T-SQL code to invoke CLR routines for debugging. Paste the following T-SQL into the Stored Procedure section:

```
EXEC GetSalesPerTerritoryByMonth
    @StartDate = '20050501',
    @EndDate = '20050701'
```

Now return to the code for the managed stored procedure and put the cursor on the first line:

```
SqlCommand command = new SqlCommand();
```

Pressing the F9 key will toggle a breakpoint for that line.

Before starting the debug session, open Server Explorer by selecting View ➤ Server Explorer, as shown in Figure 14-11. In Server Explorer, right-click the database connection being used for this project and make sure that both Application Debugging and Allow SQL/CLR Debugging are checked, as shown in Figure 14-12.

■**Caution** Allowing SQL/CLR debugging should not be done on a production SQL Server. During debugging, all managed code running within the SQL Server process will be halted if any breakpoints are hit. This can wreak havoc on a live system that makes use of CLR routines, so make sure to only debug on development systems.

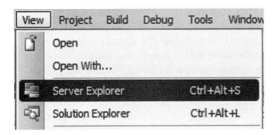

Figure 14-11. *Opening Server Explorer in Visual Studio*

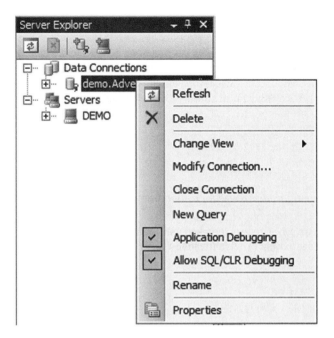

Figure 14-12. *Allowing SQL/CLR debugging for the project's database connection*

Once debugging is enabled, press the F5 key, and Visual Studio will enter debug mode. If all is working as it should, the breakpoint should be hit, and code execution will stop on the first line of the stored procedure.

Use the F10 key to step through the stored procedure one line at a time, using the Locals pane to check the value of all of the variables. Stop stepping through on this line:

```
yearsMonths.Remove(yearsMonths.Length - 2, 1);
```

Look at the value of the yearsMonths variable in the Locals pane—it's empty. No characters can be removed from an empty string!

As it turns out, this stored procedure wasn't coded properly to be able to handle date ranges in which there is no data. This is definitely a big problem, since the output requires a column per each month in the input date range that sales occurred. Without any data, there can be no columns in the output. The stored procedure needs to return an error if no data is present.

Throwing Exceptions in CLR Routines

Any exception that can be thrown from the CLR will bubble up to the SQL Server context if it's not caught within the CLR routine. For instance, the sales cross-tab stored procedure could be made a bit more robust by raising an error if yearsMonths is zero characters long, instead of attempting to remove the comma:

```
if (yearsMonths.Length > 0)
{
    //Remove the final comma in the list
    yearsMonths.Remove(yearsMonths.Length - 2, 1);
}
else
{
```

```
        throw new ApplicationException("No data present for the input date range.");
}
```

Instead of getting a random error from the routine, a well-defined error is now returned—theoretically. In reality, the error isn't so friendly. As shown in Figure 14-13, these errors can get quite muddled. Not only is the error returned as with native T-SQL errors, but the call stack is also included. And although that's useful for debugging, it's overkill for the purpose of a well-defined exception.

```
Msg 6522, Level 16, State 1, Procedure GetSalesPerTerritoryByMonth, Line 0
A .NET Framework error occurred during execution of user defined routine or aggregate 'GetSalesPerTerritoryB
System.ApplicationException: No data present for the input date range.
System.ApplicationException:
   at StoredProcedures.GetSalesPerTerritoryByMonth(SqlDateTime StartDate, SqlDateTime EndDate)
.
```

Figure 14-13. *Standard CLR exceptions aren't formatted well for readability.*

A better option might be to use a native T-SQL error, invoked with the `RAISERROR()` function. A batch can be sent using `SqlPipe.ExecuteAndSend()`, as in the following code fragment:

```
if (yearsMonths.Length > 0)
{
    //Remove the final comma in the list
    yearsMonths.Remove(yearsMonths.Length - 2, 1);
}
else
{
    command.CommandText =
        "RAISERROR('No data present for the input date range.', 16, 1)";
    SqlContext.Pipe.ExecuteAndSend(command);
    return;
}
```

Alas, as shown in Figure 14-14, this produces an even worse output. The T-SQL exception bubbles back into the CLR layer, where a second CLR exception is thrown as a result of the presence of the T-SQL exception.

```
Msg 50000, Level 16, State 1, Line 1
No data present for the input date range.
Msg 6522, Level 16, State 1, Procedure GetSalesPerTerritoryByMonth, Line 0
A .NET Framework error occurred during execution of user defined routine or aggregate 'GetSalesPerTerritoryB
System.Data.SqlServer.SqlException: No data present for the input date range.
System.Data.SqlServer.SqlException:
   at System.Data.SqlServer.Internal.StandardEventSink.HandleErrors()
   at System.Data.SqlServer.Internal.RequestExecutor.HandleExecute(EventTranslator eventTranslator, SqlConne
   at System.Data.SqlServer.Internal.RequestExecutor.ExecuteToPipe(SqlConnection conn, SqlTransaction tran, (
   at System.Data.SqlServer.SqlPipe.Execute(SqlCommand command)
   at StoredProcedures.GetSalesPerTerritoryByMonth(SqlDateTime StartDate, SqlDateTime EndDate)
.
```

Figure 14-14. *RAISERROR alone doesn't improve upon the quality of the exception.*

The solution, as strange as it seems, is to raise the error using `RAISERROR` but catch it so that a second error isn't raised when control is returned to the CLR routine. The following code fragment shows how to accomplish this:

```
if (yearsMonths.Length > 0)
{
    //Remove the final comma in the list
    yearsMonths.Remove(yearsMonths.Length - 2, 1);
}
```

```
else
{
    command.CommandText =
        "RAISERROR('No data present for the input date range.', 16, 1)";
    try
    {
        SqlContext.Pipe.ExecuteAndSend(command);
    }
    catch
    {
        return;
    }
}
```

After catching the exception, the method returns. If it were to continue, more exceptions would be thrown by the PIVOT routine, as no pivot columns could be defined. Figure 14-15 shows the output this produces when run with an invalid date range. It's quite a bit easier to read than the previous exceptions.

```
Msg 50000, Level 16, State 1, Line 1
No data present for the input date range.
```

Figure 14-15. *Catching the exception in the CLR routine after firing a RAISERROR yields the most readable exception message.*

The following is the complete code for the sales cross-tab stored procedure, including handling for invalid date ranges:

```
using System;
using System.Data;
using System.Data.SqlClient;
using System.Data.SqlTypes;
using Microsoft.SqlServer.Server;

public partial class StoredProcedures
{
    [Microsoft.SqlServer.Server.SqlProcedure]
    public static void GetSalesPerTerritoryByMonth( SqlDateTime StartDate,
                                                     SqlDateTime EndDate)
    {
        //Get a SqlCommand object
        SqlCommand command = new SqlCommand();

        //Use the context connection
        command.Connection = new SqlConnection("Context connection=true");
        command.Connection.Open();

        //Define the T-SQL to execute
        string sql =
            "SELECT DISTINCT " +
                "CONVERT(char(7), h.OrderDate, 120) AS YYYY_MM " +
            "FROM Sales.SalesOrderHeader h " +
            "WHERE h.OrderDate BETWEEN @StartDate AND @EndDate " +
            "ORDER BY YYYY_MM";
        command.CommandText = sql.ToString();
```

```
//Assign the StartDate and EndDate parameters
SqlParameter param =
    command.Parameters.Add("@StartDate", SqlDbType.DateTime);
param.Value = StartDate;
param = command.Parameters.Add("@EndDate", SqlDbType.DateTime);
param.Value = EndDate;

//Get the data
SqlDataReader reader = command.ExecuteReader();

//Get a StringBuilder object
System.Text.StringBuilder yearsMonths = new System.Text.StringBuilder();

//Loop through each row in the reader, adding the value to the StringBuilder
while (reader.Read())
{
    yearsMonths.Append("[" + (string)reader["YYYY_MM"] + "], ");
}

//Close the reader
reader.Close();

if (yearsMonths.Length > 0)
{
    //Remove the final comma in the list
    yearsMonths.Remove(yearsMonths.Length - 2, 1);
}
else
{
    command.CommandText =
        "RAISERROR('No data present for the input date range.', 16, 1)";
    try
    {
        SqlContext.Pipe.ExecuteAndSend(command);
    }
    catch
    {
        return;
    }
}

//Define the cross-tab query
sql =
    "SELECT TerritoryId, " +
        yearsMonths.ToString() +
    "FROM " +
    "(" +
        "SELECT " +
            "TerritoryId, " +
            "CONVERT(CHAR(7), h.OrderDate, 120) AS YYYY_MM, " +
            "d.LineTotal " +
        "FROM Sales.SalesOrderHeader h " +
        "JOIN Sales.SalesOrderDetail d " +
            "ON h.SalesOrderID = d.SalesOrderID " +
        "WHERE h.OrderDate BETWEEN @StartDate AND @EndDate " +
    ") p " +
    "PIVOT " +
```

```
            "( " +
                "SUM (LineTotal) " +
                "FOR YYYY_MM IN " +
                "( " +
                    yearsMonths.ToString() +
                ") " +
            ") AS pvt " +
            "ORDER BY TerritoryId";

        //Set the CommandText
        command.CommandText = sql.ToString();

        //Have the caller execute the cross-tab query
        SqlContext.Pipe.ExecuteAndSend(command);

        //Close the connection
        command.Connection.Close();
    }
};
```

Deploying CLR Routines

Once a routine is written, tested, and, if necessary, debugged, it can finally be rolled out to production. The process of doing this is quite simple: the release version of the DLL is copied to the server, and a few T-SQL statements are executed.

In order to produce a release version, change the build option on the Standard toolbar from Debug to Release, as shown in Figure 14-16. Once the configuration is set, click Build from the main toolbar, and then click Build Solution. This will produce a release version of the DLL—a version with no debug symbols—in the [Project Root]\bin\Release folder. So if the root folder for the project is C:\Projects\SalesCrossTabs, the DLL will be in C:\Projects\SalesCrossTabs\bin\Release.

Figure 14-16. *Configuring the project for a release build*

The release version of the DLL can be copied from this location onto any production server in order to deploy it. Only the DLL is required to deploy the CLR routines compiled within it.

The DLL is registered with SQL Server using the CREATE ASSEMBLY statement, which has the following syntax:

```
CREATE ASSEMBLY assembly_name
[ AUTHORIZATION owner_name ]
FROM { <client_assembly_specifier> | <assembly_bits> [,...n] }
[ WITH PERMISSION_SET = { SAFE | EXTERNAL_ACCESS | UNSAFE } ]
[ ; ]
```

The assembly_name represents a user-defined name for the assembly. Generally, it's best to use the name of the project. The AUTHORIZATION clause is optional and allows the DBA to specify a particular owner for the object. The important part of the FROM clause is the client_assembly_specifier, which is the physical path to the DLL file. The assembly_bits option is used for situations in which the DLL has been binary-serialized.

The most important clause of CREATE ASSEMBLY, however, is the optional WITH PERMISSION_SET clause. The DBA is in complete control when it comes to what CLR routines can do. Routines can be assigned to one of three permission sets, each progressively less restrictive.

- SAFE: The default SAFE permission set restricts routines from accessing any external resources, including files, web services, the registry, or networks.

- EXTERNAL_ACCESS: The EXTERNAL_ACCESS permission set opens access to these external resources. This can be useful for situations in which data from the database needs to be merged with data from other sources.

- UNSAFE: The UNSAFE permission set opens access to all CLR libraries. It is recommended that this permission set not be used, as there is potential for destabilization of the SQL Server process space if libraries are misused.

By controlling CLR routine permission, the DBA can keep a close watch on what routines are doing and make sure that none are violating system policies.

Assuming that the SalesCrossTabs DLL was copied to the C:\Assemblies folder on the SQL Server, it could be registered using the following T-SQL:

```
CREATE ASSEMBLY SalesCrossTabs
FROM 'C:\Assemblies\SalesCrossTabs.DLL'
```

Since this assembly doesn't use any external resources, the default permission set doesn't need to be overridden. Keep in mind that if the assembly had already been deployed using Visual Studio, this T-SQL would fail; assembly names must be unique within a database. If there is already an assembly called SalesCrossTabs from a Visual Studio deployment, it can be dropped using the DROP ASSEMBLY statement.

Once CREATE ASSEMBLY has successfully registered the assembly, the physical file is no longer accessed. The assembly is now part of the database in which it's registered.

The next step is to tell SQL Server how to use the procedures, functions, and types in the assembly. This is done using slightly modified versions of the CREATE statements for each of these objects. To register the GetSalesPerTerritoryByMonth stored procedure, the following T-SQL would be used:

```
CREATE PROCEDURE GetSalesPerTerritoryByMonth
    @StartDate DATETIME,
    @EndDate DATETIME
AS
EXTERNAL NAME SalesCrossTabs.StoredProcedures.GetSalesPerTerritoryByMonth
```

The parameter list must match the parameters defined on the CLR method. The EXTERNAL NAME clause requires three parameters, delimited by periods: the user-defined name of the assembly, the name of the class defined in the assembly (in this case, the default StoredProcedures class), and finally the name of the method defined as the stored procedure in the assembly. This clause is case sensitive, so be careful. Changing the case from that defined in the routine will result in an error.

Once the stored procedure is defined in this way, it can be called just like any native T-SQL stored procedure.

Summary

CLR integration allows developers to extend the functionality of SQL Server using safe, well-performing methods. Coding CLR stored procedures is an easy way to improve upon some of the things that T-SQL doesn't do especially well.

In the next chapter, we'll cover the other types of CLR objects available to developers: functions, aggregates, user-defined types, and triggers. We'll also present a more in-depth look into managing routines from a DBA's perspective.

CHAPTER 15

■ ■ ■

Programming Assemblies

In addition to the stored procedures covered in the previous chapter, SQL Server can also host a variety of other types of common language runtime (CLR) routines. These include user-defined datatypes, functions (both scalar and table-valued), aggregates, and triggers. Like CLR stored procedures, each of these types of routines can be built in Visual Studio 2005 or 2008 using C# or Visual Basic .NET (VB. NET). Also like CLR stored procedures, it's important to consider using these routines carefully, as CLR integration is not appropriate for all situations.

For the DBAs of the world, all of this functionality represents a double-edged sword. On one hand, these features provide incredible power to create functionality within the database that could never before have been imagined. On the other hand, there is quite a bit of room for abuse and misuse. This chapter will help you maneuver through the potential minefields and show how to use the features—as well as how not to use them. This chapter covers the following topics:

- *CLR user-defined types*: These allow for special compound type cases, such as point or shape datatypes that can't be modeled naturally using intrinsic scalar types. We present two user-defined type examples in this chapter: a phone number type and an array type.

- *CLR user-defined functions*: These allow developers to easily integrate any functionality provided by .NET libraries, such as data compression or regular expressions. The sample functions in this chapter show how to expose the compression capabilities of the .NET 3.5 base class library, and how to return the elements of the array user-defined type example as a rowset.

- *CLR user-defined aggregates*: These are an especially exciting feature. They allow developers to create custom aggregation functions that can be used in queries with GROUP BY clauses. Hacking with cursors and (non-CLR) user-defined functions is no longer necessary for defining custom aggregations that go beyond the built-in sum, average, minimum, maximum, count, and standard deviation aggregates. In this chapter, we show a "trimmed" mean example that calculates the average value of a column over a set of rows, disregarding the minimum and maximum values of the column.

- *CLR user-defined triggers*: These behave much like Transact-SQL (T-SQL) triggers, but they can leverage the power of the .NET libraries for more flexible operations. The example in this chapter shows how to create a CLR trigger to validate data on insert or update.

Note All of the examples in this chapter rely on Visual Studio 2008's project templates and automated deployment functionality. And while Visual Studio really does assist with creating CLR objects, it is not necessary. Keep in mind that the only things required to create these objects are a text editor and a copy of the .NET Framework. Visual Studio 2008 is only a wrapper over these.

CLR User-Defined Types

Although user-defined types have been available in SQL Server for several years, they were not an especially powerful tool for DBAs and data modelers. T-SQL user-defined types are essentially synonyms for sized type declarations. For instance, you could define a type called ZipCode that maps to a char(5), to be used for representing US five-digit postal codes. Although this can be useful in some cases, it never really caught on as a widely accepted way of defining data. Most DBAs did not bother to use the feature, and since SQL Server 2005 this functionality has been deprecated.

Slated to replace the not-so-powerful T-SQL user-defined types is a new breed of CLR types that can represent virtually any data structure, as described in the sections that follow. These types are not mere wrappers over the intrinsic SQL Server types, as are T-SQL user-defined types. Rather, these types are full-featured class structures, complete with properties and methods. Implementation of these types can and should include such niceties as data verification and string formatting, which were not possible with T-SQL user-defined types.

Applications for User-Defined Types

User-defined types are excellent candidates for representing complex data that SQL Server's intrinsic types don't deal with well. For instance, a user might want to create a type to represent postal codes, instead of using one of SQL Server's character datatypes. A postal code user-defined type could include logic for digesting and normalizing a variety of input string formats for various countries. In the United States, postal codes can be represented using five digits, with the format *XXXXX*, or nine digits, with the format *XXXXX-YYYY*. By defining logic within a postal code type to parse and process any type of input postal code format, we create a single library to deal with postal codes and thus eliminate repetition. To reduce repetition further, a series of properties or methods could be defined on the type for retrieving the postal code in various string formats.

Another application of CLR user-defined types is to extend the flexibility afforded by T-SQL from a software development perspective. For instance, many projects might benefit from an array datatype within SQL Server. In some situations it's required that small, ordered sets of data be passed between stored procedures or user-defined functions. And although developers could use a variety of hacks to achieve functionality similar to arrays in previous versions of SQL Server, starting with SQL Server 2005, developers can leverage the .NET Framework to create an actual array that operates safely and efficiently within SQL Server.

Although the ability to create and use custom datatypes brings great power, developers should avoid the temptation to use SQL Server as a serialized object store. This is conceptually possible—business objects would simply need to be decorated with the correct attributes—but it would drive no real value within the database. Member properties of serialized objects cannot be efficiently queried, so any attempt to use the properties as predicates in queries would destroy server performance. Data represented by user-defined types should be atomic from a query perspective; no individual property of a type should be required in order to filter a row containing an instance of the type.

Adding a User-Defined Type to a SQL Server Project

To start a project for user-defined types in Visual Studio 2008, choose Database, and then select the SQL Server Project template, as shown in Figure 15-1. Set the reference to a development database and click OK to launch the project.

■**Note** Although Visual Studio 2005 contains the SQL Server Project templates, at the time of this writing, Visual Studio 2008 does not come with them. The templates will be available as a separate download or in Service Pack 1 of Visual Studio 2008.

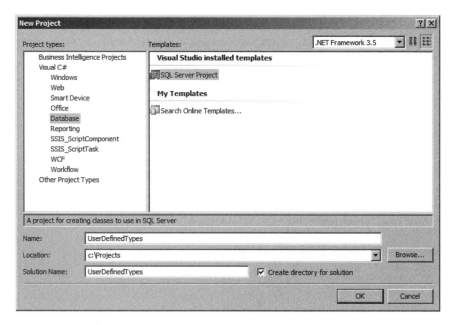

Figure 15-1. *Opening a new project in Visual Studio 2008*

Once the project has been created, right-click the project's name in Solution Explorer, and then select Add ➤ User-Defined Type, as shown in Figure 15-2. The first sample type for this chapter will be called PhoneNumber.

Figure 15-2. *Adding a user-defined type to the project*

Parts of a User-Defined Type

Upon adding a type to a project, Visual Studio 2008 will populate a stubbed version of the type with all of the pieces necessary to begin programming. The following code is the stubbed-out version of the PhoneNumber type as generated by Visual Studio 2008:

```csharp
using System;
using System.Data;
using System.Data.SqlClient;
using System.Data.SqlTypes;
using Microsoft.SqlServer.Server;

[Serializable]
[Microsoft.SqlServer.Server.SqlUserDefinedType(Format.Native)]
public struct PhoneNumber : INullable
{
    public override string ToString()
    {
        // Replace the following code with your code
        return "";
    }

    public bool IsNull
    {
        get
        {
            // Put your code here
            return m_Null;
        }
    }

    public static PhoneNumber Null
    {
        get
        {
            PhoneNumber h = new PhoneNumber();
            h.m_Null = true;
            return h;
        }
    }

    public static PhoneNumber Parse(SqlString s)
    {
        if (s.IsNull)
            return Null;
        PhoneNumber u = new PhoneNumber();
        // Put your code here
        return u;
    }

    // This is a placeholder method
    public string Method1()
    {
        //Insert method code here
        return "Hello";
    }
```

```
    // This is a placeholder static method
    public static SqlString Method2()
    {
        //Insert method code here
        return new SqlString("Hello");
    }

    // This is a placeholder field member
    public int var1;
    // Private member
    private bool m_Null;
}
```

This code is not as complex as it initially looks, and it can be broken down into a few different sections to make analysis easier.

SqlUserDefinedType Attribute

A class or structure will not be treated as a user-defined type unless it is decorated with the SqlUserDefinedType attribute, as shown in the stubbed code. This attribute has a few parameters that define the serialization behavior of the type:

- Format: This is the only required parameter, and it determines the method that will be used for serializing the type (rendering the data as binary so that it can be sent across the network or written to disk). The two choices for this parameter are Native and UserDefined. A value of Native indicates that the CLR should automatically handle the serialization, whereas UserDefined indicates that the serialization is programmed by the developer implementing the IBinarySerialize interface. Native serialization will work only if the type is defined as a structure (as opposed to a class) and all members are value types. As such, there are very few nontrivial uses for native serialization of types. The vast majority of cases will be user defined. The complete list of .NET types eligible for native serialization is as follows: bool, byte, sbyte, short, ushort, int, uint, long, ulong, float, double, SqlByte, SqlInt16, SqlInt32, SqlInt64, SqlDateTime, SqlSingle, SqlDouble, SqlMoney, and SqlBoolean.

- IsByteOrdered: For a type to be a candidate for indexing or comparison operations (equal to, less than, greater than, and so on), SQL Server must have a way of comparing one instance of the type to another instance of the type. This is implemented using *byte ordering*. If a type is byte-ordered, SQL Server will assume that comparing the raw bytes of the serialized instance of the type is equivalent to comparing the instances of the type. This is much faster than the alternative, which entails deserializing and using IComparable or a similar mechanism to compare instances of the type. Possible values for this parameter are true and false, and for a type to be considered for indexing or comparison, the value must be true. The default value is false.

- IsFixedLength: This parameter can be set to true or false. A value of true tells SQL Server that every serialized instance of this type will always be exactly the same size. The default value is false.

- MaxByteSize: This parameter tells SQL Server the maximum size the type can reach. For a fixed-length type, this parameter should indicate the length to which the type will always serialize. For other types, this size should reflect a realistic estimate on the part of the developer. The value for this parameter can be –1 or any integer between 1 and 8,000.

Remember that although a value of 8,000 can work for every non-fixed-length type, this can end up hurting performance. The query optimizer can consider a type's maximum length when determining query plans. Specifying a value of –1 means unlimited (actually the limit is now 2GB, so it's practically unlimited) and is new to SQL Server 2008.

■**Note** In SQL Server 2005, the maximum size was 8,000 bytes, so the only option was to set the MaxByteSize from 1 to 8,000. The default value in SQL Server 2005 is 8,000; in SQL Server 2008 it is unlimited (2GB).

Note that the stubbed type is also decorated with the Serializable attribute. This attribute is also necessary; an instance of a type must be serialized any time it is written to disk or sent across the network.

INullable Interface

A user-defined type must implement the INullable interface. This interface defines the Null and IsNull properties.

The IsNull property returns true if the type is null, in the SQL Server sense of the term (as opposed to the .NET sense of the term). null in C# (Nothing in VB .NET) is used to indicate that a reference type does not reference an object. In SQL Server, NULL means something different; it is a token used for unknown data, as well as uninitialized variables. Although the two are similar, it's important to remember the distinction when working between the two platforms.

The IsNull property is controlled internally in the stubbed type by the value of the m_Null private member, but developers are free to implement this property in any way appropriate to the type being developed.

The Null property returns a freshly instantiated instance of the type. This instance should be initialized such that the IsNull property will return true. The Null property will be used by SQL Server any time a new instance of the type is requested (for example, when a variable is declared of that type). SQL Server will not call new, or an equivalent of new, directly. This means that private member initialization code can be put within the Null property instead of the constructor, if appropriate.

It's important that user-defined types behave similarly to the intrinsic SQL Server datatypes. Therefore, care should be taken to make sure that the Null and IsNull properties behave correctly. Developers should make sure that these properties do not incorrectly identify null instances as non-null or non-null instances as null—doing so could severely damage the type's ability to interact properly with the SQL Server engine. This is mainly controlled within the Parse method. A simple way to handle the situation is to always return Null (that is, the Null property of the type) if the string passed in to Parse is NULL (which you can check using the IsNull property of the SqlString type).

ToString Method

Every user-defined type must override the ToString method (which is inherited from the object class by every type defined in .NET). The rationale for this is flexible client interoperability. Although some client libraries may be able to consume a serialized instance of the type, others will only be able to make sense of the type represented as a string.

It is recommended that developers code the ToString method such that the string returned is compatible with the Parse method, described next. If these two methods are compatible, the string generated by the ToString method can be later passed back to SQL Server if necessary, in order to reinstantiate the type.

Parse Method

The `Parse` method is the exact opposite of the `ToString` method. Instead of producing a string representation of an instance of the type, this method takes a string as input, returning an instance of the type generated based on the string.

`Parse` is quite important in the world of user-defined types, as it will be called any time a type's value is set using the assignment operator (equal sign). Furthermore, *public mutators* (public members or public settable properties) cannot be set on null instances; any instance that is null must first be instantiated using `Parse`.

These concepts are best illustrated using a code example. Assume the presence of a user-defined type called `PhoneNumber` that has a public, settable property called `Number`. A user might attempt to define an instance of the type and set `Number` to a value using the following code:

```
DECLARE @phone PhoneNumber
--Set the number to the Apress business phone line
SET @phone.Number = '5105495930'
```

This code will fail with the following error message:

```
Mutator 'Number' on '@phone' cannot be called on a null value
```

The following code would not result in an error, as it calls `Parse` internally:

```
DECLARE @phone PhoneNumber
--Set the number to the Apress business phone line
SET @phone = '5105495930'
```

Unfortunately, the developer may have actually wanted to set the phone number using the property. That would require first calling `Parse` with a fake value to initialize the type, and then calling the property directly.

```
DECLARE @phone PhoneNumber
--Start with a dummy value
SET @phone = '0000000000'
--Set the number to the Apress business phone line
SET @phone.Number = '5105495930'
```

In most cases, it's probably a good idea to assign the value only using the assignment operator (and, therefore, `Parse`), but in some cases it will be necessary to initialize the type to allow for more straightforward SQL coding. The `StringArray` type shown later in this chapter provides a good example to illustrate that kind of situation.

A Simple Example: The PhoneNumber Type

A common requirement in virtually every business application is storing contact information. This information usually includes, among other things, names, mailing addresses, e-mail addresses, and phone numbers. Unfortunately, problems can sometimes occur due to formatting irregularities. Some people like to write US phone numbers using parentheses and dashes, as in (510) 549-5930. Some prefer to use only dashes, as in 510-549-5930. Others feel that periods look cool and will input the number as 510.549.5930.

It's not difficult to handle these differences in format, but properly dealing with them requires that every stored procedure in the system validate the input. There should be exactly ten numerals in any valid US phone number. And preferably, those phone numbers should be stored in the database in exactly the same string format, such that they can be indexed and uniformly formatted for output purposes.

Instead of handling this validation and formatting in every stored procedure that deals with external phone number data, a CLR type can be defined. If every stored procedure uses this type, there will be no need for duplicate logic; all formatting will be handled by one central piece of code. Likewise, it will be guaranteed that the data is stored on disk in a uniform format, and output can be coded however necessary to meet business needs.

Modifying the Stubbed Code

Using the stubbed version generated by Visual Studio as a basis for defining the type, there is surprisingly little work required to develop a complete prototype. The first step is to clean up a bit and stub out the correct members for the project at hand. The following code shows the result of initial modifications:

```
[Serializable]
[Microsoft.SqlServer.Server.SqlUserDefinedType(Format.UserDefined,
IsByteOrdered=true,
IsFixedLength=false,
MaxByteSize=11)]
public struct PhoneNumber : INullable
{
    public override string ToString()
    {
            return this.number;
    }

    public bool IsNull
    {
        get
        {
            if (this.number == "")
                return true;
            else
                return false;
        }
    }

    public static PhoneNumber Null
    {
        get
        {
            PhoneNumber h = new PhoneNumber();
            h.number = "";
            return h;
        }
    }

    public static PhoneNumber Parse(SqlString s)
    {
        if (s.IsNull)
            return Null;
        PhoneNumber u = new PhoneNumber();

        //Call the Number property for assigning the value
        u.Number = s;
        return u;
    }
```

```
    // Public mutator for the number
    public SqlString Number
    {
        get
        {
            return new SqlString(this.number);
        }
        set
        {
            this.number = (string)value;
        }
    }

    // The phone number
    private string number;
}
```

The various placeholder members have been replaced with a single private member, number. This variable is a string, and it will hold the validated phone number for a given instance of the type. The public property Number has also been added. This property currently directly sets the private member to the input value; some validation logic will have to be added in order to make it workable. Parse also now internally calls the Number property; that way, any validation logic for setting numbers will need to reside in only one place.

The Null and IsNull properties have also been modified to reflect the removal of the private member m_Null. Since US phone numbers must be exactly ten digits long, the validation logic will ensure that any number persisted within the type consists of ten digits. Any other time, number will be empty, and this will represent a null value.

ToString has been modified to simply return the value of number, the member variable that contains the phone number data. Since the return type is System.String instead of SqlString, this method cannot return a SqlString.Null value if the type is null, which would be preferable to make the type behave more similarly to the intrinsic SQL Server datatypes.

Finally, the properties of the SqlUserDefinedType attribute are changed to reflect the code. The format will be UserDefined, since strings are not value types in .NET. The serialization will be byte-ordered, allowing indexing and comparison on the type (see the next section on IBinarySerialize). The type will not be fixed-length, since the empty string (null) case will occupy a single byte in serialized form, whereas properly populated phone numbers will occupy 10 bytes (1 byte per character in the phone number). Since user-defined types occupy 1 byte of overhead, the MaxByteSize parameter is set to 11. Ten bytes are allocated for the member data, and 1 byte is allocated for the type.

IBinarySerialize

If you were to compile the code as listed in Visual Studio, it would compile cleanly. And if you were to manually deploy it (using CREATE ASSEMBLY), the resultant assembly would successfully register with SQL Server. However, CREATE TYPE (and, therefore, the Visual Studio deployment task) would fail with the following error:

```
Type "UserDefinedTypes.PhoneNumber" is marked for user-defined serialization, but
does not implement the "System.Data.Microsoft.SqlServer.Server.IBinarySerialize"
interface.
```

To implement the IBinarySerialize interface, add the name of the interface to the inheritance list in the class or structure declaration.

```
public struct PhoneNumber : INullable, IBinarySerialize
```

Visual Studio 2008 has a convenient feature to assist with implementation of interfaces. Right-click the name of the interface after adding it, and a context menu will appear with an Implement Interface option. Click the suboption of the same name, as shown in Figure 15-3, to populate the type with the stubbed methods to implement the routine. Note that either Implement Interface or Implement Interface Explicitly will work. The latter explicitly prefixes methods and properties with the name of the interface to assist with multiple interface situations; however, this is not an issue with the PhoneNumber type.

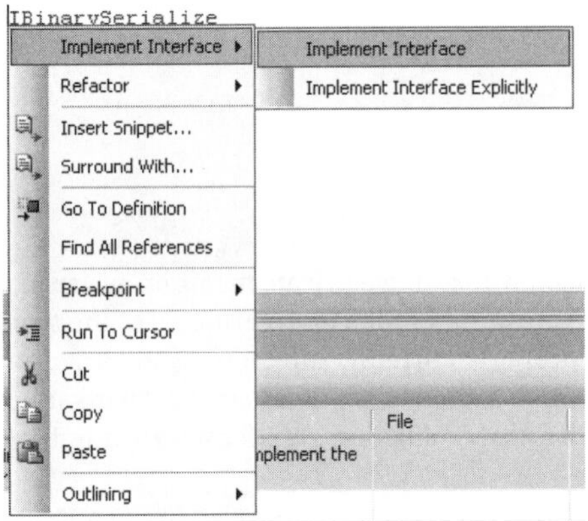

Figure 15-3. *Implementing an interface in the project*

After the interface is implemented, the code for the type will contain a new region similar to the following:

```
#region IBinarySerialize Members

public void Read(System.IO.BinaryReader r)
{
    throw new Exception("The method or operation is not implemented.");
}

public void Write(System.IO.BinaryWriter w)
{
    throw new Exception("The method or operation is not implemented.");
}

#endregion
```

The Read method is responsible for reconstituting an instance of the type from its binary serialized state; the Write method handles the serialization. Although this sounds somewhat complex, the methods of the BinaryReader and BinaryWriter classes are very simple to work with.

The BinaryReader class contains methods that can automatically handle many of the .NET types. These include ReadString, ReadInt16, ReadInt32, and others. Since the PhoneNumber type only deals with a single string (the private member number), the ReadString method alone is sufficient to rebuild an instance of the type from serialized form. The following code is the full representation of the Read method for the type:

```
public void Read(System.IO.BinaryReader r)
{
    this.number = r.ReadString();
}
```

The BinaryWriter class is even simpler than the BinaryReader class, with only a single method that developers will have to concern themselves with in most cases: Write. Several overloads are exposed for this method, such that what it offers is symmetrical to what is offered by the various Read methods of the BinaryReader. In the case of the PhoneNumber type, the overload that takes a string can be used.

```
public void Write(System.IO.BinaryWriter w)
{
    w.Write(number);
}
```

Again, this is all that's necessary for implementing the method. And since the string will be serialized as a simple binary stream, this implementation also produces the byte ordering necessary for indexing and comparison.

Although many types will end up with more complex implementations than these, the basic pattern to keep in mind is that each call to one of the BinaryReader methods should have a corresponding call to Write, and vice versa. If you keep this rule in mind when working with the IBinarySerialize interface, development can be simple and efficient.

Implementing the Validation Logic

The final step in defining the PhoneNumber type is to implement the logic to validate the input. For the sake of this exercise, the logic can be quite simplistic: strip out all nonnumeric characters from the input string. If the resultant string of numerals is exactly ten characters long, it will be considered valid. Otherwise, it will be rejected with an error.

The following code is the completed Number property for the type:

```
// Public mutator for the number
public SqlString Number
{
    get
    {
        return new SqlString(this.number);
    }
    set
    {
        //If null, don't process any further
        if (value == "")
        {
            this.number = "";
            return;
        }

        //Match groups of 1 or more digits
        Regex regex = new Regex("[0-9]*");
        MatchCollection matches = regex.Matches((string)value);

        StringBuilder result = new StringBuilder();

        foreach (Match match in matches)
        {
            result.Append(match.Value);
        }

        if (result.Length == 10)
            this.number = result.ToString();
```

```
        else
            throw new ArgumentException("Phone numbers must be 10 digits.");
    }
}
```

Note that the Regex, Match, and Matches classes are in the System.Text.RegularExpressions namespace, and the StringBuilder class is in the System.Text namespace. Appropriate using declarations need to be added before the classes to facilitate their use.

The complete code for the PhoneNumber type is as follows:

```csharp
using System;
using System.Data;
using System.Data.SqlClient;
using System.Data.SqlTypes;
using Microsoft.SqlServer.Server;
using System.Text;
using System.Text.RegularExpressions;

 [Serializable]
[Microsoft.SqlServer.Server.SqlUserDefinedType(Format.UserDefined,
IsByteOrdered = true,
IsFixedLength = false,
MaxByteSize = 11)]
public struct PhoneNumber : INullable, IBinarySerialize
{
    public override string ToString()
    {
        return this.number;
    }

    public bool IsNull
    {
        get
        {
            if (this.number == "")
                return true;
            else
                return false;
        }
    }

    public static PhoneNumber Null
    {
        get
        {
            PhoneNumber h = new PhoneNumber();
            h.number = "";
            return h;
        }
    }

    public static PhoneNumber Parse(SqlString s)
    {
        if (s.IsNull)
            return Null;
        PhoneNumber u = new PhoneNumber();
```

```csharp
        //Call the Number property for assigning the value
        u.Number = s;
        return u;
    }

    // Public mutator for the number
    public SqlString Number
    {
        get
        {
            return new SqlString(this.number);
        }
        set
        {
            //If null, don't process any further
            if (value == "")
            {
                this.number = "";
                return;
            }

            //Match groups of 1 or more digits
            Regex regex = new Regex("[0-9]*");
            MatchCollection matches = regex.Matches((string)value);

            StringBuilder result = new StringBuilder();

            foreach (Match match in matches)
            {
                result.Append(match.Value);
            }

            if (result.Length == 10)
                this.number = result.ToString();
            else
                throw new ArgumentException("Phone numbers must be 10 digits.");
        }
    }

    // The phone number
    private string number;

    #region IBinarySerialize Members

    public void Read(System.IO.BinaryReader r)
    {
        this.number = r.ReadString();
    }

    public void Write(System.IO.BinaryWriter w)
    {
        w.Write(number);
    }

    #endregion
}
```

Deploying and Testing the Type

Once the type is written, it is ready to deploy and test. The type can be deployed for debugging purposes directly from Visual Studio 2008. Right-click the project name in Solution Explorer and click Deploy, as shown in Figure 15-4.

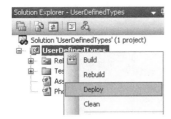

Figure 15-4. *Deploying the user-defined type*

To try out the type, open SQL Server Management Studio and connect to the database that was specified when the project was created. User-defined types, once created, are instantiated using the DECLARE keyword, just like the built-in SQL Server datatypes. Recall the example from earlier in the chapter when we discussed the Parse method.

```
DECLARE @phone PhoneNumber
--Set the number to the Apress business phone line
SET @phone = '510-549-5930'
```

This code creates a variable called @phone of type PhoneNumber. It then sets the value of the variable to the number for the Apress business phone line. Remember that this code is actually calling Parse on a null instance of the type.

To return the string representation of the type (the ten-digit phone number), the ToString method must be called, as in the following code:

```
PRINT @phone.ToString()
```

Another important thing to remember is that methods and properties on user-defined types are case sensitive, even if the server or database isn't. Note that the capitalization of ToString in the example is the same as the capitalization in the type's definition.

Selecting the type without using ToString will return the type in binary serialized form. This form may be usable from a .NET application that has a reference to the assembly in which the type is compiled, but generally speaking, ToString will be a more commonly used way of getting a type's data. Printing the type using the T-SQL PRINT statement is also possible and requires using either ToString or the CONVERT function, to convert the type into NVARCHAR.

Another Example: The StringArray Type

While the PhoneNumber type adequately illustrates the various programming nuances of working with user-defined types, it does not show off much of the power that can be gained from their use.

We'll present here a more interesting example to satisfy a common requirement in SQL Server programming projects: representing data in an array format. This usually falls into the category of a developer needing to pass more than one value into a stored procedure, but arrays can also be used to make the T-SQL language more powerful from a programmatic standpoint. CLR user-defined types dramatically change the landscape such that these hacks are no longer necessary. In this example, the power of a .NET collection (the List class) will be exposed via a CLR user-defined type, resulting in a fully functional array that can be invoked directly from T-SQL.

Wrapping the Functionality of a Generic List

Starting with .NET 2.0, the framework includes support for containers called *generics*, which are strongly typed versions of the object-specific containers available in previous versions of the .NET Framework. Using the List<T> type (which is a generic version of the ArrayList) as a basis, a CLR user-defined type can be built to deal with collections of strings.

Generics allow developers to easily implement type-safe classes, such as collections. Most of the collection types in .NET 1.*x* were collections of objects. Since every type in .NET is derived from the object type, this means that every type can be cast as an object; therefore, every type could benefit from the collections. However, this also meant that a collection could not enforce what kinds of objects it stored. A collection might be incorrectly populated with both integers and strings, for instance. This could lead to exceptions when code meant to deal with integers suddenly encountered strings.

Generics solve this problem by allowing developers to specify a type to be used by a class (or collection) at object-creation time. This allows the CLR to enforce type-safety, allowing the object to use only the specified class. The syntax for this feature is a pair of angle brackets after the type name. For example, the following code creates an instance of List that can only use integers:

```
List<int> myList = new List<int>;
```

Note that when implementing generic classes, a using directive for the System.Collections. Generic namespace should be included at the top of the source file for the class.

The actual string data will be held in a collection of type List<string>. This container will be strongly typed such that it can hold only strings. The following code defines the member:

```
// The actual array
private List<string> arr;
```

Next, the important features that make an array usable should be exposed by properties or methods such that they are accessible from T-SQL. These features include getting a count of strings in the array, adding strings to the array, removing strings from the array, and getting a string at a specific index of the array. The following block of code defines each of those features:

```
public SqlInt32 Count
{
    get
    {
        if (this.IsNull)
            return SqlInt32.Null;
        else
            return (SqlInt32)(this.arr.Count);
    }
}

public SqlString GetAt(int Index)
{
    return (SqlString)(string)(this.arr[Index]);
}

public StringArray AddString(SqlString str)
{
    if (this.IsNull)
        this.arr = new List<string>(1);
        this.arr.Add((string)str);
```

```
                    return (this);
}

public StringArray RemoveAt(int Index)
{
    this.arr.RemoveAt(Index);
    return this;
}
```

By simply wrapping the List<T>'s methods and properties, they are now accessible from T-SQL.

Implementing Parse and ToString

To instantiate an array, a developer will pass in a comma-delimited list of elements. The Parse method will handle the input, splitting up the list in order to populate the array. The ToString method will do the opposite, to return the contents of the array in a comma-delimited format.

The Parse method for the StringArray type uses the Split method of System.String. This method outputs an array of strings by splitting a delimited list. Once the array is produced, the method trims each element of preceding and trailing whitespace and puts any nonempty strings into the arr member variable. The following code implements the Parse method:

```
public static StringArray Parse(SqlString s)
{
    if (s.IsNull)
        return Null;

    StringArray u = new StringArray();

    string[] strings = ((string)s).Split(',');

    for(int i = 0; i < strings.Length; i++)
    {
        strings[i] = strings[i].Trim();
    }

    u.arr = new List<string>(strings.Length);

    foreach (string str in strings)
    {
        if (str != "")
            u.arr.Add(str);
    }

    return u;
}
```

The ToString method does the reverse of Parse, using Join, which has the opposite behavior of Split. An array of strings is input, and a comma-delimited list is output.

```
public override string ToString()
{
    // Replace the following code with your code
    if (this.IsNull)
        return "";
    else
        return String.Join(",", (string[])this.arr.ToArray());
}
```

Defining the SqlUserDefinedType Attribute

Because the private member data for this type will reside in a reference type (List<T>), the format must be user defined.

It doesn't make a lot of sense to compare two arrays for the purpose of sorting. There is no clear way to define how two arrays should sort. Should they sort based on number of elements? Based on the elements themselves? As it is nearly impossible to define how arrays would be sorted—and probably not useful for many development challenges—it also does not make sense to index a column of an array type. Indexes are generally helpful for seeking ordered data, but it is unlikely that a developer would want to perform a seek using an array as a key. For these reasons, there is no need to worry about byte ordering, so IsByteOrdered should be set to false.

And since arrays can contain any number of elements, the type is clearly not of a fixed length, nor does it have a maximum byte size (SQL Server 2008 has a byte limit of 2GB).

The fully populated SqlUserDefinedType attribute for this type is as follows:

```
[Microsoft.SqlServer.Server.SqlUserDefinedType(
    Format.UserDefined,
    IsByteOrdered = false,
    IsFixedLength = false,
    MaxByteSize = 8000)]
```

Implementing IBinarySerialize

Determining how to serialize the data for this type will not be quite as simple as doing so for the PhoneNumber type. Instead of serializing a single piece of data, serialization for this type must deal with an array containing a variable number of elements.

A simple way of dealing with this situation is to first serialize a count of elements in the array, and then loop over and serialize each array element one by one. The only open issue with such a scheme is serialization of null-valued types. This can be easily taken care of using the following code, which serializes –1 as the count if the type is null:

```
if (this.IsNull)
{
    w.Write(-1);
}
```

Non-null types, on the other hand, can be written using the following code, which first serializes the count of items and then each element in the array:

```
w.Write(this.arr.Count);

foreach (string str in this.arr)
{
    w.Write(str);
}
```

Reading back the serialized data involves doing the exact opposite. First, the serialized count of items is read back. If it is –1, there is nothing else to do; the type will already be null. If the count is greater than –1, a loop will run to read each element from the serialized binary. Remember that 0 is also a valid count. Empty arrays are not the same as null arrays.

The entire code for implementing IBinarySerialize for the StringArray type is as follows:

```
#region IBinarySerialize Members

public void Read(System.IO.BinaryReader r)
{
    int count = r.ReadInt32();
```

```
    if (count > -1)
    {
        this.arr = new List<string>(count);

        for (int i = 0; i < count; i++)
        {
            this.arr.Add(r.ReadString());
        }
    }
}

public void Write(System.IO.BinaryWriter w)
{
    if (this.IsNull)
    {
        w.Write(-1);
    }
    else
    {
        w.Write(this.arr.Count);

        foreach (string str in this.arr)
        {
            w.Write(str);
        }
    }
}

#endregion
```

Defining the IsNull and Null Properties

Implementing the INullable interface for the StringArray type is necessary in order to complete development of the type. In keeping with the theme of thinly wrapping the functionality of the .NET List<T> type, the IsNull method can be coded to determine whether the type is NULL based on whether the private member array is null—that is, whether it has been instantiated yet. Due to the fact that the array is not instantiated until data is passed into the Parse method, the Null method can simply call the default constructor and return the instance of the type. The following code implements both of these properties:

```
public bool IsNull
{
    get
    {
        return (this.arr == null);
    }
}

public static StringArray Null
{
    get
    {
        StringArray h = new StringArray();
        return h;
    }
}
```

Complete StringArray Class Sample

The complete code for the StringArray user-defined type is as follows:

```
using System;
using System.Data;
using System.Data.SqlClient;
using System.Data.SqlTypes;
using Microsoft.SqlServer.Server;
using System.Collections.Generic;


[Serializable]
[Microsoft.SqlServer.Server.SqlUserDefinedType(
    Format.UserDefined,
    IsByteOrdered = false,
    IsFixedLength = false,
    MaxByteSize = 8000)]
public struct StringArray : INullable, IBinarySerialize
{
    public override string ToString()
    {
        // Replace the following code with your code
        if (this.IsNull)
            return "";
        else
            return String.Join(",", (string[])this.arr.ToArray());
    }

    public bool IsNull
    {
        get
        {
            return (this.arr == null);
        }
    }

    public static StringArray Null
    {
        get
        {
            StringArray h = new StringArray();
            return h;
        }
    }

    public static StringArray Parse(SqlString s)
    {
        if (s.IsNull)
            return Null;

        StringArray u = new StringArray();

        string[] strings = ((string)s).Split(',');

        for(int i = 0; i < strings.Length; i++)
        {
            strings[i] = strings[i].Trim();
        }
```

```
        u.arr = new List<string>(strings.Length);

        foreach (string str in strings)
        {
            if (str != "")
                u.arr.Add(str);
        }

        return u;
    }

    public SqlInt32 Count
    {
        get
        {
            if (this.IsNull)
                return SqlInt32.Null;
            else
                return (SqlInt32)(this.arr.Count);
        }
    }

    public SqlString GetAt(int Index)
    {
        return (SqlString)(string)(this.arr[Index]);
    }

    public StringArray AddString(SqlString str)
    {
        if (this.IsNull)
            this.arr = new List<string>(1);

        this.arr.Add((string)str);

        return (this);
    }

    public StringArray RemoveAt(int Index)
    {
        this.arr.RemoveAt(Index);
        return this;
    }

    // The actual array
    private List<string> arr;

    #region IBinarySerialize Members

    public void Read(System.IO.BinaryReader r)
    {
        int count = r.ReadInt32();
        if (count > -1)
        {
            this.arr = new List<string>(count);

            for (int i = 0; i < count; i++)
            {
```

```
                    this.arr.Add(r.ReadString());
                }
            }
        }

        public void Write(System.IO.BinaryWriter w)
        {
            if (this.IsNull)
            {
                w.Write(-1);
            }
            else
            {
                w.Write(this.arr.Count);

                foreach (string str in this.arr)
                {
                    w.Write(str);
                }
            }
        }

        #endregion
}
```

Using the StringArray

The StringArray type can be used to solve development problems that might require the full power afforded by a CLR function or stored procedure, but are easier to handle using data structures that are not built into SQL Server. An instance of the StringArray can be initially populated from a comma-delimited list, as in the following code:

```
DECLARE @array StringArray
SET @array = 'a,b,c'
```

As a result of this code, the @array variable contains three elements, which can be retrieved or deleted using the GetAt or RemoveAt methods. An extension to the type might be to add a SetAt method to replace existing values in the array, but we'll leave that as an exercise for interested readers.

Interestingly, the SQL CLR engine only blocks modification of null types via public mutators—public methods that happen to perform modification are allowed. So using the AddString method is an option at any time, whether or not the type is null. The following code will have the same end result as the previous code.

```
DECLARE @array StringArray
SET @array = @array.AddString('a')
SET @array = @array.AddString('b')
SET @array = @array.AddString('c')
```

Managing User-Defined Types

If an assembly has been loaded into the database using CREATE ASSEMBLY, types can be created or dropped without using the Visual Studio deployment task, as assumed in most examples in this chapter.

To manually create a type that is exposed in an assembly, without using the deployment task, use the T-SQL CREATE TYPE statement and specify the name of the assembly and name of the structure or class that defines the type. The following code creates the StringArray type from an assembly called StringArray:

```
CREATE TYPE StringArray
EXTERNAL NAME StringArray.StringArray
```

To drop a type, use DROP TYPE. A type cannot be dropped if it is referenced by a table or function. The following code drops the StringArray type:

```
DROP TYPE StringArray
```

The sys.types catalog view exposes information about both system and user-defined types. To enumerate the data for CLR user-defined types in the database, use the is_assembly_type column:

```
SELECT *
FROM sys.types
WHERE is_assembly_type = 1
```

CLR User-Defined Functions

SQL Server 2000 introduced T-SQL user-defined functions, a feature that has greatly improved the programmability of SQL Server. Scalar user-defined functions allow developers to easily maximize encapsulation and reuse of logic. They return a single, scalar value based on zero or more parameters. These types of functions are useful for defining "black-box" methods; for instance, logic that needs to be used in exactly the same way throughout many stored procedures can be embedded in a scalar function. If the logic ever needs to change, only the function needs to be modified. Table-valued user-defined functions, on the other hand, can be thought of as parameterized views. These functions return a rowset of one or more columns and are useful for situations in which a view can return too much data. Because these functions are parameterized, developers can force users to filter the returned data.

Much like T-SQL user-defined functions, CLR functions come in both scalar and table-valued varieties. *Scalar functions* must return a single value of an intrinsic SQL Server type (an integer or a string). *Table-valued functions*, on the other hand, must return a single, well-defined table. This is in contrast to stored procedures, which can return both an integer value and one or more tables, at the same time. Also unlike stored procedures, functions do not support output parameters.

CLR functions are also similar to T-SQL functions in that data manipulation from within a function is limited. When using the context connection (covered in Chapter 14), data cannot be modified. Connecting via a noncontext connection does allow data modification, but this is not recommended in most scenarios, due to the fact that a scalar function can be called once per row of a table and the data modification could occur on each call, incurring a large performance hit compared to doing a single modification using set-based techniques.

Much like CLR stored procedures, the key to deciding when to use a CLR user-defined function instead of a T-SQL user-defined function is necessity of the power afforded by the .NET base class library. If a T-SQL user-defined function can do the job in question, T-SQL is preferred—most of the time it will deliver better performance and quicker development turnaround. However, for those cases in which additional functionality is required—such as the compression example in this chapter—CLR user-defined functions will prove invaluable.

In this section, we'll look at scalar CLR user-defined functions that enable binary data compression in the database server and table-valued CLR user-defined functions that return rowsets from various sources.

Adding a User-Defined Function to a Visual Studio Project

To add a function to a preexisting SQL Server project in Visual Studio 2008, right-click the project name in Solution Explorer and select Add ➤ User-Defined Function, as shown in Figure 15-5.

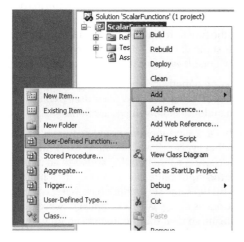

Figure 15-5. *Adding a user-defined function to a SQL Server project*

The Visual Studio 2008 User-Defined Function Template

Adding a user-defined function called NewFunction to a Visual Studio 2008 SQL Server project will produce a template similar to the following:

```
using System;
using System.Data;
using System.Data.SqlClient;
using System.Data.SqlTypes;
using Microsoft.SqlServer.Server;

public partial class UserDefinedFunctions
{
    [Microsoft.SqlServer.Server.SqlFunction]
    public static SqlString NewFunction()
    {
        // Put your code here
        return new SqlString("Hello");
    }
};
```

This template is quite a bit simpler than the user-defined type template shown previously in this chapter. A user-defined function requires nothing more than a public static method decorated with the SqlFunction attribute. The function shown here is a scalar function that returns a SqlString. A few additions are necessary to create a table-valued function. Let's first take a look at the SqlFunction attribute.

The SqlFunction Attribute

The SqlFunction attribute has several parameters, none of which is required:

- DataAccess: This parameter can be set to one of two values of the DataAccessKind enumerator. The possible values are None and Read. A value of None indicates that the function performs no data access, and this is enforced by the SQL Server engine. Attempts to perform data access will be met with an exception. Read indicates that the function is allowed to read data from the context connection (execute a T-SQL query against the database). User-defined functions cannot modify data in the context connection. The default value for this parameter is None.

- FillRowMethodName: This parameter is used to define a method for outputting rows in a table-valued user-defined function. See the section "Defining a Table-Valued User-Defined Function" later in this chapter for information on building table-valued functions.

- IsDeterministic: This parameter indicates whether a scalar function should be treated by the query optimizer as deterministic. This means that every call with the same exact input parameters will yield the same exact output. For instance, a function that adds 1 to an input integer is deterministic; the output will always be the input value plus 1. On the other hand, the GETDATE function is nondeterministic; a call with the same set of input parameters (none; it has no input parameters) can yield different output as time passes. Certain SQL Server features, such as indexed views, depend on determinism, so treat this parameter carefully. The default value is false.

- IsPrecise: This parameter allows the developer to specify whether the function internally rounds or truncates, thereby eliminating precision of the result. Even a function that does not use floating-point numbers as inputs or outputs may be imprecise if floating-point arithmetic is used within the function. Knowing whether the results are precise can help the optimizer when calculating values for indexed views and other features. To be on the safe side, always set this parameter's value to false when working with floating-point computations. The default value for this parameter is false.

- Name: This parameter is used by Visual Studio (and possibly other third-party tools) to override the name that will be used for the user-defined function when deployed. If this parameter is set, the name specified in the parameter will be used. Otherwise, the name of the method decorated with the SqlFunctionAttribute will be used.

- SystemDataAccess: This parameter determines whether the function has access to system data from the context connection. Possible values for this parameter are the two values of the SystemDataAccessKind enumerator: None and Read. If the value is set to None, the function will not be able to access views in the sys schema. The default value is None.

- TableDefinition: This parameter is used to define the output table format for table-valued user-defined functions. Its input is a string-literal column list, defined in terms of SQL Server types and/or user-defined types. This parameter is covered in more detail in the section, "Defining a Table-Valued User-Defined Function" later in this chapter.

Scalar User-Defined Functions

When most developers think of functions, they think of scalar functions, which return exactly one value. The utility of such functions is quite obvious. They can be used to encapsulate complex logic such that it doesn't need to be repeated throughout many queries in the database. By using scalar functions, developers can ensure that changes to logic can be made in a single centralized location, which can be a boon for code maintainability.

A somewhat less obvious use for scalar functions, which is made much more desirable by CLR integration, is to expose library functionality not available natively within SQL Server. Examples include such common libraries as regular expressions, enhanced encryption (beyond what SQL Server offers), and data compression. The CLR exposes a variety of very useful libraries that are now easy to consume for T-SQL programming projects.

Binary Data Compression Using a Scalar User-Defined Function

The .NET Framework 3.5 base class library exposes a namespace called System.IO.Compression, which includes classes for compressing data streams using the GZip and Deflate algorithms. The power of these algorithms can be harnessed for data applications by defining scalar functions to compress and decompress binary data. These functions can be used in document repositories to greatly reduce disk space, and moving compression into the data layer means that applications need only be concerned with the data itself, not its on-disk storage format. However, there is a downside to moving compression from the application into the data tier. Compression is expensive in terms of processor and memory utilization. Before moving compression into production databases, ensure that the servers can handle the additional load, lest performance suffer.

The first step in modifying the function template to handle compression is to add using directives for the IO and Compression namespaces.

```
using System.IO;
using System.IO.Compression;
```

The System.IO namespace is necessary, as it contains the classes that define streams. A MemoryStream will be used as a temporary holder for the bytes to be compressed and decompressed.

To facilitate the compression using the GZip algorithm, the function must create a memory stream using binary data from the SQL Server caller and pass the stream to the specialized GZipStream to get the compressed output. The BinaryCompress function is implemented in the following code:

```
[Microsoft.SqlServer.Server.SqlFunction]
public static SqlBytes BinaryCompress(SqlBytes inputStream)
{
    using (MemoryStream ms = new MemoryStream())
    {
        using (GZipStream x =
            new GZipStream(ms, CompressionMode.Compress, true))
        {
            byte[] inputBytes = (byte[])inputStream.Value;
            x.Write(inputBytes, 0, inputBytes.Length);
        }

        return (new SqlBytes(ms.ToArray()));
    }
}
```

Note that this function uses the SqlBytes type for both input and output. The SqlTypes namespace includes definitions of both the SqlBinary and SqlBytes types, and according to the .NET documentation, these are equivalent. However, the Visual Studio SQL Server Project deployment task treats them differently. SqlBinary is mapped to SQL Server's varbinary(8000) type, whereas SqlBytes is mapped to varbinary(max), which can store 2GB of data per instance. Since this function is intended for compression of large documents to be stored in a SQL Server database, varbinary(max) makes a lot more sense. Limiting the document size to 8,000 bytes would be quite restrictive.

For developers working with character data instead of binary, note that this same situation exists with the SqlString and SqlChars types. The former maps to nvarchar(4000); the latter maps to nvarchar(max). Also note that these are mappings as done by Visual Studio only. In the case of manual deployments, these mappings do not apply—SqlString will behave identically to SqlChars for any size nvarchar, and SqlBinary will be interchangeable with SqlBytes for any size varbinary.

You should also consider the use of the `using` statement within the function. This statement defines a scope for the defined object, at the end of which the `Dispose` method is called on that object, if the type implements `IDisposable`. It is generally considered good practice in .NET development to use the `using` statement when working with types that implement `IDisposable`, such that a call to `Dispose` is guaranteed. This is doubly important when working in the SQL Server-hosted CLR environment, since both the database engine and the CLR will be contending for the same resources. Calling `Dispose` helps the CLR to more quickly clean up the memory consumed by the streams, which can be considerable if a large amount of binary data is passed in.

Decompression using `GZipStream` is very similar to compression, except that two memory streams are used. The following function implements decompression:

```
[Microsoft.SqlServer.Server.SqlFunction]
public static SqlBytes BinaryDecompress(SqlBytes inputBinary)
{
    byte[] inputBytes = (byte[])inputBinary.Value;

    using (MemoryStream memStreamIn = new MemoryStream(inputBytes))
    {
        using (GZipStream s =
            new GZipStream(memStreamIn, CompressionMode.Decompress))
        {
            using (MemoryStream memStreamOut = new MemoryStream())
            {
                for (int num = s.ReadByte(); num != -1; num = s.ReadByte())
                {
                    memStreamOut.WriteByte((byte)num);
                }

                return (new SqlBytes(memStreamOut.ToArray()));
            }
        }
    }
}
```

Using the Compression Routines

The code can now be compiled and deployed using either the Visual Studio deployment task or manually with the T-SQL `CREATE FUNCTION` statement (see the upcoming section titled "Managing CLR User-Defined Functions" for more information). To compress data, simply use the `BinaryCompression` function the same way any T-SQL function would be used. For instance, to get the compressed binary for all of the documents in the `Production.Document` table in the AdventureWorks database, you could use the following T-SQL:

```
SELECT dbo.BinaryCompress(Document)
FROM Production.Document
```

And, of course, the output of the `BinaryCompress` function can be passed to `BinaryDecompress` to get back the original binary.

You should take care to ensure that the data being compressed is data that can be compressed. The nature of the GZip algorithm is such that uncompressable data will actually produce a larger output—the opposite of the goal of compression. For instance, you could use the following query to compare compressed and uncompressed data sizes for documents in the `Production.Document` table:

```
SELECT
    DATALENGTH(Document),
    DATALENGTH(dbo.BinaryCompress(Document))
FROM Production.Document
```

The results of this query show that, on average, compression rates of around 50 percent are seen. That's not bad. But trying the experiment on the photographs in the `Production.ProductPhoto` table has a slightly different outcome. The result of compressing that data show around a 50 percent increase in data size! The following query can be used to test the photograph data:

```
SELECT
    DATALENGTH(LargePhoto),
    DATALENGTH(dbo.BinaryCompress(LargePhoto))
FROM Production.ProductPhoto
```

The lesson to be learned is to always test carefully. Compression can work very well in many cases, but it can incur hidden costs if developers are not aware of its caveats.

Table-Valued User-Defined Functions

User-defined functions, as mentioned previously, come in two varieties: scalar and table-valued. The former must return exactly one value, whereas the latter can return a table of values, with many columns and rows. A table-valued user-defined function can be thought of as a parameterized view: the query logic is encapsulated within the body of the function, and parameters can be passed in to control the output. In addition, a table-valued function can be used anywhere in T-SQL queries that a view can.

CLR user-defined functions are somewhat different from their T-SQL counterparts, in that they have the capability to stream their data to the client (the calling SQL Server process) instead of writing it to a temporary table as multistatement T-SQL user-defined functions do. This can mean, in some cases, that CLR user-defined functions will be able to outperform their T-SQL counterparts. Remember, however, that as with any performance-boosting methodology, you should test both methods in most cases to ensure that you make the best choice.

Defining a Table-Valued User-Defined Function

Creating a table-valued user-defined function involves defining a function that returns an instance of a collection that implements the `IEnumerable` interface. This collection will be enumerated by the query engine, and that enumeration will result in calling a second function for each member of the collection, in order to map its attributes to a series of output parameters that map to the column list for the table.

This process is better described using a concrete example. Assume that you wish to encapsulate the following query in a user-defined function:

```
SELECT Name, GroupName FROM HumanResources.Department
```

This query can be evaluated and used to populate a `DataTable`. Since the `DataTable` class implements `IEnumerable`, it is a valid return type for a table-valued function. The following code defines a method called `GetDepartments` that retrieves and returns the data using a context connection:

```
[Microsoft.SqlServer.Server.SqlFunction(
    DataAccess=DataAccessKind.Read,
    FillRowMethodName="GetNextDepartment",
    TableDefinition="Name nvarchar(50), GroupName nvarchar(50)")]
public static IEnumerable GetDepartments()
{
    using (SqlConnection conn =
        new SqlConnection("context connection=true;"))
    {
        string sql =
            "SELECT Name, GroupName FROM HumanResources.Department";
        conn.Open();
```

```
        SqlCommand comm = new SqlCommand(sql, conn);
        SqlDataAdapter adapter = new SqlDataAdapter(comm);
        DataSet dSet = new DataSet();
        adapter.Fill(dSet);
        return (dSet.Tables[0].Rows);
    }
}
```

Aside from the fact that this method contains no exception-handling logic—and will behave very poorly if the Department table is empty—an important thing to note in this code listing is the SqlFunction attribute. Since the function is reading data from the database using the context connection, the DataAccess parameter is set to DataAccessKind.Read.

But more important, because this is a table-valued function, both the FillRowMethodName and TableDefinition parameters are used. The FillRowMethodName parameter defines the name of the method that will be used to map each member of the IEnumerable collection returned by the method to a column. The column list that the method must support is defined by the TableDefinition parameter.

In this case, the method is called GetNextDepartment. The method must have a single input parameter of type object, followed by an output parameter for each column defined in the TableDefinition parameter. The following code implements the GetNextDepartment method:

```
public static void GetNextDepartment(object row,
    out string name,
    out string groupName)
{
    DataRow theRow = (DataRow)row;
    name = (string)theRow["Name"];
    groupName = (string)theRow["GroupName"];
}
```

When the user-defined function is called, it will return a reference to the DataTable, which implements IEnumerable. The SQL Server engine will call MoveNext (one of the methods defined in the IEnumerator interface, which is required by IEnumerable) on the DataTable for each row of output. Each call to MoveNext will return an instance of a DataRow, which will then be passed to the GetNextDepartment function. Finally, that function will map the data in the row to the proper output parameters, which will become the columns in the output table.

This architecture is extremely flexible in terms of ability to define output columns. If a DataTable or other collection that implements IEnumerable does not exist in the .NET class library to satisfy a given requirement, it is simple to define a type that does. Keep in mind that the output types can be either intrinsic SQL Server types or user-defined types. This added flexibility is a sign of the tight integration provided since SQL Server 2005 for the hosted CLR environment.

The full code for the GetDepartments function follows:

```
using System;
using System.Data;
using System.Data.SqlClient;
using System.Data.SqlTypes;
using Microsoft.SqlServer.Server;
using System.Collections;

public partial class UserDefinedFunctions
{
    [Microsoft.SqlServer.Server.SqlFunction(
        DataAccess=DataAccessKind.Read,
        FillRowMethodName="GetNextDepartment",
        TableDefinition="Name nvarchar(50), GroupName nvarchar(50)")]
```

```
    public static IEnumerable GetDepartments()
    {
        using (SqlConnection conn =
            new SqlConnection("context connection=true;"))
        {
            string sql =
                "SELECT Name, GroupName FROM HumanResources.Department";
            conn.Open();
            SqlCommand comm = new SqlCommand(sql, conn);
            SqlDataAdapter adaptor = new SqlDataAdapter(comm);
            DataSet dSet = new DataSet();
            adaptor.Fill(dSet);
            return (dSet.Tables[0].Rows);
        }
    }

    public static void GetNextDepartment(object row,
        out string name,
        out string groupName)
    {
        DataRow theRow = (DataRow)row;
        name = (string)theRow["Name"];
        groupName = (string)theRow["GroupName"];
    }
};
```

References in CLR Projects: Splitting the StringArray into a Table

An important feature to be aware of when working with SQL Server's CLR integration is that assemblies loaded into SQL Server databases can reference one another. On top of that, not every assembly loaded into the database needs to expose SQL Server routines or types. A developer can, therefore, reference third-party libraries within SQL CLR classes or reference other SQL CLR classes.

To reference a third-party assembly within another assembly to be loaded within a SQL Server database, the third-party assembly must first be loaded using CREATE ASSEMBLY. For instance, assuming an assembly called MyThirdPartyAssembly was in the C:\Assemblies folder, the following code would load it into a SQL Server database:

```
CREATE ASSEMBLY MyThirdPartyAssembly
FROM 'C:\Assemblies\MyThirdPartyAssembly.DLL'
WITH PERMISSION_SET = EXTERNAL_ACCESS
```

Note that the permission set as defined on the assembly will be enforced, even if the referencing assembly is given more permission. Therefore, even if an assembly that references MyThirdPartyAssembly has the UNSAFE permission, any operation that occurs within MyThirdPartyAssembly will be limited to those allowed by EXTERNAL_ACCESS.

When working in Visual Studio 2008, a reference can be added to a SQL Server project only once the assembly to be referenced has been loaded into the database using either CREATE ASSEMBLY or a Visual Studio deployment task. To add a reference to an assembly that has already been loaded, right-click References in Solution Explorer and select Add Reference. A dialog box like the one shown in Figure 15-6 appears. Select the assembly to reference and click OK. Figure 15-6 shows adding a reference to the StringArray assembly defined earlier in this chapter.

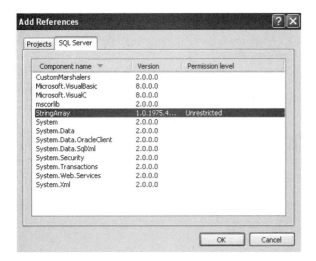

Figure 15-6. *Adding a reference to the StringArray assembly*

Once a reference has been added, the referenced assembly can be treated like any other library. A using directive can be used to alias namespaces, and any public classes, properties, and methods are available.

The following code defines a table-valued user-defined function that takes an instance of the StringArray type as input and outputs a table:

```
using System;
using System.Data;
using System.Data.SqlClient;
using System.Data.SqlTypes;
using Microsoft.SqlServer.Server;
using System.Collections;

public partial class UserDefinedFunctions
{
    [Microsoft.SqlServer.Server.SqlFunction(FillRowMethodName = "GetNextString",
        TableDefinition = "StringCol nvarchar(max)")]
    public static IEnumerable GetTableFromStringArray(StringArray strings)
    {
        string csv = strings.ToString();
        string[] arr = csv.Split(',');
        return arr;
    }

    public static void GetNextString(object row, out string theString)
    {
        theString = (string)row;
    }
};
```

The GetTableFromStringArray method retrieves the comma-delimited list of values from the StringArray using the ToString method. This is then split into an array using the String.Split method. Since all arrays are derived from System.Array, and since that class implements IEnumerable, this collection is valid for a return value without any further manipulation.

Each element of the array is nothing more than a string, so the GetNextString method merely needs to cast the row as a string and set theString appropriately. The result is a table of strings that can be joined to another table, inserted into a table, or returned to a client as a result set.

Note that in a real-world scenario, it might make more sense to define the GetTableFromStringArray method to directly consume a comma-delimited list instead of the StringArray type. This would extend the method beyond the 8,000-character limit imposed by CLR user-defined types and make it slightly more flexible. The example listed here is mainly intended to convey the utility of assembly references, and as such, it may not be the best possible solution in every case.

Managing CLR User-Defined Functions

If an assembly has been loaded into the database using CREATE ASSEMBLY, functions can be created or dropped without using the Visual Studio deployment task.

To create a function that is exposed in an assembly, use CREATE FUNCTION and specify the name of the assembly, the name of the class the function resides on, and the name of the method that defines the function. The following code creates the BinaryCompress type, from an assembly called CompressionRoutines, that contains a class called UserDefinedFunctions:

```
CREATE FUNCTION BinaryCompress(@Input varbinary(max))
RETURNS varbinary(max)
AS
EXTERNAL NAME CompressionRoutines.UserDefinedFunctions.BinaryCompress
```

To drop a function, use DROP FUNCTION. A function cannot be dropped if it is referenced by a constraint or schema-bound view. The following code drops the BinaryCompress function:

```
DROP FUNCTION BinaryCompress
```

Functions can also be altered by using ALTER FUNCTION, which is generally used to modify the input or output datatypes. For instance, you may wish to modify the BinaryCompress function, limiting the input to 1,000 bytes:

```
ALTER FUNCTION BinaryCompress(@Input varbinary(1000))
RETURNS varbinary(MAX)
AS
EXTERNAL NAME CompressionRoutines.UserDefinedFunctions.BinaryCompress
```

Although there is no dedicated view for user-defined functions, they can be enumerated using the sys.objects catalog view. To do so, use the type column and filter on FT for table-valued CLR functions or FS for scalar CLR functions. The following T-SQL will return data about both types:

```
SELECT *
FROM sys.objects
WHERE type in ('FS', 'FT')
```

CLR User-Defined Aggregates

When working with T-SQL, it's often desirable to answer various questions at different levels of granularity. Although it's interesting to know the price of each line item in an order, that information might be more valuable in the form of a total for the entire order. And at the end of the quarter, the sales team might want to know the total for all orders placed during the previous 3 months; or the average total order price; or the total number of visitors to the web site who made a purchase, divided by the total number of visitors, to calculate the percentage of visitors who bought something.

Each of these questions can be easily answered using T-SQL aggregate functions such as SUM, AVG, and COUNT. But there are many questions that are much more difficult to answer with the built-in aggregates. For example, what is the median of the total order prices over the last 90 days? What is the average order price, disregarding the least and most expensive orders? These are examples of questions that are difficult to answer with T-SQL aggregates. For instance, the standard algorithm for finding a median involves sorting and counting the set of values, and then returning the value in the middle of the sorted set. Translated to SQL Server, this would most likely mean using a cursor, walking over the result set to find the count, and then backtracking to get the correct value. And while that is a workable solution for a single group, it is not easy to adapt to multiple groups in the same rowset. Imagine writing that cursor to find the median sales amount for every salesperson, split up by month, for the last year—not a pretty picture.

User-defined aggregates eliminate this problem by giving developers tools to create custom aggregation functions in the .NET language of their choice. These aggregate functions are built to be robust and extensible, with built-in consideration for parallelism and flags that control behavior such that the query optimizer can better integrate the aggregations into query plans. User-defined aggregates can provide powerful support for operations that were previously extremely difficult in SQL Server.

In this section, we'll examine a CLR user-defined aggregate that calculates a "trimmed" mean—an average of a set of numbers minus the smallest and largest input values.

Adding a User-Defined Aggregate to a SQL Server Project

To add a user-defined aggregate to a preexisting SQL Server project in Visual Studio 2008, right-click the project name in Solution Explorer and select Add ➤ Aggregate, as shown in Figure 15-7.

Figure 15-7. *Adding a user-defined aggregate to a SQL Server project*

Once the aggregate has been added to the project, Visual Studio will add template code. The following code is the result of adding an aggregate called TrimmedMean:

```
using System;
using System.Data;
using System.Data.SqlClient;
using System.Data.SqlTypes;
using Microsoft.SqlServer.Server;
```

```
[Serializable]
[Microsoft.SqlServer.Server.SqlUserDefinedAggregate(Format.Native)]
public struct TrimmedMean
{
   public void Init()
   {
      // Put your code here
   }

   public void Accumulate(SqlString Value)
   {
      // Put your code here
   }

   public void Merge(TrimmedMean Group)
   {
      // Put your code here
   }

   public SqlString Terminate()
   {
      // Put your code here
      return new SqlString("");
   }

   // This is a placeholder member field
   private int var1;

}
```

Parts of a User-Defined Aggregate

Programming a user-defined aggregate is in many ways similar to programming user-defined types. Both aggregates and types are represented by classes or structures that are serializable. It is important to understand when dealing with aggregates that the intermediate result will be serialized and deserialized once per row of aggregated data. Therefore, it is imperative for performance that serialization and deserialization be as efficient as possible.

SqlUserDefinedAggregate Attribute

The SqlUserDefinedAggregate attribute, much like the SqlUserDefinedType attribute, functions primarily as a way for developers to control serialization behavior. However, the attribute also exposes parameters that can allow the query optimizer to choose better query plans depending on the data requirements of the aggregate. The parameters exposed by the attribute are as follows:

- Format: The Format of a user-defined aggregate indicates the method of serialization that will be used. The Native option means that the CLR will control serialization automatically, whereas UserDefined indicates that the developer will control serialization by implementing the IBinarySerialize interface. Native serialization is faster than user-defined serialization, but much more limited: it can serialize aggregates only if all member variables are value types, such as integers and bytes. Reference types such as arrays and strings require user-defined serialization. Given the performance implications of serialization and deserialization on a per-row basis, developers should try to avoid using reference types in aggregates whenever possible.

- IsInvariantToDuplicates: The IsInvariantToDuplicates parameter indicates that the aggregate is able to handle duplicate input values. Setting this parameter to true can help the optimizer formulate better query plans when the aggregate is used. An example of an aggregate that is invariant to duplicates is MIN; no matter how many duplicate values are passed in, only one is the minimum. The default value for this parameter is false.

- IsInvariantToNulls: This parameter indicates to the query optimizer whether the aggregate ignores null inputs. Certain query plans might result in extra nulls being passed into the aggregate; if it ignores them, this will not modify the aggregation. An example of an aggregate with this behavior is SQL Server's SUM aggregate, which ignores nulls if at least one non-null value is processed. The default for this parameter is false.

- IsInvariantToOrder: This property is not currently used by the query processor, so its existence is for informational purposes only.

- IsNullIfEmpty: This parameter indicates whether the aggregate will return null for cases in which no values have been accumulated. This can allow the query engine to take a shortcut in certain cases. The default value for this parameter is true.

- MaxByteSize: This parameter, similar to the same parameter on the SqlUserDefinedType attribute, controls how large, in bytes, the aggregate's intermediate data can grow. In SQL Server 2005, the maximum size and default value was 8,000. In SQL Server 2008, you can specify a value of –1, which means the maximum byte size is unlimited (actually the maximum size is 2GB).

- Name: This parameter is optionally used by the Visual Studio deployment task to name the aggregate within the target database differently than the name of the class or structure that defines the aggregate.

Init

The life of an instance of an aggregate begins with a call to Init. Within this method, any private members should be initialized to the correct placeholder values for having processed no rows. There is no guarantee that any data will ever be passed into the aggregate just because Init was called. Care should be taken to ensure that this assumption is never coded into an aggregate. An instance of an aggregate can be reused multiple times for different groups within the result set, so Init should be coded to reset the entire state of the aggregate.

Accumulate

The Accumulate method takes a scalar value as input and appends that value, in the correct way, to the running aggregation. That scalar value is an instance of whatever type is being aggregated. Since these values are coming from the SQL Server engine, they are nullable, and since the method itself has no control over which values are passed in, it must always be coded to properly deal with nulls. Remember that even if the column for the input to the aggregation is defined as NOT NULL, a NULL can result from an OUTER JOIN or a change in project requirements.

Merge

In some cases, query plans can go parallel. This means that two or more operations can occur simultaneously—including aggregation. There is a chance that some aggregation for a given aggregate of a given column will take place in one thread, while the rest will take place in other threads. The Merge method takes an instance of the aggregate as input and must append any intermediate data it contains into its own instance's member data.

Terminate

The final call in an aggregate's life is `Terminate`. This method returns the end result of the aggregation.

Programming the TrimmedMean Aggregate

T-SQL has long included the `AVG` aggregate for calculating the mean value of a set of inputs. This is generally quite useful, but for statistical purposes, it's often desirable to eliminate the greatest and least values from a mean calculation. Unfortunately, doing this in pure T-SQL is quite difficult, especially if the query also includes other aggregates that should not exclude the rows with the greatest and least amounts. This is a classic problem, and it's the kind that CLR user-defined aggregates excel at solving.

To calculate the mean value excluding the maximum and minimum values, the aggregate must keep track of four values:

- A count of the number of values processed so far
- A running sum of all input values
- The minimum value seen so far
- The maximum value seen so far

The final output value can be calculated by subtracting the minimum and maximum values from the running sum, and then dividing that number by the count, minus 2 (to account for the subtracted values). The following private member variables will be used to keep track of these values:

```
private int numValues;
private SqlMoney totalValue;
private SqlMoney minValue;
private SqlMoney maxValue;
```

The `Init` method will prepopulate each of these variables with the appropriate values. `numValues` and `totalValue` will both be initialized to 0, starting the count. `minValue` will be initialized to `SqlMoney.MaxValue`, and `maxValue` to `SqlMoney.MinValue`. This will ease development of comparison logic for the initial values entered into the aggregate. Note that the `SqlMoney` type is used for this example to facilitate taking averages of order data in the AdventureWorks database. Other applications of such an aggregate may require different types. The following code is the implementation of `Init` for this aggregate:

```
public void Init()
{
    this.numValues = 0;
    this.totalValue = 0;
    this.minValue = SqlMoney.MaxValue;
    this.maxValue = SqlMoney.MinValue;
}
```

So that the aggregate behaves similarly to intrinsic SQL Server aggregates like `AVG`, it's important that it ignore nulls. Therefore, the `Accumulate` method should increment the `numValues` variable only if the input is non-null. The following code implements `Accumulate` for this aggregate:

```
public void Accumulate(SqlMoney Value)
{
    if (!Value.IsNull)
    {
        this.numValues++;
        this.totalValue += Value;
        if (Value < this.minValue)
```

```
            this.minValue = Value;
        if (Value > this.maxValue)
            this.maxValue = Value;
    }
}
```

Implementing Merge is very similar to implementing Accumulate, except that the value comes from another instance of the aggregate instead of being passed in from the query engine.

```
public void Merge(TrimmedMean Group)
{
    if (Group.numValues > 0)
    {
        this.numValues += Group.numValues;
        this.totalValue += Group.totalValue;
        if (Group.minValue < this.minValue)
            this.minValue = Group.minValue;
        if (Group.maxValue > this.maxValue)
            this.maxValue = Group.maxValue;
    }
}
```

The final step in coding the aggregate is to define the Terminate method. Since the lowest and highest input values will be ignored, the output will be null if numValues is less than 3; it is impossible to ignore values that don't exist! Aside from that, the algorithm employed is as described previously: divide the total value by the number of values after subtracting the minimum and maximum.

```
public SqlDecimal Terminate()
{
    if (this.numValues < 3)
        return (SqlMoney.Null);
    else
    {
        this.numValues -= 2;
        this.totalValue -= this.minValue;
        this.totalValue -= this.maxValue;
        return (this.totalValue / this.numValues);
    }
}
```

Since the aggregate uses only value types as member variables, native serialization will suffice, and the default SqlUserDefinedAggregate attribute will not need to be modified. The complete code for the aggregate follows:

```
using System;
using System.Data;
using System.Data.SqlClient;
using System.Data.SqlTypes;
using Microsoft.SqlServer.Server;


[Serializable]
[Microsoft.SqlServer.Server.SqlUserDefinedAggregate(Format.Native)]
public struct TrimmedMean
{
    public void Init()
    {
        this.numValues = 0;
        this.totalValue = 0;
```

```
        this.minValue = SqlMoney.MaxValue;
        this.maxValue = SqlMoney.MinValue;
    }

    public void Accumulate(SqlMoney Value)
    {
        if (!Value.IsNull)
        {
            this.numValues++;
            this.totalValue += Value;
            if (Value < this.minValue)
                this.minValue = Value;
            if (Value > this.maxValue)
                this.maxValue = Value;
        }
    }

    public void Merge(TrimmedMean Group)
    {
        if (Group.numValues > 0)
        {
            this.numValues += Group.numValues;
            this.totalValue += Group.totalValue;
            if (Group.minValue < this.minValue)
                this.minValue = Group.minValue;
            if (Group.maxValue > this.maxValue)
                this.maxValue = Group.maxValue;
        }
    }

    public SqlMoney Terminate()
    {
        if (this.numValues < 3)
            return (SqlMoney.Null);
        else
        {
            this.numValues -= 2;
            this.totalValue -= this.minValue;
            this.totalValue -= this.maxValue;
            return (this.totalValue / this.numValues);
        }
    }

    private int numValues;
    private SqlMoney totalValue;
    private SqlMoney minValue;
    private SqlMoney maxValue;
}
```

Using the TrimmedMean Aggregate

Once deployed to the database, user-defined aggregate functions can be used just like built-in aggregates. For instance, to compare the results returned by the T-SQL AVG function to those returned by TrimmedMean for the total order amounts in the AdventureWorks database, you can use the following query:

```
SELECT
    AVG(TotalDue) AS AverageTotal,
    dbo.TrimmedMean(TotalDue) AS TrimmedAverageTotal
FROM Sales.SalesOrderHeader
```

The results of this query show a slightly lower average for the trimmed figure: $4,464.88 instead of $4,471.28 for the normal average.

Managing User-Defined Aggregates

If an assembly has been loaded into the database using CREATE ASSEMBLY, aggregates can be created or dropped without using the Visual Studio deployment task.

To create an aggregate that is exposed in an assembly, use CREATE AGGREGATE and specify the name of the assembly and the name of the structure or class that defines the aggregate. The following code creates the TrimmedMean aggregate from an assembly called Aggregates:

```
CREATE AGGREGATE TrimmedMean
EXTERNAL NAME Aggregates.TrimmedMean
```

To drop an aggregate, use DROP AGGREGATE. The following code drops the TrimmedMean aggregate:

```
DROP AGGREGATE TrimmedMean
```

There is no catalog view dedicated to aggregates, but some data is exposed in the sys.objects view. To get information about user-defined aggregates, filter the type column for the value AF.

```
SELECT *
FROM sys.objects
WHERE type = 'AF'
```

Multiple-Input User-Defined Aggregates

Up until SQL Server 2008, user-defined aggregates could allow only one input parameter, such as AVG(TotalDue) and dbo.TrimmedMean(TotalDue) in the previous examples. Now it is possible to pass more than one parameter through your user-defined aggregate.

To demonstrate, we will work through an example that uses a table called MyValue, defined formally as follows:

```
CREATE TABLE MyValue
(v1      money,
v2       money)
--Let's insert some test values as well
INSERT INTO MyValue VALUES (1,1)
INSERT INTO MyValue VALUES (2,2)
INSERT INTO MyValue VALUES (10,5)
```

We want to create an aggregate that will take the values of both columns and multiply them for each row. It will then perform a sum of the result of these products (*products* with regard to the mathematics definition—not something people buy). Our aggregate would ideally work as follows:

- For the first row, the Accumulate function will return 1 (which is 1×1).

- For the second row, the Accumulate function will return 4 (which is 2×2).

- For the third row, the Accumulate function will return 50 (which is 10×5).

- The Merge function then sums these values and will return a value of 55.

The code for this simple aggregate is as follows:

```
using System;
using System.Data;
using System.Data.SqlClient;
using System.Data.SqlTypes;
using Microsoft.SqlServer.Server;


[Serializable]
[Microsoft.SqlServer.Server.SqlUserDefinedAggregate(Format.Native)]
public struct GetTotal
{
    public void Init()
    {
       this.totalValue = 0;
    }

    public void Accumulate(SqlMoney firstValue,SqlMoney secondValue)
    {

       this.totalValue += firstValue * secondValue;
    }

    public void Merge(GetTotal Group)
    {
       this.totalValue += Group.totalValue;
    }

    public SqlMoney Terminate()
    {
       return totalValue;
    }

    private SqlMoney totalValue;
}
```

Although this example is simple and the same effect could be achieved using other programming concepts, the important point to note here is the ease of passing multiple inputs into your aggregate function. Now let's create our assembly and aggregate in SQL, as follows:

```
CREATE ASSEMBLY MyAggregates
    FROM 'C:\test_code\MyFunction.dll'

CREATE AGGREGATE SUM_ALL(@v1 money,@v2 money)
    RETURNS money
    EXTERNAL NAME MyAggregates.GetSubTotal
```

Now we can issue SELECT dbo.SUM_ALL(v1,v2) FROM MyValue and obtain our expected value.

55.0000

CLR User-Defined Triggers

Triggers are a very useful construct for T-SQL programmers. A routine can be defined that will automatically fire upon attempted data manipulation, thereby putting the onus for the required logic on the database itself, rather than every stored procedure that needs to manipulate it. An example of this would be a trigger used for auditing. By using a trigger, the logic for copying some of the modified data into another table is centralized. Without the trigger, every stored procedure that did anything with the data would need to have its own copy of this logic, and a developer might forget to include it in one stored procedure, thereby destroying continuity of the audit logs.

CLR triggers behave the same way as T-SQL triggers, bringing the same power to the table: centralization and encapsulation of logic. However, CLR triggers can be written in a .NET language and possibly take advantage of resources not easily accessible from T-SQL, such as regular expressions for data validation. CLR triggers can be used to define both DML (such as UPDATE, INSERT, and DELETE) and DDL triggers (such as CREATE TABLE). (See Chapter 13 for a discussion of DDL triggers.)

It's important to remember when working with triggers that speed is of the essence. A trigger fires in the context of the transaction that manipulated the data. Any locks required for that data manipulation are held for the duration of the trigger's lifetime. This means that slow triggers can create blocking problems, which can lead to severe performance and scalability issues. This concern is doubly important when working with the CLR. Triggers are not the place to contact web services, send e-mail, work with the file system, or do other synchronous tasks. Developers who need this functionality should investigate using technologies such as Service Broker, which is discussed in Chapter 9. Remember that if you're using CLR triggers, keep them simple!

Adding a CLR User-Defined Trigger to a SQL Server Project

To add a CLR trigger to an existing SQL Server project in Visual Studio 2008, right-click the project name in Solution Explorer and select Add ➤ Trigger, as shown in Figure 15-8.

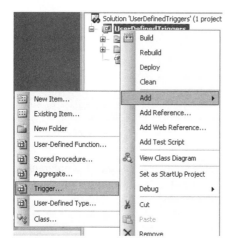

Figure 15-8. *Adding a CLR trigger to a SQL Server project*

Programming CLR Triggers

Once the trigger has been added to the project, Visual Studio will add template code. The following code is the result of adding a trigger called ValidateYear:

```
using System;
using System.Data;
using System.Data.SqlClient;
using Microsoft.SqlServer.Server;


public partial class Triggers
{
    // Enter existing table or view for the target and uncomment the attribute line
    // [Microsoft.SqlServer.Server.SqlTrigger (Name="ValidateYear", ➥
Target="Table1", Event="FOR UPDATE")]
    public static void ValidateYear()
    {
        // Put your code here
    }
}
```

This template is quite simplistic; programming a CLR trigger is very similar to programming a CLR stored procedure. The main differences between the two are the influence of the `SqlTrigger` attribute and the lack of a return value for triggers—the method that defines the trigger must return void. Aside from those differences, most programming paradigms hold true in both types of routines. CLR triggers, like CLR stored procedures, can make use of `SqlPipe` to return as many rowsets or messages to the client as the developer requires. See Chapter 14 for a complete discussion on programming with `SqlPipe`.

SqlTrigger Attribute

The `SqlTrigger` attribute's primary function is to help Visual Studio or other third-party deployment tools determine for which tables and events the trigger is written. The following parameters are available for the attribute:

- `Name`: This parameter indicates the name that should be used to define the trigger in the `CREATE TRIGGER` statement executed when the trigger is deployed. If possible, it's generally a good idea to keep this in sync with the name of the method that defines the trigger.

- `Target`: This parameter can indicate a table name in the case of DML triggers, or a database name, or the `ALL SERVER` keyword in the case of DDL triggers. This indicates the object that, when manipulated, will cause the trigger to fire.

- `Event`: This parameter indicates what event(s) to fire on and, in the case of DML triggers, whether the trigger should fire `AFTER` or `INSTEAD OF` the event in question. Another option is `FOR`, which is equivalent to `AFTER` and is included for symmetry with the T-SQL trigger options. Note that multiple events can appear in the list, delimited by commas.

TriggerContext

The `SqlContext` object exposes information about the state of the trigger via the `TriggerContext`. This object contains properties to assist with determining why the trigger fired. The most important of these are the `TriggerAction` property, which maps to an enumerator by the same name that contains every possible action that can cause a trigger to fire, and the `EventData` property, which contains XML data useful in DDL triggers.

For example, the following code fragment would be used to execute code conditionally based on whether the trigger had fired due to an update:

```
if (SqlContext.TriggerContext.TriggerAction == TriggerAction.Update)
{
    // do something
}
```

Validating a Year Using a CLR Trigger

It should be stressed once again that CLR triggers must be kept simple and quick, just like T-SQL triggers. There are few situations in which a pure CLR trigger is appropriate, given that CLR functions can be called from T-SQL triggers. As such, the example here is shown only for the sake of illustrating how to program a CLR trigger, since it represents something that should be done in a T-SQL trigger in a production environment.

An example in which a trigger (either CLR or T-SQL) can be helpful is enforcement of business rules that don't fit neatly into CHECK constraints. For instance, a DBA might want to define a rule that any new rows inserted into the HumanResources.Department table must be inserted with a ModifiedDate falling in 2005. A constraint checking the ModifiedDate column would preclude any existing rows from having a date falling in that year; a trigger can be set up to operate only on newly inserted rows and is therefore a better way to enforce the rule.

The rules for this trigger will be simple: if any rows are inserted with a ModifiedDate not falling in 2005, the transaction should be rolled back, and an error should be raised. Otherwise, nothing should happen, and the transaction should be allowed to commit.

Getting the number of rows with years other than 2005 will be accomplished the same way it could be in a T-SQL trigger: the rows will be selected from the INSERTED virtual table. Both INSERTED and DELETED are available from within CLR triggers, using the context connection, as follows:

```
SqlConnection conn =
    new SqlConnection("context connection=true");

//Define the query
string sql =
    "SELECT COUNT(*) " +
    "FROM INSERTED " +
    "WHERE YEAR(ModifiedDate) <> 2005";

SqlCommand comm =
    new SqlCommand(sql, conn);

//Open the connection
conn.Open();

//Get the number of bad rows
int numBadRows = (int)comm.ExecuteScalar();
```

If the number of "bad" rows is greater than zero, an error should be raised. Remember from the previous chapter that raising a clean error from the CLR can be tricky: it requires sending a RAISERROR, but wrapping the send in a try/catch block to eliminate a second error bubbling up. Finally, the transaction will be rolled back using the Transaction object. The code to do this follows:

```
if (numBadRows > 0)
{
    //Get the SqlPipe
    SqlPipe pipe = SqlContext.Pipe;
```

```
    //Roll back and raise an error
    comm.CommandText =
        "RAISERROR('Modified Date must fall in 2005', 11, 1)";

    //Send the error
    try
    {
        pipe.ExecuteAndSend(comm);
    }
    catch
    {
        //do nothing
    }

    System.Transactions.Transaction.Current.Rollback();
}
```

Note that to use the System.Transactions namespace, a reference to the assembly must be added. To add the reference, right-click References in Solution Explorer, click Add Reference, and select System.Transactions in the Component Name column.

The complete code for the ValidateYear trigger follows:

```
using System;
using System.Data;
using System.Data.SqlClient;
using Microsoft.SqlServer.Server;

public partial class Triggers
{
    // Enter existing table or view for the target and uncomment the attribute line
    [Microsoft.SqlServer.Server.SqlTrigger (
        Name="ValidateYear",
        Target="HumanResources.Department",
        Event="FOR INSERT")]
    public static void ValidateYear()
    {
        SqlConnection conn =
            new SqlConnection("context connection=true");

        //Define the query
        string sql =
            "SELECT COUNT(*) " +
            "FROM INSERTED " +
            "WHERE YEAR(ModifiedDate) <> 2005";

        SqlCommand comm =
            new SqlCommand(sql, conn);

        //Open the connection
        conn.Open();

        //Get the number of bad rows
        int numBadRows = (int)comm.ExecuteScalar();

        if (numBadRows > 0)
        {
            //Get the SqlPipe
            SqlPipe pipe = SqlContext.Pipe;
```

```
                    //Roll back and raise an error
                    comm.CommandText =
                        "RAISERROR('Modified Date must fall in 2005', 11, 1)";

                    //Send the error
                    try
                    {
                        pipe.ExecuteAndSend(comm);
                    }
                    catch
                    {
                        //do nothing
                    }

                    System.Transactions.Transaction.Current.Rollback();
            }

        //Close the connection
        conn.Close();
    }
}
```

Managing User-Defined Triggers

If an assembly has been loaded into the database using CREATE ASSEMBLY, triggers can be created or dropped without using the Visual Studio deployment task.

To create a trigger that is exposed in an assembly, use CREATE TRIGGER and specify the name of the assembly, the name of the class in which the trigger resides, and the name of the method that defines the trigger. The following code creates the ValidateYear trigger, from an assembly called UserDefinedTriggers, containing a class called Triggers:

```
CREATE TRIGGER ValidateYear
ON HumanResources.Department
FOR INSERT
AS
EXTERNAL NAME UserDefinedTriggers.Triggers.ValidateYear
```

To drop a trigger, use DROP TRIGGER. The following code drops the ValidateYear trigger:

```
DROP TRIGGER ValidateYear
```

The sys.triggers catalog view contains information about both T-SQL and CLR triggers. To get information about CLR triggers, filter the type column for the value TA.

```
SELECT *
FROM sys.triggers
WHERE type = 'TA'
```

Managing Assemblies

Several catalog views are available to assist with management and enumeration of assemblies loaded into the database:

- `sys.assemblies`: This view contains one row for each assembly loaded into the database.

- `sys.assembly_files`: This view contains information about the files associated with each assembly. Generally, this will be only the file that makes up the assembly (the actual DLL). However, the Visual Studio deployment task inserts all of the source files when deploying, so this table can contain many other files per assembly.

- `sys.assembly_modules`: This view contains one row per function, procedure, aggregate, or trigger created from an assembly.

- `sys.assembly_types`: This view contains one row per type created from an assembly.

- `sys.assembly_references`: This view allows developers to determine dependencies among assemblies. When an assembly references another assembly, this view shows the relationship.

Summary

When used prudently, CLR routines make powerful additions to SQL Server's tool set. Functions, aggregates, triggers, and types can each be used in a variety of ways to expand SQL Server and make it a better environment for application development. It's important to remember that some caveats exist and that careful testing is required. That said, SQL Server CLR integration should prove incredibly useful for most software shops.

SQL Server 2008 has built upon the existing functionality provided in SQL Server 2005. SQL Server 2008 adds the ability to use multiple input parameters with user-defined aggregates. It also does away with the 8,000-byte limit on user-defined types and user-defined aggregates. Developers will find these new capabilities and features a big plus when coding against SQL Server 2008.

CHAPTER 16

■■■

SQL Server and XML

$\mathbf{X}$ML is growing in usage every day. Some relational purists will look at XML and shake their heads. However, XML is complementary to relational technologies. In fact, a lot of XML is structured just like relational data. Is that good? Probably not, since the two models are best at their intended data formats: XML for semistructured data, and relational databases for relational data. Plus, the semantics of storing, querying, and modifying XML is what confuses most relational people. As you'll see, the XML query language, XQuery, looks nothing like Transact-SQL (T-SQL). However, you can use the two technologies together to solve your business problems.

In this chapter, we'll start out with the basics of XML and how SQL Server works with XML. In the next chapter, you'll see how SQL Server has evolved to include rich support for XML with the XML datatype and the XQuery language, as well as XML web services.

This chapter covers the following topics:

- An introduction to XML

- An introduction to XPath and the XPath support in SQL Server

- How to use SQLXML to extend the XML support in SQL Server

What Is XML?

For those of you who have been living in a cave for the past ten years and haven't heard the hype surrounding XML, it stands for eXtensible Markup Language. XML allows you to structure your data using a standardized schema. The standardization is the most important part, since that is the power of XML. Any other system can read or write data that adheres to the standard, with the usual caveats that different systems may interpret the data differently sometimes. XML also provides the ability for retrieving certain values from the XML using the XML Path Language (XPath) standard and transforming your XML using XML Stylesheet Language Transformations (XSLT). You'll learn about XPath later in this chapter and XSLT in the next chapter.

One interesting discussion is deciding between XML and relational data. A lot of debate goes back and forth between the value of storing your data in a purely relational model, a hybrid XML/relational model, or a purely XML model. In our opinion, do whatever makes the most sense to the problem you are solving. If your expertise is in relational technology and you are getting great performance from your relational data, there is no need to switch to XML-based storage. You can easily expose your relational data as XML to the outside world, using FOR XML statements, and you can continue to store your data internally as relational data. Don't fall prey to XML's siren song without good reason to move to it. For example, XML is text based, so it is bigger than its binary equivalents. XML is verbose since it isn't normalized like relational data, so you may have repeating sections of the same data in a single XML document. Finally, XML has a different programming model than what a relational programmer is used to using.

Let's start with some basic XML terminology. You'll hear many people refer to *documents*, *elements*, and *attributes*. The easiest way to think about this is that an entire XML structure is the document, the document contains elements, and elements can contain attributes. The sample XML document here contains one document, three elements, and two attributes:

```
<?xml version="1.0"?>
<customer>
  <name id="10">Tom Rizzo</name>
  <state region="Northwest">WA</state>
</customer>
```

XML has schemas and namespaces. You are not required to put schemas on your XML, but schemas and namespaces help to uniquely define what is valid or invalid structure and data in your XML document. In the relational world, we have our table structures and constraints. You can map some of your relational concepts to XML schemas since XML schemas have datatypes and rules that control order, cardinality, and other aspects of the XML document. Schemas allow you to share your XML data with others but still have the other people understand your XML. An XML namespace is a collection of names, identified by a URI reference, that your element types and attribute names use in an XML document. Namespaces allow you to use the same names from different sources and avoid name collisions. For example, you can use the same element called customer from two different sources if you add namespaces that identify the elements as belonging to different namespaces. Schemas and namespaces will be important when we discuss the XML datatype in SQL Server and storing your XML natively in the database.

What Are XPath and the XMLDOM?

Once you have a set of XML documents, you'll obviously want to query them in order to retrieve relevant information. XPath is a query language that enables you to define which parts of an XML document you want to select. XPath has a parser that interprets the syntax, reaches into the XML document, and pulls out the relevant parts. For example, you may want to return all customers who live in New York from an XML document. To do this, you would write an XPath statement.

Since XML is hierarchical, you can use XPath to specify the path or paths to the XML that you want to retrieve. Think of XML as a hierarchy of nodes. The root node is normally the XML document entity. Then a tree structure is created under the root node for all your XML. If we took the XML sample shown in previous section and mapped it to the XML path hierarchy, we would get the tree shown in Figure 16-1—not a very exciting tree, but a tree nonetheless. You can see that all elements, attributes, and text have nodes in the tree. There are seven node types you can access in XPath, including the root, element, attribute, namespace, processing instruction, comment, and text nodes. You'll find yourself working mostly with element, attribute, processing instruction, and text nodes in your XPath.

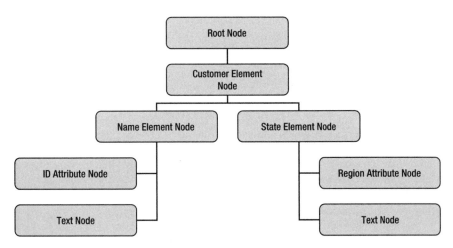

Figure 16-1. *An example of an XML document tree*

You can use XPath to navigate among these different nodes using *XPath axes*. XPath axes describe how to navigate the structure by specifying the starting point and the direction of navigation. There are 13 axes in XPath, but you'll find that you use the child and attribute axes the most. Table 16-1 lists the 13 axes.

Table 16-1. *XPath Axes*

Name	Description
Ancestor	Contains the parent node of the context node and all subsequent parent nodes of that node all the way to the root node.
Ancestor-or-self	Contains the nodes in the ancestor as well as the context node itself all the way up to the root node.
Attribute	Contains the attributes for the context node if the context node is an element node.
Child	Contains the child nodes of the context node.
Descendant	Contains the child, grandchildren, etc., nodes of the context node.
Descendant-or-self	Contains both the context node itself and all the children, grandchildren, etc., of the context node.
Following	Contains all the nodes in the same document as the context node that are after the context node in document order, but doesn't include any descendent, namespace, or attribute nodes.
Following-sibling	Same as the following axis but contains any nodes that have the same parent node as the context node.
Namespace	Contains the namespace nodes of the context node as long as the context node is an element.
Parent	Contains the parent node of the context node. The root node has no parent. This axis is the inverse of the child axis.
Preceding	Same as the following axis but instead of nodes after the context node, it will be nodes before the context node in document order.
Preceding-sibling	Same as the preceding axis except this will contain all nodes with the same parent as the context node.
Self	Contains just the context node.

XPath Syntax

XPath uses a set of expressions to select nodes to be processed. The most common expression that you'll use is the location path expression, which returns back a set of nodes called a *node set*. XPath can use both an unabbreviated and an abbreviated syntax. The following is the unabbreviated syntax for a location path:

```
/axisName::nodeTest[predicate]/axisName::nodeTest[predicate]
```

This begins with the forward slash, which refers to the root node as being the context node. Next is the axis name, followed by a `nodeTest` and an optional predicate. This all can be followed by one or more similar structures to eventually get to the nodes you are interested in retrieving. So, to retrieve all customers, we would use the following unabbreviated XPath syntax. The default axis, if none is provided, is child.

```
/child::root/child::customer
```

Most times, however, you'll use abbreviated syntax. The abbreviated version of the preceding XPath may be `//customer`. The double slash is the descendant-or-self axis. You can also use wildcards in XPath. XPath supports three types of wildcards: `*`, `node( )`, and `@*`. `*` matches any element node regardless of type, except it doesn't return attribute, text, comment, or processing instruction nodes. If you want all nodes returned, use the `node( )` syntax. Finally, the `@*` matches all attribute nodes. Table 16-2 shows common XPath expression abbreviations.

Table 16-2. *XPath Expression Abbreviations*

Name	Description
"default"	If you provide no axis, the default one used is child.
@	Abbreviation for attributes.
//	Shortcut for descendant-or-self.
.	Shortcut for self.
..	Shortcut for parent.
*	Wildcard that allows for any matches of any element node regardless of type, except it doesn't return attribute, text, comment, or processing instruction nodes.
/	Used as a path separator. Also used for an absolute path from the root of the document.

Here are examples of using abbreviated XPath syntax with the `customer` node:

- To return all the child elements of our `customer` node:

  ```
  /customer/*
  ```

- To return all the attributes only:

  ```
  /customer/@*
  ```

- To return only customers with a region equal to Northwest:

  ```
  /customer[@region = "Northwest"]
  ```

You can also use compound location paths by combining a multitude of path statements. In XPath, there is special syntax beyond the root node syntax of a single slash (/). For example, you can specify all descendants using a double slash (//). You can also select the parent node using a double period (..). Finally, you can select the current element using a single period (.). The following XPath sample selects all element nodes under the root node that have an ID of 10:

```
//[@id = "10"]
```

You may also want to access attributes. To select attributes, you use the @ syntax. For example, to select the id attribute, you would use /customer/name/@id. Sometimes you'll want to filter element nodes based on the attributes they possess. For example, if we had some customers with no region attribute on their state element, you could filter out those customers by using /customer/state[@name].

XPath Functions

XPath provides functions so that you can return values or manipulate your XML. XPath includes string, node set, number, and Boolean functions. The following are the most common functions you'll use:

- position(): This function returns the position you specify in the document order. For example, /customer[position() = 2] would return the customer element in position 2. You can abbreviate this function by leaving out the position() = portion. For example, /customer[2] is equivalent to the previous example.

- count(): This function returns the number of nodes in the node set. For example, if you wanted to count the number of customers, you would use /count(customer). Or, if customers had orders in the XML document, you could use /customer/orders/count(order).

- contains(): This function takes two strings and returns true if the second string is contained in the first string. For example, if you wanted to find out whether Tom is contained in a string, you would use /customer/name[contains(.,'Tom')].

- substring(): This function returns part of the string specified. The first parameter is the string, the second is the start position, and the final parameter is the length, such as /customer/name[substring(.,1,3)].

- sum(): This function, as its name suggests, sums numbers together. It takes a node set. For example, to sum all the prices of a set of products, you can use sum(/products/product/price).

- round(): This function rounds to the nearest integer.

The XMLDOM: XML Document Object Model

The XMLDOM is a programming interface for XML documents. With the XMLDOM, a developer can load, create, modify, and delete XML information. The easiest way to understand the XMLDOM is to see it in action. For SQL Server folks, you can think of the XMLDOM like the dataset in terms of being an in-memory representation of your parsed XML document.

When using the XMLDOM, the first thing you need to do is declare an object of the XMLDocument type. The XMLDocument type extends the XMLNode object, which represents a node of any type in an XML document. After declaring your XMLDocument, you need to load or create your XML document. To load the XML document, you can use the load or loadxml methods, as shown here:

```
Imports System.Xml.XmlDocument
Dim oXMLDOM As New System.Xml.XmlDocument

 oXMLDOM.Load("c:\myxml.xml")
 'Or if you already have it as a string
 'oXMLDOM.LoadXml(strXML)
```

Once you have the document loaded, you can traverse the nodes in the document by using an XMLNode object and the ChildNodes property of the DocumentElement. The DocumentElement property returns the XML document, and the ChildNodes property returns the collection of nodes that makes up the document. The following code scrolls through an XML document and outputs the nodes in the document:

```
Dim oXMLNode As System.Xml.XmlNode

Dim strResult As String = ""

For Each oXMLNode In oXMLDOM.DocumentElement.ChildNodes
    strResult += oXMLNode.Name & ": " & _
        oXMLNode.InnerText
Next

MsgBox(strResult)
```

As part of the XMLDOM, you can also get elements by tag name using the GetElementsbyTagName function. For example, if you had an element called customer, you could retrieve its value using this code:

```
MsgBox(oXMLDOM.GetElementsByTagName("customer").Item(0).InnerText)
```

The GetElementsbyTagName returns a node list that you can parse. The code just retrieves the first node in the list, but if you wanted to, you could loop through all the nodes and print them out. The XMLDOM has similar functions, such as GetElementsByID or GetElementsbyName.

To return a node list that corresponds to our earlier XPath statement using the XMLDOM, use the SelectNodes method. This method takes an expression that can be an XSL command or an XPath expression. You can also use the SelectSingleNode method to return just a single node rather than a node list. The code that follows runs a passed-in expression and traverses the returned nodes to print out their value:

```
Dim oNodes As System.Xml.XmlNodeList = oXMLDOM.SelectNodes(txtXPath.Text)
Dim strReturnString as string = ""

Dim oNode As System.Xml.XmlNode
For Each oNode In oNodes
        strReturnString = oNode.OuterXml
Next

Msgbox(strReturnString)
```

The XPathDocument, XPathNavigator, and XPathExpression Classes

While using the XMLDOM for rapid development is OK, if you want a scalable .NET application that uses XPath, you'll use the following classes:

- XPathDocument: This is a high-performance, read-only cache for XML documents with the explicit purpose of parsing and executing XPath queries against that document.

- XPathNavigator: This is a class based on the XPath data model. This class allows you to query over any data store. You can compile frequently used XPath expressions with the XPathNavigator class.

- XPathExpression: This class is a compiled XPath expression that you can execute from your XPathNavigator class.

The following code instantiates an XPathDocument object and loads some XML into it. Then the code creates an XPathNavigator using the CreateNavigator method. This method is also supported in the XMLDocument class. To execute our XPath expression, the code calls the Select method and passes in the expression. As you can see, the expression looks for customers with the name Tom Rizzo and then returns the state for customers matching that value.

```
'Instantiate the XPathDocument class.
Dim oXPathDoc As New System.Xml.XPath.XPathDocument("c:\note.xml")

'Instantiate the XPathNavigator class.
Dim oXPathNav As System.Xml.XPath.XPathNavigator = oXPathDoc.CreateNavigator()

'Instantiate the XPathIterator class.
Dim oXPathNodesIt As System.Xml.XPath.XPathNodeIterator = &
  oXPathNav.Select("//customer/name[. = 'Tom Rizzo']/parent::node()/state")

'Instantiate a string to hold results.
Dim strResult as string = ""

'Use the XPathIterator class to navigate through the generated result set
'and then display the selected Parent Companies.
Do While oXPathNodesIt.MoveNext
    strResult += oXPathNodesIt.Current.Value
Loop

Msgbox(strResult)
```

Getting XML into the Database

Now that you understand a bit about XML and XPath, we can start talking about how you can get XML into SQL Server. There are several different ways to do this. First, you can just dump your XML into a nvarchar column in the database using a simple INSERT statement. Using this technique is just like entering any text into a column. With SQL Server, you can use the XML datatype rather than a text column.

There are three other ways of getting XML into your database:

- Shred your XML into multiple columns and rows in a single database call. To do this, you can use the OPENXML rowset provider. OPENXML provides a rowset view over an XML document and allows you to write T-SQL statements that parse XML.

- Use *updategrams*, which are data structures that can express changes to your data by representing a before-and-after image. SQLXML takes your updategram and generates the necessary SQL commands to apply your changes.

- Use SQLXML's XML BulkLoad provider. Using this provider, you can take a large set of XML data and quickly load it into your SQL Server.

SQLXML is an additional set of technologies that include updategram support, the SQLXML BulkLoad provider, client-side FOR XML support, and SOAP support. For SQL Server 2000, SQLXML 3.0 shipped separately; it doesn't need to run on a server. With SQL Server 2005 and SQL Server 2008, SQLXML 4.0 ships with the product, but it can also be redistributed on its own. Don't confuse SQLXML with the SQL Server XML datatype.

■**Note** Don't confuse SQLXML with the SQL/XML standard, also known as the SQLX standard. SQLX is an ANSI/ISO standard that defines how to make XML data work in relational databases. Microsoft is a member of the working committee for the SQLX standard. SQL Server currently doesn't support the SQLX standard but provides equivalent functionality for the activities covered in the standard. For example, SQLX defines XML publishing, which SQL Server can do using the FOR XML statement. For the XML decomposition, you can use the XML datatype or OPENXML. Plus, there are things that the standard doesn't define that SQL Server implements, such as combining XQuery into relational queries.

Each technique for getting XML into the database has its strengths and weaknesses. If you are just looking for the fastest and highest performance way to get XML data into SQL Server, consider the BulkLoad provider. The BulkLoad provider doesn't attempt to load all your XML into memory, but instead reads your XML data as a stream, interprets it, and loads it into your SQL Server. The BulkLoad provider is a separate component, so you cannot use it inside a stored procedure or user-defined function (UDF). You could use it in an extended stored procedure (XP) by calling out to it, but that is an uncommon scenario and has its own set of issues (XPs are complex, hard to debug, and can open up your server to security issues if written incorrectly).

On the other hand, OPENXML can be used in stored procedures and UDFs, since it ships as part of the native T-SQL language. You'll pay a performance penalty for this integration though. OPENXML requires you to use a stored procedure, sp_xml_preparedocument, to parse the XML for consumption. This stored procedure loads a special version of the MSXML parser called MSXMLSQL to process the XML document and, in turn, loads the entire XML document into memory.

Updategrams are very useful for applications where you want to modify your database and you are OK with building an annotated schema and applying those changes through this annotated schema. SQLXML takes the updategram and translates it to SQL Data Manipulation Language (DML) statements. However, if you need to apply business logic to the SQL DML statements, you'll be unable to use updategrams, since you cannot access the generated DML statements.

Before we get to the details of using these techniques, we need to look at how to configure SQL Server for SOAP.

SQL Server Configuration for SOAP

With SQLXML 3.0, SQL Server 2000 required an Internet Information Services (IIS) server to listen for SQL commands using either URL queries or SOAP calls. The Internet Server Application Programming Interface (ISAPI) listener will parse out the SQL, execute it, and return a result.

Starting with SQL Server 2005, SQL Server can natively listen on a port for HTTP calls, without requiring IIS. Rather than using the IIS configuration utility from SQLXML 3.0, you can use server-side endpoint support. However, if you still want to keep an IIS server in the mid-tier, you'll need to continue to use the SQL ISAPI listener included with SQLXML 3.0 against your SQL Server back end. You can also call SQLXML from your applications, since SQLXML supports a managed object model, as you'll learn later in this chapter in the section "Programming SQLXML from .NET and COM."

As a simple setup for this chapter, we'll create an endpoint so we can send our queries and updategrams to the server. The next chapter covers full web services support.

To configure our server, we'll just issue a CREATE ENDPOINT command and allow our server to listen for T-SQL batches, as follows:

```
CREATE ENDPOINT pubs
  STATE = STARTED
  AS HTTP (
    path='/pubs',
    AUTHENTICATION=(INTEGRATED),
    PORTS = (CLEAR)
  )
  FOR SOAP(
    WSDL = DEFAULT,
    BATCHES=ENABLED
  )
GO
```

This code creates a virtual directory called pubs. Remember that this virtual directory will not show up in IIS's virtual directories. Be careful about this, since you may have an endpoint that tries to use the same port as an existing IIS endpoint. You cannot have both SQL and IIS listen on the same ports.

OPENXML

Rather than needing to parse XML into rows by loading and parsing the XML and then iterating through the XML and generating T-SQL commands, you can use the OPENXML function. The syntax for OPENXML may look difficult at first, but once you try it, you'll see that it is very approachable.

```
OPENXML(idoc int [in],rowpattern nvarchar[in],[flags byte[in]])
[WITH (SchemaDeclaration | TableName)]
```

The first parameter is the integer handle to your XML document. A *handle* is just a unique integer identifier for your document. You can retrieve this using the built-in sp_xml_preparedocument stored procedure. When you pass in your XML document as a parameter, the sp_xml_preparedocument procedure parses it and returns the integer you need to pass to the OPENXML function. The XML document you pass can be text based, or you can pass the new XML datatype starting with SQL Server 2005. You can optionally pass the namespace Uniform Resource Identifier (URI) you want for your XPath expressions. Your usage of this parameter will depend on your usage of namespaces in your XML. If you don't use any namespaces, you won't use this parameter in most of your calls to the stored procedure.

Conversely, the sp_xml_removedocument built-in procedure takes the integer handle to your XML document and removes the internal in-memory representation of your XML document that you created with sp_xml_preparedocument. You should call this stored procedure after you are finished with your XML document. If you forget, SQL Server will destroy the in-memory representation once the session that created it disconnects. However, it isn't good practice to rely on this behavior.

The second parameter to OPENXML is the XPath expression that you want to use to parse out the rows. This expression can be as simple or complex as you require.

The third parameter is optional and allows you to switch from attribute- to element-centric mapping. By default, OPENXML uses attribute-centric mapping, which is a value of 0. You'll want to switch this to element-centric mapping if your XML is element-centric by specifying a value of 2. By passing a value of 1, you are telling SQL Server to use attribute-centric mapping by default, and for any unprocessed columns, element-centric mapping is used. A value of 8 specifies to not copy overflow text to the @mp:xmltext metaproperty (see Table 16-3).

Finally, we have the WITH clause. This clause allows you to specify a schema definition for your newly created rowsets, or you can specify a table if you know your XML will map to the schema in a table that already exists. The schema definition uses this format:

```
ColName ColType [ColPattern | Metaproperty][, ColName ColType
[ColPattern | Metaproperty]...]
```

where:

- *ColName*: The name of the column in the table.

- *ColType*: The SQL datatype you want for the column. If the XML type and the SQL type differ, coercion occurs, which means that SQL Server will try to find the closest native type that can store your data.

- *ColPattern*: An XPath expression that tells OPENXML how to map the XML value to your SQL column. For example, you may want to explicitly tell OPENXML to use a particular attribute or element of the parent node for a certain column value. If you don't specify the column pattern, the default mapping you specified, attribute or element, will be used.

- *Metaproperty*: The metaproperty attribute that you want to put into the column. *Metaproperty* attributes in an XML document are attributes that describe the properties of an XML item (element, attribute, or any other DOM node). These attributes don't physically exist in the XML document text; however, OPENXML provides these metaproperties for all the XML items.

The metaproperties allow you to extract information, such as local positioning and namespace information of XML nodes, which provide more details than are visible in the textual representation. You can map these metaproperties to the rowset columns in an OPENXML statement using the ColPattern parameter. Table 16-3 shows the different values for the metaproperty attribute.

Table 16-3. *Metaproperty Values*

Name	Description
@mp:id	A unique identifier for the DOM node, which is valid as long as the document isn't reparsed.
@mp:localname	The local part of the name of a node. You could put this into a column if you need to get the node name at a later point.
@mp:namespaceuri	Returns the namespace URI of the current element.
@mp:prefix	Returns the namespace prefix of the current element.
@mp:prev	Returns the previous sibling's node ID.
@mp:xmltext	Returns a text version of the XML. This is useful for overflow processing or for handling unknown situations in your database code. For example, if the XML changes, you don't need to change your database code to handle the change if you use this metaproperty as an overflow.
@mp:parentid	Returns the ID of the parent node.
@mp:parentlocalname	Returns the local name of the parent node.
@mp:parentnamespaceuri	Returns the namespace URI of the parent.
@mp:parentprefix	Returns the parent prefix.

Let's now take a look at a couple of examples that use the OPENXML function. The XML document that we will be using is quite simple:

```
<ROOT>
  <authors>
    <au_id>172-32-1176</au_id>
    <au_lname>White</au_lname>
    <au_fname>Johnson</au_fname>
    <phone>408 496-7223</phone>
    <address>10932 Bigge Rd.</address>
    <city>Menlo Park</city>
    <state>CA</state>
    <zip>94025</zip>
    <contract>1</contract>
  </authors>
  <authors>
    <au_id>213-46-8915</au_id>
    <au_lname>Green</au_lname>
    <au_fname>Marjorie</au_fname>
    <phone>415 986-7020</phone>
    <address>309 63rd St. #411</address>
    <city>Oakland</city>
    <state>CA</state>
    <zip>94618</zip>
    <contract>1</contract>
  </authors>
</ROOT>. . .
```

■**Note** You may notice our dirty little trick in the XML. No one likes to generate sample XML data so we just used the FOR XML function, which we'll discuss shortly, on the authors table in the pubs database. The only change we made, since we're more element than attribute people, was to have FOR XML spit out our data using element-centric formatting.

First, let's just take our XML document and store it in a relational table. Since we're using pubs already, we'll take the data and store it in a new authorsXML table in pubs. We'll simply accept the defaults and not fill in any optional parameters for the OPENXML function. The code will take our XML document using element-centric mapping, parse the document, and place it into the authorsXML table.

```
CREATE TABLE [authorsXML] (
    [title] [varchar] (20),
    [au_id] [varchar] (11)
) ON [PRIMARY]
GO
DECLARE @idoc int
DECLARE @doc varchar(1000)
SET @doc ='
<ROOT>
  <authors><au_id>172-32-1176</au_id><au_lname>White</au_lname>
<au_fname>Johnson</au_fname><title>book1</title>
<phone>408 496-7223</phone><address>10932 Bigge Rd.</address>
<city>Menlo Park</city><state>CA</state><zip>94025</zip>
<contract>1</contract></authors>
  <authors><au_id>213-46-8915</au_id><au_lname>Green</au_lname>
```

```
<au_fname>Marjorie</au_fname><title>book2</title>
<phone>415 986-7020</phone><address>309 63rd St.
#411</address><city>Oakland</city><state>CA</state>
<zip>94618</zip>
<contract>1</contract></authors>
</ROOT>'
--Create an internal representation of the XML document.
EXEC sp_xml_preparedocument @idoc OUTPUT, @doc
-- Execute a SELECT statement that uses the OPENXML rowset provider.
INSERT AuthorsXML (title, au_id)
SELECT    title, au_id
FROM      OPENXML (@idoc, '/ROOT/authors',2)
            WITH (au_id    varchar(11),
                  au_lname varchar(40),
                  au_fname varchar(20),
                  title varchar(20),
                  phone    char(12)
                )
```

```
EXEC sp_xml_removedocument @idoc
```

If we tweaked the preceding statement and removed the INSERT and instead just did a SELECT on our data, such as SELECT *, SQL Server would return our parsed XML as a rowset. The results would look as follows:

au_id	au_lname	au_fname	phone
172-32-1176	White	Johnson	408 496-7223
213-46-8915	Green	Marjorie	415 986-7020

Now, you may realize that we're not storing some of the XML, such as the address, city, state, ZIP code, and contract values. If we wanted to, we could capture the XML document by creating another column and using the @mp:xmltext command in our schema definition, like this:

```
catchall nvarchar(1000) '@mp:xmltext'
```

The next example shows how to navigate an XML document using an XPath expression in OPENXML. Since OPENXML returns a relational rowset, you could actually join the results with another table and then store this rowset in your table. After calling OPENXML, your XML data can be treated just like any other relational data. Here, we'll use the returned XML rowsets to join data with the publishers table to return only authors who have the same city as a publisher.

```
DECLARE @idoc int
DECLARE @doc varchar(1000)
SET @doc ='
<ROOT>
  <authors><au_id>172-32-1176</au_id><au_lname>White</au_lname>
<au_fname>Johnson</au_fname>
<phone>408 496-7223</phone><address>10932 Bigge Rd.</address>
<city>Menlo Park</city><state>CA</state><zip>94025</zip>
<contract>1</contract>
    <books>
      <title>My book1</title>
      <title>My book2</title>
    </books>
  </authors>
```

```
     <authors><au_id>213-46-8915</au_id><au_lname>Green</au_lname>
<au_fname>Marjorie</au_fname>
<phone>415 986-7020</phone><address>309 63rd St. #411</address>
<city>Boston</city><state>MA</state>
<zip>94618</zip><contract>1</contract>
     <books>
        <title>My book3</title>
        <title>My book4</title>
     </books>
   </authors>
</ROOT>'
--Create an internal representation of the XML document.
EXEC sp_xml_preparedocument @idoc OUTPUT, @doc

SELECT    a.title, a.au_lname, p.pub_name, p.city
FROM      OPENXML (@idoc, '/ROOT/authors/books',2)
          WITH (title    varchar(20) './title',
                au_id    varchar(11) '../au_id',
                au_lname varchar(40) '../au_lname',
                au_fname varchar(20) '../au_fname',
                phone    char(12)    '../phone',
                city varchar(20) '../city'
               ) AS a
INNER JOIN publishers AS p
   ON a.city = p.city
EXEC sp_xml_removedocument @idoc
```

The results should look as follows:

title	_ au_lname	pub_name	city
My Book3	Green	New Moon Books	Boston

The best way to use OPENXML is in a stored procedure, especially if you are taking your XML from the mid-tier and putting it into the database. Rather than parsing in the mid-tier, you can send your XML as text to the stored procedure and have the server parse and store it in a single operation. This provides a lot better performance and a lot less network traffic than parsing the XML in the mid-tier and sending T-SQL commands to the server to store the data.

If you are going to use your newly parsed XML over and over again, then rather than calling OPENXML multiple times, just store the results in a table variable. This will speed up the processing and free resources on the server for other work. The sample stored procedure that follows implements OPENXML. Notice the use of the new nvarchar(max) datatype. In SQL Server 2000, you would have to use a text datatype. For all new development, use the nvarchar(max) datatype, since the text datatype may be removed in future versions.

```
CREATE PROCEDURE update_authors_OPENXML (
    @doc nvarchar(max))

AS
SET NOCOUNT ON
-- document handle:
DECLARE @idoc INT

--Create an internal representation of the XML document.
EXEC sp_xml_preparedocument @idoc OUTPUT, @doc
-- Execute a SELECT statement that uses the OPENXML rowset provider.
```

```
INSERT AuthorsXML (title, au_id)
SELECT    title, au_id
FROM      OPENXML (@idoc, '/ROOT/authors/books',2)
          WITH (title     varchar(20) './title',
                au_id     varchar(11) '../au_id',
                au_lname varchar(40) '../au_lname',
                au_fname varchar(20) '../au_fname',
                phone    char(12)    '../phone'
               )

--Execute SPROC

EXEC update_authors_OPENXML '
<ROOT>
  <authors><au_id>172-32-1176</au_id><au_lname>White</au_lname>
<au_fname>Johnson</au_fname><phone>408 496-7223</phone>
<address>10932 Bigge Rd.</address><city>Menlo
Park</city><state>CA</state><zip>94025</zip><contract>1</contract>
    <books>
      <title>My book1</title>
      <title>My book2</title>
    </books>
  </authors>
  <authors><au_id>213-46-8915</au_id><au_lname>Green</au_lname>
<au_fname>Marjorie</au_fname><phone>415 986-7020</phone>
<address>309 63rd St. #411</address><city>Oakland</city><state>CA</state>
<zip>94618</zip><contract>1</contract>
    <books>
      <title>My book3</title>
      <title>My book4</title>
    </books>
  </authors>
</ROOT>'
```

XML Views Using Annotated XML Schemas

XML Schemas define the structure of an XML document, in the same way that a relational schema defines the structure of a relational database. With schemas, you can define what makes an XML document legal according to your specifications. For example, you can define the elements, attributes, hierarchy of elements, order of elements, datatypes of your elements and attributes, and any default values for your elements and attributes. Schemas are not required in your XML documents but are recommended, especially if you'll be sharing your XML data with other applications that may not understand your XML data or how to correctly create that XML data without understanding your schema. The standard for schemas is XML Schema Definition (XSD).

With SQL Server, you can create an XML Schema that maps to your relational structure using some special schema markup. This is useful when you want to create an XML view of your underlying relational data. This view not only allows you to query your relational data into XML, but you can also persist changes using updategrams and SQLXML bulk-loading. It takes some work to create the annotated schema, but if you are going to be working extensively with XML, the extra work is worth the effort. Plus, you'll want to use annotated schemas with updategrams, which you'll learn about in the section "SQLXML Updategrams" later in this chapter.

■**Note** This chapter will assume you have some knowledge of XML Schemas. If you don't, you should read the W3C primer on XML schemas at http://www.w3.org/TR/xmlschema-0/.

Visual Studio includes a very capable XML Schema editor so that you don't need to generate XML Schemas by hand. Following is a typical XML Schema for the authors XML that we were using previously. As you can see, the XML Schema is an XML document. The system knows it is a schema document because we declare a namespace, xs, that uses the XSD namespace. This namespace is a reference to the World Wide Web Consortium (W3C) XSD namespace, which is http://www.w3.org/2001/XMLSchema. This reference is aliased to xs and then all elements use this alias as their prefix inside of the schema.

Also, notice how the schema declares an element called AuthorsXMLNew, which contains the rest of your XML data. Then there is a complex type that declares a sequence of XML elements. These elements include the ID, first name, last name, phone, and so on, of the authors. Notice how the elements also declare a type. Schemas can define datatypes for your elements and attributes. We declare some strings, an unsigned int, and an unsigned byte. You can declare other datatypes beyond what this schema has, such as dates, Booleans, binary, and other types.

```
<?xml version="1.0" encoding="utf-8"?>
<xs:schema attributeFormDefault="unqualified"
elementFormDefault="qualified"
xmlns:xs="http://www.w3.org/2001/XMLSchema">
  <xs:element name="AuthorsXMLNew">
    <xs:complexType>
      <xs:sequence>
        <xs:element name="au_id" type="xs:string" />
        <xs:element name="au_lname" type="xs:string" />
        <xs:element name="au_fname" type="xs:string" />
        <xs:element name="phone" type="xs:string" />
        <xs:element name="address" type="xs:string" />
        <xs:element name="city" type="xs:string" />
        <xs:element name="state" type="xs:string" />
        <xs:element name="zip" type="xs:unsignedInt" />
        <xs:element name="contract" type="xs:unsignedByte" />
      </xs:sequence>
    </xs:complexType>
  </xs:element>
</xs:schema>
```

Now that we have a base schema, if we want to use this annotated schema with SQLXML, we need to make some changes. First, we need to add a reference to the XML Schema mapping. To do this, we need to modify our XML Schema by first adding the namespace for SQL Server's schema mapping, which is urn:schemas-microsoft-com:mapping-schema. This schema allows us to map our XML Schema to our relational database schema. We'll alias this namespace with sql so that we can use the prefix sql: when we refer to it. Therefore, if we wanted to modify the preceding schema to support SQL Server mapping, we would use this new schema:

```
<?xml version="1.0" encoding="utf-8" ?>
<xs:schema id="XMLSchema1" targetNamespace="http://tempuri.org/XMLSchema1.xsd"
  elementFormDefault="qualified"
  xmlns="http://tempuri.org/XMLSchema1.xsd"
  xmlns:mstns="http://tempuri.org/XMLSchema1.xsd"
  xmlns:xs="http://www.w3.org/2001/XMLSchema"
  xmlns:sql="urn:schemas-microsoft-com:mapping-schema">
...
```

You'll also see the use of the `urn:schemas-microsoft-com:xml-sql` namespace in documents. This namespace provides access to SQLXML functionality that can be used in templates or XPath queries.

Default and Explicit Mapping

You may notice that the preceding schema just adds the namespace for the mapping. The schema isn't listed since SQL Server supports default mapping between your relational schema and your XML Schema. For example, the `authors` complex type would be automatically mapped to the `authors` table. The `au_id` string would automatically map to the `au_id` column, and so on.

You can also explicitly map between your schema and your SQL datatypes. For very simple applications, you can use the default mapping. In most cases, you'll use explicit mapping since your XML and relational schemas may be different or you'll want more control over how the mapping is performed or the datatypes are used. You use the `sql:relation` markup, which is part of the SQLXML mapping schema, to specify a mapping between an XML item and a SQL Server table. For columns, you use the `sql:field` markup. You can also include a `sql:datatype` to explicitly map your XML datatype to a SQL Server datatype so that implicit conversion doesn't happen. Therefore, if we were to add these markups rather than using the default mapping for our schema, our schema would change to look like the following code:

```
<?xml version="1.0" encoding="utf-8"?>
<xs:schema attributeFormDefault="unqualified"
elementFormDefault="qualified"
xmlns:xs="http://www.w3.org/2001/XMLSchema"
xmlns:sql="urn:schemas-microsoft-com:mapping-schema">
  <xs:element name="AuthorsXMLNew" sql:relation="AuthorsXMLNew">
    <xs:complexType>
      <xs:sequence>
        <xs:element name="au_id" type="xs:string" sql:field="au_id" />
        <xs:element name="au_lname" type="xs:string" sql:field="au_lname" />
        <xs:element name="au_fname" type="xs:string" sql:field="au_fname" />
        <xs:element name="phone" type="xs:string" sql:field="phone" />
        <xs:element name="address" type="xs:string" sql:field="address" />
        <xs:element name="city" type="xs:string" sql:field="city" />
        <xs:element name="state" type="xs:string" sql:field="state" />
        <xs:element name="zip" type="xs:unsignedInt" sql:field="zip" />
        <xs:element name="contract" type="xs:unsignedByte"
                sql:field="contract" sql:datatype="bit" />
      </xs:sequence>
    </xs:complexType>
  </xs:element>
</xs:schema>
```

Relationships

Since in a relational database you can relate data by keys, you can use annotated schemas to describe those relationships in your XML. However, annotated schemas will make those relationships hierarchical through the use of the `sql:relationship` mapping. You can think of this as joining a table. The relationship mapping has a parent element that specifies the parent relation or table. It also has a parent-key element, which specifies the key to use, and this key can encompass multiple columns. Also, you have child and child-key elements to perform the same functionality for the child as the other elements do for the parent.

There is also inverse functionality, so you can flip this relationship. If for some reason your mapping is different from the primary key/foreign key relationship in the underlying table, the inverse attribute will flip this relationship. This is the case with updategrams, which you'll learn about in the section "SQLXML Updategrams" later in this chapter. You'll use this attribute only with updategrams.

Imagine we had our authors and the authors were related to books in our relational schema through the use of an author ID. We would change our schema mapping to understand that relationship by using the following XML Schema. Notice how the relationship mapping is in a special section of our XSD schema.

```
<?xml version="1.0" encoding="utf-8" ?>
<xs:schema id="XMLSchema1" targetNamespace="http://tempuri.org/XMLSchema1.xsd"
  elementFormDefault="qualified"
  xmlns="http://tempuri.org/XMLSchema1.xsd"
  xmlns:mstns="http://tempuri.org/XMLSchema1.xsd"
  xmlns:sql="urn:schemas-microsoft-com:mapping-schema"
  xmlns:xs="http://www.w3.org/2001/XMLSchema">
  <xs:element name="Root">
      <xs:complexType>
        <xs:sequence>
          <xs:element name="Authors" sql:relation="Authors">
            <xs:complexType>
              <xs:sequence>
              <xsd:element name="Books" sql:relation="Books">
                <xsd:annotation>
                    <xsd:appinfo>
                      <sql:relationship name="BookAuthors"
                              parent="Authors"
                              parent-key="au_id"
                              child="Books"
                              child-key="bk_id" />
                    </xsd:appinfo>
                </xsd:annotation>
                <xsd:complexType>
                    <xsd:attribute name="bk_id" type="xsd:integer" />
                    <xsd:attribute name="au_id" type="xsd:string" />
                </xsd:complexType>
              </xsd:element>
                <xs:element name="au_id" type="xs:string"
                    sql:field="au_id"></xs:element>
                <xs:element name="au_lname" type="xs:string"
                      sql:field="au_lname"></xs:element>
                <xs:element name="au_fname" type="xs:string"
                      sql:field="au_fname"></xs:element>
. . .
                <xs:element name="contract" type="xs:boolean"
                      sql:field="contract"
                      sql:datatype="bit"></xs:element>
              </xs:sequence>
            </xs:complexType>
          </xs:element>
        </xs:sequence>
      </xs:complexType>
  </xs:element>
</xs:schema>
```

Key Column Mapping Using sql:key-fields

Now that you've seen how to build relationships, you also need to look at how to make SQL Server nest your XML data correctly. For nesting to correctly occur, you'll want to specify the key columns used in your table that make the most sense when creating XML hierarchies. To give SQL hints on the correct ordering, use the `sql:key-fields` mapping, which tells SQL which columns contain key values. The sample that follows lets SQL Server know that the `au_id` column is a key column:

```
<?xml version="1.0" encoding="utf-8" ?>
<xs:schema id="XMLSchema1" targetNamespace="http://tempuri.org/XMLSchema1.xsd"
  elementFormDefault="qualified"
  xmlns="http://tempuri.org/XMLSchema1.xsd"
  xmlns:mstns="http://tempuri.org/XMLSchema1.xsd"
  xmlns:xs="http://www.w3.org/2001/XMLSchema">
  <xs:element name="Root">
      <xs:complexType>
         <xs:sequence>
            <xs:element name="Authors" sql:relation="Authors"
               sql:key-fields="au_id">
...
```

Excluding Data from the XML Result Using sql:mapped

Using the `sql:mapped` syntax, you can specify whether to map an element or attribute in your XSD schema to a database object. If you don't want to have the default mapping occur and you don't want to have the XML appear in your results, you should use the `sql:mapped` attribute.

There may be times when there is extraneous XML that you don't want to appear in your table; for example, if you don't control the XML Schema and want to omit the data from your table since a column for the data doesn't exist in the table. This attribute has a Boolean value, with `true` meaning that mapping should occur and `false` meaning that mapping shouldn't occur.

Creating a Constant Element

If you want an element to be constant in your XML document even if there is no mapping to the underlying database, you should use the `sql:is-constant` mapping. This mapping is Boolean, and a value of `true` makes the element always appear in your XML document. This mapping is very useful for creating a root element for your XML. The following is an example of using this mapping:

```
<?xml version="1.0" encoding="utf-8" ?>
<xs:schema id="XMLSchema1"
  targetNamespace="http://tempuri.org/XMLSchema1.xsd" ...>
  <xs:element name="Root" sql:is-constant="true">
...
```

Limiting Values by Using a Filter

You may want to filter the results returned to your XML document by values from your database. The `sql:limit-field` and `sql:limit-value` mappings let you do this by allowing you to specify a filter column and the value to limit that column by. You don't need to specify the limit value if you don't want to since SQL Server will default this to null. You can also have multiple limiting values for multiple mappings. The shortened example that follows shows a schema that limits authors who live in Boston:

```
<?xml version="1.0" encoding="utf-8" ?>
<xs:schema id="XMLSchema1"
  targetNamespace="http://tempuri.org/XMLSchema1.xsd" ...>
```

```
<xs:element name="Root" sql:is-constant="true">
...
        <xs:element name="Authors"
            sql:relation="Authors"
            sql:limit-field="city"
            sql:limit-value="Boston">
...
```

Other Features in Schema Mapping

The majority of your mapped schemas will use the preceding mappings. Table 16-4 briefly summarizes the other mapping technologies. To see annotated schemas in action, take a look at the integrated example in the "the "Programming SQLXML from .NET and COM" section later in this chapter.

Table 16-4. *Other Schema Mapping Features*

Name	Description
sql:encode	Specifies whether to return a URL or binary data for a BLOB datatype. Specifying the value URL returns a URL; specifying the value default returns the data in a base-64 encoded format.
sql:identity	Allows you to specify a SQL identity column mapping. You can specify a value of ignore, which will allow SQL Server to generate the identity value based on the settings in the relational schema, or you can specify useValue, which will use a different value. Normally, you'll set this to ignore unless you are using updategrams.
sql:max-depth	Allows you to specify the depth of recursion to perform in a parent and child relationship. You can specify a number between 1 and 50. An example of using this would be generating an organizational structure where employees work for employees, and you want to go through and generate the hierarchy.
sql:overflow-field	Allows you to specify the database column that will contain any overflow information. If you have XML data that you haven't mapped into your relational database, this data will go into the overflow column. You specify the column name as the value for this mapping.
sql:use-cdata	Allows you to specify whether the data returned by SQL Server should be wrapped in a CDATA section, which will be treated by XML parsers as plain text. Specify a 1 as the value to turn on this feature.

SQLXML Updategrams

So far, you've seen how to shred data using OPENXML and how to get data out of SQL Server using an annotated schema. Updategrams build upon the annotated schema concept. Updategrams allow you to change data in SQL Server using an XML format. Rather than writing T-SQL, you specify your changes to your data using before-and-after images specified in an XML format. You can execute these updategrams from ADO or ADO.NET as you'll see in the full example in the "Programming SQLXML from .NET and COM" section later in this chapter.

The first step towards understanding XML updategrams is to understand the namespace they use, namely urn:schemas-microsoft-com:xml-updategram. This namespace is usually abbreviated to updg as part of your namespace declaration.

Every updategram must contain at least one sync element, which is an XML element that contains the data you want to change in the form of before and after elements. You can have multiple sync elements, and each element is considered a transaction, which means that everything in that sync block is either completely committed or entirely rolled back. The before element contains the data as it was before the change. You'll want to specify a key so that SQL Server can find the data that you want to change. You can modify only one row in your before element.

The after element is the changed data. You can imagine that an insertion will have an after but no before. On the other hand, a delete will have a before but no after. Finally, an update will have both a before and an after.

The following is an updategram in its simplest form:

```
<ROOT xmlns:updg="urn:schemas-microsoft-com:xml-updategram">
  <updg:sync [mapping-schema= "AnnotatedSchemaFile.xml"] >
    <updg:before>
       ...
    </updg:before>
    <updg:after>
       ...
    </updg:after>
  </updg:sync>
</ROOT>
```

You'll notice that you can optionally specify an annotated schema file that will map explicitly the elements in your updategram to columns in your tables. If you don't specify an annotated schema file, SQL Server will use default mapping, as you saw in the annotated schema mapping section. It is also important to note that you can mix and match element- or attribute-based mapping. However, for the sake of clarity, our recommendation is to select one style or the other.

To specify a null value with an updategram, you use the sync element's nullvalue attribute to specify the placeholder for the null. For example, if you wanted the value of "nothing" to be null, you would use the following updategram, which uses attribute-based syntax:

```
<?xml version="1.0"?>
<authorsupdate xmlns:updg=
    "urn:schemas-microsoft-com:xml-updategram">
  <updg:sync updg:nullvalue="nothing">
    <updg:before>
      <Authors au_id="172-32-1176"/>
    </updg:before>
    <updg:after>
      <Authors state="nothing" phone="nothing"/>
    </updg:after>
  </updg:sync>
</authorsupdate>
```

You can also use parameters with your updategrams by specifying $parametername. For example, if you wanted to create a parameter for the selection of the author, you would use the following updategram:

```
<?xml version="1.0"?>
<authorsupdate xmlns:updg=
    "urn:schemas-microsoft-com:xml-updategram">
  <updg:sync updg:nullvalue="nothing">
    <updg:before>
      <Authors au_id="$AuthorID"/>
    </updg:before>
    <updg:after>
      <Authors state="nothing" phone="nothing"/>
    </updg:after>
  </updg:sync>
</authorsupdate>
```

If you want to use identity columns and you want to pass the identity values between tables, you can use the at-identity attribute. This attribute is a placeholder that you can include, and SQL Server will provide the correct value for it when processed. If you want to pass the identity value back to the client, you can use the returnid attribute. SQL Server will then return an XML document containing the identity value after the updategram is applied successfully to the server.

An example will make this all clearer. If we wanted to insert a new author into our authors table, delete an existing author, and change the values for yet another author, we would use the following updategram against our authors table. The next section shows how to program in .NET using the SQLXML classes to execute this code.

```
<?xml version="1.0"?>
<authorsupdate xmlns:updg=
    "urn:schemas-microsoft-com:xml-updategram">
  <updg:sync updg:nullvalue="nothing">
    <updg:before>
    </updg:before>
    <updg:after>
      <Authors au_id="123-22-1232" au_fname="Tom" state="WA" phone="425-882-8080"/>
    </updg:after>
    <updg:before>
        <Authors au_id="267-41-2394"/>
    </updg:before>
    <updg:after>
    </updg:after>
    <updg:before>
        <Authors au_id="238-95-7766"/>
    </updg:before>
    <updg:after>
      <Authors city="Oakland" phone="212-555-1212"/>
    </updg:after>
  </updg:sync>
</authorsupdate>
```

XML Bulk-Loading

If you want to load a large set of XML data into SQL Server, you'll want to use the XML bulk-loading capabilities of SQLXML. Don't—we repeat *don't*—use updategrams or OPENXML. You'll find performance lacking with these two components for loading large amounts of XML data. Of course, you may be wondering what makes up a large amount of XML data. Well, it depends on a number of factors such as the size and complexity of your XML. You could be loading hundreds of small XML files, or you could be loading one big XML file. If you have fast processors, a lot of memory, and fast disks on your server, you could possibly get away with using OPENXML. Our recommendation is to run a test on your system to see which method performs acceptably with the data volume that you intend to run.

XML BulkLoad is an object that you call as part of the SQLXML object model that in turn calls the bulk-loading capabilities of SQL Server to load your data from an XML source into SQL Server. Our recommendation is to run a trace while you're bulk-loading your XML data, and you'll see the bulk-loading operations appear as part of that. This will give you insight into the commands that BulkLoad is running on your behalf and will allow you to troubleshoot any errors that occur or mis-shapen data that is imported.

XML BulkLoad leverages the mapping schema technology that we've been talking about in this chapter. The mapping schema will tell the BulkLoad component where to place your XML data in the database. The object model for XML BulkLoad is very straightforward. There is one method called Execute and a lot of properties that allow you to configure how to handle the bulk-loading, as shown in Table 16-5. The Execute method takes two parameters. The first is the path to the schema mapping file. The second optional parameter is a path or stream to the XML file you want to import.

Table 16-5. *BulkLoad Properties*

Name	Description
BulkLoad	A Boolean that specifies whether the bulk-loading of the data should be performed. If you only want to generate the schema in the database and not load the data, set this property to `false`. The default value is `true`.
CheckConstraints	A Boolean that defaults to `false` and specifies whether to check constraints such as primary key and foreign key constraints. If there is a constraint violation, an error will occur.
ConnectionCommand	Allows you to specify a command object rather than a `ConnectionString` with the `ConnectionString` property. You must set the `Transaction` property to `true` if you specify a command object.
ConnectionString	A string value that allows you to pass a connection string to your SQL Server system.
ErrorLogFile	A string value that allows you to specify a path to where you want to store errors from the bulk-loading operation. There will be a record per error with the most recent error at the beginning.
FireTriggers	A Boolean that specifies whether to fire triggers on the target tables when inserting data. The default value is `false`.
ForceTableLock	A Boolean that specifies whether to lock the entire table during the bulk-loading operation. The default value is `false`.
IgnoreDuplicateKeys	A Boolean that specifies whether to ignore when duplicate keys are being inserted into the table. The default value is `false`, which ignores duplicate keys. If you set this property to `true` and there is a duplicate key, the record will not be inserted into the table.
KeepIdentity	A Boolean property that specifies whether to keep the identity values from your XML or have SQL Server autogenerate the identity values. By default, this property is `true`, so BulkLoad keeps your identity values from your XML.
KeepNulls	A Boolean, with a default of `true`, that specifies whether to place null values in columns where there is no value specified or whether you don't want to use the default value specified for the column.
SchemaGen	A Boolean property, with a default of `false`, that specifies whether to create the underlying relational tables before performing the bulk-loading operations. You'll learn more about this property in the upcoming text.
SGDropTables	A Boolean, with a default of `false`, that specifies whether to drop and re-create tables or to retain existing tables. The property is used with the `SchemaGen` property. A `true` value drops and re-creates the tables.
SGUseID	A Boolean, with a default of `false`, that specifies whether to use an ID from the mapping schema to create the primary key in the relational table. If you set this property to `true`, you need to set one of your column's datatypes in your mapping schema to be `dt:type="id"`.
TempFilePath	A string that specifies the path to create temp files. If you leave this property blank, temp files will be created wherever the `TEMP` environment variable points to. This property has no meaning unless you set the next property, `Transaction`, to true.
Transaction	A Boolean, `false` by default, that specifies whether a single transaction should be used when bulk-loading. If you set this property to `true`, all your operations are cached in a temporary file before being loaded into SQL Server. If there is an error, the entire bulk-loading operation doesn't occur. The `Transaction` property cannot be set to `true` if you are loading binary data.
XMLFragment	This Boolean property specifies whether the XML you are loading is a fragment. A *fragment* is an XML document without a root node. Set this to `true` if your XML is a fragment; leave it alone, since it defaults to `false`, if your XML isn't a fragment.

The first property that you should understand is the `Transaction` Boolean property. Normally, you want to leave this property `false` to make the load nontransacted. This will increase your performance at the cost of not being able to roll back if there is a failure.

The next property is the `XMLFragment` Boolean property. If you set this to `true`, `BulkLoad` allows XML fragments, which are XML documents with no root element.

If you are working with constraints and you want those constraints enforced as part of your `BulkLoad`, you'll want to set the `CheckConstraints` property to `true`. By default, `BulkLoad` turns off constraint checking, which improves performance. Regardless of whether you set this to `true` or `false`, you'll want to place primary keys ahead of a table with a foreign key in your mapping schema.

If you want to ignore duplicate keys, you need to set the `IgnoreDuplicateKeys` Boolean property to `true`. This is useful if you get data feeds where the person providing the data feed may not know what data is in your database and you don't want the bulk-loading operation to fail because of duplicate keys. `BulkLoad` will not commit the row with the duplicate key, but instead just jump over that row in processing.

Many database designers use identity columns to guarantee uniqueness of keys in the table. Sometimes the XML you are loading has an identity-like element that you may want to use rather than having SQL Server generate a value using its own algorithm. To do this, set the `KeepIdentity` property to `true`. This is the default value for this property. One thing to remember is that it is a global value, so you cannot have SQL Server generate some identities and have `BulkLoad` pull from the XML for others.

The `KeepNulls` property defaults to `false` with `BulkLoad`. `BulkLoad` will not automatically insert null as the value for any column that is missing a corresponding attribute or element in the XML document. If you set this property to `true`, you must be careful here since `BulkLoad` will fail if you don't allow nulls in those columns. `BulkLoad` will not assign the default value for a column, if one is specified in SQL Server, if the property is `true`.

One interesting `BulkLoad` property is `ForceTableLock`, which locks the table as `BulkLoad` loads its data. This will speed performance of the load at the cost of locking other users out of the table. The default value is `false`, so `BulkLoad` acquires a table lock each time it inserts a record into the table.

If your target tables don't already exist, `BulkLoad` can create the tables for you. You need to set the `SchemaGen` property to `true` to have `BulkLoad` perform this functionality. `BulkLoad` will take the datatypes from your schema mapping and autogenerate the correct database schema based on those datatypes. If a table or column already exists with the same name and you want to drop and re-create them, set the `SGDropTables` property to `true`.

The next section shows using `BulkLoad` from a managed environment. `BulkLoad` supports both COM and .NET so you can program from both environments with this technology.

Getting XML Out of the Database

Many developers and database administrators (DBAs) want to keep their relational data as relational but transfer that relational data to other systems as XML due to XML's flexibility and universal support. `FOR XML` (added in SQL Server 2000) allows you to get your relational data back in an XML format without needing to store that relational data as XML.

FOR XML

You probably use `FOR XML` today, as it's the easiest way to take data in a relational format from SQL Server and put it into an XML format. A simplified form of the `FOR XML` query extension syntax is the following:

```
SELECT column list
FROM table list
WHERE filter criteria
FOR XML RAW | AUTO | EXPLICIT [, XMLDATA] [, ELEMENTS]
    [, BINARY BASE64]
```

Using FOR XML Modes

As shown in the preceding syntax, you can use FOR XML in RAW, AUTO, or EXPLICIT mode. Most people use the AUTO or RAW mode. The main reason people normally don't use EXPLICIT mode is that the other two modes meet their needs. The other reason, as you'll see, is EXPLICIT mode is an explicit pain to work with. If you can get away with using the other two modes, we recommend you do that, since you'll find yourself pulling your hair out if you do any complex XML structures with EXPLICIT mode.

RAW Mode

When working in RAW mode, the FOR XML query returns columns as attributes and rows as row elements. An example of FOR XML RAW is shown here:

```
USE pubs
GO
SELECT * FROM Authors FOR XML RAW
```

Here are the results (truncated for brevity):

```
<row au_id="172-32-1176" au_lname="White" au_fname="Johnson"
phone="408 496-7223" address="10932 Bigge Rd." city="Menlo Park"
state="CA" zip="94025" contract="1"/>
<row au_id="213-46-8915" au_lname="Green" au_fname="Marjorie"
phone="415 986-7020" address="309 63rd St. #411" city="Oakland"
state="CA" zip="94618" contract="1"/>
<row au_id="238-95-7766" au_lname="Carson" au_fname="Cheryl"
phone="415 548-7723" address="589 Darwin Ln." city="Berkeley"
state="CA" zip="94705" contract="1"/>
<row au_id="267-41-2394" au_lname="O&apos;Leary" au_fname="Michael"
phone="408 286-2428" address="22 Cleveland Av. #14" city="San Jose"
state="CA" zip="95128" contract="1"/>
```

As you can see, there is a row element for each row, and each non-null column has an attribute on the row element. If you are retrieving binary data, you need to specify BINARY BASE64. Also, if you want to retrieve an XML Data schema with the returned XML, you can specify XMLDATA.

AUTO Mode

When working in AUTO mode, the FOR XML query is the same as RAW mode in that it returns each row as an element with column values as attributes, except the name of the element representing the row is the table name. Here is an example using the authors table:

```
USE pubs
GO
SELECT * FROM authors FOR XML AUTO
```

You'll see the following results (truncated for brevity):

```
<Authors au_id="172-32-1176" au_lname="White" au_fname="Johnson"
phone="408 496-7223" address="10932 Bigge Rd." city="Menlo Park"
state="CA" zip="94025" contract="1"/>
<Authors au_id="213-46-8915" au_lname="Green" au_fname="Marjorie"
phone="415 986-7020" address="309 63rd St. #411" city="Oakland"
state="CA" zip="94618" contract="1"/>
<Authors au_id="238-95-7766" au_lname="Carson" au_fname="Cheryl"
phone="415 548-7723" address="589 Darwin Ln." city="Berkeley"
state="CA" zip="94705" contract="1"/>
<Authors au_id="267-41-2394" au_lname="O&apos;Leary" au_fname="Michael"
phone="408 286-2428" address="22 Cleveland Av. #14" city="San Jose"
state="CA" zip="95128" contract="1"/>
<Authors au_id="274-80-9391" au_lname="Straight" au_fname="Dean"
phone="415 834-2919" address="5420 College Av." city="Oakland"
state="CA" zip="94609" contract="1"/>
<Authors au_id="341-22-1782" au_lname="Smith" au_fname="Meander"
phone="913 843-0462" address="10 Mississippi Dr." city="Lawrence"
state="KS" zip="66044" contract="0"/>
```

The table name is the element for each node with the column values as attributes on that element. The nesting of elements depends on the order in your SELECT clause, so choose your order carefully. Furthermore, you cannot use a GROUP BY, but you can use an ORDER BY in your SELECT statements with FOR XML. The work-around for a GROUP BY is to use a nested SELECT statement to achieve the results you want, but this will have some performance implications. When using joins, you'll find that AUTO will nest the result set, which is most likely what you want to happen. If you don't want this to happen, you'll need to use the EXPLICIT mode to shape your XML. For example, if we join publishers and titles, and we want all titles nested under their publisher in our XML, we would run the following code:

```
USE pubs
GO
SELECT Publishers.Pub_Name, Titles.Title, Titles.Price
  FROM Titles, Publishers WHERE Publishers.Pub_ID = Titles.Pub_ID
  FOR XML AUTO
```

The following are the results (truncated):

```
<Publishers Pub_Name="Algodata Infosystems">
  <Titles Title="The Busy Executive&apos;s Database Guide" Price="19.9900"/>
  <Titles Title="Cooking with Computers:
    Surreptitious Balance Sheets"
    Price="11.9500"/>
</Publishers>
<Publishers Pub_Name="New Moon Books">
  <Titles Title="You Can Combat Computer Stress!" Price="2.9900"/>
</Publishers>
<Publishers Pub_Name="Algodata Infosystems">
  <Titles Title="Straight Talk About Computers" Price="19.9900"/>
</Publishers>
```

You can also use the ELEMENTS option with FOR XML AUTO. If you are more of an element than attribute person, you can have AUTO return back element-centric syntax rather than attribute-centric syntax. Personally, we find that element-centric syntax, while making the XML larger in text size because of all the opening and closing tags, results in XML that is easier to read and understand.

Explicit Mode

As the name implies, EXPLICIT mode allows you to completely control the way that your XML is generated. You describe what you want your XML document to look like, and SQL Server fills in that document with the correct information. You use a *universal table* to describe your XML document. This table consists of one table column for each value you want to return as well as two additional tags: one that uniquely identifies the tags in your XML and another that identifies your parent-child relationships. The other columns describe your data. An example of a universal table appears in Table 16-6.

Table 16-6. *A Universal Table*

Tag	Parent	Column1's Directive	Column2's Directive
1	Null	Data value	Data value
2	1	Data value	Data value
3	2	Data value	Data value

You use directives to describe how to display your data in the table. Directives are just special commands that you use so that SQL Server understands how to parse. The format for these directives is as follows:

Element!Tag!Attribute!Directive

The different pieces of your directive are separated by an exclamation point.

Imagine we want to display authors, but make the au_id an attribute on our XML and the rest of our data elements in our output. Well, we can't do that with FOR XML AUTO or RAW, since neither of them can be split between being attribute- or element-centric. Let's see what our query would look like to do this:

```
SELECT 1 AS Tag, NULL AS Parent,
    au_id AS [Authors!1!au_id], au_lname as [Authors!1]
    FROM authors FOR XML EXPLICIT
```

The first thing you'll notice is that in our column list we have the Tag and Parent columns. We need these columns to identify the tag of the current element, which is an integer from 1 to 255, and also the parent of the current element. In this example, we're not nesting our data, our parent is always null, and our tag is always 1, since we always refer to the same parent. You can see we use the AS clause to rename our data to describe the XML formatting we want to do. The naming for au_id tells SQL Server that we want to use the Authors element, a tag ID of 1, and the name of our attribute. Since we want the other data to be elements, we just rename them to be the element and tag name. At the end, we specify FOR XML EXPLICIT, since we don't want to get our universal table back, which describes our XML structure, but our actual processed XML structure. The results of this query are shown here:

```
<Authors au_id="409-56-7008">Bennet</Authors>
<Authors au_id="648-92-1872">Blotchet-Halls</Authors>
<Authors au_id="238-95-7766">Carson</Authors>
<Authors au_id="722-51-5454">DeFrance</Authors>
<Authors au_id="712-45-1867">del Castillo</Authors>
<Authors au_id="427-17-2319">Dull</Authors>
...
```

You can see that we get the last name returned as element data for our Authors element. We may want to make the last name an element itself nested under the Authors element. To do this, we modify our query slightly to use the element directive, as shown here:

```
SELECT 1 as Tag, NULL as Parent, au_id as [Authors!1!au_id],
  au_lname as [Authors!1!au_lname!element]
  FROM Authors FOR XML EXPLICIT
```

Table 16-7 lists all the directives you can use with a description for each.

Table 16-7. *FOR XML EXPLICIT Directives*

Name	Description
cdata	Wraps the data in a CDATA section.
element	Specifies that you want the element entity encoded (for example, > becomes >) and represented as a subelement.
elementxsinil	If you want to generate elements generated for null values, you can specify this directive. This will create an element with an attribute xsi:nil=TRUE.
ID	Allows you to specify an ID for your element. All ID directives require that XMLDATA be requested in your FOR XML clause.
IDREF	Allows attributes to specify ID type attributes to enable intradocument linking.
IDREFS	Similar to IDREF in that it allows you to create intradocument linking, but uses the IDREFS structure rather than IDREF.
hide	Hides the result from the XML rendered.
xml	Same as the element directive, but no encoding takes place.
xmltext	Useful for OPENXML overflow columns in that it retrieves the column and appends it to the document.

When using FOR XML EXPLICIT queries, many people get the error that the parent tag isn't open yet. To troubleshoot your FOR XML EXPLICIT statements, the easiest way to fix problems is to remove the FOR XML EXPLICIT statement and just render the results. This will return the universal table, and you can track down errors. The easiest way we've found to solve the parent tag problem is to make sure to include the tag column in your ORDER BY clause so that you know that no later tags will be rendered before earlier tags, which is the cause of the problem.

Let's look at a more complex example. If we want to return all our authors with their titles and author royalties, we would generate a UNION ALL query to combine together this data from disparate tables, and we would need to nest the results so that our XML hierarchy appears correctly with authors, royalties, and then titles. Notice that we define a number of parent-child relationships using the Tag and Parent columns. Also notice that we use the ORDER BY trick to make sure that the parent tags are in the XML before we process the children tags.

```
SELECT 1 AS Tag, NULL AS Parent,
  Authors.au_fname AS [Authors!1!au_fname!element],
  Authors.au_lname AS [Authors!1!au_lname!element],
  NULL AS [Titleauthor!2!Royaltyper],
  NULL AS [Titles!3!Title!element]
FROM
Authors

UNION ALL

SELECT 2 AS Tag, 1 AS Parent,
  au_fname,
  au_lname,
  royaltyper,
  NULL
FROM Authors INNER JOIN Titleauthor ON
Authors.au_id = Titleauthor.au_id

UNION ALL

SELECT 3 AS Tag, 2 AS Parent,
  au_fname,
  au_lname,
  royaltyper,
  title
FROM Authors INNER JOIN Titleauthor ON Authors.au_id = Titleauthor.au_id
INNER JOIN Titles ON Titles.title_id = Titleauthor.title_id
ORDER BY [Authors!1!au_fname!element], [Authors!1!au_lname!element],
[Titleauthor!2!royaltyper], Tag
FOR XML EXPLICIT
```

Here is the truncated universal table:

Tag	Parent	Authors!1!au_fname!element	Authors !1 !au_lnameelement
1	NULL	Abraham	Bennet
2	1	Abraham	Bennet
3	2	Abraham	Bennet
1	NULL	Akiko	Yokomoto
2	1	Akiko	Yokomoto
3	2	Akiko	Yokomoto
1	NULL	Albert	Ringer
2	1	Albert	Ringer
3	2	Albert	Ringer
2	1	Albert	Ringer
3	2	Albert	Ringer

And here are the truncated results:

```
<Authors>
  <au_fname>Abraham</au_fname>
  <au_lname>Bennet</au_lname>
  <Titleauthor Royaltyper="60">
    <Titles>
      <Title>The Busy Executive&apos;s Database Guide</Title>
    </Titles>
  </Titleauthor>
</Authors>
<Authors>
```

```
    <au_fname>Akiko</au_fname>
    <au_lname>Yokomoto</au_lname>
    <Titleauthor Royaltyper="40">
      <Titles>
        <Title>Sushi, Anyone?</Title>
      </Titles>
    </Titleauthor>
  </Authors>
...
```

As you've seen, FOR XML EXPLICIT is powerful, yet it can be hard to master. If you can get away with using FOR XML AUTO or RAW and avoid FOR XML EXPLICIT mode, your coding will be much easier. However, for those situations where FOR XML AUTO or RAW doesn't meet your needs, you can always fall back to EXPLICIT mode.

Returning Values As XML Types

To support returning values using the XML datatype, FOR XML provides an extra directive called TYPE. By passing this directive to your call, instead of generating the XML and returning it as text, SQL Server returns the result as an XML datatype. This means that you can then use XQuery on that returned value to query for information inside the result set. Also, you can assign the results to a variable or insert into an XML datatype column. Finally, you can nest FOR XML statements to generate a hierarchy, rather than needing to resort to using XML EXPLICIT. This capability allows you to quickly convert your relational data or even your data that uses the XML datatype into an XML datatype value.

The following code shows how to use the new TYPE directive and then pass the result to an XQuery, which you'll learn about in the next chapter:

```
SELECT (SELECT * FROM authors FOR XML AUTO, ELEMENTS, TYPE).query(
'count(//author)')
```

Specifying a Column's Location in the Hierarchy

The PATH mode allows you to specify where a column's value should appear in your XML hierarchy by using XPath. By having this capability, you can move away from FOR XML EXPLICIT, which is complex and burdensome, and instead generate complex XML using nested FOR XML statements and the new PATH mode.

An example of the new PATH mode is shown here. This sample renames the root element to AuthorsNew and also makes a new complex type called Names, which stores the first name and the last name.

```
SELECT au_fname "Names/FirstName", au_lname "Names/LastName"
FROM authors FOR XML PATH('AuthorsNew')
```

Generating In-Line XSD

Another enhancement is support for in-line XSD in RAW and AUTO modes. You can optionally pass the XMLSCHEMA directive in your code. The following example shows using the XMLSCHEMA directive and the results returned from the server:

```
SELECT * FROM authors FOR XML RAW('Authors'), XMLSCHEMA('urn:example.com')

<xsd:schema targetNamespace="urn:example.com"
  xmlns:xsd=http://www.w3.org/2001/XMLSchema
  xmlns:sqltypes="http://schemas.microsoft.com/sqlserver/2004/sqltypes"
  elementFormDefault="qualified">
  <xsd:import namespace="http://schemas.microsoft.com/sqlserver/2004/sqltypes"
    schemaLocation=
    "http://schemas.microsoft.com/sqlserver/2004/sqltypes/sqltypes.xsd" />
  <xsd:element name="Authors">
    <xsd:complexType>
  ...
    </xsd:complexType>
  </xsd:element>
</xsd:schema>


<Authors xmlns="urn:example.com" au_id="172-32-1176"
         au_lname="White" au_fname="Johnson" phone="408 496-7223"
         address="10932 Bigge Rd." city="Menlo Park"
         state="CA" zip="94025" contract="1" />
```

Using FOR XML on the Client Side

Up until now, we have been writing our FOR XML code so that it is processed on the server. However, using SQLXML, you can process your FOR XML code on the client side.

Rather than sending back the formatted XML results from the server, SQL Server can send back the rowsets to SQLXML, and SQLXML will format the results on the client side. You'll see an example of this in the upcoming "Programming SQLXML from .NET and COM" section.

Templates to Improve Performance

You can use templates to execute queries against SQL Server with SQLXML. Templates are just encapsulation of the technologies we've already looked at in this chapter. These templates can use SQL or XPath queries. You need to use the annotated schema that you create for your XML view with your template. The schema can be in-line or loaded via a file.

To specify your template, create a file that uses the urn:schemas-microsoft-com:xml-sql namespace. Then you can pass in your SQL or XPath queries in the template. SQLXML will cache your templates in order to improve performance. The following template executes a SQL query:

```
<Root><sql:query xmlns:sql=""urn:schemas-microsoft-com:xml-sql"">
SELECT * FROM Authors FOR XML AUTO</sql:query></Root>
```

To use an XPath query, we would change the sql:query syntax to sql:xpath-query. The sample that follows queries for all authors:

```
<Root><sql:xpath-query xmlns:sql=""urn:schemas-microsoft-com:xml-sql"">/Authors
</sql:xpath-query></Root>
```

You'll see how to use templates in the section "Programming SQLXML from .NET and COM" later in this chapter.

Working with XML Data

XSD schema collections in SQL Server 2005 allowed users to validate XML data by enforcing compliance of the XML data with a given schema definition. As discussed earlier in this chapter, a schema definition describes the permissible XML elements and attributes for a particualr XML data structure. SQL Server's support for XML is based on published XML standards. The actual implementation of XML in SQL Server 2005 was not a complete implemenation of the XML specification; rather, it was a broad subset that covered the most common XML validation scenarios. SQL Server 2008 builds on SQL Server 2005's implementation by including additional features like schema validation, date/time support, and union and list types.

Validation for "Any" Types

In SQL Server 2005, users had the ability to define XSD schemas. A schema itself defines the rules for a specific XML document, such as what kinds of elements and attributes can appear in an XML document, the number and order of child elements, and so on.

In an XSD schema, you can define a wildcard declaration via the any, anyAttribute, and anyType keywords. This gives the schema designer the flexibility to arbitrarily add information in-line, without defining it at design time. Consider the following code, which creates a schema within a schema collection object in SQL Server:

```
CREATE XML SCHEMA COLLECTION EmployeeSC AS
N'<?xml version="1.0"?>
<xsd:schema xmlns="http://schemas.apress.com/AcceleratedSQLServer2008"
            xmlns:xsd="http://www.w3.org/2001/XMLSchema">
<xsd:element name="Employee">
<xsd:complexType>
<xsd:sequence>
<xsd:element name="Name" type="xsd:string"/>
<xsd:element name="DateOfBirth" type="xsd:date"/>
<xsd:element name="Salary" type="xsd:long"/>
<xsd:any namespace="##other" processContents="skip" minOccurs="0"
 maxOccurs="unbounded"/>
</xsd:sequence>
</xsd:complexType>
</xsd:element>
</xsd:schema>';
```

Let's bind this schema with a simple table as follows:

```
CREATE TABLE Employees (emp_xml    XML(EmployeeSC))
```

In the schema, we define the elements Name, DateOfBirth, and Salary, followed by an xsd:any definition. Essentially, we are telling the processor to allow any element from any namespace at this location in the document. That makes the following XML valid:

```
<Employee xmlns:nsP="http://schemas.apress.com/AcceleratedSQLServer2008">
<Name>John Doe</Name>
<DateOfBirth>1969-03-05</DateOfBirth>
<Salary>34900</Salary>
<nsP:Picture>C:\\employees\\emp1.bmp</nsP:Picture>
</Employee>
```

One of the parameters available for an "any" type is processContents. This parameter tells the processor whether or not it should perform validation on the element. This parameter can be one of the following values:

- skip: This means don't bother validating even if the schema collection contains a declaration for the nsp:Picture element. We used this setting in the preceding example.

- strict: This means that the processor will perform validation and fail if any errors occurred during the process.

- lax: New in SQL Server 2008, this option means enforce validation for any elements that have schema declarations associated with them, but ignore any elements that are not defined in the schema.

Date and Time Support

xs:dateTime represents a date and time value, optionally including time-zone information. Those who used xs:dateTime in SQL Server 2005 may have been a bit frustrated because its implementation wasn't complete. In SQL Server 2008, the implementation of xs:dateTime aligns more closely with the W3C specification (http://www.w3.org/TR/xmlschema11-2/#dateTime) in terms of its expected behavior.

For example, consider the following schema:

```
<?xml version="1.0"?>
<xsd:schema xmlns:xsd="http://www.w3.org/2001/XMLSchema">
<xsd:element name="StockPurchased" type="xsd:dateTime"/>
</xsd:schema>
```

In SQL Server 2005, we were required to input time-zone information. Thus, the following statement would not be valid, since it fails to specify the time zone:

```
INSERT INTO DateTimeTest VALUES
  ('<StockPurchased>2008-01-27T16:11:00.813</StockPurchased >')
```

In SQL Server 2008, the time-zone information is now optional, just as defined in the W3C specification. Therefore, this statement works correctly in SQL Server 2008. If you queried the DateTimeTest table in SQL Server 2008, you would get the following:

```
<StockPurchased>2008-01-27T16:11:00.813</StockPurchased>
```

Another interesting change from SQL Server 2005 is the fact that SQL Server 2008 now preserves the time-zone information. Consider issuing the following statement to SQL Server 2005:

```
INSERT INTO DateTimeTest VALUES
  ('<StockPurchased>2008-10-10T12:00:00-04:00</StockPurchased>')
```

Notice we are specifying a time 4 hours before UTC time. If we queried this table in SQL Server 2005, we would get this result:

```
<StockPurchased>2008-10-10T16:00:00Z</StockPurchased>
```

Notice that the stored value is different than what we had originally sent to the database engine because interally it converted the time to a value based on time zone zero (Z). This behavior does not happen in SQL Server 2008, so the same query will return the same value as was input.

Union and List Types

SQL Server 2008 allows for schema declarations for unions of list types, as well as SQL list types that contain union types

As an example, suppose our company has a web site that sells shoes. The original web page design allowed only for dress shoes and sneakers to be sold. Recently, upper management has decided to broaden the product line and include slippers and other products that have sizes defined as small, medium, and large, as opposed to traditional shoe sizes like 9, 9.5, and 10. As the XML developers, we already have a simple type defined to take on the value of the shoe size, but it expects a number and not a string.

Ideally, what we would want is for the schema to accept either a numeric value or a string, depending on which shoe is being purchased. This is a great place for us to define two lists of accepted values: one our numeric shoe size and the other a string of sizes. Our new schema is defined as follows:

```
CREATE XML SCHEMA COLLECTION OrderSchema AS
N'<?xml version="1.0" encoding="UTF-16"?>
<xs:schema xmlns:xs="http://www.w3.org/2001/XMLSchema">
<xs:element name="shoesize" type="shoeSizeType"/>
   <xs:simpleType name="shoeSizeType">
      <xs:union>
         <xs:simpleType>
            <xs:list>
               <xs:simpleType>
                  <xs:restriction base="xs:decimal">
                     <xs:enumeration value="9"/>
                     <xs:enumeration value="9.5"/>
                     <xs:enumeration value="10"/>
                     <xs:enumeration value="10.5"/>
                  </xs:restriction>
               </xs:simpleType>
            </xs:list>
         </xs:simpleType>
         <xs:simpleType>
            <xs:list>
               <xs:simpleType>
                  <xs:restriction base="xs:string">
                     <xs:enumeration value="S"/>
                     <xs:enumeration value="M"/>
                     <xs:enumeration value="L"/>
                     </xs:restriction>
               </xs:simpleType>
            </xs:list>
         </xs:simpleType>
      </xs:union>
   </xs:simpleType>
</xs:schema>'
```

Now we can submit either the numeric size (for example, `<shoesize>9.5</shoesize>`) or the string size (for example, `<shoesize>M</shoesize>`), as both of these are valid.

Programming SQLXML from .NET and COM

SQLXML 4.0 provides an object model that allows you to program its capabilities from both managed and unmanaged code. For unmanaged code such as ADO, you use the SQLXMLOLEDB driver. This provider uses the new SQL Server Native Client. For managed code, you can add a reference to Microsoft.Data.SqlXml in Visual Studio, as shown in Figure 16-2.

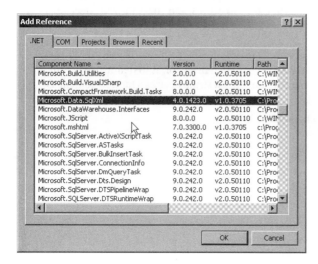

Figure 16-2. *Adding a reference to SQLXML*

The SQLXML-managed assembly has four classes: SqlXmlCommand, SqlXmlParameter, SqlXmlAdapter, and SqlXmlException. Using these classes, you can send commands to SQL Server and process the results on the client side, such as rendering FOR XML statements or executing XML templates. First, we'll look at each of the classes, and then we'll show some examples.

SQLXML Classes

SqlXmlCommand is one of the primary classes you'll interact with when using SQLXML functionality. Tables 16-8 and 16-9 list all the methods and properties for SqlXmlCommand.

Table 16-8. *SqlXmlCommand Methods*

Name	Description
ClearParameters	Clears all parameters that were created for a particular command object.
CreateParameter	Creates a SqlXmlParameter object from which you can set the name and value for the parameter.
ExecuteNonQuery	Executes the query but doesn't return any value. This is useful if you want to call an updategram that doesn't return a value.
ExecuteToStream	Executes the query and returns the results to an existing Stream object that you pass to the method.
ExecuteStream	Executes the query and returns the results back as a new Stream object.
ExecuteXMLReader	Executes the query and returns the results in an XMLReader object.

Table 16-9. *SqlXmlCommand Properties*

Name	Description
BasePath	The base directory path, which is useful for setting paths to XSL, schema mapping, or XSD schema files used in your applications.
ClientSideXML	When set to true, this Boolean property tells SQLXML to convert your rowsets to XML on the client side.
CommandStream	Allows you to set your command by using a stream. This is useful if you want to execute a command from a file.
CommandText	Gets or sets the text of the command that you want to execute.
CommandType	Allows you to get or set the command type using the following values: SQLXMLCommandType.Diffgram, SQLXMLCommandType.Sql, SQLXMLCommandType.Template, SQLXMLCommandType.TemplateFile, SQLXMLCommandType.XPath, and SQLXMLCommandType.UpdateGram.
Namespaces	Allows you to specify namespaces for your XML in the format xmlns:x= 'urn:myschema:Yournamespace'. When using XPath queries that are namespace qualified, you must specify your namespaces using this property.
OutputEncoding	Specifies the encoding for the results. By default, the encoding is UTF-8, but you could specify ANSI, Unicode, or other valid encoding values.
RootTag	Specifies the root tag for your XML document, if required. This will normally be the string value root.
SchemaPath	Specifies the directory path and filename for the schema file. If you are using relative paths via the BasePath property, SQLXML will look in the base path directory. You can also use absolute paths such as c:\myapp\myschema.xml.
XslPath	Same as the SchemaPath but specifies the path to the XSLT file rather than the schema file.

SqlXmlParameter provides the ability to pass parameters to your code. This class is very straight-forward since it has only two properties: Name and Value. You specify the name of the parameter such as customerid and the value to be the value for the parameter. You can create a SqlXmlParameter object by calling the CreateParameter method on the SqlXmlCommand object.

The SqlXmlAdapter object allows interoperability between .NET datasets and SQLXML functionality. The constructor for this object has three forms:

- The first form can take a SqlXmlCommand that is populated with the necessary information to connect to your datasource.

- The second form is the command text as a string, the command type as a SqlXmlCommand object, and finally the connection string as a string.

- The third form is the same as the second one, except you pass in a Stream object rather than a string for the command text.

Once you've created your adapter, there are only two methods on the object. The first is the Fill method, to which you pass an ADO.NET dataset. SQLXML will fill the ADO.NET dataset with whatever data your commands should return. Then you can modify your dataset using standard dataset functionality and call the second method, which is Update, with your dataset as a parameter to the method. SQLXML uses an optimistic locking scheme when updating your data in your back-end table.

The SqlXmlException object inherits from the standard SystemException object and allows you to pass back SQLXML exceptions as part of your code. There is an ErrorStream property that you use to return the error. The following code uses this property to print out any errors caught in an exception:

...

```
Catch ex As Microsoft.Data.SqlXml.SqlXmlException
    ex.ErrorStream.Position = 0
    Dim oSR As New System.IO.StreamReader(ex.ErrorStream)
    Dim strResult As String = oSR.ReadToEnd()
    System.Console.WriteLine(strResult)

End Try
```

SQLXML Coding Examples

To show you how to use this functionality, let's take a look at a sample application. The sample application allows you to bulk-load XML data into SQL Server and then try out the different functionality discussed in this chapter such as FOR XML, dataset integration, running templates, using updategrams, and also using client-side processing and XMLTextReaders. The user interface for the sample is shown in Figure 16-3.

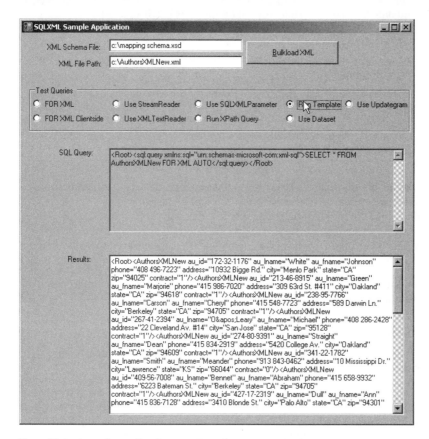

Figure 16-3. *Sample application user interface*

The sample already has a reference to SQLXML, so we don't need to perform that step again. To start working with our data, we need to load our XML data into our database and shred it into relational columns. The code could have used an OPENXML statement, but instead it uses XML BulkLoad. To start using BulkLoad, we first need to add a reference to the BulkLoad COM object in Visual Studio.

The component name is Microsoft SQLXML BulkLoad 4.0 Type Library. Next, we need to create a `BulkLoad` object in our application. The code that follows performs this task:

```
Dim oXMLBulkLoad As New SQLXMLBULKLOADLib.SQLXMLBulkLoad4Class()
```

Next, we need to set some properties for our `BulkLoad`. Since we cannot assume that the table that we are going to bulk-load into already exists, the sample sets the `SchemaGen` property to true. Also, if the tables do exist, we want to drop them, so the sample sets the `SGDropTables` to true as well. The sample sets other properties such as where to put the error file, whether our XML is a fragment, and whether to keep identities. The most important property is the `ConnectionString` property, since it tells `BulkLoad` how to connect to the server. Once we have set all of our properties, the sample calls the `Execute` method of `BulkLoad` and passes in the schema mapping file and the XML to bulk-load. You'll find all of the schema mapping files and the sample XML files included with the sample application. All this code is shown here:

```
oXMLBulkLoad.ErrorLogFile = "c:\myerrors.log"
oXMLBulkLoad.SchemaGen = True
oXMLBulkLoad.KeepIdentity = False
oXMLBulkLoad.BulkLoad = True
oXMLBulkLoad.SGDropTables = True
oXMLBulkLoad.XMLFragment = True
oXMLBulkLoad.ConnectionString = strConnectionString
oXMLBulkLoad.Execute(txtXMLSchema.Text, txtXMLFile.Text)
```

FOR XML: Server-Side and Client-Side Processing

Once we've successfully bulk-loaded our data, we can start working with it. One thing we can do is get our data back out as XML, now that it is shredded into the database. We can use the `FOR XML` construct to do this. Remember that SQLXML allows you to render your XML on the server or on the client. The example allows us to select either one. The code uses a common method for executing all queries in the example. This method takes a number of different parameters such as whether the query coming in is a SQL, template, or diffgram query. (A diffgram is an XML format that is used to identify current and original versions of data elements.) The first thing the common query method does is create a `SqlXmlCommand` object as shown here. Note the connection string is a standard connection string, such as `"Provider=sqloledb;server=localhost;database=pubs;integrated security=SSPI"`.

```
Dim oSQLXMLCommand As New _
Microsoft.Data.SqlXml.SqlXmlCommand(strConnectionString)
```

Next, it sets the command type to be the appropriate type based on the query coming in. For standard SQL queries, the command type is set to SQL, as shown here:

```
oSQLXMLCommand.CommandType = Microsoft.Data.SqlXml.SqlXmlCommandType.Sql
```

To send our `FOR XML` query to the server, we need to set the command text for our `SqlXmlCommand` object. Since we pass the query to the method, we use the `strQuery` variable for this purpose.

```
'Set our Query
oSQLXMLCommand.CommandText = strQuery
```

Since we can render our `FOR XML` on the server or client, we need to set the `ClientSideXml` property of our command object to `true` or `false`, with `true` being to render the XML on the client side. Once we've set this property, we can execute our query and retrieve the results. The following code uses a `StreamReader` to get the results and put them in our results text box. We can also use an `XMLTextReader`, which you'll see used later in this section.

```
'See if we need to render client-side
If bUseClientSide = True Then
    oSQLXMLCommand.ClientSideXml = True
End If

Dim oStream As System.IO.Stream
oStream = oSQLXMLCommand.ExecuteStream()

oStream.Position = 0
Dim oStreamReader As New System.IO.StreamReader(oStream)
txtResults.Text = oStreamReader.ReadToEnd()
oStreamReader.Close()
```

As you can see from the code, using FOR XML in SQLXML is very straightforward. The hard part is making sure that you get your FOR XML query correct and returning the correct results.

Using an XMLTextReader

There may be times when you don't want to use a StreamReader to get your results back from your SQLXML queries, but instead want to use an XMLTextReader. The XMLTextReader gives you fast access to XML data and more flexibility in navigating your XML than a StreamReader does. The XMLTextReader parses your XML and allows you to query that XML using XPath. To use an XMLTextReader, you just need to change your ExecuteStream method call to an ExecuteXMLReader method call on your SqlXmlCommand object. Once you get back the reader, you can use the methods and properties of the XML reader to navigate your XML. The following code executes the XML reader and displays the results to the user in the sample:

```
'Use XMLTextReader
Dim oXMLTextReader As System.Xml.XmlTextReader
oXMLTextReader = oSQLXMLCommand.ExecuteXmlReader()
Dim strXML As String = ""

While oXMLTextReader.Read()
  'We're on an element
  If oXMLTextReader.NodeType = XmlNodeType.Element Then
    strXML += "<" & oXMLTextReader.Name & ""
  ElseIf oXMLTextReader.NodeType = XmlNodeType.EndElement Then
    strXML += "</" & oXMLTextReader.Name & ">"
  End If

'Look for attributes
  If oXMLTextReader.HasAttributes() Then
  Dim i As Integer = 0
  Do While (oXMLTextReader.MoveToNextAttribute())
    i += 1
   strXML += " " & oXMLTextReader.Name & "=" & oXMLTextReader.Value
   If oXMLTextReader.AttributeCount = i Then
    'Last attribute, end the tag
    strXML += " />"
  End If
  Loop

  End If
  End While

  txtResults.Text = strXML
  oXMLTextReader.Close()
```

As you can see, the XML reader, for simple operations like just displaying the XML, is overkill since you must parse the XML to display it. But, if you wanted to figure out information about the XML, such as the number of attributes or elements, or if you wanted to navigate in a richer way, the XML reader is up for the task.

Using Parameters with SQLXML

To use parameters with SQLXML, we need to create a `SqlXmlParameter` object. Our query must specify that we are going to pass a parameter, and the `SqlXmlParameter` object must have its properties set correctly. The following code snippets show you how to use a parameter with your SQLXML queries:

```
strQuery = "SELECT * FROM " & strTable & " WHERE city = ? FOR XML AUTO, ELEMENTS"
. . .
Dim oSQLXMLParameter As Microsoft.Data.SqlXml.SqlXmlParameter
oSQLXMLParameter = oSQLXMLCommand.CreateParameter()
oSQLXMLParameter.Name = "city"
oSQLXMLParameter.Value = "Oakland"
...
```

Executing XPath or SQL Queries with Templates

With SQLXML, you can execute XPath or SQL queries. The sample application uses a template to execute a SQL query and a straight XPath statement for the XPath query. The sample could have used a template for the XPath query, but the sample demonstrates how to use the XPath command type. The following code sets up the SQL template query:

```
'Load up our query
strQuery = "<Root><sql:query xmlns:sql=""urn:schemas-microsoft-com:xml-sql""> _
SELECT * FROM AuthorsXMLNew FOR XML AUTO</sql:query></Root>"
```

Next, the sample sets the command type to be a template in order to run the SQL template query. The sample also specifies the root node and the path to the annotated XSD schema file.

```
oSQLXMLCommand.CommandType = Microsoft.Data.SqlXml.SqlXmlCommandType.Template
oSQLXMLCommand.SchemaPath = txtXMLSchema.Text
oSQLXMLCommand.RootTag = "ROOT"
```

The code uses a `StreamReader` to render the results. That code won't be shown here, since you've seen it already.

To perform the XPath query, again, we set up the query as shown here:

```
'Load up our query
strQuery = "/AuthorsXMLNew[city='Oakland']"
```

Since we are using an XPath query directly, we need to set the command type to be XPath for our `SqlXmlCommand` object. Just as we did for the SQL template query, we want to set our root node and also the path to our annotated XSD schema. After that, we'll again use the `StreamReader` to render our results.

```
oSQLXMLCommand.CommandType = Microsoft.Data.SqlXml.SqlXmlCommandType.XPath
oSQLXMLCommand.SchemaPath = txtXMLSchema.Text
oSQLXMLCommand.RootTag = "ROOT"
```

Interoperating with the ADO.NET Dataset

SQLXML interoperates with the ADO.NET dataset through the `SqlXmlAdapter` object. You can use the `SqlXmlAdapter` to fill your dataset. Then you can use the `DataSet` object as you normally would in ADO.NET. The following code, taken from the sample application, creates a query, executes that query using the `SqlXmlAdapter` object, and then fills a dataset with the information. To write out the value returned back, the code uses some stream objects.

```
strQuery = "SELECT * FROM " & strTable & " WHERE city =
   'oakland' FOR XML AUTO, ELEMENTS"
...

Dim oSQLXMLDataAdapter As New _
   Microsoft.Data.SqlXml.SqlXmlAdapter(oSQLXMLCommand)
Dim oDS As New System.Data.DataSet()
oSQLXMLDataAdapter.Fill(oDS)

'Display the underlying XML
Dim oMemStream As New System.IO.MemoryStream()
Dim oStreamWriter As New System.IO.StreamWriter(oMemStream)
oDS.WriteXml(oMemStream, System.Data.XmlWriteMode.IgnoreSchema)
oMemStream.Position = 0
Dim oStreamReader As New System.IO.StreamReader(oMemStream)
txtResults.Text = oStreamReader.ReadToEnd()
oMemStream.Close()
```

Programming Updategrams

The final piece of the sample application we'll look at uses updategrams. Updategrams allow you to update your SQL Server using your existing XML documents. The code creates the updategram using a `StringBuilder` object. Then the code sets the command type to be `UpdateGram`. Finally, the rest of the code is the same as the original code to execute the command and get the results, so that section is not repeated here.

```
Dim strUpdateGram As New System.Text.StringBuilder()
strUpdateGram.Append("<?xml version='1.0'?><AuthorsXMLNewupdate ")
strUpdateGram.Append("xmlns:updg='urn:schemas-microsoft-com:xml-updategram'>")
strUpdateGram.Append("<updg:sync updg:nullvalue='nothing'>" &
    "<updg:before></updg:before>")
strUpdateGram.Append("<updg:after><AuthorsXMLNew au_id='123-22-1232'")
strUpdateGram.Append(" au_fname='Tom' state='WA' phone='425-882-8080'/>")
strUpdateGram.Append("</updg:after>")
strUpdateGram.Append("<updg:before><AuthorsXMLNew")
strUpdateGram.Append(" au_id='267-41-2394'/></updg:before>")
strUpdateGram.Append("<updg:after></updg:after>")
strUpdateGram.Append("<updg:before><AuthorsXMLNew")
strUpdateGram.Append(" au_id='238-95-7766'/></updg:before>")
strUpdateGram.Append("<updg:after><AuthorsXMLNew")
strUpdateGram.Append(" city='Oakland' phone='212-555-1212'/>")
strUpdateGram.Append("</updg:after></updg:sync></AuthorsXMLNewupdate>")

strQuery = strUpdateGram.ToString()
...

oSQLXMLCommand.CommandType =
Microsoft.Data.SqlXml.SqlXmlCommandType.UpdateGram
```

Summary

This chapter introduced the XML technologies that work against SQL Server. This includes the OPENXML and FOR XML query extensions, XML BulkLoad, and also the SQLXML technologies. SQL Server 2008 adds features like lax validation and new date and time support. These are welcome additions to SQL Server's XML arsenal.

In the next chapter, you'll see how SQL Server has evolved to include rich support for XML with the XML datatype and the XQuery language. We'll also look at XML web services support, which replaces the ISAPI SQLXML web services support.

CHAPTER 17

■ ■ ■

SQL Server XML and XQuery Support

Convergence is happening all around us. Cell phones are integrating PDA functionality and cameras. PDAs are becoming cell phones. Convergence is also happening in the world of data. Customers do not want to need to deal with multiple systems to manage their unstructured, semistructured, and structured data. This is why for years customers have been looking to relational databases to manage all their data, not just their relational data.

There are a number of reasons why a relational database, rather than other technologies like the file system, is the best place to work with all your data. First, relational databases have powerful storage technologies that are more granular than what the file system offers. You can do piecemeal backups. You can break apart your data into filegroups—and now even into partitions. And you have a transacted storage mechanism underneath your data. Second, databases have powerful indexing as well as query processors, so you can ask complex questions to the system about your data. Finally, databases already store some of your most critical data that you probably want to query across to compare with your other nonrelational data. For example, you may want to show all sales for a particular customer, where your sales data is stored relationally and your customer data is XML. If you use the file system and a relational database, you must query across those technologies, and if you want to transactionally update across the two for any data changes, you need to write a lot of code. To support these new scenarios that require XML and relational data working seamlessly together, Microsoft has native XML support in SQL Server .

With SQL Server, you work with your nonrelational data in the same way you work with your relational data. The methods might be a little bit different, but the tools and environment are the same. You saw some of this in the last chapter with XPath, `OPENXML`, and SQLXML support in SQL Server. Beyond these technologies, SQL Server natively supports storage, querying, and modification of XML data. In this chapter, we will look at the following functionalities in SQL Server:

- *XML datatype*: The XML datatype brings native XML storage to SQL Server. Rather than shredding your XML data into relational columns, you can store your XML using the native XML datatype.

- *XQuery*: XML Query Language (XQuery) is a forthcoming standard from the World Wide Web Consortium (W3C) that allows you to query XML data. XQuery is to XML data what the SQL language is to relational data. You can use XQuery inside Transact-SQL (T-SQL) code, as you will see in this chapter.

- *XML indexes*: Just as you can index relational columns in SQL Server, you can also index XML columns to improve performance. SQL Server supports both primary and secondary indexes on XML columns.

- *Full-text search*: Since XML is text-centric, you may want to combine full-text indexing with the XML datatype to find XML information faster.

- *Dynamic management views for XML*: You may want to understand the usage of XML in your server, such as which XML columns are indexed and which XML Schemas you have loaded into your server. Dynamic management views provide this type of information for your XML data.

- *XML web services support*: To support scenarios for data access, such as retrieving SQL Server information from non-Windows platforms, SQL Server has native support for XML web services. Using this capability, you can get or set your data using web services, as well as call stored procedures or user-defined functions (UDFs).

Using the XML Datatype

SQL Server has an XML datatype you can use to natively store XML data in SQL Server databases. If you are still using SQL Server 2000, you can store XML, but it must be in a string-based column, or you must shred the data into relational columns using OPENXML or BulkLoad, as you saw in the previous chapter. By using a native XML type, SQL Server 2005 and 2008 can support richer operations against your XML data, such as constraints, cross-domain queries that combine relational data and XQuery, and XML indexes.

Another benefit of using the native XML datatype is that XML data is inherently different from relational data in its structure. XML data is in a hierarchical structure that can be recursive, and XML supports a different query language than relational systems.

There are many scenarios where using relational modeling is a better choice than XML, and vice versa. For example, if you have data that is very interrelated, such as customers, their orders, the products in the orders, and the stores that sell those products, you could try to implement a solution using XML, but it would be quite challenging. How do you structure your hierarchy? Do you want a customer to be a top-level node and then have orders for each customer appear underneath? How do you write a query that returns all customers with at least five orders, where each order is greater than $1,000, and the name of the store where the customers purchased the products? Another problem is that you will repeat data throughout the hierarchy, such as product names, product prices, and so on, because of the hierarchical nature of XML. Plus, if you want to delete a customer but not the products or orders under that customer, you can't do so, because the orders and products are children under the customer element. On the other hand, using a relational model as a solution, you can quickly model your data and query the information.

You may be thinking that in this scenario, you should just shred your XML data into the relational database, as you saw in the previous chapter. However, shredding has its own issues, in that you do not always get back what you put in, since you are not guaranteed the same XML when you reconstitute the shredded data. Shredding adds another layer of complexity in terms of code creation and maintenance. Also, any reasonably complex XML document will need to be shredded across many tables, requiring extensive join operations across those tables to reconstitute the XML. You'll also end up with a complex, annotated schema full of tables and many foreign key relations into which to shred that XML.

Now, there are scenarios where modeling your data using XML is very useful. First, XML can be more flexible than relational models. So, if you need a free-form structure to store data, XML can be a good choice. Also, XML is self-describing and easily portable across applications or even platforms. Plus, if your data has sparse entries or needs rich multivalue functionality, XML is a good choice as your data format. Finally, if you truly have document-centric data such as Microsoft Office documents, you will want to store this information as XML, since Microsoft Office documents lack rigid structures. XML provides the flexibility to store and query the information in the documents in a rich way.

Even if you choose XML as the format for your data, you will need to decide between using the XML datatype, shredding your XML into relational columns, and storing the XML using the (n)varchar(max) or varbinary(max) type. If you care about the order of elements, and you want the ability to use XML programming paradigms such as XPath and XQuery, you will want to use the XML datatype to store your XML data. If your XML data is best represented using a relational model, you can shred your data into relational columns using annotated schemas, just as you could in SQL Server 2000. Finally, if you need to preserve the XML data exactly as it was created, including whitespace and attribute ordering, then you will want to store the XML in an (n)varchar(max) or a varbinary(max) column. Some scenarios (such as legal documents) may require this.

Finally, SQL Server can support a hybrid model, whereby you may use the XML datatype but promote certain properties—for example, key document properties such as author, last modification time, or last save time—into relational columns, or you may shred your XML into relational columns but keep the original copy in an nvarchar column. SQL Server provides the flexibility to meet the needs of your application when working with XML data.

We want to make one thing very clear, though, since this will cause you issues in the long term if you do not remind yourself of it regularly: if your data is quite structured, in that your XML does not look hierarchical and is normalized, you should use the relational model. Do not use XML. XML is targeted at semistructured or unstructured data. If you need to dynamically add schemas or data on the fly that you never expected, XML is your best choice. Do not make the mistake of thinking everything is a nail to bang with the XML hammer in SQL Server.

Understanding How XML Is Stored by SQL Server

Before we discuss how to create a column of type XML, let's first look at how SQL Server stores XML. You may be wondering how, under the covers, SQL Server translates XML into something that is performant when running queries against the XML data. One thing we can guarantee is that XML is not stored as text!

When you create a column using the XML datatype, SQL Server takes the XML and converts it into a binary XML format. One reason for this is that it's faster to index and search binary data than plain text data. A second reason is that you can compress binary data much more easily than plain text data. SQL Server will tokenize the XML and strip out portions of the markup. If you look at many XML documents, you can see that they have redundant text throughout for element or attribute markup. With the XML datatype, this redundancy can be removed, and your data can be compressed.

The XML datatype is implemented using the varbinary(max) datatype under the covers to store the binary XML. If the converted binary XML is small enough to fit in the row, SQL Server stores the binary XML in the row. If the XML is too large, a 24-byte pointer that points to the binary XML is left in the row. With the built-in compression, you should expect an average of 20 percent compression of the XML when storing it in the XML datatype. Of course, this will depend on the number of tags you have in the document and the redundancy of your text. As you will see, using typed XML is preferable to untyped. When types are specified, you can get better performance and compression of the XML datatype because SQL Server does not need to do type conversions and can parse data faster.

If you ever want to see how much compression is achieved between storing your XML using nvarchar and using the XML datatype, you can use the DATALENGTH function. The following example compares using nvarchar and the XML datatype with the XML we use as our sample XML in this chapter:

```
select DATALENGTH(N'<?xml version="1.0" standalone="yes"?>
<people>
  <person>
    <name>
      <givenName>Martin</givenName>
      <familyName>Smith</familyName>
    </name>
. . .
```

```
') as NVARLEN,
DATALENGTH(CAST(N'<?xml version="1.0" standalone="yes"?>
<people>
  <person>
    <name>
      <givenName>Martin</givenName>
      <familyName>Smith</familyName>
    </name>
. . .
' AS XML)) as XMLLEN
```

```
Results:
NVARLEN: 1154
XMLLEN: 324
```

As you can see, we save about 3.5 times the space using the XML datatype. The reason for this is that many tags in this XML repeat, and the XML datatype can strip these tags when it stores the XML data in SQL Server. Depending on the redundancy in your XML, you should find similar savings in size.

Creating XML Columns

The following code creates a new table that contains a standard relational primary key column as well as an XML column. This example uses untyped XML:

```
CREATE TABLE xmltbl (pk INT IDENTITY PRIMARY KEY, xmlCol XML not null)
```

You can have multiple XML columns in a single table. One thing you will notice is that there is no XML schema associated with the XML column.

SQL Server supports both *untyped* and *typed* XML columns. Untyped columns have no schema associated with them. Typed columns have XML Schemas to which the XML documents inserted into the column must conform. Whenever possible, you will want to associate XML Schemas with your XML columns, so that SQL Server will validate your XML data, make better optimizations when querying or modifying your data, perform better type checking, and optimize the storage of your XML data.

As you saw earlier, SQL Server stores XML data in a proprietary binary format for speed and compression. With an index, the server can find the information more quickly, but there is a bit of a performance hit when you insert your data.

■**Note** SQL Server does not support Document Type Definitions (DTDs). DTDs define the document structure of your XML documents. You can use external tools to convert DTDs to an XML Schema Definition (XSD). SQL Server does support XSD.

Defining Typed XML Columns

To create a typed XML column, you need to load your schema into SQL Server and then associate it with the column in question. Once you've done this, only documents that adhere to your schema can be inserted into the table. You can have one or many schemas associated with an XML column.

The following code creates a new table that uses a schema on an XML datatype, so it is a *typed* XML column:

```
-- Create a new database for the samples
USE master
DROP DATABASE xmldb
```

```
IF NOT EXISTS (SELECT * FROM sys.databases WHERE name = 'xmldb')
        CREATE DATABASE xmldb
GO
--Declare the variable for the XML
DECLARE @x XML
-- Open the XSD schema
SELECT @x = s
FROM OPENROWSET (
 BULK 'C:\Customer.xsd',
 SINGLE_BLOB) AS TEMP(s)

select @x
-- Make sure the schema does not exist already
IF EXISTS(select * from sys.xml_schema_collections where name='Customer')
  DROP XML SCHEMA COLLECTION Customer
-- Create the schema in the schema collection for the database
CREATE XML SCHEMA COLLECTION Customer AS @x
GO
-- Create a table that uses our schema on an XML datatype
CREATE TABLE xmltbl2 (pk INT IDENTITY PRIMARY KEY,
xmlColWithSchema XML (CONTENT Customer))
GO
```

First, you need to load your XML Schema into SQL Server. The code uses OPENROWSET to open the XML Schema file stored in the file system. The code assigns the schema to the variable x. Next, the code drops the schema if it exists. Here, you will see the use of the dynamic management views for XML, which we cover later in this chapter. SQL Server includes views for querying the schema collections, schema namespaces, and XML indexes.

If the schema collection does not exist, the code creates the schema collection in SQL Server. Schema collections are scoped to the database where they are created. Schema collections cannot span databases or instances, so you may need to create the same schema in multiple locations if you use the same schema for multiple, different XML datatypes in different databases. You can have more than one XML Schema in your database. In addition, you can assign more than one XML Schema to a column that uses the XML datatype.

One caveat with schemas is that once you create a schema, you cannot modify or drop it until all references to it are removed from the system. For example, if an XML column in your table references a schema, you will not be able to modify that schema. SQL Server will return a message stating that the schema is in use and will include the name of the components using the schema.

Your schema is loaded into SQL Server's metadata and can be viewed using the sys.xml_schema_collections metadata view. If you want to retrieve the schema after you load it into the system, you will need to use the xml_schema_namespace function. This function takes two parameters: the first is the relational schema in which your XML Schema was created, and the second is the name of the schema you want to retrieve. The following code retrieves the Customer schema created in the previous example:

```
--Return the schema
USE xmldb
go

SELECT xml_schema_namespace(N'dbo',N'Customer')
go
```

Here is the returned XML Schema from this call:

```
<xsd:schema xmlns:xsd=http://www.w3.org/2001/XMLSchema
xmlns:t="urn:example/customer" targetNamespace="urn:example/customer"
elementFormDefault="qualified">
  <xsd:element name="NewDataSet">
    <xsd:complexType>
      <xsd:complexContent>
        <xsd:restriction base="xsd:anyType">
          <xsd:choice minOccurs="0" maxOccurs="unbounded">
            <xsd:element ref="t:doc" />
          </xsd:choice>
        </xsd:restriction>
      </xsd:complexContent>
    </xsd:complexType>
  </xsd:element>
<xsd:element name="doc">
  <xsd:complexType>
    <xsd:complexContent>
      <xsd:restriction base="xsd:anyType">
        <xsd:sequence>
          <xsd:element name="customer" minOccurs="0" maxOccurs="unbounded">
            <xsd:complexType>
              <xsd:complexContent>
                <xsd:restriction base="xsd:anyType">
                  <xsd:sequence>
                    <xsd:element name="name" type="xsd:string" minOccurs="0" />
                    <xsd:element name="order" minOccurs="0"
                     maxOccurs="unbounded">
                      <xsd:complexType>
                        <xsd:complexContent>
                          <xsd:restriction base="xsd:anyType">
                            <xsd:sequence />
                            <xsd:attribute name="id" type="xsd:string" />
                            <xsd:attribute name="year" type="xsd:string" />
                          </xsd:restriction>
                        </xsd:complexContent>
                      </xsd:complexType>
                    </xsd:element>
                    <xsd:element name="notes" minOccurs="0"
                    maxOccurs="unbounded">
                    <xsd:complexType>
                        <xsd:complexContent>
                          <xsd:restriction base="xsd:anyType">
                            <xsd:sequence>
                              <xsd:element name="buys" type="xsd:string"
                              minOccurs="0" />
                              <xsd:element name="saleslead" type="xsd:string"
                              minOccurs="0" />
                              <xsd:element name="competitor" type="xsd:string"
                              minOccurs="0" />
                            </xsd:sequence>
                          </xsd:restriction>
                        </xsd:complexContent>
                    </xsd:complexType>
                  </xsd:element>
                </xsd:sequence>
```

```
            <xsd:attribute name="id" type="xsd:string" />
          </xsd:restriction>
        </xsd:complexContent>
      </xsd:complexType>
    </xsd:element>
  </xsd:sequence>
  <xsd:attribute name="id" type="xsd:string" />
</xsd:restriction>
    </xsd:complexContent>
  </xsd:complexType>
</xsd:element>
</xsd:schema>
```

If you compare the returned XML Schema and the original file included with the sample code, you will find that they are different. SQL Server does not guarantee that it will return the same exact XML Schema document as you submitted, since it translates your schema into the server metadata catalog. For example, comments, annotations, and whitespace are removed, and implicit types are made explicit. If you need to keep a copy of your exact schema document, you should store it in a string column, an xml column, or the file system.

SQL Server defines certain schemas by default; these are common schemas that you may want to use in your XML Schemas in addition to your custom schema definitions. The following are the reserved XML Schemas with their prefixes. Note that you cannot create schemas with the same name as the existing predefined schemas in SQL Server.

```
xml = http://www.w3.org/XML/1998/namespace
xs = http://www.w3.org/2001/XMLSchema
xsi = http://www.w3.org/2001/XMLSchema-instance
fn = http://www.w3.org/2004/07/xpath-functions
sqltypes = http://schemas.microsoft.com/sqlserver/2004/sqltypes
xdt = http://www.w3.org/2004/07/xpath-datatypes
(no prefix) = urn:schemas-microsoft-com:xml-sql
(no prefix) = http://schemas.microsoft.com/sqlserver/2004/SOAP
```

An interesting predefined schema is sqltypes. This schema allows you to map your XML data to SQL types such as varchar.

You cannot modify these built-in schemas, nor can you serialize these schemas. You can use the import namespace directive to import these schemas into your own XML Schema, however, and then use the schema in your own custom schema declarations.

As we mentioned earlier, you cannot modify an existing XML schema. You can add new schemas, but then you will need to go through and modify your XML instances to use the new schema. You can drop your schemas and create new schemas, but that will untype your XML, which could be a long operation depending on the number of XML instances contained in your table.

Defining XML Columns Using a GUI

You've seen how to create columns using the XML datatype through code. However, SQL Server Management Studio allows you to work with XML in many ways. Figure 17-1 shows creating a new column of type XML. In the Properties area, you can specify the schema you want to associate with the column, if any. Beyond that, all dialog boxes that take types, such as the new stored procedure header dialog box, will take XML as a type since it is a native type in SQL Server.

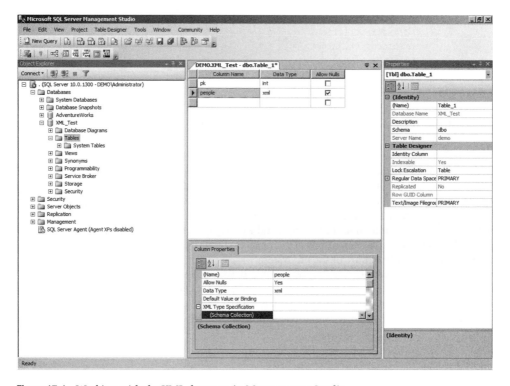

Figure 17-1. *Working with the XML datatype in Management Studio*

Setting Permissions for Schema Creation

The code you walked through earlier for schema creation assumed that you already had permissions to create XML Schemas in the server. However, that may not be the case. Since an XML Schema is like other objects in a SQL Server database, you can set permissions on schema collections. One thing to note is that users need both permissions on the relational schema and explicit permissions for XML Schema creation, since XML Schema creation modifies the relational schema as well. The different types of permissions you can grant and their effects are discussed next.

To create an XML Schema, you need to be granted the CREATE XML SCHEMA COLLECTION permission. You need to grant this permission at the database level.

When you set the ALTER permission, users can modify the contents of an existing XML Schema collection using the ALTER XML SCHEMA COLLECTION statement. Remember that users need permissions on the relational schema as well for this to work.

The CONTROL permission allows users to perform any operation on the XML Schema collection. This means that users can create, delete, or edit the schema information. To transfer ownership of XML Schemas from one user to another, you would set the TAKE OWNERSHIP permission.

To use constraints or for typing your XML datatype columns, you would add the REFERENCE permission to users. The REFERENCE permission is also required when one XML Schema collection refers to another.

The VIEW DEFINITION permission allows users to query the contents of an XML Schema collection either through XML_SCHEMA_NAMESPACE or through the XML dynamic management views. Users need to also have ALTER, CONTROL, or REFERENCES permission.

To perform validation against schemas, the EXECUTE permission is required. Users also need this permission when querying the XML stored in columns and variables that are typed.

The following code shows how to grant permissions for a user to alter the relational and XML Schema inside a database:

```
-- Grant permissions on the relational schema in the database
GRANT ALTER ON SCHEMA::dbo TO User1
GO
-- Grant permission to create XML schema collections in the database
GRANT CREATE XML SCHEMA COLLECTION
TO User1
GO
```

Constraining XML Columns

You can use relational constraints on XML columns. There may be times when you will keep your XML data untyped and use constraints instead; for example, if the constraint you want to use is not easily expressed using XML Schemas, such as executing an XPath statement. One example of this may be a constraint that makes sure that the order amount is not discounted by more than a certain amount, which is calculated dynamically, depending on the total cost of the order. Bigger order amounts may get larger discounts, but cannot exceed a certain sliding scale of percentages for discounts.

Another reason to use constraints is if you need to constrain the column based on other columns' values. For example, you may want to make sure that another value in another column is filled in before allowing users to insert data into your XML column.

There are limitations to using XML columns, though. For instance, XML columns cannot be primary keys or foreign keys, nor can they have unique constraints. However, they can be included in a clustered index or explicitly added to a nonclustered index by using the INCLUDE keyword when the nonclustered index is created.

The following example creates a table with an XML column that has a constraint.

■**Note** Since XML datatype methods are not directly supported in CHECK constraints, you need to use a UDF to perform the constraint check. This technique is shown in the sample code.

```
CREATE FUNCTION CheckCustomerName(@x xml)
RETURNS bit
AS
BEGIN
  RETURN @x.exist('declare namespace
cust="urn:example/customer";
/cust:doc/cust:customer/cust:name')
END;
GO
--Create a constraint
CREATE TABLE xmltbl3 (pk int IDENTITY PRIMARY KEY,
xmlColWithConstraint XML CHECK(dbo.CheckCustomerName(xmlColWithConstraint) = 1))
GO
```

The constraint checks to see if the XML being inserted has a customer name. You could also create constraints against other columns, different datatypes, or information contained in the XML itself. Once you create your table with the constraint, you can then try to insert data into the table. If you insert data that does not meet the constraint, you'll get the following error message:

```
Msg 547, Level 16, State 0, Line 1
INSERT statement conflicted with CHECK constraint 'CK__xmltbl3__xmlColW__0BC6C43E'.
The conflict occurred in database 'xmldb',
 table 'xmltbl3', column 'xmlColWithConstraint'.
The statement has been terminated.
```

Examining the XML Datatype Limitations

There are a number of limitations you should be aware of with the XML datatype. First, the XML datatype is limited to 2GB in size and 128 levels of hierarchy. Furthermore, the XML datatype cannot be compared, sorted, grouped by, part of a view, part of a clustered or nonclustered index, part of a distributed partitioned view, or part of an indexed view. Some of these limitations are due to the fact that XML is not relational data or that the XML datatype has its own way to create indexes or sort its data. Even given these limitations, you should be able to store the majority of your XML data in SQL Server. If you have data that exceeds these limitations, especially the 2GB size limit, we'd love to learn more about that dataset!

SQL Server stores your XML data using UTF-16 by default. If you need to use a different encoding, you will cast the results or perform a conversion in your application. For example, you could convert your XML result to a different SQL type such as nvarchar. However, you cannot convert the XML datatype to text or ntext. Your XML data will use the collation settings on your server for the result set.

XML data employs the same locking mechanism as SQL Server. This means the XML datatype supports row-level locking. This is true whether you are using T-SQL or XQuery. Therefore, if the row gets locked, all XML instances in that row are locked as well.

Inserting Data into XML Columns

Now that you know how to create XML columns, we will show you how to get your XML data into those columns. In the previous chapter, you saw how to perform this task using SQLXML BulkLoad. Beyond SQLXML, there are three common ways that you will get your data into your XML column: SQL Server Integration Services (SSIS), bulk-loading with OPENROWSET and bcp.exe, and writing queries or applications. We'll discuss each method in the sections that follow.

Using SSIS with XML Data

SSIS is probably the easiest way to move XML data between different data sources. With SSIS, you can easily take XML data and move it into SQL Server. SSIS supports pulling XML from file systems or other locations, transforming that XML, and then putting the XML into an XML datatype column in SQL Server or shredding the XML into relational columns. Figure 17-2 shows a package that pulls data from an XML source and puts the XML into SQL Server.

Figure 17-3 shows mapping the data from the XML source to the XML column created earlier.

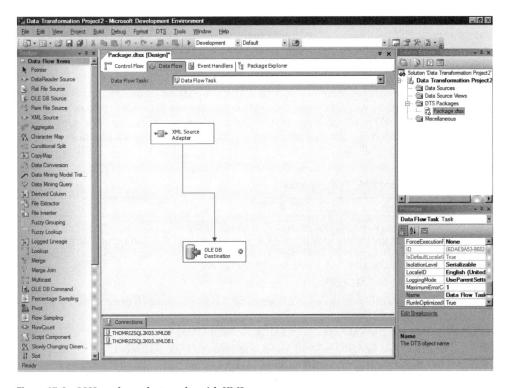

Figure 17-2. *SSIS package that works with XML*

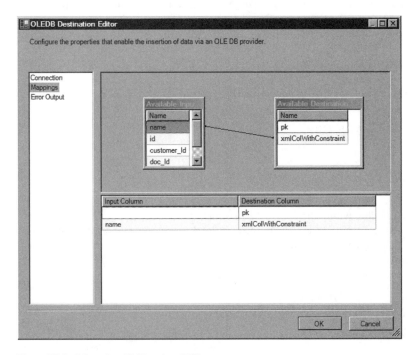

Figure 17-3. *Mapping XML using SSIS*

The XML data source adapter allows you to select any XML data source, such as XML from a file. You can specify the XSD for the XML or have SSIS infer the XSD from the XML file. You can also select your output columns for your XML just in case you do not want all columns to be imported into the SSIS pipeline. In addition, you can use the XML data source adapter to shred your XML into relational columns.

One other interesting component of SSIS with XML is the XML task. The XML task is part of the SSIS control flow and allows you to take multiple XML documents and combine them or transform the documents using XSL Transformations (XSLT). You can then put the results back into a file or into a SSIS variable that you can use through the rest of your SSIS flow. Table 17-1 outlines the tasks you can perform with the XML task.

Table 17-1. *SSIS Predefined XML Task Methods*

Operation	Description
Diff	Compares two XML documents. The source is the base document, and you specify the XML document to which to compare the source. The difference is saved into a diffgram document. The result is not a new XML document, but just the differences. To apply the diffgram, use the Patch operation.
Merge	Merges two XML documents together.
Patch	Applies a diffgram to an XML document. A new document is created with the changes applied.
Validate	Validates the XML against an XML schema or DTD.
XPath	Allows you to perform XPath queries against the XML document.
XSLT	Allows you to apply an XSLT transform to your XML document.

You may notice that XQuery is not an option in the XML task. Instead, if you want to perform an XQuery, you will need to use the Execute SQL task feature and use the XQuery methods on a stored XML datatype in your SQL Server database.

Bulk-Loading XML

Beyond using SSIS, you can bulk-load XML data into SQL Server using the OPENROWSET keyword. The following example takes the data from the file system and inserts it into SQL Server:

```
INSERT INTO xmltbl2 (xmlColWithSchema)
SELECT *
FROM OPENROWSET (
 BULK 'C:\Customer1.xml',
 SINGLE_BLOB) AS TEMP
GO
```

Using a bulk-load provider within the OPENROWSET is similar to the BULK INSERT statement, but you do not need to send the output to a table with the bulk-load provider. You can specify a format file, as you can with bcp.exe. In addition, you can specify in-line information about the file properties using the following options: CODEPAGE, DATAFILETYPE, FIELDTERMINATOR, FIRSTROW, LASTROW, and ROWTERMINATOR. You can also specify table hints using the new bulk-load provider.

Writing a Custom Query or Application

The final way to get your data into your XML columns is to write applications that insert the data. For example, your application could be a simple T-SQL script you run in Management Studio or it could be a full-blown application that inserts XML data into SQL Server using ADO.NET or ADO. No matter which method you use, you will insert XML using the INSERT INTO statement. The following code snippet demonstrates inserting XML data in-line using T-SQL:

```
--Insert XML directly using inline XML
INSERT INTO xmltbl2(xmlColWithSchema) VALUES(
    '<doc id="d1" xmlns="urn:example/customer">
      <customer id="c7">
        <name>Tom</name>
        <order id="1" year="2002"></order>
        <order id="2" year="2003"></order>
        <notes>
          <buys>gizmos</buys>
          <saleslead>Bob</saleslead>
          <competitor>Acme</competitor>
        </notes>
      </customer>
    </doc>
    ')
Go
```

As you can see, you can pass in-line XML directly using an INSERT statement. In your applications, you will either use dynamic SQL to add rows with XML data or create stored procedures.

■**Tip** There may be times when you want to preserve whitespace in your XML so that the XML data you put in is the same as you get out, with all the whitespace included. By defaut, SQL Server will discard insignificant whitespace, such as spaces between tags for elements. If you want to preserve this whitespace, you can use the CONVERT function and pass the optional style parameter with a value of 1.

Querying XML Data

Once you get your XML data into SQL Server, you may want to get it back out. The XML datatype provides four methods for you to do this: query(), value(), exist(), and nodes(). Another method on the XML datatype is modify(), which we discuss later in the section "Modifying XML Data."

These methods are based on the use of the XQuery language, so we'll start with a quick XQuery tutorial. Then we'll investigate how to use these methods to query XML data.

XQuery 101

If you currently use XPath or XSLT, XQuery should not be entirely unfamiliar to you. You're used to iterating over hierarchies of data and the semantics of the XPath language. However, if you do only relational work with T-SQL, XQuery may look like a strange new beast. The reason for this is that T-SQL works on rows and columns, not hierarchies of information. XML data is structured differently from relational data, and it will take a bit of time for relational developers to get used to XQuery or even XPath syntax. That should not stop you from starting to learn these different languages, though, since more and more information will be stored in XML over the coming years.

SQL Server 2000 supported XML shredding and XPath 1.0 expressions, and you saw some examples of these technologies in the previous chapter. However, XPath gets you only so far in working with your XML data. It lacks the ability to perform more complex operations on your XML data, as it does not support recursive XML schemas and projection and transformation syntax. XQuery is the big brother of XPath, in that the simplest form of an XQuery is an XPath expression.

Before we dive into XQuery, though, let's take a look at an XPath statement just in case you've never used XPath before or didn't read the previous chapter. We'll work with the following sample

XML document. You can follow along with the samples in this chapter by opening the file XMLSample.sql included with the sample downloads for this book, which you can find in the Source Code/Download area of the Apress web site (http://www.apress.com).

```
<?xml version="1.0" encoding="UTF-8" standalone="yes"?>
<people>
  <person>
    <name>
      <givenName>Martin</givenName>
      <familyName>Smith</familyName>
    </name>
    <age>33</age>
    <height>short</height>
  </person>
  <person>
    <name>
      <givenName>Stacy</givenName>
      <familyName>Eckstein</familyName>
    </name>
    <age>40</age>
    <height>short</height>
  </person>
  <person>
    <name>
      <givenName>Tom</givenName>
      <familyName>Rizzo</familyName>
    </name>
    <age>30</age>
    <height>medium</height>
  </person>
</people>
```

To retrieve all the names for all the people, you execute the following XPath statement:

```
/people//name
```

To move this XPath query to an XQuery, you put a curly brace around the query, which tells the XQuery processor that the query is an XQuery expression and not a string literal.

■**Note** See the previous chapter for a brief introduction to XPath. If you need more information, *Beginning XSLT 2.0* by Jeni Tennison (Apress, 2005) provides a good introduction to XPath, and you can check out the articles on sites such as http://www.xml.org.

FLWOR

While you can use XPath expressions in XQuery, the real power of XQuery is through FLWOR. *FLWOR* stands for For-Let-Where-Order By-Return. FLWOR is similar to T-SQL's SELECT, FROM, and WHERE statements, in that you can conditionally return information based on criteria that you set. However, instead of returning relational data like T-SQL, XQuery returns XML data. Let's look in more detail at each of the parts of FLWOR.

- The For expression lets you specify the XML that you want to iterate over. The way you specify your XML is by using an XPath expression. Normally, you surround your entire XQuery statement with any beginning or ending XML tags that you want. This will depend on which nodes you iterate in your document and the desired structure of the returned XML document. You can think of this expression as being similar to combining the SELECT and FROM T-SQL statements.

- The Let expression allows you to set a variable to an expression, but does not iterate over the values.

- The Where expression is similar to the T-SQL WHERE clause. This expression evaluates to a Boolean. Any value that returns True passes through, and any value that returns False is rejected.

- The Order By expression is similar to the SQL ORDER BY clause. This expression allows you to sort your result sets using the sort order you specify.

- The Return expression specifies the content that should be returned.

The following is a more complex example of an XQuery statement. The example iterates over the XML contained in a table and returns only the given name of people who have an age element in the XML document.

```
SELECT people.query(
'for $p in //people
where $p//age
return
  <person>
    <name>{$p//givenName}</name>
  </person>
'
)
FROM xmltblnew
```

The following XQuery counts the number of person elements in an XML document. It also shows how to use the query method of the XML datatype with XQuery.

```
SELECT people.query(
'count(//person)
')
FROM XMLtblnew
go
```

Beyond FLWOR, XQuery supports functions such as avg, min, max, ceiling, floor, and round. The following example shows how to calculate the rounded average age of people from an XML document:

```
SELECT people.query(
'round(avg(//age))
')
FROM XMLtblnew
go
```

XQuery has string functions such as substring, string-length, and contains. It also has date/time functions such as dateTime-equal, dateTime-less-than, dateTime-greater-than, and individual date and time functions. The example that follows shows some of these functions in use. First, you get all the nodes in the XML document under the people node that have an age. Then you return the givenName element for each person. If you wanted to return only the data for this element, you could use the data function. Instead, you want to return the full element for the givenName. Next, if there is a match on a particular name, such as Martin, you want to return True; otherwise, you want to return False. Finally, the code figures out the maximum age of all people by using the max function.

```
SELECT people.query(
'for $c in (/people)
where $c//age
return
  <customers>
     <name>
     {$c//givenName}
     </name>
     <match>{contains($c,"Martin")}</match>
     <maxage>{max($c//age)}</maxage>
  </customers>
')
FROM xmltblnew
Go
```

Table 17-2 lists the functions you can use against the XML datatype when using XQuery.

Table 17-2. *XML Datatype XQuery Functions*

Function	Description
Numeric	
ceiling	Returns the smallest integer of the values passed to the function that is greater than the value of the argument.
floor	Returns the largest integer of the values passed to the function that is not greater than the value of the argument.
round	Rounds to the nearest integer the values passed to the function.
String	
concat	Concatenates the strings passed to the function, such as concat($p//givenName[1]/ text()[1],$p//familyName[1]/ text()[1]).
contains	Returns a true value if the first argument, the string to test, contains the second argument, the string to search for. Otherwise, it returns false.
substring	Returns a portion of the first argument, the source string, starting at the location specified in the second argument and optionally for the length in the third argument, such as substring($p//givenName[1]/text()[1], 1, 2).
string-length	Returns the length of string passed as an argument.
Boolean	
not	Flips the value of the Boolean from true to false and false to true.
Node	
number	Returns a number for the value of the node passed as an argument, such as number($p//age[1]/text()[1]).
Context	
last	Returns an integer that is the count of the last item in the sequence.
position	Returns an integer that is the current position in the sequence. This is useful if you want to print the ordinal value of your sequence for identification.
Sequences	
empty	Returns true if the argument passed, which is a sequence, is empty.
distinct-values	Removes duplicates from your sequence. You must pass a sequence of atomic values to this function, such as distinct-values(data(//people/person/age)).

Function	Description
Aggregate	
avg	Returns the average of a sequence of numbers.
count	Counts the number of items in the sequence and returns an integer.
min	Returns the minimum value from a sequence of numbers.
max	Returns the maximum value from a sequence of numbers.
sum	Returns the sum of a sequence of numbers.
Constructor	
various	Allows you to create an XSD type from another type or literal. Depending on the desired type, the constructor function will be different. For example, to construct a string, you would use xs:string("Tom") or a date/time using xs:dateTime("2005-10-01T00:00:00Z").
Data Access	
data	Returns the typed value of the node. For example, data(/people/person/name/familyName) returns the family name. Data is implicit and does not need to be specified, but doing so can help readability of your XQuery.
string	Returns the value of the argument as a string. For example, to return just a string of the document node, specify string(/).

XQuery in More Depth

If you break apart the XQuery statements shown earlier, XQuery contains a *prolog* and a *body*. The prolog contains declarations and definitions that set up the necessary environment to run the body. This setup could include declaring namespaces in the prolog. The body consists of a series of XQuery expressions that will get you your desired result.

To declare a namespace in the prolog, you have two choices: put an in-line declaration in the prolog or use the WITH XMLNAMESPACES keyword. To improve readability of your queries, you will want to use the WITH XMLNAMESPACES approach, since declaring namespaces in-line can make a query very hard to understand and read. For example, take a look at the following two queries. You can decide for yourself which one is easier to understand, but most likely you will agree that it's the second one.

```
SELECT people.query(
'declare namespace peopleschema="urn:example/people";
round(avg(//peopleschema:age))
')
FROM XMLtblnew
GO

WITH XMLNAMESPACES('urn:example/people' AS peopleschema)
SELECT people.query(
'round(avg(//peopleschema:age))
')
FROM XMLtblnew
GO
```

As part of the prolog, you can also declare a default namespace. You can then omit element namespace prefixes on all your elements in that namespace. This is useful if you have only one namespace for all elements in your XML document. You would use the declare default element namespace syntax if you declared your namespace in the prolog, or you would use the WITH XMLNAMESPACES (DEFAULT 'yournamespace') syntax if you declared the namespace outside the prolog.

Note that you can use the WITH XMLNAMESPACES syntax with other operations besides XQuery operations. You can also use this syntax with FOR XML if you want to add a namespace to your FOR XML-rendered XML documents.

Once you begin working with the body of your XQuery, you will start using the literals and operators we discussed previously, such as sum, min, max, for, order by, path expressions, sequence expressions, and so on.

Always remember that comparison operators are XML-encoded, which means less than (<) is <, greater than (>) is >, and so forth.

Also note that you can use the built-in types such as xs:string and xs:date in your XQueries. Casting is supported using the CAST AS operator for explicit casting, but XQuery also supports implicit casting for types it can coerce to be other horizontal types. Numeric types are supported only when doing implicit casting.

XQuery Processing in SQL Server

Because of its modular architecture, SQL Server can leverage the existing query execution and optimization technologies to process XQuery. Rather than building a separate query execution pipeline or optimization infrastructure, SQL Server leverages the same infrastructure for XQuery that it does for T-SQL. Because of this implementation, the level of integration between XQuery and T-SQL is superior. This is what allows you to do rich cross-domain queries between the two languages. For example, when SQL Server encounters an XQuery statement, the XQuery parser is called. The results of the XQuery parser, which is a query tree, are grafted onto any existing query to generate the entire query tree, which may contain both relational and XQuery queries. In effect, the T-SQL query and the XQuery are combined into a single query. The entire query is then passed to the optimizer, and an XML Showplan is created that includes the XQuery operations, as shown in Figure 17-4.

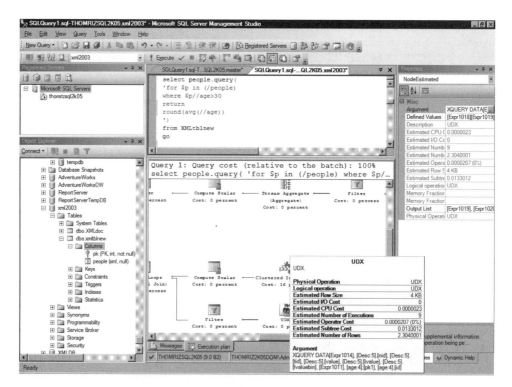

Figure 17-4. *Execution Showplan with an XQuery*

Basic XML Query Methods

Let's now examine the four methods for querying XML datatypes:

- query(): Returns the XML that matches your query
- value(): Returns a scalar value from your XML
- exist(): Checks for the existence of the specified XML in your XML datatype
- nodes(): Returns a rowset representation of your XML

query()

The query() method takes an XQuery statement and returns the XML that matches the query. The XML that is returned is untyped XML and can be further parsed if needed.

To see how this works, create a new table, xmltblnew, to store the XML. You'll use this table to learn how to query and modify XML data.

```
-- Create a new table
CREATE TABLE xmltblnew (pk INT IDENTITY PRIMARY KEY, people XML)
GO

--Insert data into the new table
INSERT INTO xmltblnew (people)
SELECT *
FROM OPENROWSET (
 BULK 'C:\peopleXML.xml',
 SINGLE_BLOB) AS TEMP
GO
```

The following example uses the query() method to look for all people who have an age, and then returns XML that identifies each person by name:

```
SELECT people.query(
'for $p in //people
WHERE $p//age
return
  <person>
    <name>{$p//givenName}</name>
  </person>
'
)
FROM xmltblnew
```

As you look at the preceding XQuery, you will notice that it maps somewhat to T-SQL in the following ways:

- SELECT is equivalent to RETURN.
- FROM is equivalent to FOR.
- WHERE is equivalent to WHERE.

The interesting part is that the semantics of the query are different. Rather than using relational types of operations, you use hierarchical path operations. The XQuery—and for that matter, XPath syntax—takes some getting used to. If you haven't thought in a hierarchical, path-based way before, you should start out with simple queries to learn the language. Once you progress from the simple queries, you will see that XQuery can be almost as complex in terms of functionality as T-SQL.

value()

The value() method returns a scalar value back from the XML instance. This method takes two arguments: the first is the XQuery you want to use to get the value, and the second is the T-SQL type that you want that value converted to. You cannot convert to a timestamp or the NTEXT, TEXT, or IMAGE types. Also, you can't convert to an XML or a sql_variant datatype.

You will want to try and match types between XML and SQL. For example, a string value in XML can be converted to any T-SQL string type. Numbers can be converted to numeric types. In addition, string values that can be coerced into numbers can be converted into numeric or money types. Date, time, or string values that can be valid datetime values can be converted into datetime types.

The following code snippet gets the age of the second person in the XML document and returns it as an integer:

```
SELECT people.value('/people[1]/person[2]/age[1][text()]', 'integer')
 as age FROM XMLtblnew
GO
```

As a quick aside, try running the following code and note the error you get:

```
SELECT people.value('/people[1]/person[2]/age[1][text()]', 'integer')
 as age FROM XMLtblnew
GO
```

You will get an archaic error telling you that the value function requires a singleton or an empty sequence and not an operand of type xdt:untypedAtomic. You may be looking at this and thinking, "But I return the text of the first age element, which is a singleton!" Well, when SQL Server goes through its evaluation, it looks at the entire expression to see if any part can return more than a single node. In the code that returns an error, the people path in the expression does not have a position predicate, so it could possibly return more than a single node. The easiest way to fix this common error is to make sure you use position predicates in your expressions.

exist()

The exist() method is used to check for the existence of an XML datatype. This method returns 1 if the XQuery expression returns a non-null result. Otherwise, this method will return 0 if the condition is not met or if the result set is null. The following example returns the columns in the SELECT statement where the givenName of the person stored in the XML document is equal to Tom.

```
SELECT pk, people FROM xmltblnew
  WHERE people.exist('/people/person/name/givenName[.="Tom"]') = 1
```

nodes()

The nodes() method returns a rowset for each row that is selected by the query. You can then work on that rowset using the built-in functionality of SQL Server. The following example returns the XML in relational form by breaking the XML into individual rows per person using CROSS APPLY. You could also use OUTER APPLY if you like. The nodes() method is similar to OPENXML, except that OPENXML requires you to prepare the document, and it uses the Document Object Model (DOM) to parse the document, which can slow down performance. The XML datatype is already parsed, so you could see better performance using nodes() than using OPENXML.

```
SELECT T2.Person.query('.')
FROM   xmltblnew
CROSS APPLY people.nodes('/people/person') as T2(Person)
```

```
Results:
Row 1: <person><name><givenName>Martin</givenName>
<familyName>Smith</familyName>
</name><age>33</age><height>short</height></person>

Row 2: <person><name><givenName>Stacy</givenName>
<familyName>Eckstein</familyName></name><age>40</age>
<height>short</height></person>

Row 3: <person><name><givenName>Tom</givenName>
<familyName>Rizzo</familyName></name>
<age>30</age><height>medium</height></person>
```

Cross-Domain Queries

There may be times when you want to combine your relational and XML data. You've already seen some examples of cross-domain queries in the previous section, whereby you combine relational queries with XML queries, or vice versa.

SQL Server provides functionality for you to use your relational data in your XQuery through the sql:variable() and sql:column() methods. The sql:variable() method allows you to apply a SQL variable in your XQuery. The sql:column() method allows you to use a SQL column in your XQuery.

The following example uses the sql:column() method to retrieve values from relational columns in the table and sql:variable to retrieve a T-SQL variable value, and it uses both of these to generate a result set:

```
USE xmldb
GO

CREATE TABLE xmlTable (id int IDENTITY PRIMARY KEY,
                       CustomerID char(5),
                       Name varchar(50),
                       Address varchar(100),
                       xmlCustomer XML);
GO
INSERT INTO xmlTable
VALUES ('AP', 'Apress LP', 'Berkeley CA', '<Customer />');

GO
DECLARE @numemployees int;
SET @numemployees=500;
SELECT id, xmlCustomer.query('
DECLARE namespace pd="urn:example/customer";
     <Customer
         CustomerID=        "{ sql:column("T.CustomerID") }"
         CustomerName=      "{ sql:column("T.Name") }"
         CustomerAddress=   "{ sql:column("T.Address") }"
         NumEmployees=      "{ sql:variable("@numemployees") }">
     </Customer>
') as Result FROM xmlTable T;
GO
```

Modifying XML Data

SQL Server includes an extension method to XQuery, the modify() method. The modify() method allows you to modify parts of your XML data. You can add or delete subtrees, replace values, or perform similar XML modifications. The modify() method includes Data Manipulation Language (DML) commands such as insert, delete, and replace value of.

SQL Server supports piecemeal XML modification. This means that when you modify your XML document, such as adding elements, changing attributes, or deleting elements, SQL Server performs just the necessary operations on the XML rather than replacing the entire XML document.

Inserting an Element

With the insert command, you can insert XML as the first or last element. You can specify whether to insert the XML before, after, or as a direct descendant of an existing XML element. You can also insert attributes using this method. Without needing to modify the entire document, you can use insert to easily put XML into existing documents. The insert command also allows the user to use a scalar T-SQL variable of type xml within the insert expression. For example, consider the following shopping list:

```
<List>
  <Item>Bananas</Item>
  <Item>Apples</Item>
</List>
```

Suppose we want to insert a value stored in a T-SQL variable into this list as another item. This can be accomplished using the following code:

```
DECLARE @GroceryList xml
SET @GroceryList='<List><Item>Bananas</Item><Item>Apples</Item></List>'

DECLARE @AdditionalItem xml
SET @AdditionalItem='<Item>Dog Food</Item>'

SET @GroceryList.modify
('insert sql:variable("@AdditionalItem")  as last into (/List)[1]')

SELECT @GroceryList
```

The result of the @GroceryList variable is as follows:

```
<List>
  <Item>Bananas</Item>
  <Item>Apples</Item>
  <Item>Dog Food</Item>
</List>
```

Deleting an Element

With the delete command, you can delete XML elements or attributes from your XML document. For example, you might remember that you don't need dog food after all.

```
SET @GroceryList.modify ('delete /List/Item[Dog Food]')
```

This invocation of the delete command within the modify method deletes the dog food item that was added to your grocery list in the preceding section.

Changing a Node Value

The `replace value of` command allows you to replace a node with a new value that you specify. You can replace only a single node at a time; you cannot select multiple nodes.

The following example inserts and changes the `favoritecolor` element for person number 3 in the XML document:

```
--First insert a new value
UPDATE xmltblnew SET people.modify(
'insert <favoriteColor>Red</favoriteColor>
  as last into (/people/person[3])[1]')
WHERE pk=1
GO

--Select the data to show the change
SELECT * FROM xmltblnew
GO

--Modify the value
UPDATE xmltblnew SET people.modify(
'replace value of (/people/person[3]/favoriteColor[1]/text())[1]
  with "Blue"')
WHERE pk=1
GO

--Select the data to show the change
SELECT * FROM xmltblnew
GO

--Now delete the value
UPDATE xmltblnew SET people.modify(
'delete /people/person[3]/favoriteColor')
WHERE pk=1
GO

--Select the data to show the change
SELECT * FROM xmltblnew
GO
```

Limitations of XML Modification

You have some limitations when you modify your XML, including the following:

- For typed or untyped XML, you cannot insert or modify the attributes `xmlns`, `xmlns:*`, and `xml:base`.
- For typed XML only, the attributes are `xsi:nil` and `xsi:type`.
- For typed or untyped XML, you cannot insert the attribute `xml:base`.
- For typed XML, deleting and modifying the `xsi:nil` attribute will fail, as will modifying the value of the `xs:type` attribute. For untyped XML, you can modify or delete these attributes.

Indexing XML for Performance

There may be times when you want to increase query performance speed at the cost of data insertion speed by creating an index on your XML columns. SQL Server supports both primary and secondary indexes on XML columns. In addition, your XML column can be typed or untyped. SQL Server supports indexes on both. SQL Server will index all the tags, values, and paths in reverse order, as path expression searches are faster when the suffix is known.

SQL Server stores the XML datatype in a BLOB field. This field can be up to 2GB in size, and parsing this field at runtime to perform queries without an index can be very time consuming. For this reason, you may want to create an index to speed performance. One thing to note is that the base table must have a clustered index to create an XML index on an XML column. You cannot modify the primary key of the table until you drop all XML indexes on the table. Once you create the XML index, a B+ tree structure is created on all tags, values, and paths on your XML data.

If you do a lot of queries but few inserts on your table with the XML column, you should consider indexing the column with one or more indexes. Also, if your XML data is large but you're often returning only a subset of the data, you will want to create an index. The index will be used when using XQuery methods, but if you retrieve the entire column using relational methods, such as SELECT xmlCOL from Table, the index will not be used.

Creating the primary index is very straightforward. You can have only one primary XML index per XML column. You can, however, have multiple secondary indexes on an XML column. The following code creates a primary XML index on an XML column called people:

```
CREATE PRIMARY XML INDEX idx_xmlCol on xmltblnew(people)
```

Understanding How XML Indexing Works

Let's take a look under the covers of SQL Server to understand how XML indexing works, since the implementation will affect your system's performance depending on what you do with the XML data after it is indexed. Once you create a primary XML index, SQL Server creates a B+ tree that contains a shredded version of your XML. The XML index does have some redundancy, so you may see your XML index grow on average to about twice the size of the XML data, which means you should plan your disk space usage accordingly.

SQL Server uses ORDPATH, which is a system for labeling nodes in an XML tree that keeps structural fidelity. The easiest way to understand what the underlying index looks like is to consider an example. If we take part of the people XML and look at the structure for the index, Table 17-3 represents the index table.

Table 17-3. *Index Table for Sample XML*

ORDPATH	Tag	Node_Type	Value	Path_ID
1	1 (people)	1 (Element)	Null	#1
1.1	2 (person)	1 (Element)	Null	#2#1
1.1.1	3 (name)	1 (Element)	Null	#3#2#1
1.1.1.1	4 (givenName)	1 (Element)	Tom	#4#3#2#1
1.1.1.5	5 (familyName)	1 (Element)	Rizzo	#5#3#2#1
1.1.3	6 (age)	1 (Element)	32	#6#3#2#1
1.1.5	7 (height)	1 (Element)	medium	#7#3#2#1

Of course, this XML is element based, so the index is not as interesting if you also have attributes and free text in your XML. The most important thing to note is not the values of the index, but the structure of the index. If you continued to draw the table out for the XML, you would find that the path ID overlaps with all XML elements that use the same path, such as all the givenName values for people use the path ID of #4#3#2#1, regardless of where they fall in the XML hierarchy in terms of document order. Also, the node type shown in the table is for illustration. SQL Server will map the value to an integer value and use only the integer value, not the string value shown in the table.

You will notice that only odd numbers are used for the ORDPATH. The reason for this is so that in the future, when insertions happen, you do not need to re-create the numbering scheme, but instead can use even numbers.

When you have an XML index, the query optimizer decides what will give the best performance when querying your XML. The optimizer can use a top-down approach, where it processes the base table rows before the XML index. Otherwise, it can use a bottom-up approach, where the optimizer does an XML index lookup and then back-joins with the base table. In the most common cases, where you are retrieving the entire XML document or using XPath expressions that retrieve most of the data, the optimizer will just shred the XML BLOB at runtime rather than using the index.

Be aware that if you insert or delete nodes that are earlier in the sibling order, you will incur significant cost if you use an XML index, since new rows must be inserted or deleted from the primary XML index. Remember that the index costs you time for insert and delete operations, but it can significantly improve query performance, depending on the types of queries.

Examining Secondary XML Indexes

Once you create the primary XML index, you may want to create a secondary XML index to speed up your applications. There are three types of secondary XML indexes: PATH, PROPERTY, and VALUE. The type of index you will select depends on the types of queries your application uses the most. If you find that you are using one type of XQuery more often than another, and there is a secondary XML index that covers your query type, consider using a secondary XML index. You will not normally gain as much performance by creating a primary XML index on an unindexed table as you will by adding a secondary index to a table that already has a primary index. You can have multiple secondary XML indexes on a single column.

If your queries are mostly path expressions to retrieve your data, you will want to use a PATH index. The most common operators that take path expressions are the query()and exist() methods. If you find yourself using the query() or exist() method regularly in your code, you will want to definitely take a look at the PATH index. Plus, if your XML documents are large and you use path expressions a lot, the primary XML index will walk sequentially through the XML, which will provide slower performance than creating a PATH secondary index.

If you retrieve property values from your XML, you will want to use the PROPERTY index. For example, if you retrieve values in your XML such as the age or name as shown in the previous example, you will want to use the PROPERTY index. Also, if you regularly use the value() method in your XQueries, you will want to use the PROPERTY index.

Finally, if you have a jagged hierarchy or you have imprecise queries using the descendant-or-self axis (//), you will want to use the VALUE index. This index will speed up value-based scans of your data. For example, you may use a wildcard search that will look at every element with an attribute of a certain value. A VALUE index will speed up this type of search.

Listings 17-1 through 17-3 show the creation of an index of each type and a query that will benefit from creating the particular index type.

Listing 17-1. *Creating a PATH Secondary Index*

```
CREATE XML INDEX idx_xmlCol_PATH on xmltblnew(people)
  USING XML INDEX idx_xmlCol FOR PATH
-- Query that would use this index
SELECT people FROM xmltblnew
  WHERE (people.exist('/people/person/name/givenName[.="Tom"]') = 1)
```

Listing 17-2. *Creating a PROPERTY Secondary Index*

```
CREATE XML INDEX idx_xmlCol_PROPERTY on xmltblnew(people)
  USING XML INDEX idx_xmlCol FOR PROPERTY
-- Query that would use this index
SELECT people.value('(/people/person/age)[1]', 'int') FROM xmltblnew
```

Listing 17-3. *Creating a VALUE Secondary Index*

```
CREATE XML INDEX idx_xmlCol_VALUE on xmltblnew(people)
  USING XML INDEX idx_xmlCol FOR VALUE
-- Query that would use this index
SELECT people FROM xmltblnew WHERE people.exist('//age') = 1
```

Full-Text Search and the XML Datatype

Beyond indexing the XML column, you can also full-text index the XML column using the built-in XML IFilter in SQL Server. You can combine the XML column index with the full-text index. However, the following differences apply to full-text indexing of XML:

- Markup is not indexed; only content is indexed. Therefore, the elements are the boundaries of the full-text indexing.

- Attributes are not indexed, since they are considered part of the markup. If you mostly store your values in attributes, you will want to use an XML index, not full-text search.

- Full-text search returns the full XML document, not just the section where the data occurred. If you want to retrieve a particular element that contained the search phrase, you need to further query the returned XML document with XQuery.

- The XQuery contains method and the full-text search contains method are different. Full-text search uses token matching and stemming, while XQuery is a substring match.

Other than these differences, the standard full-text restrictions are in effect, such as having a unique key column on the table and executing the correct Data Definition Language (DDL) to create the index. The DDL that follows creates a full-text index on a table containing an XML column. A primary key index called pkft is created in the following code:

```
CREATE FULLTEXT CATALOG ft AS DEFAULT
CREATE FULLTEXT INDEX on xmltblnew(people) KEY INDEX pkft
```

You can combine an XML column index, both primary and secondary, with a full-text index. Whether you do this depends on what your data in the tables looks like, what your application workload does, and the overhead that you want to place on the server for creating and maintaining your index. If you find that you are querying data in your XML column regularly, and a lot of the XML information is not stored as attributes, then creating both a column and full-text index may speed up your query response time. First, you will want to filter based on the full-text index, and then you can use XQuery on the returned data to filter the XML data even more.

For example, the following code uses a full-text search with the contains keyword and an XQuery that also uses the contains keyword. Remember that the full-text search contains keyword is different from the XQuery one. The full-text search is a token-match search that uses stemming, whereas the XQuery one is a substring match. Therefore, if you search for "swim" using full-text search, you will also find values for "swimming" and "swam." However, with XQuery, you will find only "swimming" and "swim," since XQuery performs a substring match.

```
SELECT * FROM   xmltblnew
WHERE  contains(people,'Tom')
AND people.exist('//familyName/text()[contains(.,"Rizzo")]') =1
```

Catalog Views and XML

Catalog views are views that wrap information stored in system tables. These views are covered in detail in Chapter 13. The XML datatype is represented in these views. For example, you can retrieve all the XML schemas registered in your database instance using the `sys.xml_schema_collections` view. You can retrieve elements and attributes that are registered by your schemas using the `sys.xml_schema_elements` and `sys.xml_schema_attributes` views.

The following code sample uses the dynamic management views to look at all the namespaces in a database instance, all the elements and attributes for a particular namespace, and also any indexes on XML columns:

```
SELECT * FROM sys.xml_schema_collections
SELECT * FROM sys.xml_schema_elements
SELECT * FROM sys.xml_schema_attributes
SELECT * FROM sys.xml_schema_namespaces
SELECT * FROM sys.xml_indexes
```

Interesting scenarios for using these views occur when you want to figure out what namespaces exist in your server, what indexes you've created for your different XML types, and what the actual XML looks like across your server using the elements and attributes views. The following example uses the dynamic management views to enumerate all namespaces in your XML schema collections on the server. The code joins together the schema collection and schema namespace views so that you can see the name of your schema namespace. Without this join, if you query the `sys.xml_schema_collections` view, you would see only the name of the namespace you defined, which may be different from the name of the namespace in your schema.

```
SELECT *
FROM sys.xml_schema_collections xmlSchemaCollection
     JOIN sys.xml_schema_namespaces xmlSchemaName
     ON (xmlSchemaName.xml_collection_id = xmlSchemaName.xml_collection_id)
WHERE xmlSchemaCollection.name = 'Customer'
go
```

Applications and XML

If you use SQLXML or ADO.NET, programming using the XML datatype is simple and does not require much explanation. However, if you use ADO together with SQL Native Client to connect with a SQL Server database, you will want to initialize SQL Native Access Client (SNAC) with the `DataTypeCompatibility` keyword in your connection string. You should set this string to be equal to 80, which specifies that you want to use features such as multiple active result sets, query notifications, user-defined types, and XML datatype support. If you continue to use Microsoft Data Access Components (MDAC), there are no required changes to use the XML datatype.

Both SNAC and MDAC will return XML as text. You could then load the text into an XML document object to parse the XML. For the richest XML experience, you will want to use .NET with SQLXML. The following code shows how to use ADO with data that uses the XML datatype:

```
Imports ADODB
Const strDataServer = "localhost"
Const strDatabase = "xmldb"
```

```
    'Create objects
    Dim objConn As New Connection
    Dim objRs As Recordset

    'Create command text
    Dim CommandText As String = "SELECT xmlColWithSchema" & _
                 " FROM xmltbl2" & _
                 " WHERE pk = 1"

    'Create connection string
    Dim ConnectionString As String = "Provider=SQLNCLI" & _
                     ";Data Source=" & strDataServer & _
                     ";Initial Catalog=" & strDatabase &
                     ";Integrated Security=SSPI;" &
                     "DataTypeCompatibility=80"

    'Connect to the data source
    objConn.Open(ConnectionString)

    'Execute the command
    objRs = objConn.Execute(CommandText)

    Dim irowcount As Integer = 0

    'Go through recordset and display
    Do While Not objRs.EOF
        irowcount += 1
        MessageBox.Show("Row " & irowcount & ":" & vbCrLf & vbCrLf &
         objRs(0).Value())
        objRs.MoveNext()
    Loop

    'Clean up our objects
    objRs.Close()
    objConn.Close()
    objRs = Nothing
    objConn = Nothing
```

XML Web Services Support

SQL Server can expose XML web services directly from the server, without IIS installed. Now, you may be wondering about security concerns, but the web services functionality is explicitly off by default, and SQL Server requires you to create the web service through some code before it turns on.

By supporting web services, SQL Server can support clients that do not have MDAC installed or other platforms that may not even have Windows installed. Through the use of the documented web services protocols and formats, you can even use development environments that may not have native drivers for SQL Server.

The web services support allows you to send T-SQL statements with or without parameters to the server, or you can call stored procedures, extended stored procedures, and scalar UDFs.

You create an *endpoint* to expose your web services functionality. The endpoint needs to have a unique URL that SQL Server will listen on. When that URL receives a request, which is routed to the kernel mode http.sys, http.sys passes this request to the correct SQL Server functionality that the endpoint exposes. By using http.sys, SQL Server does not require IIS. There may be times, however, when you will want to expose your web services through a mid-tier component. For example, if you want to scale out your solution, you may find mid-tier components are easier and sometimes cheaper to scale than your SQL Servers.

You can have multiple endpoints for a single function, or you can expose multiple endpoints for multiple functions. It is up to your application architecture how you use this technology.

Before we look at the technology, we should state that there are times when using web services does not make sense. For example, web services are more verbose than using the native Tabular Data Stream (TDS) protocol, so if size and speed are concerns for you, web services may not make sense. Also, if your application frequently works with BLOB data, you will want to avoid using web services.

Creating an Endpoint

Assume you have a stored procedure existing in your database, and you want to expose it as a web service. The first thing you need to do is create your endpoints. All endpoints are stored in the master database, and you can use the `sys.http_endpoints` catalog view to query for all the endpoints that exist. To find all the web methods you create, you can use the `sys.endpoint_webmethods` catalog view.

The DDL that follows creates a new endpoint. Note that endpoints work only on platforms that support `http.sys`, which is the kernel mode `http` listener. Windows Server 2003, Windows XP with Service Pack 2, and Windows Vista are the only platforms that support this capability. The `CREATE ENDPOINT` statement for HTTP endpoints and web services uses the following format:

```
CREATE ENDPOINT endPointName [ AUTHORIZATION login ]
STATE = { STARTED | STOPPED | DISABLED }
AS { HTTP | TCP } (
   <protocol-specific_arguments>
      )
FOR { SOAP | TSQL | SERVICE_BROKER | DATABASE_MIRRORING } (
   <language-specific_arguments>
       )

<AS HTTP_protocol-specific_arguments> ::=
AS HTTP (
  PATH = 'url'
      , AUTHENTICATION =( { BASIC | DIGEST | INTEGRATED
      | NTLM | KERBEROS } [ ,...n ] )
      , PORTS = ( { CLEAR | SSL} [ ,... n ] )
  [ SITE = {'*' | '+' | 'webSite' },]
  [, CLEAR_PORT = clearPort ]
  [, SSL_PORT = SSLPort ]
  [, AUTH_REALM = { 'realm' | NONE } ]
  [, DEFAULT_LOGON_DOMAIN = { 'domain' | NONE } ]
  [, COMPRESSION = { ENABLED | DISABLED } ]
  )

<FOR SOAP_language-specific_arguments> ::=
FOR SOAP(
  [ { WEBMETHOD [ 'namespace' .] 'method_alias'
    (   NAME = 'database.owner.name'
      [ , SCHEMA = { NONE | STANDARD | DEFAULT } ]
      [ , FORMAT = { ALL_RESULTS | ROWSETS_ONLY } ]
    )


  } [ ,...n ] ]
  [   BATCHES = { ENABLED | DISABLED } ]
  [ , WSDL = { NONE | DEFAULT | 'sp_name' } ]
```

```
  [ , SESSIONS = { ENABLED | DISABLED } ]
  [ , LOGIN_TYPE = { MIXED | WINDOWS } ]
  [ , SESSION_TIMEOUT = timeoutInterval | NEVER ]
  [ , DATABASE = { 'database_name' | DEFAULT }
  [ , NAMESPACE = { 'namespace' | DEFAULT } ]
  [ , SCHEMA = { NONE | STANDARD } ]
  [ , CHARACTER_SET = { SQL | XML }]
  [ , HEADER_LIMIT = int ]
)
```

If we look at an implementation of `CREATE ENDPOINT`, we get the following:

```
CREATE ENDPOINT SQLWS_endpoint
STATE = STARTED
  AS HTTP(
    PATH = '/sql/sample',
    AUTHENTICATION= ( INTEGRATED ),
    PORTS = ( CLEAR )
  )
FOR SOAP (
  WEBMETHOD
    'http://tempuri.org/'.'SQLWS'
    (NAME = 'xmldb.dbo.usp_SQLWS'),
    BATCHES = ENABLED,
    WSDL = DEFAULT
  )
```

As you can see in the code, you need to pass the name of your endpoint and the type of web authentication you want. You also pass the URL path for your web service, the ports used, the initial state, and finally the method name and whether you want to allow T-SQL batch statements and automatic Web Services Description Language (WSDL) generation.

Note the following about creating endpoints:

- Endpoints do not allow you to pass credentials unsecured over the wire. Therefore, if you use Basic authentication, you will have to use Secure Sockets Layer (SSL). To enable SSL, you must register a certificate on your server. Use the `httpcfg.exe` utility to register, query, and delete certificates. Also, for testing purposes, you can make self-signed certificates using the `makecert.exe` utility.

- You can use a subset of WS-Security to authenticate against the server. Specifically, SQL Server web services supports the `Username` token headers. This is used for SQL Server–based authentication.

- You can specify whether you want a complex WSDL, which will use complex XSD types (which some applications do not support), or a simple WSDL, which increases interoperability. To get a simple WSDL, just use `?wsdlsimple` at the end of your URL rather than the standard `?wsdl`.

- You can specify your own custom WSDL by passing in the name of a stored procedure that returns the WSDL. This is useful if you know that the automatically generated WSDL does not work with your applications, and you need to tweak the WSDL.

- You can specify the format of the results to return. By default, SQL Server will return all the results, including the results, row count, error messages, and warnings. This is the `ALL_RESULTS` option for the optional `FORMAT` property. If you want only the data, set this option to `ROWSETS_ONLY`. This will return a `DataSet` object rather than an object array.

Endpoints are implicitly reserved with `http.sys` when you use `CREATE ENDPOINT`. If SQL Server is running, `http.sys` will pass requests to SQL Server. However, if SQL Server is not running, other applications can be forwarded the requests rather than SQL Server. You can explicitly request a name-space from `http.sys` by using the system stored procedure `sp_reserve_http_namespace`, which takes the namespace you want to reserve. For example, if you want to reserve the `sql` namespace over port 80, you use `sp_reserve_http_namespace N'http://MyServer:80/sql'`.

Also, you can specify whether to have session support, which allows you to send multiple SOAP messages as a single session with the server. The default is no session support.

The last property that you may want to set is `DATABASE`, which specifies the default database. If you do not specify this property, SQL Server will default to the database specified for the login.

Once you create an endpoint, you can change it using the `ALTER ENDPOINT` statement. You can also drop the endpoint using the `DROP ENDPOINT` statement.

Endpoints are considered applications by SQL Server, in that you must explicitly give your users permissions to execute the endpoint. When you create an endpoint, only those with the `sysadmin` role or the `owner` role can execute the endpoint. In addition, endpoints do not skirt SQL Server security. You need permissions on the underlying SQL Server object in order to execute it. If you attempt to call an endpoint that you have permissions on without having permissions on the underlying stored procedure or UDF, you will receive an error.

In addition, endpoints have two levels of security. The first is at the HTTP transport layer, where you can specify web-based authentications such as Integrated, Basic, or Anonymous. The second is the SQL Server layer. The SQL Server layer requires that you are authenticated with SQL Server. There-fore, you could have an anonymous connection at the HTTP layer, but you would not be able to call any SQL Server functionality without passing explicit SQL Server logins and passwords.

To grant execution permissions for users on the endpoint, execute the following code:

```
use MASTER
GRANT CONNECT ON ENDPOINT::SQLWS_endpoint TO [DOMAIN\username]
```

Now that you've created your web service, let's see how to use it from Visual Studio. You can add a reference to the endpoint using the standard web reference dialog box in Visual Studio, as shown in Figure 17-5.

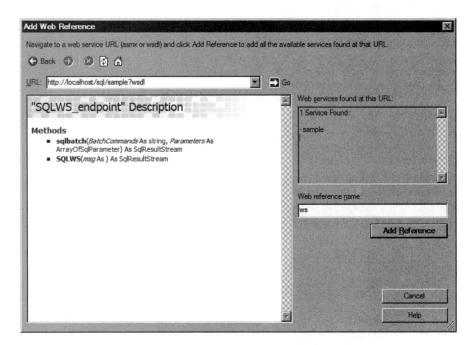

Figure 17-5. *Adding a web reference to a SQL Server web service*

Also, you can just retrieve the WSDL of your endpoint by passing in ?wsdl, just as you do for other web services. The code for getting the WSDL for the previous web service is shown here:

```
http://localhost/sql/sample?wsdl
```

Finally, you can call your web service from code using the standard functionality of Visual Studio or any other development environment that supports web services. Since XML web services use the diffgram format for their return values, you can easily load the results into a .NET dataset. The following code will call your web services and assume the web service reference is named ws:

```
//Add a reference to SQL WS
ws.SQLWS_endpoint SQLWS = new ws.SQLWS_endpoint();

//Set default credentials to the Windows one
SQLWS.Credentials = CredentialCache.DefaultCredentials;

//Call the sproc through the WS
System.Data.DataSet dsReturnValue =
(System.Data.DataSet)SQLWS.SQLWS("Calling stored proc").GetValue(0);

//Get the reader associated with our Dataset
System.Data.DataTableReader drSQL = dsReturnValue.GetDataReader();

//Get the result
string strResult = "";
while (drSQL.Read())
    {
       strResult = drSQL[0].ToString();
    }

//Display the results
MessageBox.Show("Return value from SQL call: " + strResult);

ws.SqlParameter[] sqlparams = new ws.SqlParameter[0];

//Send a batch command to SQL
System.Data.DataSet dsReturnValue1 =
(System.Data.DataSet)SQLWS.sqlbatch("SELECT * FROM
sys.http_endpoints", ref sqlparams).GetValue(0);

//Get the reader associated with the Dataset
System.Data.DataTableReader drSQL1 = dsReturnValue1.GetDataReader();

//Get the result
string strResult1 = "";
while (drSQL1.Read())
    {
       strResult1 = drSQL1[0].ToString();
    }

//Display the results
MessageBox.Show("Return value from SQL call: " + strResult1);
```

As you can see, you need to create a new instance of your web service. Then you need to set the default credentials for your web service calls. The code uses the default Windows credentials by using the CredentialCache class's DefaultCredentials property.

Once you set the credentials, you can make the call to your web service. Since you exposed a stored procedure, the code calls that first. Without casting the result, an object type would be returned by the server. Instead of just getting a generic object, the code casts the return value to a `DataSet` object. From the `DataSet` object, the code gets a `DataTableReader` object and then gets the results. The `DataTableReader` object provides a forward-only, read-only iterator over the data in your result sets.

In the second example in the code, since the endpoint allowed batch commands, the code can send T-SQL to the server to have it execute. Since the master database is the default database in this code, the dynamic management view for endpoints is queried and returned.

The code uses the built-in web services technologies in Visual Studio, but you could call this code from other environments and create the SOAP headers and body yourself. For example, you could use the Web Services Toolkit from Visual Basic 6 or the `XMLHTTP` or `ServerXMLHTTP` objects directly to make raw HTTP calls to the server. This is the flexibility and power SQL Server gives you with its web services integration.

Using Advanced Web Services

Typically, you will use the built-in capabilities of Visual Studio and SQL Server web services to do your web services programming. However, there may be times when you want to leverage the advanced functionality of SQL Server web services. For example, you may want to support sessions, transactions, SQL authentication, and other functionality.

To use the advanced functionality, you will need to dive into writing part of the SOAP envelope that will be delivered to SQL Server. The reason for this is that SQL Server uses some special extension headers to implement its functionality. Before we talk about how to achieve this functionality, let's look at a piece of a typical SOAP request (only a portion of the SOAP request is shown for space reasons).

```
<?xml version="1.0" encoding="utf-8" ?>
<soap:Envelope
    xmlns:soap="http://schemas.xmlsoap.org/soap/envelope/"
    xmlns:xsi="http://www.w3.org/2001/XMLSchema-instance"
    xmlns:xsd="http://www.w3.org/2001/XMLSchema">
 <soap:Body>
   <MySP xmlns="http://tempUri.org/">
<Param1>1</Param1>
<OutputParam />
   </MySP>
</soap:Body>
</soap:Envelope>
```

As you can see, SOAP messages are XML messages with an envelope and a body. The body contains the payload, which is the stored procedure, UDF, or T-SQL batch you want to send to the server. SQL Server extends the envelope with some special headers to achieve more advanced functionality. Table 17-4 shows the SQL Server optional header extensions. The table assumes that you have declared the namespace for the header extensions as `xmlns:sqloptions="http://schemas.microsoft.com/sqlserver/2004/SOAP/Options`. Assume `sqloptions:` appears before each header name.

Table 17-4. *SQL Server XML Web Services Header Extensions*

Name	Description
applicationName	User-defined application name. You could use this to limit applications that call your web service.
clientInterface	User-defined client interface. For example, you could limit applications to only certain interfaces, such as ADO.NET 2.0.
clientNetworkID	User-defined network ID.
clientPID	User-defined process ID.
databaseMirroringPartner	The name of the database-mirroring partner for this server. This is returned by SQL Server when you use the environmentChangeNotification("partnerChange") request.
environmentChangeNotifications	Allows you to specify that you want to be notified of environment changes. Valid environment changes include language changes using languageChange, database-mirroring changes using partnerChange, database changes using databaseChange, and transaction-usage changes using transactionChange.
hostName	User-defined hostname.
initialDatabase	Allows you to specify the initial database for your SOAP request. You can also pass the database filename using the filename attribute for this header. You must set this in your initial session request to the server if using sessions.
initialLanguage	Allows you to specify the language, similar to the SET LANGUAGE T-SQL command. You must set this in your initial session request to the server if using sessions.
notificationRequest	Allows you to use query notifications. You must specify the attributes notificationId and deliveryService, which specify the unique notification ID for the query notification already created and the delivery service that will deliver the notifications.
prepExec	Allows you to prepare and execute operations.
sqlSession	Allows you to maintain a session across multiple SOAP requests. This header has attributes, which are initiate, terminate, sessionId, timeout, and transactionDescriptor.

While just looking at the header descriptions may be confusing at first, seeing some of them in action will make the concepts clearer. Before we show you some examples, however, we need to look at non-SQL extension headers. SQL Server supports some parts of the WS-Security standard, specifically the ability to pass usernames and passwords using WS-Security. This is also the way that you specify SQL Server authentication information if you want to use that rather than Windows-based authentication. Remember that to use SQL Server authentication, you must set LOGIN_TYPE to mixed and PORTS must be set to SSL in your CREATE ENDPOINT statement. SQL Server will not let you send usernames and passwords over unencrypted channels!

To use WS-Security for your web services, you need to pass WS-Security–specific information in your headers. The following code shows how to perform a SQL Server authentication-based connection when calling a SQL Server web service:

```
<SOAP-ENV:Header>
        <wsse:Security  xmlns:wsse=
                "http://docs.oasis-open.org/wss/2004/01/
                    oasis-200401-wss-wssecurity-secext-1.0.xsd">
```

```
              <wsse:UsernameToken>
                       <wsse:Username>thomriz</wsse:Username>
              <wsse:Password Type=
                       "http://docs.oasis-open.org/wss/2004/01/
                          oasis-200401-wss-username-token-profile-
                        1.0#PasswordText">Passw0rd!@11</wsse:Password>
              </wsse:UsernameToken>
              </wsse:Security>
</SOAP-ENV:Header>
```

As you can see, you pass the username using the Username element and the password using the Password element. You can even change passwords using WS-Security with SQL Server by adding the oldpassword element as follows:

. . .

```
              <wsse:UsernameToken>
              <sql:OldPassword Type="http://docs.oasis-open.org/wss/2004/01/
                oasis-200401-wss-username-token-profile-1.0#PasswordText"
               xmlns:sql="http://schemas.microsoft.com/sqlserver/2004/SOAP">pass
               word1</sql:OldPassword>
```

...

Using Sessions and Transactions with Web Services

Since the Web is asynchronous and loosely coupled in nature, SQL Server web services are that way as well by default. When you send a request via web services, each request is a new session and transaction with the server. In fact, there is an implicit transaction created when you send your requests. There may be times, though, when you want to keep a session alive across multiple requests, or you may want to be able to do transactions across session boundaries. To support this, SQL Server has the ability to initiate sessions and transactions as part of its web services support. To enable this, you must use the SOAP extension headers discussed earlier.

Before you can start using sessions, the endpoint you create must have sessions enabled. You can also specify session timeout and header limits. The following statement alters an endpoint to enable session support:

```
ALTER ENDPOINT default_endpoint_clear
FOR SOAP  (
                               SESSIONS = ENABLED,
                               SESSION_TIMEOUT = 1200,
                               HEADER_LIMIT = 65536
)
go
```

The next step is to send a SOAP header on your first request to the server that tells the server to enable session support, which you do by using the SOAP extension headers. The following is the header you send to start a session with SQL Server:

```
<SOAP-ENV:Envelope xmlns:SOAP-ENV="http://schemas.xmlsoap.org/soap/envelope/"
xmlns:sql="http://schemas.microsoft.com/sqlserver/2004/SOAP"
xmlns:xsi="http://www.w3.org/2001/XMLSchema-instance"
xmlns:sqlparam="http://schemas.microsoft.com/sqlserver/2004/SOAP/types/SqlParameter"
xmlns:sqlsoaptypes="http://schemas.microsoft.com/sqlserver/2004/SOAP/types"
xmlns:sqloptions="http://schemas.microsoft.com/sqlserver/2004/SOAP/Options"
>
<SOAP-ENV:Header>
<sqloptions:sqlSession SOAP-ENV:mustUnderstand="1" initiate="true" />
</SOAP-ENV:Header>
```

```
<SOAP-ENV:Body>
  <sql:sqlbatch>
    <sql:BatchCommands>use Northwind
    </sql:BatchCommands>
  </sql:sqlbatch>
</SOAP-ENV:Body>
</SOAP-ENV:Envelope>
```

The response from SQL Server will contain the GUID sessionId returned in the headers. You need to retrieve that sessionId and pass it along in subsequent requests to make sure you continue over the same session. The following is the response from the server:

```
<SOAP-ENV:Envelope xml:space="preserve" xmlns:xsd="http://www.w3.org/2001/XMLSchema"
xmlns:xsi="http://www.w3.org/2001/XMLSchema-instance" xmlns:SOAP-
ENV="http://schemas.xmlsoap.org/soap/envelope/"
xmlns:sql="http://schemas.microsoft.com/sqlserver/2004/SOAP"
 xmlns:sqlsoaptypes="http://schemas.microsoft.com/sqlserver/2004/SOAP/types"
xmlns:sqlrowcount=
  "http://schemas.microsoft.com/sqlserver/2004/SOAP/types/SqlRowCount"
xmlns:sqlmessage=
  "http://schemas.microsoft.com/sqlserver/2004/SOAP/types/SqlMessage"
mlns:sqlresultstream=
  "http://schemas.microsoft.com/sqlserver/2004/SOAP/types/SqlResultStream"
mlns:sqltransaction=
  "http://schemas.microsoft.com/sqlserver/2004/SOAP/types/SqlTransaction"
xmlns:sqltypes="http://schemas.microsoft.com/sqlserver/2004/sqltypes">
<SOAP-ENV:Header xmlns:sqloptions=
  "http://schemas.microsoft.com/sqlserver/2004/SOAP/Options">
  <sqloptions:sqlSession sessionId="SESSIONIDGUID">
</sqloptions:sqlSession>
  </SOAP-ENV:Header>
  <SOAP-ENV:Body>
    <sql:sqlbatchResponse>
    <sql:sqlbatchResult>
    </sql:sqlbatchResult>
    </sql:sqlbatchResponse>
  </SOAP-ENV:Body>
</SOAP-ENV:Envelope>
```

Note that you must pass the sessionId to continue using a session. You must also continue to use the same endpoint and the same user context. If you change any of this, sessions will not work.

To terminate the session, send the terminate command and pass the sessionId to the server. Instead of showing the full SOAP request here, we show the terminate SQL header:

```
<sqloptions:sqlSession terminate="true" sessionId="SESSIONIDGUID" />
```

To use transactions, you must use sessions. However, you will want to make sure that in your headers, the transaction request comes before the session initiation. Explicit transactions are supported only with SQL batches and not when calling web methods. If you want to support transactions with your web method calls, put the transaction into the functionality called by the web method. For example, if you expose a stored procedure as a web method, put your transaction context code in the stored procedure.

The following code is a snippet of the header you will want to pass to start transactions. You need to set the transactionBoundary attribute of the environmentChangeNotifications header to true to use transactions. Then you can use the BEGIN TRANSACTION statement in your T-SQL batch.

```
. . .
<sqloptions:environmentChangeNotifications transactionBoundary="true" />
<sqloptions:sqlSession initiate="true" timeout="60"/>
. . .
<sql:BatchCommands>
        USE MyDB
        BEGIN TRANSACTION
        INSERT INTO MyTable (MyColumn) VALUES ('MyValue');
      </sql:BatchCommands>
. . .
```

The server will let you know whether or not the transaction was successfully begun and will send back a transactionDescriptor. This is similar to the sessionId in that you need to send this transactionDescriptor with every request that wants to perform an action that uses that transaction context. The following code is a snippet of the response from the server:

```
<SOAP-ENV:Body>
    <sql:sqlbatchResponse>
      <sql:sqlbatchResult>
         <sqlresultstream:SqlTransaction xsi:type="sqltransaction:SqlTransaction">
            <sqltransaction:Descriptor>BQCCCDMABCD=</sqltransaction:Descriptor>
            <sqltransaction:Type>Begin</sqltransaction:Type>
         </sqlresultstream:SqlTransaction>
      </sql:sqlbatchResult>
    </sql:sqlbatchResponse>
  </SOAP-ENV:Body>
```

The following code snippet is the next request, with the sessionId and the transactionDescriptor passed along with the request:

```
. . .
sqloptions:sqlSession sessionId="SessionGUID"
  transactionDescriptor=" BQCCCDMABCD="/>
...
```

Over one session, you can have multiple transactions. Just make sure to keep track of the different transactionDescriptor values that are sent back from SQL Server.

Adding SOAP Headers Using Visual Studio

The easiest way to add custom headers to your Visual Studio applications is to use the sample class included with SQL Server Books Online. This class makes it easy for you to take an existing SOAP call and add the headers to it. Since Books Online includes all the information you need to start using this class, we refer you there to get the sample code and the instructions for using that sample code.

Monitoring Performance of XML Web Services

The XML web services in SQL Server have a number of performance counters that you can monitor to understand how your web services are performing. The web services counters are under the SQL Server: General Statistics object. Table 17-5 lists the performance counters included.

Table 17-5. *XML Web Services Performance Counters*

Name	Description
HTTP Anonymous Requests	Number of anonymous requests per second
HTTP Authenticated Requests	Number of authenticated requests per second
SOAP Empty Requests	Number of empty SOAP requests per second
SOAP Method Invocations	Number of SOAP method invocations per second
SOAP Session Initiate Requests	Number of SOAP session initiations per second
SOAP Session Terminate Requests	Number of SOAP session terminations per second
SOAP SQL Requests	Number of batch SQL requests per second
SOAP WSDL Requests	Number of WSDL requests per second

Summary

In this chapter, you saw many examples of using XML in SQL Server. Having this native XML support within the database engine enables developers to build powerful database applications more quickly, since they can store XML data right alongside relational data, leverage the power of the XQuery language, and easily build web services that consume XML data. SQL Server definitely provides the level of XML support you need for most applications.

LINQ to SQL

Object/relational mapping (O/RM) allows developers to work with relational data in an object-oriented (OO) manner. Language Integrated Query (LINQ), released with .NET 3.5, adds the ability to query objects using .NET languages. The LINQ to SQL O/RM framework provides the following basic features, which will be covered in this chapter:

- Tools to create classes (usually called *entities*) mapped to database tables

- Compatibility with LINQ's standard query operations

- The DataContext class, with features such as entity record monitoring, automatic SQL statement generation, record concurrency detection, and much more

Object/Relational Mapping

A main goal for OO developers has been finding an easy solution to join the database world to the OO one. The former is composed by tables, columns, and a tabular way to store the data. The latter is formed by classes, relationships between them, and data stored within objects. The way to retrieve a record from the database is different from what OO developers are accustomed to with object manipulation. First of all, OO developers must know another language—SQL—to retrieve records from the database. Then they need to use the appropriate Application Programming Interface (API) to execute the queries from the code. Finally, developers must manipulate the retrieved data, looping through the collection of records.

Using the ADO.NET framework, one of the most powerful and complete APIs to manage the database from the code, these steps can be transformed into the following code snippet:

```
string connString = "Data Source=.;Initial Catalog=AdventureWorks;" +
                            "Integrated Security=SSPI";
string SQL = "SELECT ProductID, Name FROM Production.Product";

SqlConnection conn = new SqlConnection(connString);
SqlCommand comm = new SqlCommand(SQL, conn);

conn.Open();
SqlDataReader reader = comm.ExecuteReader();

while (reader.Read())
{
    Console.WriteLine(reader.GetInt32(0).ToString() + " " + reader.GetString(1));
}

conn.Close();
```

Note that for brevity, this sample code is not optimized, and it doesn't contain exception handling. It's intended to highlight some important aspects related to OO development:

- OO developers are not accustomed to using indexes to retrieve values from an object. They use properties instead. Using both the GetInt32(0) and GetString(1) methods to obtain the values from the related columns is not an OO approach.

- OO developers are accustomed to encapsulating recurrent actions into a unique class's method. For example, the preceding code could be reduced to a unique method that accepts the connection string and the SQL command, and is responsible for managing the connection to the database, executing the query, and so on.

- OO developers usually avoid the mix of different languages in the code. So mixing either C# or Visual Basic code with SQL commands is not so digestible to OO purists. Developers try to separate the code that accesses the database in classes belonging to the data layer and the code using these classes in a separate business layer.

One of the earlier OO approaches to the database world taken by Microsoft is the strongly typed dataset. With the use of the Visual Studio Dataset Designer, developers can drag tables from the Server Explorer window and drop them onto the designer surface. This operation generates a new class derived from the DataSet class, typed on source tables. Practically, this means that the class contains properties related to the table's columns, with the same name and datatype. Moreover, the class contains a DataTable-derived class for each table dropped on the designer surface and the code to select and eventually update the database. In this way, calling just one method, Update from the DataAdapter class, the database is updated. The previous code snippet can be rewritten with the use of these classes, as follows:

```
Products p = new Products();
ProductsTableAdapters.ProductsTableAdapter da =
            new ProductsTableAdapters.ProductsTableAdapter();
da.Fill(p._Products);

foreach(Products.ProductsRow r in p._Products.Rows)
    Console.WriteLine(r.ProductID + ", " + r.Name);
```

Here, the Products class is inherited from a DataSet class and is typed upon the Products class from the AdventureWorks database. The ProductsTableAdapters contains the Fill method that accepts a ProductsDataTable parameter; it is useful to fill the Products dataset with records from the Products table. The Fill method runs the query specified during the class code generation with the Visual Studio Dataset Designer.

As you can see, the code is more readable and maintainable, providing properties that have the same name as related properties. It is an OO approach to the database records!

But this is just one little step toward what OO developers would have from their classes. The preceding example shows an automatic way to manage the database but contains a trick: the Visual Studio Dataset Designer generates SQL statements for you, but they are still in the class code! A purist doesn't want to see mixed code in the class.

A pure O/RM tool allows developers to manage data without worrying about how to retrieve the data. Developers do not need to write any SQL code in their classes; they just manage classes and objects. The following pseudo-code snippet illustrates what a pure O/RM should provide:

```
Products p = new Products();
p.ProductID = 1;
p.Retrieve();

Console.WriteLine(p.ProductID + ", " + p.Name);
```

The `Retrieve` imaginary method "knows" we are looking for the `Product` record that has the `ProductID` property equal to 1 and creates the SQL command for us, filling the `Products` class fields with the related values. It's really gorgeous, isn't it?

If you believe that the LINQ to SQL framework provides something similar to this pure O/RM code to manage a database, we have to inform you that this is only partially true. In fact, the LINQ to SQL framework provides *basic* O/RM functionality. As declared by Luca Bolognese (one of the creators of the LINQ to SQL framework) during a conference, LINQ to SQL has been provided with some basic O/RM features in the first release, and it will be expanded in future releases, thanks to feedback from the developers. In this chapter, you will see these features in action, and you will be able to use them in your projects. At the end of the chapter, you will have an idea of what the LINQ to SQL framework provides and what it doesn't yet offer.

Entity-Generation Tools

O/RM is based on entities. An *entity* is a class that has its properties mapped to table columns. Usually, databases have a lot of tables and a lot of columns. An O/RM framework such as LINQ to SQL provides tools to generate entities automatically, so developers don't need to create them manually.

The LINQ to SQL framework provides two tools for generating entities: SQLMetal and the LINQ to SQL Classes Designer in Visual Studio 2008. These tools generate the same entities with the same code. The big difference is that Visual Studio's LINQ to SQL Classes Designer allows you to choose which table to transform into an entity; the SQLMetal tool does not allow you to choose. SQLMetal generates all the entities analyzing all the tables contained in the database. Also, SQLMetal can produce `.mdf`, `.sdf`, or `.dbml` files. The LINQ to SQL Classes Designer produces only `.dbml` files. A `.dbml` file contains XML tags representing the database's structure.

Using SQLMetal

SQLMetal is a command-line program that generates entities from a provided database. The executable resides in the `C:\Program Files\Microsoft SDKs\Windows\v6.0A\bin` folder, but you can easily use it from the Visual Studio 2008 command prompt, accessed from the Visual Studio Tools menu. The following is the command to use SQLMetal:

```
SQLMetal [options] [input file]
```

For [`options`], you can use the options listed in Table 18-1. The [`input file`] optional option is a SQL Server Express filename (`.mdf`), a SQL Server CE filename (`.sdf`), or a DBML filename (`.dbml`). You can provide the database filename and obtain the entities mapped on the database's structure. More interesting is the DBML file option. This file is easy to read and modify, so you can change its content and obtain a part of the whole database's structure (just as with Visual Studio's LINQ to SQL Designer) or easily re-create entities after the database has changed its structure. For example, if the database administrator (DBA) changes a table name or adds a new column to a table, you can modify the DBML file manually and execute the SQLMetal tool to re-create the entities.

Table 18-1. *SQLMetal Generation Tool Options*

Option	Description
/server:<name>	Represents the SQL Server server name to which it connects.
/database:<name>	Represents the SQL Server database name to use to produce entity classes.
/user:<name>	Represents the username to use to connect to the database server.
/password:<name>	Represents the user's password to use to connect to the database server.
/conn:<value>	Lets you specify the connection string to connect to the database. This option cannot be used together with the /server, /database, /user, or /password option.
/timeout:<value>	Lets you specify the timeout (in seconds) to use for each database command.
/views	Obtains the database views extraction.
/functions	Obtains the database user functions extraction.
/sprocs	Obtains the database stored procedures extraction.
/dbml:<filename>	Lets you specify the name of the file that will contain the .dbml file. This option cannot be used with the /map option.
/code:<filename>	Lets you specify the name of the file that will contain the entity classes and data context.
/map:<filename>	Obtains an external XML file with mapping attributes. The entities produced in the code will not contain class and property attribute decorations because they have been included in the .dbml file.
/language:<name>	Produces a file in the specified programming language. The two options are csharp and vb. If not specified, the file extension is used to understand the language to use.
/namespace:<name>	Lets you specify the namespace that will contain the generated entity classes.
/context:<name>	Lets you specify the name of the class derived from the DataContext class.
/entitybase:<name>	Lets you specify the name of the base class from which to derive the entity class. By default, entity classes don't have a base class.
/pluralize	Obtains entity class and property names with English plurals.
/serialization:<param>	Generates serializable classes. Possible values are None and Unidirectional.
/provider:<name>	Lets you specify the name of the provider to connect to the database. By default, SQLMetal will detect it at runtime.

Following is a practical SQLMetal tool usage example:

```
SQLMetal /server:.\SQL2K8 /database:AdventureWorks /pluralize /code:
AdventureWorks.cs
```

In this example, the tool connects to an instance of a SQL Server 2008 database called SQL2K8. Then it examines the structure of the AdventureWorks database and generates the entities. They will be written in the AdventureWorks.cs file with C# language code.

Here's another example:

```
SQLMetal /conn:"server=.\sql2k8;database=AdventureWorks;Integrated Security=
SSPI" /dbml:AdventureWorks.dbml
```

In this case, SQLMetal uses a connection string to connect to the database. Then it analyzes the AdventureWorks database and generates a DBML file.

■**Note** The DBML file contains XML tags describing the structure of the database. It can be read by Visual Studio's LINQ to SQL Classes Designer.

Finally, here's an example that specifies options to generate code that manages stored procedures, functions, and views other than entities:

```
SQLMetal /server:.\SQL2K8 /database:AdventureWorks /user:sa /password:admin /code:
AdventureWorks.cs /sprocs /views /functions
```

Using the Visual Studio LINQ to SQL Classes Designer

The LINQ to SQL Classes Designer, included in Visual Studio 2008, is a visual designer that allows you to drag and drop a table from Server Explorer onto the designer. In this way, you can generate entity code automatically. The designer generates DBML files.

The designer is able to recognize when tables have relations. Figure 18-1 shows the designer with a couple of tables from the AdventureWorks database. The designer has recognized one relationship, indicated by the arrow, and created the necessary classes.

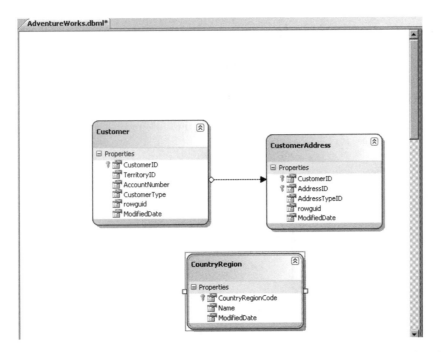

Figure 18-1. *Visual Studio LINQ to SQL Classes Designer with some AdventureWorks tables*

To add a LINQ to SQL Classes file to your project, select Project ➤ New Item to open the Add New Item dialog box. In this dialog box, select the LINQ to SQL Classes template, as shown in Figure 18-2.

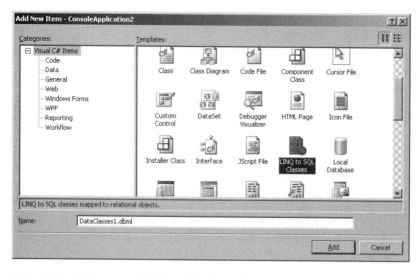

Figure 18-2. *Adding a new LINQ to SQL Classes file*

Now that you're familiar with the tools, it's time to analyze the code that they generate.

Analyzing the Generated Code

After you've used either SQLMetal or LINQ to SQL Classes Designer to create entities, you can use the classes to manage the database. But first you should understand what has been generated by the tool that you're using.

If you have used SQLMetal with the /code option, just open the file with your preferred text editor. To read the code generated by the Visual Studio LINQ to SQL Classes Designer, you need to expand the DBML file node in Solution Explorer, as shown in Figure 18-3, and take a look at the source code within the designer.cs file.

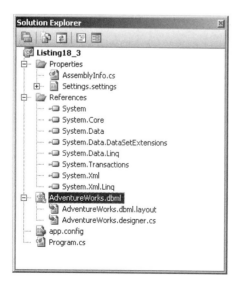

Figure 18-3. *The code generated by the LINQ to SQL Classes Designer is contained in the designer.cs file.*

In our example, the first important instruction in the code is the AdventureWorksDataContext class definition. This class derives from the DataContext class.

```
[System.Data.Linq.Mapping.DatabaseAttribute(Name="AdventureWorks")]
public partial class AdventureWorksDataContext : System.Data.Linq.DataContext
```

The DataContext class represents the database. The LINQ to SQL framework uses it to connect to the database and to manage it (as detailed in the "The DataContext Class" section later in this chapter). The DatabaseAttribute attribute specifies the database's name. Specifying the database's name is useful in two cases: the LINQ to SQL framework uses the name when you ask to create a database with the CreateDatabase method of the DataContext class, and the framework uses the name when you connect to the database without specifying the database in the connection string.

Next in the generated code, you'll see that the LINQ to SQL framework classes have been added to the System.Data.Linq namespace:

```
public System.Data.Linq.Table<Customer> Customers
{
    get
    {
        return this.GetTable<Customer>();
    }
}

public System.Data.Linq.Table<CustomerAddress> CustomerAddresses
{
    get
    {
        return this.GetTable<CustomerAddress>();
    }
}
```

This snippet of code defines a property for each entity within the class (in this case, two properties). The GetTable method provided by the DataContext class returns an instance of the entity. So, it's time to look at how an entity is defined in the class:

```
[Table(Name="Sales.Customer")]
public partial class Customer : INotifyPropertyChanging, INotifyPropertyChanged
```

Every entity in the class has a Table attribute with an optional Name property used to indicate the name of the table as specified in the database. You can omit Name when the partial class's name is equal to the table's name.

The LINQ to SQL framework has a monitoring feature that allows it to catch changes to your entities after having filled them with data retrieved from the database. This feature is provided with the help of the entity class and its implementation of both the INotifyPropertyChanging and INotifyPropertyChanged interfaces. The methods defined by these interfaces enable the framework to inform you that a property is both going to change and has changed, respectively.

Next in the generated code, you can find the declaration of a private field for each column defined in the table. The Customer entity code has these declarations:

```
private int _CustomerID;

private System.Nullable<int> _TerritoryID;
private string _AccountNumber;
private char _CustomerType;
private System.Guid _rowguid;
private System.DateTime _ModifiedDate;
private EntitySet<CustomerAddress> _CustomerAddresses;
```

And the `CustomerAddress` entity code has these declarations:

```
private int _CustomerID;
private int _AddressID;
private int _AddressTypeID;
private System.Guid _rowguid;
private System.DateTime _ModifiedDate;
private EntityRef<Customer> _Customer;
```

Every field has the related column's datatype, and a nullable datatype is used when the column defined in the database can contain a null value. Much more interesting are the `EntitySet` and `EntityRef` classes. They are provided by the LINQ to SQL framework to manage relationships between entities and data consistency. The `EntitySet` class contains items from the *many* part of the one-to-many relationship type between the entities. In this case, a customer can have more than one address specified in the `CustomerAddress` table, so an `EntitySet<CustomerAddress>` field is defined to store related records. The `EntityRef` class represents the *one* part of the one-to-many relationship type between the entities. So, if you examine the code of the `CustomerAddresses` entity, you will see the `EntityRef<Customer>` field. This is correct, because a customer address belongs to only one customer.

Continuing with the generated code, you'll next see this:

```
[Column(Storage="_CustomerID", AutoSync=AutoSync.OnInsert,
            DbType="Int NOT NULL IDENTITY", IsPrimaryKey=true,
            IsDbGenerated=true)]
public int CustomerID
{
    get
    {
        return this._CustomerID;
    }
    set
    {
        if ((this._CustomerID != value))
        {
            this.OnCustomerIDChanging(value);
            this.SendPropertyChanging();
            this._CustomerID = value;
            this.SendPropertyChanged("CustomerID");
            this.OnCustomerIDChanged();
        }
    }
}
```

Every private field has a public property that allows you to set and retrieve its value. The property is decorated with attributes that allow the LINQ to SQL framework to manage the field. Just as with the `DatabaseAttribute` attribute, these values are useful to create the database with the `CreateDatabase` method and to manage the entity. Table 18-2 shows the attributes to decorate a field. The interesting part of the preceding code snippet resides in the set accessor. The `SendPropertyChanging` and `SendPropertyChanged` methods are the implementations of the `INotifyPropertyChanging` and `INotifyPropertyChanged` interfaces, respectively. They inform the LINQ to SQL framework that the property is changing by calling the `PropertyChanging` method. They also inform the framework that the property has changed by calling the `PropertyChanged` method. Moreover, the `OnCustomerIDChanging` and `OnCustomerIDChanged` methods are *partial methods*. Partial methods are a new C# 3.0 feature that allows you to define partial classes in which to insert implementations of those methods. If you do not eventually provide implementations for partial methods, the C# compiler will exclude them from the compilation. The `PropertyChanging` and `PropertyChanged` methods use the `On[PropertyName]Changing` and `On[PropertyName]Changed` format. That format is created for each property in the entity class.

Table 18-2. *Column Attribute Properties*

Property	Description
AutoSync	Specifies if the column is automatically synchronized from the value generated by the database on insert or update commands. Valid values for this tag are Default, Always, Never, OnInsert, and OnUpdate.
CanBeNull	A Boolean value indicating if the column can contain null values (true) or not (false).
DBType	Specifies the column's datatype in the database. If you omit this property, LINQ will infer the type from the class member. This property is mandatory only if you want to use the CreateDatabase method to create a new database instance.
Expression	Defines the column as a computed column. Using this attribute, you can define the formula used to compute the result.
IsDBGenerated	Identifies a column whose value is generated by the database. Usually, you will use this property in conjunction with primary key columns defined with the IDENTITY property.
IsDiscriminator	Indicates that the member holds the discriminator value for an inheritance hierarchy.
IsPrimaryKey	Specifies that a column is part of a table's primary (or unique) key. LINQ currently works only with tables that have primary (or unique) keys.
IsVersion	Indicates the member is a database timestamp or version number.
Name	Specifies the column's name in the database. Defaults to the member name.
Storage	Specifies the name of the private field underlying a property. LINQ will bypass the property's get and set accessors and use the field instead.
TypeId	Gets a unique identifier for the attribute.
UpdateCheck	Specifies how LINQ detects optimistic concurrency conflicts. The possible values are Always, Never, and WhenChanged. If no member is marked with IsVersion=true, all members participate in detection unless explicitly specified otherwise.

The last snippet of generated code that deserves an explanation is where the entity manages the EntitySet and EntityRef fields. Here's that bit of code from our example:

```
[Association(Name="Customer_CustomerAddress", Storage="_CustomerAddresses",
                OtherKey="CustomerID")]
public EntitySet<CustomerAddress> CustomerAddresses
{
    get
    {
        return this._CustomerAddresses;
    }

    set
    {
        this._CustomerAddresses.Assign(value);
    }
}
```

Every property participating in the relationship is decorated with the Association attribute. This attribute owns properties useful to the LINQ to SQL framework to understand the name and the type of the relationship (of course, they are useful to create the relashionship in the database with the CreateDatabase method, too). Table 18-3 lists the Association attribute properties that you can use to specify the relationship between two entities.

Table 18-3. *Association Attribute Properties*

Property	Description
DeleteOnNull	When set to true, indicates to delete the object when the association is set to null. This is valid only for an association whose foreign key members are all non-nullable.
DeleteRule	Specifies the delete behavior associated with the foreign key. This property will be used only by the CreateDatabase method, so do not expect to see LINQ to SQL deleting records for you. You need to specify a CASCADE rule in your database to get automatic record deletion.
IsForeignKey	When set to true, indicates that the entity represents the relationship's side having the foreign key.
IsUnique	When set to true, indicates that there will be a 1:1 relationship between entities.
Name	Identifies the name of the relation. Usually, its value is the same as the name of the foreign key constraint relation name defined in the database. You must specify it if you plan to use the CreateDatabase method from the DataContext class to create a new database with this relation. You must use the same name in the entity class that composes the relation with this one.
OtherKey	Identifies a list of parent entity class keys separated by commas. If the keys are not specified, LINQ to SQL infers them, and assumes they are equal to the primary keys defined in the parent entity class.
Storage	Contains the name of the private field defined in the class. When specifying this property, LINQ to SQL will use the class's field to access data instead of using the related get and set accessors.
ThisKey	Identifies a list of keys of this entity class, separated by commas. If the keys are not specified, LINQ to SQL assumes they are equal to the primary keys defined in this class.

A one-to-many relationship has been defined between the Customer and CustomerAddress entities. So two Association attributes are specified: one in the Customer entity and one in the CustomerAddress entity. The preceding code is stored in the Customer entity that has the collection of addresses related to a customer. So, the Customer entity represents the *one* side of the relationship where you need to indicate which property represents the foreign key in the other entity. You indicate a foreign key by setting the OtherKey property with the name of the child entity's property. In the set accessor, the CustomerAddress object is added to the collection of the Customer's addresses by the Assign method. A way to relate a Customer object with a CustomerAddress object is using the CustomerAdresses property, as shown in the following code snippet:

```
CustomerAddress ca = new CustomerAddress();
Customer c = new Customer();

c.CustomerAddresses.Add(ca);
```

When the Add method is called, a call to the set accessor within the Customer entity is automatically done, and the Assign method is called.

In the following code snippet, you can see the code within the CustomerAddress entity, the one representing the *many* side of the relationship:

```
[Association(Name="Customer_CustomerAddress", Storage="_Customer",
ThisKey="CustomerID", IsForeignKey=true)]
public Customer Customer
{
    get
    {
```

```
        return this._Customer.Entity;
    }
    set
    {
        Customer previousValue = this._Customer.Entity;
        if (((previousValue != value)
          || (this._Customer.HasLoadedOrAssignedValue == false)))
        {
            this.SendPropertyChanging();
            if ((previousValue != null))
            {
                this._Customer.Entity = null;
                previousValue.CustomerAddresses.Remove(this);
            }
            this._Customer.Entity = value;
            if ((value != null))
            {
                value.CustomerAddresses.Add(this);
                this._CustomerID = value.CustomerID;
            }
            else
            {
                this._CustomerID = default(int);
            }
            this.SendPropertyChanged("Customer");
        }
    }
}
```

The second Association attribute is defined in the CustomerAddress entity. Here, the Customer property uses the IsForeignKey property of the Association attribute set to true to indicate that the Customer property is the foreign key. Finally, the ThisKey property indicates that the CustomerID is the name of the foreign key.

In the preceding snippet, the set accessor contains very important code because it manages the consistency of the entity object's data. The Assign method is one way to relate a Customer object to a CustomerAddress object. But using the CustomerAddresses property is not the only way to relate those objects. You can start creating or retrieving with a query to a CustomerAddress object and then use its Customer property to relate them. Using this approach, you call the code within the set accessor of the Customer property. The following code snippet demonstrates this concept:

```
AdventureWorksDataContext db = new AdventureWorksDataContext();
CustomerAddress ca = (from addr in db.CustomerAddresses
                                 select addr).First();
Customer c = new Customer();
ca.Customer = c;
```

The set accessor of the Customer property is responsible for managing the data and preventing it from becoming inconsistent. From the preceding code snippet, you can see that a CustomerAddress object is retrieved by a query. This object already contains a relationship with a Customer record, but in the code, you are going to change it because you are assigning the new Customer object to the CustomerAddress object with its Customer property. The set accessor must avoid data inconsistency, so it needs to break the relationship with the old Customer and then create the new one.

Running LINQ Queries

The LINQ to SQL framework implements LINQ's standard query operators (SQO). These operators or methods have been defined by the LINQ development team as query operators for in-memory objects. You can use SQO with arrays and collections that implement the IEnumerable interface. For example, using the Select and Where standard query operators, you can filter array items specifying a condition.

■**Note** Understanding LINQ's SQO is very important to using LINQ to your greatest advantage. Two books that we recommend on LINQ are *Pro LINQ: Language Integrated Query in C# 2008* by Joseph C. Rattz, Jr. (Apress, 2007) and *LINQ for Visual C# 2005* by Fabio Claudio Ferracchiati (Apress, 2007).

Each new technology based on LINQ must implement the functionality for each of the standard operators. Thus, frameworks such as LINQ to XML, LINQ to SQL, LINQ to Dataset, and many others yet to come all provide the same operators. That uniformity means that developers can learn just once how to write a LINQ query, and not have to deal with differences between frameworks.

Some commonly used standard operators in the LINQ to SQL framework are Select, Where, Join, and OrderBy. We'll show examples of queries with each operator using the AdventureWorksDataContext class generated by either the Visual Studio LINQ to SQL Classes Designer or SQLMetal. We use a console application to display the query results on the screen.

The Select Operator

The Select operator allows you to select either some or all records from an entity. When used in conjunction with the Join operator, it allows you to pick up field values from different joined entities.

Here is a simple LINQ query that uses only the Select operator:

```
AdventureWorksDataContext db = new AdventureWorksDataContext();

IQueryable<Customer> query = from c in db.Customers
                                              select c;

foreach (Customer customer in query)
{
    Console.WriteLine(customer.AccountNumber);
    Console.WriteLine("-=-=-=-=-=-=-=-=-=-=-=-=");

    foreach (CustomerAddress address in customer.CustomerAddresses)
    {
        Console.WriteLine(address.AddressTypeID);
    }

    Console.WriteLine("-=-=-=-=-=-=-=-=-=-=-=-=");
}
```

Let's take a close look at how this code works. After having defined an object from the AdventureWorksDataContext class to connect to the database and to execute the SQL query, the code defines the query. The definition begins with the keyword from. As you can see, the LINQ query is very similar to a SQL query, but the order of the operators is different.

In this case, the Select operator returns a collection of customers within an IQueryable<Customer> object. If you analyze the IQueryable<T> interface, you will see that it implements the IEnumerable<T>

interface. That's why it can be enumerated in the first foreach loop. The second foreach loop is very cool, because the addresses that belong to the customer are printed on the screen without your having asked for them in the query. How can that be? Recall that the code in the generated Customer entity class contains an EntitySet property called CustomerAdresses. In the exact moment you use it, the DataContext method executes the query to fill the collection automatically. That's exactly what an OO developer expects to see when managing objects! The output from this query is shown in Figure 18-4.

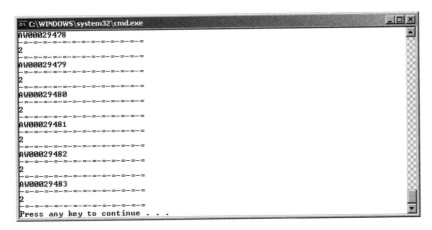

Figure 18-4. *The output of the Select operator example*

The following shows a new instruction (bolded) to help you see what happens under the DataContext hood:

```
AdventureWorksDataContext db = new AdventureWorksDataContext();

db.Log = Console.Out;

IQueryable<Customer> query = from c in db.Customers
                                            select c;

foreach (Customer customer in query)
{
    Console.WriteLine(customer.AccountNumber);
    Console.WriteLine("-=-=-=-=-=-=-=-=-=-=-=-=");

    foreach (CustomerAddress address in customer.CustomerAddresses)
    {
        Console.WriteLine(address.AddressTypeID);
    }

    Console.WriteLine("-=-=-=-=-=-=-=-=-=-=-=-=");
}
```

The Log property from the DataContext class allows you to see what is generated by the LINQ to SQL framework when the query is run. As you can see in Figure 18-5, the framework executes an initial SQL query to retrieve all the regions as required in our code. But when the code asks for territories, the LINQ to SQL framework runs a second query in which the CustomerID is used to retrieve all the addresses of the current customer.

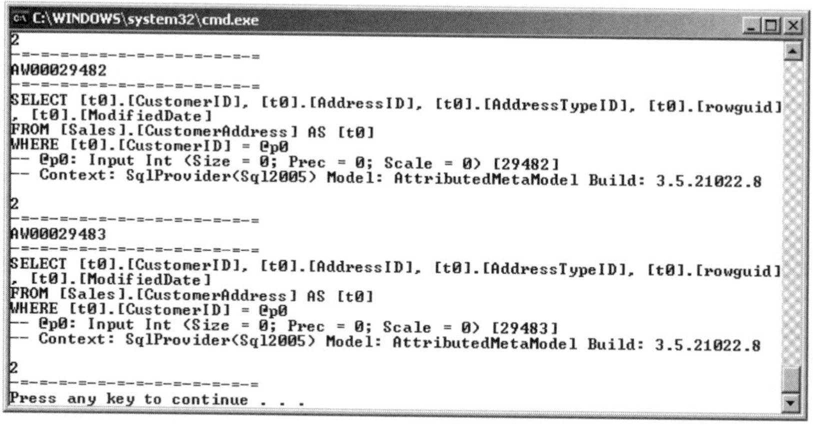

Figure 18-5. *By assigning the Log property to the console output, you can see the SQL-generated statements.*

The Where Operator

The Where operator allows you to add a condition to a query. Such conditions are similar to those in SQL's WHERE clause. The Where operator allows you to add logical operators such as or and and to link several conditions together. The important thing to remember is that you must write your conditions following your host code language syntax (C# or Visual Basic .NET), and not the SQL syntax. For example, the following code snippet retrieves the customer with a CustomerID value equal to 1.

```
AdventureWorksDataContext db = new AdventureWorksDataContext ();

IQueryable<Customer> query = from c in db.Customers
                             where c.CustomerID == 1
                             select c;

foreach (Customer customer in query)
{
    Console.WriteLine(customer.AccountNumber);
    Console.WriteLine("-=-=-=-=-=-=-=-=-=-=-=-");

    foreach (CustomerAddress address in customer.CustomerAddresses)
    {
        Console.WriteLine(address.AddressTypeID);
    }

    Console.WriteLine("-=-=-=-=-=-=-=-=-=-=-=-");
}
```

As you can see from the bolded text, the *equal* operator is the one used by the C# language, not the one supported by SQL. Figure 18-6 shows the code's output.

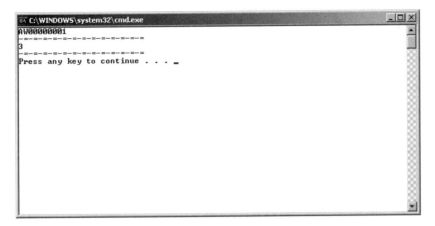

Figure 18-6. *The output from the Where operator example shows the customer with the identifier equal to 1.*

The Join Operator

The Join operator allows you to join data from two entities and eventually put the result into a brand-new result set. The Join operator's usage in the LINQ to SQL framework is very different from its usage in other LINQ frameworks, such as LINQ to Objects, because the O/RM generates code that already implements relationships between entities.

As you have seen in the first LINQ query code snippet, demonstrating the Select operator, the records of the CustomerAddress entities are automatically joined to the Customer's entity record. The Join operator allows you to add relationships that are not defined in the database schema and that are not automatically created by the O/RM tool. The following example shows the Join operator syntax, which uses some interesting new C# 3.0 features.

```
AdventureWorksDataContext db = new AdventureWorksDataContext();

db.Log = Console.Out;

var query = from c in db.Customers
join ca in db.CustomerAddresses on c.CustomerID equals ca.CustomerID into results
where c.CustomerID == 1
select new { CustomerID = c.CustomerID, NumOfAddresses = results.Count() };

foreach (var result in query)
{
    Console.WriteLine("CustomerID: {0} Count: {1}",
                      result.CustomerID,
                      result.NumOfAddresses);
}
```

In this example, the Join operator is used to join the Customer and CustomerAddress entities by the CustomerID. The into keyword is optional but it is useful to create a new identifier containing the results of the join operation. Here, it is used to obtain information similar to the information you could obtain using the GROUP BY SQL instruction. The Join operator is used to count addresses of the customer that have the identifier equal to 1.

In the example, you can see some new C# 3.0 features: the var keyword, the anonymous type, and the possibility to set property values during object instantiation. Using the Select operator, you can pick values from different entities and create an anonymous type to contain the related values. This operation avoids the need to create a new class with fields to contain the result of your query. Since the type is anonymous and created by the compiler on the fly, you need to use the var keyword to obtain a variable representing an instance from the anonymous class. The var keyword represents a generic variable, and the compiler will assign the correct datatype when it encounters this keyword. Figure 18-7 shows the result of the join operation.

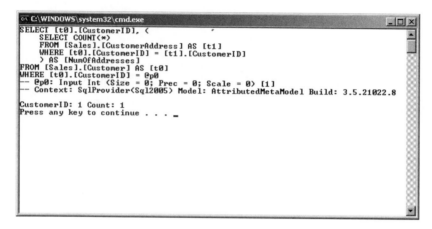

Figure 18-7. *The result of the join operation with only one address for the selected customer*

The OrderBy Operator

Use the OrderBy operator to sort the results of a query in ascending or descending order. For this example, we've added a new entity wrapped around the CountryRegion table of the AdventureWorks database. The table is pretty simple and contains the region's code and name. The following example sorts regions by their name.

```
AdventureWorksDataContext db = new AdventureWorksDataContext();

IQueryable<CountryRegion> query = from r in db.CountryRegions
                                  orderby r.Name
                                  select r;

foreach (CountryRegion result in query)
{
    Console.WriteLine("Region: Code:{0}  Name:{1}",
                                result.CountryRegionCode,
                                result.Name);
}
```

The output of this code snippet is shown in Figure 18-8.

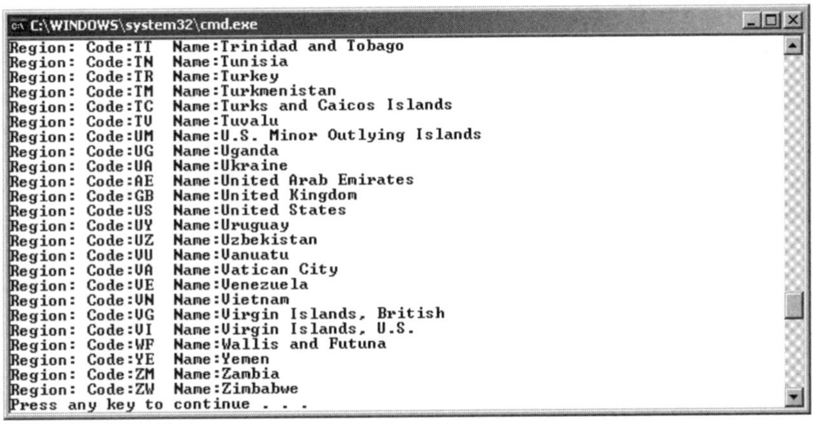

Figure 18-8. *Using the OrderBy operator, regions are sorted by name.*

To change the sorting order from ascending (the default) to descending, you need to specify the descending keyword after the entity field name used to do the sorting operation, as follows:

```
AdventureWorksDataContext db = new AdventureWorksDataContext();

IQueryable<CountryRegion> query = from r in db.CountryRegions
                        orderby r.Name descending
                        select r;

foreach (CountryRegion result in query)
{
    Console.WriteLine("Region: Code:{0}  Name:{1}",
                            result.CountryRegionCode,
                            result.Name);
}
```

Figure 18-9 shows the output from this example.

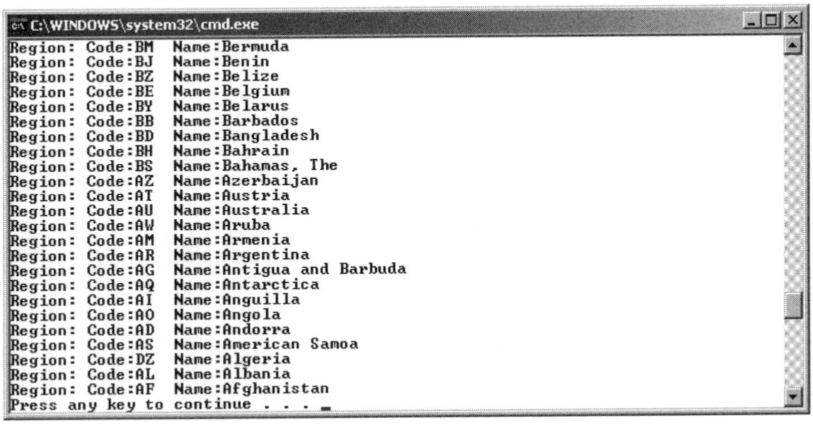

Figure 18-9. *By using the descending keyword, the CountryRegion names are sorted in descending order.*

The DataContext Class

Every operation between the database and the LINQ to SQL framework passes through either the DataContext class or a class derived from it. The DataContext class provides many properties and methods that you will find useful for managing the database. These include creating and removing a database, updating its content, querying records, executing stored procedures, and using functions and views. The DataContext class also provides a mechanism for tracking changes to your entity data and detecting concurrency conflicts.

This section covers the following aspects of DataContext:

- Insert, update, and delete operations
- Concurrency conflict detection
- Deferred query execution
- Stored procedures and functions usage

Inserting, Updating, and Deleting Records

So far, you have seen how to query the database using LINQ syntax and entities. Entities can be used to do other operations on the database, such as insert new records, update records, and delete existing records. Using the LINQ to SQL framework, these operations will be executed by the DataContext class automatically. In fact, the DataContext class uses a change-tracking feature that allows it to track every difference between data originally retrieved by a query and the current version of that data as modified by your code.

For example, if your code adds a new region by instantiating a new Region object and assigning it to the derived DataContext class's Regions collection, the change-tracking feature understands that a new record has been added and composes the related SQL statement to insert it into the database. The actual insert is accomplished when the code invokes the SubmitChanges method. Here is an example:

```
AdventureWorksDataContext db = new AdventureWorksDataContext();

CountryRegion newRegion = new CountryRegion();
newRegion.CountryRegionCode = "ZZ";
newRegion.Name = "New Region from Code";
newRegion.ModifiedDate = DateTime.Now;
db.CountryRegions.InsertOnSubmit(newRegion);

db.Log = Console.Out;
db.SubmitChanges();
```

The InsertOnSubmit method defined in each entity allows you to add a new object to the related collection. Internally, the InsertOnSubmit method informs the change-tracking feature to compose the INSERT SQL instruction. So, when SubmitChanges is called, the SQL statement is built and executed, as shown in Figure 18-10, and the database is updated, as shown in Figure 18-11.

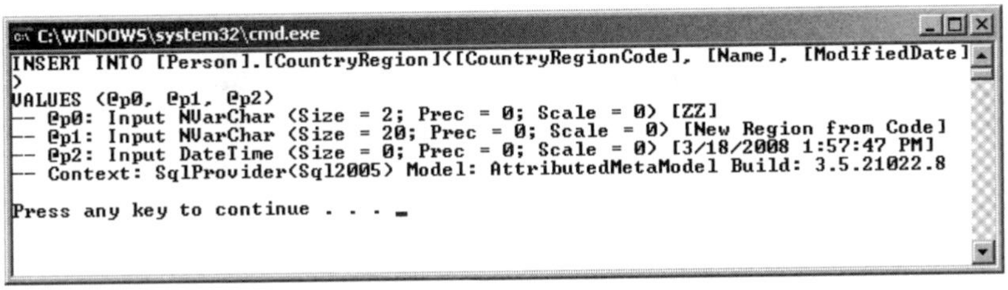

Figure 18-10. *The change-tracking mechanism builds the INSERT statement automatically.*

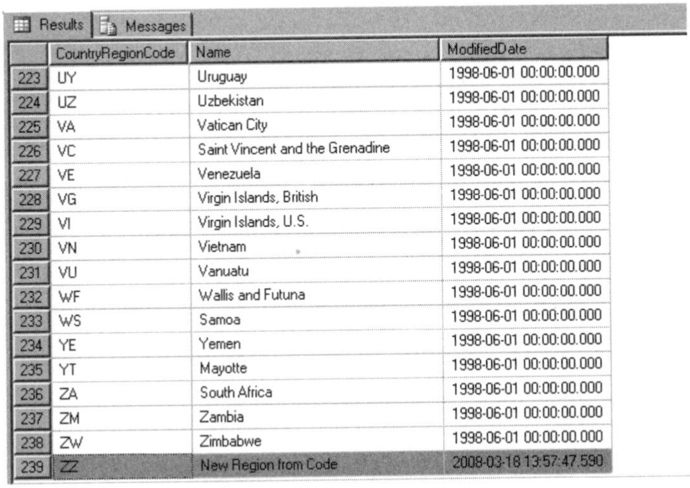

	CountryRegionCode	Name	ModifiedDate
223	UY	Uruguay	1998-06-01 00:00:00.000
224	UZ	Uzbekistan	1998-06-01 00:00:00.000
225	VA	Vatican City	1998-06-01 00:00:00.000
226	VC	Saint Vincent and the Grenadine	1998-06-01 00:00:00.000
227	VE	Venezuela	1998-06-01 00:00:00.000
228	VG	Virgin Islands, British	1998-06-01 00:00:00.000
229	VI	Virgin Islands, U.S.	1998-06-01 00:00:00.000
230	VN	Vietnam	1998-06-01 00:00:00.000
231	VU	Vanuatu	1998-06-01 00:00:00.000
232	WF	Wallis and Futuna	1998-06-01 00:00:00.000
233	WS	Samoa	1998-06-01 00:00:00.000
234	YE	Yemen	1998-06-01 00:00:00.000
235	YT	Mayotte	1998-06-01 00:00:00.000
236	ZA	South Africa	1998-06-01 00:00:00.000
237	ZM	Zambia	1998-06-01 00:00:00.000
238	ZW	Zimbabwe	1998-06-01 00:00:00.000
239	ZZ	New Region from Code	2008-03-18 13:57:47.590

Figure 18-11. *The new record appears in the database.*

Updating a record requires a different approach from inserting a new one. First, you use a query to retrieve the record you want to change. Then you can change its values. Finally, you call the `SubmitChanges` method. Thanks to the change-tracking mechanism, `SubmitChanges` is able to compose the necessary SQL to propagate your changes back to the database. The following is an example in which the country region added in the previous example is modified.

```
AdventureWorksDataContext db = new AdventureWorksDataContext();

CountryRegion zzRegion = (from r in db.CountryRegions
where r.CountryRegionCode == "ZZ"
select r).Single();

zzRegion.Name = "Updated by code";

db.Log = Console.Out;
db.SubmitChanges();
```

In this code snippet, the `Single` method provided by the `IQueryable<T>` interface is used to retrieve the single record from the collection. Then its region identifier is changed, and the `SubmitChanges` method is called. Since the `Log` property is assigned to the console output, you can see the resulting SQL statement on the screen, as shown in Figure 18-12.

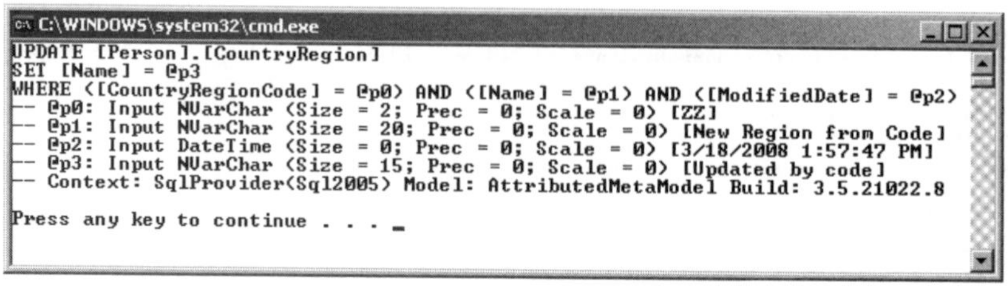

Figure 18-12. *The SubmitChanges method understands an entity is changed and generates the UPDATE statement to reverse the changes in the database.*

You take a similar approach to delete a record from the database. You retrieve the record to be deleted, and then invoke the DeleteOnSubmit method provided by the entity class. The following shows an example in which the new region added to the CountryRegion table is removed.

```
AdventureWorksDataContext db = new AdventureWorksDataContext();
CountryRegion zzRegion = (from r in db.CountryRegions
                          where r.CountryRegionCode == "ZZ"
                          select r).Single();

db.CountryRegions.DeleteOnSubmit(zzRegion);

db.Log = Console.Out;
db.SubmitChanges();
```

Running this code will retrieve the output shown in Figure 18-13.

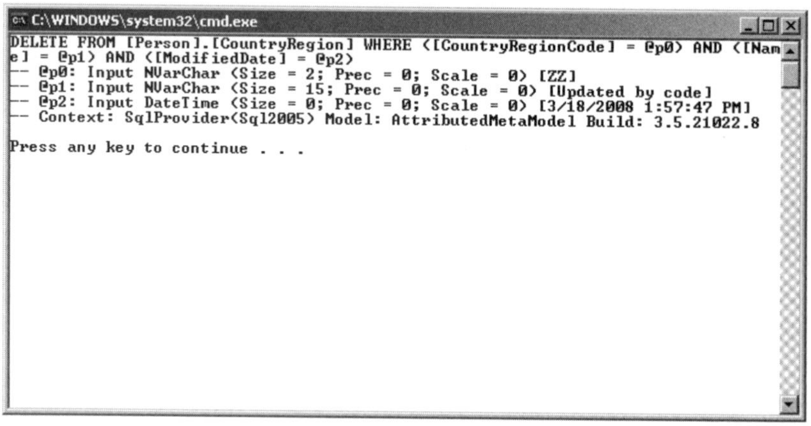

Figure 18-13. *The record is removed from the CountryRegion table.*

■Note The LINQ to SQL framework doesn't support cascade-deletion operations. In other words, if you are going to delete related records using your entities without having defined a constraint rule in your database, you will receive an exception. To learn more about insert, update, and delete operations with the LINQ to SQL framework, see http://msdn2.microsoft.com/en-us/library/bb386931.aspx.

Concurrency Conflict Detection

The LINQ to SQL framework provides for concurrency conflict detection on records retrieved by a query. Conflict detection is necessary, because from the moment you retrieve records from the database to the moment you call the SubmitChanges method to transmit your data changes to the database, one or more of those records, or related records, could be changed by some other database user. For example, another program could access the same table and update its content. In the event of a conflicting change from another user, the SubmitChanges method will raise a ChangeConflictException. You can then manage that exception and decide what your best course of action is to resolve the conflict.

The following example is similar to the update example in the previous section, but with a new instruction to wait for user input before updating the record with the SubmitChanges call.

```
AdventureWorksDataContext db = new AdventureWorksDataContext();

CountryRegion zzRegion = (from r in db.CountryRegions
                          where r.CountryRegionCode == "ZW"
                          select r).Single();

zzRegion.Name = "Updated by code";
db.Log = Console.Out;
Console.ReadLine();

db.SubmitChanges();
```

In order to raise the ChangeConflictException exception, you need to run the previous code twice. Two console applications are running now. Choose one of them and press a key, and the code will update the database. Then go to the second console, press a key again, and you will generate the exception shown in Figure 18-14.

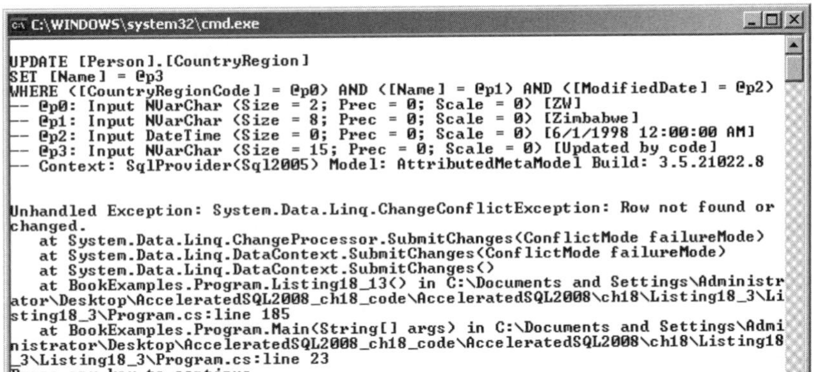

Figure 18-14. *The ChangeConflictException is thrown by the second console application.*

How Conflict Detection Works

If you look carefully at the SQL statement produced by the SubmitChanges method (see Figure 18-14), you will see that the CountryRegionCode, Name, and ModifiedDate columns are used in the WHERE clause. Usually, just the primary key is used in the WHERE condition (in this case, the CountryRegionCode column), because it is sufficient to identify the record. However, in the case of an update operation, the LINQ to SQL framework also checks whether the original record in the database has been changed.

That check is accomplished by providing the record's original values to the query as part of the WHERE condition. If the record was changed, the condition will fail, the database will report no records updated, and the SubmitChanges method raises ChangeConflictException.

You can decide which entity's fields participate in concurrency conflict detection using the UpdateCheck property of the Column attribute. You can select from three UpdateCheck values:

- Never: The column is excluded from the check.
- Always: A column is always checked. This is the default value.
- WhenChanged: The column is checked only when its value is changed.

Resolving the Conflict

Using a try/catch block, you can trap the ChangeConflictException exception. Then you can use the ChangeConflicts collection provided by the DataContext class to resolve the conflict. The ChangeConflicts collection provides the ResolveAll and Resolve methods, which you can use to specify what to do with your data. Both methods accept the RefreshMode enumeration that you can use to specify how to resolve the conflict. That enumeration provides three values:

- KeepChanges: Retrieves fresh data from the database, without changing those entity data that you have changed in the code.
- OverwriteCurrentValues: Retrieves a fresh version of data from the database, overwriting even current values modified by code.
- KeepCurrentValues: Leaves everything as is; that is, your data will not be changed.

The following example updates the code from the previous example to catch conflict exceptions and uses the ChangeConflicts collection to resolve any conflicts that occur. Again, run this code twice to have two copies running at the same time. Figure 18-15 shows the resulting output.

```
AdventureWorksDataContext db = new AdventureWorksDataContext();

CountryRegion zzRegion = (from r in db.CountryRegions
                          where r.CountryRegionCode == "ZW"
                          select r).Single();

zzRegion.Name = "Zimbabwe";

db.Log = Console.Out;
Console.ReadLine();

try
{
    db.SubmitChanges();
}
catch (ChangeConflictException ex)
{
    Console.WriteLine("An exception is occurred... ResolveAll method is called.");
    db.ChangeConflicts.ResolveAll(RefreshMode.OverwriteCurrentValues);
}
```

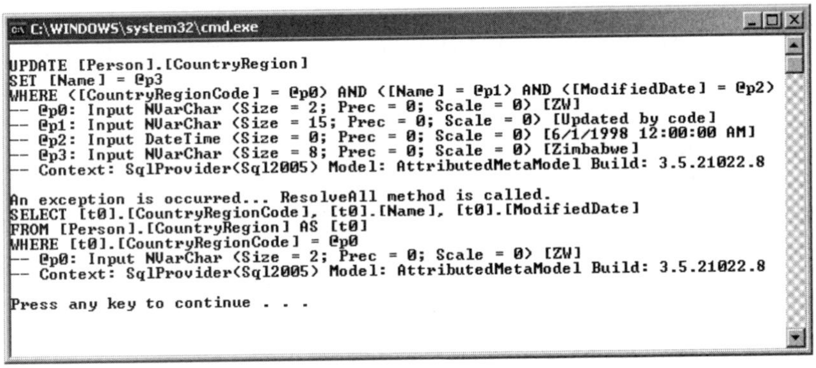

```
C:\WINDOWS\system32\cmd.exe
UPDATE [Person].[CountryRegion]
SET [Name] = @p3
WHERE ([CountryRegionCode] = @p0) AND ([Name] = @p1) AND ([ModifiedDate] = @p2)
-- @p0: Input NVarChar (Size = 2; Prec = 0; Scale = 0) [ZW]
-- @p1: Input NVarChar (Size = 15; Prec = 0; Scale = 0) [Updated by code]
-- @p2: Input DateTime (Size = 0; Prec = 0; Scale = 0) [6/1/1998 12:00:00 AM]
-- @p3: Input NVarChar (Size = 8; Prec = 0; Scale = 0) [Zimbabwe]
-- Context: SqlProvider(Sql2005) Model: AttributedMetaModel Build: 3.5.21022.8

An exception is occurred... ResolveAll method is called.
SELECT [t0].[CountryRegionCode], [t0].[Name], [t0].[ModifiedDate]
FROM [Person].[CountryRegion] AS [t0]
WHERE [t0].[CountryRegionCode] = @p0
-- @p0: Input NVarChar (Size = 2; Prec = 0; Scale = 0) [ZW]
-- Context: SqlProvider(Sql2005) Model: AttributedMetaModel Build: 3.5.21022.8

Press any key to continue . . .
```

Figure 18-15. *The exception is caught and the ResolveAll method is called.*

By default, the LINQ to SQL framework uses *optimistic* conflict detection. As the name suggests, the framework is optimistic that nothing is changed when SubmitChanges is called, so no locks are applied to the underlying database tables. You can change to *pessimistic* conflict detection using the TransactionScope class contained in the System.Transactions.dll assembly. With the pessimistic mode, the application locks the table until an update is complete. Here is an example of using pessimistic conflict detection:

```
AdventureWorksDataContext db = new AdventureWorksDataContext();

using (TransactionScope ts = new TransactionScope())
{

    CountryRegion zzRegion = (from r in db.CountryRegions
                              where r.CountryRegionCode == "ZW"
                              select r).Single();

    zzRegion.Name = "Zimbabwe_";

    db.Log = Console.Out;
    Console.ReadLine();

    db.SubmitChanges();

     ts.Complete();
}
```

By running this code twice, and then pressing a key in both console applications, you will update the database without errors from one console, while the other console will raise an exception. Figure 18-16 shows the output.

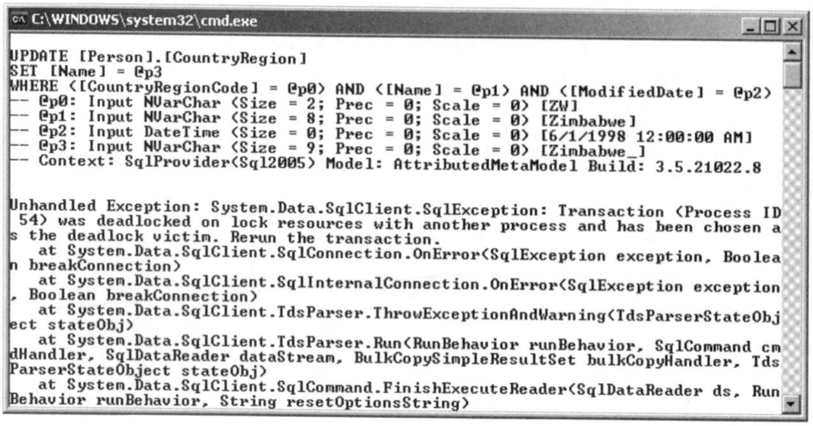

Figure 18-16. *The deadlock on the table doesn't allow the application to update the table.*

Deferred Query Execution

A very important LINQ to SQL framework behavior is *deferred query execution*. With deferred query execution, a query you define in your code is not executed until you use a loop to iterate through the IQueryable<T> collection or until you invoke particular methods, such as Single, ToList, and many others that use the collection for you. When you write the query in your code, you just define it; there is no SQL statement execution until you loop through the collection's items. To demonstrate this behavior, run the following code, putting a breakpoint just after the query definition, on the foreach statement.

```
AdventureWorksDataContext db = new AdventureWorksDataContext();

db.Log = Console.Out;

IQueryable<CountryRegion> query = from r in db.CountryRegions
                                  select r;

foreach (CountryRegion region in query)
{
    Console.WriteLine(region.Name);
}
```

Figure 18-17 shows the results.

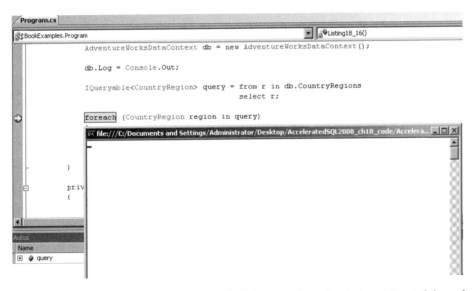

Figure 18-17. *The SQL statement hasn't been built because the code still hasn't iterated through items.*

When the code enters the foreach loop, the query is executed, as shown in Figure 18-18.

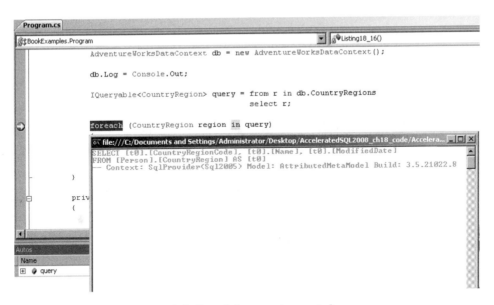

Figure 18-18. *The SQL statement is built and the query is executed.*

There are pros and cons to the deferred query execution behavior provided by the LINQ to SQL framework. Since a query is not executed until its collection is enumerated, you can change the query in your code at runtime, perhaps depending on user input choices. That's a good point! But if you iterate through a collection's items over and over, then the SQL statement is executed several times, once for each iteration. That's not so good for performance. Moreover, you will not be able to determine whether the LINQ query you wrote is good until it is enumerated. You could write a query with good syntax but containing some logical error, which you will discover only after the query is executed.

You can avoid executing a query repetitively using methods such as ToArray, ToList, ToDictionary, and ToLookup. For example, with the ToList method, you obtain a List<T> collection with data that will be cached by the LINQ to SQL framework. So, when you execute the same query again, the framework returns the cached data without running the query. The following code simulates a double query execution, and in Figure 18-19, you can see that the query is performed twice.

```
AdventureWorksDataContext db = new AdventureWorksDataContext();

db.Log = Console.Out;

IQueryable<CountryRegion> query = from r in db.CountryRegions
                                  select r;

for (int i = 0; i < 2; i++)
{
    foreach (CountryRegion region in query)
    {
        Console.WriteLine(region.Name);
    }
}
```

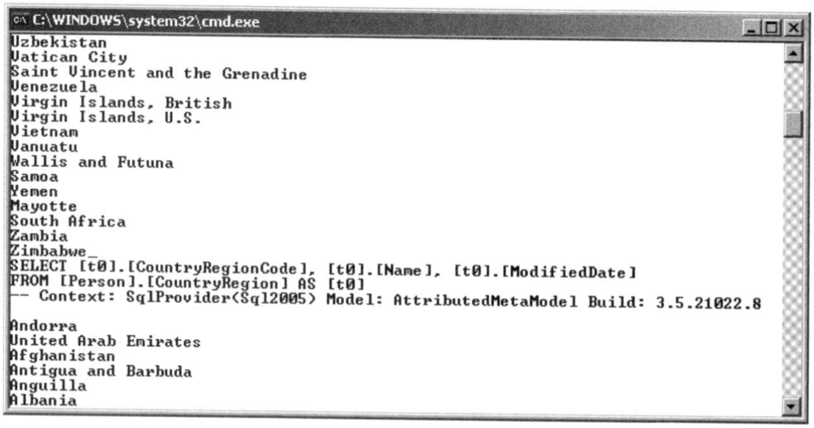

Figure 18-19. *The query is executed twice.*

In the next example, the ToList method is used to cache the records. Figure 18-20 demonstrates that the query is executed just once—not when the collection items are enumerated, but when the ToList method is called.

```
AdventureWorksDataContext db = new AdventureWorksDataContext();

db.Log = Console.Out;

IEnumerable<CountryRegion> query = (from r in db.CountryRegions
                                    select r).ToList();
```

```
for (int i = 0; i < 2; i++)
{
    foreach (CountryRegion region in query)
    {
        Console.WriteLine(region.Name);
    }
}
```

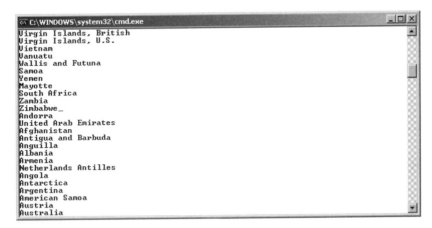

Figure 18-20. *The query is executed only one time. Record printing restarts without another query to the database.*

Deferred Loading

When you have two entities with a relationship, such as Customer and CustomerAddress, and you run a query to retrieve a customer, the CustomerAddresses collection is not populated. A second query is executed when you enumerate items of the CustomerAddresses collection. If you look carefully at the SQL generated for the earlier Select query example, shown in Figure 18-5, you will see that after a customer such as AW00000001 is displayed on the screen, a SELECT statement is executed to retrieve the address for that customer. This behavior of loading data only when needed is called *deferred loading.*

If you wish, you can change the framework's default behavior to one of *preloading.* You make that change using the DataLoadOptions class and its LoadWith method. The LoadWith method accepts a lambda expression as a parameter. You can specify which collection to load, thus preventing the DataContext class from deferring loads for that class.

The following shows a code snippet in which territories for a region are retrieved as soon as the parent record for that region is retrieved.

```
AdventureWorksDataContext db = new AdventureWorksDataContext();

DataLoadOptions dlo = new DataLoadOptions();
dlo.LoadWith<Customer>(c => c.CustomerAddresses);
db.LoadOptions = dlo;

db.Log = Console.Out;
```

```
IQueryable<Customer> query = from c in db.Customers
                             select c;

foreach (Customer customer in query)
{
    Console.WriteLine(customer.AccountNumber);
    Console.WriteLine("-=-=-=-=-=-=-=-=-=-=-=-=");

    foreach (CustomerAddress address in customer.CustomerAddresses)
    {
        Console.WriteLine(address.AddressTypeID);
    }

    Console.WriteLine("-=-=-=-=-=-=-=-=-=-=-=-=");
}
```

When the `CustomerAddresses` collection is used to print territory descriptions, no other query is executed, and preloaded data is used instead. The output in Figure 18-21 demonstrates this behavior.

Figure 18-21. *A unique query is executed to fill the Customer and CustomerAddress entities.*

Executing Stored Procedures and User-Defined Functions

The LINQ to SQL framework and its O/RM tools allow you to execute both a stored procedure and a SQL user-defined function using an entity. If you use the SQLMetal tool, you need to include the /sprocs option to generate code to use every stored procedure within the database. If you use Visual Studio's LINQ to SQL Classes Designer, you can drag the stored procedure from the Server Explorer window and drop it onto the designer surface as usual. The stored procedure's name will appear in the top-right corner of the designer. For example, drag and drop the `uspGetEmployeeManagers` stored procedure, as shown in Figure 18-22.

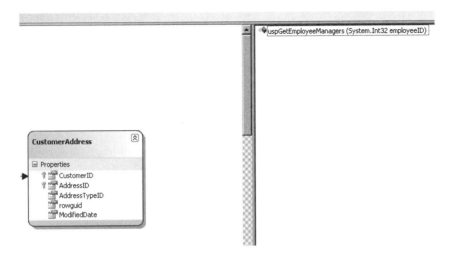

Figure 18-22. *Visual Studio designer shows the new stored procedure.*

The same approach applies for SQL user-defined functions. You can use the /functions option for the SQLMetal tool or drag and drop the function from Server Explorer onto the Visual Studio designer surface. This is what both tools generate in the code:

```
[Function(Name="dbo. uspGetEmployeeManagers")]
public ISingleResult<uspGetEmployeeManagersResult> uspGetEmployeeManagers
    ([Parameter(Name = "EmployeeID", DbType = "Int")]
        System.Nullable<int> employeeID)
{
    IExecuteResult result = this.ExecuteMethodCall(this,
            ((MethodInfo)(MethodInfo.GetCurrentMethod())),employeeID);
    return ((ISingleResult<uspGetEmployeeManagersResult>)(result.ReturnValue));
}
```

The stored procedure name has been used as a method name of the AdventureWorksDataContext class. The Function attribute decorates the method; its Name property represents either the name of the stored procedure or the user-defined function. To understand when a method needs to call the stored procedure or the user-defined function, the LINQ to SQL framework looks for the IsComposable flag. By default and if not specified, it is equal to false, indicating that a stored procedure is used by the code. On the other hand, when the flag is specified as true, the Function attribute's Name property indicates a user-defined function.

The method's return type depends on the stored procedure. For stored procedures returning single values, such as the number of affected records after an operation or the record count, the method's return type will be a standard datatype, such as int or string. In this example, the uspGetEmployeeManagers stored procedure returns all the Employee table columns of a specified Manager. So the return type is more complex, and the LINQ to SQL Classes Designer defines a new class to contain the result of the stored procedure execution: uspGetEmployeeManagersResult.

The O/RM tool is very smart. It analyzes the stored procedure code (the same is valid for user-defined functions, too), looking for what it returns. If the stored procedure returns a single column value, the method returns the related C# datatype (for example, a varchar column will be translated to the string datatype). When the stored procedure returns a record set of data (the case with this stored procedure), the ISingleResult class is used to contain the results. Finally, when the stored procedure returns more than a single result, the IMultipleResult class is used.

Calling either a stored procedure or a user-defined function from your code is just like calling a method. In the following example, the uspGetEmployeeManagers stored procedure is called and the result is printed on the screen, as shown in Figure 18-23.

```
AdventureWorksDataContext db = new AdventureWorksDataContext();

db.Log = Console.Out;

foreach (uspGetEmployeeManagersResult result in db.uspGetEmployeeManagers(21))
{
    Console.WriteLine("EmployeeID: {0} FirstName: {1} LastName: {2}",
                    result.EmployeeID,
                    result.FirstName,
                    result.LastName);
}
```

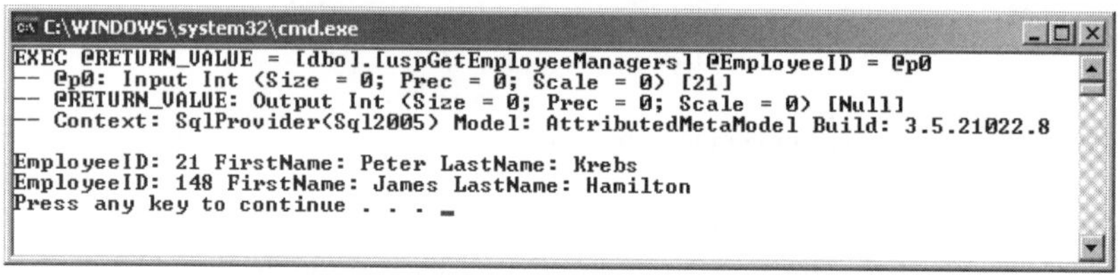

Figure 18-23. *The LINQ to SQL framework executes the stored procedure.*

The LINQ to SQL framework executed the related stored procedure, creating the EXEC statement and passing related parameters to the stored procedure (in this case, there aren't any parameters).

Summary

This chapter introduced the LINQ to SQL framework and its functionalities. However, we have just scratched the surface of LINQ's capabilities!

LINQ is not only applied to SQL but even to in-memory objects, XML, datasets, and any other class that implements the IEnumerable interface. Moreover, the IQueryable interface (which implements the IEnumerable interface, too) provides overridable properties and methods to implement your own LINQ to *something* framework. This interface provides *expression trees* containing LINQ's query parameters and values. You need to transform the expression tree into the query to obtain what the user has searched for and return the entity full of data. For example, you could use expression trees with the LDAP protocol to obtain information from the Microsoft Active Directory server or any other user repository. If you are interested in implementing your own LINQ framework, take a look at Matt Warren's blog, http://blogs.msdn.com/mattwar/default.aspx, where Matt provides a series of articles on building an IQueryable provider. If you are interested in LINQ news, take a look at the blog at http://www.ferracchiati.com.

PART 4

Business Intelligence in SQL Server

CHAPTER 19

■■■

Reporting Services

With SQL Server 2008, it is very clear that Reporting Services continues to be a major focus area and an investment area for Microsoft. It is one of the key components of the Microsoft Business Intelligence (BI) platform, which almost guarantees that this high level of focus and investment will continue into future releases of SQL Server.

Reporting Services is really in its third major release: it was introduced in 2004 as part of SQL Server 2000, completely integrated and expanded with SQL Server 2005, and now provided with major enhancements with SQL Server 2008. It is fair to say that, until SQL Server 2008, Reporting Services may have been the weakest component of the Microsoft BI platform. Integration Services and Analysis Services would consistently outperform their competitors for Windows-centric workloads. However, Reporting Services, although satisfying 75 percent of requirements, seemed to fall short in very large enterprise deployments. Having said that, and having spent some time reviewing and working with Reporting Services in SQL Server 2008, we think that Microsoft has made the required improvements to compete with the industry leaders in enterprise reporting.

Reporting Services technology allows you to design rich reports that can pull from multiple data sources; display the data from those data sources in a rich way using tables, matrices, lists, gauges, and charts; and also export your reports to a number of formats such as Word, Excel, PDF, XML, and HTML, without writing any code. Reporting Services also provides an extensibility model that lets you extend the designer, exporting formats, data sources, and delivery mechanisms for your reports. Reporting Services offers rich functionality for automating the delivery of reports on a scheduled basis, and its integration with Microsoft Office SharePoint Server continues to grow and improve. Finally, Reporting Services has an API that you can call using web services, so you can automate almost any part of your reports through your own scripts or programs.

This chapter will describe Reporting Services, focusing on what is new and changed with SQL Server 2008 such as the following:

- The new Reporting Services Configuration Manager encapsulates, in one tool, the most common configuration settings for a reporting environment.

- A new architecture eliminates the need for Internet Information Services (IIS), eases manageability, and dramatically improves the paging and caching capabilities for reports.

- Arguably the most talked about features are the new Tablix and Gauge data regions and the updated Chart data region. The new charts and gauges exist as the result of functionality acquired from Dundas Chart. The Tablix data region is a powerful feature that allows for the combination of tables and matrices in a single region. In the past, producing this type of report would certainly have required the creation of multiple reports and custom code to hide and show areas and columns.

- Reporting Services now provides improved rendering to Microsoft Excel format and new rendering to Microsoft Word format.

- The new Report Designer Preview application exposes the complete power of Report Designer, previously available only within the Business Intelligence Development Studio (BIDS) environment. Report Designer Preview is a rich client application that can be installed in power users' Windows environments to enable them to create very complex reports.

Reporting Services Components

Most companies store a vast array of data that can form the basis of many critical decisions affecting the performance and direction of the business. However, up until the release of Reporting Services with SQL Server 2000, the creation of reports based on this data involved the use of often expensive third-party tools, which frequently used proprietary formats for the definition of a report and weren't well integrated.

One of the goals of Reporting Services was to provide a single, standard platform for the design, creation, deployment, and management of all reports, and to promote interoperability between different reporting environments by adopting a standard XML-based language to define the reports, called Report Definition Language (RDL).

The underlying architecture for Reporting Services in SQL Server 2008 has fundamentally changed, removing the need for IIS and drastically increasing the scalability of the entire reporting environment. One of the limitations with the previous architecture was that there was no caching or lazy loading of very large reports. This gave the perception of poor performance and sometimes resulted in memory errors.

■Note Although huge reports that need caching or lazy loading seem totally unreasonable for human consumption, they are sometimes necessary to meet business requirements. For example, large insurance companies may produce reports with thousands of pages on a regular basis in order to satisfy regulation requirements.

The main components of Reporting Services are as follows:

- *Report Server service*: A Windows service that exposes web services and Report Manager as web-based applications. It also is responsible for processing every client request, either to render a report or to perform a management task.

- *Report Manager*: A browser-based tool for viewing and rendering reports, creating report subscriptions, modifying report properties, configuring security, and a host of other tasks. Report Manager is no longer hosted within IIS; it is now part of the core Report Server service.

- *Report Server Web Services*: A web-based programmatic interface that allows any client to initiate a report processing or maintenance task.

- *Report Server Background Processing*: The component primarily responsible for the generation and delivery of scheduled reports. It also contains functionality that maintains the report server database.

- *Metadata catalog*: Stores all of the information related to reports, such as report definitions, data sources, report parameters, cached reports, security settings, scheduling and delivery information, and report execution log information.

- *Report Builder:* A graphical client accessed through Report Manager. This client is designed to facilitate simple, ad hoc reporting by end users and is not a full-featured report development environment.

- *Report Designer:* A graphical client, embedded within BIDS and also available as a stand-alone application, that allows you to design and deploy reports in a "drag-and-drop" environment.

Figure 19-1 provides a graphical representation of the Reporting Services components.

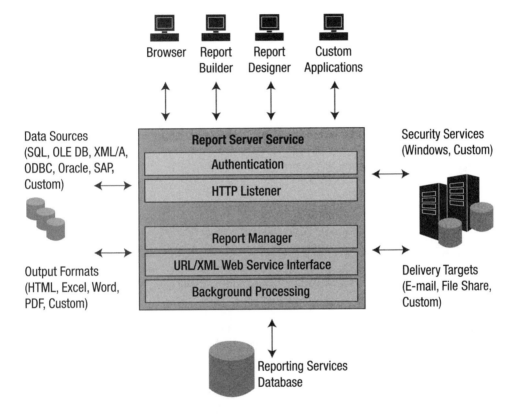

Figure 19-1. *Reporting Services components*

Report Server Service

Past releases of Reporting Services had a Windows service that provided functionality such as scheduling, maintenance, and report delivery. Reporting Services also had web applications that provided a management user interface (UI) and a web services-based API, hosted in IIS, separate from the Windows service. For many, this reliance on IIS was a concern, and the number of components within the architecture increased the risk of configuration mistakes.

With Reporting Services in SQL Server 2008, all services are combined into a single Windows service. This single Windows service hosts three application domains: Report Manager, Web Services, and Background Processes. This architecture ensures that there is no loss of functionality from previous versions. The following sections will provide details on some of the key pieces of the new service architecture.

All the other components interact with the Report Server service. For example, to deploy reports, Report Builder calls the methods exposed by web services. The Report Manager web application initiates management operations via the web service. Client or server applications could call the web service to automate Reporting Services functionality.

The Report Server service also supports URL addressability so that you can embed reports in your application using a web browser. By passing different parameters along with the URL, you can control different aspects of your reports. For example, the following URL retrieves a report called `employees`, whose RDL file is stored in the HR subfolder of the `reportserver` virtual root directory (which points to the web service) of a report server called SRS03, and instructs it to render the report (the `rs:Command` parameter) in PDF format (via the `rs:Format` parameter):

```
http://SRS03/reportserver?/hr/employees&rs:Command=Render&rs:Format=PDF
```

Native Support for HTTP.sys and ASP.NET

As mentioned earlier, IIS is no longer needed to host the ASP.NET applications of Reporting Services. Reporting Services now provides native support for ASP.NET and HTTP.sys, and therefore Report Manager and Web Services are hosted within the single Report Server service. To make this all work, the service includes an HTTP listener that listens for requests on a specific URL or URLs. The URL is registered, during installation time or through the Reporting Services Configuration Manager, with the HTTP.sys component of the underlying Windows operating system.

Improved Memory Control

It is now possible to configure memory utilization for the Report Server service. This is a very important new capability. In past releases, there was no way to limit Reporting Services so that it did not consume all available server memory. You can do this configuration by editing the underlying Reporting Services configuration file (unfortunately, the settings that control memory utilization cannot be set from within the Reporting Services Configuration Manager).

■**Note** When configuring Reporting Services memory settings, it is important to understand that the settings apply to the entire Report Server service, which consists of the Report Manager, Report Server Web Services, and Report Server Background Processing applications. Memory management cannot be configured for these components individually.

The Report Server service will act in one of four ways based on the memory configuration settings and the memory pressure on the service. There is no default memory pressure setting. Instead, the service is constantly monitoring memory utilization and adjusting between the various memory pressure modes as required. These four modes of operation are as follows:

- *No Pressure*: The Report Server service applications will be fairly liberal with the requests for memory. Each will request a set of memory before any requests are made, so that requests can be processed as quickly as possible.

- *Low*: Existing requests continue to process and new requests are accepted. The Background Processing application group is given lower priority than the Web Services application group.

- *Medium*: Existing requests continue to process and new requests are accepted if possible. Similar to low memory pressure, Background Processing is given the lowest priority. The Report Server service reduces the memory allocations from each of the three application groups (Report Manager, Web Services, and Background Processing), with Background Processing being reduced as much as possible.

- *High*: Existing requests are slowed down to reduce the chance of memory errors, and no new requests are accepted. Memory allocations continue to be reduced from the three internal application groups. Memory is paged to disk. When new requests are denied, users will receive an HTTP 503 error until existing requests complete and free up resources. In very extreme cases, the service may actually restart an application group to make memory immediately available.

So how do we control the transition of the service between the low, medium, and high behaviors? Although we can't control the actual behaviors, we can control the thresholds that the service uses to determine the level of memory pressure. Memory configuration settings are specified within the RSReportServer.config file, in the <Installation directory>\Reporting Services\ReportServer directory. The following are some sample memory configuration settings:

```
<MemorySafetyMargin>80</MemorySafetyMargin>
<MaximumThreshold>190</MemoryThreshold>
<WorkingSetMaximum>4000000</WorkingSetMaximum>
<WorkingSetMinimum>2400000</WorkingSetMinimum>
```

Table 19-1 describes the memory configuration elements in the configuration file.

Table 19-1. *Memory Configuration Elements*

Element	Description
WorkingSetMaximum	Specifies the maximum amount of memory that the Report Server service can consume. If this value is reached, new requests are denied until existing requests finish and release memory. If existing requests continue to request memory, then each of the three service application groups will be recycled. If WorkingSetMaximum is not configured, the service will set it to the amount of available memory on the computer when the service starts.
WorkingSetMinimum	Specifies the lower limit for service memory consumption. Memory will not be released if consumption is below this amount. The service does not "capture" or "reserve" this amount of memory when it starts. This is similar to SQL Server's Min and Max Memory configurations. However, if the service consumes more than this amount, the service will release only down to the WorkingSetMinimum, unless the application groups are restarted; in which case, all memory is released.
MaximumThreshold	Sets the percentage of WorkingSetMaximum that determines the boundary between medium and high memory pressure. Based on the sample configuration file, if the service consumed 190 percent of 4,000,000KB, it would go into high memory pressure mode.
MemorySafetyMargin	Sets the percentage of WorkingSetMaximum that determines the boundary between low and medium memory pressure. Based on the sample configuration file, if the service consumed 80 percent of 4,000,000KB, it would go into medium memory pressure mode. You might lower the MemorySafetyMargin value if your report server experienced extreme spikes in activity between extreme lulls in activity. This spike may not give the service enough time to adjust memory utilization and could result in memory errors. Setting MemorySafetyMargin to a lower value would give the service more time to make adjustments.

Authentication

Reporting Services is no longer hosted within IIS and therefore needs to implement authentication and authentication extensions natively. A Windows Authentication extension is provided by default. This extension supports Kerberos, NTLM, and Basic authentication types. There is also a custom authentication type, which makes it possible to develop and configure a custom authentication extension that can authenticate against virtually any environment.

HTTP Logging

Reporting Services now provides its own HTTP logging so that records of requests can be monitored and verified by external HTTP aggregation tools. The format of the HTTP log is the same as the log file format provided by IIS.

HTTP logging is not enabled by default. To enable it, you need to make changes to the `ReportServerService.exe.config` file, which, for a default installation, is located at `Program Files\ Microsoft SQL Server\MSSQL.n\Reporting Services\ReportServer\Bin`. The `http:4` setting must be added to the `Component` element within the `RStrace` section of the configuration file, as in this example:

```
<RStrace>
  <add name="FileName" value="ReportServerService_" />
  <add name="FileSizeLimitMb" value="32" />
  <add name="KeepFilesForDays" value="14" />
  <add name="Prefix" value="tid, time" />
  <add name="TraceListeners" value="debugwindow, file" />
  <add name="TraceFileMode" value="unique" />
  <add name="HTTPLogFileName"
    value="ReportServerService_HTTP_" />
  <add name="HttpTraceSwitches" value="date,time,
    activityid,sourceactivityid,clientip,
    username,serverip,serverport,host,
    method,uristem,uriquery,protocolstatus,
    bytessent,bytesreceived,timetaken,
    protocolversion,useragent,cookiereceived,
    cookiesent,referrer" />
  <add name="Components" value="all:3,http:4" />
</RStrace>
```

Table 19-2 lists the fields that can be contained within the log.

Table 19-2. *HTTP Log Fields*

Field	Description
HttpLogFileName	This value is optional. The default value is `ReportServerServiceHTTP_`. You can specify a different value if you want to use a different file-naming convention (for example, to include the server name if you are saving log files to a central location).
HttpTraceSwitches	This value is optional. If you specify it, you can configure the fields used in the log file in comma-delimited format.
Date	The date when the activity occurred.
Time	The time at which the activity occurred.
ActivityID	The activity identifier.
SourceActivityID	The activity identifier of the source.
ClientIp	The IP address of the client accessing the report server.
UserName	The name of the user who accessed the report server.
ServerPort	The port number used for the connection.
Host	The content of the host header.
Method	The action or SOAP method called from the client.

Field	Description
UriStem	The resource accessed.
UriQuery	The query used to access the resource.
ProtocolStatus	The HTTP status code.
BytesSent	The number of bytes sent by the server.
BytesReceived	The number of bytes received by the server.
TimeTaken	The time (in milliseconds) from the instant HTTP.sys returns request data until the server finishes the last send, excluding network transmission time.
ProtocolVersion	The protocol version used by the client.
UserAgent	The browser type used by the client.
CookieReceived	The content of the cookie received by the server.
CookieSent	The content of the cookie sent by the server.
Referrer	The previous site visited by the client.

Report Manager

The Report Manager web application allows you to browse, manage, and view your reports. Using the Report Manager interface, you can view the report hierarchy, select a single report to view, and then export that report to the multitude of formats that Reporting Services supports (such as HTML, Excel, TIFF, PDF, comma-delimited values, and XML). You can also manage your data sources, report parameters, execution properties, and subscriptions.

Three interesting pieces of functionality that Reporting Services provides and that you can manage through Report Manager are caching, report snapshots, and subscriptions. *Caching* allows you to increase the performance of your reporting solution. With caching enabled, a report can be added to the cache on its first execution and then retrieved from the cache, rather than the Reporting Services database, for subsequent requests.

A *report snapshot* is a point-in-time representation of both the layout of a report and its data. The rendering of a large report (one that contains a lot of data) can consume valuable resources, and you may not want to perform this action every time a different user requests the report. Instead, you can create a snapshot of the report and allow users to access that. You can also use report snapshots to keep a history of your report and see how it changes over time.

You can also create *subscriptions* to reports. Subscriptions provide a means of delivering reports to a specified location—an e-mail account, a fileshare, or a custom delivery location you code—at a specified time (for example, to the e-mail account of a department manager on the last Friday of every month). Reporting Services has two types of subscriptions:

- *Standard subscriptions*: These are statically set up for one or more users and can be created and managed by individual users.

- *Data-driven subscriptions*: These are system-generated subscriptions. Subscriber lists can be dynamically generated from multiple data source locations.

Data-driven subscriptions are great in scenarios where you have a very large list of subscribers who may want personalized data and report formats, and where the subscriber list may change over time. For example, you may want to deliver personalized reports for a thousand salespeople based on their own sales data. Some may want the report in HTML, and others may want a PDF. Rather than creating and managing a thousand individual subscriptions for these salespeople, you can create one data-driven subscription that queries a database for the list of salespeople, their e-mail addresses, and the format in which they wish to get the report.

As part of the subscription, you can select the delivery mechanism. Reporting Services supports delivering reports via e-mail or posting to fileshares. You can extend the delivery system in Reporting Services to deliver reports to other locations via a set of extensions called *delivery extensions.*

Metadata Catalog

Reporting Services requires that you have a SQL Server database to store metadata information. The metadata catalog, created as part of the Reporting Services installation, stores information such as data sources, report snapshots that contain the layout and data for a report at a specific point in time, and report history and credential information for authentication, if you have Reporting Services store that information.

This metadata catalog can be on the same server as your Reporting Services server, but most people deploy it on a separate server for performance reasons and for high availability using clustering.

Report Designer in BIDS

BIDS provides an integrated development environment (IDE) for SQL Server BI development. Using the graphical Report Designer in BIDs, you can connect to your data, write your queries, and design and deploy your reports, all in a drag-and-drop environment. Figure 19-2 shows Report Designer within the BIDS environment.

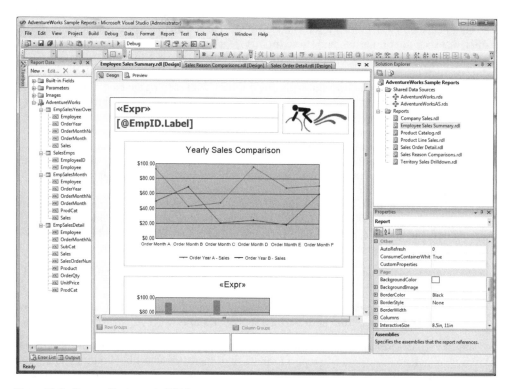

Figure 19-2. *Report Designer in BIDS*

Report Designer has a number of controls that you can use to add a UI to your form. Report Designer supports controls such as text boxes, tables, matrices, images, lines, charts, gauges, rectangles, subreports, and lists. Along with the standard Properties window, you'll find nicely redesigned Properties dialog boxes, which have been standardized throughout Report Designer, as shown in Figure 19-3.

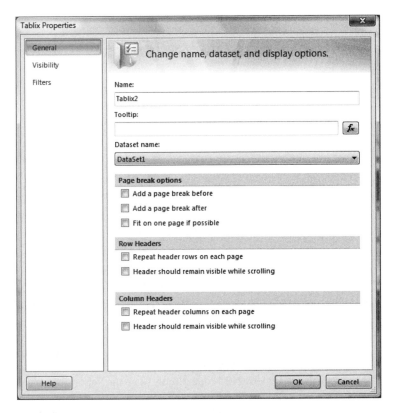

Figure 19-3. *New look for the Properties dialog boxes in Report Designer*

Report Designer allows you to extend any of your reports using expressions, or even to call code in a custom .NET assembly that you have associated with the report. Figure 19-4 shows a sample report included with Reporting Services. It demonstrates the use of an expression to dynamically set the title of a report. Expressions are based on Visual Basic .NET (VB .NET) and can be used in many different properties in Reporting Services.

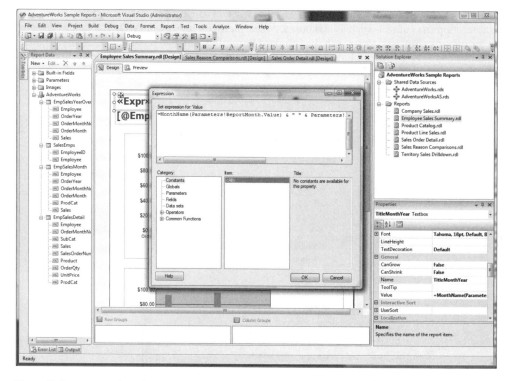

Figure 19-4. *A report that shows using controls and expressions in Report Designer in SQL Server 2008*

You can write script code using VB .NET and embed it directly in your report, or you can write a custom .NET assembly and call it from your report. Using embedded script code is the simpler of the two techniques, and you get the highest level of portability, since the custom .NET code is saved with the report definition file. To add your custom VB .NET code, simply open the Report Properties window of your report from within Report Designer and paste the code into the Custom Code section in the Code tab. Methods in embedded code are available through a globally defined Code member that you can access in any expression by referring to the Code member and method name (in other words, Code.*methodname*).

Use of a .NET assembly adds to the complexity of deployment, because assemblies are deployed as a separate file and must be on every server where the report runs. However, the payback is flexibility. The assemblies can be written in any .NET language and, once installed, are available to all reports that run on that server.

If you look at the source for your report, you will see that the report definition is an XML file. This XML file uses RDL (see SQL Server Books Online for the complete report schema definition). You could edit your report's XML by hand, but Report Designer is a much better interface to create your reports! Since RDL is a published format, third-party tools can create RDL, and Reporting Services will consume that RDL.

Report Designer Preview

In addition to Report Designer within BIDS, we have Report Builder, which is available via a ClickOnce installation from within Report Manager. You've seen how Report Designer provides a very rich set of functionality, and it is loved by application and database developers. Report Builder, on the other hand, provides fairly high-level functionality and uses a semantic data model, called the Report Model, to mask the complexities of report building from the user. This allows users the ability to build simple ad hoc reports when needed, as discussed in more detail in the "End-User Ad Hoc Query and Reporting" section later in this chapter.

Well, it turns out that some users are much smarter than we thought, and they are looking for something as powerful as Report Designer in BIDS to use within an environment that they are familiar with, such as Word, Excel, or PowerPoint. To address this need, the Microsoft Office team developed just such a tool, currently called Report Designer Preview.

■**Note** The tool is called Report Designer Preview in the February Community Technology Preview (CTP) release of SQL Server 2008. It is not clear what the final name will be, although simply Report Designer is likely. We also are not sure how the component will be distributed. I would be nice if this functionality were added as an add-in to Microsoft Office, similar to the Data Mining component for Excel. Regardless, there will be some tool for power users to develop very rich reports.

Figure 19-5 shows a fairly complex report being edited within the new Report Designer Preview application. You can see that Report Designer Preview provides a ribbon and bubble menu, which is consistent with the new Microsoft Office 2007 UI. Also notice the Data menu on the left, which provides access and allows the creation of built-in fields, parameters, images, data sources, and datasets.

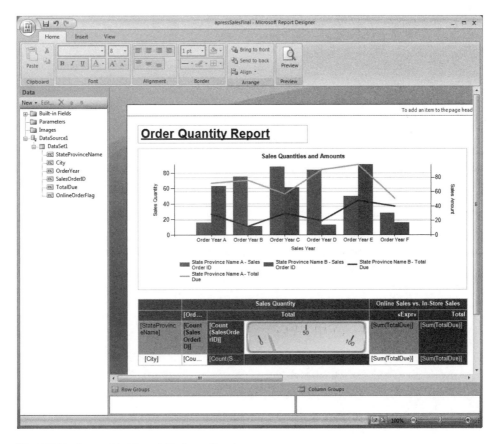

Figure 19-5. *A report in Report Designer Preview*

Along the bottom of the screen are the row and column grouping panes, which allow for manipulation of value groupings within the new Tablix data regions. There is also a Properties window (not shown in Figure 19-5), which is very similar to the BIDS Properties window.

SQL Server Management Studio Integration

In SQL Server 2008, a number of Reporting Services features have been removed from SQL Server Management Studio. Management Studio is no longer used to manage folder hierarchies, report content, or user permissions. Those tasks are left to the Report Manager application or SharePoint Server, if running in SharePoint integrated mode.

Management Studio is used to manage jobs, shared schedules, roles, and system roles. Figure 19-6 shows browsing report server jobs, security, and schedule objects from Management Studio.

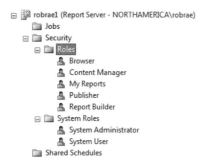

Figure 19-6. *Browsing Reporting Services objects from SQL Server Management Studio*

Reporting Services Configuration Manager

Because of all the architectural changes for Reporting Services, it was only natural that the Reporting Services Configuration Manager would need some upgrading. The new Configuration Manager includes panes for defining the Report Manager and Web Services URLs, and an upgraded wizard for creating Reporting Services databases. The Configuration Manager can be used to configure the settings of both remote and local servers.

The following are details for some of the main areas within the Configuration Manager:

- *Web Services URL*: This is the URL that is used by client applications for connecting to Report Server Web Services. This setting defaults to ReportServer, as shown in Figure 19-7, for a URL of http:\\servername\reportserver.

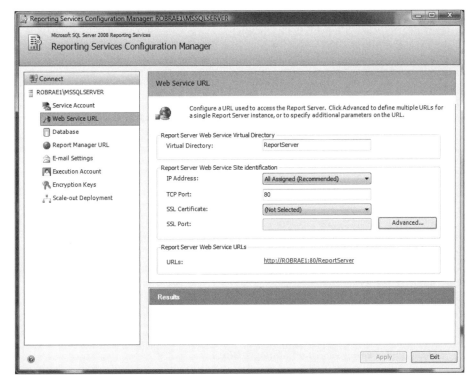

Figure 19-7. *Setting Report Server Web Services URL information*

- *Database*: The Database pane allows you to set the Reporting Services database and credentials. This pane also provides access to the Database Configuration Wizard, as shown in Figure 19-8, which allows for the creation or specification of a new Reporting Services database.

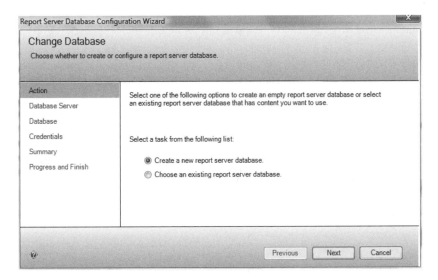

Figure 19-8. *Updated Database Configuration Wizard*

- *Report Manager URL*: This pane allows you to configure the URL to use when accessing the Report Manager application. By default, it is `Reports`, as shown in Figure 19-9, for a URL of `http\\servername\reports`.

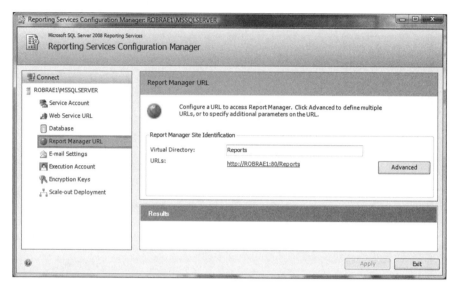

Figure 19-9. *Setting the Report Manager URL*

Reporting Services Security

The final piece of Reporting Services architecture that we will discuss is security. Reporting Services supports role-based security. The default roles in the server are as follows:

- *Browser*: Users assigned to the Browser role may only view reports, folders, and resources. They may also manage their own subscriptions.

- *Content Manager*: Administrators are assigned to the Content Manager role by default. This role allows a user to perform every task available for objects such as folders, reports, and data sources.

- *My Reports*: When the My Reports feature is enabled, this is the role that is automatically assigned to a user. It creates individual report folders specific to each Windows user, and allows those users to create and manage their own reports.

- *Publisher*: Typically, this role is used for report authors who work with Report Designer to create and deploy reports. It provides the privileges required to publish reports and data sources to the report server.

- *System User*: This role allows a user to view the schedule information in a shared schedule and view other basic information about the report server.

- *System Administrator*: This role can enable features and set defaults. You can set sitewide security and define role definitions. This role can also manage jobs on the server.

Building a Basic Report

Let's build a basic report that lists all employees from the AdventureWorks database, so that you can see Reporting Services in action. This is just a simple example to get you started. Later in this chapter, you'll learn how to use more advanced features and the new data regions available with Reporting Services in SQL Server 2008.

Launching the Designer

Your Reporting Services report design will begin in BIDS. After launching BIDS, you should create a new project. In the project type list, you should see Business Intelligence Projects, as shown in Figure 19-10. Select that project type, and then select Report Server Project as the template. Enter `BasicReport` as the name, and then click OK.

Note If you do not see Business Intelligence Projects listed as a new project type, you need to install Report Designer for Reporting Services, which you can do by running the SQL Server setup.

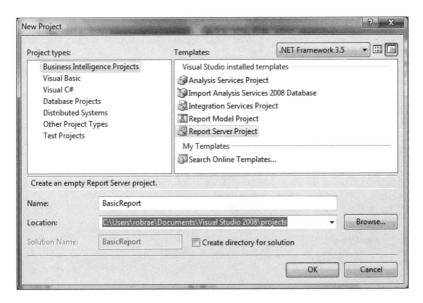

Figure 19-10. *Creating a new Report Server project*

Working with Data Sources and Datasets

Now that you have your project, you need to add a data source to your report. Without data, you will not have very much to report on! To do this, right-click the Shared Data Sources node in Solution Explorer and select Add New Data Source. For this example, in the dialog box that appears, type in your server name for your SQL Server and select the AdventureWorks database from the drop-down list. Click OK, and you now have a data source.

However, you can't stop here. The data source defines what data you want to connect to, but you really haven't defined the data on which you want to report. You need to create a dataset from your data source. To do this, add a new report to your project by right-clicking the Reports node in Solution Explorer and selecting Add ➤ Add New Item. In the dialog box, select Report and click Open. Report Designer should launch in the main window, and you should see a link in the middle of the design surface that you can click to create a data source and dataset. In the Data Source Properties dialog box, select Use Shared Data Source Reference, and then choose DataSource1 from the drop-down list.

Reporting Services drops you into the generic Query Designer by default, which is used for writing your queries. Paste the following SQL statement into the Query Designer window:

```
Select FirstName, LastName, EmailAddress From Person.Contact
```

■**Note** In the final version of SQL Server 2008, there will be a graphical query designer similar to the graphical designer in SQL Server 2005. This component of Reporting Services was not available in the CTP used for this book.

To test your query, click the Run button on the toolbar, represented by the exclamation point icon. The Query Designer window should look similar to Figure 19-11 at this point. As you build more and more reports, you will appreciate the Query Designer and the ability to execute your queries to see what data is returned. This report has a simple query, but you could write distributed queries across multiple data sources that will work with Reporting Services.

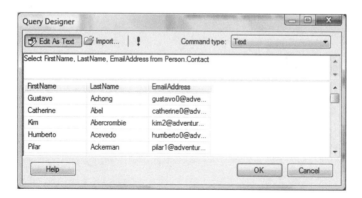

Figure 19-11. *Query Designer with sample results*

Laying Out and Previewing the Report

The next step is to lay out your report. Click the Design tab at the top, and a blank surface should appear. This is your report body. Creating the layout is a matter of dragging report controls, such as tables, lists, and matrices, onto the report body. These are available in the Toolbox window on the left, along with many other report controls. Drag and drop a Table control onto your report.

Next, select the Report Data tab on the left side of the IDE. Reporting Services creates fields for the data that is returned in your dataset. You can also create calculated fields, which do not exist in the dataset but instead are created by writing VB .NET expressions. For example, you could have created a FullName field that combines the first and last name together.

Drag and drop your fields onto your table. Drag FirstName into the detail cell in the first column. Drag LastName into the middle detail cell. Finally, drag EmailAddress into the last detail cell. Notice how headers are automatically created as you do this.

Now that you have your simple report laid out, preview it. To do this, click the Preview tab at the top of the designer. The report should look similar to Figure 19-12.

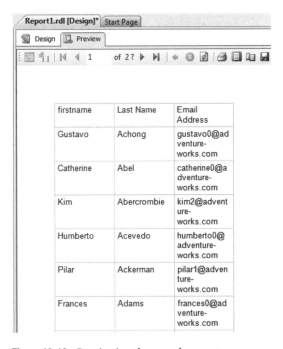

Figure 19-12. *Previewing the sample report*

Working with Expressions

The final touch for your report is to add a little splash of color using VB .NET expressions. You will alternate row colors so that the rows are easier to read, making even rows a different color than odd rows. Reporting Services supports expressions on many different properties in your reports. One such property is the background color for your detail row in your report.

The Expression Editor allows you to build expressions, using an expression language based on VB .NET. With the Expression Editor, you can easily write expressions and combine items such as constants, globals, operators, and common functions.

Go back to your design by clicking the Design tab. Select the entire detail row by clicking the leftmost icon for the row, which looks like three bars. Next, in the Properties window, find the BackgroundColor property, click its drop-down list, and select <Expression . . .>. In the Expression Editor, paste the following expression, as shown in Figure 19-13, and then click OK:

```
=iif(RowNumber(Nothing) Mod 2,"LightGreen","White")
```

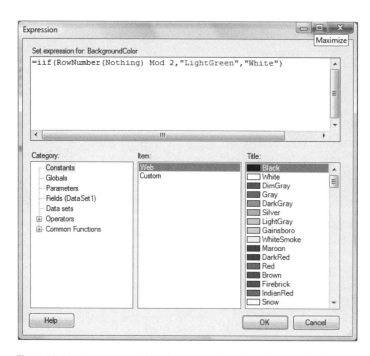

Figure 19-13. *Expression Editor being used to set background color*

This expression will check the row number in your report. RowNumber is a built-in function, and if it's an odd row number, the BackgroundColor will be LightGreen; otherwise, the color will be White.

Click the Preview tab at the top of the form to view the report. You should see a lovely green-bar report, reminiscent of the old green-bar printer days, similar to that shown in Figure 19-14.

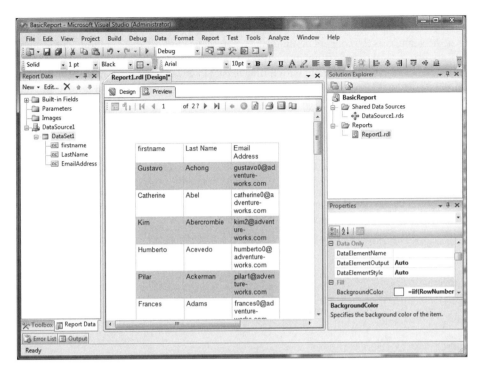

Figure 19-14. *Basic report with expression for row highlighting*

Deploying Your Report

You'll want to deploy your report to your server so that other users can use your report. To do this, you need to set some properties on your project to define where to place the report.

Right-click the BasicReport solution in Solution Explorer and select Properties. In the dialog box, enter the path to your server in the TargetServerURL text box. This path should be something like http://servername/reportserver/. Click OK.

To deploy your report, select Build ➤ Deploy BasicReport. You will see status information at the bottom of your screen on how the deployment is progressing. Once deployed, your report is ready to be used by all users who have permissions for viewing the report.

Report Design Advanced Features

As you've seen, it is fairly easy to create a basic report. But by no means should this lead you to believe that very complex reporting solutions can't be built with Reporting Services. It is possible to have multiple master detail reports, subreports, charts, gauges, and advanced formatting—all within a single report. Reporting Services also provides the ability to generate totals and aggregates on the fly when needed (although if you need this type of functionality on a larger scale, Analysis Services is probably the proper tool for the job). Here, we'll review some of the more advanced Reporting Services features. The Tablix, Gauge, and Chart data regions are discussed in the "Data Regions" section later in this chapter.

Multivalued Parameters

Reporting Services supports the concept of multivalued parameters for report generation. Multivalued parameters are very useful in reporting applications. Imagine the scenario where you want to be able to select sales based on the state in which they exist. However, you may have sales reps who cover multiple states, so they want to access their customers from multiple states at once. With multivalued parameters, you can provide this capability.

To create a multivalued parameter, you create your parameters as you normally would, except you also check the Allow Multiple Values check box in the Report Parameter Properties dialog box, as shown in Figure 19-15.

■**Note** Also notice the new Internal option in the Report Parameter Properties dialog box. This is to support parameters that cannot be changed at runtime. They do not appear anywhere in the report or in the URL, unlike hidden parameters. These parameters appear only in the report definition.

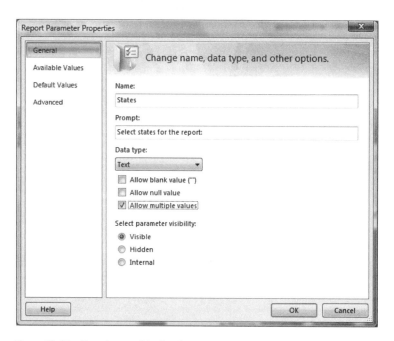

Figure 19-15. *Creating multivalued parameters*

Once you have specified that your parameter will be multivalued, the Reporting Services runtime takes care of displaying the parameters as check box options in the UI for users to select the different values, as shown in the example in Figure 19-16. There is even a Select All option that will select and deselect all parameter values.

Figure 19-16. *Runtime UI for multivalued parameters*

When a user selects a multivalued parameter, Reporting Services returns the selected values as a comma-delimited list. If you want to use that list in an expression, you will need to parse that list into its different values. You can also pass values for parameters within a URL to Reporting Services using a comma-delimited list.

Multivalued parameters have the following restrictions:

- They cannot accept null values.
- They are always returned as strings, so you need to make sure your stored procedures or logic can understand and parse the strings.
- You cannot use them in filters since they are not deterministic.
- You cannot use them with stored procedures.
- Your query must use an IN clause to specify the parameter, such as SELECT * FROM table WHERE name IN (@NameMVParam).

If you want to use multivalued parameters in expressions, you can use the Join and Split functions to join together or split apart the values for your multivalued parameter. With multivalued parameters, you can use the Label, Value, and Count functions to return the names of the parameter values. The Value function returns the values for the selected parameters that might be different from the label. Count returns the count of the values for the parameter. For example, the following expression returns the values for a multivalued parameter named Cities:

```
=Join(Parameters!Cities.Value, ", ")).
```

Finally, as with any parameters, make sure to not overdo the number of options you allow in your parameter. Limit it to the list that is required for the user to make the right selections; otherwise, performance will suffer.

DatePicker for Date Values

To make it easier for end users to select date values used in parameters, Reporting Services includes a DatePicker runtime control. But note that the parameter must use a datetime type. Also, it cannot be selected for a multivalued parameter. If you specify a multivalued parameter, you will get a drop-down list for your parameter value selection, not a DatePicker control. Figure 19-17 shows selecting a parameter that uses the DatePicker control.

Figure 19-17. *Runtime UI for date parameters*

Interactive Sorting

Interactive sorting is done through text box properties. This means that you do not select an entire column to view the interactive sort properties, but instead click the text box that is the column heading in a table. Interactive sorting works with tables, lists, and matrices, as well as grouped or nested data in those containers. In addition, you can sort different multiple columns using this technology. Figure 19-18 shows the Properties dialog box for interactive sorting.

Figure 19-18. *Setting interactive sort settings at design time*

You can specify the data region or grouping to sort, or where to evaluate the scope of the sort expression. This is useful if you want independent sorting based on grouping. For example, you could have a sales report grouped by country and then by city. By default, changing the sort order of countries does not affect the sort order of the cities in those countries. However, you could make re-sorting the countries affect the sorting of the cities as well.

The UI element for the sort is an up arrow or a down arrow, depending on the sort order. When you do the sort inside the UI, a request is actually sent back to the server to redo the sort. It is not a client-side sort only, so you must be careful about performance implications of users re-sorting on many columns in your report.

Analysis Services Integration

Reporting Services provides tight integration with Analysis Services via the BIDS environment. By having Reporting Services integrate with BIDS, you now have one place where you can create and manage your Analysis Services technologies, such as cubes, key performance indicators (KPIs), and data-mining settings. Finally, you can create and deploy your reports from BIDS. Figure 19-19 shows the interface for the Analysis Services in BIDS.

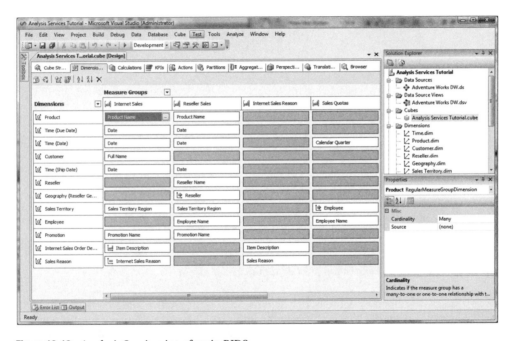

Figure 19-19. *Analysis Services interface in BIDS*

With Reporting Services, you can easily add your Analysis Services cubes to a report. Let's walk through the creation of a new report that uses Online Analytical Processing (OLAP) technologies in SQL Server to give you a better understanding of how the Analysis Services integration works. The walk-through assumes you already have an existing Analysis Services cube. For the purposes of the example, we'll use the AdventureWorks sample database and cubes.

First, create a new Business Intelligence project and select Report Server Project as the template. Once you select the report project and give it a name, you're dropped into Report Designer within BIDS. In Solution Explorer, right-click the Shared Data Sources node and select Add New Data Source. For the provider, you will use the .NET Framework Provider for Microsoft Analysis Services. Select Microsoft SQL Server Analysis Services as the data source, and enter the path to the AdventureWorks Analysis Services environment.

■**Tip** This exercise assumes that you have installed the AdventureWorks Analysis Services database from the SQL Server 2008 samples. For SQL Server 2008, the samples are not shipped as part of the installation. Instead, they are available as a download from `http://www.codeplex.com`.

If you double-click your data source after you create it, you will see that Analysis Services appears as a top-level data source, just like SQL Server, Oracle, OLE DB, and ODBC. The Properties dialog box for the data source is shown in Figure 19-20.

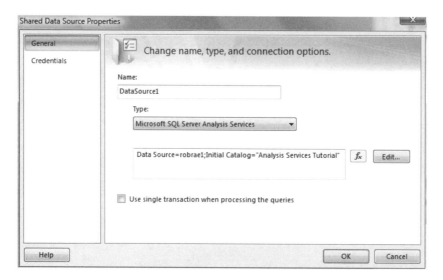

Figure 19-20. *Analysis Services as a top-level data source*

Next, add a new report by right-clicking Reports and selecting Add ➤ Add New Item ➤ Report, which creates a blank report. Type in your report name, such as `Report1.rdl`, and click Add. Once the report is created, you can add a new dataset to the report by clicking the link on the report surface. This new dataset will be based off your Analysis Services data source. After you select the shared data source you created earlier and click Next, you are dropped into the Analysis Services Query Designer, as shown in Figure 19-21. Instead of having to write Multidimensional Expressions (MDX) by hand, you can drag and drop measures in the Query Designer. The MDX is automatically generated for you based on your interaction with the Query Designer. If you are a power MDX user, you can still go into the generic Query Designer and write your own MDX.

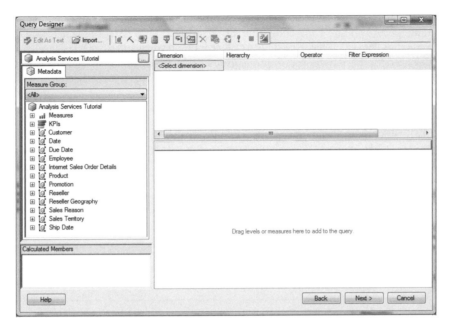

Figure 19-21. *The Analysis Services Query Designer in Reporting Services*

Since you want to create a quick sales report that shows reseller sales by geography and fiscal year, you need to drag and drop items from your measures, KPIs, or Analysis Services hierarchy over to the right side of the Query Designer window. The first level in the hierarchy that you'll add to the report is Geography. When you drag and drop, the Query Designer executes the query to return a preview of your result set, as shown in Figure 19-22, once you complete the steps that follow.

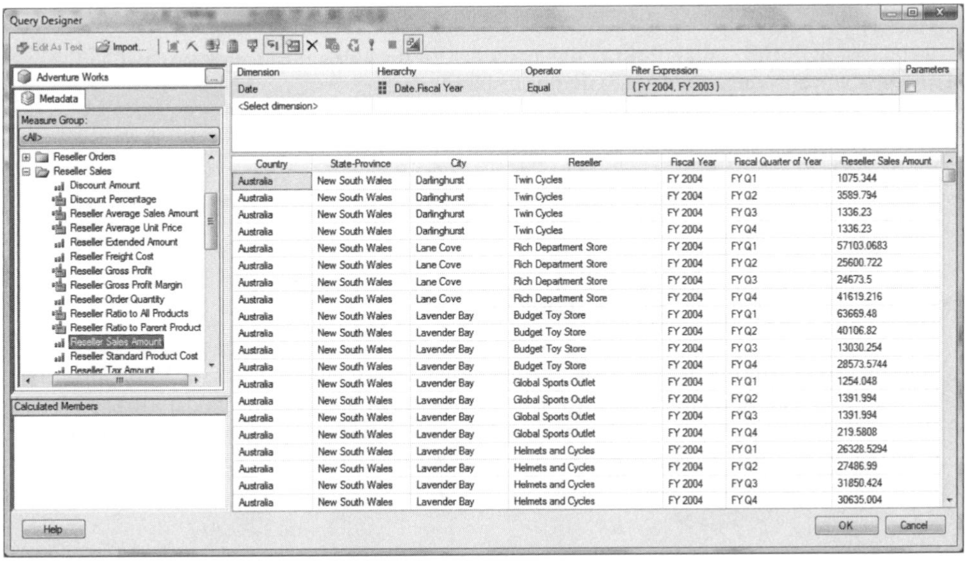

Figure 19-22. *Previewing the result set in the Query Designer*

First, drag and drop the dimension called Geography onto the grid on the right. You can find this dimension under the AdventureWorks cube. This will create the Country, State-Province, City, and Postal Code columns. You can remove the Postal Code column if you want, since it is a level of detail that we don't need for this report. Next drag and drop just the Reseller name from the Reseller dimension onto the grid. Then drag and drop the Date.Fiscal Year and Date.Fiscal Quarter of Year dimensions from the Date dimension under the Fiscal grouping.

Next, you need to drag and drop some measures. The first one is the Reseller Sales Amount measure. You can find this under the Measures hierarchy, then under Reseller Sales. Drag and drop the Reseller Sales Amount measure onto the grid. Then drag and drop the Reseller Order Quantity measure from the same hierarchy.

Right now, this returns all fiscal years. Let's refine the query a bit to return only two fiscal years. To make this change, you just need to select the dimension on which you wish to filter in the top filter dialog box, the hierarchy in that dimension that you want to use, the operator, and finally the value. Here, select the Date dimension, the Date.Fiscal Year hierarchy, and check to see whether the Fiscal Year is equal to FY 2004 or FY 2005, as shown in Figure 19-23.

Note Optionally, you can make the filter expression a parameter to the report by clicking the check box called Parameters (this option may be off the screen to the right in some cases).

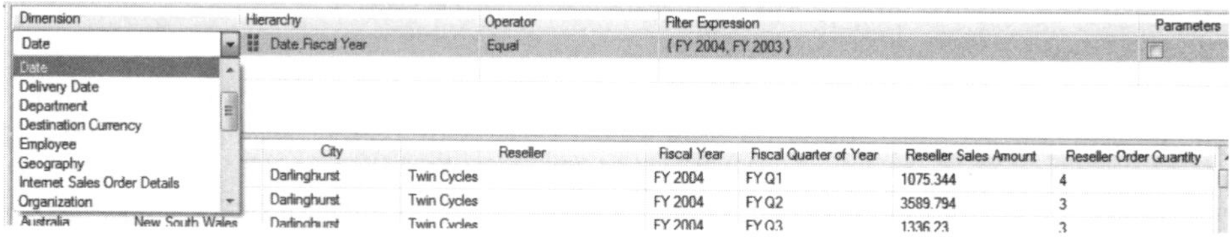

Figure 19-23. *Creating filters in the Query Designer*

If you look at the MDX that the designer generates for the entire query, as shown in Figure 19-24, you can see that you would not want to do this by hand!

```
SELECT NON EMPTY { [Measures].[Reseller Sales Amount], [Measures].[Reseller Order Quantity] } ON COLUMNS, NON EMPTY { (
[Geography].[Geography].[City].ALLMEMBERS * [Reseller].[Reseller].ALLMEMBERS * [Date].[Fiscal Year].[Fiscal
Year].ALLMEMBERS * [Date].[Fiscal Quarter of Year].[Fiscal Quarter of Year].ALLMEMBERS ) } DIMENSION PROPERTIES
MEMBER_CAPTION, MEMBER_UNIQUE_NAME ON ROWS FROM ( SELECT ( { [Date].[Fiscal Year].&[2004], [Date].[Fiscal Year].&[2003]
} ) ON COLUMNS FROM [Adventure Works]) CELL PROPERTIES VALUE, BACK_COLOR, FORE_COLOR, FORMATTED_VALUE, FORMAT_STRING,
FONT_NAME, FONT_SIZE, FONT_FLAGS
```

Figure 19-24. *MDX generated by the Query Designer*

Now that you have your dataset, switch to the design view of Report Designer by clicking the Design tab. You will notice that the fields from your cube are available in the field list to the left of the design surface. You can drag and drop your fields onto controls that you add to your report. You'll use the Table and Chart controls to display your data.

Drag a Table control from the Toolbox onto the design surface. You can use this control to add your information to the report. (You could also use the Matrix control if you want to have expanding columns as well as expanding rows.) In the table, you'll just drop some fields from the Dataset tab into the details: Country, State_Province, City, Reseller, Fiscal_Year, Fiscal_Quarter_of_Year, and Reseller_Sales_Amount. Right-click the Reseller_Sales_Amount column and select the text box properties. Within the Number section of the Text Box Properties dialog box, set the Category value to Currency. Also select the Use 1000 Separator (,) check box and choose to Show Zero as - . By default, Reporting Services will render two decimal places in a currency value. Figure 19-25 shows the form design with just the table added.

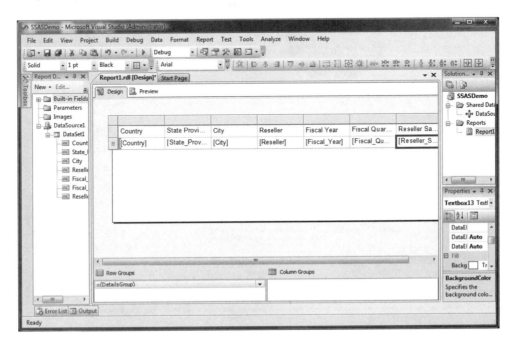

Figure 19-25. *A table layout with OLAP information*

Next, you may want to chart the information to see how each reseller is doing. The charting technology has been significantly updated in SQL Server 2008 and will be covered in detail in the "Updated Chart Data Region" section later in this chapter. Adding OLAP fields to a chart is another drag-and-drop operation. Drag and drop a Chart control from the Toolbox onto your report. Select 3D-Pie as the chart type. From the Report Data tab, drag and drop the Fiscal_Year field onto the category field drop target on the chart. Drag and drop the Reseller_Sales_Amount field onto the data field drop target on your chart. Figure 19-26 shows a simple chart that will show yearly sales.

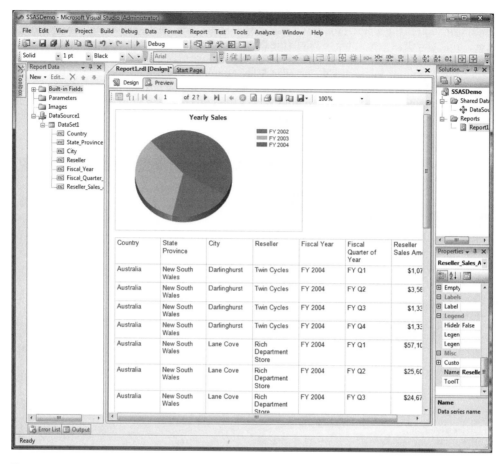

Figure 19-26. *A chart with OLAP information*

You can then preview or deploy your new report using the built-in previewing or deployment support of BIDS.

In this walk-through, you've seen how you can leverage your OLAP information as easily as your relational information in SQL Server 2008 Reporting Services.

Reporting Services Data Sources

Reporting Services provides, out of the box, connectivity to a vast array of data sources, such as XML/web services, Hyperion, SAP, Oracle, ODBC drivers, and OLE DB drivers. The SQL Server Integration Services (SSIS) data source connects to and runs an SSIS package and returns the results so you can report on them. There is also the option to derive the values used within a data source using expressions. We'll cover some of the more interesting data sources here.

Data Source Expressions

To use a data source expression, you should create your data source as you normally would using a static connection string. Expression-based connection strings work only with nonshared data sources.

Lay out the report the way you want, and then add a parameter that will specify your data source. You can make this parameter use static values or pull from a data source to get its values. Once you have set the parameter, you can go back to your data source definition and replace the static value with a parameter. An example of a connection string using a data source expression is shown here:

```
="data source=" & Parameters!Datasource.Value & ";initial catalog=AdventureWorks"
```

Figure 19-27 shows setting a data source using an expression.

■**Note** Remember that you must use a report-specific data source and not a shared data source in order for expression-based data sources to work.

Figure 19-27. *A data source that uses an expression*

XML/Web Services Data Source

The XML/web services data source (called XML in the data source drop-down list) allows you to connect to an XML document, a web service, or a web application that returns XML data. You simply specify the endpoint URL to which you wish to connect. For example, if you wanted to connect to a web service, you would input the URL to the ASMX or WSDL file for the web service.

Reporting Services supports connecting to web services like SQL web services using the new native web services technology in SQL Server, as well as the Google, Amazon, and eBay web services. You can also use web services that you've created using Visual Studio or other IDEs,

You can also connect to just pure XML data sources. This means that if you have a web application that you can address via URL and that returns an XML document, you can use that application to retrieve information to your report.

> **■Note** The XML data source does not work with `file://` URLs. You must use `http://` URLs.

SAP Data Source

The SAP data source lets you report directly from an SAP data source so that you can provide rich reporting for SAP applications, without needing to extract the data into another intermediary data source.

SQL Server provides an SAP ADO.NET provider in the Enterprise Edition. You can download the provider from `http://msdn.microsoft.com/downloads`. Once you have downloaded the provider, you can start executing queries against your SAP system from any environment that uses ADO.NET, including Reporting Services. There are two query commands you can send to this data source. The first executes RFCs/BAPI, which is the API for SAP. The second executes SQL queries against SAP tables. Refer to SQL Server Books Online for details on using the SAP data source.

Custom Report Items

Custom report items are primarily targeted at partners who want to extend Reporting Services with custom controls that are processed when the report is processed, and then output an image onto the report. These controls allow the enterprise developer to build custom controls in any .NET language and deploy them.

> **■Note** Do not confuse custom report items with the ability to drop custom controls, like .NET controls, onto a report.

For example, if you wanted to add a new chart type that Reporting Services does not support, such as one that shows advanced financial or statistical analysis, you can write a custom report item (sometimes called a custom ReportViewer control) that integrates with the design-time and runtime Reporting Services experience. With the image you produce on the report, you can create an image map so that you can provide interactivity with your control. Most likely, you will not create custom report items, but you will probably consume them in your reports from third-party providers.

Visual Studio Integration and ReportViewer Controls

One of the big questions that customers and partners always ask is how they can embed reports in their applications. Reporting Services includes both a WebForm and a WinForm rendering control that can be embedded inside custom web or Windows applications. The controls take an RDL source and some data, and perform the processing on the local machine, rather than having to go back to the report server to process the information. The controls support background processing and will start streaming the report onto the screen as the report is processed.

When users want to view reports offline using a report snapshot, or a developer needs report rendering but can't guarantee that the customer has Reporting Services, the controls are very useful. However, when the workload of the application gets too large for the controls to handle, moving the controls from local processing to using a report server is very easy.

The controls support both local execution and server-side execution against a Reporting Services server. At times, you may want to switch between the different execution modes. For example, your application may need to work both online and offline. When online, you may want to leverage the Reporting Services infrastructure, but when you're offline, you may want to render from a snapshot, since you may not have a connection to the report server.

The main differences between using these controls and customizing Reporting Services using URLs are as follows:

- The controls do not support exporting to all Reporting Services formats when working with client-side reports. Only HTML and Excel are supported through client-side reports. With server-side reports, all formats are supported.

- The controls do not prompt for parameters in local execution mode—you must pass parameters programmatically to the controls.

- The controls do not support the advanced features of Reporting Services such as caching and subscriptions.

Using WinForm Controls

If you've seen the preview pane in Report Designer, the WinForm control will look familiar. It's pretty much the same control, but has the ability to run outside of the Report Designer environment. Plus, the control has an object model that you can program against. We're going to cover the WinForm control here. The WinForm and WebForm controls have very similar object models.

Adding the control to your application is a drag-and-drop operation. In Visual Studio, just drag and drop the ReportViewer control, which you can find in the Data group in the Toolbox for your WinForm application. Figure 19-28 shows the WinForm control in an application.

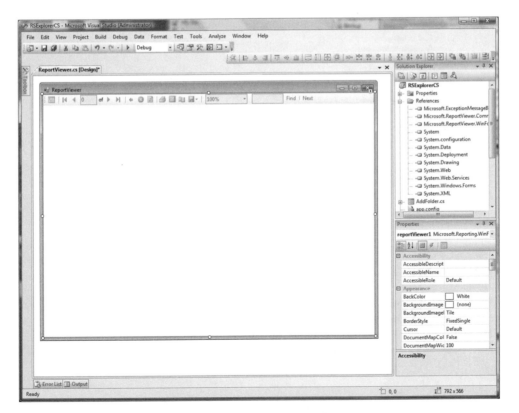

Figure 19-28. *A WinForm application with the WinForm ReportViewer control*

Once you have the control on the page, you need to set some properties, either through the IDE or programmatically. Using the smart tags in Visual Studio, you can select your report location. The controls allow for either creating a new report or rendering from an existing server report.

If you select an existing report on the report server, you need to pass the URL and report path to the control in order for the rendering to work. If you select a new report, you will be creating a client-side report, denoted by an .rdlc extension to specify client side, which will use a different data source mechanism than what server reports use. If you want to move this report to the report server, you will need to perform some work to do this, since the data source and query mechanisms differ. The main benefits of using the local data source vs. the server is that you can pass arbitrary ADO.NET data tables to the ReportViewer controls and they do not require a report server to work, which means that the ReportViewer controls can work offline.

When using local, client-side processing, the control takes ADO.NET data tables or objects that implement the IEnumerable interface as data sources to the report. The easiest way to get the data for your report is to use the Data Source dialog boxes and wizards in Visual Studio. Using the wizards, you can select your data source and the actual data that you want returned to your report. Figure 19-29 shows using the Data Source Configuration Wizard.

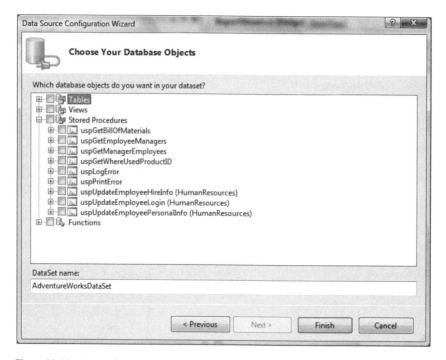

Figure 19-29. *Using the Data Source Configuraion Wizard*

As part of Visual Studio, you get Report Designer, discussed earlier in this chapter, so that you can design reports for the controls. After you create your data source, you can use Report Designer to drag and drop your fields onto your report. You will notice that the extension for your local report is .rdlc, not .rdl. This is how it is differentiated from the server-side RDL code.

Once you have created your data source, designed your report, and dragged and dropped the ReportViewer control onto your application, you are set to go. To try out your application, just run the application as you normally would from Visual Studio. You may notice that in the load event for your form, Reporting Services adds some code to load your data and render your report. We will explore how to programmatically perform the same steps in the next section. Figure 19-30 shows running a simple form with a ReportViewer control and a report displayed.

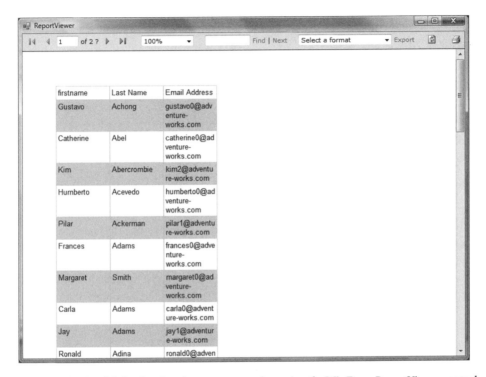

Figure 19-30. *Combining local and remote processing using the WinForm ReportViewer control*

Working with the ReportViewer Control Programmatically

Rather than doing everything through the IDE, you may want to programmatically pass your data and render the report from code inside your application. The ReportViewer controls support a rich API to allow you to do this.

If you want to perform the same steps we just did in the IDE, first pass your data through the Datasources collection of the control. Next, pass the RDL for the report that you want to render. This can come as an embedded resource from the project itself by just passing the fully qualified project and then report name, with underscores replacing spaces, or it can be read from the file system. Then you can set some of the properties on the control, such as whether to display the toolbar, document map, context menu, or parameters. Finally, you need to render the report. One thing to note is if you already have a data source in the report, make sure to name your data source programmatically with the same name as your existing data source. Otherwise, you will receive errors from the control.

Table 19-3 outlines the most common properties you will use with the ReportViewer control.

Table 19-3. *Properties of the WinForm ReportViewer Control*

Name	Type	Description
CurrentPage	Int32	Gets or sets the current page displayed in the report
LocalReport	LocalReport	Returns a LocalReport object from which you can load report definitions, set data sources, perform actions such as document map navigation, and render reports
ShowDocumentMap	Boolean	Gets or sets whether the document map is visible
ShowParameterPrompts	Boolean	Gets or sets whether the parameters area is visible
ShowCredentialPrompts	Boolean	Gets or sets whether the credentials area is visible
ShowToolbar	Boolean	Gets or sets whether the toolbar is visible
ShowContextMenu	Boolean	Gets or sets whether the context menu is visible
ShowDocumentMapButton	Boolean	Gets or sets whether the Document Map button is visible
ShowExportButton	Boolean	Gets or sets whether the Export button is visible to export to other formats
ShowPageNavigationControls	Boolean	Gets or sets whether the page navigation controls are visible
ShowPrintButton	Boolean	Gets or sets whether the Print button is visible
ShowProgress	Boolean	Gets or sets whether the progress animation is visible when rendering
ShowRefreshButton	Boolean	Gets or sets whether the Refresh button is visible
ShowZoomButton	Boolean	Gets or sets whether the Zoom button is visible
ServerReport	ServerReport	Returns a ServerReport object, which allows you to perform similar tasks as the LocalReport object, except in the context of a server report (for example, you cannot add new data sources with the ServerReport, but you can retrieve the list of data sources)
ZoomMode	Enum	Gets or sets the zoom factor such as FullPage, PageWidth, or ZoomPercent
ZoomPercent	Int32	Gets or sets the zoom percentage

Table 19-4 shows the methods available for the WinForm ReportViewer control.

Table 19-4. *Methods for the WinForm ReportViewer Control*

Name	Description
Back	Goes back if the report is a drill-through report
Clear	Clears the report
Find	Searches the report for the given text
FindNext	Continues the search for the given text from the current search point
GetPrintDocument	Returns a print document for printing the report
PrintDialog	Brings up the Print dialog box and then prints the report
Refresh	Refreshes the report, which reprocesses the report with any new data
Render	Processes and renders the report
RenderStream	Returns a stream associated with the report
SaveSnapshot	Saves a snapshot
Stop	Stops background processing of the report

The ReportViewer controls also support events, so your application can listen for events such as page navigation, printing, drill-through, searching, zooming, and other activities in the control.

LocalReport and ServerReport Objects

Beyond learning the ReportViewer controls' methods and properties, you should also look at both the LocalReport and ServerReport objects. Here, we discuss the common LocalReport methods and properties. You retrieve this object from the ReportViewer control using the LocalReport property. The ServerReport object is simpler in its design and has less functionality because you are using the control just as a rendering engine and not passing data sources to it.

Tables 19-5 and 19-6 show the most common properties and methods for the LocalReport object.

Table 19-5. *Properties for the LocalReport Object*

Name	Type	Description
Datasources	ReportDatasourceCollection	Returns the Datasource collection so you can get and set data sources for your report.
ReportEmbeddedResource	String	Name of the embedded report within the application. This must be a fully qualified name with the project and report name. Replace all spaces with underscores.
ReportPath	String	Fully qualified path to the report definition in the file system.

Table 19-6. *Methods for the LocalReport Object*

Name	Description
GetDocumentMap	Returns a DocumentMapNode object so you can traverse your document map in your report.
GetParameters	Returns a ReportParameterInfoCollection so that you can then get information about parameters in your report. Use this in conjunction with SetParameters.
GetTotalPages	Gets the total number of pages in the report.
ListRenderingExtensions	Lists the rendering extensions that are available.
LoadReportDefinition	Loads the specified RDL file, which you pass either as a TextReader or a Stream object.
LoadSubReportDefinition	Loads the specified RDL file for subreports, which you pass either as a TextReader or a Stream object.
PerformBookmarkNavigation	Navigates to the specified bookmark that you pass the ID and name for.
PerformDocumentMapNavigation	Navigates to the document map node that you specify the ID for.
PerformDrillThrough	Performs a drill-through to another report, which you specify in the call to this method. You can also listen for drill-through events in the control and perform the correct actions to drill to another report.
Render	Renders the report and returns either a byte array or a stream, which is the end result. You need to pass in the format, device information, MIME type, and encoding.
SetParameters	Allows you to pass an array of ReportParameter objects, which will set the parameters for your report. ReportParameter objects are effectively just a named key/value pair.

In this overview, you've seen how you can get started with the ReportViewer controls in your own applications and leverage the power of Reporting Services, even without the report server.

SharePoint Integration

Reporting Services is integrated with SharePoint. Most of the details of that integration matter more to SharePoint users than to Reporting Services users. The main thing to note, however, is that the Reporting Services web parts for SharePoint—the Report Explorer and Report Viewer—are implemented as IFrames that wrap Report Manager. A more interesting implementation may be using the ReportViewer controls in SharePoint web parts to display report information. However, if you are just looking for the ability to drag and drop web parts from your SharePoint web part gallery onto your page, set some properties, and have reports appear, the web parts that ship with Reporting Services should easily meet your needs.

Reporting Services includes support for the following deployment modes relevant to SharePoint integration:

- *Native mode:* This is the default mode for Reporting Services and enables the Reporting Services Report Manager for tasks such as administration, scheduling, report viewing, and security configuration.

- *SharePoint integrated mode:* The advantage of this mode is the ability to leverage all the rich SharePoint application pages and data stores. For example, in SharePoint integrated mode, it is possible to leverage SharePoint's document versioning against your RDL files. It also becomes possible to manage, list, and view Reporting Services reports alongside other content within the SharePoint portal, and even drive the content of other web parts based on a selected report. In this mode, the Report Manager application is not available.

- *Native mode with SharePoint web parts:* Report Explorer and Report Viewer continue to provide access to Reporting Services from within SharePoint when not running in integrated mode.

SharePoint integration has come a long way in the last couple of releases of Reporting Services. It is pretty clear that this trend will continue, with Reporting Services integration into SharePoint getting the lion's share of the SQL Server product team's focus over the Reporting Services Report Manager.

End-User Ad Hoc Query and Reporting

While BIDS is a great place for a developer or database administrator (DBA) to create reports, and the stand-alone Report Builder is a great place for the power user, most end users will not understand those environments. This is why the Report Builder client exists. From a technology standpoint, Report Builder uses Reporting Services on the back end to create and show the reports. What is actually produced by Report Builder is RDL that is executed on the server. For this reason, Report Builder works only when a user is online.

Report Builder uses a metadata model, called the Report Model, which sits between the end users and the data they access. So, the different pieces of the Report Builder architecture are the Report Builder client, the Report Model and its designer, and the server side of Reporting Services.

The Report Builder Client

The Report Builder client is a report designer that creates RDL on the fly, and this RDL gets passed to the server. Since most end users do not understand relational databases or sometimes even OLAP structures, the semantic data model takes the complexity of the database and puts it in terms that the end user understands, such as entities, relationships, and aggregates. This means that the full power of the relational database and your OLAP systems is used, while reducing the complexity of getting the data needed for the report. Plus, end users do not have to depend on information technology folks or developers to build reports for them; they can self-service their needs through the Report Builder client.

The Report Builder client is a Windows Form application built using .NET. You may be wondering how you could deploy this application to all your different end users, since it is Windows-based. Well, the Report Builder client actually leverages some deployment technology in .NET called ClickOnce. ClickOnce provides Windows-based interactivity and applications, with the deployment model of web applications. When end users click the Report Builder button in Report Manager, ClickOnce checks their machine to make sure that the system has the .NET 2.0 Framework (or higher) and also that the latest version of the Report Builder client that is published on the server. If the system does not have these components, they are downloaded and installed, making for a very easy deployment experience. You could also deploy the client via standard mechanisms, though, such as Systems Management Server (SMS), and when the end user clicks, if the versions match, nothing will be downloaded.

Note You can have different versions of the client on the same machine. For example, you may have Service Pack 1 of Report Builder on one server and just the RTM version on another. Since Report Builder data sources are server-dependent and the client bits are installed from the server, one end-user machine may have both versions of the client. This is OK and no cause for alarm. When the other server is updated to Service Pack 1 and the end user clicks the Report Builder button, the new version will be downloaded.

Realize that the Report Builder client is not Report Designer. It does not have all the power and flexibility that Report Designer has. There is a good reason for this, since that power and flexibility is a liability for an end-user tool that is supposed to be simple and easy to use. Therefore, you may be frustrated by the perceived lack of flexibility in the tool, but end users will find it easier to create reports because it is structured and works only in a certain way. However, you can open a report created with the Report Builder client in Report Designer. In that case, you will be working against the semantic data model and not the data source underneath. Any reports that you modify in Report Designer may not be able to go back to Report Builder due to the differences in functionality. It is usually a one-way street between the two.

The Report Model and Semantic Model Definition Language

A Report Model is built using the Semantic Model Definition Language (SMDL), which is an XML-based grammar that describes your data sources in human-readable terms. Think of it as a universal translator for your data sources from geek to end user. Building a Report Model uses the other pieces of SQL Server that both SQL Server Integration and Analysis Services use, which are data sources and data source views.

Data sources are straightforward. The only caveat is that currently Report Models support only SQL Server and Oracle as data sources. The reason for this is that the queries in SMDL must be translated to data-specific queries for the underlying source. However, the query translator that is built into Reporting Services is pluggable, so that in future versions, Microsoft could add more data sources. Also, only one data source—in fact, if you are working with databases, only one database— is supported per model. So, you cannot query relational and OLAP data sources together; you can query only OLAP or relational databases in a single model.

Data source views (DSVs) allow you to separate physical schema from virtual schema. Think of it this way: you may have underlying schema in your relational database that you cannot modify, but in order to make the schema better for end users, you need to add schema or modify schema. With DSVs, you can perform these actions in the metadata for the DSV rather than in the underlying data source. You can create calculated columns, virtual tables, and other schema changes in DSVs without modifying the original data source.

SMDL is made up of entities, folders, attributes, expressions, perspectives, and roles. Entities correspond to a table or query view in the underlying data source. For example, you may have a product entity that maps to the product table in your database. Folders are just containment vehicles for entities. If you want to group entities together, put them in a folder. Attributes correspond to columns or named calculations on an entity. For example, the price attribute on the product entity could just be the price column in the products table, or it could be a calculated aggregate that exists only in the DSV.

Expressions are what they sound like: calculated fields in your model. You can create expressions that create aggregates, do string manipulation, perform conversions, and perform other functions. You control the creation of expressions while the Report Model creates attributes for you automatically.

Perspectives provide the ability to break a large model into smaller models. You can create perspectives that contain a subset of an existing model. End users can then see the perspectives they have permissions on from the client. You can think of perspectives like relational database views. With views, you can hide your underlying tables and display information only to users who have permissions on the view.

Roles define relationships among your data. For example, an employee has an address or a customer has orders. You can define roles to have a one-to-one, one-to-many, or many-to-many relationship. Customers do not have one order but have many orders. The way roles are surfaced in the client is through the navigation.

■**Note** SMDL roles should not be confused with role-level security in Reporting Services. Report Builder does support role-level security so that you can lock down parts of the model based on user roles. This is useful to secure sensitive and confidential data such as salaries, Social Security numbers, and so on.

The reason for having the Report Model, beyond the simplicity it presents to the end user while still providing a powerful model for the DBA and developer, is the ability to provide rich relationships and infinite drill-through. Say you enable infinite drill-through on your data model, and you own the Enterprise Edition of SQL Server (since infinite drill-through is only supported there). When a report is rendered, if there is a path through the model, users can click attributes that send queries, which in turn generate drill-through reports. End users do not need to create each individual report themselves, and DBAs do not need to manually link together reports, since they can just mark relationships in the model.

Report Rendering

Reporting Services has always done a fairly good job of rendering reports and maintaining formatting between different export formats. With Reporting Services in SQL Server 2008, exporting to Microsoft Excel has been significantly enhanced, and there is a new capability to export to Microsoft Word. Very significant changes have also been made to the underlying paging architecture of the report server.

Exporting Reports

Reporting Services now supports the ability to export reports to Microsoft Word format. Similar to Microsoft Excel, Microsoft Word will render reports with soft page breaks, which will ensure the report layout and format are maintained. Figures 19-31 and 19-32 show a sales report rendered in Microsoft Excel format and Microsoft Word format, respectively.

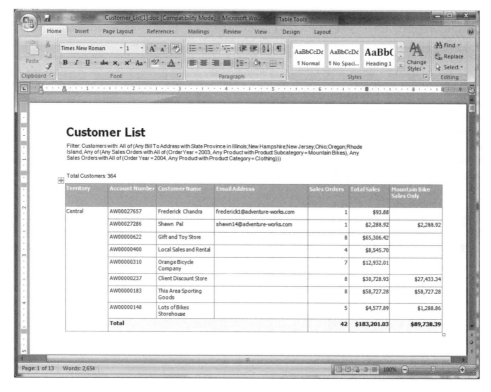

Figure 19-31. *Report rendered in Microsoft Excel*

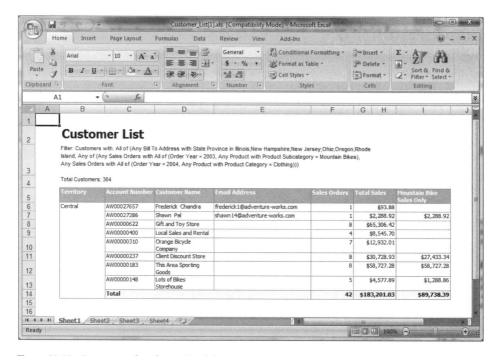

Figure 19-32. *Report rendered as a Word document*

One thing to keep in mind is that Excel will maintain column and row drill-downs, whereas Word will not. Look for + signs beside row and columns labels in Excel to determine if there is some hidden detail data within your Excel report.

Rendering Large Reports

Rendering very large reports within a reporting client introduces some very interesting memory challenges. This was a particular area of frustration in previous versions of Reporting Services, as users sat waiting for their 100-page report to generate. With Reporting Services in SQL Server 2008, this problem is eliminated because of the underlying caching mechanism within the Report Server service.

When viewing a very large report, only the first couple pages of the report are rendered and returned to the client. Behind the scenes, remaining pages are loaded only as they are requested. In Figure 19-33, notice that the page is shown as *3 of 4?*. This is because we have not moved past the third page of the report, and the fifth and later pages have not been loaded; therefore, an accurate page count cannot be generated.

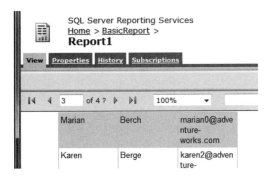

Figure 19-33. *New paging capabilities for large reports*

Data Regions

Data regions are one of the key components of Reporting Services and allow for entire datasets to be displayed, summarized, grouped, sorted, filtered, and so on. This is unlike the functionality of a single text box, line, or image, which can be used to show only a single value. For those familiar with other reporting platforms such as Crystal Reports, the data region can be thought of as the body portion of the report. The differences are that it is very easy to add multiple data regions to a report and the data regions can be placed in any configuration required to achieve the desired output.

Reporting Services in SQL Server 2008 introduces the Tablix data region, which combines the matrix and table, and the Gauge data region. Furthermore, the Chart data region has been significantly upgraded, with 3D rendering capabilities and many more chart types.

Tablix Data Region

Awesome is the word that comes to mind when we think about the new functionality introduced by the Tablix data region. Its main features are as follows:

- *Combination of multiple tables and matrices within a single region*: In the past, we were able to easily build tables of data that allow for dynamically expanding rows based on the underlying data of the report. We were also able to build matrices that allow for dynamically expanding rows and columns based on the underlying data. However, we have never been able to easily combine multiple matrices or tables within a single data region. The Tablix control provides this capability. This means that two matrices that have the same row grouping but different column grouping and totaling could be combined together side by side. An example is a sales matrix by region being combined with a sales matrix by time. The data regions within each matrix can also be different. One data region could display sales dollars, and the other could display sales quantities.

▪Note In fact, through some ingenious UI trickery, all lists, tables, and matrices are actually templates on top of the Tablix control.

- *Multiple levels of grouping on both columns and rows*: The Tablix data region also provides the ability to create stepped columns. For example, instead of having separate columns for country, state, and city data, you can have a single column, with each value indented a specified distance from its parent. The Tablix data region maintains the ability to group and subtotal on each individual value, even though the values are combined into a single column.

The Tablix region offers very powerful functionality that will eliminate the need to develop custom solutions for building very complicated reports. To demonstrate, the following examples provide a walk-through of creating some Tablix-based reports.

Hierarchical Rows and Dynamic Headers

In this example, we'll build a report that displays yearly sales totals by state and city. The report will provide stepped rows and the combination of total values within a group header row. We will also use advanced formatting to provide a drill-down effect. The finished report, DataRegions – Step1 – Hierarchical Rows and Dynamic Headers.rdl, can be downloaded from the Source/Downloads area of the Apress web site (http://ww.apress.com).

Setting Up the Data Source and Dataset

Follow these steps to set up for the report:

1. Open the new Report Designer Preview application from within the Reporting Services section of the Microsoft SQL Server 2008 program group.

2. Add a data source by selecting the "Click here to create a data source and data set for your report" link. The Data Source Properties dialog box appears.

3. Leave the default type set to Microsoft SQL Server and click the Edit button. The Connection Properties dialog box appears. Set the server name to the name of your server and set the database name to AdventureWorks. Click the Next button.

4. In the Query Designer window, enter the following SQL statement:

```
select pprov.Name as StateProvinceName, paddr.City,
datepart(yy, sheader.OrderDate) as OrderYear,
sheader.SalesOrderID, sheader.TotalDue
from Sales.SalesOrderHeader as sheader
  inner join Person.[Address] as paddr
```

```
   on sheader.BillToAddressID = paddr.AddressID
 inner join Person.StateProvince as pprov
   on paddr.StateProvinceID = pprov.StateProvinceID
where pprov.StateProvinceCode = 'AL' or pprov.StateProvinceCode = 'AZ'
order by pprov.Name, paddr.City
```

5. Test the query by clicking the Run Query in the Query Designer window. The results should look something like those in Figure 19-34.

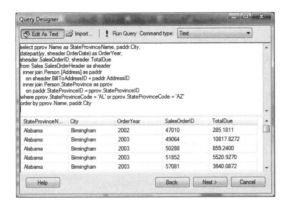

Figure 19-34. *Query Designer with reults preview*

6. Click Next. A new data source and dataset are created within the report.

7. Add a Matrix data region to the design surface of the report. You can add this region by selecting the Insert menu and double-clicking the Matrix icon, by right-clicking anywhere within the design surface of the report and selecting Insert ➤ Matrix, or by dragging the Matrix control from the Toolbox if you're using Report Designer within BIDS. At this point, you have an empty Matrix region, along with a data source and a dataset, as shown in Figure 19-35.

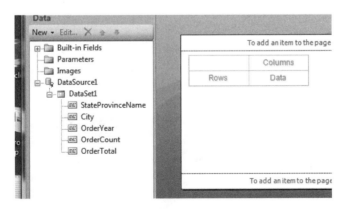

Figure 19-35. *Report Designer with the data source, dataset, and empty matrix*

Adding Values

We are now in a position to start building our report. We'll start out by adding row, column, data, and total values.

1. Add StateProvinceName to the Rows section of the matrix.

2. Add the City value to the right of StateProvinceName within the Rows section of the matrix. This creates a hierarchical group that will show all the cities within each state.

3. Drag and drop SalesOrderID to the Data region. Notice that the expression [Sum(SalesOrderID)] is automatically entered within the cell text box. We'll change this later.

4. Add OrderYear to the Columns area of the matrix.

5. Right-click the [City] cell (second row, second column) and select Add Total ➤ Before. This will create a total row for each StateProvinceName.

6. Right-click the [OrderYear] header (first row, third column) and select Add Total ➤ After. This will create a new column within the report that will provide the total for [OrderYear] within each row.

At this point, the report should look similar to Figure 19-36 when previewed.

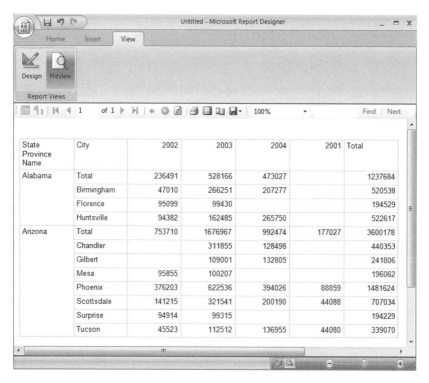

Figure 19-36. *Preview of report*

Clearly, there are some problems:

- The columns are not ordered properly.
- We are calculating the sum of OrderID when we really want the count of OrderID.
- The state and city need to be combined into one column, with the city slightly indented from the state value.
- Our total line does not need the Total heading.
- We cannot easily distinguish between headers, totals, or data values.
- Our report doesn't have a title.

So, let's go ahead and take care of these issues.

Adding a Report Title

First things first—let's add a text box that will contain the title for this report.

1. In design mode, reposition the Matrix data region so that you can add a new text box above it.
2. Right-click the design surface and select Insert ➤ Textbox.
3. Reposition and resize the text box to align with the Matrix data region. Notice the new guidelines feature within the designer, which helps you align report items. The guidelines are shown in Figure 19-37.

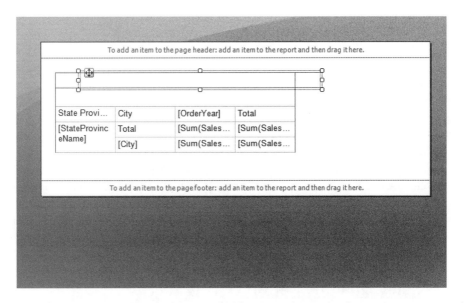

Figure 19-37. *The new alignment feature enables easier placement of report items.*

4. Enter **Sales Quantity Report** in the text box.
5. Set the font size to 20, make it bold, and underline the text.

Updating the Formulas

Now we'll update the sales formulas to use the Count function instead of the Sum function.

1. Right-click the City data cell (third row, third column) of the matrix and select Expression.

2. We want to count the number of sales orders within each city not summarize the value of the SalesOrderID values. To do this, we modify the expression to use the Count function instead of the Sum function. Take this opportunity to review the various operators and common functions available within the Expression Editor. The final expression should be =Count(Fields!SalesOrderID.Value).

3. We now need to update all the total fields with the new expression. Simply copy and paste the new expression over the old expression within the total fields. You should be working with cells 3 and 4 within the second row, and cell 4 within the third row of the data region. Your report should look similar to Figure 19-38.

Sales Quantity Report

State Provi...	City	[OrderYear]	Total
[StateProvinceName]	Total	[Count(Sale...	[Count(Sale...
	[City]	[Count(Sale...	[Count(Sale...

Figure 19-38. *Report with title and updated expressions for data and totals*

Creating Stepped Row Headings

We will now create the stepped row headings by combining the Province and City values into the same column.

1. The cell within the second row and second column has the heading Total in it. This cell is directly above the [City] data field and directly below the City column title. Select the StateProvinceName Total heading (row 2, column 2), click the field picker that appears in the upper-right corner of the field, and select StateProvinceName.

2. Right-click the first column and select Delete Columns.

3. Right-click the City row heading (row 3, column 1) and select Textbox Properties. On the Alignment tab, set the Left property under Padding Options to .125in and click OK. This causes the City values to be indented 0.125 inch when displayed underneath the State value.

4. Delete that text for the City heading (row 1, column 1). The report should look similar to Figure 19-39 when in design mode. Also take this opportunity to preview the report to see how things look.

Sales Quantity Report

	[OrderYear]	Total
[StateProvi...	[Count(Sale...	[Count(Sale...
[City]	[Count(Sale...	[Count(Sale...

Figure 19-39. *Report with stepped column headings for StateProvince and City*

Sorting the Rows

Let's take care of the row-sorting issue. We need the values for year to be sorted from oldest to newest (2001–2004).

1. In design mode, select the Tablix data region.

2. Right-click the [OrderYear] group within the Column Groups section at the bottom of the designer and choose Edit Group.

3. Select the Sorting section within the dialog box.

4. Click the Add button and choose OrderYear within the Sort By drop-down. Leave the Order as A to Z. Click OK.

■**Note** All of the dialog boxes within Report Designer have been updated and are consistent across all areas of the report. This makes for a very consistent and productive UI.

Formatting Numeric Values

We need to format the numeric values so that they don't display decimals or zero values.

1. Right-click the cell that represents the StateProvinceName total for each OrderYear (second row, second column) and select Textbox Properties.

2. Within the Number section, choose Number for the Category value.

3. Set the Decimal places to 0. Check Use 1000 Separate (,). Set the Show Zero As option to -.

Repeat these steps for each of the other three cells that contain the formula [Count(SalesOrderID)].

Creating a Drill-Down Effect

Creating a drill-down effect within your report is pretty easy, assuming that you have used useful names for the text boxes to be used in the grouping. We want our report to open with the individual city values for each state hidden. The user would then select a + icon next to the state to see the city detail.

1. Update the Name property for the StateProvinceName text box (second row, first column) to StateProvinceName.

2. Within the Row Groups area at the bottom of the design surface, select the City group, right-click, and select Edit Group.

3. In the dialog box, select the Visibility section and set "When the report is initially run" to Hide. Select the check box for "Display can be toggled by this report item" and select the StateProvinceName text box from the list.

4. Preview the report. You should see the result of your changes, as shown in Figure 19-40.

Sales Quantity Report

	2001	2002	2003	2004	Total
⊞ Alabama	-	5	10	7	22
⊞ Arizona	4	16	32	15	67

Figure 19-40. *Drill-down enabled for State/City details*

Final Touches

Finally, we can make some formatting changes to highlight the various totals and sections of our Tablix data region.

1. In design mode, set the background color for the first row to Blue-Gray, bold the text, and set the text color to White.

2. Bold the text of the StateProvinceName row heading (second row, first column).

3. Set the background color for the StateProvinceName row (second row) to Ocean.

4. Set the background color for the Total column (third column) to Blue-Gray, bold the text, and set the text color to White.

The final report should look similar to Figure 19-41, which shows the City details for Alabama displayed.

Sales Quantity Report

	2001	2002	2003	2004	Total
⊟ Alabama	-	5	10	7	22
Birmingham	-	1	5	3	9
Florence	-	2	2	-	4
Huntsville	-	2	3	4	9
⊞ Arizona	4	16	32	15	67

Figure 19-41. *Final report showing city details for Alabama*

Parallel Dynamic Groups

The new Tablix data region allows for the combination of two matrices within the same data region. Previously, this was next to impossible without some tricky coding. Now it is as simple as adding some parallel groups and adjusting subtotals. Note that both the dynamic column value and the data value can be different between the two side-by-side matrices.

To demonstrate this feature, we'll continue with our previous example by adding a column group to indicate online sales, and for each column, we'll provide the dollar value of the sales by state and city. A completed version of this report, DataRegions- Step2 - Parallel Dynamic Groups.rdl, can be downloaded from the Apress web site.

1. Open the report that you created in the previous example (alternatively, open the report named DataRegions - Step1 - Hierarchical Rows and Dynamic Headers.rdl that you downloaded). It may be a good idea to save the report with a new name before making the changes for this example. That way, you can always start over if things get messy.

2. We need to add a new value to our dataset. Open the properties for DataSet1 and open the Query Designer. Modify the query so that it returns the OnlineOrderFlag value from the Sales.SalesOrderHeader table, as follows and as shown in Figure 19-42.

```
select pprov.Name as StateProvinceName, paddr.City,
datepart(yy, sheader.OrderDate) as OrderYear,
sheader.SalesOrderID, sheader.TotalDue, sheader.OnlineOrderFlag
from Sales.SalesOrderHeader as sheader
  inner join Person.[Address] as paddr
    on sheader.BillToAddressID = paddr.AddressID
  inner join Person.StateProvince as pprov
```

```
       on paddr.StateProvinceID = pprov.StateProvinceID
where pprov.StateProvinceCode = 'AL' or pprov.StateProvinceCode = 'AZ'
order by pprov.Name, paddr.City
```

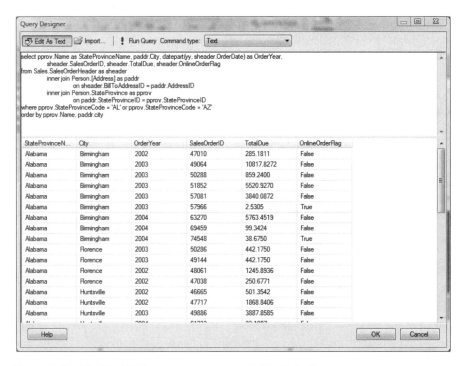

Figure 19-42. *Modified SQL statement to return OnlineOrderFlag*

3. Right-click the Total column (first row, third column) and select Add Column Group ➤ Adjacent Right. Select the OnlineOrderFlag as the Group Expression.

4. Add the TotalDue data value to the detail row (third row, fourth column) for this group. In this case, the default expression (Sum) is the correct function to use.

5. Copy the expression from the detail row and paste it into the cell directly above (second row, fourth column) for the StateProvinceName row group.

6. Add a total for the new column group by right-clicking the OnlineOrderFlag header (first row, fourth column) and selecting Add Total ➤ After. Preview your report.

7. In order to get some familiarity with a more detailed expression, let's convert the True/False that displays for OnlineOrderFlag to Online or In-Store, based on the value. In design mode, right-click the OnlineOrderFlag header (first row, fourth column) and select Expression.

8. We will modify the expression to use the Immediate If (IIf) function to do the conversion between the values True/False and Online/In-Store. The final function looks like this:

```
=IIf(Fields!OnlineOrderFlag.Value, "Online", "In-Store")
```

9. To provide some clarity, let's add some static headings within the Tablix region. Right-click the first row and select Insert Row ➤ Outside Group - Above. The Tablix region allows for cells to be merged. In the new row (first row), select cells two and three, right-click, and select Merge Cells. Do the same for the last two cells. Enter **Sales Quantity** as the first heading and **Online Sales vs. In-Store Sales** as the second heading. Columns may need to be resized at this point to fit the heading text.

10. Before previewing, let's change the formatting of the TotalDue cells to currency. For each of the cells that uses the expression [Sum(TotalDue)], change the Number section of the text box properties to have a category of Currency, to use the 1000 separator, and to show zero as -.

11. Update the formatting of the new columns to match that of the Sales Quantity section with regard to coloring, and then preview the report.

Your report should look similar to that shown in Figure 19-43.

Sales Quantity Report

	Sales Quantity					Online Sales vs. In-Store Sales		
	2001	2002	2003	2004	Total	In-Store	Online	Total
⊞ Alabama	-	5	10	7	22	$60,286.88	$41.21	$60,328.08
⊞ Arizona	4	16	32	15	67	$1,938,291.19	$2,324.94	$1,940,616.13

Figure 19-43. *Sales report showing sales quantities and online sales volume*

Gauge Data Region

With the KPI quickly becoming a staple of almost every business intelligence project, it only makes sense that Reporting Services would start to provide more support in this area. The introduction of the Gauge data region is a step in this direction. It provides a one-dimensional view into a single key value. The Gauge region is very useful for displaying KPIs within your reports, but gauges can also be grouped together in tables, matrixes, and panels to provide functionality over and above reporting on a single KPI.

▪**Note** The Gauge data region is made available as an acquisition of technology from Dundas Chart. Microsoft has licensed both the Chart and Gauge controls from Dundas and made them available within Reporting Services in SQL Server 2008. Let's hope that this continues and that Microsoft makes Dundas Map available as well.

As an example, let's walk through adding a gauge to an existing report. The finished report for this exercise is provided as DataRegions - Step3 - Gauge Data Region.rdl.

1. Use Report Designer to open the sales report that we created in the previous exercise (alternatively, open the report named DataRegions - Step2 - Parallel Dynamic Groups.rdl that you downloaded).

2. It is possible to insert a gauge within a cell in a Matrix data region. In this example, we'll add a gauge to the Sales Quantity Total column to visually indicate which state has the greatest sales. Resize the StateProvinceName row (second row) group to about four times its current height.

3. Right-click the Sales Quantity Total column (second row, third column) and select Insert Column ➤ Right. This adds a new column within the Total section of the report. Merge the Sales Quantity heading (row 1, column 2) with the new column. Merge the Total heading for Sales Quantity (row 2, column 3) with the new column.

4. From the Insert menu, or Toolbox if you're using BIDS, select Gauge. The Select Gauge Type dialog box appears, as shown in Figure 19-44. Select the Radial Meter gauge type and click OK. Cut and paste the Gauge data region from the design surface into the new StateProvinceName Total cell (row 3, column 4). At this point, you should be comfortable enough with Report Designer to be able to resize the cells to get a professional-looking gauge.

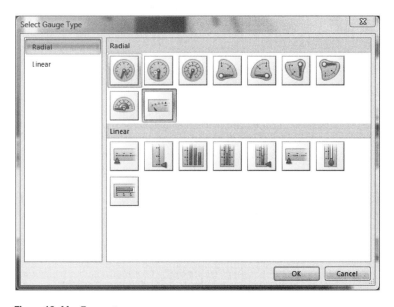

Figure 19-44. *Gauge types*

5. Once inserted into the proper cell, drag and drop the SalesOrderID data value onto the RadialPointer1 data value, which will become visible when you drag the SalesOrderID over the gauge. Note that the expression will default to [Sum(SalesOrderID)]. You will need to view the pointer properties and edit the formula to use the Count function instead of the Sum function.

Preview the report. As shown in Figure 19-45, the report will show the gauge side by side with the sales totals for each state.

Order Quantity Report

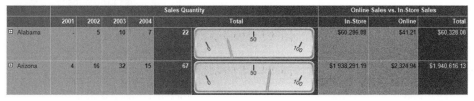

	2001	2002	2003	2004	Total	In-Store	Online	Total
⊞ Alabama		5	10	7	22	$60,286.88	$41.21	$60,328.08
⊞ Arizona	4	16	32	15	67	$1,938,291.19	$2,324.94	$1,940,616.13

Figure 19-45. *Sales order report with an embedded meter Gauge data region*

Updated Chart Data Region

The Chart data region has existed for some time, but in many ways, the charting capabilities in Reporting Services in SQL Server 2008 provide so much richness and flexibility that they could almost be thought of as a new component. It is now possible to create charts with multiple data regions, scale breaks, and detailed labeling. Furthermore, Reporting Services has a number of new chart types, such as shape, stock, polar, and range. These dramatically enhance your ability to provide proper visualizations in BI applications. Table 19-7 provides brief descriptions of the various chart types.

Table 19-7. *Reporting Services Chart Types*

Chart Type	Description
Area	Similar to a line chart, in that it displays a series of points connected by a line. The difference is that the area chart fills the space below the line with a specified color. Area chart types are stacked, percent stacked, and smooth.
Bar	Displays data in horizontal bars. The bar chart is able to present its data horizontally, which, for many datasets, provides a more natural visualization. Bar chart types are stacked, percent stacked, 3D clustered, and 3D cylinder.
Column	Similar to the bar chart, but presents data vertically instead of horizontally. Column chart types are stacked, percent stacked, 3D clustered, 3D cylinder, histogram, and pareto.
Line	Displays points connected by a line on a horizontal axis. Line chart types include smooth and stepped.
Pie	Displays separate regions of a circle or pie that, combined, make up a whole. Pie chart types include exploded pie, doughnut, exploded doughnut, 3D pie, and 3D exploded pie.
Polar	Provides a 360-degree view of data; commonly referred to as radar chart. Polar charts are commonly used when comparing multiple sets of data to identify deficiencies in things like functionality, operations, and sales.
Range	Similar to the area chart type, in that it displays a series of points connected by a line. However, unlike the area chart, which simply fills the area below the line, the range chart allows for a lower limit (range) to be identified. In this way, the thickness of the line indicates the size of the range.
Scatter	Plots individual values as points on a graph. It can be useful for visualizing aggregated data and identifying sales trends or support call volume spikes. Scatter chart types are bubble and 3D bubble.
Shape	Displays values from highest to lowest in the shape of a pyramid or funnel. Commonly, the funnel chart is used to express opportunities within a sales pipeline. Where there are typically many opportunities or leads in the early phases of the sales process, as leads are qualified and progress through the sales process, the number of opportunities typically becomes smaller. (In fact, if this were not the case, and there were more opportunities almost complete and less lead opportunities, the chart would indicate that marketing activities were needed to generate more leads.)
Stock	Typical stock chart that we have all become used to over the past years. It is designed for financial data and can provide indicators for four values per data point. This is useful for showing things like a sale range, current bid, lowest bid, and highest bid.

The best way to become familiar with the new charting capabilities is to walk through an example of creating a chart. This exercise will provide less detail, based on the assumption that you are now somewhat familiar with Report Designer. A completed version of this report, DataRegions - Step4 - Chart Data Region.rdl, can be downloaded from the Apress web site.

1. Open the report that you have been building for the data regions examples (alternatively, open the report named DataRegions - Step3 - Gauge Data Region.rdl that you downloaded).

2. Move the Matrix data region down the report a good distance to make room for a chart between it and the title. Insert a new column chart between the report title and the Tablix data region. Resize the chart to be the same width as the matrix by using the guidelines.

3. Drag the OrderYear to the Category Fields section of the chart designer. Then edit its sort properties so that it sorts in ascending order. To do this, right-click the field, select Category Group Policies, select the Sorting section of the Category Group Properties dialog box, and then add a new sort on OrderYear.

4. Add the StateProvinceName field to the Series section of the chart designer.

5. Add the SalesOrderID field to the Data Fields section of the chart designer. Modify the expression for this field to use the Count function instead of the Sum function. A preview of the report should look similar to Figure 19-46.

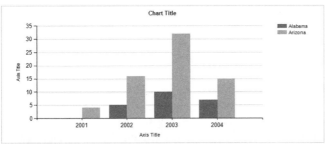

Figure 19-46. *Sales report with a Chart data region*

6. Now we want to add order amounts within the same Chart data region. In design mode, add the TotalDue field to the Data Fields section of the chart.

7. Right-click the new data field and select Change Chart Type to display the Select Chart Type dialog box. Change the chart type to Line.

8. Right-click the TotalDue series and open the Series Properties dialog box. In the Axes and Chart Area section, set the value axis to Secondary. This will enable the sales quantity value to display on the left axis and the sales amount values to display on the right axis. Preview the report and check that it looks similar to Figure 19-47.

Order Quantity Report

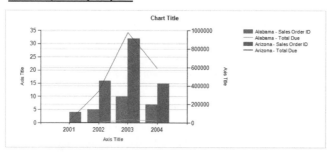

Figure 19-47. *Chart with two data series with primary and secondary axes*

9. Because sales in Alabama are substantially lower than those in Arizona, it is very hard to see the SalesAmount line series for Alabama. Enabling scale breaks for the secondary axis will take care of this problem. In design mode, right-click the secondary axis series (the right axis) and select Axis Properties. In the Axis Options section of the Secondary Value Axis Properties dialog box, select Enable Scale Breaks.

10. Now we just need to add some finishing touches. Set the Chart Title to **Sales Quantities and Amounts**.

11. Right-click the legend and set its position to bottom-middle. Figure 19-48 shows the various legend position choices.

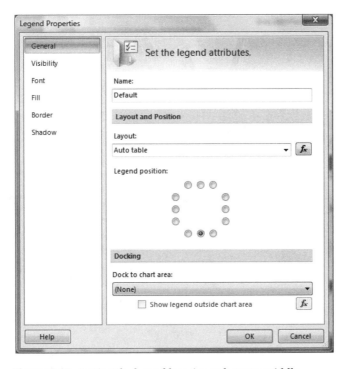

Figure 19-48. *Setting the legend location to bottom-middle*

12. Set the left-axis title to **Sales Quantity**.

13. Set the right-axis title to **Sales Amount**.

14. Open the properties for the TotalDue series. In the Border section, set the line width to 2pt.

15. Set the horizontal axis title to **Sales Year**.

And now we're finished. Preview the final report, which includes Chart, Gauge, and Tablix data regions. Figure 19-49 shows the final report.

Order Quantity Report

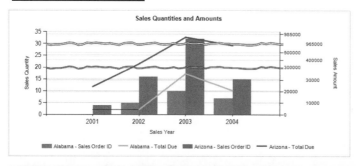

Figure 19-49. *Final report containing Chart, Gauge, and Tablix data regions*

Summary

As you have seen, Reporting Services in SQL Server 2008 is well worth the price of admission. We believe that the enhancements that Microsoft has made with this release will only increase the, already spectacular, adoption of the entire Microsoft BI platform. In the future, expect continued integration with SharePoint, new rendering formats, the ability to design reports within any Microsoft Office application, and the introduction of Reporting Services as a service in the cloud. We don't think that it will be a challenge for you to put Reporting Services to good use in any of your BI projects.

CHAPTER 20

■ ■ ■

Analysis Services

Databases store data, but they are truly effective as a business tool when used to support business decisions. These decisions may be strategic (should a firm expand into new territories?), tactical (what pricing strategy is best?), or operational (which customer do I call on and what discount should be offered?). However, all of these decisions require the right data, at the right time, in the right format. We call the process of preparing, delivering, and interpreting this data *business intelligence (BI)*.

SQL Server 2008 includes a suite of technologies that support the development and administration of BI applications. SQL Server Reporting Services and Integration Services are elements of BI, but the cornerstone is SQL Server 2008 Analysis Services (SSAS). Analysis Services includes technologies for Online Analytical Processing (OLAP) and data mining. OLAP and data mining are really subjects in their own right, with data mining being the most specialized. Therefore, in this chapter, we will review OLAP, the more commonly used technology.

Any Analysis Services endeavor can be broken down into tasks associated with application administration and with application development. For administration, SQL Server 2008 ships with SQL Server Management Studio. This tool supports application administration, including viewing data and creating Multidimensional Expressions (MDX), Data Mining Extensions (DMX), and XML for Analysis (XML/A). For development, Business Intelligence Development Studio (BIDS) supports application development by enabling you to define the core components of an Analysis Services project (data sources, data views, dimensions, value, cubes, and so on). With this tool, you can also view data within the analyzed environment from a variety of perspectives.

When installing SQL Server 2008, the option is available to install or not install Analysis Services. You can also choose whether the Windows service associated with Analysis Services should start by default. In order for Analysis Services to function, this Windows service must be running. It is not necessary to run the Analysis Services Windows service on a developer's machine. Ultimately, Analysis Services would run on a production host. Developers could connect to a server on which Analysis Services is installed and running. For ease of development, it is simplest to install and run Analysis Services locally on the development machine, and publish Analysis Services projects to staging or production hosts after they have been developed and debugged.

In this chapter, we will cover the following topics:

- New features in Analysis Services in SQL Server 2008
- Analysis Services fundamentals
- OLAP concepts
- Analysis Server projects in BIDS
- Analysis Services Scripting Language

New Analysis Services Features in SQL Server 2008

Users of Analysis Services in SQL Server 2005 will be anxious to know what is new in the latest release. For these users, we'll quickly review some new features, before examining the Analysis Services architecture and helping new users get started with this exciting technology. For novice users, this section may be rather redundant, since all features are new to you, by definition. Nevertheless, it will be useful to see that Analysis Services is far from a static technology, but rather one in which Microsoft is constantly developing and innovating new ideas.

The improvements in Analysis Services in SQL Server 2008 fall into three categories: improvements to design, monitoring, and runtime operations.

Improvements in Design Tools

In Analysis Services in SQL Server 2005, Microsoft made significant advances in the usability of the design tools for building OLAP databases. However, user feedback indicated that users needed help and guidance on how to build best practices into their applications. Therefore, in Analysis Services in SQL Server 2008, the design experience now includes comprehensive best practices alerts. These alerts appear as blue and red "squiggly" lines in the user interface, which draw attention to warnings and errors, respectively. Think of these as being like the warnings displayed in the Microsoft Word environment to show spelling or grammar errors. This technique enables the user to continue working—it does not require any action on the part of the user—while flagging important issues. In this chapter, you will see these alerts in action in the "Configuring Dimensions" section later in this chapter.

In addition to these alerts, Microsoft has also radically revised some of the designers. You will find the Cube Wizard, described in the "Defining Cubes" section later in this chapter, to be much simpler than previously. In addition, the Dimension Designer now includes a special interface for developing attribute relationships. This is also described in the "Configuring Dimensions" section.

In this chapter, we describe some of the basics of MDX, the language used with Analysis Services. For the more advanced MDX user, Microsoft has introduced dynamic named sets. A *named set* is, in essence, a predefined subset of data values, such as "Top 10 Customers," which can be used in an expression. In SQL Server 2005, named sets were always static—the top 10 customers were selected when the cube was processed. This meant that running a query such as "find the top 10 customers over 70 years old" would actually return the subset of the original top 10 customers who were over 70, which could be none of them. Dynamic named sets enable you to return the top 10 customers in the context of the query. Therefore, you can now easily and dynamically query for your top 10 septuagenarian customers.

Improvements in Monitoring Tools

For the advanced user, who already has cubes designed and in production, new features in SQL Server Management Studio help to monitor the performance of deployed databases. You can think of the monitoring features as being equivalent to dynamic management views for the SQL Server relational database engine. An Analysis Services administrator, working in Management Studio, can now issue an MDX query such as this:

```
SELECT
    session_spid,
    session_user_name,
    session_last_command,
    session_start_time,
```

```
    session_CPU_time_MS,
    session_reads,
    session_writes,
    session_status
FROM $system.discover_sessions
WHERE session_status = 1
```

The results give a detailed view of which sessions are running on the server and the resources they are using. Similar schemas exist for connections, sessions, commands, and objects touched by commands, affording a very comprehensive resource-monitoring solution.

Runtime Improvements

The improvements in Analysis Services in SQL Server 2008 are not just in the user interactions—whether for designers or administrators. The runtime engine has also seen substantial enhancements. Some of these are deeply technical.

For example, a technology known as *subspace* (or *block*) computation offers remarkable performance improvements for queries that return sparse result sets. Take the case of a query returning sales of all products in all stores on all dates. Typically, only a relatively small subset of all products are sold in all stores on all dates, so the result from this query will include many null (or default) values. Subspace computations optimize the engine operations required to answer this query, and they can show performance improvements up to 20 times faster in some cases.

Another significant runtime improvement for the advanced user is the ability to write back to a Multidimensional OLAP (MOLAP) partition (rather than a Relational OLAP partition). For users building interactive budgeting and planning applications, this again offers substantial performance gains.

Analysis Services Fundamentals

In this section, we will look at the architecture of Analysis Services, as established in SQL Server 2005 and continued in SQL Server 2008. We will also explore some of the fundamental features of Analysis Services.

Architecture

Figure 20-1 gives a high-level view of the Analysis Services architecture. A main component is the Unified Dimensional Model (UDM), which is a cohesive dimensional model representing relational and multidimensional data repositories. The UDM provides a bridge (standard representation) from a client such as Excel or SQL Server Reporting Services to a diverse set of heterogeneous data sources. Rather than accessing the data sources in their native languages (such as specific SQL dialects), the UDM enables client applications to issue commands against the UDM.

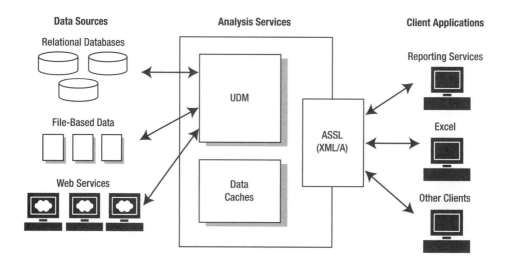

Figure 20-1. *Analysis Services architecture*

A large number of Analysis Services features build on the UDM. These include hierarchies, categorizations, time representations, language translations, and perspectives. Even advanced functionality such as proactive caching and analytics are intrinsically part of the UDM and therefore available to Analysis Services.

As XML and web services become ever more important, Analysis Services supports these contemporary technical mainstays in a comprehensive manner. An Analysis Services server behaves as a web service, and it should come as no surprise that the language for administering this server is XML-based. All client communication with the Analysis Services server is via the standards-based XML/A protocol.

Microsoft is continuing to support a variety of technologies aimed at backward compatibility with the functionality provided by XML/A (ADOMD, ADOMDB.NET, OLE DB for OLAP, and Win32). XML/A is actually a subset of the Analysis Services Scripting Language (ASSL), where XML/A sends action commands such as Create, Alter, and Process (to create a cube, alter a cube, and process a cube). ASSL is also the language used to specify the objects within Analysis Services. XML/A handles commands, while the rest of ASSL is a Data Definition Language (DDL) for Analysis Services objects.

BIDS, the development environment for SQL Server BI, uses Visual Studio's development style (solutions, projects, and source files). The source files associated with a BIDS Analysis Services project contain the metadata associated with Analysis Services objects. You can check these files in to standard source code control (such as Visual SourceSafe or Visual Studio Team Foundation Server). The metadata language is XML and is stored in files. SQL Server Management Studio and BIDS use XML/A to communicate with Analysis Services.

Microsoft introduced proactive caching in Analysis Services in SQL Server 2005 to empower low-latency applications with minimal managerial overhead. The primary purpose of proactive caching is the management of data obsolescence. For example, you can configure the proactive cache to update when the underlying data changes. If the cache is in the process of updating, Analysis Services is sophisticated enough to direct a query not to the cache, but instead to run the query against the underlying data source. Proactive caching works optimally against a relational database that provides notifications when the underlying data has changed.

Analysis Services in SQL Server 2008 does not cache entire dimensions in memory. Just as an operating system keeps certain pages in memory and has certain pages swapped out to disk, Analysis Services uses physical memory and disk space. The benefit of this approach is that Analysis Services now supports unlimited dimension sizes. For example, Analysis Services in SQL Server 2000 hit constraints depending on the physical RAM available. Analysis Services can now take advantage of caching (keeping results partially on disk) and is therefore not RAM-bound.

Development Environment

BIDS is the primary environment for Analysis Services development. This application is actually a version of Visual Studio 2008 that ships at no extra cost with SQL Server 2008.

BIDS supports offline development before the developer deploys an Analysis Services project to a server. This offline development is possible because BIDS works with snapshots of the schemas from the data sources accessed. The Analysis Services objects it creates (cubes, dimensions, fact tables, and so on) are just local copies of these objects. The developer must deploy them to a specific Analysis Services server. The true benefit of this is that development can take place even if the Analysis Server is not running locally and even if a developer is not connected to the network.

On top of offline development, BIDS provides administrative dialog boxes and wizard-based support for the creation of computations. These user interface enhancements automate the manipulation of computations ranging from time manipulation and interpretation, to account intelligence, financial aggregation, support for multiple currencies, and semi-additive measures. The alternative to using the dialog box and wizard-based support would be hand-coding computations.

■**Note** Understanding the term *semi-additive measures* requires some understanding of Analysis Services objects. Computations run over cubes composed of dimensions. Fully additive measures are computed against all dimensions of a cube. Semi-additive measures are additive across some but not all dimensions of a cube.

Another benefit of BIDS is support for multiple configurations. This enables you to deploy projects against multiple instances of Analysis Services. Also supported are localized objects and translations, so Analysis Services supports deployments in multiple languages.

Analysis Services Objects and Concepts

Analysis Services includes many features of interest. Here, we will review some of the most important objects and concepts that are especially useful for effective BI implementations. We'll cover some more concepts that are particular to OLAP applications in the next section.

Data Source Views

Data source views (DSVs) form a virtual layer on top of a data source and contain a subset (just the pertinent elements) of the objects associated with a data source. For example, a DSV could contain a subset of the tables and views pertaining to payroll processing. This virtualization enables developers to rename objects, and to create calculated columns and named queries. An added benefit of named query support is developers gain access to what are fundamentally views without requiring a user to have CREATE VIEW permissions on the data source.

Multidimensional Expressions

As noted earlier, MDX is the language supported by Analysis Services for calculations and security rules. Developers use MDX to query Analysis Services and to build calculations and key performance indicators.

Key Performance Indicator Framework and Perspectives

Key performance indicators (KPIs), introduced in SQL Server 2005, are server-side objects that can graphically represent a value, a desired goal for that value, the status of the indicator (good, bad, and so on), and the trend of the measure.

For example, a brokerage house could use a thumb-is-up or thumb-is-down graphic to indicate whether a stock should be purchased or sold. The underlying algorithm to determine this could be quite complex (value, goal, status, and trend), but the KPI (the corporate measure) can be quite simple: buy (thumb-is-up graphic) or sell (thumb-is-down graphic).

A trend is directional behavior, which can be associated with a graphic, such as a thermometer, a fuel gauge, or an arrow pointing up or down. For example, a car might be winning a race (the status of the KPI), but another car could be gaining rapidly (the trend). Developers define the value, goal, status, and trend of a KPI using the MDX language.

Another feature that supports a user-specific context of information is perspectives. A *perspective* is a logical collection of attributes, user-defined hierarchies, actions, and measure groups optimized to provide a given category of user a highly sophisticated, customized view of the underlying data. You can think of perspectives in Analysis Services as being rather like a view in the relational engine.

Common Language Runtime (CLR) Integration

At times, the Analysis Services developer may still need to take advantage of computations per-formed in a high-level language such as the common language runtime (CLR) languages C# and VB .NET. In SQL Server 2008, SQL Server objects such as user-defined functions can be created using such CLR languages. This CLR language support extends not only to user-defined functions, but also to stored procedures and triggers.

You can develop such CLR add-ons to SQL Server using Visual Studio 2008. It would be possible for the same Visual Studio solution to contain both an Analysis Services project and the C# or VB .NET project for the user-defined functions utilized by the Analysis Services project—one application and one development environment.

Analysis Management Objects (AMO)

From an administrative standpoint, Analysis Management Objects (AMO) expose an API for creating and maintaining Analysis Services objects. AMO can handle administrative tasks including security and processing, and even backup and restore.

OLAP, OLTP, and Data Warehouses

Imagine that you are a developer working for AdventureWorks (as in the SQL Server 2008 demo database). Someone from accounting stops at your office and asks for a breakdown of product sales. Therefore, you write a query in Management Studio, joining the Production.Product table to the Sales.SalesOrderDetail table, as shown in Figure 20-2.

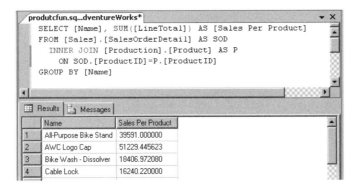

Figure 20-2. *Query and result: total sales by product*

With this task completed, you start your real work again, but then someone from manufacturing stops by and wants to see a sales breakdown by Production.DaysToManufacture, soon followed by a design team member who wants to see sales by Production.Color. Just as you're about to start writing these queries, the accounting guy returns, wanting to see a further breakdown of the product sales according to sales period (by month, quarter, and year) and also wanting you to include a breakdown by SalesPerson, Product, ProductCategory, ProductSubCategory, and Customer. Rather than writing custom query after custom query, the solution is to use Analysis Services.

These examples of data interpretation are considered OLAP. An OLAP database is optimal for analysis and decision making. However, before analyzing and interpreting data, there must be data to analyze. This source data is often created, updated (and deleted when necessary) in a database environment known as an *Online Transaction Processing* (OLTP) system. For example, a retail establishment needs to record purchases, process returns, add new products, and receive new inventory. All this falls into the category of an OLTP system, and AdventureWorks is an example of a typical OLTP database.

After the store closes, the IT of the AdventureWorks database will typically copy the data to a separate, structured, repository or a *data warehouse*. Business users can query the data warehouse to determine if denim jackets are profitable to sell and if plaid skirts sell more than striped shorts.

One of the best sources of data for learning SQL Server 2008 is the AdventureWorksDW database, a sample database optimized for OLAP or data warehousing. You can download this at no cost from http://www.codeplex.com, where all the SQL Server code samples are now hosted.

OLAP and OLTP Configuration

Given their different characteristics, OLAP and OLTP environments require different configurations. Within an OLAP environment, it might make sense to have more indexes to optimize data for reading. In an OLTP system, each additional index can negatively affect the performance of insert, delete, and update operations. In order to make data simpler to interpret, an OLAP data system could have denormalized data. As we have all learned the hard way, fully normalized data can get extremely complex. In an OLAP environment optimized for ease of analysis, it is simpler to know an employee is part of the accounting department rather than knowing the employee belongs to DepartmentID=398. In addition, OLTP would favor normalization for performance and design clarity reasons.

As we mentioned, when you have a separate repository for analysis-centric data, we typically refer to this as the *data warehouse*. Such repositories are often large (terabytes) and optimized for the delivery and analysis of copious amounts of information. OLAP does not require a data warehouse, but OLAP is often associated with data warehouses because OLAP is the technique for interpreting copious amounts of data. Integration Services facilitates populating the data warehouse. Analysis

Services organizes and places the data in accessible constructs. Reporting Services presents the data in a meaningful form targeted to those who need to make the business decisions based on this data.

OLAP Concepts

Working with Analysis Server requires the understanding of certain key OLAP terminology including *cubes*, *dimensions*, and *measures*. These concepts correspond to objects used within Analysis Services and its related technologies.

Cubes

Core among the OLAP and Analysis Services concepts is the *cube*. Figure 20-3 shows an example of this derived from the AdventureWorksDW database.

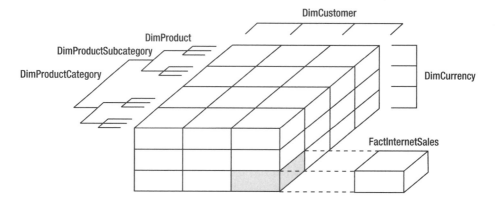

Figure 20-3. *AdventureWorksDW Internet sales cube*

A cube is a multidimensional representation of the quantitative values for analysis. The analytic data is contained in the FactInternetSales table. The elements within this fact table include OrderQuantity, SalesAmount, DiscountAmount, and TaxAmount. The mechanisms for administering and accessing these values are what Analysis Services provides.

In conventional terms, we think of a cube as containing three dimensions: height, width, and depth. Within Analysis Services, a cube is not limited to three dimensions. Sales and Quantity are measures that could readily be associated with five dimensions: DimProduct, DimCustomer, DimSalesPerson, DimCreditCardType, and DimCurrency. The cube diagram in Figure 20-3 contains three dimensions (DimProduct, DimCustomer, and DimCurrency) because they are simpler to draw, but this in no way means that an Analysis Services cube is limited to three dimensions.

Cells

Regardless of the number of dimensions, a cube is composed of cells. A *cell* is the atomic unit of an Analysis Services cube. We specify a cell by identifying its position within the cube in terms of dimensions. For example, we may identify a measure of Sales uniquely by its Customer, Sales Person, Credit Card Type, Currency, and Product.

Measures and Fact Tables

Within a cube, measure groups such as FactInternetSales include quantitative values like OrderQuantity and SalesAmount. These assess business activity. By managing and enabling the manipulation of measures, Analysis Services allows a score to be associated with data (much like a football match has a score associated with it). Often numeric in value, measures tend to be aggregated (show sales aggregated by product category, sales by product color, or sales by customer). Date/time, monetary units, and quantity are examples of potential measures.

Measures are contained in a fact table, which is a database table with one or more measures. The aptly named table FactInternetSales is the fact table of the cube shown in Figure 20-3. The term *measure* is synonymous with the term *fact*; hence the terms *fact table* or *measure group*.

A measure may not only be a database column but could be a calculation (sales less commission, sales plus tax, and so on). Within Analysis Services, MDX can generate calculated measures.

Dimensions and Attributes

The sample cube in Figure 20-3 has three dimensions (DimProduct, DimCustomer, and DimCurrency). What is a dimension? The formal definition of an Analysis Services dimension is "a dimension categorizes measures." The DimCurrency dimension categorizes the measures in the FactInternetSales fact table by Hong Kong dollar, ruble, and euro. The DimCustomer dimension is completely independent of the DimCurrency dimension and categorizes based on which customer purchased the product.

In a more traditional database sense, dimensions are often the foreign keys of a fact table. Each dimension is composed of descriptive characteristics. For example, a DimProduct may be red in color. Color is an attribute of the dimension. You can use it to select data within that dimension.

Hierarchies

We order dimensions by hierarchies. In a product dimension, the levels of a hierarchy may be category, subcategory, and product. The tables associated with category, subcategory, and product compose all levels of the DimProduct dimension. Hierarchies are broken down into *balanced hierarchies* and *unbalanced hierarchies*.

In order to understand hierarchies, consider the Category, Subcategory, and Product levels shown in Figure 20-4. At the base of this hierarchy are specific products (such as Logo Cap and Stock Vest, S). These values represent the leaves of the hierarchy. Each leaf is the same distance from the root level of the hierarchy, which means it is a balanced hierarchy. Results can show Internet sales for all products, Internet sales by category, Internet sales for category starting with the letter Q, or product sales by category and subcategory.

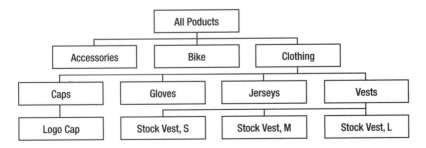

Figure 20-4. *Production dimension: balanced hierarchy*

Unbalanced hierarchies are also possible, such as the geographic hierarchy shown in Figure 20-5 (which is quite different from the cube diagram in Figure 20-3). In the example, the leaf nodes are cities, and the city of Washington D.C. is separate from any state. The distance between this leaf node and the root level of the hierarchy differs from that of the other leaf nodes.

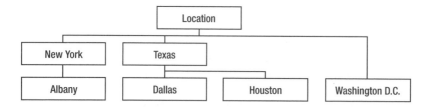

Figure 20-5. *Location dimension: unbalanced hierarchy*

Why this emphasis on balanced and unbalanced hierarchies? Analysis Services in SQL Server 2008 supports both types of hierarchies; this is not the case with comparable tools from other database vendors.

Analysis Services Projects

In order to create Analysis Services objects (cubes, dimensions, measures, and so on), a developer could code natively in ASSL, the XML-based language used by client applications to communicate with Analysis Services. However, writing raw XML (regardless of how well designed) is tedious and error-prone.

The BIDS integrated development environment (IDE) supports Analysis Services projects. This project type is ASSL under the covers (the source files of the project are ASSL XML), but the BIDS IDE streamlines development by generating ASSL while developers get to work with a sophisticated user interface.

■**Note** The types of projects available in BIDS depend on whether you installed SQL Server on a host with or without Visual Studio 2008. If you installed Visual Studio 2008 on the same host as SQL Server, then BIDS will contain all projects installed with Visual Studio 2008 (Window Application, Console Applications, and so on). The examples in this chapter assume that you installed SQL Server 2008 without Visual Studio 2008.

Starting a New Analysis Services Project

The cube diagram in Figure 20-3 included the dimensions of DimProduct, DimCurrency, and DimCustomer. This cube also contains a fact table, `FactInternetSales`. We can implement this cube using an Analysis Services project in BIDS, in order to show off BIDS capabilities in the Analysis Services arena. Let's modify the cube in Figure 20-3 to add a fourth dimension, DimTime.

To create a new Analysis Services project, open BIDS (Microsoft SQL Server 2008 ➤ Business Intelligence Development Studio) and select File ➤ New. You will see the New Project dialog box, as shown in Figure 20-6. Navigate it as follows: Other Languages ➤ Business Intelligence Projects (this sequence is slightly different on a host with both SQL Server and Visual Studio 2008 installed on it). In the Templates pane, select Analysis Services Project.

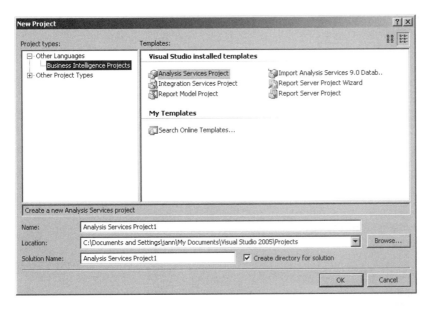

Figure 20-6. *Creating a new Analysis Services project*

By default, the name of the project and solution will contain a generic name such as Analysis Services Project1. To identify the project, enter Internet Sales in the Name text box. Then click OK to close the New Project dialog box.

The model used by BIDS is that of a solution containing one or more projects. For this scenario, there is one solution and one Analysis Services project. It would be possible within the same solution to create additional projects such as a Reporting Services project and an Integration Services project.

Defining Data Sources

Once you create an Analysis Services project, you must create a data source to do useful work. This data source refers to the database from which your project will access data. This data source may be associated with SQL Server or could be any flavor of data source accessible as a managed provider, OLE DB, or ODBC.

In order to create a data source, within Solution Explorer (View ➤ Solution Explorer), right-click the Data Sources folder within the Internet Sales project and select New Data Source from the context menu, as shown in Figure 20-7.

Figure 20-7. *Choosing to create a new data source*

Selecting the New Data Source option starts the Data Source Wizard. Click Next to move past the welcome screen. The second screen of the Data Source Wizard, shown in Figure 20-8, enables you to create the data source.

Figure 20-8. *Defining the data source*

A data source is associated with a data connection (data provider, host, database, security credentials, and so on). To create a data connection, thus enabling a data source to be created, click the New button. You will see the Connection Manager dialog box, as shown in Figure 20-9.

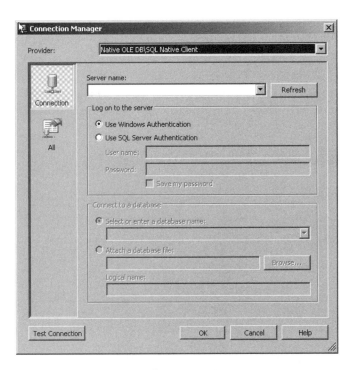

Figure 20-9. *Creating a new data connection*

When the Connection Manager dialog box initially displays, it selects the Native OLE DB\SQL Native Client by default. OLE DB is the data access technology that predates .NET and managed providers. In order to access SQL Server most efficiently, select the .Net Providers\SqlClient Data Provider from the Provider combo box. Under Server name, a drop-down list will appear of all available hosts running SQL Server. You can enter localhost (or a period, for shorthand) to indicate that the machine on which BIDS is presently running contains the instance of SQL Server to which you wish to connect.

At this point, you should select the type of security required. You can choose either Windows authentication or SQL Server authentication. Microsoft advocates using Windows authentication. SQL Server authentication has one minor advantage over Windows authentication: developers do not need to submit a formal request with their information technology department to get their Windows accounts associated with specific SQL Server roles/permissions. However, the consistency and security of Windows authentication make this the preferred choice. The connection name displayed in the dialog box will take the following form if you create it using Windows authentication: Hostname.Databasename. If you create the connection using SQL Server authentication, the connection will be in the form Hostname.Databasename.Username.

One clue that your security is set up correctly is that when you select the database name from the drop-down list, it will display all accessible databases on the server for the specific user credentials. From the drop-down list, select the database AdventureWorksDW. As a check, click the Test Connection button in order to verify that the server, security credential, and database all combine to make a valid database connection. Once the connection validates, click OK to create a data connection.

■**Tip** If the database name drop-down list is empty, the first place to check is your credentials. Perhaps you have not been provisioned with access to the databases you need.

After the data connection is created, click Next in the wizard. You'll see the Impersonation Information screen, as shown in Figure 20-10. This is where you specify the credentials that are used by Analysis Services to connect to the specific data source.

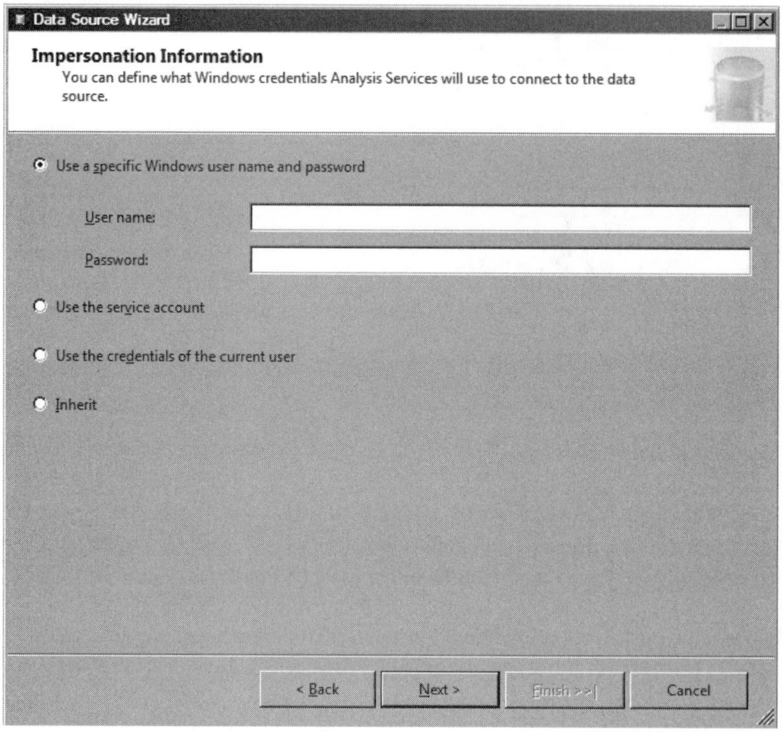

Figure 20-10. *Providing impersonation information*

The Impersonation Information screen is important because the Analysis Services server, and not the user currently working with BIDS, ultimately connects to the data source. It is best not to select the Use the Credentials of the Current User option. Under certain circumstances (such as when a data source is used for training data-mining structures/modules), it is not permissible according to the documentation to use this impersonation mode. For the purposes of this exercise, choose the Use the Service Account option. Selecting this option assumes that the account under which Analysis Services runs (the service account) has access to the data source.

There is no mandate that the data source point to a SQL Server 2008 database. The purpose of the Analysis Services UDM is to enable access to heterogeneous data sources in a manner seamless to the end user. For the sake of convenience, we use AdventureWorksDW, a SQL Server 2008 database, for this example. The data source could have easily been a SQL Server 2000 database such as Northwind or a Jet database named Pubs. The data source could have been DB2, Oracle, Excel, or any heterogeneous data source supported by a managed provider, OLE DB, or ODBC.

Editing a Data Source

After you've created a data source, you can double-click it in Solution Explorer to launch the Data Source Designer, shown in Figure 20-11. Using this designer, you can edit the data source.

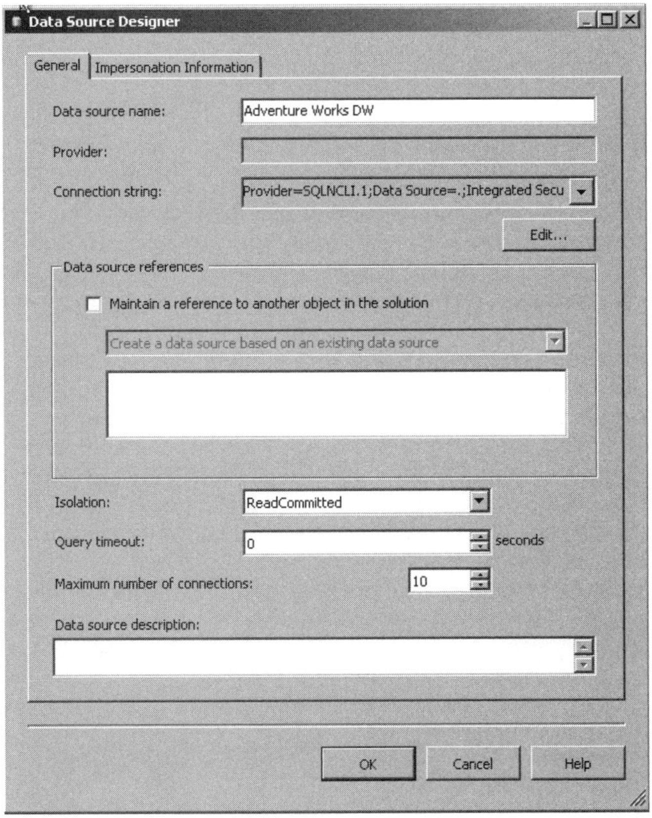

Figure 20-11. *Editing a data source with the Data Source Designer*

Using the Data Source Designer, you can change the name of the data source, alter the connection string, or modify other properties associated with the data source. In fact, the designer has access to features not exposed by the wizard. The Edit button is useful if the underlying host, data, or security credentials change for the data source. Each top-level object within BIDS (DSVs, cubes, and dimensions) has a wizard and a designer associated with it.

Defining Data Source Views

A core premise of Analysis Services for many developers is that if they can get the metadata correct, then the data will fall into place for them. In keeping with this philosophy, the DSV is a very important requirement within an Analysis Services project. A DSV is an offline version of the metadata associated with tables or views used by the Analysis Services project. The idea is to enable development to proceed by enabling access to the required metadata without having to maintain a persistent connection to the data source.

To create a DSV, right-click the Data Source Views folder for the Analysis Services project within Solution Explorer and choose New Data Source View, as shown in Figure 20-12. This starts the Data Source View Wizard. Click Next to move past the welcome screen.

Figure 20-12. *Choosing to create a new DSV*

The second screen of the wizard allows you to select a data source. For this exercise, select the data source previously created, AdventureWorksDW. Then click the Next button to bring up the Select Tables and Views screen, as shown in Figure 20-13. Here, you select the tables and views for your DSV. For this example, double-click the `DimProductCategory`, `DimProductSubCategory`, `DimProduct`, `DimCustomer`, `DimCurrency`, `DimTime`, and `FactInternetSales` tables, to move them to the Included Objects list. Although not used in this example, the Add Related Tables feature can prove quite useful. Clicking this button moves tables from the Available objects list that have a foreign key relationship with the tables and views of the Included Objects list.

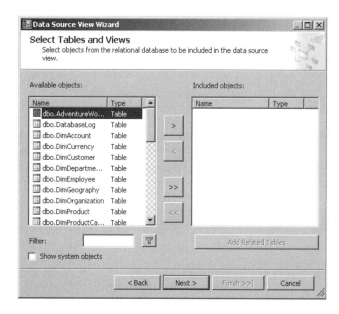

Figure 20-13. *Selecting tables and views for a DSV*

Once you have selected the tables for the DSV, click Next. When the final screen of the wizard appears, change the default name of the Data Source View from Adventure Works DW to **Adventure Works Internet Sales**, and then click Finish to create the DSV. The purpose of the view is to isolate a pertinent subset of the information. In our case, this was a set of tables from the AdventureWorksDW database related to sales generated via the Internet.

A data diagram appears in the design view associated with the newly created DSV, as shown in Figure 20-14.

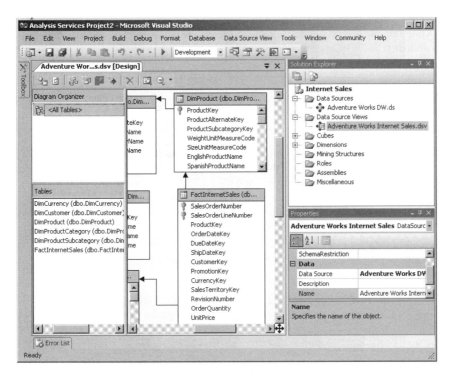

Figure 20-14. *Data Source View Designer*

In the Data Source View Designer, you can select a table. You can change the properties of a table (such as FactInternetSales) in the Properties window. For example, you might associate a friendly name with an otherwise cryptically named table/view. It is also possible to drag one table/view on top of another to create a relationship between these entities.

Right-clicking the design window displays a context menu that enables additional manipulation of the DSV:

- *Add or remove tables and views*: As an example, if we had forgotten the DimProduct table when creating the new DSV, a significant piece of the model would be missing. You could correct this oversight using the context menu's Add/Remove Tables option.

- *Specify a named query for the data source*: Recall that a named query is a query associated with a specific data access command (a SELECT in SQL terminology). This named query would show up in the designer as a table. A named query does not reside in the underlying data source and therefore does not require CREATE VIEW permission on the data source. It also could be the case that the underlying data source is not a relational database, and therefore does not even support the concept of a view. The named query resides in the local metadata associated with the DSV.

- *Create new relationships*: This might prove useful if the foreign key relationships do not exist in the underlying data source, or if the underlying data source does not provide access to its metadata, preventing the BIDS wizard from automatically setting up the table relations. This latter scenario is quite common where a user has access to data but not to metadata definitions for constructs such as indexes, foreign keys, and view definitions. Creating a new relationship is a necessity when using a named query. A named query has no underlying metadata defining its relationship to the other tables in the data source. Creating a new relationship provides this missing critical information.

Tip You can also create a new relationship by dragging a foreign key from one table and dropping it onto the primary key of the table referenced by the foreign key.

- *Toggle between design and code view*: Code for any object in an Analysis Services project object is just the XML representation of the object. This XML is the ASSL, as discussed earlier in the chapter. The code view is handy for globally changing names within an Analysis Services project object. For example, if a developer mistakenly used *Sails* as the friendly name for each sales-related object, a global replace operation in the code can easily remedy the mistake. For developers who need to work directly with ASSL, the various source files of an Analysis Services project can serve as a tutorial.

Defining Cubes

There are many changes to the Cube Wizard in SQL Server 2008, but it is still remarkably easy to use. Creating a new cube is a matter of right-clicking the project's Cubes folder within Solution Explorer and selecting New Cube from the context menu. Cubes are highly configurable, but the new user will typically just choose the default on the Select Creation Method screen, Use Existing Tables, as shown in Figure 20-15.

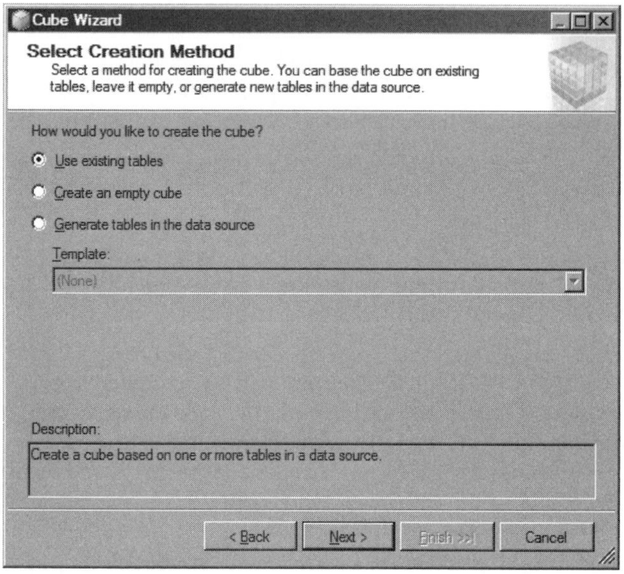

Figure 20-15. *Selecting a cube creation method*

Clicking Next takes you to the Select Measure Group Tables screen, as shown in Figure 20-16. Here, you can select several fact tables or just one. In this example, select the `FactInternetSales` table, which contains the potential measures (OrderQuantity, UnitPrice, SalesAmount, TaxAmount, Freight, and TotalProductCost). A fact table contains one or more measures.

Tip If you are not sure of which tables to select, or even which tables are fact tables, you can click the Suggest button in the Select Measure Group Tables dialog box. The wizard will select candidate fact tables for you to review.

Figure 20-16. *Selecting measure group tables for a cube*

After specifying the fact tables, click Next. You'll see the screen used to select the measures associated with a cube, as shown in Figure 20-17. For this example, select Order Quantity, Sales Amount, Tax Amt, and Freight. (The Sales Amount column is the total cost of the goods sold, taking into account quantity, price, and discount.) All other columns should be unchecked. Click Next to continue.

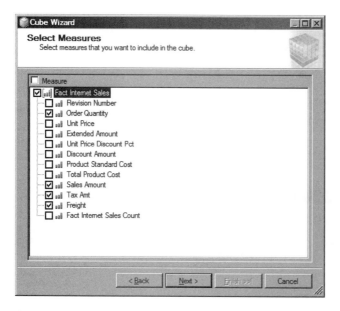

Figure 20-17. *Selecting measures for a cube*

The next screen enables you to select your dimensions, as shown in Figure 20-18. Here, we have selected the DimCurrency, DimCustomer, and DimTime tables to serve as dimensions. These do not contain a hierarchy, as their dimension contains just one table. The fourth dimension, which is hierarchical in nature, is composed of DimProductSubcategory, DimProductCategory, and DimProduct tables. The Cube Wizard discovered this hierarchy for us. Also, note that we unchecked the FactInternetSales table, as we do not want that to play any dimensional role, although fact tables sometimes can serve as a dimension in special circumstances.

Figure 20-18. *Selecting your dimensions*

To complete the Cube Wizard, click Next, and then click Finish. The cube picks up the name of the DSV by default, so this cube is `Adventure Works Internet Sales.cube`, as can be seen in Solution Explorer, as shown in Figure 20-19.

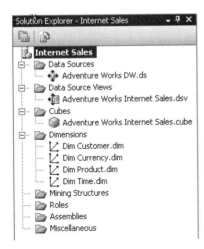

Figure 20-19. *Solution Explorer with the cube and dimensions*

Configuring Dimensions

Now that you have completed the Cube Wizard, it has created dimensions for you. The wizard has also added the database dimensions to the new cube, creating cube dimensions. You must now configure your dimensions. You can do this using the Dimension Designer. The Dimension Designer enables you to configure properties, add dimension attributes, define new hierarchies, design attribute relationships, and add localized translations if needed.

■**Note** It is also possible for advanced users to create dimensions from scratch by using the Dimension Wizard. If you create dimensions in this way, you must add them to the cube manually using the Cube Designer.

To configure a dimension, right-click the dimension in Solution Explorer and select Open. For this example, open the DimTime dimension in the Dimension Designer, as shown in Figure 20-20.

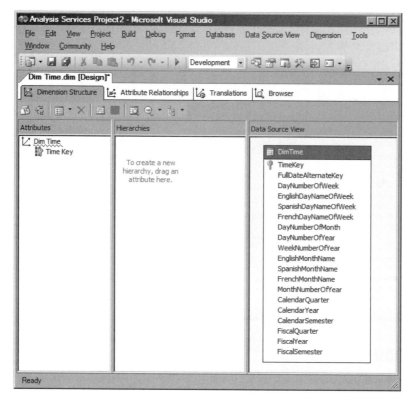

Figure 20-20. *The Dimension Designer*

The Dimension Designer has four tabs:

- *Dimension Structure*: Here, you can select dimension attributes and arrange these attributes into hierarchies.

- *Attribute Relationships*: In this tab, you specifically manage the relationships between attributes. These relationships help you navigate through your dimension hierarchies.

- *Translations*: Use this tab to add and edit dimension metadata in multiple languages.

- *Browser*: Use this tab to view a processed dimension.

When you first look at the Dimension Structure tab (Figure 20-20), you will see a blue squiggly line under the name of the Time dimension, Dim Time. This is a best practices warning, which we described earlier in the chapter. Move your mouse pointer over the line, and a tooltip will show you the warning "Create hierarchies in non-parent child dimensions." Generally, you will want to heed these warnings, and you should work through your cube and dimension designs to eliminate as many as possible. They really do help you to build a better design.

Adding Attributes

In this example, before we can create useful hierarchies, we need to add more attributes. By default, the only attribute that the wizard adds to the dimension is the dimension key.

Add new attributes by dragging them from the Data Source View pane on the right side of the Dimension Designer to the Attributes pane on the left side. For now, drag over the following attributes:

CalendarYear, Calendar Semester, CalendarQuarter, and EnglishMonthName. You can drag them over in any order, or you can multiple-select them in the Data Source View pane and drag them all at once.

You can rename the EnglishMonthName attribute to a more friendly form by right-clicking it in the Attributes pane and selecting Rename. For example, you may just want to call this attribute Month. While you are at it, you can also rename the dimension key from TimeKey to simply Date. These friendly names make it much easier for business users to browse the cube and to understand the data.

Creating a Hierarchy

Now that you have added the attributes to the dimension, it is time to create a hierarchy. As you can see in Figure 20-20, the Hierarchies pane tells you to drag attributes there to create these objects. As soon as you drag an attribute to the Hierarchies pane, a new Hierarchy object appears, named Hierarchy by default. You can drag more attributes above or below the first one you added in order to create levels of the hierarchy. It is a good idea to pay attention to the order at this stage, although you can rearrange levels later by dragging and dropping them, if you like.

Drag all the attributes over, one by one, to create the hierarchy shown in Figure 20-21. You can also right-click in the header space of the new Hierarchy object, select Rename, and give it a friendly name, such as Calendar.

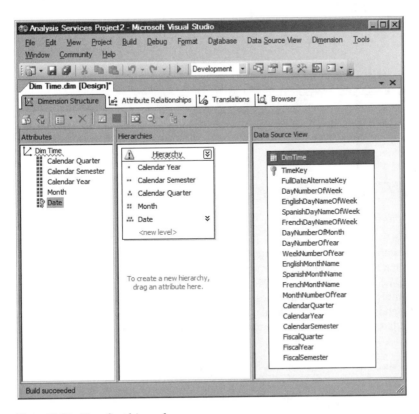

Figure 20-21. *Your first hierarchy*

Creating Attribute Relationships

You will notice that your new hierarchy has some warning signs: a yellow triangle and a blue squiggly line. Again, these are best practices warnings. You can mouse over them to see what the advice is. In this case, the warning is "Attribute relationships do not exist between one or more levels of this hierarchy. This may result in decreased query performance." Good advice! Let's navigate to the Attribute Relationships tab, shown in Figure 20-22, and start to create these.

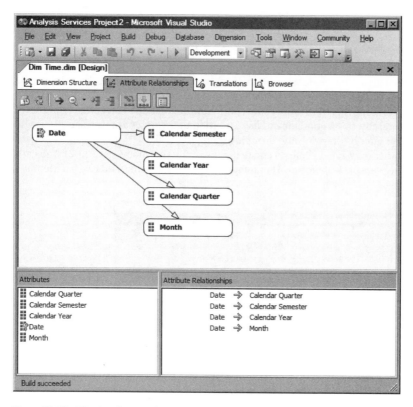

Figure 20-22. *The Attribute Relationships tab in the Dimension Designer*

In this figure, you can see that all the attributes relate to the dimension key, Date, but none of them relate to each other. This would make the dimension difficult to navigate. You could drill down from CalendarYear to Date, but not from CalendarYear to CalendarSemester. To create relationships to improve navigation, simply drag and drop attributes in this view onto the attribute that you want to be the parent. So, drag CalendarSemester onto CalendarYear, CalendarQuarter onto CalendarSemester, and Month onto CalendarQuarter. Now your hierarchy should look like Figure 20-23.

Figure 20-23. *Attribute relationships*

We are not quite finished here yet. To see why, navigate back to the Dimension Structure tab for a moment. You will see that there is still a blue squiggly line under the name DimTime in the

Attributes pane. The warning is "Define attribute relationships as 'Rigid' where appropriate." This tells us that all our attribute relationships are flexible, but we expect that some should be rigid. A *rigid* attribute relationship is one that we do not expect to change. For example, in our Time dimension, the month January will always be part of CalendarQuarter 1.

Return to the Attribute Relationships tab, where you can modify these relationships. At the bottom right of the Attribute Relationships tab, you will see the Attribute Relationships pane, as shown in Figure 20-24.

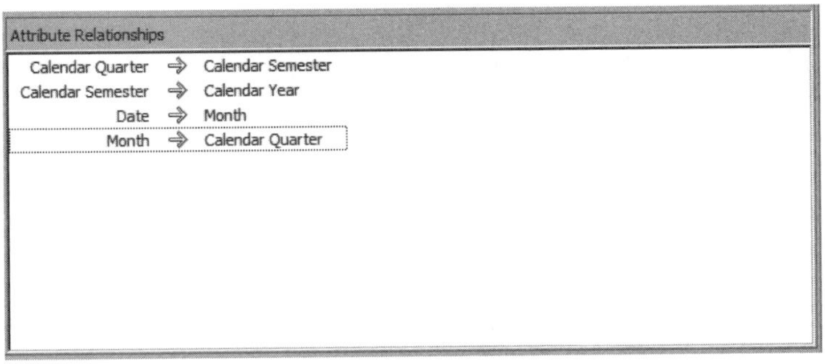

Figure 20-24. *Listed attribute relationships*

You can multiple-select all the relationships here, right-click, and then select Properties. In the Properties window, change the RelationshipType property from Flexible to Rigid. All the attribute relationships here should be set as Rigid.

■**Note** If you do not set a relationship to Rigid, then after an incremental update of the data, Analysis Services will drop the aggregations. You need to process them again manually. However, Analysis Services saves rigid aggregations, so reprocessing is not required.

Making Attribute Hierarchies Invisible

We have nearly completed our dimension configuration. All that remains is to return to the Dimension Structure tab. Here, you will still see the blue squiggly line under the dimension name, but this is the last one—promise! The warning is "Avoid visible attribute hierarchies for attributes used as levels in user-defined hierarchies." This warning is because users may be confused if dimension attributes are visible in different ways. However, sometimes this is acceptable. For example, business users may like to look at all sales in November or December, across all years, to evaluate holiday season sales. Yet they may also like to browse by December 2004, December 2005, and so on. To enable this scenario, we will make all the attribute hierarchies invisible, except for Month.

To do this, multiple-select all the attributes in the Attributes pane, except Month. Right-click and select Properties. In the Properties window, set the value of the AttributeValueVisible property to False.

Dismissing Best Practices Warnings

Are you still worried that there is a warning under the dimension name? Fortunately, it is possible to dismiss warnings, both globally and for a specific instance. In this case, we want to dismiss only the warning for the Month attribute. This is quite easy to do.

Select Build ➤ Build Solution in BIDS. When the build has completed (you can see "Build succeeded" in the status bar at the bottom of the screen), open the Error List window by selecting View ➤ Error List. As you can see in Figure 20-25, there are several errors relating to other dimensions. You should fix these later, in the same way as we have done for the Time dimension. For now, let's clear up our immediate concerns.

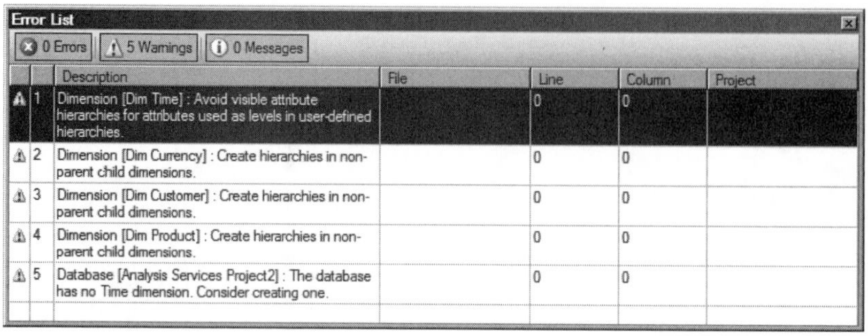

Figure 20-25. *The Error List window showing best practices warnings*

Right-click beside the error that reads "Dimension [Dim Time]: Avoid visible attribute hierarchies for attributes used as levels in user-defined hierarchies" and select Dismiss. In the Dismiss Warning dialog box, you can dismiss this particular instance of the warning by clicking OK. However, before doing so, it is useful to add a note about why you are dismissing the warning—for your own reference or for others who may review the cube design. Add a short note, such as "Allowing multiple views of Month," and then click OK to dismiss the warning. You will notice that the blue warning line under the dimension name (in the Attributes pane of the Dimension Structure tab) disappears as soon as the object model validates the cube metadata.

Look again at Figure 20-25. You may also have been surprised to see the warning "The database has no Time dimension. Consider creating one." Surely, we have been creating a Time dimension? Indeed, we have, but Analysis Services does not know that. To mark our dimension as a Time dimension, right-click the dimension name (DimTime) in the Attributes pane of the Dimension Structure tab and select Properties. In the Properties window, find the Type property and change it from Regular to Time. To see that this has been effective, you can select Build ➤ Build Solution and look at the Error List window again. The warning has disappeared, and our dimension is now in good shape. Remember to configure your other dimensions in the same way.

■**Note** It is also possible to dismiss warnings globally, for any instance of the warning. Do this with care, because you could end up hiding useful warnings. To dismiss a warning globally, select the Analysis Services project in Solution Explorer, right-click, and select Edit Database. You can navigate to the Warnings tab, where you will see all the possible warning listed. Dismiss warnings here and add notes for reference. You can also reenable warnings if you or others have previously dismissed them, whether globally or locally.

Deploying Projects

We must deploy our sample project in order to demonstrate some advanced features of cube development. It is important to recognize that a project is a local metadata representation of the objects that Analysis Services will manage. Deploying a project makes constructs such as cubes become visible to the Analysis Services server.

Configuring a Project for Deployment

In a real-world situation, developers might deploy to their local machine or a training/development host in order to debug their project. Once a project was behaving correctly, developers may then deploy it to a staging or production server. To change the deployment host machine, select Project ➤ Properties. In the Property Pages dialog box, select Configuration Properties, then Deployment. In the Target section, specify the server to which the project should be deployed, as shown in the example in Figure 20-26.

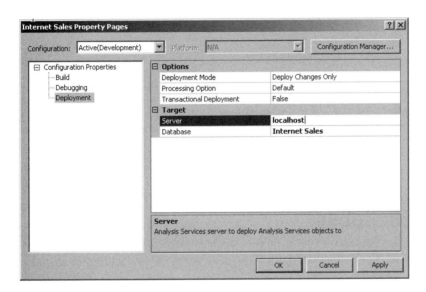

Figure 20-26. *Internet Sales Property Pages dialog box*

In this dialog box, you will see a button labeled Configuration Manager. C# and VB .NET developers will recognize what this button does. Clicking Configuration Manager enables a BIDS developer to create a production configuration (for example) in addition to the standard development configuration associated with the project. The development configuration could utilize localhost, while the production configuration could access BigMainCorporate host.

The standard toolbar of BIDS has a drop-down list that displays the current configuration, which is set to Development by default, as shown in Figure 20-27. You can select an alternate configuration from this drop-down list, which allows you to deploy an Analysis Services project to an alternate host without needing to make the change through the Property Pages dialog box for each alternate deployment.

Figure 20-27. *BIDS standard toolbar with configuration drop-down list*

Deploying a Project

You can deploy a project by selecting Build ➤ Deploy Solution of Build *project name*—Build Internet Sales for our example. Alternatively, you can right-click the project within Solution Explorer and choose Deploy from the context menu.

Deployment is not an instantaneous process. You can watch the status of the deployment using the BIDS Output window (View ➤ Other Windows ➤ Output). The process of deployment could involve more than just the Analysis Services project. When you select Build ➤ Deploy Solution, all deployable projects within the solution will be deployed. This could include Analysis Services projects, Reporting Services projects, Integration Services projects, and CLR projects such as a C# or VB .NET DLL that contains user-defined functions used by the Analysis Services project. In the case of a CLR project, deployment will be to the SQL Server on which the user-defined function is to reside. In the case of other project types (Analysis, Reporting, and Integration Services), deployment is to their respective servers.

Processing a Project

The BIDS Build menu and context menu accessed by right-clicking a project within Solution Explorer include options to either deploy or process a cube. Thus far, we have discussed deployment, which is the process of pushing the project and its objects (data sources, dimensions, cubes, and so on) to a specific Analysis Services server. Simply deploying does not make the underlying data associated with the cube visible. For example, the data associated with a cube will not be browsable until it is *processed*. When an object such as a cube is processed, Analysis Services copies data from the underlying data source or data sources into the cube objects.

Working with Cubes

When you view the design window for a cube, a set of tabs are available to enhance the cube. The contents of these tabs will not be accessible until a project is deployed. Here are the most commonly used tabs:

- *Cube Structure*: The tab includes Measures and Dimensions windows, which identify the fundamental structure of the created cube.

- *Calculations*: Calculations are MDX scripts or expressions. Calculations define entities such as computed members (e.g., a member computed using arithmetic expressions) and name sets (e.g., a set of dimension members).

- *KPIs*: As discussed earlier, KPIs are graphical representations of a value, goal, status, and trend.

- *Actions*: An action is an MDX statement used by client applications. An action is capable of running a command or other style of operation. An action can return a dataset, rowset, or report. Reporting actions return reports after submitting a URL to the report server.

- *Partitions*: Partitions allow you to manage the data and metadata for the aggregations of measure groups.

- *Perspectives*: As discussed earlier, a perspective is a per-user (simplified) view of the cube's information.

- *Translations*: Translations facilitate client applications that localize content such as presenting the data for English Canadian and French Canadian.

- *Browser*: On this tab, you can browse the contents of the cube, meaning the actual data associated with each element within a cube.

Viewing Cube Structure

By default, the Cube Structure tab is selected in the Cube Designer. This tab contains the Measures and Dimensions windows, as shown in Figure 20-28.

Figure 20-28. *Measures and Dimensions windows*

In the Measures window, you could click Fact Internet Sales and add new measures, such as Unit Cost and Total Product Cost, using the context menu. Using the Measures context menu, you could add measure groups, which are an organizational approach to categorizing what could potentially be hundreds of attributes (cost measure groups or tax measure groups or income measure groups).

Through the Dimensions window's Hierarchies tab, you could access DimCustomer. If you like, you can use the Geographic key of the DimCustomer table to create a geographic layer in the hierarchy of the dimension. By adding the DimGeography table to the DimCustomer hierarchy, new types of aggregation would be available to the developer, such as to aggregate the data in the cube by a customer's state, city, or postal code.

The Attributes tab of the Dimensions window allows you to see the attributes of the dimension. The attributes include the columns within each member of a dimension. For the DimProduct dimension, the product-related columns would be available, as well as the columns associated with the category and subcategory members of the product hierarchy.

Browsing Cubes

In order to see the data associated with a cube, the cube must first be processed (select Build ➤ Process, or right-click the project in Solution Explorer and select Process). Once the cube processes successfully, you can browse the data.

Browse the cube by clicking a cube instance to display the designer for the cube. From the Cube Designer, select the Browser tab, and you will see the measures and dimensions of the cube displayed in the navigation pane on the left side of the Browser window, as shown in Figure 20-29.

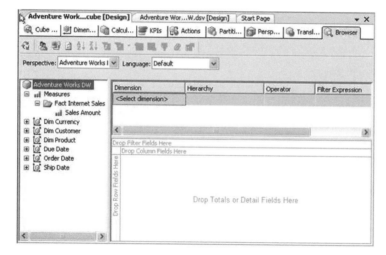

Figure 20-29. *Browser window before displaying data*

Displaying a Cube's Data

To demonstrate the Browser window's ability to display a cube's data, open the DimProduct dimension, drag the English Product Name attribute from the navigation pane on the left, and drop the product on the Drop Row Fields Here region of the Browser window. Then drag from Measures ➤ Fact Internet Sales ➤ Sales Amount to the Browser window's region labeled Drop Total or Detail Fields Here, as shown in Figure 20-30.

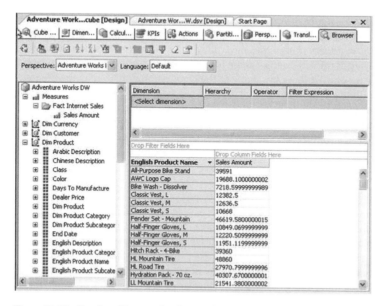

Figure 20-30. *Product.Name sales figures for AdventureWorksDW*

The information displayed in the Browser window is actually the information initially requested by the chap in accounting. Recall that your coworker from the design team wanted to see sales based on product colors. From within the Browser window, select Products and then hit the Delete key. Products are no longer the value used to interpret the sales measure. Drag Product ➤ Color and drop it on the Drop Row Fields Here region of the Browser window, as shown in Figure 20-31.

■**Note** Remove dimensions and measures from the Browser window using the Delete key. The Browser window is for display purposes only. This delete action in no way deletes or alters the underlying data associated with the cube.

Color	Sales Amount
Black	8838411.9576015
Blue	2279096.28000007
Multi	106470.740000006
NA	435116.689999853
Red	7724330.52400018
Silver	5113389.08160051
White	5106.31999999993
Yellow	4856755.62750044
Grand Total	29358677.2206503

Figure 20-31. *Product.Color sales figures for AdventureWorksDW*

With a click, a drag, and a drop, you have answered the question raised by the design department. There was no SQL used at all in this manipulation of how the data was displayed (at least not SQL visible to the developer). Best of all, the UDM displayed the data without a data store-specific command being executed. There was no Transact-SQL, PL/SQL, or any other homogeneous language required to access the cube data.

Browsing Cubes with Hierarchies

Let's now look at how to browse more complex data structures.

1. From Solution Explorer, right-click the Adventure Works DW DSV and select the View Designer option from the context menu. This displays the relational diagram of all the tables in the DSV.

2. Right-click in an empty space in the DSV Designer and select Add/Remove Tables. In the Add/Remove Tables dialog box, double-click DimGeography to move this table from the Available Objects list to the Included Objects list. Click OK to add the DimGeography table to the DSV.

3. Visually inspect the DimGeography table to make sure that the foreign key was created such that the table's GeographyKey columns are one-of-many columns in the DimCustomer table. This relationship should be set up automatically. If not, you will need to manually create it.

4. Just because the DimGeography table is part of the data source does not mean that it is automatically part of the DimCustomer dimension of the cube. In order to add this new table to the DimCustomer dimension, double-click the Adventure Works Internet Sales cube and select the Cube Structure tab. In the navigation pane on the left, expand the DimCustomer dimension, thus exposing a rather useful link, Edit Dim Customer, as shown in Figure 20-32.

Figure 20-32. *The Edit Dim Customer link launches the Dimension Designer.*

5. In the Dimension Designer, right-click in the Data Source View pane on the right side and select Show Tables. Select both DimCustomer and DimGeography. Now you can drag and drop attributes from both tables in order to build a Customer dimension with Geography hierarchies. After making these changes, remember to redeploy the project so that the Cube Designer can access the new data.

■**Tip** Sometimes after successful deployment, the design window for a cube may say that it cannot verify that the cube has been deployed. In such cases, close the Cube Designer window (click the X in the upper-right corner) and then double-click the cube in Solution Explorer in order to display the Cube Designer again. This refreshing of the Cube Designer will enable you to manipulate the cube.

---

6. It is now possible to drag items from the Customer hierarchy English Country Region Name and Last Name onto the Drop Row Fields Here region of the Browser window. Drag the measures Sales Amount and Order Quantity to the Browser window region labeled Drop Total or Detail Fields Here, as shown in Figure 20-33.

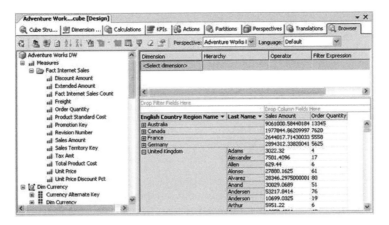

Figure 20-33. *Adding Customer Country and Customer Last Name measures*

This example demonstrated the simplicity with which the Cube Designer's Browser window can display hierarchical data aggregations. Based on the nodes you choose to expand within the Browser window, you were able to see totals for Sales Amount and Order Quantity based on customer country or customer country and last name.

Filtering Cube Data

The Browser window still has more tricks. For example, drag Customer Birth Date on the Drop Filter Fields Here region. The results in the Browser window can now be set up to include or exclude ranges of birthdays. Using this approach, you can cluster the septuagenarian customers in preparation for a marketing campaign aimed at active senior citizens, as shown in Figure 20-34.

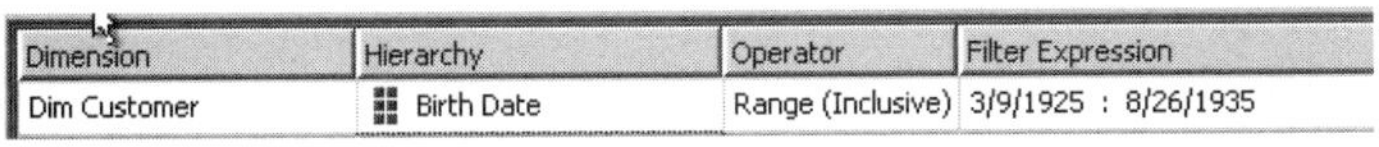

Dimension	Hierarchy	Operator	Filter Expression
Dim Customer	Birth Date	Range (Inclusive)	3/9/1925 : 8/26/1935

Figure 20-34. *Filtering data*

Thus far, the Browser window has behaved like a Tree View control (like the Folder View in Windows Explorer). By dragging dimension members onto the Drop Column Fields Here region of the Browser window, the Cube Designer can now show detailed information across the horizontal dimension, much as Windows Explorer does when configured to show details (View ➤ Details).

You can apply even finer-grained filtering by clicking the headings along the top of the Browser window to select zero or more dimensions, hierarchies, operators, and filter expressions. For example, when browsing product-related data, you could see only product categories whose names begin with *C* (such as clothing and components), as shown in Figure 20-35.

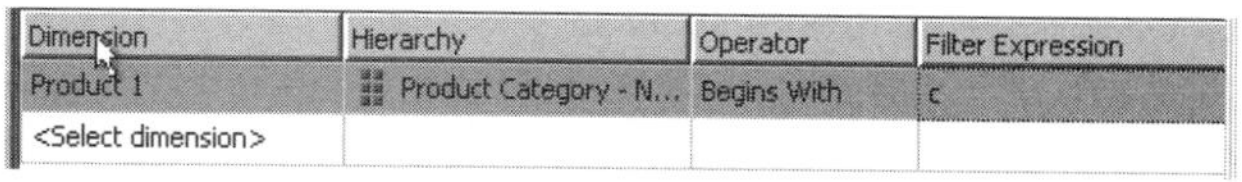

Dimension	Hierarchy	Operator	Filter Expression
Product 1	Product Category - N...	Begins With	c
<Select dimension>			

Figure 20-35. *Filtering category, subcategory, and product sales data for AdventureWorks*

This filtering can become quite sophisticated, given multiple cube dimensions with intricate hierarchies. The operators supported include Not Equal, In, Not In, Contains, Begins With, Range (Included), Range (Excluded), and MDX.

Managing Displayed Data

The Browser window provides a good deal of functionality, but perhaps you thought that some aspects were a little rough; for example, that the measures were not particularly well formatted. You may have noticed that Sales Amount is a currency, but contains no currency symbol (the dollar sign), and the column is left-justified instead of right-justified. Order Quantity is also a numeric value, but it is left-justified instead of right-justified. You can format data through the Properties window accessible from the Code Structure tab, as well as through the Command and Options dialog box accessible from the Browser tab.

Setting Properties

The remedy to the numeric maladies in our example is to select the Cube Structure tab for a given cube. The Cube Structure tab contains a navigation pane that enables you to select an individual measure or dimension member, as shown in Figure 20-36. Expand this navigation pane and select Sales Amount.

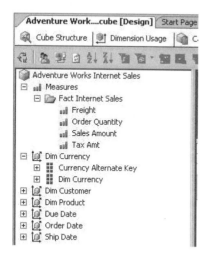

Figure 20-36. *Exploring cube structure*

Once Sales Amount is selected, display the Properties window for this measure (View ➤ Properties), as shown in Figure 20-37.

Figure 20-37. *Viewing the properties of the Amount measure*

In the Properties window, the FormatString property of the Sales Amount has been set to Currency. The other FormatString options are Percentage, Short Date, and Short Time. A format taking into account thousands separators and/or decimal places (# or #, #.0 or #, #.00) can also be specified.

The AggregateFunction property is set to Sum, which makes sense since this value represents the sales figure over a category or subcategory or product aggregation. For measures such as UnitPrice or UnitDiscount, Sum is not an appropriate aggregate function. The choices for the AggregateFunction property include Sum, Count, Min, Max, DistinctCount, None, FirstNonEmpty, and LastNonEmpty.

After modifying any of these properties, or any measure/member properties for that matter (for example, it might make sense to set the Name property to Sales), the project must be deployed again. If you do not redeploy the project, the Browser window will generate errors.

■**Note** When the Browser tab is visible, you will see there is also a navigation pane that contains measures including Sales Amount. Displaying the Properties window (View ➤ Properties) will show the properties for the cube. In order to select per-measure or per-member properties, you must select the Cube Structure tab.

Using the Commands and Options Dialog Box

Using the Properties window to format measures or members does not handle all display-related issues. Within the Browser window, you can alter the data's appearance. In the Browser window, right-click the item to be formatted (measure or member) and select Commands and Options. This menu item displays a dialog box that is rather like a mini word processor, capable of formatting the data, as shown in Figure 20-38. You can right-justify numeric values and change other formatting such as font, color, and column width.

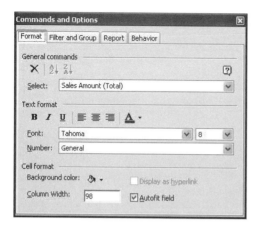

Figure 20-38. *Commands and Options dialog box for Sales Amount measure*

Viewing Many-to-Many Hierarchies

Thus far, when discussing hierarchies, each child in the hierarchy has had one parent, such as each product belonging to at most one subcategory and each subcategory belonging to at most one category. There are hierarchies, called *many-to-many* hierarchies, where this is not the case. In order to understand this, consider a product such as a yogurt breakfast drink. If we categorize this, it might fall under beverage and breakfast. The category is "beverage" because the yogurt is a drink, but it is also "breakfast" because the yogurt serves as a meal. If AdventureWorks sold this yogurt drink, how would it compute, given that it could reside in two categories? It would not make sense to include the data twice. The sales figures would be in error.

For many-to-many relationships in dimensional hierarchies, a useful property is MeasureExpression. Using this property, a weighting can be given to any computation involving a jointly parented product (say 50/50). These numbers would be used in weighting the computations performed against each of these separately aggregated categories, since they frankly cannot both be 100 percent. This same weighting concept and the use of the MeasureExpression property can apply to any many-to-many hierarchy.

Performing Calculations

The dimensions and measures of a cube provide one view of the data. It is often useful to perform a calculation on this data in order to create a data value that is easier to interpret. For example, the Customer dimension contains LastName and FirstName, which could be represented as a calculated member, FullName, whose calculation is LastName + ", " + FirstName. Calculations can be performed on the members of dimensions or measures.

Calculations are MDX, which you can easily set up using the Calculations tab of the Cube Designer. As an example, we will walk through setting up a calculation to determine the average cost per product sold. Figure 20-39 shows the completed setup in the Calculations tab.

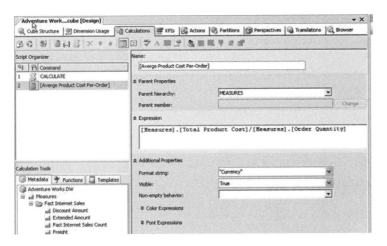

Figure 20-39. *Creating an Average Product Cost Per-Order calculation*

We create the Average Product Cost Per-Order calculation as follows:

1. Right-click in the Script Organizer window and select New Calculated Member. This displays a window like the one in Figure 20-39 (without the data).

2. In the Name text box, enter **[Average Product Cost Per-Order]**. In order to be able to use spaces and special characters (the dash is a special character as it is an operator), you need to enclose the name in square brackets.

3. By default, the Measures parent hierarchy is selected. If, for example, the computation had been FullName, then we would have picked a parent hierarchy such as DimProduct. Since this computation is a measure, leave the Parent Hierarchy drop-down list set to Measures.

4. From the Calculation Tools window, select the Metadata tab and expand the Measures node and its child node, Fact Internet Sales.

5. From the list of measures displayed in Fact Internet Sales, drag Total Product Cost and drop it in the Expression text box of the Calculations window.

6. From the list of measures displayed in Fact Internet Sales, drag Order Quantity and drop it in the Expression text box after the Total Product Cost text.

7. Place the division operator, **/**, between the Total Product Cost and the Order Quantity members, thus creating the calculation expression.

8. From the Format String drop-down list, select Currency (since the average product cost per order is a monetary value).

In order to work with the calculated member, you need to deploy the project. Once deployed, calculated members will appear under Calculation Tools ➤ Metadata under their appropriate parent. For example, Average Product Cost Per-Order will appear under the Measures node, as this was the parent of this calculation.

It is possible to use a calculation as part of other calculations. It is also possible to use the calculation in the computation of KPIs and to browse the contents of the calculated member using the Cube Designer's Browser tab.

In this example, we used the division operator. As far as MDX goes, there are more elaborate operations, including string concatenation, cross-joins, multiplication, greater than, and Boolean XOR. MDX even includes the standard SQL comment operators (/* paired with */ and --).

Using Functions

In addition to operators, the Calculations window supports all of the functions associated with MDX. These functions are accessed using the Functions tab of the Calculation Tools window, as shown in Figure 20-40. You can drag functions from the Functions tab and drop them in the Expression text box.

Figure 20-40. *Functions tab of the Calculation Tools window*

Using the Functions tab, functions, including those that manipulate and expose key performance indicators, hierarchy navigation, statistics, and string/time manipulation, can be used as part of your calculations. You can see that the Calculation Tools window (including the Metadata and Functions tabs) provides significant assistance in creating and maintaining MDX.

Using Templates

The Calculation Tools window contains one more tab: Templates. This tab offers a variety of standard template computations, including topics such as Analytics, Budgeting, Financial, Forecasting, Internet, and Time Series. For example, the Internet topic includes templates for computing average page loads, distinct visitors over time, downloads over time, and so on. When a template is selected by double-clicking the template name, the fields in the Calculations window are filled in with seed values (calculation name, expression, format string, and so on). For example, clicking Financial ➤ Net Income fills the Expression text box with the following:

```
<<Gross Profit>> - (<<Operating Expenses>> + <<Tax Expense>> + <<Interest>>
+ <<Depreciation>>)
```

This snippet is simply a template. A developer is responsible for filling in the dimension members that are used to compute values, such as gross profit, operating expense, tax expense, interest, and depreciation. A crafty developer might use techniques such as named queries, aliased member names, and calculations (such as a calculation for gross profit) in order to already have values for gross profit, operation expenses, and so on precomputed so they could simply be plugged into the template.

Scripting with MDX

The Calculations tab of the Cube Designer hid a tremendous amount of the complexity associated with the MDX language. In a formal sense, the MDX scripting language is used to populate a cube with calculations. The specific form of the language is that it is composed of statements separated by semicolons. The MDX scripts are actually parts of cubes, just like dimensions and measures.

As a scripting language, MDX is broken down into scripting statements (such as CALCULATE, CASE, FREEZE, and IF), data definition statements (CREATE CUBE, ALTER CUBE, CREATE SET, CREATE DIMENSION, CREATE MEMBER, and so on) and data manipulation statements (INSERT INTO, SELECT, UPDATE, and so on). As is the case with any language, MDX exposes operators (mathematical, comparative, Boolean, and join manipulations) and an incredible suite of functions encompassing metadata manipulation, set operations, statistical computation, date/time computations, string manipulation, and so on. As you saw earlier, you can access these functions through the Functions tab of the Calculation Tools window.

In order to see the raw MDX of a calculation, click the Script View icon in the Calculations window toolbar. When you select the Script View icon for the Average Product Cost Per-Order calculation, you see the following:

```
CALCULATE;
CREATE MEMBER CURRENTCUBE.[MEASURES].[Average Product Cost Per-Order] AS
[Measures].[Total Product Cost]/[Measures].[Order Quantity],
FORMAT_STRING = "Currency", VISIBLE = 1  ;
```

This MDX script is composed of two statements:

- CALCULATE: Computes the value of a subcube or determines the order of how the dimensions in a subcube are computed.

- CREATE MEMBER: A data definition statement in MDX used to create a calculated member.

To return the friendly user interface that facilitates the creation of calculations, click the Form View icon.

The benefits of using BIDS should be clear when compared to the alternative of raw MDX scripting. Extremely sophisticated developers can code directly in MDX. This can be accomplished using the Script View icon in the Calculations window, or within SQL Server Management Studio using File ➤ New ➤ Analysis Services MDX Query.

Working with Key Performance Indicators

Surf to any web site that evaluates stocks, and you will be immediately exposed to a KPI, namely that a given stock is rated based on Strong Buy, Buy, Hold, Sell, and Strong Sell. To add some spice to the web site, rather than simply saying Strong Buy, we can display a thermometer that is fiery red and shooting through the top. Rather than simply saying Strong Sell, we can display a thermometer with the line sunk down to the bottom and the thermometer covered in cold, blue ice. These visual hints often make even mundane analyses more compelling.

A KPI as a quantifiable value (such as Strong Buy or Strong Sell) used to assess a business's performance. From an Analysis Services standpoint, a KPI is a set of computations performed using MDX. These computations are associated with additional information indicating how their results are to be displayed. When the computations determine a company's stock is a Strong Buy, display that bursting red thermometer. Although visual in nature, a KPI is a server-side object. This means that the company web site developed in C# and ASP.NET would get the same thermometer displayed as the company's annual report, which was put together with Microsoft Word and VB .NET. There is a single version of the KPI on the server, and it is accessible to different clients (such as ASP.NET or Microsoft Office).

Within an Analysis Services project, you can work with KPIs by selecting the Cube Designer's KPIs tab.

Creating KPIs

To create a new KPI, click the New KPI icon on the KPIs window's toolbar (hovering your mouse over the toolbar icons displays tooltips showing their functions). You will see the dialog box shown in Figure 20-41.

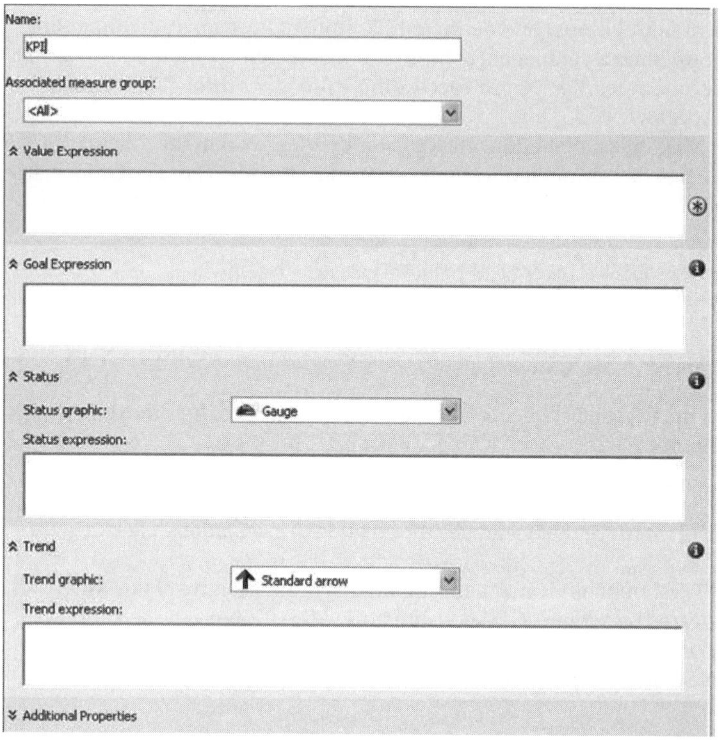

Figure 20-41. *Creating a new KPI*

For demonstration purposes, we will walk through creating a KPI that can measure the profitability of a product. For example, software has a fixed cost and costs next to nothing to manufacture (potentially high profitability). A game console sells at cost or near cost for competitive reasons, and hence has a low profitability. For the purposes of simplicity, profitability is a measure of the sales compared to cost. We will name this KPI Profitability.

A KPI is associated with all measure groups or a specific measure group. Potentially, there could be measure groups for sales, marketing, and human resources. These measure groups are set up in advance and are just categorizations of measures targeted to a specific audience (such as the accounting department or the human resources department). This example will be associated with all measure groups, so we choose <All> from the Associated Measure Group drop-down list.

A useful KPI contains at least two expressions: value and goal. We use MDX to specify these expressions. The value expression is a physical measure, while the goal expression is objective. For our example, we define the value expression as profitability:

```
(
   ([Measures].[Sales Amount] -[Measures].[Total Product Cost])
   / [Measures].[Sales Amount]
)
```

Like the Calculations tab, the KPIs tab contains a Calculation Tools window. We can drag the measures Sales Amount and Total Product Cost from the Calculation Tools window to the Value Expression text box. (The formula here is not sophisticated.) If the cost equals the amount of the sale, the profit is zero (0 percent profit). If the cost is zero, then the profit is 1 (100 percent). The Goal Expression text box is set to 0.80, which means that it is desirable that costs represent no more than 20 percent of a sale.

BIDS provides a set of status graphics that include a traffic light, a gauge similar to a car's fuel gauge, a thermometer, and faces with various expressions (ranging from smiling to indifferent to sad). Each graphic gauges business performance across a range of values from −1 (e.g., WorldCom, Enron) to 1 (e.g., Berkshire Hathaway, Microsoft). For the purpose of this example, we can select the smiley face.

A certain type of expression, called a status expression, generates the values used by the status graphic when displaying the KPI. Given that a range of values from −1 to 1 needs to be produced for the status expression, MDX's CASE scripting statement is ideal, as it behaves just like CASE in standard SQL. The status expression for our example is as follows:

```
CASE
  WHEN /* 60% looking good so 1 */
    ((([Measures].[Sales Amount] -  [Measures].[Total Product Cost])
        / [Measures].[Sales Amount])> 0.60) THEN 1
  WHEN /* between 30 and 60 percent profit, okay but not great  so zero */
    ((([Measures].[Sales Amount] - [Measures].[Total Product Cost])
        / [Measures].[Sales Amount])> 0.30) THEN 0
  WHEN /* between 10 and 30 percent profit, okay but not great  so -0.5 */
    ((([Measures].[Sales Amount] - [Measures].[Total Product Cost])
        / [Measures].[Sales Amount])> 0.10) THEN -0.5
  ELSE -1 /* less 10% or less profit or maybe even a loss so -1 */
END
```

The comments in this status expression explain what each WHEN clause of the CASE statement is looking to indicate. For example, 60 percent profit is good, while less than 10 percent profit is extremely bad.

An additional measure is useful with a KPI, namely a trend expression. This expression represents the current behavior of the value expression as compared to the goal expression. The trend expression helps the business user to determine quickly whether the value expression is getting better or worse relative to the goal expression. You can associate one of several graphics with the trend expression to help business users to understand the trend. Consider a soccer game. One team might be leading 3 to 1 (hence the status expression is a smiley face); however, having 5 players on the team in the lead start to feel poorly would result in a trend expression indicated by a down arrow, as there could be 11 players facing only 6 opponents. The trend would indicate that a 3-to-1 lead might not be safe if half the players on the team in the lead are unable to play due to illness.

For a trend graphic for our example, we will select the standard arrow. Indicating how a trend behaves requires comparing the past values to the present values, which you can see in the following trend expression for our example:

```
CASE
  WHEN
    (((([Measures].[Sales Amount] - [Measures].[Total.Product Cost]) >
(((([Order Date].[Fiscal Time].PrevMember, [Measures].[Sales Amount]) -
      ([Order Date].[Fiscal Time].PrevMember, [Measures].[Total Product Cost]))
  THEN 1
  ELSE -1
END
```

Browsing KPIs

The KPIs window's toolbar also contains an icon for the Browser view. Clicking this icon, which looks like a magnifying glass in front a stack of folded towels, displays the current status of the KPI and enables filters to be associated with the KPI (to fine-tune the range of value over which the KPI applies). Figure 20-42 shows the Profitability KPI created in the previous section in the Browser view.

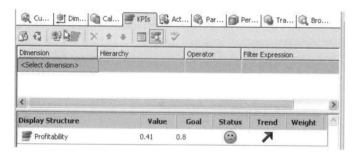

Figure 20-42. *KPI Browser view*

It should be evident from the sad face that the status of profitability goal is not being met. Over time, the trend is positive (meaning we are becoming more profitable). Still, the goal is 0.80 (80 percent) and the present profitability is 0.41 (41 percent).

It might benefit the AdventureWorks Bicycle Company to jettison their least profitable products (accessories, bikes, clothing, and so on). Using the Dimension column above the displayed KPI, we can create a filter to explore the profitability of each catalog, subcatalog, or profit. The behavior of these filters directly parallels that of the Cube Designer's Browser window functionality, described earlier in this chapter.

Using Analysis Services Scripting Language

ASSL is the scripting language used by clients to communicate with Analysis Services. SQL Server Management Studio and BIDS both use ASSL and its command subdialect, XML/A. ASSL may be used by developers as a means to programmatically communicate with Analysis Services.

To examine an ASSL command, we will create an object whose underlying representation is ASSL. As each object type within a project (data source, DSV, dimension, cube, and so on) is represented by ASSL, using BIDS to manipulate ASSL will enable us to explore the complexities and power associated with this language. For this example, we will add a named query to a DSV.

Creating a DSV with a Named Query

When browsing data, a customer's LastName displays in conjunction with Sales Amount. It would be possible to display both the LastName and the FirstName columns, but this is an inconvenient way to view named data, such as "Show me all people named Patel who bought bike helmets." It might make more sense to include a full name (LastName + ", " + FirstName) so customers could be uniquely identified, say, Preshant Patel vs. Baiju Patel. We can use a named query for this.

A named query in a DSV is similar to a view within a relational database. The benefit of a named query is that it does not require changes to the source system because the expression defining the named query is stored within Analysis Services.

Create a named query by double-clicking a DSV within Solution Explorer to open the Data Source View Designer (or select View ➤ Designer), which shows the database diagram of tables and named queries for the DSV. To create a named query, right-click an empty region in the designer and select the New Named Query option. You will see the Create Named Query dialog box.

In the Name text box, enter the name of the named query, **DimCustomerMaster** in this example. Enter the code associated with generating the named query at the bottom of the dialog box, as shown in Figure 20-43. After you click OK, the named query will be added to the Data Source View Designer.

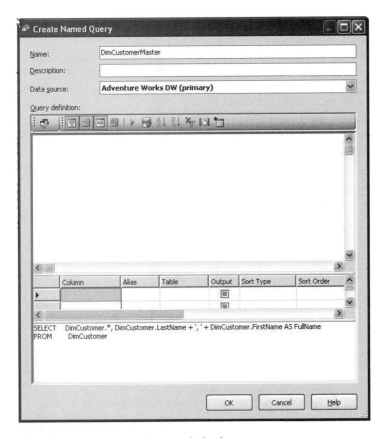

Figure 20-43. *Create Named Query dialog box*

684 CHAPTER 20 ■ ANALYSIS SERVICES

The new named query added to the designer still needs some work before it can be used. Specifically, the named query does not contain a primary key and does not have relationships set up to other tables in the diagram. To add these missing entities, do the following:

1. Right-click the CustomerKey column of the DimCustomerMaster named query and select Set Logical Primary Key. This causes this named view to mirror the primary key of the DimCustomer table.

2. Drag the DimCustomerMaster.GeographyKey column and drop it on the like-named column in the DimGeography table. This sets up the GeographyKey foreign key in the DimCustomerMaster named query.

3. Drag the FactInternetSales.CustomerKey column and drop it onto the primary key for the DimCustomerMaster named query (DimCustomerMaster.CustomerKey).

In order to use this newly created named query, either a new cube must be created or a dimension of an existing cube must be edited. If every cube in the Analysis Services project used the named query instead of the underlying table, DimCustomer, it would be possible to delete the source table from the DSV. It is better to remove the table, if using a named query in its place, so that you have no superfluous entities hanging around.

Viewing the ASSL

The best way to experience the power of ASSL is to select the DSV in Solution Explorer and display the code window (select View ➤ Code). Figure 20-44 shows the code for the DSV we modified in the previous section.

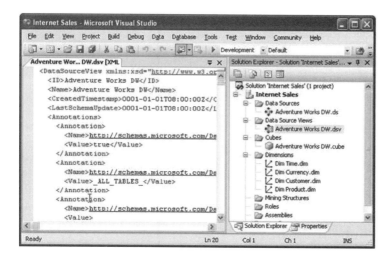

Figure 20-44. *ASSL for a DSV*

Given the readability of XML, the ASSL snippet should be understandable because it is composed of elements such as <DataSourceView>, <ID>, and <Name>. Each of these elements is fully documented in SQL Server Books Online, along with aptly named elements such as <DataSource>, <Cube>, <Dimension>, and <Measure>. Looking through the file for our named query, you can find the name DimCustomerMaster inside the hierarchy of a <Diagram> element, representing the designer view associated with the DSV:

```
<xs:element name="DimCustomerMaster"
  msprop:QueryDefinition="SELECT CustomerKey, GeographyKey,
      CustomerAlternateKey, Title, FirstName,
```

Like most XML formats, ASSL is simple to understand but lengthy to write. You can use SQL Server Management Studio to develop such code (File ➤ New ➤ Analysis Services XMLA Query). Clearly, this highly granular type of development is designed for a very narrow group of applications.

In all, the AdventureWorksDW DSV has more than 1,100 lines of XML in it. The cube developed for the Analysis Services project has more than 1,000 lines. The time it would take to work programmatically with raw XML at the ASSL level, including XML/A to pass commands to Analysis Services, is far greater than working with the graphical environments such as Management Studio and BIDS. Developers requiring a low level of granular access to Analysis Services and companies such as CA, which makes data-modeling software, are candidates for using ASSL and XML/A.

Summary

This chapter introduced the key concepts of Analysis Services, including the architecture, enhancements in SQL Server 2008, and the core objects and concepts used by Analysis Services. We looked at Analysis Services projects within BIDS. It is common for developers to be somewhat overwhelmed by the number of features exposed by Analysis Services projects within BIDS. The best advice for Analysis Services users is to start simply and gradually build up to projects that are more complex.

We also presented the administration of Analysis Services and touched on ASSL and XML/A. You saw that ASSL is extremely powerful and may be useful to developers who need precise, programmatic administration of their Analysis Services environment. Similarly, we touched on MDX in the context of calculations and KPIs. Like ASSL, MDX is an extremely powerful and complex language. BIDS dramatically simplifies development using MDX scripting, and where possible, BIDS should be used to save time.

BI development, which encompasses Analysis Services, Integration Services, and Reporting Services, is a complex but greatly rewarding arena. The previous chapter covered SQL Server Reporting Services. The next chapter covers Integration Services.

■ ■ ■

Integration Services

Starting with SQL Server 2005, SQL Server Integration Services (SSIS) replaced Data Transformation Services (DTS) as Microsoft's enterprise class Extract, Transform, and Load (ETL) tool. The key goal of SSIS is to bring user productivity, scalability, and advanced transformation logic to those building ETL solutions on the Microsoft platform.

As you'll learn in this chapter, Microsoft's investments in SSIS have continued in SQL Server 2008, with the addition of capabilities such as caching transformations, enhanced lookup transformations, data profiling, and a set of expanded data sources.

This chapter covers the following topics:

- An overview of SSIS features and uses
- SSIS fundamentals—control flow, data flow, and event handling
- Control Flow Designer and Data Flow Designer tasks
- The new Change Data Capture feature
- SSIS logging
- The Package Configuration Organizer
- Variable creation and configuration
- Precedence constraints and checkpoints
- SSIS transaction support
- SSIS package deployment, migration, and scheduling

An Overview of SSIS Features

In SQL Server 2008, SSIS continues to be the Swiss army knife of the ETL world by enabling you to perform many tasks, including the following:

- Importing and exporting data between SQL Server instances and heterogeneous data sources
- Applying sophisticated transformations against data
- Automating SQL Server maintenance tasks and business processes
- Executing scripts
- Sending e-mail notifications
- Cleansing, duplicating, and profiling data (to ensure data quality)
- Interacting with message queues and FTP sites

- Launching Analysis Services processes

- Submitting data-mining queries

- Processing and manipulating XML files

- Querying your computer using Windows Management Instrumentation (WMI) queries and responding to events accordingly

Many of us have spent the past several years converting or rewriting our packages from DTS into SSIS. It is probably pretty safe to say that most of us had mixed emotions about our first experiences with SSIS; things seemed so easy with DTS. However, after spending a few days getting used to the SSIS development environment, the separation of control flow from data flow, the greatly expanded list of built-in transformations, and the advanced package configurations, most people have found that they are much more productive with SSIS than they were with DTS. Some of the added sophistication comes with the fact that SSIS is truly an enterprise ETL tool. Moving forward, you'll be happy to know that most, if not all, investment of time that you have made in SSIS will transfer nicely into the SQL Server 2008 version of SSIS.

When Can You Use SSIS?

With SQL Server 2008, Microsoft has added several new features, improved existing features, and removed problem areas. Database administrators (DBAs) and developers alike can use SSIS to address a wide variety of business solutions. The following are some scenarios in which SSIS can be used:

- A real estate company is building a property search web site that allows users to search for properties by city and county. It receives several denormalized flat files from third-party multiple listing services. Each of the third-party providers produces flat files differently, so the solution must be flexible. Each of these files must be imported, scrubbed, and put into the same normalized tables in the database. SSIS is used to import the files via FTP, scrub them using transformations, and load them into the production tables.

- A manufacturing company trains new plant managers on how to use a parts-tracking maintenance application. During training, trainees are allowed to connect to their own test database, where they can modify the data without doing harm to the production data. Nightly, an SSIS package is scheduled to refresh the data in the training databases, based on real data from a production database.

- A financial services company uses legacy systems to track an individual investor's transactions to his or her savings plan. These legacy systems allow simple OLE DB connectivity to the raw transactional data. A reader-friendly reporting database isn't available. Executives want to be able to view aggregated transaction data grouped by investment and time period. SSIS is used to extract data from the legacy systems into a SQL Server database.

- An information technology company wants to automate the extraction and reporting on the condition of its SQL Server environment. The company wants to maintain a central reporting database in SQL Server that will contain various statistics about all SQL Server machines (SQL Server Agent jobs, SQL Error and Agent logs, database file locations, and the last time each database was backed up). SSIS is used to query each server and extract the data to the centralized reporting database.

- A human resources (HR) department in a small regional office receives daily "new employee" files from corporate headquarters. Each file contains a single record of data for each new employee. Included in this record is a BLOB image containing the photo of the new employee. The HR department uses SSIS to import the character data into one table and output the image BLOB into a separate image file (using the Export Column transformation).

What's New in SSIS?

The foundational components of SSIS haven't changed from SQL Server 2005 to 2008. However, there have been many enhancements made to ensure that SSIS can scale to meet the needs of the most advanced data warehousing scenarios, to ensure that SSIS continues to be easy to use and a very productive environment, and to expand the number of data sources supported out of the box. Some SQL Server 2008 feature highlights include the following:

- An enhanced lookup operator supports more flexible levels of caching.

- Improvements in thread utilization ensure that machine resources are put to their best use and that the maximum number of pipeline components are running in parallel.

- The new Change Data Capture feature and merge (upsert) capabilties are supported within the core SQL Server 2008 relational engine. The introduction of these capabilities has many ETL designers very excited, because they will greatly simplify what, in the past, has been a complex problem to solve.

- New data profiling (data quality) functionality provides advanced algorithms for identifying patterns within data values.

- Visual Studio Tools for Applications (VSTA) support has replaced the Visual Studio for Applications (VSA) engine and provides more advanced .NET scripting capabilties.

- Improvements in package logging and diagnostics make debugging package problems and production issues much easier.

- Full ADO.NET support has been added, along with Office 2007 ACE provider support and LOB adapters for Oracle, Teradata, and SAP.

- Enhancements to the Import/Export Wizard include more intuitive error messages, which are helpful to those who aren't intimately familiar with SSIS.

- Full support is provided for DTS packages running within SQL Server 2008. More advanced upgrade functionality will further assist those individuals with dozens of DTS packages to convert to SSIS. Often, very complex DTS packages become fairly trivial within SSIS because of the separation of control flow from data flow and the inclusion of advanced transformations.

We'll discuss these new features and improvements throughout this chapter.

The SSIS Integrated Development Environment

If you've worked with Visual Studio, you'll be familiar with the layout of the SSIS integrated development enviroment (IDE), which, like SQL Server development for Reporting Services and Analysis Services, exists within Business Intelligence Development Studio (BIDS). In fact, BIDS is just a scaled-down version of Visual Studio, and therefore employs the Visual Studio concepts of projects and solutions. (A *project* is a container that groups related files and can contain one or more packages, and a *solution* is a container that groups and manages projects used to develop business solutions.)

Another advantage of developing within BIDS is that developers are typically much more comfortable with this environment and therefore much more productive. Any investment in application lifecycle management (ALM) technologies, such as Visual Studio Team Foundation Server, can now be leveraged not only for .NET application development, but also for SQL Server development. The source files for SSIS packages are all XML, so versioning within your source control system is possible.

Within this environment, development is performed in BIDS, and the management of SSIS packages becomes the realm of the SSIS command-line utility, SQL Server Agent jobs, and SQL Server Management Studio (the Integration Services node). Management Studio allows you to import packages to and export packages from the msdb database and file system; start, stop, and monitor both local and remote packages; and change package configuration settings.

> ■**Note** A common misssconception is that SSIS requires the SQL Server database engine in order to function. In fact, SSIS is a totally independent component of the SQL Server product. It does not require any other component of SQL Server to be installed on the server. For example, it is possible, and quite common, to install SSIS and perform integrations between a DB2 database and an Oracle database.

Connecting to SSIS in Management Studio

After you have installed SSIS (typically, during the installation of SQL Server 2008) and started the service, you can connect to it from Management Studio. You can manage SSIS settings and its running status within the SQL Server Configuration Manager under SQL Server Services.

With the service running, here are the steps to connect from within Management Studio:

1. In Object Explorer, click the Connect button and select Integration Services.

2. In the Connect to Server dialog box, type in the name of the server where the Integration Services service is located (the machine name). SSIS doesn't support the notion of named instances as does the SQL Server database engine.

3. The Integration Services node will now appear in Object Explorer. Expand the Running Packages folder. Unless SSIS packages are currently running, you won't see any packages.

4. Expand the Stored Packages folder. Notice the File System folder and MSDB folders, as shown in Figure 21-1. By right-clicking either of these folders, you can create subdirectories for storage of your packages, and execute, rename, or perform other package operations. We'll review how you create and edit packages in the next section.

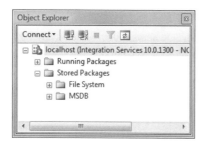

Figure 21-1. *The Integration Services node in Object Explorer*

Notably missing from Management Studio functionality is the ability to create, modify, debug, test, and deploy an SSIS package. For these tasks, you must use BIDS.

Creating a New SSIS Project in BIDS

To create a new SSIS project, open BIDS and select File ➤ New Project. In the New Project dialog box, under Project types, select Business Intelligence Projects, and under Templates, select Integration Services Project. In the Name field, type a name for your project—MyFirstSSISProject for the examples in this chapter. Leave the check box for Create Directory for Solution checked, and click OK.

You'll notice that there are many windows and design surfaces in BIDS. In the next section, we'll review each of these design surfaces and windows, describing what they are and how they are used.

SSIS Fundamentals

If you used SSIS in SQL Server 2005, you shouldn't have a problem transferring those skills to SSIS in SQL Server 2008. The core of SSIS remains the *package*. A package is a collection/container of tasks, connections, subcontainers, and workflow that can be executed via a command-line utility (DTEXEC), scheduled as a SQL Server Agent job, or designed and debugged from BIDS.

As a review for those who are just beginning the transition from SQL Server 2000's DTS to SSIS, the DTS Designer had a single design surface on which were placed all DTS tasks, connections, workflow (precedence constraints), and transformations. For simpler packages, this was acceptable; however, as the packages increased in complexity, it became more difficult to discern what activities the package was actually performing. To address this, the SSIS Designer, shown in Figure 21-2, divides the workspace into five new areas: the Control Flow design surface, the Data Flow design surface, the Event Handlers design surface, the Package Explorer window, and the Connection Managers area. You'll also see Toolbox, Solution Explorer, and Properties windows.

■**Note** The DTS design surface layout matched very closely to the execution flow of the runtime code. Think back to your DTS packages and try to determine where parallel processing was performed. The separation of control flow from data flow within SSIS allows for a clean delineation between areas of the package that can be run in parallel. This new architecture has allowed SSIS to efficiently handle the largest enterprise data warehousing solutions in the world and to take full advantage of all hardware resources.

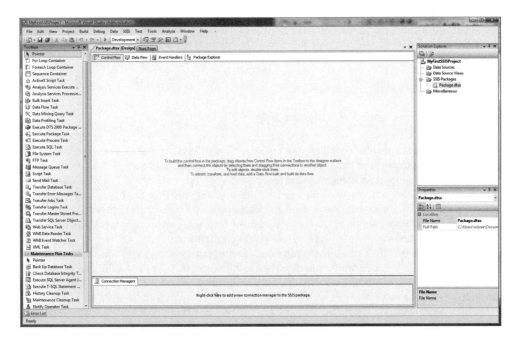

Figure 21-2. *SSIS Designer interface*

An Overview of the SSIS Designer

You use the Control Flow design surface to place tasks, containers, and precedence constraints (which define package workflow). An SSIS package can contain one or more *tasks*. A task is a unit of work performed during the runtime of an SSIS package execution. Tasks perform various activities such as moving data, executing Transact-SQL (T-SQL) commands, using File Transfer Protocol (FTP), sending mail notifications, and much more. SSIS provides several out-of-the-box tasks that perform various operations. (We'll review some of these tasks in the "Control Flow and Data Flow Designer Tasks" section later in the chapter.)

SSIS also introduces a new type of object and concept, the *task container*, of which there are four kinds: the Sequence container, the Foreach Loop container, the For Loop container, and the Task Host container. These containers are used to hold other tasks or containers, providing hierarchical (parent/child container) control to the package. Containers group tasks together into a meaningful unit of work, allowing you to, for example, participate in an SSIS transaction (described in the "Transactions" section later in the chapter). Depending on the type of container task, you can also perform iterative and conditional loop processing against the tasks held within the container. Figure 21-3 shows an example of a Sequence container on the Control Flow design surface. Containers are described in detail in the "Control Flow Containers and Tasks" section later in the chapter.

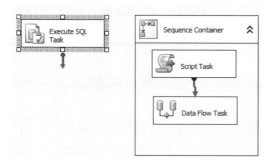

Figure 21-3. *A Sequence container that contains tasks*

Packages and tasks are also considered to be containers in SSIS. A package is a container that can contain other containers or tasks. A Task Host container encapsulates a single task, which you configure by setting properties specific to that task.

Using the SSIS Designer, you can add a task within your SSIS package by simply dragging the selected task from the Toolbox window (by default, located on the left side of the IDE) onto the Control Flow design surface. After placing a task on the design surface, you can proceed to set the various properties and settings unique to the type of task you're configuring.

Once you've defined the tasks that should execute within the package, you'll most likely want to define their workflow. For example, you may wish to run a specific task only if the preceding task succeeds. Other workflow possibilities include executing a task only if the preceding task fails or regardless of failure or success.

On the Control Flow design surface, you can define both the order of operation and workflow by using *precedence constraints*. Precedence constraints are used to connect executables in the package, helping to order the workflow as well as define the conditions under which the tasks run. If no precedence constraints are defined, during package execution (runtime), all tasks will attempt to run simultaneously (or in no particular order). Figure 21-4 shows the On Success and On Failure precedence constraints between tasks. The left arrow (which is green in the designer) defines the On Success precedence, and the right arrow (which is red in the designer) defines the On Failure precedence constraint. A blue arrow indicates an On Completion precedence constraint. We'll discuss precedence constraints in more detail in the "Precedence Constraints" section later in this chapter.

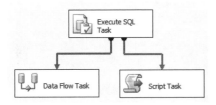

Figure 21-4. *On Success and On Failure precedence constraints between tasks on the Control Flow design surface*

Annotations are text labels that can be added to the Control Flow and Data Flow design surfaces, allowing you to self-document the SSIS package. You can add an annotation by right-clicking the design surface and selecting Add Annotation. Figure 21-5 shows an example of an annotation added to the Control Flow design surface.

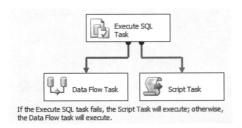

Figure 21-5. *Adding an annotation to the Control Flow design surface*

When you add at least one Data Flow task to the Control Flow design surface, you can access the Data Flow design surface. Data Flow tasks consist of source adapters (where data is extracted from), destination adapters (where data is imported into), and transformations (actions taken against the data before being passed to the next transformation or destination adapter). These objects are available from the Toolbox on the Data Flow design surface. We'll discuss these components in detail in the "Data Flow Designer Tasks" section later in this chapter.

When working with Data Flow components, you use *paths* to connect them together. A path connects the output of one component to the input of another. A path allows two workflow options: a "success" (green) path or an "error" (red) path.

Once connected by a path, the resulting set of connected data flow components is called a *graph*. In the example in Figure 21-6, an OLE DB source is used as a source adapter, connected to a Character Map transformation, which writes data to an OLE DB destination adapter. (The Character Map transformation allows you to apply string functions to character data—for example, to change the source data from lowercase to uppercase.)

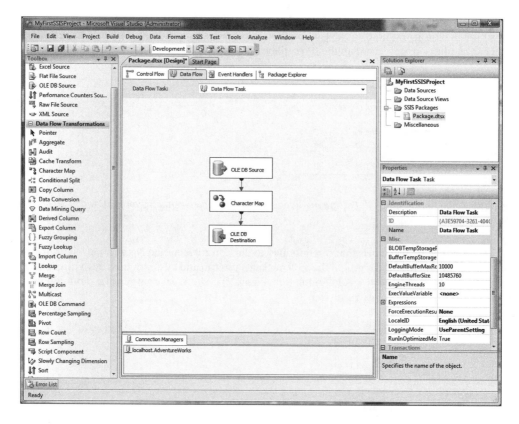

Figure 21-6. *Sample data flow graph*

Package Explorer is a separate tab that allows you to view the various elements of the SSIS package in a hierarchical fashion, as shown in Figure 21-7. You can use Package Explorer to view many elements of the SSIS package, including variables, executables, precedence constraints, event handlers, connections, and log providers. We'll discuss all these elements in more detail in later sections of this chapter.

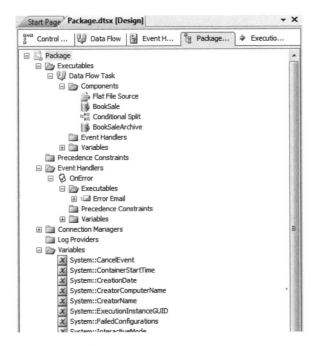

Figure 21-7. *Examining a package in Package Explorer*

Beneath the Control Flow, Data Flow, and Event Handlers design surfaces is the Connection Managers area. An SSIS connection manager is used to connect to data sources. Some of the available sources include a flat file, OLE DB, Excel, ODBC, cache, and FTP. By default, for a new package, this area is empty. To create a new connection, right-click anywhere within the empty Connection Managers area.

■**Note** Connections are not the end-all, be-all when it comes to transferring data. A connection can be used in conjunction with Data Flow or other Control Flow tasks. For example, if you were to create a connection to a specific SQL Server instance, that connection will be available for use within the Execute SQL task and Data Flow task.

Solution Explorer allows you to view and manage packages within your SSIS project, as shown in Figure 21-8. By right-clicking the SSIS Packages folder, you can choose to create a new package for the solution, launch the Import/Export Wizard, or migrate DTS packages from SQL Server 2000.

Figure 21-8. *Solution Explorer in SSIS*

The Properties window allows you to view and modify the properties of the SSIS package and its objects (tasks, containers, and connections), as shown in Figure 21-9. This window is context sensitive and will display properties based on the selected object.

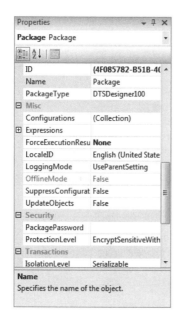

Figure 21-9. *Properties window for an SSIS package*

At this point, we have briefly discussed the major components of an SSIS package. Let's take a step back and review before beginning an example. The highest level unit of work within SSIS is the *package*. Each package can contain exactly one *control flow* and zero or more *data flows*. Each control flow contains one or more *tasks* and *task containers*. A particular type of task is the Data Flow task. Adding one or more of this particular task type to a control flow is how you create data flows. Each Data Flow task gets its own design palette and can contain one or more *data sources*, *transformations*, and *data destinations*. In all cases, the various executable components (tasks, sources, transformations, and destinations) are linked together with *precedence constraints*, as is the case with control flows, or with *paths*, as is the case with data flows. Figure 21-10 illustrates these concepts.

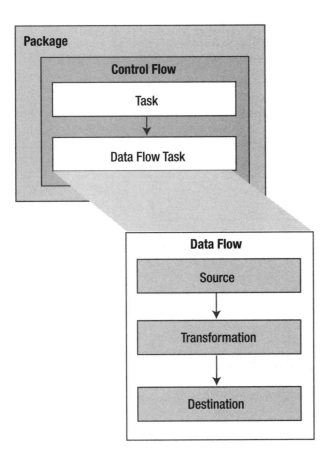

Figure 21-10. *Package hierarchy and data flow in the SSIS Designer*

■**Tip** Even though the SSIS Designer contains separate areas for control flow and data flow, it is still best practice to separate very large ETL applications into multiple smaller packages within an SSIS solution. This allows for multiple developers to work on separate pieces in parallel more easily. It can also facilitate a shorter test cycle, depending on the nature of your testing process.

A Data Flow Example

The example in this section will give you a preview of the SSIS Data Flow design surface functionality. Don't worry if you don't understand all the steps you're performing—the purpose of this exercise is just to familiarize you with the primary concepts before diving into the details later in the chapter.

SSIS is commonly used to import data from external flat files into SQL Server database tables. Flat file integration is often an easier data exchange solution than attempting to move data directly between different relational database or mainframe systems. A DB2 system DBA, for example, may find it easier to dump out data into flat files for the SQL Server DBA to consume, rather than attempting to connect via native methods.

As an example, we'll use SSIS to import data from a single BookSales.txt file. We'll import this data into two tables in the BookSale database (which we'll create in this exercise). Data from the year 2008 will be imported into the BookSale table. Book sales from before 2008 will be put into the BookSaleArchive table.

Creating the Sample Data Source and Destination

In Management Studio, open a new query window connected to your SQL Server instance and execute the following script (to create the BookSeller database and tables):

```
-- Create the BookSeller database with default settings
CREATE DATABASE BookSeller
GO


USE BookSeller
GO


-- The BookSale table is for current-year sales
CREATE TABLE dbo.BookSale
    (BookSaleID int IDENTITY(1,1) NOT NULL PRIMARY KEY,
     ISBN char(10),
     SoldDate datetime NOT NULL,
     SoldPrice money NOT NULL)
GO


-- The BookSaleArchive table is for previous-year sales
CREATE TABLE dbo.BookSaleArchive
    (BookSaleArchiveID int IDENTITY(1,1) NOT NULL PRIMARY KEY,
     ISBN char(10),
     SoldDate datetime NOT NULL,
     SoldPrice money NOT NULL)
GO
```

For the source data, we'll use the BookSales.txt comma-delimited file, which you can download from the Source Code/Download area of the Apress web site (http://www.apress.com). Create a new directory on your SQL Server instance called C:\Apress\, and then download the BookSales.txt file to that directory. The columns included in the file are ISBN, SoldDate, and SoldPrice, in that order:

```
1700670127    2007-10-13 12:23:54.890000000    31.434
2190414452    2007-12-11 12:23:55.080000000    91.5634
9163370433    2007-10-23 12:23:55.080000000    93.8803
8240890662    2007-11-02 12:23:55.080000000    72.5189
9724485384    2007-11-01 12:23:55.080000000    42.3559
3818073842    2007-10-10 12:23:55.080000000    35.5185
4354109840    2007-11-07 12:23:55.080000000    77.4156
3841883691    2007-10-19 12:23:55.090000000    5.2721
8248344093    2007-11-23 12:23:55.090000000    27.8866
7742829934    2007-09-29 12:23:55.090000000    96.8699
3972918159    2007-11-30 12:23:55.090000000    80.8913
3387357000    2007-11-05 12:23:55.090000000    37.0749
3020951299    2007-10-31 12:23:55.090000000    55.7052
5062025755    2007-10-01 12:23:55.090000000    25.1956
7794466091    2007-12-15 12:23:55.090000000    79.8708
```

3613708504	2007-11-09 12:23:55.090000000	17.2435
7033565864	2007-10-22 12:23:55.090000000	92.4496
4632544057	2007-10-08 12:23:55.090000000	89.7585
5004909486	2007-09-23 12:23:55.090000000	31.6866
1916341917	2007-12-02 12:23:55.090000000	42.531
9828905102	2008-03-12 12:24:05.837000000	31.4099
4401326876	2008-02-01 12:24:05.837000000	29.9687
4439395032	2008-02-14 12:24:05.837000000	13.013
6062292933	2008-02-12 12:24:05.837000000	5.6384
2497442656	2007-12-29 12:24:05.837000000	92.9495
4405919414	2008-02-19 12:24:05.837000000	39.628
7499038595	2007-12-29 12:24:05.837000000	55.5942
799884766	2008-03-02 12:24:05.837000000	32.4062
7137023232	2008-01-04 12:24:05.837000000	64.077
9857116326	2008-03-25 12:24:05.837000000	21.5201
6858375361	2008-02-04 12:24:05.837000000	79.6188
2811816672	2008-02-07 12:24:05.837000000	77.5774
6066791506	2008-02-17 12:24:05.837000000	51.4393
8398729596	2008-02-15 12:24:05.837000000	27.2878
6016191510	2008-03-28 12:24:05.837000000	15.7501
5739941273	2008-01-19 12:24:05.837000000	71.9712
2507570361	2008-03-12 12:24:05.837000000	56.2592
6272684851	2008-03-13 12:24:05.847000000	93.4991
388103114	2008-04-03 12:24:05.847000000	76.8347
9602390361	2008-02-15 12:24:05.847000000	2.4937

Creating a Connection to SQL Server

This next set of steps shows you how to create a connection to SQL Server, which you can then use as a data source and destination.

1. Within BIDS, select File ➤ New Project.

2. In the New Project dialog box, under Templates, select Integration Services Project. In the Name field, type BookSalesImport. Leave the check box for Create Directory for Solution checked. Click OK.

3. By default, the BookSalesImport project is created with a single package named Package.dtsx. In Solution Explorer, right-click Package.dtsx and select Rename. Change the name to BookSalesImport.dtsx.

4. From the Toolbox, drag the Data Flow task onto the Control Flow design surface.

5. Double-click the Data Flow task to switch to the Data Flow design surface.

6. In the Connection Managers area, beneath the Data Flow design surface, right-click a blank area and select New OLE DB Connection.

7. Click the New button to create a new data connection manager. The Connection Manager dialog box appears.

8. In the Server Name field, select or enter the name of your SQL Server instance and select the logon method. For the database, select BookSeller. Your dialog box should look like Figure 21-11.

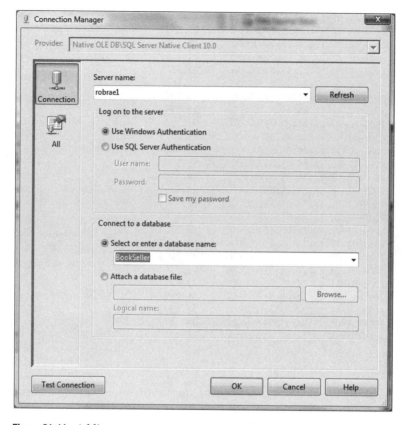

Figure 21-11. *Adding a new connection manager for an OLE DB connection*

9. Click OK, and then click OK again to select the new data connection manager.

Your new connection manager should now appear in the Connection Managers area of the SSIS Designer.

Creating a Data Source

Next, we'll create a connection manager for the BookSales.txt text file, which will be used to pull the data into a transformation.

1. In the Connection Managers area, click a blank spot and select New Flat File Connection.

2. In the Flat File Connection Manager Editor dialog box, type BookSales.txt in the Connection Manager Name field. In the File Name area, select the location of the BookSales.txt file, as shown in Figure 21-12. Take this opportunity to get an initial look at the general configuration options for the flat file connection. Notice that SSIS has full support for Unicode text and also supports various code pages for non-Unicode text. Various formats (fixed, delimited, and ragged right) and other information about the qualifiers, delimiters, and header rows can also be specified within this dialog box.

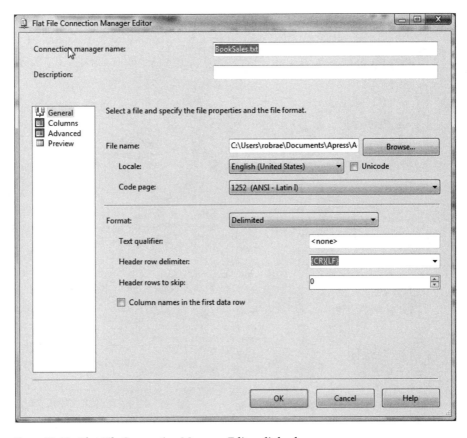

Figure 21-12. *Flat File Connection Manager Editor dialog box*

3. Click the Columns selection in the left navigation pane. This will show the default row and column delimiters identified by the application (tab delimited should be selected). You should see that the three columns were identified, as shown in Figure 21-13.

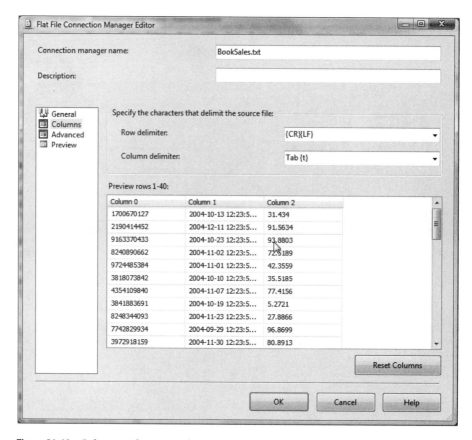

Figure 21-13. *Columns selection in the Flat File Connection Manager Editor*

4. Click Advanced in the left navigation pane. This will show the properties of each column. You need to ensure that each column is interpreted as the proper datatype. Column 0, which is the ISBN column, is already set properly to the string [DT_STR] datatype, as shown in Figure 21-14. For Column 0, change the OutputColumnWidth property to a value of 10.

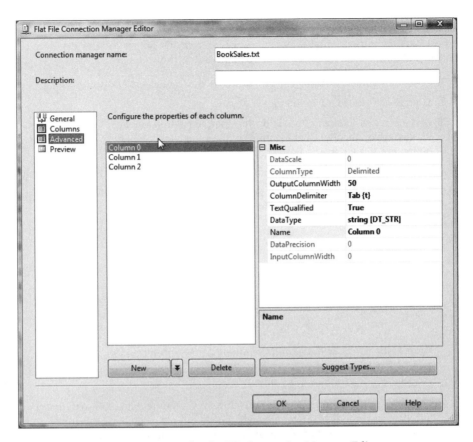

Figure 21-14. *Advanced settings in the Flat File Connection Manager Editor*

5. Click Column 1 (SoldDate) and change its datatype to date [DT_DATE].

6. Click Column 2 (SoldPrice) and change its datatype to currency [DT_CY].

7. Click OK to accept the settings.

Creating the Data Flow

The next steps demonstrate how to use the connections to SQL Server and the text file to create a data flow, allowing you to import the values of the text file into a table.

1. From the Toolbox, drag the Flat File source to the Data Flow design surface.

2. Double-click the Flat File source.

3. In the Flat File Source Editor dialog box, the Connection Manager field should default to the BookSales connection. Click Columns in the left navigation pane. Notice the three checked columns. Click OK to accept the defaults.

4. From the Toolbox, drag the Conditional Split transformation to the Data Flow design surface.

5. Click the Flat File source so that a green arrow appears. Click and drag the green arrow to the Conditional Split transformation, as shown in Figure 21-15.

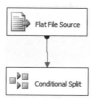

Figure 21-15. *Flat File Source and Conditional Split transformation*

6. Double-click the Conditional Split transformation.

7. The Conditional Split transformation allows you to route data rows to different outputs based on a condition/expression you define. In this case, you'll use this transformation to route book sales rows that belong to the year 2008 to the BookSale table, and rows from previous years will be routed to the BookSaleArchive table. Begin by clicking Columns in the left navigation pane. Notice that available columns from the Flat File source are listed.

8. Click in the Condition cell in the bottom pane and enter the following expression:

```
YEAR( [Column 1])==2008
```

9. Press Enter. Notice that the default output name is Case 1. This expression evaluates Column 1, the SoldDate column, to confirm whether the row belongs to the year 2008.

10. Write a second expression beneath Case 1 that evaluates if a row belongs to a year prior to 2008, as shown in Figure 21-16.

```
YEAR( [Column 1])<2008
```

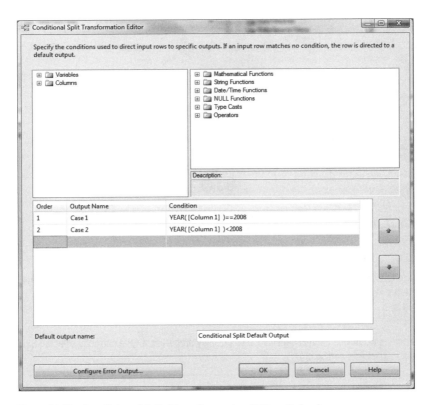

Figure 21-16. *Conditional Split Transformation Editor dialog box*

11. Click OK.

■**Note** YEAR([Column 1])<2008 is an example of an SSIS *expression*. Expressions are used within the Conditional Split and Derived Column transformations, and within variables, precedence constraints, and loop containers. If you have used T-SQL before, some of the functions and operators in the expressions may be familiar to you; however, there are several differences, too. For more information about SSIS expressions, see the SQL Server Books Online topics "Using Expressions in Packages" and "SSIS Expression Concepts."

---

12. From the Toolbox, drag the OLE DB Destination to the design surface of the Data Flow tab.

13. Connect the Conditional Split transformation to the OLE DB Destination by dragging the green connector (which appears when you click the Conditional Split). You will be prompted in the Input Output Selection dialog box to select an output. Select Case 1, as shown in Figure 21-17, which evaluates rows belonging to the year 2008.

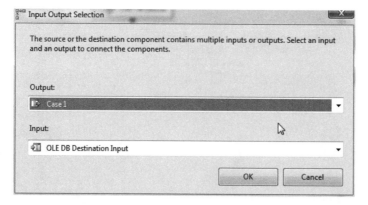

Figure 21-17. *Input Output Selection dialog box*

14. Click OK. Notice that Case 1 now appears by the green path.

15. Click the OLE DB destination, and in the Properties window (the lower-right window), rename it to BookSale, as shown in Figure 21-18.

■**Note** The Properties window is context sensitive. It will display properties for the currently selected SSIS object (task, transformation, package, and so on).

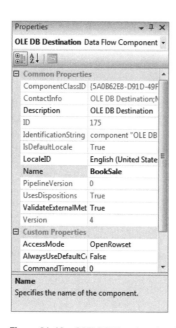

Figure 21-18. *OLE DB Destination Properties window*

16. Double-click the BookSale destination.

17. Change the name of the table or the view to [dbo].[BookSale].

18. Select Mappings from the left navigation pane. This is the screen where you define which input columns (from the Conditional Split transformation) are mapped to which destination columns. Click and drag the input columns to the output column mappings, mapping Column 0 to ISBN, Column 1 to SoldDate, and Column 2 to SoldPrice, as shown in Figure 21-19.

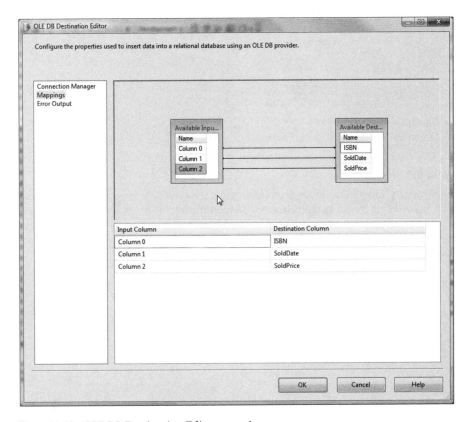

Figure 21-19. *OLE DB Destination Editor mappings*

19. Click OK.

20. From the Toolbox, drag the OLE DB Destination to the design surface of the Data Flow tab.

21. Connect the Conditional Split transformation to the OLE DB destination by dragging the green connector (which appears when you click the Conditional Split). You will be prompted in the Input Output Selection dialog box to select an output. This time, select Case 2, which evaluates rows belonging to the years less than 2008.

22. Click OK. Notice that Case 2 now appears by the green path.

23. Click the OLE DB destination, and in the Properties window, rename it to BookSaleArchive.

24. Double-click the BookSaleArchive destination.

25. Change the name of the table or the view to [dbo].[BookSaleArchive].

26. Select Mappings from the left navigation pane. Click and drag the column mappings, mapping Column 0 to ISBN, Column 1 to SoldDate, and Column 2 to SoldPrice.

27. Click OK when you've finished. Your design surface should look something like Figure 21-20.

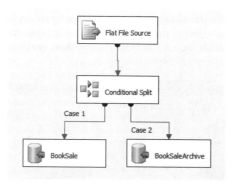

Figure 21-20. *Finished Data Flow design surface*

Running the SSIS Job

To run the SSIS job, select Debug ➤ Start Debugging. Data will flow from the flat file (40 rows), into the Conditional Split transformation, routing 18 rows (belonging to 2008 year sales) to the BookSale table, and 22 rows (belonging to pre-2008 sales) to the BookSaleArchive table, as shown in Figure 21-21. After execution has completed and you are finishing viewing the row counts, select Debug ➤ Stop Debugging.

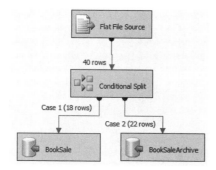

Figure 21-21. *Data Flow design surface after debugging*

Now that we've walked through an example of a simple implementation of data flow, let's try another example, this time using the Event Handlers design surface.

Event Handlers Design Surface

The Event Handlers design surface allows you to create programmatic reactions to specific package or task events. For example, if an error occurs within the package, you can use the Send Mail task to issue a warning to a particular user. Events are organized by executable (the package or other tasks/containers). Each executable has its own event handlers, capturing errors, status changes, failures, and more.

Let's take a look at an example. We'll add an event handler that will e-mail us when the package encounters an error. This example requires you to have a valid SMTP server on your network or on your local machine. In order for this exercise to work, your SMTP server must have relay access.

1. Create a new SSIS project and package. You'll add an event handler that will respond to any errors within the package.

2. In your new package, click the Event Handlers tab.

3. Under the Executable drop-down, select Package. Under the Event Handlers drop-down, select OnError. Click the "Click here to create an 'OnError' event handler for executable 'Package'." A blank design surface (similar to the Control Flow and Data Flow design surfaces) appears.

4. In the Connection Managers area, right-click the surface and select New Connection.

5. In the Add SSIS Connection Manager dialog box, select SMTP and click Add.

6. In the SMTP Connection Manager Editor dialog box, enter the name of your SMTP server. Then click OK.

7. Drag a Send Mail task onto the Event Handlers design surface.

8. Double-click the Send Mail task.

9. In the General section, change the Name field text to **Error Email**, and the Description field text to **Emails on Package Errors**, as shown in Figure 21-22.

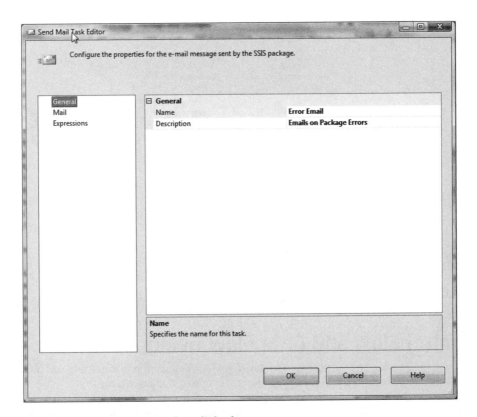

Figure 21-22. *Send Mail Task Editor dialog box*

10. From the navigation section, select Mail. Select the SmtpConnection you created earlier. Type in the e-mail addresses for From and To. In the Subject field, type **Example Package Error**. In the MessageSource area, type **There has been an error in the package**, as shown in Figure 21-23.

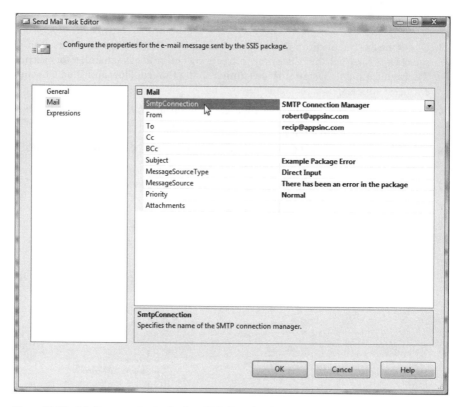

Figure 21-23. *Mail properties in the Send Mail Task Editor*

11. Notice that the MessageSourceType is equal to Direct Input. This means you manually enter the body of the text. Keep in mind that the body of the e-mail can also be derived from a package variable (variables are described in the "Variables" section later in this chapter) or an external file. Click OK.

12. To test the error event handler, right-click the Error Email task and select Execute Task. If successful, the task should turn green, and the e-mail should be sent.

13. Select Debug ➤ Stop Debugging to exit the event handler test.

Control Flow and Data Flow Designer Tasks

As mentioned earlier, an SSIS package is defined by tasks, connections, containers, and precedence constraints. A package can contain one or more tasks (also called *executables*).

SSIS has added several new tasks and enhanced others, and we will briefly review some of these tasks in this section. Different SSIS tasks will appear in the Toolbox window depending on the current design surface.

Control Flow Containers and Tasks

Figure 21-24 shows the Toolbox when you're working in the Control Flow design surface. Let's look at the available containers and tasks.

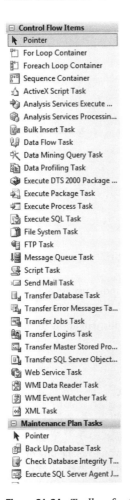

Figure 21-24. *Toolbox for the Control Flow design surface*

Containers

Containers provide a way to logically group tasks together for readability or dependency purposes. SSIS provides three Control Flow containers: the For Loop container, the Foreach Loop container, and the Sequence container.

Sequence Container

The Sequence container can contain one or more tasks, or other containers, allowing you to logically group tasks together. Because these tasks are contained within a Sequence container, they can be managed as a unit. This task provides visual benefits as well—by selecting the upper-right corner of a container, you can expand or collapse the detail of the tasks within, further enhancing readability of the package, as shown in Figures 21-25 and 21-26.

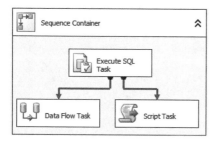

Figure 21-25. *An expanded Sequence container*

Figure 21-26. *A collapsed Sequence container*

Using a Sequence container also allows you to do the following:

- Enable or disable all tasks within the container (e.g., if you are debugging the package and do not wish to fire off the tasks within this container).

- Isolate workflow by container (e.g., have a container that is executed upon success of the previous task, or a different container that is executed on failure of the previous task).

- Define scope for a transaction, meaning that the rollback of a transaction can apply to all tasks within the Sequence container.

- Connect to other containers or other tasks by precedence constraints. Tasks within a container can also be connected to each other in the same way.

For Loop and Foreach Loop Containers

Two containers allow for repeating control flow within a package:

- *For Loop*: Like the Sequence container, the For Loop container allows you to place one or more tasks within it. Unlike the Sequence container, the For Loop container executes the tasks within it repeatedly, based on an evaluation condition. Once the condition returns false, execution of the tasks within the container ceases.

- *Foreach Loop*: This container executes the tasks based on an iteration statement. The iteration statement can be based on rows in an external table, files in a folder, objects within a variable, Server Management Objects (SMO), or even an XPath expression.

Let's look at an example that uses the Foreach Loop container. Suppose that we wish to have a nightly process that evaluates error logs generated by SQL Server (under the C:\Program Files \Microsoft SQL Server\MSSQL\LOG directory). In our hypothetical scenario, an external application will evaluate each error file in that directory. After the external process is finished, it will delete the row from the table. Our process is responsible for letting the application know which files need to be processed. In this exercise, we will explore this directory (in real time), finding each file within it and adding the filenames to a table of files pending processing.

█Caution Your directory may be different from the one listed in this section. You should change it to match your own path. As with the other exercises, use a safe test environment.

1. Create the `PendingFileProcess` table in a test database:

   ```
   CREATE TABLE PendingFileProcess
   (FileID int IDENTITY(1,1) NOT NULL PRIMARY KEY,
    FileNM nvarchar(1000) NOT NULL)
   ```

2. Create a new SSIS project called `Foreach loop example`.

3. In the new SSIS package, right-click the Control Flow design surface and select Variables. The Variables window will appear. (We will review variables in more detail later in this chapter, in the "Variables" section.)

4. Click the Add Variable button (the one showing a function symbol with an orange star in the upper-left corner) (see Figure 21-27).

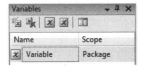

Figure 21-27. *Adding a variable*

5. A new package variable appears. Change the Name field text to **FileName** and the Data Type field text to **String**.

6. From the Toolbox, drag a Foreach Loop container onto the Control Flow design surface.

7. Double-click the Foreach Loop container.

8. In the Foreach Loop Editor dialog box, change the Name field to **Error Files**.

9. In the left navigation pane, select Collection.

10. Change the Enumerator value to Foreach File Enumerator. This means your task will loop through each file contained within a specified folder. Change the Folder field to the directory where your SQL Server error logs (or, for the purposes of this example, any directory where readable text file logs) are located, as shown in Figure 21-28.

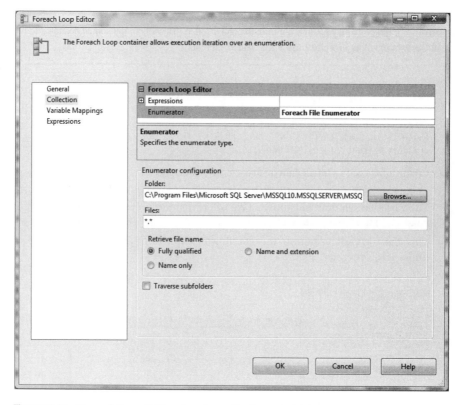

Figure 21-28. *Foreach Loop Editor showing collection properties*

11. In the left navigation pane, select Variable Mappings.

12. In the Variable section, from the drop-down list, select the variable User::FileName, which you created earlier. This variable will contain each filename found in the specified folder. The Foreach loop will loop through each file, changing the variable value at each pass.

13. Click OK to exit the Foreach Loop Editor.

14. In the Connection Managers area, create a new connection that points to the test database where you created the PendingFileProcess table in step 1.

15. Drag an Execute SQL task into the Foreach Loop container named Error Files, as shown in Figure 21-29.

Figure 21-29. *Foreach Loop container*

16. Double-click the Execute SQL task.

17. In the Execute SQL Task Editor dialog box, change the Name field to **Insert Error Files**. In the Connection drop-down list, select the connection you created in step 14. Set the SQLStatement property to the following statement:

```
INSERT dbo.PendingFileProcess
(FileNM)
VALU6ES (?)
```

The question mark is a placeholder for a parameter mapping. In this case, you will map the FileName variable to this parameter.

18. In the left navigation pane, select Parameter Mapping and click the Add button.

19. Select the User::FileName variable from the drop-down list. Change the Data Type value to nvarchar (matching the FileNM column in the PendingFileProcess table). Change the ParameterName value to @P1.

20. Click OK.

21. Select Debug ➤ Start Debugging. This will execute the SSIS package, looping through each file in the error log directory. For each file, a new row will be inserted into the PendingFileProcess table. Check this table in Management Studio to confirm that the table was populated:

```
SELECT FileID, FileNM
FROM dbo.PendingFileProcess
```

22. Select File ➤ Save All.

You will use this package in the upcoming Scripting task exercise.

Analysis Services Tasks

If you use Analysis Services, you'll want to be aware of three tasks:

- *Analysis Services Execute DDL*: This task allows you to submit Data Definition Language (DDL) statements to the selected Analysis Services connection.

- *Analysis Services Processing*: This task processes Analysis Services objects (such as cubes and dimensions).

- *Data Mining Query*: This task allows you to submit prediction queries based on Analysis Services data-mining models.

Data Flow Task

A Data Flow task represents an instance of the SSIS data flow engine executable. This executable is responsible for calling the data sources, data destinations, and any transformations that have been added to the Data Flow task.

As you saw in our first example in this chapter, when you add the Data Flow task to the Control Flow design surface and double-click it, you are directed to the Data Flow design surface. A Data Flow task can contain one or more Data Flow tasks (which we'll review in the "Data Flow Designer Tasks" section later in this chapter). You can also have more than one Data Flow task on the Control Flow design surface.

As noted earlier, the Data Flow tasks describe how data moves from a data source (*source adapter*), and how the data is modified and mapped (*transformation*) to a destination (*destination adapter*). In other words, you take data from somewhere, change it in some way, and then store the results somewhere else.

This mapping of source to transformation to destination is called a *graph*. A graph is a set of connected Data Flow components. One graph represents, for example, the data population of one table from another table. Unlike DTS 2000's Transform task, a single Data Flow task can also update multiple tables (which is to say, multiple graphs).

Data Profiling Task

As SQL Server is used more and more for the largest enterprise data warehousing projects in the world, it becomes increasingly important for the core product to provide the majority of data-quality functionality required for these implementations. The new Data Profiling task helps to deliver this functionality. It provides support for eight different profiles: five that profile at the column level and three that provide profiling between columns.

The Data Profiling task provides the following data profiles for individual columns:

- *Column Length Distribution*: Provides the distinct lengths for string values with the table, along with the percentage distribution for each length. This profile can help identify data-length problems that are common when migrating data from legacy systems that may not have enforced column lengths properly. Alternatively, this profile could be used to determine the required column lengths for a new table that will hold data from many different sources.

- *Column Null Ratio*: Provides the percentage of null values within a column.

- *Column Pattern*: Generates regular expressions for a percentage of rows within a table. This can be used to identify the number of different formats within a column for things like phone number, postal codes, and Social Security numbers. For example, if profiling a ZIP code column, you may be interested in how many entries have the expanded ZIP code format (with four extra digits). The likely regular expressions might be \d{5}-\d{4}, \d{5}, and \d{9}. Getting an expression like \d{15} would cause you to want to do further research.

- *Column Statistics*: Provides statistical values for the selected column, such as standard deviation, minimum, maximum, or average. For example, this could be used to do bounds checks for test scores, where no score should be less than 0 percent or greater than 100 percent. You could also use this profile to check date ranges during a data warehouse load. For example, you probably wouldn't expect an active employee to have a start date greater than the current date.

- *Column Value Distribution*: Provides all the distinct values within the column along with their percentage distribution. If you were profiling a column that contained US states, then you would expect 50 or 54 distinct state values, depending on what is considered a state. If you received 70 distinct state values, then obviously there would be a data-quality problem.

The Data Profiling task provides the following data profiles for multiple columns:

- *Candidate Key*: Indicates whether a particular column, or set of columns, can be used as a key or an approximate key.

- *Functional Dependency*: Provides an indication of the dependency of one column on another. For example, if there is a product category and product subcategory relationship, this profile can determine whether a particular subcategory exists only within the product category. It wouldn't be expected that the subcategory exists within many product categories.

- *Value Inclusion*: Indicates the overlap between a set of columns. Continuing with the previous example, when profiling the product subcategory column within the product table, all values should exist within the product subcategory table.

The Data Profiling task generates an XML file that contains the results. This file can then be further parsed and used within a package, or the stand-alone Data Profile Viewer, available within the SQL Server program group, can be used to view the profile output externally from the package.

Execute Package Tasks

SSIS includes two separate tasks for executing SSIS packages: the Execute Package task and the Execute DTS 2000 Package task. Unfortunately, the upgrade path for packages created in SQL Server 2000 is less than perfect. Although best efforts to upgrade are attempted by the upgrade wizard, certain features have changed too significantly in SSIS to provide a smooth upgrade path from prior versions. This is not as bad as it may seem—many very complicated DTS packages are now far simpler to create within SSIS. However, to address compatibility issues, SSIS includes the Execute DTS 2000 Package task.

The Execute DTS 2000 Package task will allow the execution of a DTS 2000 package from within an SSIS package. This way, you can continue to use your older packages until you have an opportunity to rewrite them in the new version. The Execute Package task is used to execute other SSIS packages as part of the workflow. Both tasks allow you to encapsulate and reuse existing packages, rather than creating task or data flow redundancy within your package.

Bulk Insert Task

The Bulk Insert task imports text files into SQL Server tables. Although you cannot validate, scrub, or transform data using this task, it is usually the fastest method for importing data from a text file into SQL Server. Consider using the Bulk Insert task when data file import (to SQL Server) performance is important. We will demonstrate this task in the next exercise.

Execute SQL Task

The Execute SQL task allows you to run SQL statements or call stored procedures against a SQL-compliant connection. For example, you can use this task to create a table, and then populate it with data based on a query.

In the following example, we'll use both the Execute SQL and Bulk Insert tasks. We'll demonstrate deleting data from a staging table and populating data from a text file into a SQL Server table using the Bulk Insert task.

The following exercise uses the BookSeller database and BookSales.txt file from earlier examples in this chapter.

1. Create a new staging table (in Management Studio) in the BookSeller database:

```
USE BookSeller
GO

-- The BookSale table is for current-year sales
CREATE TABLE dbo.Staging_BookSale
    (ISBN char(10) PRIMARY KEY,
    SoldDate datetime NOT NULL,
    SoldPrice money NOT NULL)
GO
```

2. In BIDS, create a new project called Import Book Sales.

3. In the new SSIS package, create two new connections: one for the BookSeller database and the other for the BookSales.txt file.

4. Drag an Execute SQL task onto the Control Flow design surface. Double-click the Execute SQL task.

5. Under Connection, select the connection for the BookSeller database. For the SQLStatement property, type the following:

```
DELETE dbo.Staging_BookSale
```

6. Click OK.

7. Drag a Bulk Insert task onto the Control Flow design surface. Double-click the Bulk Insert task.

8. Change the Name property to **Import BookSales file**.

9. In the left navigation pane, select Connection.

10. Under Connection, select the BookSeller database connection. For the Destination table, select the dbo.Staging_BookSale table. Change the column delimiter to a comma-based delimiter. For the File property, select the BookSales.txt connection. Click OK.

11. Click the Execute SQL task and drag the green arrow to the Import BookSales file task, as shown in Figure 21-30. The green arrow means that the first task (deleting data from the dbo.Staging_BookSale table) must execute successfully before the BookSales.txt data is imported.

Figure 21-30. *Execute SQL and Import BookSales tasks*

12. Select Debug ➤ Start Debugging.

13. Select Debug ➤ Stop Debugging.

14. From Management Studio, within a new query window, execute the following query to confirm that the rows were loaded:

```
SELECT ISBN, SoldDate, SoldPrice
FROM BookSeller.dbo.Staging_BookSale
```

Execute Process Task

The Execute Process task allows you to execute a Win32 executable or a batch file within an SSIS package. For example, you could use this task to call a third-party application that performs business functions unrelated to SSIS task functionality. Be careful not to call executables that require user feedback; otherwise, your package execution may hang.

File System Task

The File System task allows you to perform several different file-based operations, all without needing to create custom code (for example, in DTS 2000, if you wanted to rename a file you would be required to either use xp_cmdshell or write an ActiveX script). The File System task allows you to copy a folder from one location to another, copy a file from one location to another, create or delete a folder in a specified location, delete all files and folders in a folder, delete a file in a specified location, move a file or directory from one location to another, rename a file in a specified location, and change file or directory attributes.

FTP Task

The FTP task allows you to both send and receive files using FTP. With the FTP task, you can send files, receive files, create or remove a local directory, create or remove a remote directory, delete local files, and delete remote files—all without writing a bit of code.

Maintenance Plan Tasks

SSIS includes a set of tasks designed to assist in the maintenance of your SQL Server database environment. These tasks are found under the Maintenance Plan Tasks group in the Toolbox. as shown in Figure 21-31. They provide a flexible and enhanced alternative to manually creating plans within SQL Server Agent.

Figure 21-31. *Maintenance Plan tasks in the Toolbox*

Maintenance Plan tasks allow you to back up databases, check database integrity, defragment (using `ALTER INDEX, REORGANIZE`) or rebuild indexes (using `ALTER INDEX, REBUILD`), execute SQL Server Agent jobs and T-SQL statements, clean up database history (backup and restore history, SQL Server Agent Job history, and database maintenance plan history), notify operators, shrink databases, and update table statistics.

■**Tip** One particularly helpful new feature provided with the Mainenance Plan tasks is that each provides a View T-SQL button, so you can see exactly what each task is doing.

Message Queue Task

The Message Queue task is used to send or receive messages between SSIS packages or custom application queues using Microsoft Message Queuing (MSMQ) functionality. These messages allow asynchronous communication between systems and applications, meaning that messages can be delivered to a queue, where they will await pickup and processing from the MSMQ service on the server or workstation. Once the message is received, the receiving SSIS package can process and act upon the received message. Messages can be sent in text, file, or variable format.

Send Mail Task

The Send Mail task relies on a valid SMTP server to send e-mail messages. If you have a valid SMTP server on your network, you will be able to use this task to send e-mail notifications on package failures or successes, specific task events, or reporting of SQL Server data (for example, reporting on the status of database file sizes). This task lets you define an e-mail's To line, From line, CC line, BCC line, Subject line, and priority level, as well as include file attachments. The e-mail body (called the *message source*) can be directly entered text, or it can be based on the value of a variable or an external file.

Scripting Tasks

SSIS includes two separate scripting tasks: the ActiveX Script task and the Script task. The ActiveX Script task is a carryover from DTS 2000. It allows you to write scripts using the VBScript or JScript language to define logic within packages, write functions, access data using ActiveX Data Objects, perform computations, and set variables.

■**Note** In SSIS, you are no longer able to manipulate the DTS package object model. This is to prevent behind-the-scenes package manipulation, which often made DTS 2000 packages difficult to troubleshoot (e.g., hidden ActiveX scripts in the workflow disabling or overriding workflow success or failure).

The ActiveX Script component will be removed from the next version of SQL Server, so you should remove it from your packages as soon as possible. The Script task should be used in its place. Unlike the ActiveX Script task, the Script task allows you to write your scripts with the full-featured Visual Basic .NET or C# programming languages. Scripts are written in the VSTA environment, which includes IntelliSense, debugging, Object Explorer, and integrated help modules. Using the .NET Framework and COM objects offers obvious performance and functionality benefits.

In the following example, you will use the Script task to combine multiple files in a directory into a single file (so that it can be imported by the hypothetical application). You will reuse part of the project and package you created for the earlier example demonstrating the use of the Foreach Loop container. As you recall, this package looped through each error file in the C:\Program Files\ Microsoft SQL Server\MSSQL\LOG directory. For each file it found, a row was inserted into the PendingFileProcess table.

With the Script task, you can now perform actions that are not natively available within the SSIS environment. In this example, you have been asked to loop through each error file and merge them into a new, single, separate file. This way, the external (hypothetical) application can instead load all errors from a single file.

■**Tip** While you proceed through this exercise, consider the different uses for this particular script. For example, SQL Server DBAs and developers often use Visual SourceSafe (VSS) to store their stored procedures and other database objects. When asked to migrate changes, the VSS object checkout process creates several separate files. These files must be separately executed within a query window. You could, however, use a script like the one presented in this exercise to combine all SQL files into a single file.

---

1. In the SSIS package from the earlier exercise, delete the Execute SQL task contained within the Foreach Loop container.

2. Drag a Script task into the Foreach Loop container.

3. Double-click the Script task.

4. Change the Name field to **Merge Files**, as shown in Figure 21-32.

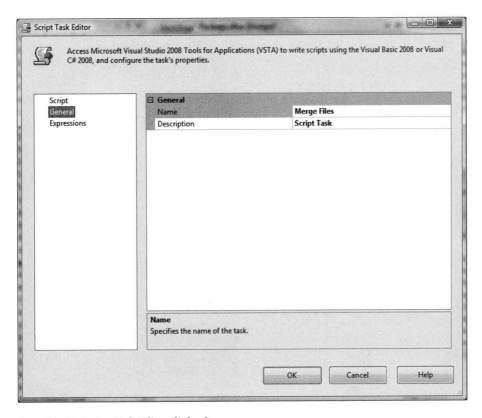

Figure 21-32. *Script Task Editor dialog box*

5. In the left navigation pane, select Script and change the ScriptLanguage property to Microsoft Visual Basic 2008.

6. Click the Design Script button.

7. In the Imports area of the script, add the following line:

```
Imports System.IO
```

This will allow you to access file-streaming functionality.

8. Within the `Public Sub Main()` procedure, add the following code:

```
Public Sub Main()

    Dim sw As StreamWriter
    Dim variables As Variables

    'Check for the existence of the FileName variable
    If Dts.VariableDispenser.Contains("FileName") = True Then
        Dts.VariableDispenser.LockOneForRead("FileName", variables)
        Dim FileName As Object = variables("FileName").Value
```

```
        End If

        'Populate the source variable with the FileName variable value
        Dim source As String = variables("FileName").Value.ToString

        'The name and location of the merged error log
        Dim dest As String = "c:\Apress\MergedErrorLog.txt"

        ' Creates the MergedErrorLog.txt file if it doesn't already exist
        If File.Exists(dest) = False Then
            ' Create a file to write to.
            sw = File.CreateText(dest)
            sw.Flush()
            sw.Close()
        End If

        ' Creates a visual divider within MergedErrorLog.txt between file data
        sw = File.AppendText(dest)
        sw.WriteLine("----------------------------------------")
        sw.Flush()
        sw.Close()

        ' Opens the current file and writes it into MergedErrorLog.txt
        Dim sr As StreamReader = File.OpenText(source)
        Dim s As String
        sw = File.AppendText(dest)
        Do While sr.Peek() >= 0
            s = sr.ReadLine()
            sw.WriteLine(s)
        Loop
        sr.Close()
        sw.Flush()
        sw.Close()
        Dts.TaskResult = Dts.Results.Success
    End Sub
```

This code is commented so you can better understand what it does. In a nutshell, the script grabs the value of the FileName variable (which will be populated by the Foreach Loop container task). This is the file that will be combined into the single C:\Apress\MergedErrorLog.txt file.

9. Select File ➤ Save to save the script.

10. Select File ➤ Close and Return.

11. Click OK to exit the Script task.

■**Tip** This example assumes that you are merging log files not currently open in other processes. Since you are merging SQL Server log files, if the SQL Server service is running, one of these log files will, of course, be running. To test this, one option is to copy off the inactive log files to a separate location and then merge them accordingly. For the clarity of this example, however, the script merges all files directly from a single directory of a SQL Server instance that is *not* currently running.

---

12. Select Debug ➤ Start Debugging to test the package.

If the package succeeded, both the Foreach Loop container and the Script task will turn green, as shown in Figure 21-33. You should also find a populated C:\Apress\MergedErrorLog.txt file containing the contents of all error logs from the error log directory.

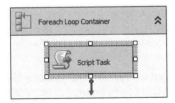

Figure 21-33. *Foreach Loop container and script example after execution*

Web Service Task

The Web Service task executes a web method using an HTTP connection. Within the task, you designate the HTTP connection and the Web Services Description Language (WSDL) file (which specifies the location of the service and the functionality of the web service).

Web Service task input parameters can be specified through strings within the task or, preferably, by using variables. Similarly, the results from a Web Service task can be written to a file or to a variable.

WMI Tasks

WMI is the programmatic interface provided by Microsoft to allow users to monitor and control Windows system resources. SSIS includes two tasks that tie into the WMI interface: the WMI Data Reader task and the WMI Event Watcher task.

The WMI Data Reader task allows you to execute a WMI Query Language (WQL) query against a specific system (for example, retrieving the application event log file). The WMI Event Watcher task allows you to execute a WQL query that watches for a specific event to happen (for example, being notified when logical disk space falls beneath a certain threshold). The WMI Event Watcher task can also be used to monitor for the existence of a file or files within a specific directory. This is a common requirement to make nightly batch-loading a little more flexible.

XML Task

The XML task allows you to perform operations against XML documents. Some of the operations include the ability to compare XML documents (writing the differences to an XML diffgram document), merge two XML documents into one document, query and evaluate an XML document using the XPath language, and transform an XML document based on an XSLT style sheet.

Data Flow Designer Tasks

Before using the Data Flow design surface, you must first add a Data Flow task to the Control Flow design surface. Once you have added the Data Flow task, you can begin adding items (from the Toolbox) to the Data Flow design surface.

Data Flow components fall into three categories:

- *Source adapters*: These access data from different types of data sources, making the data available to the Data Flow task. Source adapters produce outputs, meaning they feed output columns and rows to the receiving destination adapter or transformation.

- *Transformations*: These are tasks used within the data flow of a package to modify data per your particular business needs. Transformations require *inputs*, meaning they expect an input of columns and rows from either another transformation or a source adapter. Transformations also provide outputs that contain columns and rows, making them available to other transformations or destination adapters.

- *Destination adapters*: These write data in a data flow to different types of data sources. Destination adapters use inputs to receive columns and rows from source adapters or transformations.

Source Adapters

Source adapters define the source of the data; the specific table, query, or view when applicable; and the specific columns that need to be extracted. In SSIS, you extract data using the data source adapters listed in Table 21-1.

Table 21-1. *SSIS Source Adapters*

Source Adapter	Description
ADO NET	Works with ADO.NET connections to deliver data to either a transformation or destination adapter.
Excel	Allows you to read data from a Microsoft Excel spreadsheet. For Excel 2007 data, an OLE DB source adapter must be used.
Flat File	Allows you to read from a delimited, fixed-width, or mixed-format (ragged-right) text file.
OLE DB	Allows you to extract data using any valid OLE DB provider such as DB2 or Oracle. This is the adapter you will use to extract SQL Server data. If selecting a SQL Server data source, you'll have the option of reading data based on a table or view, reading based on a variable referencing a table or view, or using a SQL query.
Raw File	Used to read raw data files generated from the Raw File destination adapter. The Raw File destination adapter is used to write intermediary results of partly processed data. The data is stored in a "raw" or native format, which requires little processing from the Raw File source adapter. Raw data can be exported via the Raw Data destination adapter so it can be processed by a different (or the same) SSIS package.
XML	Allows you to extract data from an XML document source.

Destination Adapters

Destination adapters define the endpoint of extracted data, receiving it either directly from a data source adapter or from a transformation. In SSIS, you can extract data using the data destination adapters shown in Table 21-2.

Table 21-2. *SSIS Destination Adapters*

Destination Adapter	Description
ADO NET	Similar to the ADO NET source adapter, can be used to write data to a variety of databases.
Data Mining Model Training	Trains one or more data-mining models within SQL Server Analysis Services.
DataReader	Works with ADO.NET connections to export data to the selected ADO.NET destination data source.
Dimension Processing	Processes dimensions in data warehouse tables, allowing for incremental, full, or update processing. This adapter is available only in SQL Server Enterprise and Developer Editions.
Excel	Allows you to export data into a Microsoft Excel spreadsheet. To export data to Excel 2007, use the OLE DB destination adapter.
Flat File	Uses a flat file provider to write data to the destination text file. You can designate how the text file is formatted using a delimited, fixed-width, or mixed format.
OLE DB	Writes to a variety of OLE DB-compliant destinations, such as DB2 or Oracle.
Partition Processing	Processes Analysis Services partitions and allows for incremental, full, or update processing. This adapter is available only in SQL Server Enterprise and Developer Editions.
Raw File	Writes data to a raw data file, which can then be read by a Raw File source adapter.
Recordset	Creates and uses an in-memory ADO record set that can be stored within a package variable and used within other areas of the package, outside the current data flow.
SQL Server Compact Edition	Allows you to write to a table in Microsoft SQL Server Compact Edition 3.5 SP1.
SQL Server	Allows you to import into SQL Server using the high-speed Bulk Insert interface. This adapter provides the performance advantages of the Bulk Insert task, with the added benefit of being able to transform the data as well.

Transformations

SSIS provides several new and enhanced transformation tasks, shown in Table 21-3, that are used to modify data as it moves from the source data adapter to the destination data adapter.

Table 21-3. *SSIS Transformations*

Transformation	Description
Aggregate	Applies aggregate functions (group by, sum, average, count, count distinct, minimum, and maximum) against column values provided by the source adapter.
Audit	Allows you to capture and include environmental data within the data flow. With this task, you can designate additional fields to be captured during the data flow (such as the package name, version, and execution start time) and send them to the destination adapter (or as an input to the next transformation).
Cache Transform	Enables the storage of data from a connected data source into a cache connection manager. This data can then be used by a Lookup transformation within a Data Flow task.
Character Map	Allows you to apply character modifications to existing string datatype columns or to a separate copy of an existing column. Modifications include changing text to all uppercase or lowercase, byte reversal, and other language conversions.
Conditional Split	Allows you to route data rows to different outputs based on a condition/expression you define. For example, you can use this task to route all employees who belong to the "East" sales territory to their own table and those belonging to the "West" sales territory to their own table.
Copy Column	Allows you to create new columns in the output by copying input columns. The new copies are added to the transformation output and can be modified without changing the original column data.
Data Conversion	Modifies the datatype of the input column and copies it to an output column.
Data Mining Query	Used to perform prediction queries against data-mining models, using Data Mining Extensions (DMX). This transformation is available only in SQL Server Enterprise and Development editions.
Derived Column	Creates a new column by using expressions against input columns and variables. The expression can be built using the original input column, variables, functions, and operators.
Export Column	Used to read data from the data adapter to generate a file for each row. For example, if your Employee table contains a BLOB image column, you could use the Export Column task to extract the BLOB into an individual file for each Employee row.
Import Column	Does the reverse of the Export Column; it reads data from separate files and adds the data columns to the existing data flow.
Fuzzy Grouping	Uses an algorithm to identify duplicate rows of data within a data source. This would be particularly useful if you were interested in creating a single customer master by combining many customer files from divisions of a large multinational organization, for example. This transformation requires a connection to SQL Server to create the temporary tables and indexes it needs to perform its operations. This transformation is available only in SQL Server Enterprise and Development Editions.

Transformation	Description
Fuzzy Lookup	Performs a lookup against a lookup result set, but rather than using an equi-join, it uses a fuzzy matching algorithm, allowing lookups to return matches on exact or close matches from the reference table. This transformation also outputs a similarity and confidence score (both decimal values between 0 and 1, where 1 is an exact match) for the overall match and also for each column within the match. The similarity score indicates the mathematical difference between the input and a lookup record, whereas the confidence score calculates the likelihood that a given looked-up value is the best match compared to other matches found in the lookup table. This transformation is available only in Enterprise and Development Editions.
Lookup	Used to perform a join of the source data against a cache file, table, view, new table, or SQL query. The lookup uses an equi-join and must match exactly between the two values. A *lookup* operation involves referencing a value from a separate dataset, based on the value of a source column or columns. The Lookup transformation can be a little confusing in that it can return different results depending on the caching level being used. If the reference dataset is loaded into the cache before the transformation runs, then SSIS is responsible for the lookup. If the reference data is not loaded into the cache, then a SQL Server query is used for the lookup logic. The caching options for the Lookup task are as follows: The reference data is generated from a table, view, or query and is loaded into the cache. This happens before the transformation is run. The reference data is generated from the data source within the data flow or from the cache file using a cache connection manager. The reference data is generated and cached before the transformation is run. The reference data is generated while the transformation is run and the cache is populated while the transformation runs. An individual lookup is done for every record, and the data is not cached.
Merge	Used to combine two sorted datasets based on values in their key columns, outputting the results into a single result set to the next transformation task or data adapter.
Merge Join	Creates a single result set based on the joining of two sorted result sets. Like a T-SQL query, a Merge Join transformation can use varying join types to combine result sets, including INNER, FULL, and LEFT joins.
Multicast	Takes a single result set and distributes it to multiple destinations (transformations or data adapters). This task allows you to spread out your data (e.g., across different servers at the same time).
OLE DB Command	Executes an individual SQL statement for each row in the data flow.
Percentage Sampling	Generates a sample dataset by selecting a percentage of the transformation input rows.
Pivot	Used to transform a normalized dataset into a less normalized version by pivoting the input data on a column value.
Row Count	Used to capture row counts as they move through the data flow, allowing you to store the results into a variable.

Continued

Table 21-3. *Continued*

Transformation	Description
Row Sampling	Creates a sample dataset by selecting a specified number of the transformation input rows.
Script Component	Allows you to write your own .NET-coded transformation, destination adapter, or source adapter. The script is created in Microsoft VSTA using either the Visual Basic .NET or C# language.
Slowly Changing Dimension	Allows you to update and insert into data warehouse dimension tables.
Sort	Sorts the input data prior to sending it to the next transformation or data destination adapter. This can potentially improve table load performance if you match the sort of this transformation to the destination table clustered index sort order.
Term Extraction	Provides the ability to extract individual words or phrases from input columns. For example, if you wanted to derive the individual street names from an Address column, the Term Extraction transformation searches the column and extracts the individual address names. This transformation can extract words only, phrases only, or both. Exclusion tables can be referenced to not reextract existing terms (if you are, for example, populating a search-term table based on common text field values). This transformation is available only in SQL Server Enterprise and Development Editions.
Term Lookup	Allows you to take an input result set, reference it against a term reference table, and output those rows that associate to each term. For example, if you wanted to see the frequency of search terms within an Address column, the output result set will return the search term from the reference table, the address column where it was identified, and a reference count of 1. The resulting data can then be grouped in later queries, to identify the frequency of search-term matches. This transformation is only available in SQL Server Enterprise and Development Editions.
Union All	Like the T-SQL UNION ALL command, gathers outputs from multiple data sources or transformations and combines them into a single, unsorted dataset. If you need sorted outputs, use the Merge transformation.
Unpivot	Does the opposite of the Pivot transformation, taking the pivoted data and reversing it into a more normalized version (moving values from columns into multiple records with the same value in one column).

Export Column Transformation Example

For this example, imagine you've been asked by a hypothetical third-party catalog provider to generate thumbnail image GIFs for all of the products in the AdventureWorks application, for use in the third party's online sales application.

1. Create a new project and package in BIDS.

2. Create a new OLE DB connection manager to the AdventureWorks database.

3. Drag a Data Flow task onto the Control Flow design surface. Double-click it.

4. From the Toolbox, drag an OLE DB source onto the Data Flow design surface. Double-click it.

5. In the OLE DB Source Editor dialog box, under Connection, select the SQL Server instance containing the AdventureWorks database. For the Data Access Mode option, select SQL command. For the SQL command text, enter the following query:

```
SELECT ThumbNailPhoto,
        'C:\Apress\' + ThumbnailPhotoFileName AS PhotoFileName
FROM Production.ProductPhoto
```

■**Tip** Notice that the query designates the actual file directory where you'll be placing the thumbnail images. In a real-life situation, you could designate either a local or a UNC path.

6. Click OK.

7. From the Toolbox, drag an Export Column transformation onto the Data Flow design surface.

8. Click the OLE DB source and drag the green precedence constraint to the Export Column task.

9. Double-click the Export Column task.

10. In the Export Column Transformation Editor, under Extract Column, select ThumbnailPhoto. This table column will define the actual name of each file generated. Under File Path Column, select PhotoFileName. Figure 21-34 shows these selections.

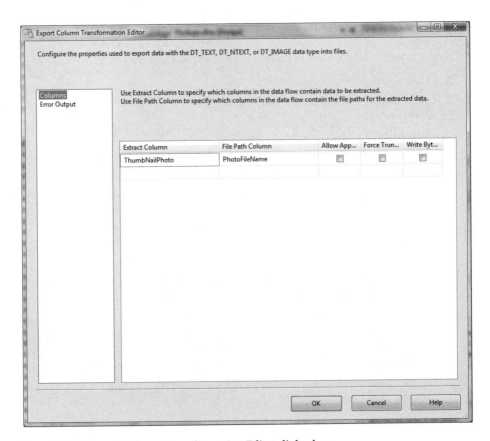

Figure 21-34. *Export Column Transformation Editor dialog box*

11. Leave the other options unchecked, and click OK.

12. Select Debug ➤ Start Debugging.

You should see that 101 rows were processed by the Export Column task, as shown in Figure 21-35.

Figure 21-35. *Export Column package after execution*

The files should have been generated to your C:\Apress directory. You can then use the FTP task to send the files to the client.

Row Sampling Transformation Example

For this example, your company's HR department would like you to generate a text file containing a random sampling of 20 employees who will be asked to participate in an employee survey. You'll use the AdventureWorks table HumanResources.Employee for the SQL Server source data, and you'll use the Row Sampling transformation to export the sampling to a text file.

1. Create a new project and package in BIDS.

2. Create a new connection manager to a SQL Server instance set to the AdventureWorks database.

3. Drag a Data Flow task onto the Control Flow design surface. Double-click it.

4. Drag an OLE DB source to the surface area. Double-click it. For the name of the table or the view, select HumanResources.Employee.

5. Select Columns from the left navigation pane. In the Available External Columns check box list, deselect all fields except EmployeeID, ManagerID, and HireDate. Click OK.

6. Drag a Row Sampling transformation onto the Data Flow design surface.

7. Click the OLE DB source and drag the green precedence constraint to the Row Sampling transformation.

8. Double-click the Row Sampling transformation. In the Row Sampling Transformation Editor, change the number of rows to 20. Then click OK.

9. Drag a Flat File destination onto the design surface.

10. Click the Row Sampling transformation and drag the green precedence constraint to the Flat File destination. In the Input Output Selection dialog box, select Sampling Selected Output (this feeds the 20 rows selected, rather than the remaining rows *not* selected). Click OK.

11. Double-click the Flat File destination. Click the New button next to the Flat File Connection Manager drop-down.

12. In the Flat File Format dialog box, select Delimited. For the filename, select `C:\Apress\`
    `EmployeeSampling.txt` (it doesn't need to already exist). Check the "Column names in the
    first data row" check box. Click OK.

13. Back in the Flat File Destination Editor, in the left pane, select Mappings. Verify that the
    input columns map to the destination columns appropriately. Click OK.

14. Select Debug ➤ Start Debugging.

After debugging the package, check the contents of the `C:\Apress\EmployeeSampling.txt` file
for the 20 sampled employees. Also, if you debug the package again, you'll notice that you get a different
set of employees exported to the file.

Change Data Capture

Data within our systems changes over time, and it has been notoriously difficult to capture change
information for further processing. Certainly, we are able to create backups and snapshots of data,
but these techniques don't really allow us to easily determine changes to data values within tables.

We've tried adding metadata columns such as `UpdateDate` and `CreateDate` to all of our tables or,
in the worst-case scenario, we've just reprocessed all data every time we ran our ETL process. The
insert and update dates allowed us to make comparisons against a processing date in order to
determine data that needed to be processed. However, this technique did not give us the before and
after picture of data that so many applications require. Therefore, triggers were typically used to
track more detailed change information. These triggers provided a way to capture the before and
after data values, and write them to another table or to create versioned records within the same
table. For the vast majority of applications, this functionality worked very well. But wouldn't it be
nice to have this type of functionality natively provided by SQL Server?

With SQL Server 2008, the ability to determine changes to data values within tables has been
provided, and it is called Change Data Capture (CDC). CDC provides the necessary foundation for
easily tracking changes to data within specific tables, and removes the requirement for application
developers to create triggers and tables to capture changes.

■**Note** You may be wondering why the CDC topic is covered in a chapter about SSIS. From a pure functionality
implementation point of view, it really doesn't have anything to do with SSIS. When the authors of this book were
discussing the value that CDC provides, we couldn't decide where it should live within the overall book. CDC was
developed by the replication team within the SQL Server product group at Microsoft, so our initial thinking was to
cover it in the chapter about high availability. However, as it exists today, CDC really isn't a high availability/data
recovery capability per se. The next logical area would have been within one of the development-focused chapters.
In the end, we considered that the primary use case for CDC is within ETL processes that extract delta change
information for a line-of-business system into a data warehouse. Therefore, we decided to place the CDC topic
within the SSIS chapter.

CDC works by capturing insert, update, and delete information and automatically storing it in change data tables for future retrieval. Metadata regarding the type of operation performed (insert, delete, and update) and log sequence (which can be translated to time) is stored along with the column data from the table. Once enabled, CDC captures changes to the source tables by monitoring the database transaction log. The changed data is then written to corresponding change tables. External applications can use the change tables to perform various types of processing.

In this section, we will work through an example of implementing CDC. This example will demonstrate one of the primary use cases for CDC, which is within ETL processes to extract changed data from a line-of-business system. This changed data will then typically be inserted into a data warehouse.

Enabling Change Data Capture

Before individual tables can be configured for CDC, an administrator must enable the database for CDC. Then the database owners can enable individual tables for CDC. Here are the steps for enabling CDC for this example:

1. Open SQL Server Management Studio and run the following query in the context of the database for which you want to enable CDC (sysadmin permissions are required to make this change):

```
USE AdventureWorks
EXECUTE sys.sp_cdc_enable_db_change_data_capture
```

2. Enable CDC on the Production.Product table by running the following DDL:

```
EXECUTE sys.sp_cdc_enable_table_change_data_capture
@source_schema = N'Production'
,@source_name = N'Product'
,@role_name = N'cdc_Admin'
,@supports_net_changes = '1'
```

This will create the cdc.Production_Product_CT change table in the AdventureWorks database. Along with the table, two table-valued functions are created: cdc.fn_cdc_get_all_changes_Production_Product and cdc.fn_cdc_get_net_changes_Production_Product.

3. The sys.databases and sys.tables catalog views can be used to ensure that CDC is properly configured for the database and table. Issue the following query:

```
SELECT name, is_cdc_enabled FROM sys.databases
```

You should see that the is_cdc_enabled column for the AdventureWorks database is set to 1.

4. Issue the following query:

```
SELECT name, is_tracked_by_cdc FROM sys.tables WHERE name = 'Product'
```

You should see that the is_tracked_by_cdc column is set to 1.

Extracting Change Data with SSIS

Once CDC is enabled for the AdventureWorks database and for the `Production.Product` table, SQL Server will automatically start to populate the `cdc.Production_Product_CT` with all data changes. We could now start building an SSIS package that would use the `fn_cdc_get_net_changes_Production_Product` or `fn_cdc_get_all_changes_Production_Product` to extract data from the change table and perform the appropriate action within the data warehouse table.

SQL Server Books Online contains a very detailed example of configuring CDC, under the title "Improving Incremental Loads with Change Data Capture."

Logging

SSIS includes advanced logging functionality that can be configured to track various runtime events. It is also possible to generate custom messages from within a running package. SSIS provides the following logging options (see Figure 21-36):

- Log events to text files
- Log events that can be captured by SQL Profiler
- Log events to a SQL Server table
- Log events to the Windows Event Log
- Log events to an XML file

The following exercise demonstrates how to access these options.

Figure 21-36. *SSIS logging options*

You can control which events are logged for each executable within the control flow. SSIS can log events such as errors, execution status changes, informational events, postexecution events, postvalidation events, preexecution events, prevalidation events, progress notifications, task failures, variable changes, and warnings.

You can also determine which columns are logged, including the date the log event occurred, the computer name where the log event occurred, the user who launched the package, the name of the container or task where the log event occurred, the package's unique identifier, the unique identifier of the package execution, the event message text, the start time of the task/container execution, the end time of the task/container execution, and the elapsed time based on the start and end time.

In this example, you will set up an Execute SQL task that will generate an error. You will enable error logging for the task, execute the package, and then examine the resulting Windows Event Log entries.

1. In a new SSIS package, create an OLE DB connection manager to the SQL Server instance containing the AdventureWorks database.

2. Drag an Execute SQL task onto the Control Flow design surface. Double-click the Execute SQL task.

3. For the Connection property, select the AdventureWorks connection. In the SQLStatement property, type the following SELECT statement (the statement will cause a divide-by-zero error):

```
SELECT 1/0
```

4. Click OK.

5. In the Control Flow design surface of the SSIS package, right-click an empty area and select Logging.

6. In the Configure SSIS Logs: Package dialog box, enable logging by selecting the check box under Containers in the left pane (based on the name of your package), as shown in Figure 21-37.

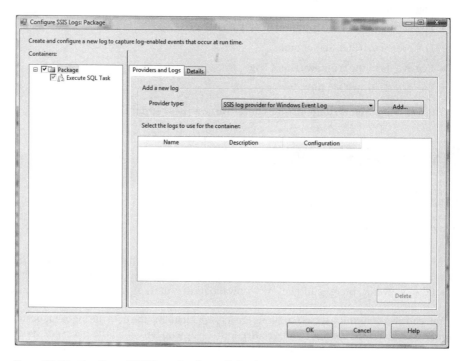

Figure 21-37. *Configure SSIS Logs: Package dialog box*

7. In the "Add a new log" section, select SSIS log provider for Windows Event Log from the Provider type drop-down list, and then click the Add button.

8. In the "Select the logs to use for the container" section, select the check box of the new logging item, as shown in Figure 21-38.

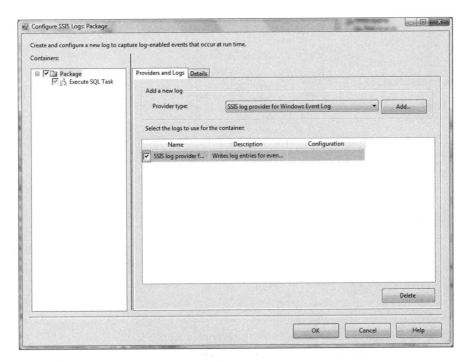

Figure 21-38. *Adding Execute SQL task logging*

9. Click the Details tab and check the OnError event.

10. Click the Advanced button. Notice that the events are preselected, as well as the associated columns that will be logged for each event, as shown in Figure 21-39. Click OK to set the defaults.

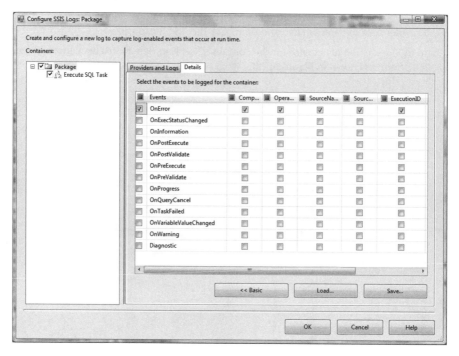

Figure 21-39. *Details tab of the Configure SSIS Logs: Package dialog box*

11. Select Debug ➤ Start Debugging. You will see the Execute SQL task fail.

12. From Windows, select Start ➤ Run. Type **eventvwr** and click OK.

13. In Event Viewer, select Application Log. You will see three errors of varying granularity for the failed task. Click through each. Within the description of each, look for the error with a source name of Execute SQL Task. It is here you will see the "Divide by zero error encountered" error message that caused the task (and package) to fail, as shown in Figure 21-40.

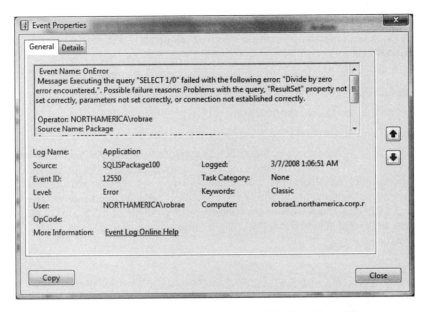

Figure 21-40. *Example of event logging from SSIS in Windows Event Viewer*

Dynamic Package Configuration

The Package Configuration Organizer allows you to dynamically set package properties based on machine environment variables, XML configuration files, registry entries, a SQL Server table, or parent package variables (sent by the calling the Execute Package task).

Setting configurations dynamically allows you to change important connections or settings without needing to hard-code them within the package. For example, if you have a development, staging, and production environment where you port your SSIS packages, you can use the Package Configuration Organizer to dynamically set the source server connections based on the local machine name environment variable. These settings are applied when your SSIS package is loaded (for example, if you add an existing package to a different project). Settings are *not* applied during execution time, unless the configuration is set through a parent package variable.

■**Tip** You'll most likely use the Package Configuration Organizer functionality prior to setting up a package in the Package Deployment Wizard, so that deployments are able to run from different computer contexts.

In this example, you'll create a package configuration that can be used to update the SQL Server instance and database based on an XML file.

1. In BIDS, create a new SSIS project called PackageConfigExample.

2. In the default Package.dtsx package, create a new data connection to the SQL Server AdventureWorks database.

3. Right-click the Control Flow design surface and select Package Configurations.

4. In the Package Configurations Organizer dialog box, select Enable Package Configurations.

5. Click the Add button to add a new configuration.

6. Click Next on the Package Configuration Wizard welcome screen.

7. On the Select Configuration Type screen, for the configuration type, select XML Configuration File, as shown in Figure 21-41. Keep "Specify configuration settings directly" selected. This means the configuration will expect the XML file to be in the same file location wherever the package is loaded. Use the other option, "Configuration location is stored in an environment variable," if you expect this location to change. For the configuration filename, type C:\Apress\test.dtsConfig. A new file will be created if one does not already exist. Click Next to continue.

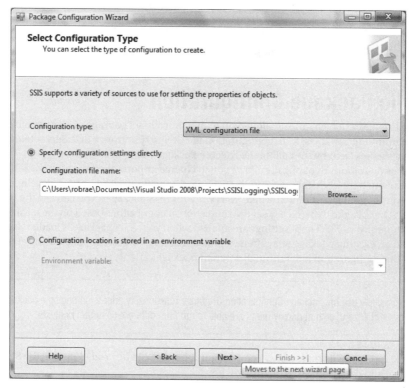

Figure 21-41. *Selecting the configuration type in the Package Configuration Wizard*

8. On the Select Properties to Export screen, under the \Package\Connections folder, expand your SQL Server instance connection. Expand the Properties folder, check the Connection-String, InitialCatalog, and ServerName properties, as shown in Figure 21-42. Then click Next.

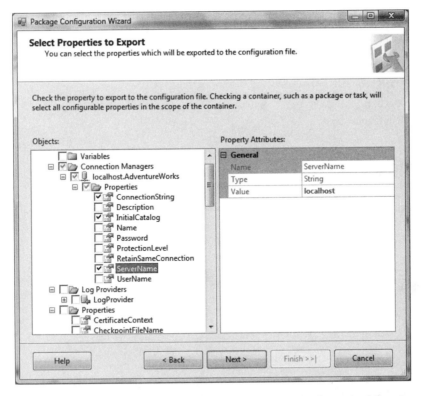

Figure 21-42. *Selecting properties to export in the Package Configuration Wizard*

9. On the Completing the Wizard screen, type **SQL Server Connection Change** in the Configuration Name text box. Click Finish.

10. Your new configuration will now appear in the Package Configuration Organizer. Click Close.

11. Open the configuration file from the location you specified. Here, you can change the three property values. As shown in the following code, the ConfiguredValue tags outline the values for each configurable property. If you change the property in the XML file and then load the package to a new project, the SSIS package will inherit the properties based on the XML file.

```
<?xml version="1.0"?>
<DTSConfiguration>
  <DTSConfigurationHeading>
    <DTSConfigurationFileInfo
GeneratedBy="JOEPROD\Owner" GeneratedFromPackageName="Package"
GeneratedFromPackageID=
"{FA099B09-C230-4688-AF93-E88C73C8683F}" GeneratedDate="1/1/2005 9:28:29 PM"/>
    </DTSConfigurationHeading>
    <Configuration ConfiguredType="Property"
Path="\Package.Connections[{C2FB43E4-2DD7-44D0-B616-
D9EF80D60901}].ConnectionString" ValueType="String">
<ConfiguredValue>Data Source=localhost;Initial Catalog=AdventureWorks;
Provider=SQLNCLI10.1;Integrated Security=SSPI;
Auto Translate=False;</ConfiguredValue>
    </Configuration>
    <Configuration ConfiguredType="Property" Path="\Package.Connections
```

```
[{C2FB43E4-2DD7-44D0-B616-D9EF80D60901}].InitialCatalog" ValueType="String">
    <ConfiguredValue>AdventureWorks</ConfiguredValue>
  </Configuration>
  <Configuration ConfiguredType="Property" Path=
"\Package.Connections[{C2FB43E4-2DD7-44D0-B616-D9EF80D60901}].ServerName"
ValueType="String">
    <ConfiguredValue>localhost</ConfiguredValue>
  </Configuration>
</DTSConfiguration>
```

Variables

SSIS variables allow you to store values for use during package execution. Variables can be used to update package properties during runtime, store integer values used for controlling container looping, provide lookup information, store values for use within a T-SQL statement or Script task, and build expressions. Figure 21-43 shows the Variables window.

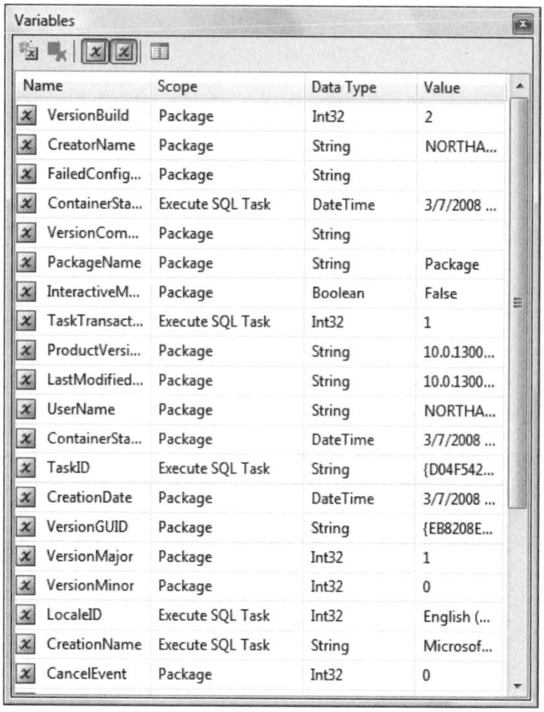

Figure 21-43. *Variables window*

A variable is defined by its namespace (either *system* or *user-defined*). You can create new user-defined variables, but you cannot create new system variables.

A variable is also defined by its scope, variable datatype, and value. *Scope* defines where the variable can be seen from within the package. A variable with package-level scope can be viewed by all objects within the package, whereas variables defined within a task's scope can be viewed only by the task. Allowed variable datatypes include Boolean, byte, char, datetime, DBNull, double, int16, int32, object, sbyte, single, string, and Uint32.

Configuring Variables

To configure variables within your SSIS package, follow these steps:

1. Within the SSIS Designer of a new SSIS package, right-click the Control Flow design surface and select Variables.

2. The Variables window will appear. To view system variables, click the Show System Variables button (the one with the *X* in a gray square). System variables will now appear.

3. To create a new user-defined variable, click the Add Variable button (which shows a function symbol with an orange star in the upper-left corner). This will create a user variable with the name `Variable` and a scope of your SSIS package.

4. To create a variable scoped at the task level, click and drag a File System task from the Toolbox to the empty Control Flow design surface.

5. To create a task-scoped variable (in this case, based on a File System task), simply create a new variable while the task is selected in the Control Flow design surface.

Now that you know how to configure variables, let's run through creating a variable for a business scenario.

Creating Variables

Say that your company's HR department has an application that uses the AdventureWorks table `[HumanResources].[JobCandidate]` to track job candidates in the queue. Once a week, the HR group wishes to evaluate the number of candidates in the queue, to determine whether or not to pull the job advertising campaign from the local newspaper.

In this example, you will create a variable called `JobCandidateCount`, populate it from the table, and e-mail an advertising update to HR based on the variable value.

1. In a new package, add a new connection to the AdventureWorks database.

2. Create a new user-defined variable called `JobCandidateCount` with a datatype of `Int32`.

3. Drag an Execute SQL task onto the Control Flow design surface. Double-click the Execute SQL task.

4. In the General properties, in the SQL statement section, change the Connection property to use the AdventureWorks connection. Change the SQLStatement property to use the following query:

```
SELECT COUNT(*) as 'CandidateCount'
FROM HumanResources.JobCandidate
```

5. Change the ResultSet property to Single row.

6. From the left navigation pane, select Result Set and click the Add button. Change the Result Name to **CandidateCount**. In the Variable Name field, make sure `JobCandidateCount` is selected. Click OK to exit the Execute SQL Task Editor.

7. Create a new SMTP connection manager (use a valid SMTP server in your network or on your desktop).

8. Drag a Send Mail task onto the Control Flow design surface. Double-click it.

9. In the Send Mail Task Editor, under the General properties, change the Name property to **Pull Advertising**. Under the Mail properties, for the SmtpConnection property, select the SMTP connection manager. Since this is just an exercise, for the From and To properties, select your own e-mail address. In the Subject line, type **Pull Advertising**. This will be the notification to remove advertising if the job candidate queue exceeds ten candidates. Click OK.

10. Copy the Pull Advertising task and paste a copy on the design surface. Double-click it.

11. On the General tab, rename the Name property to **Retain or Start Advertising**. In the Mail properties, change the Subject property to **Retain or Start Advertising**. Click OK.

12. Create a precedence constraint from the Execute SQL task to the Retain or Start Advertising task. Double-click the green arrow to configure the constraint.

13. In the Precedence Constraint Editor, change the Evaluation operation to Expression. In the Expression field, type the following expression:

    ```
    @JobCandidateCount<11
    ```

    This expression evaluates your user variable, testing to TRUE if the variable is less than 11. Click OK. Notice that a small function symbol appears by the Retain or Start Advertising task.

14. Create a precedence constraint from the Execute SQL task to the Pull Advertising task. Double-click the green arrow to configure the constraint.

15. In the Precedence Constraint Editor, change the Evaluation operation to Expression. In the Expression field, type the following expression, and then click OK.

    ```
    @JobCandidateCount>10
    ```

16. Select Debug ➤ Start Debugging to test the package.

Since the candidate count is more than ten, you'll see the Execute SQL task turn green, and then the Pull Advertising task will turn green afterward. The Retain or Start Advertising task is not run, as the variable value was *not* less than ten.

Precedence Constraints

In the previous example, you applied a precedence constraint that used an expression to determine which e-mail should be sent. As we've discussed, precedence constraints are used to define package workflow, determining if and when specific tasks are executed and in what order. Tasks (including containers) can be connected to other tasks or to other containers.

The following example reviews how to configure precedent constraints within the Control Flow design surface. You will add tasks but not configure their properties, since we're focusing on how precedence constraints work.

1. In the SSIS Designer, using a new package, drag and drop a File System task onto the Control Flow design surface.

2. Drag and drop a Send Mail task onto the Control Flow design surface.

3. To make sure that the File System task executes first, click the File System task and drag the green arrow onto the Send Email task. The arrow defaults to green, meaning that the Send Email task will execute only if the File System task executes successfully.

4. Double-click the green arrow to open the Precedence Constraint Editor. The Evaluation operation drop-down list designates whether or not a constraint is evaluated, an expression, an expression and a constraint, or an expression or a constraint. When Constraint is selected, the Exception result drop-down lists whether the next task executes on success, failure, or completion of the preceding task.

   • If Expression is selected as an evaluation operation, the Expression dialog box becomes available. Expression evaluation was demonstrated in the previous exercise, when you evaluated the value of the JobCandidateCount user variable.

   • The Multiple Constraints section applies to multiple constraints referencing the *same* task.

5. Keep the Evaluation operation selection of Constraint. Change the Execution result to Failure and click OK. Notice that the green arrow has turned to red. The Send Mail task will now be fired only if the File System task fails.

Checkpoints

For the majority of enterprise integration scenarios, it is very desirable to have a package restart where it left off in the case of a failure. Being able to start where a particular failure happened, as opposed to from the beginning of package, could save hours of unnecessary rework.

SSIS provides this support through the implementation of *checkpoints*. When an SSIS task fails, the new checkpoint functionality allows you to restart the package, beginning from the point of failure.

To enable checkpoints for an SSIS package, follow these steps:

1. In the SSIS Designer, click an empty area in the Control Flow design surface to focus the Properties window on the SSIS package.

2. In the Properties window, type in a filename for the CheckPointFileName property. This file does *not* need to exist already.

3. Enable checkpoint usage for the package by selecting Always for the CheckpointUsage property.

The checkpoint file will be used to save all completed tasks, package configurations, containers, system variables, and user-defined variable information. When the SSIS package runs successfully, it deletes the checkpoint file it originally created. If you select the Always option, the SSIS package will *not* execute unless the checkpoint file exists. If you select the IfExists option, the package will use the checkpoint file if a previous execution failed, but if the previous execution succeeded, it will execute as normal.

■Note During the checkpoint process, a unique package identifier is written to this file, preventing the use of a checkpoint on a modified SSIS package. To restart successfully from the point of failure, the SSIS package design must not be modified between the initial failure and the restart.

Transactions

SSIS packages support *transactions*, which combine a group of tasks into a logical unit of work that is either wholly committed or rolled back. If two tasks are enlisted within a transaction, and the second task fails, the first task will roll back database changes previously made to a consistent state before the package executed.

To enable transactions for your SSIS package, follow these steps:

1. In the SSIS Designer, right-click an empty area on the Control Flow design surface and select Properties.

2. In the Properties window, change the TransactionOption property to Required. The Required option means that the SSIS will start a transaction. The Supported option does not actually start a transaction; rather, it joins any transaction already started by the package or its parent container.

3. To enlist a specific task or container within the package transaction, click the task on the Control Flow design surface. In the Properties window, change the task's TransactionOption property to Required.

Debugging

With SSIS, Microsoft provides several debugging and troubleshooting features, including control flow and data flow visual debugging, data viewers, breakpoints, and other debug windows.

Control Flow and Data Flow Visual Debugging

While creating your SSIS package, as you add and configure tasks, containers, or data flow objects, you will see real-time warning icons within them, as shown in Figure 21-44. These warning icons contain tooltips that describe which properties are either missing or configured incorrectly.

Figure 21-44. *File System task with a warning icon*

During package debugging, the SSIS Designer also displays task color-coded progress reporting. Without waiting for the SSIS package to finish executing, you can watch the task icons change colors, indicating their current status: gray indicates waiting to run, yellow indicates executing, green indicates success, and red indicates failure.

You can also monitor progress during package execution by viewing the Progress tab (called the Execution tab when the package is not debugging) in the SSIS Designer, as shown in Figure 21-45. From here, you can monitor the start and finish times of tasks and containers, as well as view any events, errors, and warnings.

■**Tip** The Progress tab is an easy way to identify the cause of errors within your package. You can scroll through the various tasks and search for red *X*s. If there is, for example, a divide-by-zero error in a SQL task or a missing property in a Send Mail task, the Execution/Progress tab will indicate this.

Figure 21-45. *Progress tab in the SSIS Designer*

In the SSIS Designer, during package execution all Data Flow paths display the number of rows that have passed through them on the design surface, saving you from needing to validate the actual row counts after the package finishes executing.

Data Viewers

Data viewers allow you to watch data as it moves through a path, enabling you to identify transformation issues or bugs. You can add a data viewer to the Data Flow design surface by right-clicking the path between two Data Flow components and selecting Data Visualizer. In the Data Flow Path Editor dialog box, add one or more viewers, which allow you to view data in a grid, histogram, scatter plot, or column chart format.

During runtime, a Data Viewer window will appear, as shown in Figure 21-46, enabling you to continue moving the data, copy the data to a clipboard, truncate all data from the table, or reconfigure the data viewer.

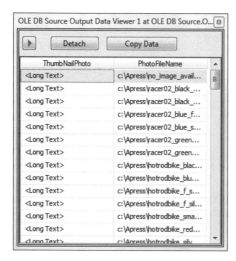

Figure 21-46. *Data Viewer window during runtime*

Breakpoints

The SSIS Designer allows you to set *breakpoints* (a point in the SSIS package at which the task can be interrupted for manual intervention) within SSIS tasks, containers, or Data Flow components. As shown in Figure 21-47, you can configure breakpoints for various events, including OnPreExecute, OnPostExecute, OnError, OnWarning, OnInformation, OnTaskFailed, OnProgress, OnQueryCancel, OnVariableValueChanged, and OnCustomEvent.

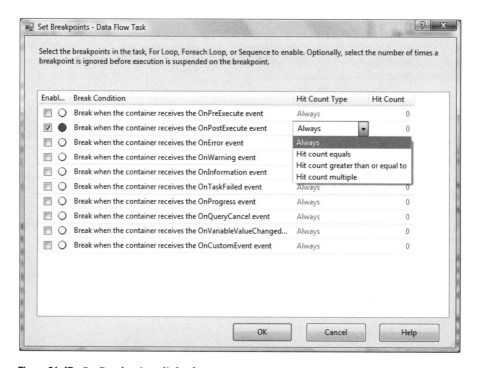

Figure 21-47. *Set Breakpoints dialog box*

During package runtime, you can view the Breakpoints window, which lists all enabled breakpoints within the SSIS package.

Other Debug Windows

In addition to the Breakpoints window, Microsoft includes other windows useful for debugging runtime of the package:

- *Call Stack*: This window shows SSIS objects that are currently running during debug mode.

- *Command*: This window can be used for executing commands directly into the BIDS environment (for example, if you wanted to exit debug mode during the execution of an SSIS package, you could type Debug.StopDebugging and press Enter). The Command window uses IntelliSense and allows you to browse through the various IDE commands.

- *Immediate*: This window is used for executing commands in order to debug expressions, statements, and variables.

- *Watch*: This window allows you to read, edit, and save variables.

- *Output*: This window displays status errors related to project compilation and validation.

SSIS Package Handling

After you've completed your SSIS package, you can easily deploy and install it with SSIS wizards. You can also schedule SQL Server Agent jobs to execute SSIS packages. And if you have SQL Server 2000 packages, you may be able to use the Data Transformation Services Migration Wizard to map their tasks to the equivalent tasks in SSIS.

The SSIS Package Deployment Utility

BIDS creates a package deployment utility that you can use to deploy your packages to any computer. After building the package deployment utility, you can use the DTSInstall.EXE executable (created in the folder of your deployed project) to install packages using the SSIS Package Installer Wizard, which guides you through the process of installing files on either the file system or SQL Server.

The following steps will create a simple deployment utility for a completed SSIS package:

1. In the Solution Explorer window of an open SSIS project, right-click the project and select Properties.

2. In the Configuration Properties window, select Deployment Utility. In the Properties window, change the CreateDeploymentUtility property to True. Click the OK button.

3. Right-click the project in Solution Explorer and select Build. This process will create the SSIS deployment manifest file under the bin\Deployment directory, with its name based on the deployed project.

4. Double-click the SSIS deployment manifest file (e.g., BookSalesImport.SSISDeploymentManifest) to launch the SSIS Package Installer, where you are able to deploy your package(s) to the file system or to a SQL Server instance.

Migrating SQL Server 2000 DTS Packages

SQL Server 2000 packages can be migrated by using the Data Transformation Services Migration Wizard. The wizard maps tasks within the SQL Server 2000 package to their equivalent DTS tasks in SSIS. For those tasks that do not map to SSIS, the new package structure will encapsulate non-SSIS-compliant functionality within an Execute DTS 2000 task.

■**Caution** DTS object model references within a SQL Server 2000 ActiveX task are no longer allowed in SSIS.

To launch the Migration Wizard, in BIDS, within an SSIS project, right-click the SSIS packages folder in the Solution Explorer window and select Migrate DTS 2000 Package. The wizard will step you through the migration process.

It is also possible to run DTS packages within the SQL Server 2008 environment as legacy components. This ensures that the conversion process of a large number of DTS packages does not disrupt any plans to migrate to SQL Server 2008. There is also a DTS package editor, contained in the SQL Server Feature Pack available from Microsoft.com, which you can use to edit legacy DTS packages.

Scheduling an SSIS Package

SSIS packages can be scheduled using SQL Server Agent jobs in SQL Server Management Studio. Jobs can be scheduled to execute SSIS packages stored in SQL Server, on the file system, or in the SSIS store.

■**Note** The *SSIS store* is simply the default folder on the file system used to store packages deployed with the Package Deployment Wizard. The SSIS service looks for packages in this folder, rather then searching the entire file system for DTSX files.

This exercise shows you how to schedule an SSIS package that is stored within SQL Server (in the msdb database).

1. In SQL Server Management Studio, expand the SQL Server Agent node and Jobs folder in Object Explorer.

2. Right-click the Jobs folder and select New Job.

3. Enter the name and owner of the job.

4. Select the Steps page from the "Select a page" pane on the left.

5. Click the New button to create a new step.

6. Enter the step name and select the type of SSIS package from the drop-down list.

7. Under the Package Source area, keep the default of SQL Server. Under the Server area, type in or select from the drop-down the SQL Server instance name.

8. In the Package field, type the package name or select it by clicking the ellipsis button and selecting the name from the Select an SSIS Package dialog box. Then click OK.

■**Note** If the SSIS package is nested within a folder, use the naming convention of /Foldername/PackageName.

9. Select the Schedules page from the "Select a page" window. Click the New button to define your job schedule, and then click OK.

10. Click OK in the Steps dialog box, and click OK again in the main New Job dialog box.

Many people don't actually use the SQL Server Agent for scheduling database activities. Instead, they prefer to use other scheduling tools. Typically, integration with these enterprise scheduling tools is accomplished through command-line utilities and batch files. SSIS provides full support for running packages from the command line. After working through the preceding example, you can view the Command Line tab within the job step that actually runs the SSIS package. This will give the exact syntax required to run the package with all the appropriate configuration settings.

Summary

With SSIS in SQL Server 2008, Microsoft continues its push into the enterprise ETL space. More and more, people will continue to migrate from competitive ETL tools because of the tremendous value that SSIS provides as an integral part of the overall SQL Server product.

In this chapter, you learned about some of the key capabilities in SSIS and became familiar with the SSIS development environment (BIDS). You learned about the division of labor within the SSIS Designer: control flow and data flow. You examined all the tasks and features available for use both in the Control Flow and Data Flow design surfaces. You were introduced to the advanced logging features, variables, and debugging features. We reviewed how you can deploy and schedule SSIS packages as SQL Server Agent jobs. This chapter also covered the new CDC feature, which lets you determine changes to data values within tables.

This chapter just barely scratches the surface of SSIS. Coverage of SSIS could easily fill an entire book of its own (and has certainly done so in previous versions), so be on the lookout for a future Apress title devoted to SQL Server 2008 SSIS.

Index

You Need the Companion eBook

Your purchase of this book entitles you to buy the companion PDF-version eBook for only $10. Take the weightless companion with you anywhere.

We believe this Apress title will prove so indispensable that you'll want to carry it with you everywhere, which is why we are offering the companion eBook (in PDF format) for $10 to customers who purchase this book now. Convenient and fully searchable, the PDF version of any content-rich, page-heavy Apress book makes a valuable addition to your programming library. You can easily find and copy code—or perform examples by quickly toggling between instructions and the application. Even simultaneously tackling a donut, diet soda, and complex code becomes simplified with hands-free eBooks!

Once you purchase your book, getting the $10 companion eBook is simple:

❶ Visit **www.apress.com/promo/tendollars/**.

❷ Complete a basic registration form to receive a randomly generated question about this title.

❸ Answer the question correctly in 60 seconds, and you will receive a promotional code to redeem for the $10.00 eBook.

THE EXPERT'S VOICE™

2855 TELEGRAPH AVENUE | SUITE 600 | BERKELEY, CA 94705

Offer valid through 12/02/08.